Joel
JOHNSON

W9-CNG-792

April 2012

ALSO BY ED SIKOV

ON SUNSET BOULEVARD:
THE LIFE AND TIMES OF BILLY WILDER

MR. STRANGELOVE:
A BIOGRAPHY OF PETER SELLERS

LAUGHING HYSTERICALLY:
AMERICAN SCREEN COMEDY OF THE 1950S

SCREWBALL: HOLLYWOOD'S MADCAP ROMANTIC COMEDIES

DARK
VICTORY

DARK
VICTORY

THE LIFE OF BETTE DAVIS

ED SIKOV

A HOLT PAPERBACK

HENRY HOLT AND COMPANY ◆ NEW YORK

Holt Paperbacks
Henry Holt and Company, LLC
Publishers since 1866
175 Fifth Avenue
New York, New York 10010
www.henryholt.com

Permission to quote portions of the "Playboy Interview: Bette Davis," July 1982, © 1982, has been generously granted by *Playboy*.

Ogden Nash verse on p. 311 copyright © 1952 by Ogden Nash. Reprinted by permission of Curtis Brown, Ltd.

Distributed in Canada by H. B. Fenn and Company Ltd.

Library of Congress Cataloging-in-Publication Data

ISBN-13: 978-0-8050-8863-2
ISBN-10: 0-8050-8863-6

Henry Holt books are available for special promotions and premiums.
For details contact: Director, Special Markets.

Originally published in hardcover in 2007 by Henry Holt and Company

First Holt Paperbacks Edition 2008

Designed by Meryl Sussman Levavi

Printed in the United States of America

10 9 8 7 6 5 4 3 2 1

FOR CHRISTOPHER BRAM

Players should be immortal, if their own wishes or ours could make them so; but they are not. They not only die like other people, but like other people they cease to be young, and are no longer themselves, even while living. . . . Their life is a voluntary dream; a studied madness. The height of their ambition is to be beside themselves.

—William Hazlitt
(English literary critic, 1778–1830)

She insisted that I see *Hush . . . Hush, Sweet Charlotte* with her. So she had a screening set up—it was just the two of us. I was really more interested in watching her than the movie, and it didn't take much to do that because she talked all the way through it. And she kept talking about herself in the third person. She kept saying, "Look at that dame up there on the screen! Isn't she *great*?" She would criticize and compliment her performance, always in the third person, as if it were some other actress performing. I have no explanation for the psychological underpinnings of people who talk about themselves in the third person, but it has a regal ring, doesn't it? "She's *great*, she's *fabulous, oh look what she's doing now!*" It's also kind of mad.

—Mart Crowley
(American playwright, 1935–)

CONTENTS

DARK
VICTORY

PROLOGUE

Adark, square-cut mink jacket and matching hat frames Bette Davis's face and neck, the fur lent an extra touch of sparkle by virtue of its glamorous silver tips. She is seated at a table at an elegant restaurant—a violin is playing in the distance—and she is angry. It's a seething, bitter anger, and so she is systematically getting drunk, having discovered in the previous scene two devastating pieces of information: she is dying, and, far worse, she has been lied to. She is talking to her two dinner companions, one of whom is her neurosurgeon and fiancé, the other her best friend—it is they who are the liars—and while she's not slurring her words exactly, neither is she not; they're coming out as warm bursts of gin-scented mist.

Her friends, having arrived late enough to have missed the first few rounds of cocktails, are growing anxious and urge her to order some food, and she promptly obliges by yanking a menu out of a visibly startled waiter's hand. Cut to a front-and-center medium shot. A martini glass sits prominently on a plate before her. The dark frosted fur surrounds her face. She looks righteous, dangerous, divine. And while the flat, white menu serves nominally as the focus of her gaze, it's clear that she's putting on a performance of reading it. Bette Davis and her character, the equally willful Judith Traherne, have each been mentally drafting and redrafting the delivery of one of the greatest lines of their joint lifetime, and as they look up together in perfect superimposition, they fire it with precise aim and flawless timing: "Well, I—I think I'll have a large order of *prognosis negative!*"

Bette's enormous eyes widen even further at the end of the sentence. She glares off to the right and draws in a sharp intake of breath as a mark of emotional punctuation.

The film is *Dark Victory*, the year 1939. The director is Edmund Goulding, and the two other actors are George Brent and Geraldine Fitzgerald.

But the scene, and the film, belong to Bette Davis in the supreme and certain way that the Vatican and all of its paintings and sculptures and manuscripts and chapels and plazas belong absolutely to the Church. Davis's artistic possession of almost all of her films is just as incontrovertible (though the financial realm is precisely where the analogy fails). Goulding made some decent pictures, Fitzgerald was a proficient actress, Brent kept working . . . but Bette Davis was, and remains, as singular and commanding a figure as world cinema has ever produced.

She was a trained actress but a purely self-styled one. And her style—the cinematic answer to the peaty pitch of a fine scotch or three, the smoke curls of cigarettes by the thousands, the effortless fashion in which a huge square-cut mink sits on her smallish shoulders, her peculiar way with breathing and vocal stresses—that style is what made Bette Davis.

She was magnificent and exasperating, luminous and bellicose in equal measure. Her longtime boss, Jack Warner, called her "an explosive little broad with a sharp left."[1] Humphrey Bogart once remarked, "Unless you're very big she can knock you down."[2] She was a force of nature, a blazing talent. She defined and sustained stardom for over half a century. She worked like a dog.

Pretty enough to be given the glamour treatment in her early twenties, she developed by middle age into weathered, thick-featured boniness graced by a slash of red lipstick. Later, when she was elderly, crippled by a stroke and weakened by breast cancer, she still compelled the world to look at her, just as she compelled herself to keep acting. Some stared, some cackled, and others no longer cared, but Bette Davis proudly remained a working actress until the day she died. Much more than family or friends or hobbies or, God forbid, idleness (as she would have snapped, "Oh, *brother!*"), acting was the only thing that really mattered in the end.

Her friend Ellen Hanley stated it simply: "Bette Davis was one of the major events of the twentieth century."[3]

Imitating her vocal delivery and broadest physical gestures is actually quite easy as long as getting your audience to recognize who you're imitating is your goal. You snap the words out between your teeth and swiftly bite them off while holding an imaginary cigarette between the index and middle fingers and cranking the hand around by your waist in an inexplicable circular gesture, as though you're spinning a small wheel or turning a dial made of air. For longer lines of dialogue, you lay stresses eccentrically throughout the sentences and take breaths at odd places, all the while continuing to wave the cigarette around. The biggest laughs come from leaving off the last syllable of any sentence you choose, pausing for half a beat, and then bleating it in too high a tone.

With a minimal amount of practice and a taste for camp you can pull some laughs out of some of the stories in this book. But mimicking Bette Davis without reverence is (to revive the metaphor) like staring at the Sistine Chapel without awe.

Hollywood in the 1930s is unthinkable without Mildred Rogers, Davis's scenery-chewing harridan in *Of Human Bondage*; Julie Marsden, the southern bitch of *Jezebel*; and her self-knowing, self-reliant Judith Traherne in *Dark Victory*. The 1940s are unimaginable without *The Letter*, in which she's a remorseless killer, and *Now, Voyager*, in which she's a growing, healing survivor. Her Margo Channing in *All About Eve* set the bar so high in 1950 that the rest of the decade was bound, for Davis at least, to be a letdown. By 1962, Bette, a working actress for thirty-four years, gladly turned herself onscreen into the crazy gargoyle known as Baby Jane Hudson in the ghastly masterpiece *What Ever Happened to Baby Jane?* With *Baby Jane*, the razor's edge that separates the tragic from the ludicrous is sharp enough to have cut a lesser actress to bloody ribbons. And all of it—*all of it*—was a battle.

Dark Victory is the story of Bette Davis's life as focused through her art. I write more about her films than about, say, her marriages because I care about them a great deal more and because they define her legacy in a way a series of failed husbands cannot. She had four of them, all of whom found her difficult, cantankerous, sniping, rude. Prone to picking fights. Apt to drink too much. So did many of her directors and costars, screenwriters and producers. So did many of her friends. Davis is not an admirable, role-model heroine in *Dark Victory* except in terms of her thundering talent, which is, I think, what counts. That's why her victory was dark: with some unquantifiable degree of self-knowledge, she sacrificed her personal life for the sake of her work, and it hurt. She fought people. Belligerence was in her blood. Painting her as a vivifyingly independent woman who battled Hollywood men in the name of Cinema is fair only to the extent that she battled everything she encountered, from Hollywood producers to the tarnished brass doorknobs in her many houses. Only some of it was worth fighting, a fact even she appeared to realize at times. Davis was an angry woman for reasons nobody who knew her ever adequately explained to me and for reasons I still cannot fully understand.

You may grow to hate her. I did not. Because I love her performances—most of them, anyway. Even after three years of researching her life; watching her movies; interviewing people who knew her and worked with her; brooding darkly; thrashing through sporadic fits of writer's block and bitterly, exasperatedly blaming her for them; and slipping half-consciously and rather morbidly into several of her vices (though I never smoked), I remain entranced by her when she's onscreen. She had, more than any performer I have ever studied, a blazing ability to imprint herself onto every character she ever played—to make me believe in those fictive characters while never letting me forget that I was watching *her*, a calculating actress, an intuitive star. Bette Davis forces audiences to notice her as Bette Davis even when she is most deeply immersed in her roles. Always the Yankee, she wants us to appreciate how hard she's working.

It's not that she's unsubtle. Throughout her film career a simple but well-timed intake of breath is enough to take one's own breath away. The imitators get the drastic parts right in a clownish sort of way, but nobody can mimic her unique sense of restraint: Bette Davis's face in repose is as dramatic as her broadest gestures. Her most discreet facial expressions are among her most affecting. Think of the wry and knowing look on Margo Channing's face as Eve Harrington prepares to accept the Sarah Siddons Award in *All About Eve*; the shy fear in Charlotte Vale's ugly-duckling eyes in the beginning of *Now, Voyager*; the set of the jaw Leslie Crosbie effects in *The Letter*. Davis immobile and silent is as emotionally resonant as Davis in full throat and motion.

It's a cliché, but the cliché happens to be not only true but historically decisive: they don't make movie stars like Bette anymore. So it's difficult to gauge her influence on succeeding generations of actors other than to state the obvious: there would be no Meryl Streep or Charles Busch without Bette Davis. These are flamboyant performers who, like Davis, demand to be recognized and applauded as such, putting on characters and wearing them like the finest couture gowns, their audiences always knowing that at the end of the show the dresses will come off and be placed on hangers while the actors go home. The legacy Davis left to Streep and Busch—and Marlon Brando, for that matter—is this: never let anyone forget or deny that you, the emoting human with the colossal talent, are creating the art. Make them watch you *act*.

It's a showy style, but with Davis in particular it brought with it a corollary: if the part required the audience to hate her, then she made them hate her. Many actors claim to enjoy playing villains and thugs, bitches and tramps, but few have ever equaled Davis's capacity to risk generating an audience's thoroughgoing contempt, let alone openly invite it. As talented as Meryl Streep is, one gets the sense that, deep down, she wants her characters to be loved a little—and that she herself requires the affection of millions of strangers. Bette Davis didn't give a goddamn. She dares us to hate her, and we often do. Which is why we love her.

A word of defiant advice to those who hope to grow fond of the people whose biographies they are reading in the same genial way they grow fond of their friends: by the end of this book you may well be disappointed with Bette Davis and angry with me. But Miss Davis taught me something. After all the boozing and the bristling, the struggling to get it right, I have to admit it: I don't give a good goddamn either.

EARLY
SKIRMISHES

An Infant's Album

 *S*HE WAS A LIFELONG SAVER OF THINGS: clippings, thank-you notes, family snapshots, daybooks, opening-night telegrams, marketing lists, studio stills, scripts. Here is her baby book, carefully archived, the earliest private record of a most public life:

An angular father holds a baby swathed in an immense, flowing blanket; Ruth Elizabeth Davis is four days old.

Her baby gifts are itemized in a florid, practically indecipherable Victorian hand. They include a blue rattle, a pink rattle, a hairbrush and comb, a diamond ring from (illegible), and a silver spoon. The book itself was a gift from the baby's nursemaid, a Mrs. Hall of Augusta, Maine.

April 6, 1908: on the day after she was born, Ruth Elizabeth weighed six pounds. At three months, eight pounds. At nine months, a diary entry notes, she was caught amusing herself by imitating her humorless father and laughing.

The baby began to crawl at fourteen months. At seventeen months she stood alone.[1]

There is a small grayish envelope glued to one of the album's pages, and from it you can extract a lock of Ruth Elizabeth's baby hair. It's strawberry blonde, or, better, raspberry—more floridly pink than you would imagine, though it may have discolored, the result of age and longtime storage. From another box in the Bette Davis Collection at

Boston University you can dig out, sniff, and even taste (if you dare) the stubbed-out cigarette butt that some demented queen snatched off the floor of the Lincoln Center garage on the night the Film Society presented Miss Davis with a lifetime achievement award in 1989, but that would be skipping ahead.[2]

Whether it's Ruth Elizabeth's precocious imitation of her father or a lipstick-stained cigarette butt plucked from a garage floor and preserved in its own tiny Baggie, it is hard not to read what you already know about this woman into everything you discover about her. Take the snapshots her nanny affixed in the baby album. Here's one of her dour father, Harlow, looking down his beaklike nose at the child as though he was examining a zoological specimen of minor but still appreciable importance. Of course, you say; she had lifelong trouble with men, four failed marriages, various affairs, an insatiable rage . . . it must have started here. But does a distant daddy fully explain an affair with the nutty Howard Hughes? More important, what does any of this have to do with her fiery talent?

Here's another shot of father and daughter taken at Ocean Park on October 1, 1909, the day Ruth Elizabeth—called Betty—took her first step. Given Harlow Davis's reportedly icy nature, the photo seems out of character—too relaxed and full of everyday familiarity. Father and daughter look comfortable with each other; that can't be right. But you cannot deny the camera's ability to record a split second's worth of emotional honesty. Ruth Elizabeth's difficult, severe father may indeed have loved her, however momentarily. The key is that she herself demanded that the world think that he hadn't.

Scattered throughout the scrapbooks and photo albums in the archive are photos of the mother, Ruthie. They show a proper if plain young woman with eyes set slightly widely apart, a gently dimpled chin, and a rather flat but appealing face.[3] Ruthie, the driving, indulgent force behind the superstar. Ruthie, who may have been the one who originally preserved these volumes of clippings and reviews and photographs and keepsakes until they hired a service to take over when the publicity onslaught began in the early 1930s. Nobody, not even the adoring Ruthie Davis, could ever have kept up with press coverage of that magnitude, let alone the magpie preservation of diaries, snapshots, telegrams, and other assorted ephemera.

In her fine autobiography, *The Lonely Life*, Davis characterizes Ruthie as the artistic one, her father as the intellectual. Ruthie was flight, passion, theatrics, decorating. Harlow was all focus and analysis, as clear and precise as a magnifying glass. He had a stinging temper, too, in a way that Ruthie did not. When Harlow took a good-natured faceful of rice moments after his wedding, he wheeled around to the well-wishers and roared, "Goddamn you! I'll get you for this!"[4]

He could not forgive his wife for her sex, either. Harlow Morrell Davis married Ruth Favor on July 1, 1907.[5] Three days later, the newlyweds were lodging at Squirrel Island, Maine, where a water shortage kept Ruthie from douching after a bit of honeymoon intercourse. Harlow flew off the handle at this female breach of a gentleman's trust and, according to Ruthie, brought the whole hotel into his intimate uproar.[6] Betty Davis was born nine months and one day later in Lowell, Massachusetts.

In her unpublished memoirs, Ruthie recalls the "lovely April shower" that "heralded" Betty's birth on April 5, 1908.[7] Davis, in *The Lonely Life*, turns it into a Homeric squall: "The gods were going mad and the earth was holding its head in a panic. . . . I happened between a clap of thunder and a streak of lightning. It almost hit the house and destroyed a tree out front. As a child I fancied that the Finger of God was directing the attention of the world at me. Further and divine proof—from the stump of that tree—that one should never point."[8]

Appalled at the baby she bore, at least at first, Ruthie said, "Is that what I've got? Take it away! It's horrible!"[9] She changed her mind later, though she maintained a vigilant criticism lest Ruth Elizabeth ever commit the sin of resting on her laurels. No matter what Ruth Elizabeth's achievements and fame, her mother taught her that she could always do better.

Harlow was not cut out for fatherhood, a fact that should have been clear from the start. He was cut out for dissecting infants, not nurturing them. Nevertheless, as Ruthie described it, "Bette's sister Barbara came along eighteen months later to keep Bette from being spoiled."[10] If that was indeed the rationale for bearing a second child, it didn't work.

With Barbara, called Bobby, it was all about Betty from the start. Bobby was in her crib when Betty, according to Ruthie, waited until Bobby's nurse was out of the room. She then removed Bobby from the crib Betty considered her own, trundled her across the room, and deposited the usurper on the couch in an act of reclamation and revenge.[11]

Betty was driven in a way Bobby never was, an innate trait that her parents reinforced with firm Yankee expectations. Their soil was rocky, their winters were harsh; for generations they had been brutalized into enduring. Betty's grandfather once bullied her into climbing a flight of stairs. Betty faced him from the bottom. She was barely able to walk. "Come on, climb!" he commanded from the top. "You can do it. One step at a time." According to Davis, she made it, bruised but triumphant.[12] It was the first of many painful successes.

There were strict rules in the Davis household, as there generally were in the New England families from which the Davises and Favors descended. Harlow Davis was a man who believed that children ought not to dine at table until they could conduct a worthy conversation, so Ruth Elizabeth and Barbara were exiled to the kitchen or nursery. Father's rule didn't apply on Sundays, but he often banished them in tears anyway after they committed some infant infraction or other.[13]

Of the sisters, Ruthie remembered, "they were always close. Bette once cut off Barbara's hair, but on the whole they lived amicably together."[14] "Now she isn't going to be pretty," Ruthie heard Betty declare moments after the shearing. "She isn't going to be pretty any more."[15]

Throughout her life, everybody liked Bobby. Most felt sorry for her.

A scrapbook photo has both girls stripped to nothing but bandanas tied around their very blonde hair, sitting on a blanket on a hot summer's day.[16] Another poses them with Harlow: the girls are wearing large Mother Goose–like bonnets and sitting on his lap. Betty engages the camera, caught in a half smile, seemingly about to remark upon something of importance. Bobby sports a determined pout. Harlow is sour beyond words, staring glumly at the camera with an admonishing expression on his face. Wire-rimmed glasses perch slightly down on his nose. There's a high, bony, recognizable forehead on a longer, thinner face. Why he feels such a powerful urge to reprimand remains unclear.[17]

Harlow graduated from the Harvard Law School in 1910. Obsessive-compulsive before the condition had been diagnosed, he found his calling as a meticulous patent attorney with the United Shoe Machinery Company of Boston.[18] In *The Lonely Life* and elsewhere, Davis describes him using words like *brilliant, cruel,* and *sarcastic.* She tells a story so frigidly exact in its rendering of her father's logic that you immediately see and understand her psychological profile as well as his. She was enchanted by a clear summer nighttime sky, as any romantic, unstunted child would be. "Do you see all those stars up there?" the father asked his little girl. "There are millions and millions of them. Remember that always and you'll know how unimportant you are."[19]

Still, the portrait Bette Davis draws of her father is complicated by one most unexpected detail: "Christmas should have exacted a loud 'bah humbug' from Harlow M. Davis," Davis writes, but "it was Daddy's favorite holiday." The sour, distant father decorated their Christmas tree every year. Then he played Santa.[20] He could be generous with money and special-occasion cheer, if not his affections, of which he had few, though the exception to that rule took the form of his brutal dog, a chow, which terrified Bette with its constant snapping.

Harlow's menacing presence to the contrary notwithstanding, Davis maintained that her childhood—spent mostly in Winchester, Massachusetts, a suburb of Boston about ten miles to the northwest—was essentially happy. (Never dwell on adversity; a Yankee creed. One with true strength of character should barely acknowledge it.) Her thanks went entirely to Ruthie.[21] She cited the wedding Ruthie threw for her sister Mildred, complete with Japanese lanterns dangling from the yard's trees. She recalled sliding with Bobby down the snow-covered hill behind the house, swinging on the swings by the kitchen door, baking pies with her cheery mother in the kitchen.[22] But she also remembered running dreamlike through the woods while being chased by a pack of dogs. One of them caught her hair in its teeth until she broke free.[23]

Was Bette Davis really chased by wild dogs as a child? Or was she having a clear premonition of her career in the movie business?

BARBARA STANWYCK ONCE said of Davis that "she had the kind of creative ruthlessness that made her success inevitable." It's a marvelous turn of phrase, suggesting that it was her fierce drive that was creative rather than the other way around.[24]

Ruth Elizabeth Davis mastered the fine art of emotional manipulation at an early age. It comes naturally to children, but particularly so to nascent performers. "If I could never win my father, I completely conquered Ruthie. I became an absolute despot at the age of two." She sensed her mother's weakness and exploited it: "The tantrum got me what I wanted. My demands were frightening and unusual." Indulgence was Ruthie's favored response. Still, little Ruth Elizabeth was Harlow's daughter, too: "My passion for order and perfection were unheard of in a child so young. An untied lace on a shoe, a wrinkle on a dress, drove me into a fury."[25] Harlow escorted the girls to the circus one afternoon. Betty, once she noticed it, could not shake away her itchlike awareness that the long carpet runner on which the animals made their entrances was ruined by a crooked seam. It wasn't just a crooked seam to Betty but a fatal, ceaselessly distracting flaw that threatened to take the whole world down into chaos with it.[26] Even as a child, Davis was an odd combination: part hysteric, part obsessive-compulsive, a blend seen as well in some of her most dedicated fans.

Harlow menaced, Ruthie pandered. Bobby, aiming to please, attempted to win Harlow's love by conforming to his expectations, an impossible task for a five-year-old, and a strategy that almost certainly led to her lifelong battle with mental illness. Betty's goal was to steer clear of him on a practical level, though emotionally she never got over the longing—for love, approval, stability, and male control, which of course she also felt compelled to reject, dismiss, ignore, or mock.[27]

When Betty was seven, Ruthie packed their things for a trip to Florida. On their way to the train station, they stopped at the Copley Plaza in Boston. A string orchestra played. Harlow was unusually gentle. Ruthie didn't talk much. Betty was surprised to see her father kiss her mother farewell.

Harlow did not accompany them onto the train. When they arrived in Florida, Ruthie announced that when they returned North they would no longer be living with Daddy. Bobby cried. Betty was relieved and announced, "Now we can go on a picnic and have a baby."[28]

It's not that this Yankee child had no idea about the facts of life that's striking; one assumes she had no such knowledge. No, it's her guileless lack of innocence—that and the joyous sense of a harsh world opening up to its fullest creative potential. Life without Father had become a luscious rose blooming unexpectedly from a bush full of thorns.

After returning from Florida, Ruthie and the girls left Winchester for Newton, another Boston suburb, this one to the west of the city, where the previously impractical mother learned that Harlow's support payments would not be enough to live on. She had to go to work. Grandmother Favor not only made the choice of boarding school for the girls after seeing an ad in the *Atlantic Monthly* but went ahead and enrolled them without telling Ruthie: Crestalban, a farm school in the Berkshires that operated without the benefit of electricity. (The word *Yankee* does not begin to describe the spartan ethos of this school. Crestalban girls took naked snow baths every winter morning and stayed outside most of the day.[29] In the New England mind, this was thought to build character.) Ruthie moved to New York City and became a governess for three Upper East Side boys.[30]

In one of the scrapbooks, two photos of little girls dressed as winged wood sprites in a school play illustrate Crestalban's rustic theme.[31] This might have been Betty Davis's first theatrical performance.

For each of the three years she spent at Crestalban, Betty played Santa Claus in the Christmas pageant. The third year she caught fire. Lacking any twentieth-century source of power, the Crestalban Christmas tree was lighted, of course, by candles. Betty, dressed in red flannel that was pillowed out by a lot of cotton wadding, disobeyed the order not to get near the tree, and her sleeve, then her beard, snagged the flames. Quick-thinking teachers wrapped her in a blanket and put the fire out, but something else ignited: despite her blistering skin, Betty Davis was seized with the dramatic impulse and, for the sake of the effect, kept her eyes closed when they took the blanket away from her face. "I heard one of the teachers wail, 'She's blind! Oh God, she's blind!' I didn't know whether I was blind or not. But I do remember feeling with thrills and chills of morbid pleasure that this was my moment, my big dramatic moment. And I deliberately kept my eyes tight closed and groped helplessly about with my hands until the full savor of that moment was extracted."[32]

Betty Davis's first starring role came to a hasty end when Margery Whiting, the headmistress, insisted that the burned child simply buck up. At Crestalban, it was the better part of puritanical valor not to spoil everyone else's Christmas party by moaning in agony.[33]

Ruthie failed to recognize Betty when she arrived at Grand Central Station for the holiday break, because her face was covered in blisters. An intern at the hospital to which Ruthie sped insisted that the only way to prevent lifelong facial scarring was to keep Betty's skin greased and bandaged round the clock for several weeks.[34] There's a scrapbook photo showing Betty wearing what appears to be a wimple. This was the dramatic effect that the ever inventive Ruthie created by merging acres of facial bandages with a large white bow.[35]

In the 1930s, Margery Whiting, asked about her by-then-famous former pupil, was far too much a New Englander to gush. The crusty lady remembered Ruth Elizabeth Davis as having performed in school plays "capably," but her acting was "not inspired." Miss Whiting characterized the eleven-year-old Betty as much more self-conscious than the other girls, and, said the headmistress, her high-pitched and squeaky voice did not help matters at all. On the plus side from Miss Whiting's perspective was the child's sharp memory and, it might go without saying, young Betty Davis's extraordinary drive.[36]

Belief in herself above all others was the central tenet of Davis's life-long faith, and her mother was the first votary. But in the fall of 1921, Ruthie decided to do something for herself rather than for her head-strong daughter and her younger sister, the afterthought. She pulled the girls out of Crestalban and used what would have been their tuition money for her own: she enrolled herself in the Clarence White School of Photography in New York City. The girls' transition was harsh—from the Berkshires to a tacky apartment on Broadway and 144th Street, from a tiny rustic farm school to P.S. 186 with fifty children in every class.[37]

Ruthie, intent on making something out of nothing, taught the girls how to entertain themselves by spying on neighbors—a sort of *Rear Window* game, free urban entertainment.[38] By December the girls were happily sledding down a hill toward the Hudson, adjusted to life in the city.[39] And Ruthie, seeing a future for herself in commercial art, was learning the intricacies of lighting, shading, composition, and chemical developing. The pictures she took before her formal training already demonstrated a natural flair, but with training Ruthie could do more than simply *be* a visual artist. She could support her family as one.

In New York, Ruth Elizabeth Davis became a Girl Scout. Vehemently. As you would expect, she rose rapidly to the rank of patrol leader and commanded her girls like a drill sergeant. There was a contest—a competitive dress parade for Mrs. Herbert Hoover at Madison Square Garden—and Ruth Elizabeth's patrol necessarily won. When she entered a citywide cooking contest sponsored by the Board of Education, naturally she earned first prize.[40] Nothing else would do.

A home economics notebook survives in the archives.

Betty Davis, PS 186.
530 West 144th St.
13 1/2 years old
5' 2.5"
97 pounds. What I should weigh: 107 pounds.
How to keep ourselves and others strong:

1. Keep body clean inside and outside.
2. Eat the right kind of food.

3. Exercise regularly in the open air.
4. Care of teeth, etc.

The notebook also contains recipes for cream soups and chocolate pudding as well as instructions on the proper care of babies.[41]

Ruthie had a friend in New York, the improbably named Myrtis Genthner. Myrtis Genthner was reading a French novel at one point and casually suggested to Ruth Elizabeth that she change the spelling of her nickname, and with that, Betty turned into Bette. "The fact that M. Balzac's Lisbeth Fischer was a horror didn't come to my attention until I read the book some time later," Miss Davis observed. Bette wrote a letter to her father soon thereafter and employed the new spelling when she signed her name. Harlow mocked the change, of course, and by dismissing it, he hammered it into permanence.[42] Of course.

The novelist and critic Brigid Brophy remarked of Bette Davis's rechristening, "Perhaps the change of name has as much ritualistic significance in the psychology of a star as in that of a dictator—or of a nun taking the veil."[43] Betty is everyday, Bette eccentric. Betty is a homey dessert. Bette is resplendent, all but unique. With the change to Bette, an even more dramatic persona began to emerge.

THE FOLLOWING SUMMER, Ruthie sent the girls to Camp Mudjekeewis in Fryeburg, Maine, close to the New Hampshire border, for the first of three summers. It was considered a wholesome dose of brisk northern air—swimming, hiking, canoeing. The camp, named for Hiawatha's father, was operated by the Misses Perkins and Pride. The latter, a piano teacher from East Orange, New Jersey, was so impressed by Bobby Davis's native talent as a pianist that she convinced Ruthie to move to New Jersey at the end of the summer so that Bobby could continue her lessons. [44] For once excited by her younger daughter's talent, Ruthie moved them all into an East Orange boardinghouse.

Bette, shocked at finding herself out of the spotlight, made a point of being bored and obnoxious. Bobby was getting the attention she believed was owed solely to her, and she resented it.

Ruthie was, as she herself described it, "petrified" of Bette. Bossy and unmanageable in East Orange, Bette took everything out on her mother. The slightest suggestion—what to wear, how to behave—provoked piercing, theatrical glares. Bette held Ruthie's nervous giggle in severe condescension, and she let Ruthie know it. Even the doting Ruthie grew exasperated to the point that she suggested a new game one day: she and Bette would exchange clothes and personalities for the evening. Bette was mildly entertained until the accuracy of Ruthie's performance struck her. She had to admit that the glum sulks and furious scowls were hers. Ruthie was especially shrewd in that she played this game out in front of the other boarders at the communal dining table, which only added to Bette's shameful self-recognition: Bette learned that the way she presented herself to the world was at least as important as how she actually felt.[45]

According to Bette, her behavior improved somewhat, but she remained essentially miserable in New Jersey. So Ruthie placated her. Mother terminated Bobby's piano lessons with Miss Pride, and they moved again—this time to the Boston suburb of Newton, where Ruthie's sister Mildred lived.

There was another reason for the move: Ruthie had to quit her job at Pierie MacDonald's photography studio in Manhattan because she developed osteomyelitis of the jaw, an incapacitatingly painful bone inflammation, and she needed her sister's help in caring for the children.[46] Bette neglects to mention this detail in The Lonely Life. How odd that Davis chose to represent herself as selfish and manipulative instead of legitimately citing her mother's illness as the rationale for their move back to Massachusetts.

The soundstage is set. One of the sisters went crazy from time to time. The other became an actress.

Bette's first school dance at Newton High School: a disaster. Clad in a corduroy jumper and having given no thought to her hair, shoes, or dancing ability, she was not the ball's belle. One boy danced with her for mercy's sake but soon began gesturing frantically to the other boys in an effort to convince one of them to cut in. Nobody did; Bette thought perhaps the boy was spastic. When she figured it out, she rushed home in tears. For the next dance, Ruthie came to the rescue with a new white chiffon dress with turquoise trim and a daringly low neckline. Bette was fourteen at the time. When she put her hair up, she realized—to her horror, she later claimed—that she was pretty.

The young Bette Davis was a prude and remained so until she got to Hollywood and saw how much fun other people were having and finally decided to join in. She attributed this straitlaced self-denial to her family's strict Protestant nature, which her parents had inherited from *their* parents, and back through the generations. When a boy first kissed her, she became convinced that she was pregnant.[47] After all, she descended, she claimed, from a Pilgrim, James Davis, who accused a fellow member of his community of witchcraft. (The Favors, on the other hand, were originally Huguenots—French Protestants who, unlike the Puritan Pilgrims, left room for the arts. Still, there was a strong strain of righteousness on the Favor side. Bette's great-great-grandmother's tombstone reads "Bearing the White Lily of an Unsullied Life.")

In the fall of 1924, Ruthie uprooted the girls once more by putting them in boarding school again. Stability was not a feature of Bette Davis's upbringing, which led to an unresolvable ambivalence: a powerful longing to settle and an equally strong compulsion to move.

This time Ruthie chose the Northfield Seminary for Young Ladies, which had the dual benefit of being the only fully integrated private school around and also cheap.[48] Bette and Bobby both hated the seminary's overly religious nature, and having gotten used to public school, they resented the amount of time they spent on housekeeping (never a problem at Crestalban). The food, too, was awful. At the end of the first semester Ruthie yanked them once more. They adjourned to Uncle Myron's for Christmas, and after the holidays, Ruthie packed them off to Cushing Academy in Ashburnham. It was the school Ruthie herself had attended.[49]

Cushing Academy was, and remains, a classic New England preparatory school, having none of the eccentricity of Crestalban, none of the racial integration of Northfield, and certainly none of a public school's working class. One day early on at Cushing, Bette was called in by the headmaster's wife, who began extolling Ruthie's self-sacrificial virtues to a perplexed Bette, who at first comprehended the woman's praise of her mother as a reflection of her own fine nature. "And she is blessed in having a lovely and generous daughter," the woman continued, only to add an unexpected stinger at the end: "I think it would be splendid if you would help her with your expenses by waiting on table." Bette was mortified: "My face burned with indignation but, fortunately, I held my tongue, for instantly I realized that mother would not permit me to demean myself by becoming a waitress." She wrote to Ruthie with the news, fully expecting to receive the kind of self-martyred mothering response to which Bette had grown accustomed. But Ruthie, evidently tired and struggling, was for once willing to share the burden: "That's very sweet of you," she wrote. "Go ahead."

Bette was, as she later described herself, "humiliated and admittedly belligerent" when she reported to the dining room. She was hardly an experienced server in any sense of the word, and the first few days were hell. It was never easy for Bette Davis to be brought down a peg or two, but after the bruises healed, such experiences came to serve as self-defining life lessons, parables for the less fortunate. In this case, Bette smugly became less of a snob.[50]

Bette Davis's day at Cushing Academy, 1925–26: Rising bell at 7:00 a.m., breakfast at 7:30. Chapel at 8:30, though attendance may not have been required. English IV at 8:50, Latin IV at 9:45, Math IV at 10:30. After lunch: Ancient History at 1:15, at 2:00 French III, and, on Fridays, Bible II at 2:50.[51]

On June 12, 1926, Bette Davis appeared onstage at the Cowell Chapel in the play *The Charm School*, presented by Cushing's senior class in conjunction with the Drama Club. Bette played the part of Elise, the president of the senior class at a school much like Cushing. Harmon O. "Ham" Nelson's Syncopators provided the music.[52]

From the Cushing Academy *Breeze*, June 1926:

> *One of the fairest girls we know*
> *Is Bette Davis—"Ham" says so.*

Bette may be the busiest girl in the senior class, but she is never too busy to help out when she is asked. Her giggle is a delight far more pleasing than the "laughing" record on the "vic." Bette's talents are numerous, for she has a lovely voice, is the best actress, and the class beauty—what more could anyone wish? She is undecided about what she is going to do next year, but the school she picks out will be lucky! Minervian; Vice-President; President, Comrade Club; Glee Club; Student Council; *Breeze* staff; Expression Play; "Vanities"; Senior Play.[53]

More from the *Breeze*:

Harmon O. Nelson, Jr. "Ham." July 5, 1907. Ham came to us from Northbridge High School, wherever that may be. . . . We know his acting in *Seventeen* was superb, and we also know a certain girl who likes "Ham" without the eggs.

Harmon Oscar Nelson's nickname was clearly the subject of much hilarity around the halls of Cushing. For her senior gift, Bette's classmates presented her with a sixteen pound, twelve ouncer, the wrapping of which she carefully preserved in one of the scrapbooks now archived at Boston University: "Armour's Skinned Ham—'the ham what am.'"[54]

As she knew better than anyone (although those who felt the lash might disagree), Bette Davis held fast to a set of righteous beliefs, a roster of strict and unshakable values that saw her through from childhood to old age. With the unyielding tenacity of her Yankee forebears, she bore what the writer James McCourt called a "desire for rectitude" that was based on a bedrock of puritanism. The parameters of right living began to stretch in the 1930s, but even after her liberalization by Hollywood, Bette Davis lived her life as though her ancestors had placed an heirloom yardstick against her spine and demanded that she stand up straight at all times. Bad posture in others was scarcely tolerated either. And yet, McCourt added, "she was so expansive."[55] In other words, Davis was an upright bluenose but a flamingly theatrical one, her passions burning as fiercely as her stringent sense of probity.

Hers was an upbringing of stern but detached pressure, although (or maybe as a consequence) she was possessed with pent-up drives that eventually found expression onstage, onscreen, and in bed. The latter was the last of the three to emerge. She let loose as a performer well before she unleashed herself sexually, and even so she ended her life as she began it—by demanding but inevitably distrusting male control.

As so often is the case, the cliché that begs most loudly to be disproved turns out to be unavoidably true: her father set the course for Bette's relationships with men. The problematic star of the defining first scene, Harlow M. Davis was, as Bette's uncle, Paul Favor, once wrote, a "man who revealed his deepest feelings to few people and who wore a habitual mask of indifference."[56] Although Bette claims to have expressed delight at his departure from her family at the time and certainly did so consistently for decades to come, her father's abandonment resonated throughout her life in ways she herself never fully understood, let alone acknowledged. A lifelong sense of loss and a thorough ignorance of sex in her youth combined to forge her uneasy development from a hurt little girl who necessarily if unconsciously blamed herself for her father's departure to an angry and defiant woman who necessarily blamed everyone else for everything.

Harlow was a distant, unapproachable man whose rare physical contact with his daughter took such a grudging form that even the single incident of physical punishment wasn't his idea: "Daddy spanked me only once and at Ruthie's request," Bette writes in *The Lonely Life*. She and Bobby had eaten some unripe grapes, an infraction that Ruthie felt required an unusual degree of discipline. "I gave them castor oil," Ruthie told the head of the house. "*You* can give them a spanking."[57] The abuse Bette's father doled out at other times was emotional, not physical, and it resulted in lifelong bruises that couldn't possibly heal because they were so rarely acknowledged.

Harlow was cold, detached, glacial—and yet this asthmatic man of pure reason had been caught having an affair with his nurse. That was why the marriage ended. Her name was Minnie Stewart, and she became the second Mrs. Davis.[58] Only late in life did Bette acknowledge Ruthie's role in Harlow's abandonment; at that point she was able to recognize her mother's behavior as her own. As she told James McCourt in the 1980s, "Of course she drove him mad; I see that. I did the same."[59]

Ruthie's brother Paul took Harlow's place as a paternal figure. From patent lawyer to pastor, Uncle Paul gave sermons for a living. "In our early years we were very much under the influence of our uncle, Dr. Paul Favor, an Episcopalian minister, and we attended church and Sunday school with the fidelity of Puritans. We were reared in the strict New England manner, with one eye always to God."[60] The other eye, in similar Yankee style, was earnestly focused on high principles of a mortal variety.

Failure to live up to standards could be cause for panic. She got a kiss on the way home from a drugstore soda counter one summer in Southwest Harbor, Maine, where Ruthie had taken a rental. "Every day I walked to the pharmacy, not necessarily for an ice cream soda." She was walking for a boy named Francis Young. "Every day, he would come to where I was sitting and ask if I wanted an ice cream soda. I would order one and just look across the counter at his beautiful brown eyes. He walked me home one day and kissed me."[61] This innocent gesture was the occasion of the pregnancy scare: after the kiss, Bette became hysterical and clinically so, her belly actually swelling in response to her guilt-ridden pleasure.[62]

Later, there were Newton High School dances and invitations to bridge parties and socials.

To meet Miss Virginia Day
Miss Virginia Farnum
Requests the pleasure of your company
At a Bridge Party
On Friday the twenty-eighth of December
At two-thirty o'clock
Eleven Gibson Road, Newtonville[63]

This was the way things were done; this was the world whose strict rules of etiquette she adopted. The twenties may have roared elsewhere, but not in Newton or Ashburnham, and not for Bette Davis, who continued to employ *Miss* and *Mr.* throughout her life, well after the rest of Hollywood was on a first-name basis with stars and directors they'd never met.

Rectitude aside, there was the conventional boy-crazy phase. Before Ham Nelson, there was "Gige" (George J. Dunham), the son of the president of Standard Steel Motor Car Co. in Boston; and during Gige there was Warren (J. Warren Blake). Before any of these boys there were the senior football players at Newton High whose advances Bette spurned and who retaliated by leaving her, in the seniors' will, "two dozen handkerchiefs to blow her 'no's' with." "I cried for hours in humiliation," Davis later wrote, but her humiliation wasn't enough to make her say yes to anyone but Ham, and that was only on their wedding night in 1932.[64]

At Cushing, Ham gave Bette his pin, which she kept until the summer Ruthie took the girls to Perkins Cove on the Maine coast, where Bette fell for a Yalie named Fritz Hall, at which point she returned the pin to Ham.[65] But it wasn't Fritz with whom Bette went on her first unchaperoned date that summer. An unnamed youth took her to a dance in Kennebunkport with some of his friends, and they all got roaring drunk, including the driver. Ruthie, said by Bette to have possessed "great psychic powers" but who was actually more of a magnificent worrier whose fears were periodically founded, begged one of Bette's young friends to rush to Kennebunkport and spirit Bette home to safety. According to Bette, the boy who took her on the date arrived the next morning to report that the driver had indeed crashed the car on the way home. "Bette would most likely have been killed!" the boy is said to have declared.[66]

Another young man, an aspiring actor, recalled meeting Bette in

1927. His friend Hunter Scott, whom he described as "a typical F. Scott Fitzgerald character [who] never bothered to get engaged," picked up the actor outside the Ziegfeld Theater one afternoon in a Packard convertible. In the car were "a Mrs. Davis and her two daughters." Hunter was courting Bobby Davis at the time and invited them all down to Princeton for the weekend. Scott suggested that he and the actor, Henry Fonda, score their experiences, despite the fifth-wheel presence of their pal Frank "Worms" Grubbs. The following evening, Hunter asked Ruthie for permission to take Bette and Bobby to the Princeton stadium for a moonlight tour. Ruthie, described by Fonda as "a stern New England lady," acquiesced. Hunter led Bobby off into the darkness, leaving Henry and Bette in the car—and Worms unaccounted for.

Fonda wrote in his autobiography,

> I sat there thinking, "I've got to kiss her. I've got to!" She looked up at me with those enormous saucerlike eyes and what the hell. [I] sort of leaned over and gave her a peck on the lips—not a real kiss, but what a relief to me. One point! I felt like Casanova.
>
> [Later,] I received a letter that my date had written on the train. . . . It said, "I've told Mother about our lovely experience together in the moonlight. She will announce the engagement when we get home." It was signed, "Bette Davis."
>
> "Holy shit," I thought. "One kiss and I'm engaged." That's how naïve I was. And that's what a devil Bette Davis could be at seventeen. For years, whenever I saw Bette Davis I'd give her a wide berth.[67]

Bette herself recalled the scene somewhat differently, or maybe she was just exercising Yankee discretion: "Perhaps we discussed, that night, our hopes for the future. Perhaps we necked. I don't remember."[68] A calling card affixed in one of Davis's scrapbooks reads simply "Henry Jaynes Fonda."[69]

2

LESSONS

John Murray Anderson—Robert Milton School of the
Theatre and Dance
128-130 East 58th St.
Plaza 4524
New York

Owned and operated by the Park Avenue Theatre
Corporation

October 19, 1927

Enrollment Contract

I hereby enroll in the Anderson-Milton School of the
Theatre and Dance as a Dram. (Jr.) Student for a course of
four months (less 3 weeks) beginning on Oct. 24. 1927 and
terminating on Jan. 31. 1928.

Miss Bette Davis, age 19
c/o Rev. Paul G. Favor
22 Westminster Court
New Rochelle, NY

(Signed) John Murray Anderson[1]

JOHN MURRAY ANDERSON WAS *COMME*
ça—a beautifully dressed, finely mannered man of the theater in the
style of Clifton Webb. The composer Sheldon Harnick tells a classic
story about him: Anderson was once directing a rodeo out West when
someone let the wild bulls out of their pen before their proper cue. "*No,
no, no!*" Anderson shrieked. "Get back in the pens! It's not *time* yet!" In
Anderson's theatrical imagination, charging bulls and errant chorus
girls were essentially the same animal.[2]

The Anderson-Milton School was not Bette Davis's first choice for dramatic education in New York City. She held it against Eva Le Gallienne
until the day she died that Le Gallienne rejected her application to attend
the august actress's Civic Repertory Company, on Fourteenth Street in
Manhattan, where young actors received free tuition in exchange for taking roles in the company's productions. According to Davis, she was pan-
icky at her first professional audition—and especially so in her skittish,
electric youth, when life was a series of high-voltage moments on which
existence itself depended. Le Gallienne asked her to read the part of a
sixty-five-year-old Dutch woman. It was a showy, stupid request meant to
intimidate rather than teach, and Bette sensibly replied that that was why
she wanted to go to drama school—"to learn how to play a part like this."
Le Gallienne reacted with stony silence. Bette performed as well as she
could, and Le Gallienne thanked her with forced politeness and promptly
dismissed her, calling her "a frivolous little girl."[3] (One of Davis's other biographers, Barbara Leaming, insists that it was Le Gallienne's secretary
who actually conducted the audition, but no matter.)[4]

Davis had been treated much better, and received far more nurturing,
during the summer she spent in Peterborough, New Hampshire, where
Ruthie had opened a photography studio, the Silhouette Shop. This was
between her junior and senior years at Cushing—the summer of 1925.
There were two summer dance and theater programs in Peterborough at
the time: Mariarden, where the exotic Roshanara taught dance, and the
cheaper Out-Door Players, run by Marie Ware Laughton.[5] Bette was accepted at Mariarden, but Ruthie couldn't afford the tuition, so she began
her studies at the Out-Door Players, where she learned, as she later put
it, "nature dances à la Isadora Duncan."[6] But Roshanara attended one of
Bette's early performances and was so impressed by the girl's natural
gift for movement that she agreed to take her on as a student at

Mariarden—provided that Bobby Davis would earn Bette's tuition by playing the piano for rehearsals.

"Bobby was thrilled with the opportunity to contribute to the family exchequer and very expertly played for Roshanara's classes that summer," Bette writes in *The Lonely Life*, achieving on paper a balance of admission and denial so precarious that one wonders if she sustained it equally unstably in her mind. As it actually happened, Bobby didn't play for Roshanara herself at Mariarden but rather for one of Roshanara's protégées in the dank basement of a church twenty miles away in Keene.[7] Bluntly stated, Bobby was now working for Bette, as she would continue to do on and off for the rest of her life.

There are scrapbook photographs of Roshanara, who was in fact a round-faced Irishwoman named Olive Craddock. In one, she's bareheaded and wrapped in layers of sarilike silk; in another, she's got a nunlike Mother Teresa scarf over her head. In still another, she's clad in a drastically wide-sleeved cloak and a turban.[8] Still, Olive Craddock came by her adopted Indian identity honestly; she was born in Calcutta, the daughter of an officer in the British army.[9]

Roshanara, who died the following year, gave Bette her first formal lessons in the art of bodily motion, the use of one's physical being to express fluid, ephemeral emotions that words would be incapable of pinning down. Any mildly proficient performer can utter the line "*I don't mind,*" as Davis does in *Of Human Bondage*, but without the particular stretch of the neck and cock of the head, the line would lack its irritating, brittle authority. Even in her first moment in her first movie, *Bad Sister*, Davis holds a stack of plates just a bit too high, an essentially choreographic strategy that not only compels her audience's attention but reveals, clearly but nonverbally, the primness of her character.

At Mariarden, Davis's lessons in motion had a more graphic, less narrative end. One of Ruthie's art photos shows Bette performing as "The Moth": a swirl of white fabric, angular at the top as the material flies straight out like a plate, but rounds itself and swirls at the bottom, like a fluent wing.

After the Le Gallienne rejection and Bette's brief period of despair in Norwalk, Connecticut, Ruthie marched into the Anderson-Murray School and told Hugh Anderson, the director's brother and the academy's manager, "My daughter wants to go to your school. I have no money. You'll have to let me pay her tuition as I can."[10] According to Davis, Anderson "was so stupefied by Ruthie's guts that before he knew it he had said yes." They returned to Norwalk, packed their things, and moved to the city the following day.[11]

By the time she got to Anderson's school, Bette Davis possessed some basic dramatic skills and an even more basic natural flair. At eighteen, she was a small, odd beauty. Standing at five feet, two inches, she had a dynamic presence far greater than her physical stature. Ruthie's high school graduation portrait of Bette shows a smart white fur collar framing an improbably boyish face that's sharply feminized by two huge, magnetic eyes directed slightly off to the left. Her hair is styled in waves and parted on the right, a single curl jutting provocatively over her cheek. In Davis's physicality alone, Anderson saw what Le Gallienne (or her secretary) missed, and so Bette Davis began her formal dramatic education sympathetically.

Claiming he could never remember anybody's name, Anderson called everyone by the nicknames he bestowed upon them. Staunch New Englander that she was, Bette's was "the little Southern girl."[12] Perhaps she earned the nickname because of the successfully subtle accent she perfected in imitation of her new best friend, Marie Simpson, the West Virginian she met at Ogunquit, Maine, the previous summer. Simpson, who was working as a waitress at Ogunquit and who later changed her name to Robin, remained an almost lifelong friend.

After installing Bette in an East Fifty-eighth Street rooming house next to the Anderson-Milton academy, Ruthie took a job as housemother of St. Mary's School in Burlington, New Jersey, on the other side of Trenton.[13] Bobby was removed from Cushing and sent back to Newton High to save the tuition. She lived with her aunt.

George Currie, one of the faculty at the Anderson school, began his instruction appropriately with a pedagogy of hopelessness. He told his class on the first day of school, as Bette later wrote, "that we were heading for the toughest, least glamorous life imaginable. His picture of the artist's life was a pointillism whose dots of color were sweat, jealousy, competition, disillusionment, insecurity, and more sweat."[14] "Any artist who doesn't know that the greatest reward is his own satisfaction in work should choose an easier way of life," Currie told his impressionable students.[15] The theme of dashed dreams formed the backbone of Currie's syllabus. As Davis described him, "George Currie did little other than lecture his class on the futility of the theater. Day after day he emphasized what a dreadful place it was. By the time the semester ended, fully thirty pupils had dropped out."[16]

Other faculty at Anderson's school included Michael Mordkin, Robert Bell, John Murray Anderson himself, and a dance instructor, Martha Graham, whose technique, which became famous as "contraction and release," focused on the back and shoulders, all toward the goal of precise expression and startling, percussive movements.[17] "What she said to us," Bette told James McCourt, "was: 'Think of acting exactly like a ballet' . . . by which she meant that acting had to have a continuity of movement in both voice and body—everything smoothly connected."[18]

"To act is to dance," said Graham to her students. Bette adored her. "She was all tension—lightning! Her burning dedication gave her spare body the power of ten men. If Roshanara was a mystic curve, Miss Graham was a straight line—a divining rod." Later, after Davis became a movie star, Graham is said (by Davis) to have admired Davis's ability to express "an emotion with full body, as a dancer does. If this be so, I would like to remind her that it was she who made it possible. Every time I climbed a flight of stairs in films—and I spent half my life on them—it was Graham, step by step."[19]

As for Bette's voice, the high squeal decried by Crestalban's Margery Whiting lowered considerably thanks to an elocution class. As Anderson himself declared, "Remember that voice a month ago? Well, listen to it now!"[20]

Because Hollywood called in late 1930, Davis never got a chance to become the grand dame of the theater she imagined in her youth. And she quickly accustomed herself to the brief but intense bursts of acting—and long stretches of setup time—required by the camera, the cinematographer and electricians, the sound crew, the makeup artists, the director, and everyone else involved in the construction of a film. Between drama school and the Universal and Warner Bros. lots, Bette Davis got only a taste of the physical, live, do-it-all-again-tomorrow reiterations of the theater. Her relative inexperience with the paradoxical exhilaration and tedium of performing on a stage in front of an audience would come back to haunt her.

As one might expect with Bette Davis, there was drama with the dramas. "It was a dark and stormy night in Macdougal Street," the critic Robert Garland wrote of March 5, 1929, the evening of Bette Davis's Off-Broadway debut in *The Earth Between*. Produced by the Provincetown Playhouse, the play, as Garland felicitously described it, "deals with the jolly old Oedipus complex in two acts and eight scenes." "Bette Davis did well as Floy," he noted; "Miss Davis is nice to look at, too." The critic Burns Mantle of the *Daily News* called her "a wraith of a child with true emotional insight." But it was Brooks Atkinson of the *New York Times* who offered the most astounding assessment—astounding in retrospect, that is: "Miss Bette Davis, who is making her first appearance, is an enchanting creature *who plays in a soft, unassertive style*."[21]

The Earth Between is about a Nebraska farmer's incestuous desire for his sixteen-year-old daughter, played by Bette. She was just shy of twenty-one at the time and had to have the theme spelled out for her. "It did seem to me when I read the play that the widowed father's compensative demands on the child were excessive, but it never occurred to me for one moment just how fully he wanted her to replace her mother. I had never bumped into Oedipus at dear old Cushing—and certainly never in Winchester. *My* father didn't even like me!"[22]

Even the most benign form of paternal love may not have been prominent in Harlow Davis's emotional repertoire, but he was dutiful on the occasion of Bette's opening night. He sent a bouquet of flowers and a note. Her uncle, Paul Favor, who attended the opening-night performance with Ruthie, noted in a letter that "she had enough flowers for a funeral, including a large basket of roses, jonquils, etc. from Harlow and a telegram from him." The Reverend Favor went on: "I met some of the so-called leaders of the stage, producers, managers, and so on, and one of them assured me that Betty was considered to have a great future. She seems well but is thin and looks frail."[23]

Bette received her first fan letters thanks to *The Earth Between*. "One was from an unholy student at Holy Cross," she wryly commented.[24]

The Earth Between was the reason Bette left drama school before completing her full course of study. In fact, she turned down a scholarship at the Anderson-Milton academy to prepare for the play, and she did so with the full blessing of Hugh Anderson, who thought the opportunity to make her professional debut at the Provincetown Playhouse was a risk worth taking. But as it happened, the production of *The Earth Between* was postponed for a full year after Bette dropped out of school. For Bette, it was a year of struggle, frustration, despair, and terror, with intermittent fits of glory. It was a high-strung twenty-year-old girl's first exposure to professional theater.

With the help of Mariarden's Frank Conroy, Bette first found acting work in Rochester, New York, where George Cukor, then in his late twenties, was directing a show called *Broadway* and needed someone for a tiny role. Ruthie, once again credited by Bette with the possession of clairvoyance, advised her at the train station on April 27, 1928, to take pains to learn the role of Pearl, because she, Ruthie, sensed that something wonderfully dreadful would happen to the actress playing that part. "Monday and Tuesday were uneventful," Davis later wrote of the first week of *Broadway*'s run. "By Wednesday we had slipped into the routine of the performance. Then, during the matinee, it happened. Miss Lerner fell during the second act. . . . She played that night on crutches." Cukor replaced her with Bette.

Pearl had one great moment: she got to fire two gunshots at her lover, who was then to stagger offstage and die, neatly and safely, in the wings. But Bette, who was particularly jittery one night, her fear of guns compounding her stage fright, kept pulling the trigger so quickly and repeatedly that she practically machine-gunned the poor fellow, who had no actorly choice but to drop dead in the middle of the stage and hold his breath for the rest of the act.[25] On a more serious note, Barbara Leaming reports that Cukor was impressed with Bette's performance and its "many heightening touches, such as the odd dancelike rhythm that made it seem almost as if she were willing her victim to die."[26]

When *Broadway*'s run ended, Bette returned to New York. She found no acting work there, but she did convince a man who was connected with the Cape Playhouse, a summer stock company in Dennis, Massachusetts, to hire her. She, Ruthie, and Bobby sped to Cape Cod only to be informed that the guy in New York lacked the authority to hire actors and that all the acting slots were full. But, they told her, she could be an usher if she wanted. And so Bette Davis spent most of the summer of 1928 showing patrons to their seats and watching other actors do what she knew she could do at least as well herself.

The season was nearly over when Laura Hope Crews showed up to appear in A. A. Milne's *Mr. Pim Passes By*. Crews told Bette—who had made it naggingly clear to everyone all summer long that she would be much happier onstage than handing out programs—that she would be granted a small role in the show if she learned to play the song "I Passed By Your Window." The only trouble was that nobody but Crews knew the song, and Crews wasn't singing. Spurred by a pleading and histrionic Bette, Ruthie scoured the Cape and found what may have been the only copy of the obscure melody in the possession of a church organist in Hyannis who agreed to teach it to Bette on his piano. "We stayed there until three in the morning while I learned the music," Bette recalled.[27] Crews (who went on to achieve her greatest fame as Aunt Pittypat Hamilton in *Gone with the Wind*) found Bette to be fidgety onstage—no surprise there—and commanded her to keep her arms at her sides, still. Immobility was impossible for Bette Davis, especially in the earliest stage of her career. "Came the day of dress rehearsal and its accompanying excitement. The play ran off well and I kept myself in hand until the third act. Then, involuntarily, I moved my arm perhaps twelve inches. A slap brought my arm down to its proper limp position and I turned to see [Crews], impassive and unconcerned, continue with her lines. My face burned, and I must have counted to ninety-five before I regained control of myself. . . . The blow may have been a major tragedy when it was delivered. Time and a degree of success have made it seem awfully unimportant," though not so immaterial as to escape retelling in several of Davis's memoirs.[28]

Bette returned to Rochester in the fall of 1928, this time with Ruthie and their atrociously named dog, Boogum, the three of them having deposited Bobby at Denison College in Ohio on their roundabout trip from Cape Cod to upstate New York. Cukor and his producing partner, George Kondolf, had formed the Temple Players, named after the Rochester theater in which their plays were to be performed, and they hired Bette to appear in the company's first production: a vaudeville story called *Excess Baggage*. In Bette's words, the play was about "a tightrope walker and his pretty wife, who stood about in spangles."[29] Wallace Ford played the tightrope walker; Miriam Hopkins was the pretty wife.

Bette was enchanted with Hopkins—at first. "Miriam was the prettiest golden-haired blonde I had ever seen," Davis later wrote. "I will never forget her before a performance—emerging from a shower and simply tossing her curly hair dry. She was the envy of us all."[30] But Davis soon grew resentful of Hopkins, as the other actors also did, for Hopkins had an annoying compulsion to steal scenes by whatever means necessary. An actor would speak, and Hopkins would pointedly move during the middle of the line; an actress would build to an important gesture, and Hopkins would beat her to it—anything to distract the audience's attention from her fellow performers.

Hopkins didn't particularly take to Bette, either. One day during a rehearsal, she stopped in midscene, pointed to Bette, and screeched, "She's stepping on my lines! The bitch doesn't know her place! *I'm* the star of this show—not that little nobody!"[31]

Other productions at the Temple Players included *Cradle Snatchers* (one Rochester newspaper printed a photo of "the little blonde who is seen in this week's production"); *Laff That Off*; *The Squall*; *The Man Who Came Back*; and *Yellow*, which had a cast of forty and starred Louis Calhern. Bette played Calhern's girlfriend—an odd bit of casting on Cukor's part, since Calhern was six foot four and thirteen years older than Bette. As Calhern put it, "She looks more like my kid than my mistress." Other trouble was brewing as well. As Bette herself admitted, "I was apt to be a know-it-all. When Mr. Cukor criticized my work, I would always have a reason as to why I did it my way. I alibied."[32] There was still another problem: Bette's puritanical rectitude. She grew into a famously and frankly foulmouthed woman, a cigarette-dragging, liquor-swilling curser, but even at the age of seventy-four, and speaking to *Playboy* (of all publications), she couldn't bring herself to speak of the publicly unspeakable: "I didn't live up to what was expected in those days of a stock company ingénue, who had *other* duties—you know what I'm talking about. Socializing. Socializing very seriously, let us say, with people in the company. That was just not my cup of tea."[33]

And so, during a final rehearsal for *Yellow*, "the stage manager came to me and said, 'We won't need you after this show.' It was so abrupt, so without warning, that I did not have time to be angry. All I could do was ask a simple, 'Why?' 'Cukor says you won't be needed any more,' he repeated, and nothing I said brought additional information."[34]

Louis Calhern saw no need to mince words. Bette Davis, he said, just wouldn't "put out."[35]

It obviously wasn't George Cukor who expected sexual favors from Bette. It was his straight producer, George Kondolf. But long after the actress had become a movie star and the director one of Hollywood's most successful creative forces, Bette continued to blame Cukor for her dismissal. And Cukor grew increasingly cranky at the mention of it. "She does not let me forget it," he once complained to the gossipmistress Sheilah Graham. "She keeps telling the story! I find it a great bore."[36]

Bette returned to New York and found a tiny apartment on Eighth Street in Greenwich Village with her friend from Ogunquit, Robin Simpson. "Bette's mother was around, too, I remember," Robin's sister Reggie later recalled. "It must have been a little crowded."[37] The two young women later moved to midtown: an apartment on East Fifty-third Street.

The comedy *Broken Dishes* served as Bette's Broadway debut: harried husband Donald Meek grows a backbone after he gets plastered enough to square off against what one critic described as his "brigadier-general wife," with Bette playing his sympathetic daughter. After tryouts on Long Island and at Werba's Brooklyn (a theater at the corner of Flatbush and Fulton), *Broken Dishes* opened at the Ritz Theatre on West Forty-eighth Street on November 5, 1929. "Miss Davis was easy on the eyes," wrote the reviewer for the *Evening World*.[38] "Bette Davis, a young actress who would be a better one if she elected to spell her Christian name less self-consciously, is a member of the cast," another critic opined.

The *Evening Graphic*'s "Daily Physical Culture Page" of November 5, 1929, featured a triptych of Bette and Ellen Lowe, one of her cast mates, demonstrating a series of exercises. "Should a man propose to a girl on his knees?" Lowe asks in a bubble in the first frame as Bette suspends herself in a sort of a crab posture with her back and torso flat. "I should think the girl would like it." Bette, now upright and stretching her left leg out, replies. "But if the man doesn't?" "Then he can ask her to get off, can't he?" Ellen bizarrely answers as Bette shifts legs.[39] "Physical culture" indeed. It was a glorified skin show. Broadway's publicity was every bit as crass as Hollywood's.

In January 1930, *Broken Dishes* shifted to the Theatre Masque (later renamed the Golden) on West Forty-fifth Street and continued running for a total of 178 performances before closing in April 1930 to prepare for a tour. The production moved in May to the Wilbur Theatre in Boston and then went on hiatus for the summer, which Bette spent doing stock at the Cape Playhouse.

Broken Dishes picked up again in September 1930, with performances in Baltimore and Washington, D.C. On September 25, the cast made a personal appearance at the Rosedale Airport. "The entire company is enthusiastic about aviation," an ad declared.

During the play's run in Washington, Bette got a call from the play's producer, Oscar Serlin, who wanted to replace the ingenue in his new production, *Solid South*, starring Richard Bennett, a notoriously temperamental actor (and the father of Constance, Joan, and Barbara). She took the job.[40]

Directed by Rouben Mamoulian, *Solid South* opened on October 14, 1930, at the Lyceum Theatre. Bette played "Alabama" Follensby; Bennett was her grandfather, the major. Jesse Royce Landis played her widowed mother. "Richard Bennett Called Bette Ham, Got Face Slapped," a later gossip headline trumpeted. "Are you another of these young ham actresses?" Bennett reportedly asked Bette when they met, so she slapped him.[41] Davis herself tells a much more benign version in *The Lonely Life*: Bennett said, "So! You're one of those actresses who think all they need are eyes to act. My daughters are the same." "Mr. Bennett," Bette properly responded, "I'm very happy to return to Washington immediately." "You'll do," Bennett replied, laughing. According to Bette, "from then on in, he and I were the best of friends."[42]

Solid South was not so solid. The critic John Mason Brown wrote that the play "came bearing no more direct relation to actuality than a cartoon does to life." Burns Mantle called the play "a somewhat ironic, deliberately satirical, fairly extravagant study of a slightly demented major."[43] The critics were especially hard on Bennett, but Davis wasn't spared either. "This attempt to learn a Southern speech fell very flat with Miss Bette Davis, sweet Broadway child that she may be," the *New Republic* observed. "She [and Owen Davis Jr.] struggled with the problem of how to be interesting as nobodies. . . . Miss Davis achieved that cereal quality that the roles of pure girls on Broadway are taken to represent."[44]

Solid South closed in November, and Davis didn't appear again on Broadway for another twenty-two years. After all, as a gossip columnist had noted a few months earlier, "Talkies want Donald Meek of *Broken Dishes*. Also want Bette Davis."[45]

3

A Yankee in Hollywood

A CHUBBY, OVERLY CHEERY FATHER from the Booth Tarkington Midwest takes a newspaper from the paper-boy at the front door of his house at Universal Pictures and walks into a large dining room. The camera swings back and to the left to reveal a very blonde, very young Bette Davis carefully setting plates on the table, her elbow cocked, her hand placing the plates on the table just so. "He's up all right," Davis carefully intones in a voice deeper and a pace more measured than one expects. "I dumped him out of bed." And out of the scene she goes.

Aside from some lost screen tests, this is Davis's first appearance on celluloid. The moment is electrifying—not because of her performance's inherent artistry (she's going through the paces of a secondary character's entrance, though with the extreme focus of bright sunlight hitting a prism), but because a glorious fifty-eight-year film career radiates out from it. All the characters she played, and all the characters she became, bloom from this single generative bud. The film is called *Bad Sister*.

She arrived in Hollywood in December 1930, along with Ruthie and Boogum the dog, having been promised the lead in Universal's adaptation of Preston Sturges's hit Broadway comedy *Strictly Dishonorable*, or so she later said, and when she was cast instead as the good sister in *Bad Sister*, Universal having changed its mind, she necessarily took it personally.

With the sting of this rejection still raw, *Bad Sister* (then called *Gambling Daughters*) began filming on the cusp of the new year. Mousy Laura Madison (Davis) plays second fiddle to her wild sibling, Marianne (Sidney Fox), who is courted not only by rich, dumpy Wade Trumbull (Bert Roach) but also by Dr. Dick Lindley (Conrad Nagel, top billed). The coquettish Marianne toys with Wade, draws Dick in her sights, then cuts a date with Dick short when Humphrey Bogart shows up as the flashy Val Corliss. Marianne runs off to Columbus with Val, who ditches her in a cheap hotel; she returns home to find demure Bette/Laura engaged to Dick and, contrite in her state of sin, gratefully marries fat Wade in the end.[1]

Conrad Nagel reported that Universal's Carl Laemmle Jr. didn't see what we all now see—we can't help but see—in *Bad Sister*. Laemmle, said Nagel, called Davis and Bogart into his office "one at a time, and told them they had nothing to offer. They were colorless. No fault of theirs. They just didn't photograph. He suggested they go back to New York."[2] Young Laemmle's advice was lunacy, obviously, but how could he have foreseen the rich, smoky history these two then-inexperienced actors would create over time? When Hobart Henley, the film's director, cuts to a grinning Bogart after Val's lengthy roadster cuts Marianne and Dick off at the curb, it causes a jolt equal to Bette's own first shot. Bogart's face, with its newly emerging contours, shocks with sheer familiarity, as does Bette's.

A *Bad Sister* legend casts Bette as the naive young puritan she certainly was. ("I was the Yankee-est, most modest virgin that ever walked in," she once said.)[3] There's a scene in the film in which Bette's character, Laura, diapers her other sister Amy's newborn son, Amy having died melodramatically in childbirth. Bette, sensing trouble over her absolute inexperience with bodies unlike her own—she was a prim twenty-two at the time—asked whether the prop baby was a boy or a girl. The camera wasn't going to get close enough to care, but she was, and did. It was a boy—not surprising, since the script drives home the baby's sex with a scene of Grandpa running down the street yelling, "It's a boy! It's a boy!" But according to Bette, she had no idea what the baby would turn out to look like under its diaper, and the cast and crew lined up to watch in sophisticated amusement as the Yankee-est virgin who ever walked in reacted with a deep blush at her first sight of a penis.

If Conrad Nagel was right, it was Bogart who put them all up to it. "That dame is too uptight," Bogart told Nagel, adding, "What she needs is a good screw from a man who knows how to do it."[4] Bette, also in Nagel's telling, thought Bogie was "uncouth."[5] She was correct.

The problem with this entertaining tale, even in Davis's own version, is that the scene itself is explicitly about Laura's sexual awakening and the embarrassment it causes her. Dick enters the room as Laura adjusts the diaper and, revealing his love for her for the first time, bends down and kisses her on the lips. And she blushes—not from the shock of seeing the baby's penis, but from the first stirring of her own sexuality. If there is any meaning at all to this anecdote, it lies not only in the fact that Bette Davis saw her first penis while a 35mm camera was running and lights were blasting in her face but also that she used her personal humiliation for the sake of her character, something she would do throughout her film career.

"She has about as much sex appeal as Slim Summerville." This was Laemmle Jr.'s response to Bette Davis's screen debut. Davis claimed actually to have heard him make the remark.[6] Mean, yes; funny, terribly. Slim Summerville, the former Keystone Kop who plays one of Laura's father's business associates in *Bad Sister*, was a skinny, bent beanpole with a large comedy nose. But what the twenty-two-year-old Laemmle thoroughly missed was Davis's carnality. It comes out even in the restrained Laura of *Bad Sister*. Beneath the surface of Davis's New England reserve is raw, unsatisfied appetite—physical drive as well as emotional ambition. *Variety* got that point early on in its review of *Bad Sister*: as Laura, the anonymous critic wrote, Davis was "the very essence of repression."[7] Barely suppressed rage would become Davis's stock-in-trade, but her bottled-up frenzies were as sexual as they were emotional.

By the time she shot *Bad Sister*, she'd already been run through the gauntlet of Universal men in a demeaning episode that hammered home a sad fact she hadn't expected at all: that Hollywood moviemaking was largely about whether the men who made the pictures wanted to fuck the women they paid to act in them. Davis was suspicious when they told her she was to appear for yet another screen test, this one for an unnamed part in a likewise unspecified project. They told her to lie down on a couch, after which a succession of fifteen of Universal's contract actors got on top of her. Then they acted. "I wasn't even a woman," Bette later wrote; "I was a mattress."[8] Gilbert Roland gave Bette second thoughts, if only for the sake of a joke she could employ many years later on talk shows: "I must say, after he kissed me I thought, 'This is not so bad.'" Roland also reportedly said something on the order of: "Don't worry—we've all gone through it," though one doesn't imagine that Universal's pretty starlets ever lined up to lay a piece of freshman veal-cake in front of a screen test crew.[9]

This, along with the *Strictly Dishonorable* disappointment, was Davis's welcome to Hollywood.

*B*AD *SISTER* ATTRACTED little notice, and neither did Bette Davis. But Karl Freund, who shot the picture, told Carl Laemmle that Davis's eyes were marvelous. This, according to Bette, was the only reason Universal renewed her contract when her first three-month option came up.[10]

By that point she had made her second movie, *Seed*. Adapted from what was called a "novel of birth control" by its author, Charles G. Norris, *Seed* actually has little concern with contraception. The only trace of it is the fact that Bart Carter, a frustrated writer, has five children who create such a racket that he can't work on his novel. Bette plays one of his daughters. Rather than moving her toward prominence, *Seed* only pushed her farther into the background.

Davis didn't come any farther forward in her third film, *Waterloo Bridge*. An elegantly conceived and beautifully executed melodrama, *Waterloo Bridge* was the director James Whale's first film with Universal; he went on to make the great horror trio *Frankenstein*, *The Old Dark House*, and *Bride of Frankenstein* at that studio, not to mention the glorious musical *Show Boat*. *Waterloo Bridge* takes place in London during World War I. An expatriate American, Myra (Mae Clarke), can find no more work as a chorine and starts turning tricks. She picks them up on the bridge. During an air raid, she meets a kindly, callow soldier (Kent Douglass) when both of them stop to help an old lady pick up her spilled potatoes. Roy, nineteen, blond, and upper crust, gives Myra money to pay her overdue rent; she takes it, but in a fit of pique and guilt throws it back at him. They make up, but Myra—especially in Mae Clarke's twitchy performance—becomes increasingly troubled to the point of a marvelous histrionic breakdown scene in her sleazy apartment.

Bette, who plays Roy's petite sister, makes her first appearance with her back to the camera and generally stays that way until the end of the scene, when she shouts in her deaf father's ear that Roy wants to bring his new girlfriend up to the manor for a visit. She has a few more lines in the film—"Oh! You must come to Camden with us! It's perfectly lovely!"—and disappears.

(We know Myra is doomed at the end when Whale cuts to a bird's-eye shot of her strolling across Waterloo Bridge while the low buzz of zeppelins plays on the soundtrack. Within seconds, Myra gets hit by a perfectly aimed bomb, thereby freeing our boy Roy from having to marry the deranged hooker after he returns from the war.)

Davis made the papers during the production of *Waterloo Bridge*, but not because of her talent. According to the June 29 *Boston Traveller*, Bette was "rushed to her home from the studio last week" with an attack of appendicitis, though she wasn't operated upon.[11] Her absence from the set necessitated some rescheduling, with Whale working nights, as well as the need for a few retakes in July.

Waterloo Bridge was released in September. And Laemmle was still unimpressed. "Her sex appeal simply *ain't*," he said.[12]

In August 1931, Universal sent Davis on loan to RKO for the cornball *Way Back Home*. Based on the popular radio program *Seth Parker*, which chronicled the benign meddlings of a wise Maine farmer, the film is a strenuously homespun morality tale. Bette plays a country ingenue with a harsh father; Seth, with his jutting little white beard and folksy insights, sets things right at a festive taffy pull.

One might assume that none of this bunk was quite Bette's speed. The hard-bitten image we have of her is true, but only partly so; she had a sentimental streak, too. Bette actually liked *Way Back Home*. Her director, William Seiter, treated her well, something she hadn't necessarily experienced in Hollywood at that point, or beyond, and she appreciated the way J. Roy Hunt photographed her. Perhaps the most important aspect of the production was the makeup department's innovative treatment of her features. Bette Davis came away from *Way Back Home* with a new mouth and, consequently, a reformed face. Because RKO's makeup artist Ern Westmore decided to eschew the glamorous bee-stung convention of the period—this movie was, after all, set in backwoods Maine—he instead drew Davis a more linear set of lips, with the lower lip a bit fuller and wider than its natural shape. The result of the new, straight mouth was clear—a fresh emphasis on her greatest features: two enormous, captivating eyes.

Davis was growing frustrated with Universal. Her cattlelike casting, combined with the relative lack of care and craft in the picture making (she underappreciated *Waterloo Bridge*, probably because her part was so tiny), fed into her lifelong impatience in the face of mediocrity and half-assedness. She also resented the fact that the studios traded their contract players to other studios without the players' consent to play characters they didn't want to play at the whim of bosses who didn't care.

"There was something lower than bottom," Bette later wrote, "and Mr. Laemmle sent me there"—specifically as a loan to Bennie F. Zeidman of B. F. Zeidman Productions. Undirected by Howard Higgin, *Hell's House*—the original title of which was, appropriately enough, *Misguided*—begins with a touching scene between a country mother and her son, Jimmy (Junior Durkin), but swiftly turns mawkish when Mother steps away from the camera for a moment and gets run over by a car. Freshly orphaned, Jimmy heads for the city, where he meets the slick bootlegger Kelly (Pat O'Brien), who hires him to take liquor orders. Jimmy gets arrested after literally one minute on the job and gets shipped off to a perfectly dreadful reform school, where he meets the sickly Shorty (Junior Coghlan—there was a vogue for "Juniors" in 1931). Naturally, Shorty dies. Unnaturally, Shorty speaks to Jimmy from beyond the grave at the end when Jimmy, sprung from the reform school, asks rhetorically, "How is it now, Shorty?" and, much to his amazement, Shorty answers him in voice-over: "Okay, big boy!" Fade out.

It's ghastly. Davis plays the bootlegger's moll, Peggy. Fighting her way upstream in this filthy creek, she manages to play Peggy with a breezy self-confidence and, of all things, a kind of transparent naturalism that contrasts markedly with Pat O'Brien's early-talkie stiltedness. One rarely thinks of Bette Davis in terms of the naturalism of her performance style, so deeply has Davis's cigarette-waving, dialogue-chopping delivery been etched in the public imagination. But what Davis brought to the screen in 1931, even in the lousy *Hell's House*, was a fresh, unblinkered vitality, a kind of see-through stylization that allows us to know the character while appreciating the actress's craft.

Then Universal loaned her out to Columbia for *The Menace*. "I was a corpse!" Davis declared to Dick Cavett many years later. "All I did was fall out of a closet!"[13] She gets the gist right but the details wrong: Ronald Quayle (Walter Byron) undergoes extensive plastic surgery, including the removal of his fingerprints and the installation of an entirely new face, and returns to England under an assumed name to avenge his father's killing. Bette plays his girlfriend, who faints after finding a cadaver hanging on a hook in a closet.

The Menace is preposterous. Bette later said, "I looked like an ostrich through the whole thing—ungainly, sad, and startled. We made it in thirteen days."[14] In truth, she looks nothing like an ostrich. A bored starlet with too much talent for the dreck in which she's stuck, yes. But not an ostrich. She's right about the production's swiftness, though; *The Menace* filmed from October 30 to November 16, 1931, and there was no work on Sundays.

JACK L. WARNER CAME from nothing, which is to say Youngstown, Ohio. The enormous family—two parents, twelve children—took cold-water baths in a tub on the front porch. They pawned the family horse to buy a Kinetoscope: a four-foot-high cabinet with an eyepiece on top through which customers who paid the customary nickel could watch a moving picture. A few years later, Jack and his brothers bought a movie theater in Beaver Falls, Pennsylvania. One led to several; some failed. They began making their own product—stuff to project on the screen so the people who bought tickets would have something to look at. This business led them to Southern California.

Warner had, one would have to say, a strong personality. When Al Jolson accepted a special Oscar for *The Jazz Singer,* he remarked, "I don't know what Jack Warner's going to do with this statue. It can't say yes.' "[15]

By 1931, Warner, then thirty-nine, together with his brothers Harry and Albert, ran the most factory-like of the five major Hollywood studios, a compact lot in Burbank where, in the words of the producer David Lewis, "films were edited, previewed, and shipped like sausages" to theaters that were, conveniently enough, mainly owned by the Warners.[16] They were rich tightwads in a town of rich tightwads. *Fortune* once called Jack "a bargain-counter dictator," a description Warner himself repeated with pride.[17] Warners' pictures were usually inexpensive to set up and easy to shoot. *And they moved.* One producer remembered that Warners' editors would cut out single frames from every scene, just to make them play that much quicker.[18] Another recalled being told at a meeting that Warners couldn't possibly compete with MGM, for instance, because of MGM's huge roster of stars, "so we had to go after the stories—topical ones, not typical ones. The stories became the stars. . . . We used to say 't-t-t: timely, topical, and not typical'—that was our slogan. . . . We were all searching frantically, looking through papers for story ideas."[19]

Personally, Jack Warner was a bit of a dandy—a failed stand-up comic in blue yachting blazers, ascots, white flannels, and brilliant patent leather shoes, always with the one-liners, which often dropped like lead. When he met Albert Einstein, he made a joke about his relatives. With Madame Chiang Kai-shek and a roomful of Chinese, it was about forgetting to pick up his laundry.

He and his brother Harry, who ran the finances, were as different as two brothers can be. Jack was vulgar, Harry was subdued; Jack was crass, Harry was contained. Harry was devoted to his wife and children; Jack, who was married to the beautiful and patrician Ann, still screwed around on the side. Jack and Harry detested each another.

At Warner Bros., pretty much the only prestige pictures the studio sent out in the very early 1930s starred George Arliss, an unlikely movie star with a face like that of a misshapen orangutan—the cheeks too wide, the jaw too narrow, the lips too thin, nothing on one side matching anything on the other. Arliss was also getting on in years; in 1931 he was a well-seasoned sixty-three. But two of Arliss's sober, ennobling biopics—*Disraeli* (1929) and *Alexander Hamilton* (1931)—were good moneymakers for the studio, and for that reason alone Arliss was respected by film critics and studio bookkeepers alike. He'd made a silent picture in 1922 called *The Man Who Played God*, and in late 1931 he was preparing a sound version:

A celebrated concert pianist (Arliss) suffers sudden deafness after an explosion. Sequestered and miserable in his apartment high above Central Park, he begins spying on people with the aid of binoculars; reading their lips, he learns of their troubles and solves them from above, at first in mockery of God, but later in redemptive imitation. (One of the people Arliss assists is an especially boyish Ray Milland.) Davis plays his protégée, who lets herself become engaged to him out of an oddly appealing kind of pity, though he nobly sets her free at the end.

Bette, in high melodramatic mode in *The Lonely Life*, claims that she was reeling from the demeaning tawdriness of the corpses, closets, and offscreen screams of *The Menace* and hovering on a crumbling brink of despair and a defeated retreat to the East when, lo, the saving clarion bell of her telephone rang. The caller identified himself as George Arliss. Bette, believing him to be a prankster friend, responded with a fake British accent until she became convinced that it was, in fact, the great actor himself calling her in for an audition. Bette, according to Bette, had been recommended to Arliss by the actor Murray Kinnell, with whom she had appeared in *The Menace*.

Jack Warner later said no, that wasn't what happened at all. According to Warner, a midlevel executive named Rufus LeMaire (né Goldstick) "dropped in one morning with his familiar scowling and battered face and said: 'Jack, there's a very talented little girl over at Universal named Bette Davis. I first saw her in some New York shows, and I caught her in a bit in *Bad Sister*.'" Bette retorted by pointing out that her role in *Bad Sister* was more than a "bit"—it was the second lead—and by insisting that Kinnell, not LeMaire/Goldstick, was indeed the pivotal figure in her hiring by and eventual ensconcement at Warner Bros. Never one to be left out of a praise-earning situation, Darryl Zanuck took some of the credit for moving Bette Davis to Warner Bros. as well. Zanuck was a Warners executive at the time: "We sent [Arliss] a newcomer named Bette Davis—I didn't think she was very beautiful—and he called back and said, 'I've just heard one of the greatest actresses.'"[20]

By the time this who-gets-the-credit contretemps played itself out years after the fact, Bette Davis and Jack Warner had been snapping and squawking at each other for decades—two headstrong supersuccesses who'd grown to depend on each other for nurturing hatred and backhanded support.

Warner Bros.' legal files tell a less passionate story of *The Man Who Played God* and Bette Davis's formal relationship with the studio:

Davis's first contract with Warners is dated November 19, 1931, and specifies her salary at three hundred dollars per week. There's an addendum designed to put little starlets in their place: "Where black, white, silver, or gold shoes and hose will suffice, artist is to furnish same at her expense."[21]

An interoffice memo specifies that *The Man Who Played God* officially began production on November 27; Davis, however, had already been on the payroll as of November 18, and she finished shooting her role precisely one month later.[22] The film required no retakes.

"He certainly was my first professional father," Bette later claimed of the benign George Arliss, though given her own father's nature the honor might as well be shared by Arliss's doppelgänger, Jack Warner.[23]

Davis gives a surprisingly giggly performance at first, but she tones it down for her first serious scene with Arliss. She knows when to move from girlish naïveté to a woman with the presence of mind to be loved by a genius. Later in the film, when she squares off with her character's new beau at the edge of a brook, Davis's edgy neurosis first breaks through. "Harold" makes his obvious move, but Bette rears back, grabs at her hair, and releases it—suppressed tension bursting out in a flashing spasm—and lunges at him.

Later, in a scene set in Central Park in full binocular view of Arliss, Davis speaks in a newly clipped delivery, and one finally begins to hear the voice that sustained her stardom well after she stopped making quality pictures: "He's *put* his *faith* in *me*! And I *won't* be a *quit*-ter!"

It's not just Bette's platinumed hair that makes her seem modern in these early films. It's her stance and spiky attitude—the skittish physical energy and sharp, staccato speech. Bette enters her first scene in her next film, *The Rich Are Always with Us*, in constant motion—shifting her body, biting her lines, not exactly twitching but scarcely standing still. It was partly a conscious performance, but it also resulted from real intimidation. The film's top-billed star, Ruth Chatterton, was then in the Hollywood pantheon, and Bette was terrified of her.

Davis's bitchy description of Chatterton's entrance onto the set the first day of shooting is well worth quoting: "Miss Chatterton swept on like Juno. I had never seen a real star-type entrance in my life. I was properly dazzled. Her arrival could have won an Academy Award nomination. Such authority! Such glamour! She was absolutely luminous and radiated clouds of Patou and Wrigley's Spearmint."[24]

The scene takes place in a restaurant, and Bette's character comes up to the table Chatterton shares with her costar, George Brent. Bette was so flustered by her proximity to America's reigning glamour queen that she simply couldn't get her lines out. Brent, too, was jittery, his coffee cup rattling on its saucer. Bette then blurted to Chatterton, "I'm so damned scared of you I'm speechless!"[25] But Bette's jumpy energy endures today as a unique performance style, while Chatterton's *too-too* glamour diction has long grown musty. Referring to a game of roulette, Chatterton announces, "With this wheel—and this gamblah—you haven't got a chaunce!" "I cahn't help it," Chatterton's character later intones, and that was precisely the problem with Chatterton's career.

Davis started shooting *So Big* the day after she began *The Rich Are Always with Us*. Davis later said she filmed *Rich* during the day and *So Big* at night. She finished her work in both films in all of a week and a half.

Directed by William Wellman, *So Big* is Warners' adaptation of Edna Ferber's Pulitzer Prize–winning novel.

But Davis's role in *So Big* is so small. The film belongs to Barbara Stanwyck. Poor Selina (Stanwyck), left destitute by the death of her gambler father, becomes a country schoolteacher in a Dutch farming community outside of Chicago. She marries stolid Pervus and bears a son, Dirk, whom she calls "So Big." ("How big is my son?" "*So big!*") Young Roelf, a neighbor boy she has tutored, feels stultified by farm life and runs off to become a world-famous sculptor in Europe. Pervus dies. Dirk grows up to be a snob; he's humiliated by his mother's having become an asparagus magnate. He hires Dallas O'Mara (Davis), an elegant and high-priced graphic artist, to come up with an ad campaign for his bond trading company and falls in love with her. Roelf returns from Europe as George Brent, and in a final speech, Dallas explains to Dirk that his mother is noble, a subject worthy of great art.

Davis's delivery of the closing moral is peculiar. "*There*," Dallas says. "That's what I mean when I say I want to do portraits. Not portraits of ladies with pearls . . . but portraits of men and women who are really distinguished looking—and distinguishedly American, like your mother." Dallas is sitting at a slight angle and facing to the right (where Selina and Roelf are standing by the window, Selina's face hit by a convenient ray of sunshine). Davis's manner of speaking matches her dialogue in confidence and grace. But Bette can't help herself: she's wringing her hands furiously as she speaks, unable to keep them from contradicting what she's saying. These jangled, barely suppressed nerves are Davis's own, not Dallas's.

It doesn't matter. The speech as written is less convincing than it might be, especially because Stanwyck's Selina is nothing if not agriculturally noble throughout the film. But Davis's own, uncontrollably anxious hands give her character's words a surprising and unsettling dimension—that of an artist's irrepressible self-doubt.

AFTER *So Big* and *The Rich Are Always with Us*, she shot *The Dark Horse*, a lame political satire, in March and early April 1932. Warren William engineers the rise of a buffoon politico. The bizarre Guy Kibbee is the buffoon, and Bette wastes her time as William's wise-gal girlfriend. Then, over the vocal, heavily accented objections of the director

Michael Curtiz—"Goddamned nothing no good sexless son of a bitch!"—
Jack Warner and Darryl Zanuck cast Bette in her first truly great role:
that of the southern belle Madge in *Cabin in the Cotton*.[26] Madge is the
flashy, spoiled daughter of the plantation owner for whom Richard
Barthelmess's well-meaning Marvin works. Marvin has a peckerwood
girlfriend, but the dazzling and aggressive Madge quickly takes Marvin's
mind off fidelity.

Curtiz, whom the critic Neal Gabler describes as "feral," was abusive
to Bette personally, barking at and needling her in heavily Hungarian-
accented tones, but he lights her with great finesse. Her face seems to be
the source of sunshine rather than its target, and her brilliant blonde hair
radiates hot energy.[27] In the context of this glowing heat, Davis turns to
Barthelmess on the dusty porch of the general store, her eyes tilt appre-
ciatively down his body and back up again, and she says, "Cute! I'd like
to kiss ya, but I just washed my hair. Bye!"

In later years, Davis used this line as a comedy routine—a piece of
supposedly nonsensical Hollywood dialogue she could trot out on talk
shows and in interviews to get the interviewer and audience on her side.
But as she delivers it in the film, it's not silly at all. And its meaning
couldn't be clearer: Bette's sex-hungry Madge is suggesting to the
shocked but susceptible Marvin that a kiss from her would lead to much
more—that they'd end up rolling around in the road. There would be
dirt involved.

Warners certainly kept its actors busy. Davis worked on *Cabin in the
Cotton* from May 17 through June 9. The following day she began shooting *Three on a Match* with the director Mervyn LeRoy; she finished that
one on the thirtieth.

Three childhood friends—Vivian, Mary, and Ruth—meet in New
York after ten years. Vivian (Ann Dvorak) has married well, Mary (Joan
Blondell) has become a showgirl after serving time in a reform school,
and Ruth (Davis) is an earnest secretary without much to do. The film's
title—drawn from the World War I superstition that the third soldier to
light a cigarette from a single match would be shot, the flame's duration
enabling German soldiers to draw an accurate bead—spells doom for
one of the characters. Davis never liked *Three on a Match*, calling it a
"dull B-picture."[28] But how dull can it be to watch Ann Dvorak turn from
a Park Avenue matron into a derelict hophead in little over an hour?

True, Davis's part is by far the smallest and least meaty of the three.

Ruth stands on the sidelines as Vivian degenerates. Making matters worse for Davis, *Three on a Match* is the film that inspired Mervyn LeRoy to utter a prediction he came to regret: "I made a mistake when the picture was finished. I told an interviewer that I thought Joan Blondell was going to be a big star, that Ann Dvorak had definite possibilities, but that I didn't think Bette Davis would make it." It was remarks like that which prompted Davis to dispatch unbelievers to an icy hell of contempt.[29] LeRoy never reemerged.

4

An Actress in Motion

I
T COMES AS NO SURPRISE TO LEARN THAT
Hollywood was a terrifying place—even for Bette Davis, whose rocklike
spine belied a most insecure mental framework, especially about her
erotic impulses. The boy-madness of Newton High School, Cushing
Academy, and the various boyfriends and would-be fiancés in New York
and Rochester to the contrary notwithstanding, young Bette Davis was
profoundly inexperienced sexually, as her humiliating exposure to a
naked baby boy revealed to the cast and crew of *Bad Sister*. Add to this
the tremendous pressure of shooting film after film for directors who
had neither the time nor the inclination for nurturing, and the tension of
never knowing exactly who her new friends were, and her mother's om-
nipresence, and her sister's instability, and her own fears about her
mind, family, money, and art, and Davis's first marriage begins to make
more sense.

Davis once described Ham Nelson as "tall, lean, dark curly-haired,
with a funny nose and beautiful brown eyes." By "funny nose," she
meant that it was a too-broad mismatch for his otherwise preppy-cute
face. Barbara Leaming goes so far as to call him an "Ichabod Crane sort
of fellow," but he was nothing of the sort. Ham was a pleasantly slim,
boyish man with a narrow waist, a hairless chest, a handsome head of
very dark hair, and those deep brown eyes.

At Cushing, the young musician had learned to play the trumpet and serenaded Bette with an odd, all-too-prophetic tune: "Taps." "By then, of course, I was wading in those velvety brown eyes. I was truly in love. So was he," she writes. But when Bette was at drama school in New York, within striking distance of Yale, she ditched him in favor of Fritz Hall—that is, until John Murray Anderson announced in the press that Miss Bette Davis was "the perfect modern Venus," which displeased both her father and her Ivy League beau, who was looking for a more wifely type to accompany him into his family's business.[1] Ham, on the other hand, found the Venus remark hilarious and wrote to her "with appropriately irreverent remarks that made [her] roar."[2]

In 1929, while performing with George Cukor's company in Rochester, she took still another new boyfriend, a businessman named Charles Ainsely. Of Ainsely, Bette cryptically writes, "He would always park at the end of the street, but other than that, we couldn't have been more satisfied." But the satisfaction was brief; the relationship didn't last terribly long, since Bette didn't last long in Rochester. (Ainsley reappeared rather briefly shortly after Bette finished filming *The Dark Horse*. She and Charlie—and Ruthie and Bobby—traveled to Palm Springs and Yosemite National Park in April 1932. But Ainsley went back to Rochester, and the second phase of the affair turned out to be no more productive than the first.)

And then there's the mysterious telegram in one of the scrapbooks: addressed to Bette, then living at Carlton Terrace at Broadway and 100th Street in New York and dated September 27, 1930, it reads in its entirety, "Goodby forever—Pierre."

When Bette moved to Los Angeles three months after Pierre's terse farewell and found herself separated from her past by the vast breadth of the continent, Harmon Nelson began to be more than just her high school sweetheart. He was a comfortable, true friend in a world of pressure, paranoia, and other people's sexual hijinks—a link to a past that may have seemed stable by comparison and that promised a similar, familiar future. "Only Ham's letters kept me sane through this period," Bette writes of her first year in Hollywood.[3] So when Ham Nelson decided to move west after he graduated from Massachusetts State College (later renamed the University of Massachusetts at Amherst), they soon married, as much to be able to have sex with each other right away as to build a sustainable life together over the long haul.

Their reunion was put off by several weeks by the fact that while Ham was traveling west, Bette was heading east on a Warner Bros. promotional tour with Warren William, her *Dark Horse* costar. They crisscrossed the country "like curtain pulleys," Davis writes.[4] Tensions with the studio were beginning to build. Her manager, Arthur Lyon, told Warners that Bette was making the trip grudgingly, considering it a "gratuitous concession." And in a telegram to the Warners executive Rufus LeMaire, Davis herself sarcastically noted the studio's cheapskate nature: "Just to show you that I am a pal of the Warners have not been drinking fifteen chocolate milks per day at their expense."[5] To top it off, she had to spend a good deal of time and energy fending off the sexual overtures of Warren William.[6]

While Bette was in New York, Ham took a job as a trumpeter for the orchestra of the Tenth Olympiad, which began on July 30, 1932, at the Los Angeles Coliseum. Bette returned to Los Angeles, and on August 18, Bette and Ham and Ruthie and Bobby and Aunt Mildred and cousin Donald and two poodles piled into a car and drove to Yuma, Arizona. They left the city after midnight. Bette picks up the story for the reporter Gladys Hall of *Modern Screen*.

> Came dawn and we were still a hundred miles from Yuma, which was hundreds of miles more than we had thought. The thermometer registered 107 in the shade! Ham and I had not spoken one word the whole way. It was on the tip of my tongue to say, "This is horrible—I won't go on." Ruthie stopped me. She sensed the furies boiling and said, "Let's not go on," which was, of course, the one divinely inspired thing to say, for the mule in me immediately gave a back kick of the heels and told Ham to step on the gas. We arrived in Yuma. Everyone was soaked to the skin. . . . I kept muttering, "This is so awful it's funny!" When asked whether this was my first marriage, I said, "My third." That got back to the studio! . . . I wore a two-piece beige street dress that resembled the sands of the Arizona desert after the rain it never gets, brown accessories, and two limp gardenias. I kept thinking of the picture I'd always had of myself as a bride—dewy and divine in white satin and orange blossoms, coming up a white-ribboned aisle to the strains of Mendelssohn.[7]

In *The Lonely Life*, Bette asserts that she and Ham spent their honeymoon helping Warner Bros. plug its big, modern, glossy musical *42nd Street*. Warners' publicist Charles Einfeld had cooked up a brilliant cross-promotional deal with General Electric: the *General Electric 42nd*

Street Express, a gold- and silver-foil-wrapped train that crossed the country displaying Warners' movie stars and the latest GE home products. The train was outfitted, as the *Boston Post* put it, with "perfect General Electric housekeeping equipment and Malibu Beach sun lamps, platinum blondes, and Tom Mix's new horse, King."[8] (Aside from King and Mr. Mix, other stars on board included Bette, Glenda Farrell, Laura La Plante, Joe E. Brown, Lyle Talbot, Leo Carrillo, and the Olympic swimming gold medalist Eleanor Holm.) Taking off from Los Angeles, the train chugged through San Francisco, Salt Lake City, Cheyenne, Denver, Kansas City, St. Louis, Chicago, Cleveland, Pittsburgh, and Baltimore; made it to Washington, D.C., in time for Franklin D. Roosevelt's inauguration; then headed to Philadelphia and Boston. It ended up in New York City.

Despite the luxurious trappings of the train, Warners worked its stars hard as they made their way across the continent. Along the route, the actors, actresses, and horse had to make personal appearances in department stores, show up at parades, open model General Electric kitchens in appliance stores. "We visited 32 cities in 32 days and felt like monkeys in a zoo," Davis writes.[9]

She arrived in Boston as a hometown heroine on March 8, 1933; a crowd of 10,000 people braved a driving rain to greet her at the station. When she emerged from the train, her hair "a long gold bob curled at the ends" (according to the *Post*), an especially loud cheer erupted.

It made a good story to say that the *General Electric 42nd Street Express* served as the couple's honeymoon venue, but in point of fact, Bette Davis made four films between wedding and honeymoon: *20,000 Years in Sing Sing*, which she began shooting as a newlywed on August 25, one week after the wedding, and finished on September 14; *Parachute Jumper* (September 21 to October 17); *Ex-Lady* (December 12 to 31); and *The Working Man* (January 14 to February 1, 1933).[10] She also—finally—had her appendix removed. From the *Illustrated Daily News*, October 22, 1932: "After being ill for years, Bette Davis, blonde actress, will be operated on this morning at Wilshire Osteopathic hospital for appendicitis."* It was

---

* It's unclear that Davis actually had acute appendicitis in June 1931, when she had to leave the set of *Waterloo Bridge*; the left-lower-quadrant pain she felt may simply have been presumed to be appendix related. It's worth noting, however, that the risk of dying from a surgically acquired infection was higher in those days, and her doctors may have taken a watch-and-wait approach rather than risk surgery. There is also the possibility that she had what is known as chronic appendicitis, in which the body is able—for a time, at least—to contain the inflammation.

soon after wrapping *The Working Man* that the *42nd Street Express* honeymoon began. And Bette Davis was beginning to get tired.

But at last she had a sex life. And she loved it. Sex didn't have to be about procreation or even obligation, Bette discovered. It was healthy exercise—a way to get rid of nervous tension. Before the wedding, she writes, Ruthie had "found me more high strung than ever. 'You can't go on like this. You and Ham have been in love for years. Marry him!'" Ruthie had spent years dissuading Bette from engaging in casual sex with this sage advice: "A stiff prick has no conscience."[11] Mother may have been an upright Yankee, but apparently she could be as salty as seawater.

In her later life, Bette regretted that Ruthie hadn't just given her approval for the young couple to go ahead and have sex: "Would that she had been that wise. Would that Ham and I had been." The latter sentence, the afterthought, is shocking as such, for by adding it, Bette ranks her mother's control ahead of Ham's, let alone her own. "I was hopelessly puritan, helplessly passionate, and, with Ruthie, decided that I had better marry before I became Hester Prynne." Ham, being Ham, went along: "He was not against the idea."

It came as a surprise to Bette that making love was fun and relaxing: "The lust I had feared was natural and beautiful. I was released." But Davis doesn't dwell on her sexual liberation in *The Lonely Life*. Instead, she quickly sketches in a few storm clouds on the horizon: "I now had the work and the man I loved—the best of two worlds. It never occurred to me that they would or could collide."[12]

Did Bette really imagine that the quiet and unassuming Ham Nelson, by osmosis—by simply becoming her husband—would develop a powerful professional libido to match her own? She registers disappointment that he didn't. His Olympics trumpeting job ended with the Olympics, and no other work was forthcoming. Ham was still unemployed by mid-October, and Bette was supporting her husband along with her mother and sister. In fact, she couldn't afford the appendix surgery without help from Jack Warner, who personally approved a kind of loan: "Due to financial difficulties, surgeon's bills, and the necessity for Miss Davis to carry the entire burden of her family upkeep, Mr. Warner has approved our advancing Miss Davis during the period that she is laid off her weekly salary" (which was then $400 a week) beginning October 22.[13] By the end of November, Bette owed the studio $1,800, which was taken out of her salary at $150 a week. The raise to

$550 she got in December was thereby rendered meaningless for the duration.

Added to the financial stress was the domestic: the wife would return home fiery from a day of high-pressure Hollywood filmmaking and find the husband relaxing in his slippers and smoking a pipe.[14] She resented it. And he resented that she resented it.

DAVIS BEGAN SHOOTING *20,000 Years in Sing Sing*, with gowns by Orry-Kelly, at the end of August 1932. Stark and hard-edged to a point—the gowns are lovely—the film tells the story of a criminal's redemption, which he achieves perversely by taking the rap for a murder he didn't commit. James Cagney was originally to have starred, but he was spending the summer on suspension from Warners while he fought for a better deal: $3,000 a week instead of the $1,250 he was then being paid.[15] Spencer Tracy, on loan from Fox, was cast in Cagney's stead.

The title refers to the cumulative number of years served by all the prisoners at Sing Sing, not to an abnormally long sentence meted out to Spencer Tracy, whose character, Tommy Connors, has been sent up the river for five to thirty. It's a measure of the era's social realism and Warner Bros.' particular brand of it that there's no question about Tommy's guilt. He's a thug, albeit a charming one, and his rap sheet proves the point with a string of armed robberies and assaults behind him. Bette plays his moll.

Tracy already admired Davis—he'd actually seen *Hell's House*—and he told her so when they met. He went even further, saying that he thought she was the most talented actress in town. "Damn right," Bette answered with characteristic bravado, "but who are we against so many?"[16] "We were an awful lot alike," Davis later said of Tracy. "We weren't the best-looking people on the lot, but we knew we were talented and we weren't getting the parts we deserved. We also weren't just going to sit back and take it."[17]

James Cagney, never one to sit back and take it either, saw a rather less flattering similarity: "They were both incipient thyroid cases. Early in life Spence did have a serious thyroid problem, and anyone with thyroid trouble *is* in trouble. Spence's problem was a slightly unsettled personality. He was a most amusing guy, a good companion who told great stories beautifully—but there was always the tension that was tangible. You can *feel* the stress in such people."[18]

Davis's oddball looks in *20,000 Years in Sing Sing* made a great impression on a young James Baldwin, who recalled seeing the film with the immediacy of a fresh slap in the face: "So, here, now, was Bette Davis, on that Saturday afternoon, in close-up, over a champagne glass, pop-eyes popping. I was astounded. . . . For, here, before me, after all, was a *movie star*: *white*: and if she was white and a movie star, she was *rich*: and she was *ugly*. . . . Davis's skin [had] the dead-white greenish cast of something crawling from under a rock, but I was held, just the same, by the tense intelligence of the forehead, the disaster of the lips: and when she moved, she moved just like a nigger."[19]

Baldwin is wildly excessive in his description of Davis's skin tone. The cinematographer, Barney McGill, is no Ernest Haller or Sol Polito, but his lighting doesn't turn Davis even close to sickly. Still, Baldwin gets her physicality to a tee: the coordinated, full-body energy as well as the unexpected, even dreadful beauty of her face.

20,000 Years in Sing Sing is hard and fast-moving, exactly what one thinks of when someone mentions Warner Bros. in the 1930s. But as tough as this prison drama is—and as much as Michael Curtiz complained about Davis's lack of common sex appeal—Warners and Curtiz simply could not bring themselves to depict their leading lady as anything other than glamorous, even when her character has been physically brutalized. The result is unintentionally comical. The story has Sing Sing's warden releasing Tommy (Tracy) on his own recognizance so he can visit Bette's said-to-be-dying Fay, who, resisting the advances of a goon, has leaped from a speeding car. Curtiz's men are real. He understood that prisoners sweat when they pound boulders into pebbles in the yard; their uniforms are soaked with it. But his women are trumped-up, one-dimensional dream images—even "goddamned nothing no good sexless son of a bitch" Bette Davis. Absurdly, Tommy bursts into Fay's room to find a remarkably scar-and-contusion-free Fay lying calmly in bed, bathed in gentle light, with an Isadora Duncan–like white satin scarf wrapped around her neck to serve as a bandage and matching white satin wrist wraps to complete the ensemble. Warners' grittiness had its limits.

It's easy to mock a Bette Davis movie called *Parachute Jumper*. Had John Wayne starred in *The Tiniest Ballerina*, it would seem similarly ludicrous. But *Parachute Jumper* turns out to be one of Davis's better pictures of the period, a fast-moving Hawksian buddy movie, though without Hawks's character-building intelligence and visual grace. Davis, of course, didn't see it that way. "Damn it," she bitterly remarks in *The Lonely Life*. "I was good as the moll [in *Sing Sing*] and my notices made that clear. My reward was a little epic called *Parachute Jumper*."[20] Her costar, Douglas Fairbanks Jr., shared Bette's derision. For Fairbanks, it was a "punishment" meted out to him by Warner Bros. for not being a good little studio toiler. Davis "thought director Al Green's sense of humor as infantile as the story we were obliged to act out," Fairbanks went on. "She was always conscientious, serious, and seemed devoid of humor of any kind. But then, there was not much to be humorous about. It was a job, and she attacked it with integrity. . . . Our only interest was to get the damned thing over with."[21] They started shooting *Parachute Jumper* on September 21, 1932, and finished three and a half weeks later.

It's true that Davis isn't stretched in any way in *Parachute Jumper*. Her wisecracking character's southern accent comes straight from *Cabin in the Cotton*. And Al Green doesn't give her much worthwhile physical business. Still, the film has energy. It's funny and irreverent, and it benefits from its hard-edged pre-Code amoralism: two drug- and booze-runners, the heroes of the piece, shoot down the border patrol and escape without punishment.*

"AN ECSTASY OF poor taste." "A piece of junk." "My shame was only exceeded by my fury."[22] To hear Davis rant, her next picture, *Ex-Lady*, is a tawdry, smirky skin show—a sixty-five-minute leer. But that's Davis's puritanism enunciating itself retrospectively. Warner Bros.' pressbook, as not-to-be-believed as it may be, is more to the point. Referring to her randy, sexually liberated character, Davis is said to have said, "What she wants, of course, is freedom. She will never be satisfied until she has every right that a man has. . . . The exceptional woman should have the same opportunities and the same freedom to develop them that the exceptional man has."

The decision to cast Davis in *Ex-Lady* was one of Darryl Zanuck's last

---

*Beginning in July 1934, Hollywood studios were forced to submit all scripts to a central censoring agency, the Production Code Administration, for approval. The first general principle of the Production Code sums up the nature of the enterprise: "No picture shall be produced which will lower the moral standards of those who see it. Hence the sympathy of the audience shall never be thrown to the side of crime, wrongdoing, evil, or sin."

at Warner Bros.—he and Harry Warner had battled over the latter's Depression-based decision to cut employee salaries by half—and Zanuck was gone by the time shooting began. It cost $115,000 and took all of three weeks to film, from December 12 through 31, 1932.[23] But the picture took in more $283,000 and can only be considered a success.[24]

Davis's scorn for *Ex-Lady* might be inexplicable if there wasn't such a notable rift between the movie's appreciation of free love and the impossibly conventional domesticity she was attempting to achieve while filming it. She believed she could be a Hollywood star during the day and head home to be a transplanted Yankee wife every evening.

Davis couldn't resolve a related set of dueling expectations, this one about housing. She claimed to want to settle down, but in practice she did everything she could not to do so. Several years later—1941, to be exact—Bette, Ruthie, and Bobby Davis sat down one evening and enumerated the total number of apartments and houses that they had lived in: there were more than seventy-five of them. When they moved to Hollywood in December 1930—having done time in Lowell, Newton, Peterborough, various towns on Cape Cod, East Orange, Norwalk, and New York City—they first rented a Tudor cottage on Alta Loma Terrace near the Hollywood Bowl. Their occupancy didn't last long.[25] By the summer of 1931, the Davises had moved into a Hollywood Hills house owned by Douglas Fairbanks's cameraman. "It happened to be the first shown the Davises by an agent," wrote Mayme Ober Peake of the *Boston Globe*. "They looked no further, but leased it on the spot." Peake was fascinated by Bette's bedroom, "with its little rustic balcony—a cloistered cell in its simplicity compared with the average movie star's boudoir! I saw more books—good books—than anything else."[26] Davis was, indeed, an avid reader, a characteristic Ham Nelson failed to admire. According to Ham, books took precedence over him.

By mid-April 1932, Bette, Ruthie, and Bobby were living just around the corner from the Warners' lot in Charles Farrell's house at 9918 Toluca Lake Avenue, an expansive Tudor number with a large yard leading down to the water. By the end of June, they'd moved again—this time to 135 Zuma in Malibu.[27] This was what Bette considered her "honeymoon house," though soon after the wedding she and Ham and Ruthie and Bobby moved into a house at 1217 Horn Avenue, just north of Sunset Boulevard in West Hollywood.

At least the Horn Avenue house actually comprised two buildings— as Bette describes it, "a white, ivy-covered little English house" in front for the newlyweds and a guesthouse in the back for the bride's mother and sister. It appears to have been a mix of need and obligation that kept Bette Davis from setting her mother and sister up in their own house somewhere across town. As she puts it in *The Lonely Life*, "It was undeniable that I preferred being a captive, rebellious Palomino to a free one. Ham was in a most awkward situation."[28]

Luckily for Ham, Bobby had another nervous breakdown and moved back East with Ruthie, the strain of Bette's marriage having triggered something more or less obvious in the sad and dependent younger sister. Bobby's face, always favoring Harlow to its own detriment, was beginning to look drawn and strained. Barbara Leaming describes Bobby's emotional state: "Bobby's eruptions often began by her becoming almost catatonic, as she curled up in the fetal position. Then, suddenly, she would leap to her feet and rush about, screaming uncontrollably at the top of her lungs until someone restrained her."[29] Ruthie felt that she and Bobby needed the support of family—family who weren't fighting to become movie stars, that is—and so they headed back to Massachusetts.

Bette and Ham moved again and again—first to one of Greta Garbo's old residences on San Vicente Boulevard in Brentwood, then to a sizable Spanish Colonial Revival house at 906 North Beverly Drive in Beverly Hills, and then to an unassuming but comfortable house at 5346 Franklin Avenue in Los Feliz.[30]

She and Ham were still living in the house on Horn Avenue when she made *Ex-Lady* in December 1932. The film finds Davis cast once again as a glamorous illustrator: Helen Bauer is Dallas O'Mara from *So Big*, yanked away from Hardie Albright and his mother's asparagus farm and reaching even greater success in New York, where she belongs. Her boyfriend, Don (Gene Raymond, whose hair is nearly as bleached as Bette's), has a key to her apartment; that's the first sign of Helen's radicalism. As she explains in a late-night conversation with Don, "Nobody has any rights about me except me." ("How about a Welsh rarebit!" she immediately offers in a brilliant non sequitur.) There's some melodramatic filler involving Helen's unctuous, unrequited suitor, Don's married girlfriend, and other distractions, and in the end the marriage survives. But *Ex-Lady*'s pleasure lies not in its story or its secondary characters but rather in the cool, matter-of-fact sophistication of Davis's performance: her elegance of movement, her hips slung slightly forward as she strides; the expression of exquisite boredom she affects in a dull dinner party scene; the slow, deliberate way she chews in that scene while listening to her tablemate drone on.

With *Ex-Lady*, Davis got the billing (over her costar Gene Raymond). She got Tony Gaudio's lavish cinematographic attention. She even got writing punchy enough to stand up to her rapidly clarifying screen persona: the independent woman who triumphs on brain power as much as on how she looks in Orry-Kelly. But her emerging life theme was that what she got was never good enough, and not being good enough, it was to Bette's mind dreadful, shameful. Each indignity was another dark blossom on a weedy vine of rage.

W<small>HEN</small> D<small>AVIS</small> <small>WORKED</small> with George Arliss again, he found her less compliant, more creatively self-assertive. "My little bird has flown, hasn't she?" he observed between takes on the set of *The Working Man*.[31] Her artistic growth was scarcely surprising, since she'd made eight pictures since *The Man Who Played God*. But his turn of phrase was not entirely accurate, since she was still tightly tethered to Warner Bros., whose nest was simultaneously commodious and confining. The studio system gave Davis consistent opportunities to work, but she had no control over any of her pictures, directors, costars, costumes, makeup designs, hairstyles, or publicity obligations.

She has little to do in *The Working Man*, which centerpieces Arliss as a beneficently cantankerous shoe magnate who takes over his late rival's company in order to morally improve the rival's madcap son and daughter (Davis). Bette plays Jenny as spoiled but charming, as comfortable in her entitlement as an heiress on the family yacht. There's none of the brattiness that would have given her character some bite. Forcing her to fall helplessly in love with an especially priggish Hardie Albright is a final indignity.

Next: a drowning here, a poisoning there, a guy whose face is rendered pulp by a subway train, the vanished wife of a slaughterhouse worker—*Bureau of Missing Persons* is Warner Bros.' idea of light entertainment. Davis only turns up after about thirty-five minutes—it's really Pat O'Brien's film, though Davis got top billing. A two-fisted mug of a detective (O'Brien) lands in the missing persons department. The transfer is supposed to teach him a lesson, but he needs no education in coming up with clever insults. As "Butch" suggests to his estranged wife, "Why don't you break out in hives and scratch yourself to death?"

Bette shot her scenes from June 26 to July 10, 1933. Her character, Norma, seeks the police's help in finding her missing husband, except he's not her husband but rather the man she's killed, only she hasn't killed him—it's his idiot brother who's the corpse—and he's not her husband but someone named Therme. (*Therme?*) "And then I looked more closely at the body," Bette cries, "and I realized it wasn't Mr. Roberts at all, but that of his insane brother dressed in Mr. Roberts's clothes! And Therme Roberts was gone!" It doesn't much matter.

Pat O'Brien thought as little of the movie as Davis did, but he liked and respected her as a colleague: "I made a new friend in Bette. She was vital, high-strung, biting, so alive, so able to eat her way into a part."[32] O'Brien is right: there really is something devouring about the way Davis approached her roles, even one as ill-defined as this one. She was not only a hungry performer in the sense of being ambitious and craving fame. Her hunger was more idiosyncratic. She feasted on the process of creative make-believe. The essential lie at the heart of fiction making was, for Bette Davis, gratifying on a gut level.

With such drive becoming part of her emerging screen persona, it's jarring to see Bette turn up behind a drugstore soda counter in *The Big Shakedown*, so little does the role of a neighborhood pharmacist's moralistic wife suit her. Charles Farrell plays the druggist who gets involved in a counterfeit digitalis racket run by shady Ricardo Cortez. According to the great character actor Allen Jenkins, who plays yet another in a series of dumb clucks in the film—Jenkins once described himself as having the face of an oyster—Davis was unhappy during the production because she'd wanted to play the role of the racketeer's moll. That role featured tough talk, ratting, and going down in a hail of bullets. It went to Glenda Farrell, while Davis was relegated to the sidelines selling aspirin and doing a lot of tsk-tsking. *The Big Shakedown* is based on a story called "Cut Rate" and has an ending that fits the bill: the gangster falls conveniently into a vat of nitrohydrochloric acid. And Bette's character, Norma, is such a compliant little wife that she forgives her husband for producing the fake digitalis that causes her to lose her baby during childbirth.

For Warner Bros., pictures like *The Big Shakedown* were staple entertainments—"programmers," products to be planned, manufactured, shipped, shown, and forgotten except as numbers on a balance sheet. But for Bette Davis, each programmer was hideously special: one by one, they offered all the full-throttle anxieties of Hollywood moviemaking with none of the high-inducing creative satisfaction. After shooting eighteen pictures in three years, Davis was still clocking in as per her contract, putting in long days under hot lights, taking orders she didn't respect, watching lesser actresses get meatier roles in better movies.

Davis's driven imagination extended to her recollections, especially when there was scorn involved. "In *Fashions of 1934*, I played a fashion model in a long blonde wig and with my mouth painted almost to my ears," Davis wrote in a *Colliers* magazine article in the mid-1950s. "Imagine *me* as a fashion model! It was ridiculous. My leading man, William Powell, thought so, too."[33] She went a little further in *The Lonely Life*: "I was glamorized beyond recognition. I was made to wear a platinum wig. . . . The bossmen were trying to make me into a Greta Garbo."[34]

Actually, Davis plays a dress designer in *Fashions of 1934*, not a model; it's her eyes, not her mouth, that Warners' makeup department decided to elongate; her hair had been platinum for most of the pictures in this early phase of her career; the *Fashions* wigs aren't particularly long . . . and nobody at Warner Bros. could possibly have been under the delusion that Bette Davis was to be the new Garbo.

Fashions of 1934 doesn't suit Davis well; in that she was correct. But that's because she has next to nothing to do. Her role is a lackluster reprise of the graphic designers she played in *So Big* and *Ex-Lady*, except that this time she's drawing knockoffs of women's gowns and standing in the background looking glum. William Powell plays a debonair schemer who gets Davis's character involved in a counterfeit couture business.

Fashions of 1934 comes to delirious if incomprehensible life in a musical number. Wrapped in one of Orry-Kelly's less successful designs, an oversized wing-framed cape constructed out of black feathers (the effect is that of a hefty hunchbacked vulture), an ersatz grand duchess launches into a tortured solo, "Spin a Little Web of Dreams." A chorus girl backstage falls asleep after opening a window next to a pile of ostrich feathers. A tiny bit of feather drifts in the air until it is caught onstage—another stage, a much grander stage—by one of twenty or thirty befeathered blonde harpists plucking the rhinestone strings of human harps. Stone-faced women dressed in white ostrich feathers serve as the columns. And with this, the drab functionality of the director, William Dieterle, gives way to the gloriously demented genius of Busby

Berkeley. Huge feather fans pump and sway on a series of vast, multi-tiered sets. Overhead shots turn feather-armed women into gigantic, undulating chrysanthemums. Brilliant lights glare off the coifs of identical chorines dressed in ostrich feather bikinis as the camera swings around them, unrestrained by mundane considerations like story logic or character development. A battalion of white-feathered oarswomen row a galley—with feathered oars—across a fabric sea. Then the backstage chorine wakes up, and it's all over, and unfortunately, Bette Davis is nowhere near any of the fun while it lasts.

Bette's own black Scottie, Tibby, makes a cameo appearance sitting on a hatbox and being carried into a cab, but beyond getting her dog on-screen, Bette's performance in *Fashions of 1934* is one of her most rote.

JIMMY THE GENT, Davis's next picture, is a lopsided screwball comedy, with Jimmy Cagney's character far outweighing Bette's in both screen time and narrative interest. Jimmy Corrigan (Cagney) is a shady private investigator who specializes in finding the heirs to unclaimed millions. Bette plays his former employee who has moved on to a nominally more respectable firm. It's a Warner Bros. comedy, which is to say it's purposefully dark and blunt. The film opens with a grimly comical montage of various millionaires violently dying: a motorboat wrecks, a ship capsizes, a plane crashes, a jockey breaks his neck, all entertainingly illustrated by spinning newspapers heralding the lurid and exciting deaths.

Davis was never particularly fond of *Jimmy the Gent*—neither she nor most critics ever appreciated her genuine if offbeat talent for comedy—but the movie has found its share of fans. The critic Otis Ferguson wrote, "If this wasn't the fastest little whirlwind of true life on the raw fringe, then I missed the other one."[35] And the critic and screenwriter Andrew Bergman (*Blazing Saddles*) called it "simply a great American comedy" and "the funniest film of Cagney's career." *Jimmy the Gent* may not be *Bringing Up Baby* or *The Awful Truth*, but it has its moments, one of which Cagney himself engineered in irritated response to his own casting. As Bergman noted, Cagney's head resembles that of Sluggo:[36]

Cagney: "When I heard I was going to play another one of *those* guys, I said to myself, 'They want another of those mugs, I'll really give them a mug.' So I had my head shaved right down to the skull except for a little top knot in front, and I had the makeup man put bottle scars all over the back of my head. The opening shot was of my back to the camera, with all those scars in sharp focus. . . . Hal Wallis, who was running that part of the studio at the time, took my haircut as a personal affront. 'What is that son-of-a-bitch trying to do to me now?' he said. To *him*, for God's sake."[37]

Both Cagney and Davis tend to speak quickly even in the most laconic of movie circumstances. In *Jimmy the Gent*, they spit their lines like bullets. "They got a stiff down there that sounds swell," says Cagney. Says Bette, "You can go down deeper, stay under longer, and come up dirtier than any man I've ever known!" Smartly, she delivers this screwball line not in outrage but as cold fact.

Cagney recalled Davis as being unhappy during the filming of *Jimmy the Gent*: "Her unhappiness seeped through to the rest of us, and she was a little hard to get along with."[38] Cagney's biographer, Doug Warren, went further, describing her personal reaction to her costar as one of "contempt."[39]

A convoluted murder mystery, *Fog Over Frisco* introduces Davis in a racy nightclub where criminals aren't unfamiliar. The men at the bar hear several loud bangs and instinctively duck. The director, William Dieterle, cuts to a bunch of balloons, behind which Bette's face emerges in close-up as she pops them one by one with a pin. She's a good-time girl, this Arlene Bradford—socialite, fashion plate, and trafficker in stolen bonds. Her staid financier father (Arthur Byron) is appalled simply by her nightlife: "You promised to turn over a new leaf after your last scandalous escapade," he chastises over the breakfast table the next morning, faux-elegantly pronouncing the last word to rhyme with *act of God*. But the leaf never turns. All too soon—the whole movie runs all of sixty-eight minutes—Arlene turns up as a corpse in her own rumble seat, and by the end, her responsible stepsister, the extraordinarily named Valkyr (Margaret Lindsay), fresh from a kidnapping, has to explain the whole tangle in voice-over. The suspicious, snooping butler is really a cop; both a fiancé and a yacht each have two names; there's something about a secret code. . . .

Fog Over Frisco was fun for Davis, who had kind things to say about it in retrospect. For one thing, its production was supervised by Henry Blanke, whom she admired. He was, she later wrote, "a producer of infinite taste, an understanding man, whatever our problems. He was a great contributor to the Warner product during the great Hal Wallis years at Warner Bros. He was an enormous contributor to my personal career. The part in *Fog Over Frisco* was one I adored. It also was a very good script, directed superbly by Dieterle."[40] The film was shot with characteristic Warner Bros. efficiency from January 22 to February 10, 1934.

Two days before shooting began, Bette Davis underwent her first abortion. Ham told the studio that she was suffering from sunstroke and the flu and needed a few days' rest.[41]

WHILE SHOOTING 20,000 *Years in Sing Sing*, in the late summer of 1932, the screenwriter Wilson Mizner handed Bette a W. Somerset Maugham novel called *Of Human Bondage* and suggested she read it with an eye toward playing the disreputable antiheroine.[42] Mizner was himself a colorful character. His voice was thin, his dentures were loose, and his hands were battered into stumps, a condition he attributed to "hitting whores up in Alaska."[43] He evidently appreciated Maugham's Mildred Rogers from several perspectives.

A few months later, when the director John Cromwell screened *Cabin in the Cotton*—he was thinking of casting Richard Barthelmess in something—he saw Davis if not for the first time then at least from a fresh perspective.

The trouble was, it was RKO that would be making *Of Human Bondage*, not Warner Bros. Davis claimed to have shown up at Jack Warner's office every day along with Warner's shoeshine boy: "I spent six months in supplication and drove Mr. Warner to the point of desperation—desperate enough to say 'Yes'—anything to get rid of me."[44] When Warner at last relented and agreed to the loan, he did so with a certain you've-made-your-bed attitude, not comprehending why any of his actresses would ever want to play a dislikable creature like Mildred. As Bette later noted, "If my memory is correct, he said, 'Go and hang yourself.'"[45]

It's pure speculation, but one wonders whether Bette Davis would have had the January 1934 abortion had *Of Human Bondage* not been presenting itself imminently as her first potential masterpiece. "Harmon didn't even know she was pregnant," insists Anne Roberts Nelson, Ham's second wife. "It was Ruthie who talked her into it. If Bette couldn't work because she was pregnant, the meal ticket was gone."[46] But it wasn't just Ruthie's financial support that was at stake, though Mother's comfort—all her housing, clothing, food, and entertainment expenses, not to mention her mad money, for after she moved with Bette to Hollywood in 1930 she didn't work another day in her life—did indeed rest squarely and heavily on Bette's shoulders. At stake was something even more central to Bette's life than her mother: her art. Mildred Rogers was the first truly important role Bette wanted.

Of Human Bondage began shooting toward the end of February 1934, at RKO's studios in Hollywood on the corner of Melrose and Gower, and continued through April 9. At first, Leslie Howard and his English friends were snobby toward the little loaner from Warner Bros. "There was lots of whispering in little Druid circles whenever I appeared," she later noted.[47] But Howard's agent at the time, Mike Levee, took Howard aside in his dressing room and said, "If you're not very careful, that girl will steal the picture," to which Howard rather self-servingly responded, "Do you know something, Mike? If I am very careful, she will steal the picture," thereby giving himself much of the credit for Bette's eventual triumph.[48]

Davis's eagerness for audiences to hold her character in contempt is not the only turning-point aspect of *Of Human Bondage*. It's here that Bette really begins to deliver her lines like punches. We're introduced to Mildred in the restaurant where she works as a waitress. Philip (Howard), who has a club foot and walks with a pronounced limp, is seated at a table with a friend. Philip makes a smart remark when Mildred strides over to his table, and Mildred responds, "I *don't* know *what* you *mean*."

Bette's Cockney accent is layered, impure—a low-class twang unsuccessfully masked by pretension. But beyond the skillful inflection, the moment is historic because Bette Davis (to borrow the novelist Blanche McCrary Boyd's marvelous phrase) has started to speak in italics, in this case highly imitable iambs.

Throughout the film, Mildred replies to each of Philip's invitations with, "*I* don't *mind*," a line Bette reads with increasingly irritating condescension, a vocal recognition of what we're asked to see as Mildred's pathetic attempt to rise above her station. It's an accent noticeable as an actress's impression of Cockney, not a accurate mimic's impersonation. Bette Davis demands to be recognized as Bette Davis, the stresses her vocal signature writ large.

Vocalization aside, Mildred is also about movement—a display of physical, one could even say carnal, confidence. It's the swing and strut of a particularly common whore. In the initial flirting conversation with

Howard, Bette cocks her head back and forth in opposing diagonals, shifting her shoulders as she does so. "I *don't* know *whether* I *will* or *whether* I *won't*," she announces (in response to Philip's invitation to let him find her a reason to smile). When Philip walks away from the table, Cromwell dwells on his limp not for the audience's sake but for Mildred's. There's a shot of Philip walking past her, a shot of Mildred casting her eyes downward, a shot of Philip's legs walking away against a bare checked floor, and finally a shot of Mildred's reaction. "*Ha*," she says with a knowing cluck, but Davis undermines Mildred's superiority by shifting her eyes away to the left, a minute register of her own self-consciousness and a subtle recognition of Mildred's as well.

Davis herself claimed never to have understood Philip's fierce attraction to Mildred. She believed in Mildred's vile nature, of course; one has no doubt that Davis nailed this character so squarely because she saw something of herself there—the manipulative ambition, if nothing else. But for Davis, Philip's "whimpering adoration in the face of Mildred's brutal diffidence" was unfathomable. As an actor's issue, this was "Howard's problem and not mine," she later wrote, but it's telling that Davis refused to acknowledge in herself what Maugham treats as essential to the human condition: self-destructive desire.[49] The "bondage" of the title is the helpless submission of drastically unreturned love. Could it possibly be that Davis never felt such an emotion? Or is it that she just refused to own up to it in public?

When Davis cuts loose in the film's climactic scene, it's scenery chomping—loud, attention grabbing, histrionic. She gives Mildred the feral rage of a cornered animal, and the scene is justifiably famous. But it makes full sense only because Davis has been willing to debase herself all along. To set up Philip's revelation, Cromwell cuts to a close-up of Mildred from Philip's point of view: her eyes are languid; her mouth is slightly gaping. She is leaning forward in the drearily inviting stance of a cheap hooker. Philip has good reason to tell Mildred at last that she disgusts him; Bette Davis had never before been allowed to make herself so repulsive onscreen.

"*Me?*" she says, rolling her shoulders. "I disgust *you*? You. You! You're *too fine!*" She begins to turn away from him but reels back and spits, "You won't have none of me, but you'll sit here all night looking at your naked females! You cad! You dirty swine!" She's clutching her hands together just below the bottom of the screen, then jerks her right arm out briefly. "I never cared for you—not once! I was always making a *fool* of ya. Ya *bored me stiff*! I *hated* ya! It made me *sick* when I had ta let ya kiss me. I only did it because ya *begged* me!" Davis is doing all of this with piercing vocal rage but very little physical action; she's once again gripping her hands together to contain herself physically—to fire it all out through her voice. "Ya hounded me—*ya drove me crazy*!" She wheels around but returns to face him again. "And after ya kissed me I always used to wipe my mouth. *Wipe my mouth!*" This is when she chooses the precise physical gesture: grossly, even obscenely, she employs the back of her arm to demonstrate the wiping. "But I made up for it! For every kiss I had a laugh . . . ! We laughed at ya, because you were such a *mug, a mug, a mug!*" She hurls a plate to the floor. "You know what you are, *you gimpy-legged monster*?!"

Unfortunately for Bette, Cromwell cuts away from her at the height of her wrath to Howard to get his stricken reaction: "You're a *cripple*! A *cripple*! A *cripple*!"

As the film critic Martin Shingler observes, "This is not Davis in a rage but an actress in motion, presenting fury through her shoulders, neck, torso, her arms and hands, her eyes and her mouth, through her voice and her breathing."[50] Davis is one of melodrama's greatest dancers.

In the following scene, a knife cuts through a painting, and the camera pulls back to reveal Mildred in a garish black outfit with feathered collar. She's breathing heavily, having laid the room to waste. Her mouth is lolling. "You *love* these *things*. You *love* what they're *meant* to *be*." Davis snarls the words with rancid sarcasm. "*You want to be a doctor!*" she snaps as she rips pages out of his medical textbook. Then she goes through the desk drawers until she finds Philip's bonds. Throughout all of this, remarkably, Davis's face is entirely obscured by a jauntily louche hat with a tacky oversized fabric flower, but she's performing with her whole body so her face doesn't need to be visible. "This'll take ya through medical school," she says as she sets the bonds on fire and leaves them burning in an ashtray. She stomps out of the room, leading with her shoulders.

Of Human Bondage is the first defining moment in Bette Davis's career, and it's psychologically perverse, to say the least. Motion pictures finally gave her the sweet chance to force millions of people to despise her.

THE FIRST OSCAR

"**D**EAR GOD! WHAT A HORROR!" IS
Davis's description of the picture Jack Warner stuck her in after she returned to the studio after shooting *Of Human Bondage*. *Housewife* was yet
another Warners programmer—something to fill the screen for the allotted seventy minutes while the audience finished its popcorn.[1] George
Brent and Ann Dvorak are young marrieds, Bill and Nan, with a son
named Buddy; Bette is the sophisticated advertising copywriter who
tries to break them up. They're all old friends, but ambitious Pat (Bette)
has gone off and seen the world and returned a successful and sophisticated career woman. At lunch with Nan, Pat sends back her duck because the dressing is made with sauterne rather than Chablis. "It's not
nearly as good as the *canard sauvage* I had in Paris," she casually drops
to an intimidated-looking Nan. Of course she steals Bill away, but Bill
becomes so hardened and distracted by his affair with the modern Pat
that he runs Buddy over with the car. That changes his tune but quick.
He returns to Nan, leaving Pat to go off and drink her dinner with an
aging cosmetics executive named Duprey.

Buddy recovers.

The film was shot from April 11 to May 7, 1934, though Bette, most
displeased by the lackluster role she was being forced to play after Mildred Rogers, didn't show up until April 18. She was inspired to appear

only after a series of hostile telegrams from Warner Bros. that pointed out that she did not in fact have script approval and was forced to play any damned role the studio put her in.[2]

Adding insult to insult, Warners immediately assigned Bette to a secondary role in *The Case of the Howling Dog*. Bette rebelled again, this time refusing to appear at all. She stuck to her refusal even after a slew of wires and phone calls from the boys in the front office. At one point, Jack Warner himself telephoned her at home. Ham answered and told the head of the studio that Miss Davis was busy. She'd call him back, Ham said. She didn't.[3]

The Case of the Howling Dog, the first film adaptation of an Erle Stanley Gardner legal-mystery novel, was to feature Warren William as Perry Mason and Mary Astor as the defendant, Bessie. It's all about multiple wives and dogs and corpses buried under the garage. Bette was supposed to be Della Street, Mason's ever-competent, mostly-in-the-background secretary.

And so she walked out. That Warners easily replaced her with a first-timer named Helen Trenholme indicates the meatlessness of the role. Trenholme made only one more film before retiring from the screen.

Davis was refusing to honor the terms of her contract, so the studio slapped her on suspension. Had *Of Human Bondage* not opened on June 27, 1934, to rave reviews, Davis might have remained on suspension for the rest of her tenure at the studio. But it was quite humiliating to Jack Warner to be widely seen as a clueless vulgarian and artless hack who kept sticking a brilliant actress—who, according to *Life*'s review of *Of Human Bondage*, had given "probably the best performance ever recorded on the screen by a U.S. actress"—in silly parts in silly movies or, in her current situation, kept her sequestered from the camera altogether.[4]

Bordertown was the result. Warner took Bette off suspension and paired her with the magnetic Paul Muni, who was an even bigger Warners star than James Cagney. Warner seemed to be getting the point at long last.

The film began shooting on August 17, 1934. Johnny Ramirez, fresh out of a storefront law school in downtown Los Angeles, swiftly gets disbarred after punching out the opposing counsel. He abandons his weeping *mamacita* and resurfaces, far to the south, as the bouncer, later the co-owner, of a bordertown casino run by good old Charlie Roark (Eugene Pallette). A ritzy white sedan pulls up at the curb. "Hello, Johnny!"

says a familiar voice—Bette is Mrs. Marie Roark. She's one hot number, and visually, too: the cinematographer, Tony Gaudio, is fond of bouncing intense light off of Marie's brilliantly blonde hair. When Charlie heads off to L.A. to see his dentist, Marie makes her move on Johnny, but he spurns her. So when Charlie gets back with his new dentures, she bumps him off by leaving him drunk in the garage with the motor running.

After a brief interlude of guilt-free serenity, Marie starts to crack up, and Bette plays it up with flitting eyes and hair-clutching fingers. But Hal Wallis thought she wasn't going nutty enough quickly enough. After seeing rushes of the scene in which Marie visits the construction site of Johnny's new casino, Wallis was annoyed: "It's about time she's starting to crack. . . . She plays it like Alice in Wonderland."[5]

There was a lengthy, loud fight on the set. The subject: cold cream. One scene finds Marie waking up in the Roarks' vast baroque bed, and Bette decided to play it with an eye toward realism by smearing cold cream all over her face and applying curlers to her hair. The film's tubby director, Archie Mayo, threw a fit. Fits being contagious, Bette threw one, too, as did Hal Wallis. In Bette's words, they "screamed at each other for four hours."[6] "You can't look like that on the screen!" Wallis roared. Bette replied, equally loudly, that she looked precisely the way her character would look in bed in the morning. "Muni stood up for me," Bette later claimed, but she lost the fight anyway.[7]

She won a more important one, however. In a courtroom scene late in the film—mad Marie has falsely accused Johnny of forcing her to murder Charlie—Mayo directed Bette to go completely bonkers in what she later described as "the fright-wig, bug-eyed tradition."[8] Davis dug in her heels and refused. Wallis was again summoned to the soundstage to mediate. "If you want me to do it obviously, silent picture style, then why don't we bring back silent picture titles, too?" Bette argued. Her idea was to play her scene on the witness stand all but catatonically at first and grow increasingly distracted as the scene progressed. Although her performance isn't especially subtle, it works. Given the twitches and spasms of her earlier scenes, for Davis to have ratcheted up Marie's looniness to the shrieking level demanded by a hack like Archie Mayo would have provoked derisive hoots. Davis held her audiences to a higher standard, and they appreciated it.

From *Bordertown*, Warners pushed Davis into an odd, small movie—*The Girl from 10th Avenue*—which finds Bette as a shopgirl who distracts a jilted society fellow, Geoffrey (Ian Hunter), from his misery. One night they get both drunk and married. They plan to move to South America. His friends treat her like a golddigging whore. They fight and make up. That's it. The most remarkable aspect of *The Girl from 10th Avenue* is that it was the fourth filmed version of the property. This one was shot in March 1935.

Her next film was no masterpiece, but it wasn't embarrassing, either. In 1931, United Artists and Howard Hughes made *The Front Page*, a speedy newspaper comedy with Pat O'Brien and Adolphe Menjou. In 1935, Warner Bros. made *Front Page Woman*, with Bette Davis and George Brent—a proto–*His Girl Friday* with Brent in the Cary Grant role and Davis in Rosalind Russell's. Like the original *Front Page*, two rival reporters threaten to best each other, and like *His Girl Friday*, they're a guy and a gal in prickly love. As a hard-headed 1930s newspaperwoman (though she faints after witnessing her first electrocution), Davis gets to develop her independent, driven persona: the career woman who doesn't give a damn if she ends up single. And she even manages to wear one of those skinny, weasel-like furs with the head still on it without looking camp.

Front Page Woman began shooting in mid-April 1935 and was released in July, around the time *Special Agent* started up. "I like you," says the eponymous agent (George Brent) to Davis over a dinner table. "You don't ask asinine questions at a ball game, you don't get lipstick on a guy's collar, and you carry your own cigarettes." That's the way he proposes to her. Since her character is just that kind of gal, she takes him up on the offer.

George Brent is a star whose luster has faded over the decades to the point that his popularity in the 1930s verges on the inexplicable. Brent was handsome but not sharply or memorably so. What once seemed dashing is now dulling. His masculinity, dependable and solid in the 1930s, looks merely stolid in retrospect. *Special Agent* was the fifth film Davis made with the affable if wooden star. She'd go on to make six more, and although two of them are among Davis's finest (*Jezebel* and *Dark Victory*)—and as much as she liked him personally—Brent ended up hampering her films more than he helped them. Davis once said that Brent's onscreen energy never matched his real-life vigor. After all, this man was a trained pilot and used to buzz the studio for laughs. Still, Brent's virile charm rarely registered on celluloid, where it mattered most.

In *Special Agent*, Davis plays a gangster's bookkeeper. It's a mark of the early post–Production Code era in which the film was scripted and produced that Davis's Julie remains entirely above reproach despite the central role she plays in the criminal activities of a vicious, murdering thug (Ricardo Cortez). Julie is yet another in a string of Davis's smart women with jobs, apartments, and Orry-Kelly wardrobes. That her lifestyle comes by way of concealing a gangster's profits from the government is an issue *Special Agent* both takes for granted and downplays; Warners wouldn't abandon its down-and-dirty scenarios entirely, but the imposition of the Code in 1934 meant that the studio couldn't flaunt them either.

There's a blandness to Davis's performance in *Special Agent*, however, that goes beyond the Code's repressive moralism. She makes Julie a bit too comfortable with the bind she finds herself in as both a thug's Gal Friday and a G-man's stoolie-fiancée. "Maybe I won't end up in the morgue," she glibly observes toward the end of the movie. Then again, *Special Agent*'s writing—the screenwriters are Laird Doyle and Abem Finkel—is fairly low-grade even for a studio never known for its literary aspirations. With Davis and Brent each tied up with string inside the hideout, a cop outside actually utters the line "Whatever you do, keep your men under cover, or those kids in there are goners!"

It is time to introduce Joan Crawford's broad-shouldered silhouette to the drama, if only to pry her quickly away from it, Bette Davis's life and art being far more compelling than her overworked feud with Crawford. Davis's next picture, *Dangerous*, costarred Franchot Tone, to whom Bette was quite attracted but who was in love with Joan, who over the years generated increasing friction with Bette, friction that led to the triumph of *What Ever Happened to Baby Jane?* but that proceeded to get so out of hand that Joan fled the production of *Hush . . . Hush, Sweet Charlotte* midway through filming, and witty Bette pasted an eight-by-ten glossy of Joan with her eyes whited out and her teeth blackened in her 1964 scrapbook. . . . Forget the resurrection of Christ. For gay men of a certain age, *this* is the greatest story ever told.

This particular reiteration begins with *Dangerous*'s supervisor, Harry Joe Brown, supposedly witnessing a sexually liberated Bette Davis giving Franchot Tone a blow job in one of their dressing rooms. Brown told

Crawford's biographers Lawrence Quirk and William Schoell that "when they saw me they didn't seem to give a damn."[9] At the same time, everyone connected with *Dangerous* noticed that Tone kept showing up after lunch covered in Crawford's lipstick, and that Bette was terribly jealous. Moreover, Joan was really bisexual and always wanted a piece of Bette, and the virgin-est Yankee who ever walked in could, by 1935, give adulterous head to her male costar but Bette would have no part of a lesbian affair for the rest of her life, and that is supposedly one of the foundations of the Homeric feud.

Moving on. Davis didn't like the script for *Dangerous*, at least at first. "It was maudlin and mawkish with a pretense at quality, which in scripts, as in home furnishings, is often worse than junk."[10] It was the work of Laird Doyle, who called it *Hard Luck Dame*. Davis's derision notwithstanding, it's one of Doyle's better efforts. But as was often the case, Davis's lack of respect for the script, even misplaced, only served to fuel the fire of her performance. Some actors need, as they say, to believe in the material—to maintain the touchingly naive faith that the characters they play are not in fact fictitious. Davis, a supreme stylist, often did better when she thought the script was crap and the characters phony. Her Yankee ethos was sturdy and effective: she believed that it was her duty to make a bad script or a shaky character work, so she pushed herself all the harder and made her artistic decisions all the more adroitly. As Brigid Brophy writes, "She is actually good in *bad* parts. . . . Miss Davis needed her bad scripts as sorely as they needed her; they were what she needed to wrestle through in pursuit of that 'truth' and 'realism' (her words) which to her are 'more than natural.' "[11]

The story of a once superb, now derelict Broadway actress—what Jeanne Eagels might have become if she hadn't overdosed on chloral hydrate in 1929—*Dangerous* won Davis her first Academy Award.[12] This Oscar is usually considered to be just the consolation prize for not even having been nominated for *Of Human Bondage*. (The 1934 winner was Claudette Colbert for *It Happened One Night*, one of the record-breaking five Oscars awarded to that film; the other nominees were Norma Shearer for *The Barretts of Wimpole Street* and the opera singer Grace Moore for *One Night of Love*.) But *Dangerous* also has something else going for it in terms of Academy tastes: this time, Davis's calculating schemer finds salvation in the end. Mildred Rogers dies a pitiful, disgusting death—syphilis barely disguised as consumption. The hard-luck dame of *Dangerous*, on the other hand, finds redemption not only from alcoholism but from egocentrism as well—quite a feat for any actress, and consequently one the Academy found Oscar-worthy.

Don Bellows (Franchot Tone), a successful society architect, goes slumming downtown one night with his indefatigably cordial fiancée, Gail (Margaret Lindsay), and notices the on-the-skids actress Joyce Heath sitting alone in the corner downing her thirtieth shot of gin. He gives Gail the slip and takes Joyce to his magnificent upstate farm for a week of rehabilitation, and soon he's financing Joyce's triumphant return to Broadway and ditching Gail, who takes her rejection with perfect poise. But Joyce's jinx, the hard luck of the original title, returns in the form of a secret husband who won't give her a divorce, so she hustles him into Don's car, speeds into the night, and crashes into a convenient tree.

One might assume that such desperate melodrama would entice Bette Davis into a paroxysm of scenery chewing in an attempt to distract her audience from the plot's preposterousness. But, if anything, she underplays almost every scene, a strategy that gives Joyce Heath a measure of dignity that isn't inherent to the material. Here, Davis's struggle is to make it all look easy. There's a moment toward the end, when Joyce must selflessly act selfish for Don's own good: "You're no longer important to me. Your importance ended when the show closed," she says. The lines are cruel, but Davis plays the scene so coolly that there's only the barest indication that Joyce is being duplicitous. Or is she? Ernie Haller's lighting is flattering to Davis but not unduly glamorizing, and Bette relies on it to catch the glint in her eyes—the shine that reveals the performance behind the performance, the lie Joyce tells that convinces Don to leave her. It's the seasoned performance of a twenty-seven-year-old actress with twenty-seven films under her still-tiny belt.

Robert E. Sherwood's gangster melodrama, *The Petrified Forest*, opened on Broadway on January 7, 1935, and starred Leslie Howard as an effete British writer who has actually written nothing at all. Humphrey Bogart costarred as a grim killer heading for an existential as well as geographic border. By October, Charles Kenyon and Delmer Daves's adaptation was in production at Warner Bros.

The studio bought the property for Howard and Edward G. Robinson, Bogart having all but abandoned Hollywood after his minor role in

Three on a Match, Warners having forgotten him, never really having seen him in the first place. Robinson, perhaps out of pride, later claimed that he didn't relish the idea of playing yet another gangster and purposely backed out of the project. But of greater impact was Leslie Howard's incessant lobbying for Bogart to play the role of Duke Mantee again. "No Bogart, no deal," reads one cable from Howard to Jack Warner.[13]

It was a slow-going production, especially for Warner Bros., where actors and technicians alike were essentially human sprockets whose chief purpose was to yank movies through production as briskly as the front office could spur them. Shooting began on October 14.[14] By the end of the month the production was three days behind schedule, and Hal Wallis was becoming aggravated. Wallis was a man of exacting taste and had a nagging compulsion to care. Unlike some of his colleagues at Warners, Wallis understood that crafting a motion picture could take time, that getting it right was as important as getting it in the can. But even Wallis was losing patience after hearing reports that Leslie Howard had been showing up on the set anywhere from thirty to ninety minutes late every day and feeling no particular need to explain himself. Then Bette got a sore throat on a Friday, skipped that day's shoot, and refused to come in on Sunday to make it up. She sprained her ankle on the morning of November 22.

The Petrified Forest went into overtime for another reason, too: its director, Archie Mayo, shot a great deal of unusable footage, the most ludicrous of which was a close-up of Bogart with a mounted moose head in the background. Mayo had framed the shot in such a clumsy way that the moose appeared to be growing out of Bogart's head. Wallis was especially enraged by this boo-boo because Mayo really had only had one interior set to work with—the roadhouse dining room—and should have known his way around it. The production finally closed on November 30, a full eleven days behind schedule.

Aside from some lunar-looking desert locations, which were filmed at Red Rock Canyon near Las Vegas, *The Petrified Forest* takes place at a last-chance gas station/barbecue joint somewhere in the pasteboard Southwest of a Warners soundstage in Burbank, with strategically rolling tumbleweeds indicating the raw timelessness of artificiality. Bette's character, Gabby, yearns to leave this drab middle-of-nowhere for the excitement and vibrant culture of France, but she's stuck there with her ineffectual father and a fidgety old coot named Gramps—stuck, that is, until Leslie Howard's Alan Squier appears out of nowhere and discovers the means for her to depart. The agent of her exit is Duke Mantee, a can-do American man of action who, in this perversely modern work, takes the form of Bogart's morbid, murdering criminal, a refreshing contrast to Howard's tired but florid uselessness.

> HOWARD: I began to feel the enchantment of this desert. I looked up at the sky, and the stars seemed to be mocking me, reproving me. They were pointing the way to that gleaming sign and saying, "There's the end of your tether! You thought you could escape and skip off to the Phoenix Palace, but we know better!" That's what the stars told me. And perhaps they know that carnage is imminent, and that I'm due to be among the fallen. Fascinating thought!
>
> BOGART (snarling): Let's skip it.
>
> GRAMPS: It certainly does feel great to have a real killer around here again!

Davis is in muted form again in *The Petrified Forest*, understating her naively romantic Gabby to an extraordinary degree. It's her most modest and generous performance to date. She employs no tics, displays no dynamism. Her Gabby is a girl of not particularly profound dreams who may or may not make it to Europe in the end, so lacking is she in the ambition and drive that were essential to Bette's own personality. It's safe to assume that underplaying Gabby was a conscious decision on Davis's part, a deliberate act of actorly generosity that kept the central drama of the piece between Howard and Bogart—beautiful Old World fatigue and manly, pointless New World achievement. Sol Polito, the film's cinematographer, takes a similar view of the drama. He's fascinated by Bogart's crags and scruff and doesn't do much to overemphasize Bette's porcelain-like complexion.

"I hope you don't mind my staring at you like that," Davis said to Michael Caine many years later, around the time of *Alfie* (1966). "But when I saw you I thought of Leslie Howard. You remind me so much of him." "I was very slim in those days," Caine reports, "with long blond hair, and other people had told me before that I resembled him." Bette continued: "Did you know that Leslie screwed every woman on every movie he was ever in, with the exception of me? I told him that I was not going to be plastered on the end of a list of his conquests." ("I made what I considered to be a sort of approving moral grunt," says Caine. "The reason I was staring at you," Davis continued, "was that I was thinking what difference would it have made now if I had." Caine describes the last part as having had "a sort of a wistful tone about it.")[15]

BETTE LEFT THE set of *The Petrified Forest* on Friday, November 29, 1935, and sent her lawyer to Jack Warner's office the following day. The reason: she had just received a letter ordering her to appear three days later for wardrobe discussions for the next picture the studio had pitched her into: *The Man in the Black Hat*, Warners' second attempt at making a murder mystery of one of Dashiell Hammett's novels. Warner declined to be in his office on Saturday when the lawyer arrived, so Bette fired off a telegram: she had worked for six weeks straight on *The Petrified Forest*, she noted, and she felt that she needed two or three weeks to recuperate rather than start another film on Monday. "I have been ill several times on the picture as it is," she told Warner, and so really she had no choice but to refuse to appear at all in *The Man in the Black Hat*.

Warner responded by insisting that the studio's own doctor verify the state of Bette's health and sent him to her house on Franklin Avenue at 6:00 p.m. on Monday. Bette found it simply impossible to be home at the time, and in any event, she tartly observed in a subsequent communication with her boss, she refused to be examined by Warners' doctor on the grounds that she had not actually claimed to be sick but had merely requested a rest, having been sick previously. Warner slapped her on suspension as of Tuesday. The contretemps was resolved in Warner Bros.' favor on Friday when Bette reported to the wardrobe department for costume discussions for *The Man in the Black Hat*, whereupon she was promptly taken off suspension.[16]

The Man in the Black Hat went through several title changes before it was released in late July 1936—*Hard Luck Dame, Men on Her Mind, The Man with the Black Hat,* and finally *Satan Met a Lady*. Hammett's original title—*The Maltese Falcon*—would have been better, but Warners had already used it for the first go-round in 1931 with Bebe Daniels and Ricardo Cortez. Besides, in this version they'd changed the eponymous falcon into a treasure-filled ivory horn, Roland's Trumpet, which would have made a poor title. (Roland's Trumpet has to do with an ancient instrument, Charlemagne, Saracens, a cache of invaluable jewels. . . .)

Satan Met a Lady is terrible. The *New York Times* appears to have had the inside track on the mess when it called the film "merely a farrago of nonsense representing a series of practical studio compromises with an unworkable script."[17] However poor the original script may have been, though, Warners' editor Max Parker assembled an initial cut that Warners' executives—at least one of whom had approved the script, after all—found particularly incomprehensible, so they brought in Warren Low to recut the picture.[18] (*Satan Met a Lady* was the first of eight Bette Davis films Low edited. According to Davis, Low was "the greatest editor at Warner Bros. I owe him a lot. He used to fight for me when something of mine was going to be cut that would hurt my performance."[19]) But the end result was still a fiasco. Attempting to ride the coattails of MGM's *The Thin Man*, the director, William Dieterle, makes feeble attempts at blending mystery with comedy, but they don't work. With the spectacle of Bette whipping a gun out of a smart, tailored jacket and forcing Warren William out of her luxe apartment—not to mention Arthur Treacher stabbing a couch to death with a dagger and busty Alison Skipworth turning up as the notorious Madame Barabbas—the whole enterprise should have been a lot more fun.

In late 1935 and early 1936, while Warner Bros. was shoehorning Bette Davis into *Satan Met a Lady*, John Ford, at RKO, was preparing a much more elegant picture: *Mary of Scotland*, with Katharine Hepburn as Mary. Bette coveted the role of Elizabeth, Mary's rival. One of her lawyers, Martin Gang, went so far as to tell Warner Bros. that RKO was ready to cast her in *Mary of Scotland* if Warners would agree to the loan, but Warners turned down the request. Ford's biographer Scott Eyman astutely ascribes the decision to Warners' "corporate ego" not being able to "risk another Davis success at another studio" after her triumph in *Of Human Bondage*. That said, Ford himself wanted Tallulah Bankhead to be Elizabeth but ended up choosing Fredric March's wife, Florence Eldridge. (A much more unlikely candidate for Elizabeth I—Ginger Rogers—also campaigned for the role.) Bette's own account of her disappointment puts the blame on Ford, not Jack Warner. Davis claimed she was granted a meeting with Ford, who (in the words of Whitney Stine, another of her biographers) gruffly "told her she talked too much and ended the appointment."[20]

So instead of playing Elizabeth of England for one of the greatest directors in the world, Davis ended up having to turn herself into an ersatz cosmetics heiress for Alfred E. Green in *The Golden Arrow*, yet another film she despised.

The Golden Arrow is a screwball comedy about an heiress and a reporter, only the heiress isn't really an heiress but a working girl plucked out of the "cashier's cage of a hick town cafeteria" in order to pose as the madcap Daisy Appleby of the face cream Applebys. Davis could play comedy well when asked to, and personally she was a very funny lady, but she never *got* comedy in the way Hepburn or Jean Arthur or Irene Dunne did. These other actresses were willing to demean themselves for laughs; Davis was only willing to do it for drama's sake. She found screwball comedy unbecoming on principle in ways other screwball stars never did, and it hampered her ability to let loose.

Davis and George Brent each acquire black eyes near the end of the film, then get into a cab. "The international hilarity this was supposed to provoke was further insured by a three-shot in which the hackie himself had not one but two shiners," Davis writes in *The Lonely Life*. "The whole affair was a black eye as far as I was concerned."[21]

It's brittle, perhaps, but not bad. Screwball comedies are often about the irrepressible theatricality of life and the enchanting impossibility of love—the black eyes lovers inevitably get in pursuit of each other. But at this point in her tenure at Warner Bros., Bette Davis wasn't inclined to find such stuff funny. She wanted tougher meat to chew. She saw herself as a serious actress, not a clown. And to her, the makeup department's black eye was just another symbol of Jack Warner's abuse.

The Golden Arrow began shooting on Monday, January 20, 1936.[22] "Am dead," Davis telegrammed to Hal Wallis at the end of the third week of filming. She called in sick on Friday, February 7, citing "eye strain shooting in blazing sun and glare of water and reflectors."[23] (There are several scenes set on a yacht.)

Fighting with Warner Bros. was becoming integral to Bette Davis's life, as necessary as acting and more satisfyingly vital than her husband. Although the Academy nominated her for the Best Actress award for *Dangerous*, Davis's increasing compulsion to turn everything into an iron-clad bone of contention led her to issue a threat: she would not attend the awards dinner as one of Warners' shining lights, the studio's Best Actress nominee, but would instead fly off to Honolulu for a vacation with Ruthie. Davis eventually agreed to attend the dinner and go to Hawaii two days later. Still, it must have rankled her that she had specifically to request permission for the trip from Jack Warner.[24] (As it turned out, she ditched Ruthie in Honolulu but traveled to New York instead, prompting Ruthie to send a guilt-tripping three-word telegram to her daughter: "Anyone love me?")[25]

O N MARCH 5, 1936, in a banquet hall at the Biltmore Hotel in Los Angeles, D. W. Griffith announced that the winner of the Academy of Motion Picture Arts and Sciences' award for Best Actress was Bette Davis for *Dangerous*. "There was a shout from my table and everyone was kissing me," Davis writes in *The Lonely Life*. But as she walked to the stage to accept the award, self-doubt erupted. She *knew*: "*It's a consolation prize*. This nagged at me. It was true that even if the honor had been earned, it had been earned *last* year. There was no doubt that Hepburn's performance [in *Alice Adams*] deserved the award."[26] In those days, the Academy released the results of the voting after all the awards were presented. The president of the Academy, Frank Capra, revealed later that evening that Katharine Hepburn had in fact come in second, with Elisabeth Bergner coming in third for the British drama *Escape Me Never*.[27]

A genius well on his way down, Griffith was stern as he handed the statuette to Bette: "You don't know how lucky you are, young lady." "I do," Bette replied. Griffith, not convinced, kept on going: "At your age, to be where you are—making all that money, fame, and everything!"[28]

Bette later claimed to have christened Oscar Oscar; according to her, he had no name before she bestowed one upon him. She observes hilariously in *The Lonely Life* that the statuette was "a Hollywood male and, of course, epicene." (The book is generously spiced with references to Hollywood pretty boys as "sisters.") The golden statuette's ass, however, "was the spit of my husband's. Since the O. in Harmon O. Nelson stood for Oscar, Oscar it has been ever since."[29]

Davis's claim startled Margaret Herrick, the Academy's former director and its first librarian, who thought she'd named it after her uncle. The veteran Hollywood scribe Sidney Skolsky, too, was under the impression that he'd done the naming two years earlier in one of his columns.[30] So, in her annotations to *Mother Goddam*, Whitney Stine's first biography of Davis, Davis withdrew her claim: "A sillier controversy never existed. I don't feel my fame and fortune came from naming Oscar 'Oscar.'

I relinquish once and for all any claim that I was the one—so, Academy of Motion Picture Arts and Sciences, the honor is all yours."[31]

According to Mayme Ober Peake, Bette wore to the ceremony "a simple navy blue frock with white polka dots and pique trim."[32] According to Bette, "It was very expensive." But a fan magazine reporter took the occasion of the Best Actress's trip to a Biltmore ladies' room to berate her for her atrocious lack of sense, let alone taste: "How could you? *A print!* You could be dressed for a family dinner. Your photograph is going round the world. *Don't you realize? Aren't you aware?'*"[33]

What she *was* aware of was her relatively low income and her strict contractual obligations to Warner Bros. She was acutely cognizant of the lack of control she exerted over her persona; the relentless conveyer belt of thirty-one films she had cranked out in only six years in Hollywood; and the fact that Warners wasn't giving her the best scripts, the best directors, the best anything. Jack Warner seemed—to Bette—to have no idea how to manage her increasingly successful career, and she begrudged it, ever more feverishly.

She knew she wasn't being cast in the best of the studio's productions. In 1935, for instance, Michael Curtiz tested her for the haughty Arabella Bishop in his swashbuckling epic *Captain Blood*, which starred the unearthly beautiful and athletic newcomer Errol Flynn. She was enraged when Olivia de Havilland got the role instead. The producer Robert Lord had suggested Bette for the lead in *Give Me Your Heart*, a melodrama, but Warners cast Kay Francis instead. Davis was actually announced for the role of Julia in *Another Dawn*, but again Kay Francis took the role, this time opposite Errol Flynn; it was a melodrama about a woman who marries a British pilot after the love of her life is killed in a plane crash. (Coincidently, the screenwriter, Laird Doyle, died in a plane crash shortly before the film was released.)[34]

According to Stine, Bette craved the lead in *Anthony Adverse*, but Olivia de Havilland landed the part.[35] Stine also quotes *Silver Screen's* "Projections—Bette Davis": "She would like to play the Helen Mencken role in *Congai* some day, and the Miriam Hopkins role in *Jezebel*, and the Florence Reed role of Mother Goddam in *The Shanghai Gesture*— although she is quite sure that if by any fluke this stage play ever reached the screen, she would be called Mother Goodness Gracious. In other words, our little Bette craves something with guts, and wishes to leave the sweets to the sweet."[36]

What Warners bought for her was something called *Mountain Justice*, a convoluted story about a woman's crusade against ignorant hillbillies.[37]

Warners also bought the rights to C. S. Forester's 1935 novel *The African Queen* as a vehicle for Bette, but the studio quickly forgot about the project, and it's not even clear whether Davis ever knew the studio had ever had her in mind for it.[38]

Over the course of the previous year, Davis and her agent, Mike Levee, had been fighting with Warner Bros. over Bette's right to perform on radio dramas. Jack Warner, who called Levee "a little dynamo . . . who had once had a job as an assistant cameraman at Paramount and had lately turned agent,"[39] took the firm position that the studio had the contractual right to approve everything Davis did, including radio broadcasts.[40] For example, she didn't want to do a radio adaptation of *Dangerous* but, instead, an adaptation of Aesop's fable *The Lion and the Mouse*. After much back and forth, Warners finally agreed to let Bette perform *The Lion and the Mouse* but only with the understanding that there would be a big plug for *Dangerous* both before and after the broadcast.[41]

In addition, it was Warner Bros. and the studios that controlled the advertising racket—stars plugging cigarettes, stars hawking soft drinks, stars shilling for Max Factor or Buick or BO-busting Mum—and the stars whose pictures graced these products in print ads had nothing to say about what they were peddling. As the Oscar historians Mason Wiley and Damien Bona report, Jack Warner responded to Davis's winning the highest award in world film acting by "leasing her face to Quaker Puffed Rice." "Breakfast fit for a queen of the screen," the ad trumpeted.[42]

And then there was the question of money.

In 1935, at Warner Bros., Kay Francis made $115,000. Paul Muni got $50,000 per picture; approval rights for story, role, and script; sole star billing onscreen and in all advertising; loan-outs only on consent; and the right to appear onstage whenever he chose.[43]

Jimmy Cagney made just under $150,000. And Cagney was grousing about it—for good reason. His films were raking it in at the box office, but Warners still had him bound to a contract that paid him only a small percentage of the studio's take. Audiences were paying to see Cagney's pictures not because Warner Bros. made them; they were paying to see Cagney. For Cagney, $150,000 was a paltry fraction of what he deserved.

Bette Davis made all of $18,200 that year. Even toothy Guy Kibbee earned more than two and a half times what Bette Davis did.[44]

The major studios were under attack on other fronts as well. Cagney filed his suit on February 7, 1936. Two weeks later, the attorney general of the United States filed suit in federal court against Warner Bros., Paramount, and RKO on the grounds that the studios were conspiring to monopolize interstate commerce in motion pictures by controlling not only the production and distribution of their films but also their exhibition by their outright ownership of theaters or the bullying contracts they forced on independently owned houses. This was a limited suit involving only a few theaters in St. Louis; the government's major victory didn't come until 1948 with the U.S. Supreme Court's decision on *United States v. Paramount Pictures, Inc., et al.*, which effectively killed the studio system by forcing the majors to divest themselves of their theaters. Still, the government scored a significant victory in late April 1936 when the studios agreed to the government's demand that they stop preventing their competitors from doing business, and the suit was dropped.[45]

The stars, however, were still seething—over salaries, over control of their public images, over the long-term contracts that once seemed to offer security but that in practice turned them into indentured servants. Every time Jack Warner unilaterally slapped Bette Davis or James Cagney on suspension for perceived infractions, that time was tacked onto the end of their contract. It was like punishing a child by telling him he couldn't listen to his favorite radio program for a week, and if the child was especially temperamental, a week would easily turn into a month, a month into a year, and eventually the eight-year-old would find himself banished from the family radio until he was twenty-seven. To Davis and Cagney and others, this was an absurd way to treat the very artists whose names and talents brought in the bucks in the first place. It was time for a fight.

6

UP IN ARMS

*S*ATAN MET A LADY; THE GOLDEN ARROW;
the Best Actress award as a consolation prize for not winning for a picture produced by a studio other than Warner Bros.; a restrictive contract; shilling unwillingly for cereal; working; working harder; earning less than Guy Kibbee . . . this is the context in which Jack Warner told Bette Davis that her next role would be that of a lady lumberjack.

The film was to be called *God's Country and the Woman*. Jo Barton, the owner of Barton Logging Co., falls in love with Steve Russett (George Brent), a rival logger who has taken a menial job at Barton. Forest greenery would play a major role; there would be, in the words of *Sunset Boulevard*'s Joe Gillis, "a lotta outdoors stuff."

"I won't do it!" Bette roared. "*Satan Met a Lady* was bad enough, but this is absolute tripe!"[1]

But it will be in Technicolor, Jack Warner said.

No, said Bette.

"The heroine," Bette writes in *The Lonely Life*, "was an insufferable bore who scowled while everyone kept yelling 'Timber!' . . . If I never acted again in my life, I was not going to play in *God's Country*. It was now a matter of my own self-respect."[2]

Bette never knew it, but it might have been far worse. Warner Bros. memos reveal that in April, when Mike Levee was pushing hard for a new contract for Bette with new terms and payments and end dates, Hal Wallis was advising Jack Warner to stick her in a picture—any picture—as quickly as possible and not even wait for *God's Country and the Woman*. Wallis wanted Davis and Levee to know precisely who was boss.[3] It was like a bad joke: "Why would Hal Wallis stuff his studio's most talented actress into a throwaway quickie directed by a hack?" Answer: "Because he could."

Warner didn't take Wallis's advice, but he wasn't about to be pushed around by any little Best Actress winner either: "The shiny new Oscar she had won for *Dangerous* began to look like the Statue of Liberty to her, and she said she wouldn't work for us any more unless she had story approval," he later wrote.[4]

"As a friend of Bette, I hope she won't cut off her nose to spite her pretty face," Louella Parsons opined.[5]

Bette Davis was not about to take career advice from a gossip columnist, however powerful Parsons may have been been. She knew she worked hard, which in Hollywood terms meant not only that she performed before the camera in film after film, month after month, year after year, but that she performed before the stills photographer for every film, too. And showed up for wardrobe fittings. And makeup tests. She obliged the studio's publicists when they set up interviews; she obliged the journalists and made nice with professional tattlers like Parsons. What she had little knack and less inclination for, however, was socializing with the in crowd. She preferred to go home and read. She and Ham would, from time to time, go out to nightclubs and restaurants, but she wasn't the type of movie star who strove to be photographed out on the town. She was careful not to make enemies, but she didn't go out of her way to make friends with big shots for the sake of her career.

And her mouth grew increasingly big. In late March 1936, Bette took her trip to New York instead of joining Ruthie in Honolulu. Upon her arrival on the twenty-fifth, she immediately mouthed off in the press about the National Legion of Decency, the Catholic watchdog organization that devoted itself to protecting the morals of the nation's moviegoers by rating movies on a scale from A to C, A being acceptable for all, C being condemned. Infamously, the Legion had condemned Charles Laughton's *The Private Life of Henry VIII* because it saw the picture as sanctioning divorce.[6] Right-wing religious zealots were trying to put clamps on artistic freedom, and Bette Davis—an increasingly liberal Roosevelt Democrat who actually believed in the practice of liberty as well as the concept—was outraged. From the *New York World-Telegram*: "They would make all the women marry all the men in the movies. There would never be any illegitimate children on the screen—even if the story is based on a great classic. And there would be very little real life in the movies if they had their way. We aren't making pictures for children. We're making them for adults."[7]

For the *New York Times*, she pitched a marvelous script: "Her idea is to have Laughton and herself cast as costermonger and fishwife in a scummy waterfront hovel, with the domestic air filled with Billingsgate and dead fish. Florence McGee or maybe Bonita [Granville] would be their child—and a mean, no-account brat, too, according to the script Miss Davis has in mind. Anyway, after the necessary hour or so of un-mitigated nastiness all around on the screen, daughter would knock off both her parents by stabbing them with a broken gin bottle in a moment of pique and then dope herself to death in an opium den at the screen age of about 13."[8] Freed from the shackles of Warners' press office, Bette Davis was having herself a marvelous time.

The *Times* also reported, obviously getting its information directly from Bette, that she was refusing to do retakes on *The Golden Arrow* and was planning to send her studio a series of wires: "am in jail as danger-ous character stop," "quarantined stop have measles stop," "and a few more just saying 'stop.'"

She headed to Boston on April 3, arriving at Boston's South Station at dawn. She thought she'd be making a quiet entrance, but Warner Bros. had arranged a rather more public greeting: the platform was teeming with reporters. "Smile, Miss Davis!" a photographer shouted. "Now wave your hand!" Bette was having none of it. "Oh, *please!*" she snapped. "*Do* let's be original! Suppose you take a picture of someone leaving a train without waving a hand—*just this once*."

That afternoon, a thousand guests attended a special luncheon in her honor at the Brae Burn Country Club in Newton.[9] (A telegram in the Davis archives notes the contact she made with her father: "Congratula-tions and best wishes thank you for calling—Harlow M. Davis.")[10]

She was back in New York by April 7 when she received a message from Mike Levee, who told her that he'd notified Warners in writing of their demands but that he didn't put in writing the fact that she was threatening to refuse to return to work without changing her contract because this would have been what he called "exceedingly bad strat-egy." Levee advised her to stay in New York as long as she wanted, but he suggested that she rethink her refusal to do retakes for *The Golden Arrow*. As to her willingness to work for Warner Bros. beyond those retakes, however, Levee told Bette that it was entirely her choice.

By the time she left for New York, Davis had been trying to get Warners to agree to a new contract for at least a month. Her lawyer, Martin Gang, had met with Jack Warner in March with no success. What she wanted was reasonable—to her: a limit to the number of Warner pictures she would make in a given year; a vacation for three consecutive months; and, by the way, the right to do pictures for other studios during that time.[11]

In their memoirs, both Davis and Warner are clear about the situation regarding *God's Country and the Woman*—perhaps too clear. The reality is more nuanced. On May 24, Bette did a radio interview with Edwin Schallert and told his listening audience that her next film would indeed be *God's Country and the Woman*, that it was going to be in Technicolor, and that she was eager to see herself in color onscreen.[12] On June 6 and again on June 8, Bette requested meetings with Jack Warner. She told the Warners executive Roy Obringer that she wanted to be on the Shell Chateau radio program on June 20—and she willingly agreed to plug *God's Country* as part of the agreement.[13]

Warner sent her the continuity script on June 18 and told her to report to Orry-Kelly the following day for costume discussions.[14] Bette's response—a telegram to Warner—suggests that it wasn't *God's Country* that stuck in her craw; it was Warner's refusal to give her a new and more favorable contract. That, not "Timber!" is what really kept her from playing the lady lumberjack: "It has just come to my attention that Mike Levee has heretofore assured you that I would do the forthcoming picture without a change of contract. There has just been delivered to me a letter from Mr. Levee to that effect and I assume that a copy of it will come to your attention. Such representation to you by him was unauthorized and irrespective thereof a review of my actions since February would certainly be inconsistent with any such alleged promise. Bette Davis."[15]

The taste of crow in his mouth, or worse—familiar flavors on the Hollywood palette—Levee told Roy Obringer later about his role in the whole affair. As Levee replayed it for Obringer, he'd advised Bette not only to do *God's Country* but to put herself in an "amiable" frame of mind. This, he believed at the time as well as in retrospect, was a far better tactic to use than Martin Gang's hostile and demanding one, and so he, Levee, had dismissed Gang by letter on May 21. According to Levee, Bette had told him personally that she'd go ahead and do *God's Country* as long as Levee would see to it that her cooperation led to a new contract. But as soon as she got home that day, Levee claimed, she sent Levee a wire ordering him to take no further action. Bette Davis planned to handle the matter herself.[16] "This was an independent revolt of my own," Davis later wrote. "I was forced into some very definite action for the future of my career."[17] As she acknowledged to Dick Cavett many years later, "I never was one to go for advice much."[18]

On June 19, another of Davis's lawyers, Dudley Furse, sent a letter to the studio setting out Bette's terms for a new contract: five years, with one original year and four options to follow; the first year at $100,000, the second at $140,000, the third at $180,000, the fourth at $200,000, and the fifth at $220,000; a limit on the number of films per year set at four; three consecutive months of vacation, with the right to do a fifth picture on her own during that vacation; the right to do four radio programs of her own choosing; the right to be photographed by her favorite cinematographers, Tony Gaudio, Ernie Haller, or Sol Polito, "if reasonably possible"; a 6:00 p.m. quitting time; her name above the title and the first to be listed in the credits if the film was principally a woman's story; if the film was mostly a man's story, then she would grant her leading man the right to first billing.[19]

Jack L. Warner would have none of it. On June 20, he slapped Bette on suspension and gave away her role in *God's Country*; the suspension would last as long as it took her replacement, Beverly Roberts, to complete the film. Bette, covering her legal tracks as well as displaying good New England manners, replied briefly and promptly: "I am sincerely sorry we could not get together. I would have enjoyed very much playing Jo Barton."[20]

A longer, more passionate letter followed the next day: "When I saw you in your office the other day you assured me you would do all the things I wanted anyway with the exception of the loan-out, so it is hard for me to understand why you won't put it in writing." Davis discussed her ambition—to become "a great actress"—and she simply asked to be able to take good parts when they came along. She'd even take less money than she asked for, she told Warner, if only "you would give me my 'rights.' You have asked me to be level headed in this matter. As a happy person, I can work like hell. As an unhappy one, I make myself and everyone around me unhappy."

A lack of self-knowledge was never Bette's Davis's chief problem. "I am an essentially high-strung person," she noted. She went on: "I know and you do, too, [that] in a business where you have a fickle public to depend on, the money should be made when you mean something, not when the public has had time to tell you to 'go to hell.'" She concluded reasonably: "If you can see your way to giving me my rights clauses, the loan-out, you see, would balance the decrease in what you pay me. I am sure we can get together on the money."[21]

In the middle of all of this, she asked Warner for permission to do *The Rudy Vallee Hour* in Texas on July 9. The Warners executive Roy Obringer advised Jack Warner not to give Bette permission to do anything at all.[22]

On June 23, 1936, Davis and her business manager, Vernon Wood, met with Warner, Wallis, and Obringer at the studio. Warner told Bette that he would consider a new seven-year contract for her if she agreed to perform in *God's Country and the Woman*—Beverly Roberts, the replacement, could easily be replaced—and that the terms of this contract would be $2,000 per week for the first year, with options covering the following years at $2,500 for the second year, $2,750 for the third, $3,000 for the fourth, $3,250 for the fifth, $3,500 for the sixth, and $4,000 for the seventh. Davis objected primarily to the contract's duration and requested that it be for only five years. According to Obringer, Bette left the meeting saying she would think about it and she wasn't heard from again.[23]

That wasn't entirely true. Bette called the studio at some point and told a functionary that she'd be happy to let someone else use her dressing room while she was on strike. But Jack Warner refused. "I want it left just as it is," the boss said.[24]

One of the key points Bette Davis failed to grasp in her noble, quixotic rebellion was the sheer might of the corporation she was bucking. The massive amount of material in the Warner archives at the University of Southern California—the vast number of pieces of paper, let alone the verbal content of the pages—silently but powerfully demonstrates not only that Bette's was a steeply uphill battle on legal grounds alone but also that the entire machinery of Warner Bros.' legal, business, and records departments was ready to be deployed against her. It wasn't only the Burbank studio and its paper pushers, either. The corporation men in New York, the people Billy Wilder used to call "the money boys," were turning their guns on her as well.

No American producer would possibly be willing to take on Warner Bros. by contracting with Bette Davis to star in a film. Enter the colorful impresario Ludovico Toeplitz, whom Davis called an "Anglo-Italian mogul," the uncredited producer of Laughton's *The Private Life of Henry VIII* (credit went to the film's director, Alexander Korda) and, most recently, Maurice Chevalier's *The Beloved Vagabond*. Toeplitz was a bearded, round-faced man who resembled the actor Sebastian Cabot.[25] Jack Warner called him "Mephistopheles."[26]

Toeplitz flew to Los Angeles, met with Bette, and offered her the leads in two films: *I'll Take the Low Road*, to be filmed at Ealing Studios in London, and a film with Chevalier to be filmed in France. *I'll Take the Low Road* was to costar Kent Douglass—the callow soldier in *Waterloo Bridge*, who was now performing under the name Douglass Montgomery—and Nigel Bruce. The director was to be Monty Banks, the story that of an American woman who tries to land a title by marrying an English nobleman (Bruce) but ends up marrying a Yank (Montgomery).[27] Bette would be paid in pounds—£20,000 per film, to be exact, which was in the neighborhood of $50,000. She accepted.[28]

Fearing the service of an injunction barring her from acting in anything but a Warner Bros. production, she and Ham stealthily flew to Vancouver late on a Saturday night, took a Canadian Pacific train to Banff, played a round of golf—Bette shot a 125—got back on the train, and chugged across the Canadian plains to Montreal, where they boarded the *Duchess of Bedford* and set sail for Scotland.[29] They arrived at the Firth of Clyde, an estuary outside Glasgow, on August 18.

Bette was immediately accosted by reporters. Wearing "white flannel trousers, white sandal shoes, and a camel hair coat," she told the assembled journalists of her status: "At the moment I am one of the unemployed." Ham said he wanted to play golf at St. Andrews.[30] Bette said she wanted to buy a West Highland terrier.

They headed for London, where they checked into Claridge's and where Bette was served with an injunction; Warner Bros. had offices in the United Kingdom, so the matter could—and would—be decided in the British courts.[31]

On Wednesday, September 9, Toeplitz threw a party in Bette's honor—press included—at Claridge's. Monty Banks told one of the reporters about *I'll Take the Low Road*: "This picture needs five children, and one of them's got to be a baby that can hold its breath."[32]

"I've just realized my life's ambition!" Bette blurted to the *Sunday*

Express. "*I've just spoken to Noël Coward!*" "I didn't exactly meet him," she had to admit. "I spoke to him on the telephone. I told him how much I admired his work. He roared with laughter—seemed to think I was kidding!"[33]

She and Ham tooled around the kingdom. As the *Daily Express* reported, "She has drunk beer, played darts in a public bar in Garstang, exchanged philosophies with a pig drover, John Weston, on the road to the lakes, driven about in a second-hand car, bought a pair of clogs to practice clog-dancing, and declared to all she met, 'This is the life!' "[34] Bette found the lake district pretty but wasn't especially impressed. "We've got some far bigger mountains in America," she rather too competitively told a reporter. The Nelsons leisurely drove as far as Torquay on the southern coast of Devonshire, which Bette particularly loved, and back to Somerset. From there they headed south to Rottingdean, a village on the coast of East Sussex, then left for Paris for costume fittings.[35]

William Randolph Hearst, dissuaded from traveling to Berlin to try to talk some sense into Hitler, went instead to his castle at St. Donats in Wales, where he was joined by Jack and Ann Warner. Warner and Toeplitz had already met in Venice. The meeting ended in shouting; Hearst's Welsh castle was a relief. But as Warner later wrote, "And it was in this peaceful haven that the process servers handed me the bad-news paper from Bette Davis. She had filed suit in London and had retained a distinguished barrister, Sir William Jowitt. Ann and I moved into a London hotel, and she suggested in her own diplomatic way that it might be wise to settle the case. She was very fond of Bette—so was I—and she could foresee a great flood of perhaps unpleasant publicity. But there was a principle at stake—whether a highly paid star could dictate to a studio, and make only those pictures that pleased him or her. If Bette were to win, all the studio owners and executives in Hollywood would get trampled in the stampede."[36]

Bette and Ham moved into the Park Lane Hotel, whereupon Ham decided he'd had enough and announced that he was departing for New York to find work as a musician. Bette was surprised and upset. "It wasn't often I needed him," she writes with brutal honesty in *The Lonely Life.* "This was the only time."

One gets the sense that Ham Nelson appreciated his own expendability better than Bette did. Hence his departure. "I saw Ham off at Southampton and stood bewildered on the dock as his ship pulled away. . . . His salary, assuming he was to get work, would be negligible in comparison to the moral support I craved at that moment. I was never so wretched as when I crawled back to my cell at the Park Lane."[37]

THE HIGH COURT of Justice, King's Bench Division. *Warner Bros. Pictures, Inc., v. Nelson*. October 14, 15, and 16, 1936.

Sir William Jowitt for Bette Davis, Sir Patrick Hastings and Mr. Norman Birkett for Warner Bros., Mr. Justice Sir George Branson on the bench.

Davis, through Sir William, argued that it was in fact Warner Bros. who breached the contract—that, as the *Times* described it, the studio had "required her to play unsuitable parts and had frequently required her to work for excessive periods in the day, such periods constantly exceeding 14 hours; and that they had further required her to make an unreasonably large number of films in 1935," and this breach by Warners freed her to "tender her services to persons other than the plaintiffs."[38] Sir William described the contract as "a life sentence." The restrictions on her activities were absurd, he argued. For example, the contract gave the studio the exclusive right to photograph her: "That means that she ought not to allow her husband to take a snapshot of her in the garden," though Sir William hastily noted that Warner Bros. had never attempted to enforce its rights in this regard. Sir William himself veered into the absurd by contending, as the *Daily Telegraph* related, "that as the contract stood Miss Davis could not become a waitress at a restaurant, an assistant in a hairdresser's shop in the wilds of Africa—if they had hairdressing establishments there—and could not engage in any other occupation, whether for love or money."[39]

Sir Patrick took a different stance. "I think, m'lord, this is the action of a very naughty young lady," he said. "There is a gentleman whose name I cannot pronounce—a Mr. Toeplitz, I think. I suggest that Miss Davis has been bribed and has been unwise enough, flattered by the offer, to say, 'I will take it if I can get away from Warner Bros.' "[40] (Toeplitz's lawyer was displeased by Sir Patrick's accusation of bribery—a criminal offense, after all.) Sir Patrick went on to argue that contracts like Davis's were standard in the film industry. He ridiculed Bette's claim of "slavery" by citing her steadily increasing salary at Warners, which, by 1942, would be nearly £600 pounds a week. "If anybody wants to put me into perpetual servitude on that basis of remuneration, I shall prepare to consider it," he said.[41]

Alexander Korda took the stand as an expert witness. "If a film star walks out during the making of a picture, the loss is considerable," the producer testified.

> MR. BIRKETT: Take a production like, say, *Romeo and Juliet*. If Juliet "walks out," is it possible to continue the picture exactly where she "walks out," or do you have to start it all over again?
>
> MR. KORDA: We have to start all over again.

But of course Bette had never appeared before the cameras on *God's Country and the Woman*, so the entire exchange was irrelevant.

Sir William, on cross-examination, asked Korda, "If a producer transfers an actress against her will, it would be hard on her?" "An actress does not always understand her will or what she wants to do," Korda replied, much to the amusement of the spectators and, one assumes, the seething rage of Bette Davis.[42] "But sometimes she does?" Sir William countered. "Yes," Korda acknowledged.

When Jack Warner took the stand, Bette almost felt sorry for him, so intimidated did he appear by the formality and gravity of a British courtroom. One exchange between Sir William and Warner is especially curious.

> SIR WILLIAM: You have every reason to believe she is very happily married?
>
> MR. WARNER: Yes.
>
> SIR WILLIAM: When she was married, did your company present her with a document which she was to sign, giving an undertaking not to divorce her husband for three years?
>
> MR. WARNER: I have never heard of it.
>
> SIR WILLIAM: You have a brother, Harry Warner?
>
> MR. WARNER: Yes.
>
> SIR WILLIAM: Was there a proposal that a photograph should be taken of the lady, her husband, and Harry Warner, with the lady handing over to Mr. Harry Warner the undertaking saying that she would not divorce her husband for three years?
>
> MR. WARNER: I can't believe that anything of the kind occurred.

SIR WILLIAM: Did Miss Davis indignantly decline to do anything of the sort?

MR. WARNER: I am sure my brother never made any such
proposal, or ever thought of it.

Could Bette have made up this belittling incident out of whole cloth,
or did Jack Warner commit perjury?

Sir William did get Warner to acknowledge one key point: "I admit
that an actress could become heartbroken if she had to play parts that
were not fitted to her," the mogul testified.[43]

Bette was not called to the stand.

The Associated Press, dateline London, October 19, 1936: "Bette
Davis, the American film actress, was enjoined today from making an
English movie. Justice Sir George Branson in King's Bench Division
decided in favor of Warner Bros. of Hollywood in an injunction suit to
prevent Miss Davis from working in a future picture for Toeplitz Productions, Ltd., a British organization."

"When the news came I was walking on the beach in utter melancholy. Jack Warner had won a three-year injunction or the duration of
my contract (whichever was the shorter). I was his, and if he exercised
his options, my inhuman bondage stretched to 1942."[44] Bette and Sir
William were expecting at the worst an injunction limited to one year;
the three-year term of the injunction shocked them.[45]

Warner, always the jokester, claimed that after his court victory Sir
Patrick pitched his son-in-law for a screen test and then handed him
a screenplay written by himself.[46]

The outcome was no surprise to Ludovico Toeplitz, who had tried to
bail out as early as the end of August. Almost two months before the
case went to court—and, strangely, a week before he threw the party at
Claridge's—the producer wrote to Bette, who was then staying at the
Tudor Close Hotel in Rottingdean, and informed her that, having heard
the opinion of both his British and American counsel, "we are advised
emphatically that the contract between yourself and Warner Bros. is
valid. . . . Warner Bros. will certainly be able to obtain an injunction in
the English courts restraining you from performing. . . . You are not and
never have been in a position legally to enter into any contract to play for
us . . . and we must proceed at once to recast the part contemplated to be
played by you."[47]

One scarcely needs to paint Bette Davis's rebellion against Jack

Warner in broad Oedipal strokes to make the point that it was driven as much by irrational passion, a deep-seated need to prove an impossible invincibility against a Goliath-like adversary, as it was by practical, professional concerns. Her defeat was a personal humiliation played out on a worldwide stage, and it was doubly devastating for her to lose her case against Jack Warner the man as well as Jack Warner the head of the studio. But there was one key reversal to the Freudian theme. Harlow successfully abandoned her; Warner accomplished what was, for her, even more excruciating: he kept her tethered to him.

The paternal nurturing she craved arrived in the form of George Arliss, who visited her in Rottingdean. A man of great personal charm, Arliss was also a seasoned veteran of the theater and cinema. He was consoling, but he was also practical. She was compelled to return to Warner Bros., he told her. But she was an actress, and it was her choice as to how she played the scene. He sent a note a few days later:

"Dear Miss Davis . . . I was so happy to have that little visit with you. I admire your courage in this affair, but when you have found out just what you *can* do, then I would suggest that you review the thing dispassionately and choose the course that is likely to be best for you in the long run." Thoughtfully, he sent her a gift along with the card—a slew of cigarettes from Lewis of St. James Street.[48]

"This was the last time I ever saw Mr. Arliss," Davis writes in *Mother Goddam*. Arliss's paternal role was lost neither on Davis nor on Arliss himself: "He was a wise and beautiful man. I think he loved me as a father hopefully would. I have a signed photograph of him. The inscription reads: 'with adopted fatherly affection.' "[49]

Sɪʀ Wɪʟʟɪᴀᴍ Jowɪᴛᴛ had made the point in court that it would be difficult for both parties to resume their creative relationship: "If Mr. Warner and Miss Davis both had the tact and consideration of angels, it would be putting a very great strain on them if, after all this, she is going back to work for them."[50]

Sir William was right; it was a terrible strain. For Bette, if not for Jack Warner. Bette met with one of Warners' British lawyers, who reported back to the studio that she had respectfully offered several suggestions on how to proceed. Convinced that Arthur Edeson's cinematography for *The Golden Arrow* wasn't as good as it might have been, she once again asked that Sol Polito, Ernie Haller, or Tony Gaudio photograph her films if at all possible. She asked the studio, in the lawyer's words, "to let her appear in two good substantial parts as her next two films"— not an unreasonable request from the year's Best Actress winner, let alone one of Bette's caliber. She "seriously suggests that the maximum advantage can be obtained from her acting if her appearances are limited to four films a year." (As a point of comparison, Meryl Streep hasn't appeared in four films in a single year since 1979, the year she won an Oscar for her performance in *Kramer vs. Kramer*.) Bette mentioned her desire to be loaned out to other studios more frequently, but Warners' lawyer cut off that part of the conversation. And finally, she asked if the studio would waive its claim against her for the costs of the trial. She hadn't yet paid her own counsel's fees, which amounted to £3,000, and she didn't have the money.[51] (Whitney Stine calculates "a mean total of $103,000.")[52]

Jack Warner had no intention of waiving the studio's claim against Davis. After all, she lost. And now she had to pay. He and his staff sought a "collectable amount equivalent to a judgment . . . which we can, if we so desire, enforce against her here," meaning back in Burbank when Davis returned to work.[53] As for Bette's own legal costs, she urged her solicitors not to approach Toeplitz for payment. The solicitors' idea was to have Warner Bros. pay them directly out of Bette's weekly salary, though they did timidly float the idea that Warner Bros. might pay their fees in addition to its own, an idea Warners' counsel found "preposterous" and "impertinent."[54]

Interviewed at her hotel in Rottingdean, Davis, wearing blue beach pajamas and smoking a cigarette, called her defeat "a sock in the teeth." "I'm a bit bewildered," she went on. "I didn't make any plans for a hundred percent defeat. I thought at least that it would have been a partial victory for me and for everybody else with one of these body-and-soul contracts. Mind you, I didn't fight it as a test case for the whole film industry. I fought it for myself and for my career. . . . Instead of getting increased freedom, I seem to have provided—at my own expense—an object lesson for other would-be 'naughty young ladies.' "[55]

She got a cable two days later: "Clock in steeple strikes one come home love Ham."[56]

The episode turned out not to be the total loss Davis felt it to be at the time. It provided her with vital publicity, the key element of which was precisely that it was not dictated by Warner Bros.' publicity department. She had despised not only the apparent indifference of her casting but also the way she had been marketed. She hated the early fashion shoots, the dyeing of her hair, the cereal ads. . . . It was hardly her idea to present herself as Constance Bennett's secondhand look-alike. Even Warners' best promotions for Davis were in some ways more damaging to her psyche than her worst scripts because they tried to sell her as being someone she wasn't. So although she lost the case, by taking such a belligerent stance against Warners in the full, bright glare of the English-speaking press, she adroitly bypassed the studio's publicity machine and created a new persona for herself on her own terms: a strong-willed independent thinker as confrontational as any man.[57]

It worked. Not only did Warners give her better, more suitable scripts upon her return to Burbank, but the studio's publicists began to exploit her pugnacious, ready-to-erupt persona themselves—to the studio's advantage as well as to Davis's.[58] Contentiousness became her legacy. As the *Economist* put it on the occasion of her death, "The two cigarettes lit by Paul Henreid in *Now, Voyager*—one for him, one for her—were as nothing compared to the two fingers she gave to the head of the studio, Jack Warner, in the high court in London in 1936."[59]

But once again, that's skipping ahead. When the Cunard White Star RMS *Aquitania* departed Southampton on Wednesday, November 4, bound for New York, one of the passengers listed on the roster was "Mrs. R. E. D. Nelson."[60] And Mrs. Nelson wasn't very happy.

7

"In the Warner Jail"

"I Love My Husband Because He Doesn't Treat Me Like a Star!"—the title of a 1936 fanzine article illustrated with photos of the Nelsons' modest vine-covered, two-story house on busy Franklin Avenue. There were gables, striped awnings, and a picket fence. A driveway ran on the side. During the course of the reporter's visit, Bette turned to her modest husband, Harmon, and said, "Aren't you getting just a little tired of all this racket?"

"Not yet," he replied.[1]

But by the end of the year Ham Nelson was indeed getting sick of the racket—his wife's emotional clatter more than the traffic on Franklin—and when Bette checked into a suite at the Algonquin after disembarking from the *Aquitania*, she found her husband less than enthusiastic about returning with her to Los Angeles. He'd found work with Tommy Dorsey's band and planned to stay in New York.[2] It was with Ruthie that Bette would travel west, Mother having gotten as far as New York on her way to rescue Bette from Great Britain when Bette cabled that she was coming back to the States on her own.

Davis didn't put an especially good face on things in New York. Unbowed if not downright belligerent, she bluntly told the reporters who collected at the Algonquin that she was heading back to Hollywood to "serve five years in the Warner jail." She explained her sense of anxious resignation: "When I was a young thing and not very wise I signed the contract which ties me up to 1942. I'll be an old woman by 1942, but I'm going back, and I'll be there in a week or so, and all I can say is the hell with it."[3]

By "old woman," Bette Davis meant that in 1942 she would be thirty-four.

"She told me that her main worry for years in Hollywood was paying the rent," said the writer Dotson Rader, who got to know Davis in the 1980s.

> First and foremost, it was a job to her. The whole fight she had with Jack Warner was over the fact that she felt that the parts she was being forced to play were destroying her future ability to make money—*to get work.* The point at which she rebelled against Warner was the point at which women in Hollywood, then and now, were beginning to age—late 20s, early 30s. She was aware of that, and she wanted to establish to her audience that her appeal was not based on sex. All [Warners] looked at was the short term—what the box-office was *on this picture.* They weren't interested in what the star of the picture might be making ten years later, or if the picture was going to help the star find work in ten years. [Hollywood is] a completely short-term-driven industry, so it's in conflict with the real long-term interests of individual actors or directors—the creative people. Bette Davis was one of the first people not only to realize it but to act on it—to try to protect herself.[4]

Mrs. Davis and Mrs. Nelson arrived in Los Angeles on the Santa Fe *Chief* on Wednesday, November 18.[5] Having had the width of the continent to consider her public image, Bette was less hostile in the press this time around. She wasn't chastened. She may have been twenty pounds thinner after her legal and emotional ordeal, but she'd never be chastened.[6] She was politic: "I'm just a working girl—not a crusader," she told the L.A. scribes. " 'Work, work, and more work' is my motto from now on." She wrote a personal note to Jack Warner saying that she was "ready, willing, and able" to return to the lot and expressed her hope that she would be put back on salary as soon as Warner received the letter, which, reflecting a characteristic sense of urgency, she had hand-delivered. The boss's response was to order her to be back at the studio on Monday, November 23, at 11:30 in the morning.[7] Her next picture, *Marked Woman*, was already in preproduction.

TIMELY, TOPICAL, AND atypical, *Marked Woman* is generic Warner Bros. at its tense, 1930s best. It's the fictionalized story of the gangster Lucky Luciano and his notorious prostitution ring, though thanks to the Production Code the ladies are nominally hostesses at a shady if glamorous nightclub. The real Lucky, whose name was originally Salvatore Lucania, moved to New York from Sicily with his family at the age of nine; he was only a year older than Bette.[8] Luciano was a gangster's gangster and had the underlings to match—thuggish men with nicknames like Cockeyed Louis and Charlie Spinach.[9] Warner Bros., always looking for an angle, actually hired one of Luciano's former goons, Herman "Hymie" Marks, to play a bit part as a gangster, though Hal Wallis worried that Hymie didn't look nearly menacing enough to play one onscreen.[10]

There's a scene in *Marked Woman* in which Bette, as Mary Dwight, convinces Humphrey Bogart's self-righteous prosecutor (based on Thomas Dewey) that she's ready to sing. It's a duplicitous gesture, since Mary is still protecting the Luciano character (renamed Vanning for the film, though he retains a thick Italian accent). Vanning has not yet thrown her kid sister down a flight of steps, an act that finally gives Bette's Mary a good reason to turn on him. At this point she's still the tough nightclub hostess in the employ of the mob, which is to say that she's a Code-approved hooker. And this smart whore is putting on an act, though we're not yet aware of that fact. Her voice pitching toward feverishness, Bette hurls herself into a chair and bursts into tears, but rather than daubing at her nose with a petite piece of lace as a lesser actress would do, she digs into her nostrils with a decidedly unladylike fury. Lloyd Bacon, the director, films her from an unflattering angle: Mary is bending over the desk, using it as support in her moment of breakdown, and Bacon shoots the top of her head straight on, making her nose the primary focus. It's purposely ugly looking, but the electricity of the scene comes from Bette, who certainly could have played it more demurely and with fewer excretions. In exhaustion and apparent defeat, Mary leans back in her chair, cleans her nails on the now-wet handkerchief, and agrees to testify against Vanning. But the moment Bogart moves safely out of range, she shifts her eyes to their edges, and we see that Mary is actually a cool and cunning liar planning to commit perjury and wreck the prosecutor's case. This, it turns out, has been Davis performing a performance of hysteria, a redoubled acting job and one of the best scenes in her career.

"So long, chump," is her exit line to Bogart after the trial.

Later in the film, Mary turns against Vanning for real, kid sister having been tossed down said steps. She threatens him: "I'll get you," she spits, fixing him with a stare more sharp than bug-eyed, "even if I have to crawl back from my grave to do it!" Vanning responds by having his boys rough her up—badly. A newspaper headline roars from the screen: "Clip Joint Hostess Near Death from Attack!" You want to laugh—and you may, because it's mid-1930s Warner Bros. distilled to its entertainingly blunt essence—but the driven and artful actress who plays the clip joint hostess makes something valid out of it by shocking us with her character's injuries. On the day she filmed the scene, Bette decided that she'd had enough of the type of glamorous beating she'd endured under Michael Curtiz's timorous eye in *20,000 Years in Sing Sing*. From Bette's perspective, a new year had turned. It was 1937, and Warners' executives, producers, directors, and makeup artists still didn't get it. She alone did. The script called for Mary to be thrashed and knifed and scarred for life, but as Bette later described herself after she came out of makeup that morning, "I don't think I ever looked so attractive. Lilly Daché herself could have created that creamy puff of gauze at the peak of her inspiration. It was an absolute gem of millinery." According to Davis, she "smiled sweetly" and left the studio, supposedly for lunch.[11]

She went instead to her physician, Dr. F. Le Grand Noyes, to whom she explained the plot turn and who she asked to bandage her as though she had, in fact, been kicked hard, punched repeatedly, and knife-gashed in the cheek.

Bette may have added a few contusions of her own before showing up at Hal Wallis's office, where Wallis greeted her at the door, saw her swollen eyes, outrageously broken nose, brown abrasions, and acres of bloody gauze, and burst into laughter. "Okay, you get your way," the producer told her—"all except that broken nose. You can't have that."[12]

Bette Davis looks proudly, defiantly ghastly onscreen in this scene in *Marked Woman*. A bandage is taped to her right cheek, another wrapped around her head; there are blackened eyes looking out through hollow sockets and bruises everywhere, and she holds the left side of her mouth morbidly rigid. This was the antithesis of Hollywood convention. It was a radical blend of stylization and brutal realism—Bette Davis pulling a majestic, disturbing stunt for the sake of art, all the while demanding to be recognized as Bette Davis, a creative force of nature. Her ghastliness must have registered even more powerfully at the time because nobody in 1937 expected it, especially on the face of an Oscar-winning female movie star who was expected to look glamorous no matter what.

When *Marked Woman* was released in April, Warners' head of publicity and advertising, S. Charles Einfeld, was ecstatic. Writing to Jack Warner, Einfeld went on and on about how well audiences, particularly women, were responding to Davis in the picture: "You hear women say, 'There's a gal who doesn't need a lot of junk all over her face,' and 'Bette Davis is a female Cagney.'" Einfeld warned Warner against continuing to attempt to further glamorize his strange, bullheaded star but instead to let her play up her strengths: her nervous vitality, her bold decision making, her refusal of convention and inappropriate lip gloss.[13]

Marked Woman wrapped on January 19, 1937, two days behind schedule, and Bette immediately went into her next picture, *Kid Galahad*, which wasn't nearly as challenging. A grinning hunk of blond beefcake, a bellhop named Ward (Wayne Morris, in his film debut), doubles as bartender at a party thrown by a boxing manager, Donati (Edward G. Robinson), and his girlfriend (Davis), whose nickname, no kidding, is "Fluff." Donati's rival is played by Humphrey Bogart and is saddled with the nickname "Turkey." One of Turkey's boys insults Fluff, and Ward chivalrously decks him. So begins his career as the boxer Kid Galahad. Fluff is a singer, which leads to a delightful scene in which Bette, cigarette in hand and draped on a piano in a black sleeveless top and big-sequined skirt, lip-synchs "The Moon Is in Tears Tonight." Aside from the fight scenes, it's the highlight of the film.

Although they were two of the more intelligent and liberal actors in town, there was no love lost between Davis and Robinson. "All of us girls at Warners hated kissing his ugly purple lips," Bette said in retrospect.[14] Privately she called him "mush mouth."[15] As for Robinson, he reportedly told Hal Wallis, "This Davis girl—she's hopeless! She's an amateur. She's totally out of place in this picture." Robinson got the first part wrong, but he may have had a point about Davis's casting, which once again relegated her to the sidelines.[16] "Neither recognized the other's talent," Wallis later observed.

There was still friction between Davis and Michael Curtiz. Davis has a particularly damning story to tell in *The Lonely Life*: "I will never forget Wayne's knocking out a fighter in a take. 'Fake fight! Retake! Fake fight—awful!' Curtiz screamed—but it was difficult to redo because Wayne's opponent was unconscious. He had knocked him out cold."[17]

Another tale finds Bette stopping in the middle of a take and barking at her director, "Mike! Watch *me*! Stop watching the camera!"[18] She was mistaken, of course. Film direction isn't solely about monitoring performances. But soon enough she would learn that a director—a real director, one with ideas to express and the stubborn dynamism to get them on celluloid—would care as much about where the camera was moving as he would about the actress toward whom it happened to be pointing at the moment. After that, everyone else would look like hacks.

"IT WAS A farcical comedy," Davis writes dismissively of *It's Love I'm After*, "but Leslie [Howard] and I had a romp, and I was out of the gutter and in Orry-Kelly's latest gowns."[19] She goes on to say that she would have preferred to do humor of a higher nature—a Philip Barry or S. N. Behrman property, a *Holiday* or *The Philadelphia Story* or *No Time for Comedy*.

But she's wrong. As great as they are, those films don't have the purposefully uncomfortable bite of *It's Love I'm After*, with the admitted exception of the opening punch in *The Philadelphia Story*. In fact, Davis and Howard are both superbly prickly, not to mention eminently believable, as scene-hogging actors embroiled in a long and thorny affair. It's a shame that Davis failed to appreciate her own knack for getting complicated laughs onscreen.

In screwball comedies, characters' fluid identities lead to emotional liberation as they discover that lying pretense reveals its own higher truth. Playacting lets Cary Grant and Irene Dunne fake their way back to two happy marriages in *The Awful Truth* and *My Favorite Wife*. In *It's Love I'm After*, the fact that Joyce and Basil are both hammy actors is what enables them to rediscover their love. They see each other for what they are—and aren't. Their squabbling recalls the great Carole Lombard–John Barrymore fights in *Twentieth Century*, though here there's an added complication: a mooning young heiress played by Olivia de Havilland. While Davis's Joyce and Howard's Basil look at each other and see nothing but greasepaint, which they love, de Havilland's naive Marcia looks at Basil and sees nothing but love, which Basil quickly grows to despise.

Although the part of a tempestuous actress seems to have been tailor-made for Bette Davis, Casey Robinson, one of Warner Bros.' better screenwriters, said that it was only fortuitous casting: "We just happened to cast Bette in *It's Love I'm After*. It wasn't written for her."[20] But it certainly could have been.

The film was shot in June 1937. As *Variety* reported on the ninth, Bette was slightly injured when she fell into the orchestra pit between takes of the *Romeo and Juliet* death scene, during which the two hams snipe at each other not-so-sotto voce while laboriously dying. Luckily for Bette, she was padded for the real-life pratfall: her "heavy wig absorbed part of the shock."[21]

WHAT WITH THE frequent moves and absent father, neither of the Davis sisters had had an easy time of it, but at least the older daughter had gotten her mother's attention. Ruthie and the girls' old apartment in Newton featured innumerable photos of Bette, taken by an adoring Ruthie, but not a single one of Bobby. Mother and daughters spent the summer in Provincetown before the girls went to North-field Academy. Bobby, walking on the beach after a storm, found a broken toy sailboat and spent the next few days painstakingly repairing it, only to watch, heartbroken on the beach, as the infinitely more self-assertive Bette grabbed it and launched it into the surf, where it vanished. Bobby, a family friend once declared, was treated as though she was "the little stepchild."[22]

For reasons that aren't entirely clear, Bobby transferred from Denison to the University of Wisconsin at Madison, but her emotional state drove her to drop out and move out West with Bette and Ruthie; this was during the early days at the house on Alta Loma. Ellen Bachelder, a friend of the Davises at that time, recalled that Bette held a tight grip on herself at the studio and kept it all in until she got home, whereupon she would blow up at Ruthie and Bobby. After the Davises moved to the Tudor-style house on Toluca Lake, Bachelder arrived one day to find Bette furiously sweeping out closets, enraged that neither Ruthie nor Bobby had done the housework properly. Bobby told Bachelder that Bette would come home from a day under the lights and in front of the cameras, put on a pair of white gloves, and run her fingers along the furniture and woodwork to assess the degree of meticulous dusting that had, or hadn't, occurred during her absence.

The strain of life, let alone life with her overachieving sister, became too much for Bobby. She would periodically become violent instead of simply melancholy, shouting at both Ruthie and Bette and even slapping and punching them. Her energy spent, Bobby would then suddenly become silent and sullen again.[23]

In 1934, Ruthie moved Bobby back East—specifically to a sanitarium in Massachusetts—where she received various treatments including electroshock therapy. Ruthie returned to Los Angeles on April 5, Bette's birthday, and stayed for about a month; Ham wisely moved out for the duration.

Bobby returned to Los Angeles later that year and touchingly told the press, "I want to be an actress, just like my sister."[24] Her ambition appears to have been mainly for show, for as Bette herself noted, "Bobby, now fully recovered and with infinite lucidity, had started to call me the Golden Goose."[25]

In 1935, to her own relief more than her mother's or sister's, Bobby, then twenty-five, fell in love for the first time. Like her sister, she picked someone she knew from back East, someone familiar—in her case "little Bobby Pelgram" from Ogunquit, Maine. He was now the dashing Robert Cole Pelgram, twenty years old, a handsome socialite and flier. When Pelgram asked Bobby to marry him, Bobby had no hesitation. But she was still not her own woman: she chose her older sister's anniversary as the day of her own wedding. Bobby, Pelgram, Ham, and Bette drove down to Tijuana on August 18 for the ceremony.

The *Los Angeles Examiner* reported in mid-June 1937 that Mr. and Mrs. Robert Cole Pelgram had recently departed on a belated honeymoon, setting sail on the SS *Virginia* for a seven-month cruise through the Panama Canal to Europe, Egypt, India, China, Japan, and Hawaii. Bette thoughtfully had their stateroom adorned with gardenias and sweet peas.[26]

As much as it must have relieved Bette of the financial burden of supporting her sister as well as her mother and her husband, Bobby's marriage appears to have sparked some resentment on Bette's part; the grudging Lady Bountiful was no longer the center of Bobby's dependent life, as troubled as it sometimes was. Moreover, Bobby never had to work. Bette did.

As for Ruthie, she believed her work was done and expected to be supported in increasingly grand style. Bette writes, "She, who had worked for me like a demon—had known no sacrifice great enough— now relaxed into luxury. . . . To Mother, Hollywood was a playground and movie actresses spent their days floating through an atmosphere of Chanel-scented flattery, adoration, and glamour. I don't believe that Ruthie ever believed I worked once I arrived."[27] This was a problem.

In 1937, money—along with husband, sister, and mother—continued to impress itself on Bette's everyday psyche. She downplays it in her various memoirs, but this was a time of continuing financial panic on her part. Warners "greeted me with open arms," Davis writes in *The Lonely Life,* and "graciously relieved me of their share of the damages. I didn't have to pay the King's ransom to Sir Patrick, and Sir William's retainer was shared by my employers who fulfilled Mr. Arliss' prophecy and bent over backwards to be nice."[28] But in point of fact, Jack Warner used Bette's debts as a sword of Damocles. He was not in the mood to forgive anything, especially lucre. On January 6, 1937, Bette wrote a note to Warner asking for an advance of $14,000 to cover her legal bills. Rather than "relieving" her of her share of the damages, Warner arranged for a Bank of America loan that Bette would pay back in weekly installments against her salary.[29] Also in January Warners refused to waive its legal costs, which included internal billing from Warners' New York office: New York charged Burbank over $15,000 for the time it spent on Bette's case.[30]

She was still being paid far less than her peers, and insultingly so. Leave aside the fact that Louis B. Mayer personally took in almost $1.3 million in 1937; he was the boss of bosses and earned accordingly. But major talent wasn't doing too badly either. According to the *Hollywood Citizen Examiner,* Greta Garbo earned $472,499 that year. Irene Dunne made $259,587, Katharine Hepburn $238,703. If the *Citizen Examiner's* figures are correct, Bette Davis made only $53,200—about $155,000 less than the ice skating queen Sonja Henie.

For the most part, Warner Bros. learned its lesson from Bette's infamous walkout, and the studio offered her parts that suited her or, at least, failed to enrage her. But in the summer of 1937, Warners announced that her next picture would be Busby Berkeley's *Hollywood Hotel,* costarring Dick Powell. Bette rebelled. Vociferously. Not coincidental to her rage was that she was being forced to play the dual role of a temperamental movie star who disappears after being denied a role she coveted and the double who takes over for her to serve the studio's publicity needs.[31]

That she did not play Scarlett O'Hara in *Gone with the Wind* was one of her most bitter disappointments, and she rankled at the mention of the film for the rest of her life. According to Bette, Warner Bros. optioned the rights to Margaret Mitchell's novel just before it was published in June of 1936, and Jack Warner offered to cast her as Scarlett if only she'd just "be a good girl" and play the lady lumberjack in *God's Country and the Woman*.[32] Bette writes she hadn't yet heard of *Gone with the Wind* and left Warner's office with the exit line "I bet it's a pip."[33] Warner's own account differs slightly: "For some reason that now seems obscure to me, I was not too eager to make this picture, although I had an opportunity to bid on the film rights of Margaret Mitchell's novel, and could have had it for a mere $50,000. It may be that the anticipated $5,000,000 cost cooled my enthusiasm. . . . In any case, I did not nail down an option, and Selznick got it. This was Bette's first setback, for I would have given her Scarlett."[34]

Whether Bette's walkout and the studio's lawsuit was the absolute cause or just a contributing factor, Jack Warner lost interest in making *Gone with the Wind* precisely while Davis was wrangling with him in the British courts. By August 1936, Selznick had picked up the rights, and by September he'd chosen a director: George Cukor. "Shades of Rochester," Bette later complained. "He still saw me as the girl in *Broadway*, and whatever his ancient grievance, his thumbs were still down."[35]

Selznick's memos and contemporary news items indicate that Selznick was strongly considering Miriam Hopkins (God forbid), Tallulah Bankhead, and Joan Crawford, but not particularly Bette Davis. At one point Tallulah was the front-runner and was screen-tested. Paulette Goddard was tested as well, as was Vivien Leigh. Other stars and starlets were considered, too, if only by their press agents and acquiescent Hollywood reporters: Jean Arthur, Diana Barrymore, Joan Bennett, Marguerite Churchill, Claudette Colbert, Frances Dee, Ellen Drew, Irene Dunne, Jean Harlow, Katharine Hepburn, Carole Lombard, Susan Hayward, Boots Mallory, Jo Ann Sayers, Norma Shearer, Margaret Sullavan, Margaret Tallichet, Lana Turner, Claire Trevor, Arleen Whelan, and Loretta Young. Even less likely candidates included Mrs. Jock Whitney, Betty Timmons (Margaret Mitchell's niece), and Lucille Ball.[36] In June 1937, *Cinema Arts* joked that the only two actresses who hadn't been mentioned as serious contenders for the role of Scarlett O'Hara were Martha Raye and Shirley Temple.[37]

"Everybody's second cousin was tested, and I was used as the touchstone," Bette claimed. "That was how right I was. It was insanity that I not be given Scarlett. But then, Hollywood has never been rational."[38]

The *Hollywood Citizen News* asked various directors to voice their opinions on the matter: Mervyn LeRoy, evidently having changed his mind about Bette's prospects, picked her as Scarlett and Clark Gable as Rhett Butler, with Irene Dunne as Melanie; George Stevens suggested Katharine Hepburn and Cary Grant; Archie Mayo wanted Miriam Hopkins and Gary Cooper.[39] Bette herself received a telegram: "We are delighted to inform you we have unanimously voted you the ideal choice [for] Scarlett O'Hara." Unfortunately for Davis, the telegram was not signed "David O. Selznick and staff" but rather "Associated Cinema Fans of Westchester, Inc."[40] Davis was indeed the choice by public acclamation: of all the women mentioned over the course of the casting contest, Davis scored highest in the fan magazine polls cited by Gavin Lambert in his essay on the making of *Gone with the Wind*: "Bette Davis was easily the most popular candidate, with 40 percent of the vote."[41]

She had one more chance, and—for once—both Davis and Warner agreed on the circumstances. Warner: "Before Selznick decided on Vivien Leigh, he came to me with a proposition to lend him Bette Davis and Errol Flynn as a costarring package for the picture. Bette was fond of Errol . . . but she was also realistic about Errol's limited acting talent. She refused to have any part of the deal, and that was her last chance for the part."[42] Davis was more succinct: "The thought of Mr. Flynn as Rhett Butler appalled me. I refused."[43]

Davis and Warner may have agreed about Selznick's proposal, but Selznick himself took a rather different view of who refused whose proposal about what. The producer wrote a lengthy letter to Ed Sullivan, then the Hollywood columnist for the *New York Daily News*, correcting the supposed misreporting on his beloved project, the crown jewel of his career: "Certainly you ought to know that Warner Bros. wouldn't give up Bette Davis for a picture to be released through MGM, even had we wanted Miss Davis in preference to a new personality. Warner Bros. offered me Errol Flynn for Butler and Bette Davis for Scarlett if I would release the picture through Warners—and this would have been an easy way out of my dilemma. But the public wanted Gable."[44] (Unlike Flynn, the magnetic Clark Gable had both looks and substance; audiences adored his rugged insouciance in such hits as *It Happened One Night* and *Mutiny on the Bounty*, and when *Gone with the Wind* was published, it was Gable's name that was on everybody's lips to play Rhett Butler.)

Whether Bette Davis had a real shot at Scarlett O'Hara is therefore debatable at best, but the crucial fact is that she believed she did, and this was the context in which she was told to appear as a loser movie star in *Hollywood Hotel*.

The film was scheduled for production from early August to early November, after which she would go directly into *Jezebel*, which was exactly the kind of meaty, dramatic picture she had been demanding all along. In July, after learning of her casting in *Hollywood Hotel*, Bette and Ham took a beach vacation to Carpinteria, just south of Santa Barbara, but Bette did not relax. On July 17, she wrote a lengthy handwritten letter to Jack Warner begging him not to force her to do *Hollywood Hotel*. She was exhausted, she wrote. The picture was a comedy—"a farce"— and she wasn't right for it. She suggested her old friend Joan Blondell. She was getting only four weeks' vacation after doing four "very hard pictures." She weighed only 104 pounds. Surely he understood.[45]

Chatter ensued; memos flew. Roy Obringer told Warner he'd talked to her lawyer, Dudley Furse, who told him that Bette was up North somewhere suffering from a bad case of sunburn, but that her business manager, Vernon Wood, had talked to her and advised her to do the film on the theory that she should get away from all the heavy roles she'd done. According to Wood, Bette was planning to plead one more time, but after that she'd go ahead and do it if that's what Warner wanted.

Bette did her second-round pleading the following week. The role was no good, she wrote. "There is no living actress such a fool," she declared. And she'd have to do a musical number in the Hollywood Bowl sequence—it was, after all, a Busby Berkeley film—and she knew she'd be terrible at it.[46] Warner Bros. responded that day. There would be no further discussion; Bette Davis would do *Hollywood Hotel*.

The following day, G. Horace Coshow, M.D., of Carpinteria telephoned the studio. Bette had come down with sunstroke, he said, and he was taking her to the hospital. She would require one month to recover. A few days later, Warners slapped Bette on suspension.

Her secretary, Bridget Price, took over the conversation with the studio. (The critic Janet Flanner described Price as "a tall, intaglio-faced English lady, an old friend of Mrs. Davis."[47] *Intaglio:* a design carved into the surface of metal or stone.) She had seen Bette, Bridget wrote to Jack Warner, and could honestly report that Bette was suffering from second-degree burns. She was assured, however, that Bette would recover over time. By the way, Bridget wrote, she had told Bette that she had seen the previews for *It's Love I'm After* and loved them but was surprised to see that Bette had been given second billing to Leslie Howard when, after all, she had been billed equally with Mr. Howard above the title on previous occasions. Bette agreed that Bridget should write to Mr. Warner about this problem immediately. Bette would do it herself, of course, but for the fact that Dr. Coshow had ordered her to rest.[48] Warner waited several weeks before replying that Miss Price was mistaken: Bette Davis was in fact billed above the title on the same line as Leslie Howard and Olivia de Havilland.

But she never did *Hollywood Hotel*.

By November, Bette was back at work beginning to film *Jezebel* when the gossip columnist Radie Harris reported—in an article called "The Fear That Is Haunting Bette Davis"—that Bette had in fact suffered "a complete nervous collapse" over the summer in addition to a bad case of sunburn.[49] Bette took the occasion of her own nervous breakdown and her fear of losing her mind completely to reveal her sister Bobby's recurring mental illness. This was an unusually frank admission from a movie star, but it wasn't very nice to Bobby.[50]

B ETTE'S WEDDING RING had been stolen after only a week of marriage. Ham bought her a new one at Christmas 1932—"a very lovely band of platinum and diamonds," according to Mayme Ober Peake—but the loss of the original one was portentous.[51] The marriage wasn't working. "There was no equity in our drives nor in our sense of sovereignty. That was the core of all our troubles," Bette admits in *The Lonely Life*.[52] There was another problem, too: "It is small wonder that Ham was both dazzled, bewitched, and then exhausted with my crises. I always had one."[53]

Ham Nelson was a sporadically employed musician married to a dynamic, overwrought, increasingly famous movie star who operated under emotional and professional strains he couldn't alleviate. When he took a job in San Francisco in 1934 and earned one hundred dollars a week, he found housing in a low-rent bungalow—10 Mission Auto Court, to be exact.[54] (On one trip to visit him, Bette got a speeding ticket for going seventy miles an hour in a forty-five-mile zone near Livermore.)[55] It was all very amusing for the press to run stories about how the movie star visited her husband in an auto court, but Ham found the attention paid to the couple's income disparity more difficult to stomach.

He also experienced the classical jealousy of the star's spouse, forever having to sit through movies watching richer, better-looking, more famous men make love to his wife. Michael Curtiz overheard the couple bickering at a screening of *Front Page Woman*, with Ham accusing Bette of being a little too believable in her onscreen attraction to George Brent and stomping off hissing "Horseshit!" after Bette explained that she was simply doing her job.[56] He may or may not have known about the fling with Franchot Tone, but he became enraged when he learned that the male starlet Ross Alexander was attempting to cover his attraction to men by ostentatiously proclaiming his attraction to Bette. "I'll kill him," Ham is said to have responded and promptly beat Alexander up in a studio men's room. Alexander didn't let up on his quest for Bette, though, and Bette replied by ridiculing his masculinity, leading Alexander to call her "a merciless bitch." Shortly thereafter, in late December 1936, Alexander picked up a hitchhiker for sex. The hitchhiker tried to blackmail him, and the studio had to intervene. Haunted by this humiliation, Alexander committed suicide on January 2, 1937. Bette was wracked with guilt.[57]

Her relationship with Ham was also strained by two pregnancies, both aborted. "I had two during my first marriage," Davis acknowledged to *Playboy*'s Bruce Williamson in 1982. "I don't want to talk about my marriages, but—well, that's what he wanted. Being the dutiful wife, that's what I did. And I guess I will thank him all my life. Because if I'd had those two children. . . . I see myself at 50, with the children all grown up, wondering whether or not I ever would have made it. I think there's nothing sadder, and I'm sure I'd have given it all up if I'd had children earlier."[58] Bette may have been sure, but Ham Nelson surely wasn't. And it was Ham Nelson who saw his wife's fierce ambition and rock-bottom dedication to acting at the closest possible range.

Bette and Ham moved—again—in 1937, this time to 1700 Coldwater Canyon Drive in Beverly Hills, a hacienda-style house complete with a swimming pool, a tennis court, and an acre of land.[59] But by the time

Jezebel went into production in November, Ham was spending most of his time in New York, having taken a job as an agent.[60] "He was too honorable to trade on my position in pictures, which would have been easy for him to do, and I know the gulf between our earnings discouraged him," Bette later wrote. "That, more than anything else, licked him."[61]

VICTORIES

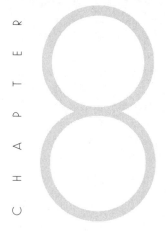

THE SECOND OSCAR

ALLING BETTE'S SPOILED, HEAD-
strong Julie Marsden "Jezebel" is a bit harsh. The biblical Ahab's Baal-
worshipping wife slew a variety of perfectly decent prophets and thus
offended the Lord so mightily that He arranged for her to be hurled out
of a window by eunuchs and her corpse to be devoured by dogs. Julie
Marsden just wears the wrong dress to a southern society ball. Still, in
the humid and overwrought New Orleans in which William Wyler's
elegant film is set, an inappropriate gown is a breach so damning that
Julie must dispatch herself to a leper colony to regain her honor.

To say that *Jezebel* is vintage Bette Davis is to praise what vinophiles
love in a fine old wine—not the bright, fresh berry but the subtle rank-
ness of controlled decay. The fact that *Jezebel* was adapted from a Broadway bomb is as key to the film's appeal as Wyler's meticulous direction.
In the first of their three collaborations, Wyler and Davis extract an
essential, rich spirit from an essentially inferior grape.

Wyler first encountered the property in December 1933, when he
saw Miriam Hopkins star in one of the thirty-two performances of the
ill-fated play. He saw it neither as fine theater nor as a project for Davis,
whom he'd dismissed and forgotten two years earlier. For Wyler, *Jezebel*
stood poised as a potential vehicle for his then-wife, the volatile Margaret Sullavan. Wyler suggested to his distant cousin, Carl Laemmle Jr.

at Universal, that the studio buy the rights and possibly even turn the play, a melodrama about a headstrong antebellum belle, into a musical of the old South. But the play quickly closed, and Junior ignored Wyler's proposal.[1]

Warner Bros. expressed interest in *Jezebel* in 1935, but the studio wasn't thinking about starring either Sullavan or Hopkins but rather the Patou-infused, spearmint-emitting Ruth Chatterton. The rights to the play, by Owen Davis Sr., were held jointly by Guthrie McClintic, its producer, and Miriam Hopkins, its star. McClintic was eager to cash in, but the sensibly pigheaded Hopkins was willing to sell only if Warners promised her the lead. Walter McEwen, of Warners' story department, got around that little problem by employing a time-honored Hollywood strategy: he simply lied. McEwen told Hopkins she'd get first crack at the role once the studio had a screenplay, all the while pushing the picture not for Chatterton but for Davis, whom Hopkins now despised.[2] Miriam had been jealous of Bette as early as Rochester; with Davis now an Oscar winner, Hopkins's enmity had only grown.

By the time Hopkins sold the rights in January 1937, McEwen was actively developing the role for Davis. He enthusiastically told the head of production, Hal Wallis, that Bette would "knock the spots off the part of a little bitch of an aristocratic Southern girl."[3] It's not particularly curious that various forms of the word *bitch* keep popping up in Warner Bros. memos on *Jezebel*; the term is not unrelated to Bette's emerging persona, both onscreen and off-, let alone the character of Julie Marsden. The director Edmund Goulding, handed the script for comment and possible employment as director, responded that "although it is quite possible to put a vivid picture upon the screen, that picture can only tell the story of the triumph of bitchery. . . . Julie is rather like one of some naughty children writing obscene things on a wall, and then when the other runs away, she will stay there and tell you that she did it, and so what?" Goulding had ideas for improving the evolving script according to his own tastes, but a Warners producer, Lou Edelman, told Hal Wallis in July 1937 that Goulding's ideas were pointedly old-fashioned and would result in "the biggest and most complicated piece of tripe that has ever been put on the screen."[4]

With Goulding out, Wallis approached Wyler, then under contract at Goldwyn, with an offer: $75,000 and a twelve-week shooting schedule. Wyler, dissatisfied with what he felt was the lackluster way Goldwyn had been promoting him, was especially interested in Warners' promise of extensive personal publicity.[5]

Bette reacted with mixed feelings to Wyler's hiring for *Jezebel*. As pleased as she was by his stature—Wyler was by far the most highly regarded director she'd been asked to work with so far—his reputation for high craftsmanship didn't erase the lingering humiliation she felt after their first meeting. In 1931, Universal had called Davis in for a screen test with Wyler for his film *A House Divided*. The wardrobe department stuck her in a tight and tawdry number with a too-revealing top. As Davis later wrote, she felt she looked "common": "Hot and embarrassed, I was rushed down to the set where the dark little director stopped brooding long enough to glare at me and say to one of his assistants, 'What do you think of these girls who show their tits and think they can get jobs?'"[6] Obviously Wyler didn't think much of these "girls"; Davis didn't get the role.

"I was now in a position to refuse to work with Mr. Wyler," Davis wrote in *The Lonely Life*. "I asked for an appointment to talk to him. Revenge, they say, is sweet. It has never been thus for me. Mr. Wyler, not remembering me or the incident, was, to put it mildly, taken aback when I told him my grim little tale of woe. He actually turned green. He was genuinely apologetic, saying he had come a long way since those days. I could not help but believe he was sincere."[7] Filming began on October 25, 1937.[8]

Jezebel begins with a simple but breathtaking display of grandness and scope, as Wyler lengthily tracks his camera down a New Orleans boulevard, past shops, street carts, carriages, passersby, buildings, and still more street stalls and carriages, until it comes to rest facing the imposing facade of a large and busy hotel. Graceful and subtle, the shot demonstrates what the great theorist of film realism André Bazin so admired about Wyler's style: the image's continuity reveals the luxurious entirety of a city block, lending weight and authenticity to what audiences would otherwise perceive, however unconsciously, as cut-apart wooden backlot construction in Burbank.

Wyler was equally painstaking with Davis's entrance as Julie Marsden, though it's not nearly as grand a sequence. The scene occurs at Julie's plantation, where—much to the delighted shock of her guests—she is late to her own party. ("Her own party! In her own house!") Wyler cuts from the interior, with all the guests atwitter, to the street outside. A dark, skittish horse rides up at a gallop. The rider, a woman clad in a tight-waisted, big-cuffed habit and feathered hat to match the spirited horse, brings it to a halt outside the gate, forces it—against its will—to turn and enter, and rides into the courtyard. Handing the horse off to a child slave, she heads to the door only to turn back at the sound of the horse struggling against the boy's nervous handling. She advises the boy not to be scared. "Yes'm, Miss Julie, but he bites!" "Then you just plain bite him back," she declares—apparently an act she wouldn't hesitate to commit herself. Julie scoops her hem up from the back with her riding crop, turns toward the camera in an arrogantly premature curtain call, and sweeps into the mansion.

Bette looks supremely confident catching the hem with her crop, but in fact the scooping bit nearly did her in. Over and over Wyler made her repeat it, and she had no idea why. She'd practiced it beforehand, after all, and she thought she had it down. Concerned, Bette begged Wyler to tell her precisely how to do it, what he wanted, would he just explain it to her, *please*? But the autocratic Wyler refused specificity. "I'll know it when I see it" was his terse response. Only when Wyler did eventually see it on take 48 did he move on to the next shot. Trying hard to understand what had occurred, Davis demanded to see the rushes. According to her, when she saw the approved take she realized that Wyler was right; the one he used was the most naturally self-possessed, the least studied. "He wanted a complete establishment of character with one gesture," she later explained. He got what he wanted.

Wyler was an expressive director, but only onscreen. The man himself gave little coaching to his actors, and Bette, who thought she required his approval, grew alarmed. Having dismissed most of her earlier directors as workmen at best, hacks at worst, she rarely needed their endorsement; she didn't respect them enough to care what they thought of her. But with Wyler, she was thrown. Here was *a director*—a creative picture maker who was carefully, technically piecing *Jezebel* together, shot by shot, in a manner Davis had never seen before. And he gave her nothing.

Being Bette, she said something. "After about a week, I went up to him and said, 'I may be very peculiar, Mr. Wyler, but I just have to know if what I'm doing pleases you in any way. I just have to know, after every scene if possible.' So the entire next day, he went, 'Marvelous! Marvelous!' And I couldn't stand it. I said, 'Please—go back to your old ways.' "[9]

Wyler recognized some of Davis's mannerisms for what they were: itchily nervous and beyond her control, expressions not of a character's psychology but of her own anxiety. So he compelled her to stand still when Julie had no reason to move. His order was reminiscent of Laura Hope Crews's, but he was male, so Bette took it better. "Do you want me to put a chain around your neck?" he barked one day during filming. "Stop moving your head!"[10] Wyler also coaxed her out of playing too many scenes at full throttle. Regarding many of her earlier films as deficient—shallow scripts, artless directors—Davis often tried make up for their lack by pumping her characters harder, substituting adrenaline and tics for the substance she knew was missing from the material. Wyler, in contrast, radiated confidence in both himself and the film he was making, and he encouraged Bette to play Julie with more moderation. "She comes in during the morning eager to do it right, maybe to overdo it," Wyler wrote in a memo to Hal Wallis and the associate producer Henry Blanke, "and I tell her to take it easy. I tell her a scene is impor-tant, but not *every* scene, so she learns not to act everything at the same pressure, as though her life depends on it."[11]

William Wyler successfully dominated Bette Davis, so naturally she fell in love with him. Ham was conveniently in New York.

"Her love affair was the talk of the studio," Wallis later declared.[12] It was clear to everyone around Warner Bros. that *Jezebel*'s star and director were acting out their passion. One night the editor Warren Low and the assistant director Rudy Fehr were waiting in the projection room for Davis and Wyler to arrive and see the day's rushes. The two were late. Low grew impatient and was about to leave when the director and his star finally showed up—with "lipstick smeared all over their mouths," Fehr recalled. "They looked ridiculous. They should have looked in the mirror before they came in. This happened practically every night after that. They obviously were doing some heavy petting in somebody's dressing room before they came to review the rushes."[13]

"Our romance was doubly difficult because we could not be seen in public," Davis once said, the Warners lot evidently not counting as a public space.[14] When they weren't at the studio working, they were es-sentially housebound and spent many evenings together at Wyler's place, where his assistant, Sam, made home-cooked dinners for them.

The love affair didn't lead Wyler to ease up on Davis at work. "That handsome, homely dynamo, Wyler, could make your life a hell," she wrote in *The Lonely Life*. "I met my match."[15] She quoted him admiringly (in retrospect) as saying, "I want actors who can act. I can only direct actors—I can't teach them how to act."[16] Wyler trusted that Davis and her costar, Henry Fonda, could act, and his faith left him free to pursue an indescribable, undirectable quality in every shot, no matter how many takes it took. His efforts put a strain on both Davis and Fonda.

In fact, Wyler demanded even more retakes of Fonda's shots than he did of Davis's. The production began to drag; costs were rising, as were rumors. A concerned Hal Wallis asked Henry Blanke, "Do you think Wyler is mad at Fonda or something because of their past? It seems that he is not content to okay anything with Fonda until it has been done ten or eleven takes. After all, they have been divorced from the same girl [Margaret Sullavan], and bygones should be bygones." Some people even proposed, wrongly, that Bette was enjoying affairs with *both* men and that Wyler was demanding Fonda's retakes out of jealousy.[17]

Wallis, accustomed to Warners' relatively compliant and workmanlike directors—men who, unlike Wyler, didn't have much of a vision—grew increasingly exasperated as Wyler kept shooting more and more footage. Wallis was himself a master craftsman, but this was ridiculous; Wyler was wasting celluloid. He complained about Wyler's multiple takes of Donald Crisp leaving the house and Davis coming down the stairs: "The first one was excellent, yet he took it sixteen times. What the hell is the matter with him anyhow—is he absolutely daffy? . . . Wyler likes to see these big numbers on the slate. Maybe we could arrange to have them start with the number six on each take, then it wouldn't take so long to get up to nine or ten."[18] Bette, on the other hand, appreciated the care Wyler was putting into *Jezebel*, as much as her own retakes unnerved her. Compared to all the *Special Agent*s she'd made, let alone the *Hell's House*s, *Jezebel* was bliss—artistically, at least.

Dissatisfied with Clements Ripley and Abem Finkel's screenplay, Wyler brought John Huston on to do some rewriting. The production was under a specific time constraint, too: Henry Fonda signed his *Jezebel* contract with the provision that he would be finished filming by December 17 so he could travel to New York to be with his wife for the birth of their first child. What with Wyler's seemingly endless shooting, that deadline was fast approaching, and the picture had fallen nearly a month behind schedule. As Wallis unpleasantly remarked, "The little nigger boy will be a full-grown man by the time Wyler finishes the picture."[19]

Jezebel's centerpiece is the fifteen-minute Olympus Ball scene, an elaborate and largely dialogue-free spectacle during which Julie's engagement to Preston Dillard (Fonda) crumbles in the face of the couple's conflicting but mutual obstinacy. The ball, to which all New Orleans society women are expected to wear virginal white, slams to a halt when Julie arrives in flaming red. As written, the scene took up but a few lines of description. This verbal brevity led an assistant director to schedule it for half a day's work. But as Davis later remembered it, "Willy took five days!"[20] They began on November 9 and finished on the fifteenth.[21]

The gowns for *Jezebel* are credited to Orry-Kelly, but he didn't design the key dress. "Milo Anderson told me that he did the red dress in *Jezebel*," said the costume expert David Chierichetti. "Orry-Kelly was an Australian citizen, and while his immigration was being processed he had to go back to Australia and stay there for a while. So Anderson finished *Jezebel*, including that famous dress. I said to Anderson, 'Didn't it bother you that Kelly was given credit for your work?' And he said, 'No, it's quite a compliment, isn't it? They kept renewing my contract, and that's all I cared about.' "[22]

Wyler begins the Olympus Ball sequence with a reverse crane shot that begins on the reigning king and queen of the ball and travels over the heads of the orchestra and the dancers on the dance floor and ends on an immense crystal chandelier, with a balcony packed with people watching the spectacle in the background. Its precision reflects the gracious regimentation of the partygoers, who are all dressed according to the rigidly refined standards of New Orleans society. A subsequent shot taken from just above the floor reveals swirling hoop skirts, all in white, and the martial steps and black trousers of the men. It's into this arch, uniformed gentility that Julie makes her brazen entrance with Preston.

Davis plays it birdlike—part peacock, part vulture. Wyler's camera tracks with them as they make their way through the ballroom, Pres glaring, Julie gliding with an air of haughty triumph tinged with increasing surprise and chagrin as she senses the magnitude of her miscalculation. She asks to leave. "We haven't danced yet," the priggish Pres responds.

Wyler cranes above them as they waltz, the crowd slowly making space around them. Julie, who loses her composure and self-possession entirely while being yanked around the dance floor, suddenly looks homely and small in high angle. "Pres," she begs. "Let me go. Take me out'a heah!"—complete with a touch of whimpering in Davis's line delivery. Pres stays silent.

On the surface, the tensions of the Olympus Ball seem absurd and arcane. Julie's dress is truly strumpetlike, but the other women's pristine, lacy gowns look more like babies' christening outfits than something an adult would wear. By my standards, Julie's rebellion is worthy of praise, not condemnation. But the underlying psychology of the scene is still bracing, particularly in light of Bette's own combustible nature. Julie, after all, has chosen the outrageous red dress in malicious anger—specifically to spite Pres for not having left a business meeting in order to accompany her to a fitting. In this way Julie plays out Bette's own ambivalence toward male authority. Like Davis herself in both her marriage and her work, Julie insists that a man offer his opinion, and when he contradicts her, she acts out against her own self-interest—in Julie's case by impulsively choosing precisely what Pres would have rejected, just to prove a point, however damning it may be to her. Julie is as sure of her belief in the scarlet gown as Bette was of her decision to leave Warner Bros. for Ludovico Toeplitz.

The pressure of making *Jezebel* for a domineering man she loved took its toll on Davis. She became depressed and frightened. Somatic symptoms appeared early on. She was sick on November 2 and 3. She had a charley horse on one of the days scheduled for the Olympus Ball. After shooting exteriors on the back lot in the rain, she developed bronchitis and a bad cold. While attempting to film the shot in which Julie, seated at her bedroom vanity, employs the old southern trick of tapping her cheeks with a hairbrush to make them blush, Bette was so overly energetic with the bristles that her slaps caused bruises and she had to take several days off while her face healed.

The Warner Bros. archives at the University of Southern California contain an all-too-lengthy discussion between executives of how Bette opened a pimple one weekend and had put some kind of salve on it, but then realized that this was the wrong thing to do, so she consulted a specialist who worried that there might be a hole left in Bette's cheek, so the physician began applying solutions to wash it out. He "will attempt to remove the core tonight, sterilize it, and apply a salve so that makeup can be applied," a detail-oriented memo writer noted on November 30.[23]

.Wyler wasn't shooting *Jezebel* in sequence, either. Eschewing continuity for the sake of convenience or artistic interest was, and remains, standard filmmaking practice, but Davis wasn't used to it and it disrupted her sense of Julie's development. "Davis had hysterics last night because we were shooting so much out of continuity," a production manager noted on December 21. On December 29, after eleven hours of shooting a number of shots out of sequence, Bette became panic-stricken and broke down in tears.[24]

Jezebel was so far behind schedule that the company spent New Year's Day working. That's when Bette received word that her father had died at his home in Belmont, Massachusetts.

"BIOGRAPHY IS THE medium through which the remaining secrets of the famous dead are taken from them and dumped out in full view of the world," Janet Malcolm writes in *The Silent Woman*, her masterful book-length essay on Sylvia Plath, Ted Hughes, and the imperfect craft of writing about other people's lives. "The biographer at work, indeed, is like the professional burglar, breaking into a house, rifling through certain drawers that he has good reason to think contain the jewelry and money, and triumphantly bearing his loot away. . . . The reader's amazing tolerance (which he would extend to no novel written half as badly as most biographies) makes sense only when seen as a kind of collusion between him and the biographer in an excitingly forbidden undertaking: tiptoeing down the corridor together, to stand in front of the bedroom door and try to peep through the keyhole."[25]

For Bette Davis's biographers, one of the most evocative and resonant scenes in Davis's life plays itself out in a luxury suite called *The Wild Duck*, 1929. It's just down the hall from the musty and rarely opened *Broken Dishes*, but it is to *Broken Dishes* what the queen's bedchamber is to a crawl space next to the servants' quarters. In the literary lives of Bette Davis, *The Wild Duck* is especially well-trodden terrain, its bureau drawers ransacked several times over, its mirrors imprinted by many sets of examining fingertips. The temperature and humidity are kept permanently high, for Ibsen's play is about a father who cruelly abandons his daughter.

After a performance of *The Earth Between* in March 1929, the director and actor Cecil Clovelly sent Bette a card requesting her to meet the actress Blanche Yurka the following morning at 11:00 a.m. uptown at the Bijou Theatre, where she was appearing in Ibsen's *The Lady from the Sea*. Yurka, who had just directed as well as starred in Ibsen's *The Wild Duck* in a successful revival at the Forty-ninth Street Theatre, was preparing to take both shows on the road, and Linda Watkins—who had played Hedvig, the sacrificial innocent in *The Wild Duck*, and Boletta, the awkward elder daughter in *The Lady from the Sea*—was leaving the company. Yurka wanted to cast Davis in both roles.[26]

To Bette, Yurka "seemed like a giant bird of prey. Her long neck pressed forward and her glowing eyes devoured everything around her."[27] The audition was brief. Bette read a few lines from *The Wild Duck* but was quickly interrupted by Yurka, who said, "That's fine, my dear. We'll have one week of rehearsal after you close in *The Earth Between*."[28] An Actors' Equity contract dated April 4, 1929, survives in the Davis archives: Bette was paid seventy-five dollars per week to play the roles of Boletta, Hedvig, and understudy "in the Ibsen Repertoire."[29]

Bette may have been a superb Boletta, but no one cares. It's her Hedvig on which everyone focuses, mainly because Bette herself made such a fuss about it, even—or especially—at the time. *The Wild Duck* sparked a severe attack of hysteria, a "malady by representation," as Freud described it: Bette broke into a violent and all-consuming rash the day she was cast. At the time, she and Ruthie assumed it was measles, but in retrospect Davis understood it to be a physical manifestation of an extreme emotional response. She was reacting explicitly to the fear and stress of her casting, and on a deeper level—however little she owned up to them—to the parallels between Hedvig's family and her own. The red flaming rash that spread over Bette's body had an even more immediate cause: Harlow, the father who had left her, was to attend *The Earth Between* that very evening.

Davis reported that she "collapsed," sick, in her dressing room after the show. That's when Harlow made his entrance. "He was as formal as ever and even more elegant," she wrote in *The Lonely Life*. Characteristically, Bette's father complimented the play and the other actors but said nothing about her or her performance.[30] "I didn't realize then how captive he was in *his* role," Bette went on, rather too benignly. "I didn't realize how inarticulate he could be, for all his brilliance. His voice became even more formal, more impersonal. He was always the gentleman. 'Would—would you care—to go out with me and have a little supper?'" She declined his offer and sent him on his way, a pitiless reaction she described with vague regret.[31]

Having paid her father back with a harsh rejection of her own, she turned on her mother.

Bette had to learn both roles while suffering through the hysterical measles, and she was never one to suffer in silence: "I have always loathed being read to, and Ruthie sat at my bed and read [the scripts] over and over until I thought I'd go mad. I couldn't eat. I was weak, irritable, and Mother became my victim. I threw the scripts across the room, howling in despair."[32]

Ruthie, the object of Bette's unconscious blame all along, responded by doing a bit of acting out herself: she neglected to set the alarm clock on the first day of rehearsals for *The Wild Duck*, a not-so-subtle act of sabotage. Bette, plied full of Ruthie's odd measles remedy—milk and Virginia Dare wine—responded by taking her hysteria to a more feral level: "I went berserk. I bit Mother on the shoulder. My teeth dug into her flesh right through her woolen dress."

They arrived at the rehearsal an hour late. Cecil Clovelly greeted them in a cold rage. "Get out, Mother! *And stay out!*" Bette shrieked.[33]

Biographers thrive on episodes like this—tight incidents that pull together the essential strands of our subjects' psyches into a rope strong enough for us to hang them with it. And we tend to characterize the hanging not as a murderous impulse on our part—we're never at fault—but as an act of suicidal self-exposure on the part of our subjects. In this case, Bette herself supplied the facts; we simply present them. With *The Wild Duck*, Davis hands us a situation so clinically exact, so dramatically telling, that the interpretation forms itself. To return to Janet Malcolm's metaphor, it's Davis who parades herself naked before the keyhole, and all we are doing, her chroniclers and readers, is crouching down in a spying posture and watching in titillated awe as she makes a spectacle of herself for our entertainment. If anything, the moment when she bites her mother and draws blood is our cue to stand up from our squatting position at the keyhole and brazenly peer into the room because our subject has thrown the door wide-open for us.

There is no doubt that the role of Hedvig held especially painful consequence for Bette. She and Ruthie had actually seen Blanche Yurka perform *The Wild Duck* in Boston in January 1926, with the ill-fated Peg Entwistle as Hedvig.* The play certainly struck a chord in her, and Bette later claimed that she decided then and there that the role would be hers someday.[34] "He'll never come home to us again," Hedvig cries. "I think I'll die from all this! What did I do to him? Mother, you've got to make him come home! . . . Yes, I'll be all right—if only Daddy comes back."[35]

The resonances between *The Wild Duck* and Bette's own family go beyond the paternal abandonment that sends the girl into a paroxysm of guilt and self-recrimination. Hedvig's father is a professional photographer, but it is her mother, Gina (played by Yurka), who does the careful,

---

* After a disappointing career, Entwistle committed Tinseltown's most symbolic suicide by jumping off the letter *H* of the "Hollywoodland" sign in 1932.

painstaking work of retouching. Hjalmar, like Harlow, believes that he sees the world with the clarity of a lens, but Gina understands not only the need to turn raw reality into a more beautiful fantasy but that this artistic process requires hard, straining work. She teaches this skill to Hedvig.

What Bette Davis made of Hedvig's breakdown scene is legendary. "Bette Davis was by no means an accomplished actress at the time," Yurka once recalled. "Her mother, frankly, was a pain in the neck, and it's a miracle she didn't sink Bette's career from the outset. She was endlessly and sentimentally fussing over her. She was a weak, silly creature. . . . The show-biz mother to end all! Even Bette, overeager and full of tears and tantrums, was a maddening handful. But one gets an instinct in this business. I knew Bette would be a great Hedvig. She would attack the part—not with technique but with her nerves and her heart."[36]

Yurka underrehearsed Bette in Hedvig's breakdown scene. "It was a risky thing to do with such an inexperienced youngster," Yurka said, "but I followed my hunch and merely told her to let herself go when she came to the spot. But on opening night, even I was not prepared for the torrent of emotional intensity which rocked that frail body as she lay downward on the sofa, crying her heart out."[37]

But one is mistaken to think that Bette was crying out to Harlow in that scene; Hedvig is not pleading with her father because her father has already left. She's crying out to her mother and, more important, blaming herself.

Harlow's reaction to Bette's casting was equally overheated. The routinely unemotional Harlow is said to have panicked at his daughter's imminent appearance in a play that so closely mimicked their own lives. All three members of the fractured Davis triangle felt the magnitude of the moment. Ruth Elizabeth Davis was giving the performance of her life.

As electrifying as these revelations may be, the most significant aspect of Bette's appearance in *The Wild Duck* is precisely that: her appearance. No one—not her director, not the other actors, not the audience, and perhaps not Bette herself—was prepared for the firestorm of anguish that Bette threw at them on opening night. That degree of raw naturalism was extreme, shocking. It was an outpouring of deeply personal agony that, as the critic Martin Shingler has noted, Bette had long tried to hold in check. But as Shingler pointed out, this was the theater, and through the repetition of theater Bette learned to formalize her own despair: "Having to do this night after night for the entire run of the play, Davis developed the technique of drawing upon her own contained neurosis, hysteria and paranoia, channeling them into her performances."[38] Davis had performed before, but now she was an actress. Like the burning episode at Crestalban, it took an extreme situation to bring out her essential nature.

Bette Davis maintained throughout her public life that her father's abandonment meant little to her, that she never grieved his absence, and that her initial response to her parents' separation—"Now we can go on a picnic and have a baby"—was not only artlessly childlike but essentially honest.[39] Ibsen provides the key to Davis's denial in *The Wild Duck*: Dr. Relling, the Ekdahls' downstairs neighbor and the play's voice of compassion, maintains an unshakable belief in what he calls "the life-lie," the fantasy that enables one to go on in the face of empty despair: "The life-lie, don't you see? That's the animating principle of life." It was this denial that enlivened Bette Davis and enabled her to turn hurt into art. It was a lie deeply dug and all-but-fully covered, and it drove her to act. Ceaselessly.

Harlow showed up for the opening night in Boston, as did Uncle Myron and Aunt Mildred, Ruthie's longtime friends the Woodwards, and a number of Bette's old schoolmates. (Her beau Charlie Ainsely chose that moment to give her a fresh taste of abandonment by having a note delivered to Bette breaking off their brief engagement. As Bette described it, Ainsely's father was blamed: "disapproved of actresses . . . we were too young . . . knew I would understand . . . and forgive . . . helpless against them . . . so sorry!" This before the curtain went up.) At the end, there was a curtain call for Yurka, then the whole cast, after which Yurka took Bette's hand and brought her to the edge of the stage, and exited, leaving Bette alone onstage. She was in tears: "I was alone—onstage and everywhere; and that's the way it was obviously meant to be. . . . This was the true beginning of the one, great, durable romance of my life."[40]

Bette was either unable or unwilling to leave the set of *Jezebel* to attend Harlow's funeral, which was held on January 3 at the Mt. Auburn Crematory Chapel in Cambridge, though she did request that she be allowed not to return to work until later that afternoon.[41] She was always the proper Yankee. (The *Boston Post* misunderstood the rent, fraught nature of Harlow's family when it announced that "Miss Davis wired her mother, Mrs. Minnie Stewart Davis, from Hollywood to say that she would not be able to attend the services. . . .")[42]

One particular studio memo—the one about Bette's late call on the third—also contains this alarming addendum: "I hope to get some definite information today regarding a second unit from Blanke, and also if and when Dieterle is to take this picture over." Warners' front office had been growing increasingly disturbed by Wyler's budget-killing pace. "Wyler has averaged a little better than 2 pages per day for 25 days," the production manager Bob Fellows wrote on November 24. "He has shot approximately 56 pages of script up to yesterday. . . . Not quite a third of the script. . . . I do not believe anyone is aware of just how slow Mr. Wyler is." "Wyler made one of his screwy shots last night," Fellows ratted on December 9—"13 takes on a scene—a long shot of Brent [sic]— purpose being to show Brent swatting a mosquito on his wrist, which was very ridiculous."[43] (Actually, it's Fonda, not Brent, who gets the mosquito bite, and it was scarcely ridiculous for Wyler to have striven for perfection because it is precisely the moment when Fonda's character gets infected with yellow fever.) The budget was rising: from an initial $783,000 to $1,073,000.[44]

It was for this reason that an exasperated Jack Warner threatened to take Wyler off *Jezebel* and install the journeyman but essentially vision-free William Dieterle in his place. Bette, emotionally fragile under the best of circumstances and coping, however obliquely, with Harlow's death, was hardly in the mood to stand back and let the malignant father figure Warner fire her benevolently domineering lover, so she stomped into Warner's office and threw a fit. Wyler was retained, though Warner did bring John Huston in on January 8 to film some second-unit stuff involving Julie's trek through the swamps with Eddie Anderson. The film wrapped on January 17, 1938, though some additional footage was shot on February 4.

Already overheated, *Jezebel* ends with Preston, feverish with yellow jack, preparing to be quarantined on the island of the lepers along with his healthy, dutiful, dull-as-soap Yankee wife, Amy (Margaret Lindsay, still indefatigably gracious). There's a pivotal scene on the staircase of Julie's mansion in which Julie convinces Amy to let her, Julie, escort Pres to the leper colony on the grounds that only Julie is tough enough, and vicious enough, to ensure Pres's survival. Amy is unconvinced. "Help me make myself clean again, as you are clean," Julie embarrassingly begs, her dignity all but gone.

Amy demands to know if Preston still loves Julie. And Julie, still the essence of duplicity in Bette's expert performance, replies: "We both *know*. . . . Pres loves his *wife*. . . . *Who else would he love?* Not me, surely. I've done too much against him."

This response is convincing only to the new Mrs. Dillard, the dullard. We see that Julie is still the lying, manipulative bitch we have admired all along, however little the desperate Julie herself may be aware of the fact. It's a spectacular performance on Davis's part, one of the most vocally nuanced and subtly emoted she ever gave. The final shots of the film, book-ending the opening tracking shot, find Julie on a cart full of wretched, feverish bodies, Pres's head on her lap, the camera moving with her as she heads in Pyrrhic triumph through the torchlit streets toward her perfectly selfish self-sacrifice.

Bette's affair with William Wyler ended soon after *Jezebel* wrapped in early February 1938. Davis was too high-strung for Wyler; she reminded him too much of his ex, Margaret Sullavan. "We fought and made up and fought and made up and fought and made up," Bette later confessed. "We were both miserable." For Davis, Wyler became the great man who got away: "Looking back, I should have married Willy after my divorce . . . and then taken the chance that it would work out. It just well might have, but of course that's hindsight. After four husbands, I know that he was the love of my life. But I was scared silly. As good as we were together, I was afraid that I couldn't handle the bit at home. I was in no way the hostess that he wanted a wife to be."

Bette appears not to have perceived her own rejection, at least not in public. In point of fact, Wyler wasn't at all interested in marrying Bette. It was he who ended the affair; she was abandoned once again. According to Wyler's biographer, Jan Herman, Wyler and his friends, the agent Paul Kohner and his wife, Lupita, would be spending a quiet evening at Wyler's house when Davis would call. "Many times we would be having dinner with Willy," Lupita Kohner recalled to Herman—"just the three of us—Paul, Willy, and myself. The telephone would ring. Sam would come in and say to him, 'Miss Davis is calling.' Willy's answer was, 'Later.' He would ignore the call."[45]

Bette was descending once again into a state of nervous exhaustion. Her physician, Dr. Noyes, told Warner Bros. that she was in no shape to start another picture in the near future. "She is going on grit alone," Noyes said. "She is not actually medically ill," he went on to add, "but her general physical and emotional makeup is such that if we rush her into another picture she will be in danger of collapse." Jack Warner wisely gave her some time to herself.

Jezebel opened at Radio City Music Hall on March 10, 1938. Business was brisk, and the reviews were mainly positive, particularly in terms of Bette's performance. Some critics carped at the ending, deriding Julie's self-sacrifice, but Davis herself emerged not only unscathed but enhanced in the public eye. The film made money; *Jezebel* took in $1.5 million on its initial release. She even made the cover of *Time*. But Davis, characteristically, credited Wyler: "Willy really is responsible for the fact that I became a box-office star."[46] Warners continued to exploit Bette in ways that must have galled her. For instance, *Photoplay* featured an early promotion for *Jezebel* in the form of a product ad in which Davis offered a purported but patently inane quote: "The easiest, most delightful way I know to protect daintiness is to bathe with Lux Toilet Soap!"[47]

When the Oscar nominations were announced in early 1939, Bette found herself in the company of Margaret Sullavan, among others, in the Best Actress category. *Jezebel* was nominated as Best Picture (along with nine other films, including Jean Renoir's *Grand Illusion*).[48] Wyler didn't make the cut in the Best Director category, and neither did Henry Fonda for Best Actor. Fay Bainter, however, was a double nominee: first for Best Supporting Actress for *Jezebel* and then for Best Actress for *White Banners*.

The ceremony was held at the Biltmore Hotel on February 23. Bette arrived with an eight-man escort that included Wyler. Having been chastised for the pedestrian dress she wore to accept her Oscar for *Dangerous* three years before, Bette took more care this time. Mayme Ober Peake was ecstatic: "Bette, wearing her new short, softly-waved haircut for the first time in public, was a stunner in brown net, made with a very full bouffant skirt and tight bodice. Across the front of the bodice was inset a bird of paradise!"[49]

Jezebel—and *Grand Illusion*—lost the Best Picture award to Frank Capra's bland *You Can't Take It With You*. Fay Bainter won for Best Supporting Actress; and finally, at the tail end of the awards, Sir Cedric Hardwicke announced that the Best Actress of 1938 was Bette Davis.

She thanked the Academy but singled out William Wyler and insisted that he stand and take a bow. "I earned the Oscar I received for *Jezebel*," Davis later wrote. "The thrill of winning my second Oscar was only lessened by the Academy's failure to give the directorial award to Willy. He made my performance. He made the script. *Jezebel* is a fine picture. It was all Wyler."

Onstage, in front of her peers, Bette's nervous exhaustion vanished. She was confident, radiant, proud. "I was never surer of myself professionally than at this moment."[50]

"A GIRL WHO DIES"

*T*HE *SISTERS* WENT INTO PRODUCTION ON the morning of Monday June 6, 1938, and continued for almost nine weeks, ending at 3:00 a.m. on Saturday August 6.[1] Bette was paired for the first time with the magnificent Errol Flynn, a man far more gorgeous than any of the actresses playing the title characters.

By the age of twenty-nine, Flynn had lived a life that would have been considered delinquent if it hadn't been so exotic and enviable and Flynn himself had been homely. He was born in Hobart, Tasmania. Sent to Australia's finest prep schools, he was inevitably expelled; sailing to New Guinea at sixteen to take a government job, he embarked instead on a private quest for gold ore. The gold hunter then turned sailor, then tobacco plantation overlord, after which he became the most naturalistic of actors because he never knew quite what he was doing other than compelling audiences to gaze upon him in a kind of dazzled wonder.

By the age of twenty-four, he was in England with the Northampton Repertory Company. At twenty-six, he was a movie star in Hollywood with *Captain Blood*. By the time *The Sisters* went into production, he was Warners' baddest bad boy—thrilling audiences by swashbuckling his way through hits like *The Charge of the Light Brigade* and *The Adventures of Robin Hood*, all the while pulling off his tights offscreen for a series of many women and even a few men on a frighteningly tight timetable that led to the expression "in like Flynn," the suggestion being that it took him mere moments to get where he wanted.

Flynn wasn't afraid to offend his directors and producers, not to mention Jack Warner himself, with his chronic lateness and unpredictability, nor was he reluctant to pick fights on the set, the most notorious of which was his refusal on the set of *Captain Blood* to let the makeup department shave Ross Alexander's hairy armpits for Alexander's spread-eagled flogging scene because he, Flynn, took too much sexual pleasure in them offscreen, a point Flynn pursued loudly and in the most colorful language until the director, Michael Curtiz, backed down and left Alexander's armpits alone.

Where Bette was methodical as a worker, Errol was anarchic and devil-may-care. For Davis, filmmaking was work, and work was good, and good was virtue and practicality in equal measure. For Flynn making movies was a sport of no more consequence than a good athletic screw. One might assume that there was immediate friction between the two stars, but there wasn't. "The most beautiful person we've ever had on the screen" is how Davis described him years later. "He openly said he knew nothing about acting, and I admired his honesty because he was absolutely right."[2]

Bette's confidant, Warner's makeup chief, Perc Westmore (Perc being pronounced as in Percival), was amazed at the rapport between the two stars. According to his nephew, Frank Westmore, "It baffled Perc when Bette Davis, the queen supreme of the Warner Bros. lot, raved about 'Errol's charm and enchanting ways' all during the filming of their first movie together, *The Sisters*, but Bette later explained that she adored working with Flynn 'because he never really *worked*. He was just *there*.' "[3]

The Sisters is a competent and reasonably involving melodrama punctuated by surprisingly effective if archaic special effects. The story begins in 1904 in Silver Bow, Montana, where three sisters—Louise (Davis), Helen (Anita Louise), and Grace (Jane Bryan)—prepare to marry under the seemingly watchful but effectively impotent eyes of their parents (Beulah Bondi and Henry Travers). Louise meets the dashing writer Frank (Flynn) at a Teddy Roosevelt election-night party; they're married within the week, and off they go to San Francisco, where Frank finds work as a low-level sportswriter while trying to write his cherished novel. But his interests really lie in drink. (The makeup department's effort to make Flynn look like a down-at-his-heels drunk is not a success. His smooth, painted-on five-o'clock shadow fails to soften his chiseled jaw and cheekbones, and what with the delicate, derelict-suggesting darkening under his eyes he ends up looking sexier than ever.) Louise miscarries. Frank takes a slow boat to Singapore, leaving Louise alone just as the 1906 earthquake hits. She winds up in a kindly Oakland whorehouse but returns quickly to her job as a department store owner's assistant. The boss (Ian Hunter) falls in love with her, but she returns to Montana on a family emergency, and at a Taft inaugura-tion ball Frank shows up, she forgives him, and they reconcile, though the actual ending of the film is a stilted shot of the three overly illumi-nated sisters standing in a row in the middle of a crowded dance floor gazing blankly off into nowhere as the camera cranes back and up.

Like Leslie Howard before him, Flynn made overtures to Davis, but once again she spurned them. "I confused him utterly," Davis wrote in *The Lonely Life*. "One day he smiled that cocky smile and looked directly at me. 'I'd love to proposition you, Bette, but I'm afraid you'd laugh at me.' I never miss the rare opportunity to agree with a man. 'You're so right, Errol.' He bit his lip, waved his arm through the air and bowed in mock chivalry like Captain Blood. He was extremely graceful in re-treat."[4] She failed to explain why she turned him down.

There was the inevitable dustup with the director, Anatole Litvak, a personally dashing womanizer but just an average-Joe director. What the critic David Thomson writes of Litvak's late career applies equally to some of his early work: "Litvak solemnly puts his actresses through the motions of ordeal."[5] In the earthquake scene in *The Sisters*, he told Bette to stand in position in her upper-floor apartment set, and, at his com-mand, the set fell to pieces around her as she screamed, flailed her arms, and stayed precisely on target. "If I had been a fraction of an inch off my position, that would have been that," Bette later wrote. "As it was, a splinter from a crystal chandelier flew in my eye." Bobby Davis Pelgram happened to be on the set that day, "knitting serenely in a corner" until the earthquake hit. "Tola Litvak!" Bobby screamed after he called "Cut." "You are a son of a bitch!"[6]

Oddly, Bette and Bobby decided that Litvak had gotten personal by pulling this stunt; he was out to get her, Bette believed. And in the man-ner of all paranoiacs, she came up with what was, to her, a plausible rea-son: the cheap bastard was saving money by not hiring a stunt double.[7] It's curious that throughout her life Davis claimed to be striving for truth and realism but remained, in this instance at least, so resistant to performing physical action in its real, spatial context. Litvak films the collapse of the building mostly in master shot. The camera is far enough away from Bette that we continually see the full extent of the devastation, but it's close enough to register the fact that it's Bette Davis herself who risks being hurt or even killed by a shifting floor or falling bricks. That's what gives the scene its tension and bite, and Litvak was wise not to spoil the effect by shooting a stand-in's faceless form from so far away that it wouldn't matter who she was.

O NE OF THE most lurid sections of Charles Higham's *Bette: The Life of Bette Davis* concerns her brief affair with Howard Hughes, the peculiar and fantastically wealthy aeronautics designer, flier, filmmaker, and, at the time of Bette's affair, on-again off-again lover of Katharine Hepburn. Hughes, Higham asserts as we return to our demeaningly squatting position at the bedroom door's keyhole, "suffered from recurrent ejaculatory impotence," and Bette, "who was not beautiful and thus was not threatening, told her friends she managed to help him overcome his impotence. She was sweet and kind and good to Hughes—she set his mind free of anxiety."[8]

Higham goes on to tell what seems to be an over-the-top story involving a jealous and maddened Ham Nelson returning from New York, wiring their bedroom on Coldwater Canyon Drive for sound—"with the aid of a well-known private detective"—and sitting alone in a sound truck up the road listening to his wife and Hughes making what was, for Hughes at least, psychotherapeutic love. As Higham reports, Ham "suddenly could endure no more. He raced down to the back door, let himself in with a key, and burst into the bedroom. Hughes tried to punch Ham in the face. He flubbed it." The enraged Ham then threatened to blackmail both Bette and Hughes—Bette by revealing her adultery to the press, Hughes by hawking the aural evidence of Hughes's sexual dysfunction to the highest bidder. Bette, Higham writes, "became hysterical as Ham ran out."

The story turns even more thrilling when Higham asserts that Hughes "hired a professional gangster to kill Ham but then learned that Ham had advised the police that if he were murdered, Hughes would be responsible for the killing" and called the goon off. Hughes is said to have paid Ham $70,000 to destroy the recording, Bette is said to have repaid Hughes by taking out a loan, and Hughes—by all accounts, the multimillionaire actually took her money—was kind enough to send her a flower every year on the anniversary of the blackmail loot's repayment.[9]

Lawrence Quirk, in *Fasten Your Seat Belts: The Passionate Life of Bette Davis*, and James Spada, in *More Than a Woman: An Intimate Biography of Bette Davis*, supply more details of the affair: Bette met Hughes while she was selling raffle tickets at a benefit for the Tailwaggers, an organization that cared for lost or abandoned dogs, at the Beverly Hills Hotel in September 1938. Bette had headed the Tailwaggers since June. ("All my life I've been animal crazy, especially over dogs," Bette said around this time. "But only when I became president of the Tailwaggers did I become acutely aware of the problems of dogdom.")[10] They began their affair at Hughes's Malibu beach house, where Hughes once romantically "covered his bed with gardenias and made love to her amid the intoxicatingly rich aroma of the exotic flower."[11]

Spada provides the exact date of the stealth recording—September 22, 1938—but claims that instead of Higham's "well-known private detective," Ham enlisted the aid of his turncoat brother-in-law, Robert Pelgram. In this version there is no sound truck with its cumbersome (and consequently suspect) trail of wires leading out of the house, across the lawn, up the street, and into a parked vehicle. Instead, according to Spada—who got his information from Bobby and Robert Pelgram's daughter, Fay—the crafty brothers-in-law drilled holes in the floorboards and ran wires from the bedroom to the basement, where they installed the recording device, all during the day while Bette was distracted at the studio. Spada also provides the detail that the flower Hughes sent every year was a red rose.

Although it seems so out of character for Ham Nelson to have become a frenzied blackmailer, Vik Greenfield, Bette's personal assistant in the late 1960s to mid-1970s, swears that the incident really took place as Quirk and Spada described it. "It's true," Greenfield stated. How did he know? "Because Bette told me," he placidly answered.[12]

The Hollywood press knew only about the tension in the marriage, not the affair with Hughes or the blackmailing. A clipping dated August 30, 1938, almost a month before the crisis, already finds Bette and Bobby (amusingly called Mrs. Pilgrim) at a Glenbrook, Nevada, divorce resort. Another quotes Bette in "righteous wrath" saying, "I am in Nevada for a *vacation*—not a *divorce!*" Another reports, erroneously I imagine, that Ham had actually joined her at Glenbrook. Still another touchingly reveals that Ham called his wife "Spuds."

By September 17, the rumors hadn't abated. The columnist Harrison Carroll quoted Ham as saying, "We'll just have to wait for developments." On September 20, Bette said, "There is no use denying that we are having difficulties." If Spada's date is correct, the difficulties worsened considerably on the twenty-second, and on September 27, Carroll reported that the couple had separated, with Ham moving out of the Coldwater Canyon house and into the home of "L. Linsk, a fellow associate in the Rockwell-O'Keefe Agency." Bette was still calling it "a marriage vacation."

Mayme Ober Peake weighed in. She quoted Bette: "I found one thing in England I hope to keep forever—peace of mind. A good licking is good for the soul."[13]

Ham filed divorce papers on November 22, alleging among other things that Bette was prone to give more attention to her books than to her husband. From the Complaint for Divorce, dated November 22, 1938, Harmon Oscar Nelson Jr., plaintiff, versus Ruth Elizabeth Nelson, defendant: "Defendant has insisted on occupying herself with reading to a totally unnecessary degree, and upon solicitation by plaintiff to exhibit some evidence of conjugal friendliness and affection, defendant would become enraged and indulged in a blatant array of epithets and derision."[14] When the matter came before Judge Thurmand Clarke on December 6, the proceedings contained the following snippet of dialogue:

> JUDGE CLARKE: Did she do a great deal of reading?
>
> HAM: Yes. To an unnecessary degree.

Judge Clarke granted the divorce.

Bette received an unsigned letter from an irate woman. Because of Bette's divorce, the former fan wrote, her husband and sons refused to see any more of her movies ever again. "They all hate you and I think you belong in hell and I hope you go there," she explained.[15]

Bette saved this letter for the rest of her life.

How would *you* feel if you were told you had only six months to live? This was the reporter Gladys Hall's question to Bette Davis at the time of *Dark Victory*'s release. "I would resent it horribly," Bette replied before shifting from decorous indignation to out-of-control rage: "I'd hate to! I'd scream, 'Why should this happen to *me*?' I'd go crazy, wild, mad! I'd try hard to deaden my agony with insane sedatives. I'd try to forget by any means I could lay my frantic hands to—drinking, love affairs, noisy nightmares, anything to dull the edges of the essential nightmare."[16] No doubt the increasingly histrionic Davis would have reacted precisely as she said she would at the time. Her divorce from Ham had made her especially vulnerable to the emotional shakes she barely restrained even at the best of times. But, as almost always, the actress in her won out. In *Dark Victory*, she plays her character's impending death much more delicately. Judith Traherne is a marvelous blend of nobility and the jitters, and Bette related to her intensely. Many years later, with the critical distance afforded by age and experience, she called Judith Traherne "my favorite—and the public's favorite—part I have ever played."[17]

The original play, by George Emerson Brewer Jr. and Bertram Bloch, starred the gravel-throated Tallulah Bankhead and ran for only fifty-one performances late in 1934. Although the critics loved Bankhead, the play got emphatically mixed reviews. Brooks Atkinson, for instance, called it "a curious stew of mixed vegetables."[18] Still, the melodrama was appealing enough to Gloria Swanson, who pitched it to Columbia's Harry Cohn as a vehicle for herself. Cohn wasn't as impressed as Swanson was and took a pass.[19] At around the same time, David O. Selznick bought the rights with an eye toward casting Greta Garbo and Fredric March; the two stars were about to make *Anna Karenina*, a project Selznick considered too similar to Garbo's other costume dramas. When Garbo turned him down, he offered the role to Merle Oberon, but *Dark Victory* stayed dormant.[20]

Davis learned of the property early in 1938, and in characteristic fashion, she made a nuisance of herself over it with the front office. She cajoled to no avail until, finally, one Warners producer expressed interest: David Lewis, an associate producer of *The Sisters* and the boyfriend of the director James Whale. Together, they approached Edmund Goulding, who had made *Grand Hotel*. His old-fashioned treatment of *Jezebel* to the contrary notwithstanding, Goulding knew the value of a good melodrama. The threesome of Davis, Goulding, and Lewis convinced Jack Warner to buy the rights from Selznick for $50,000, though Warner himself couldn't understand why anybody would "want to see a picture about a girl who dies."[21]

It's telling that Bette Davis received the most sympathetic responses from Lewis and Goulding, a gay man and a bisexual, rather than Jack Warner or Hal Wallis. If there is such a thing as a gay sensibility, however imprecise and indefinable it may be, *Dark Victory* embodies it, at least in part. The writer Jeff Weinstein once offered a definition that stands the test of time: when asked whether there was such a thing as a gay sensibility and whether it had any influence on mainstream culture, Weinstein answered that, no, there is no such thing as a gay sensibility, and yes, it has had an enormous influence on popular culture. *Dark Victory* is a classic case in point.

Judith Traherne is already gay in the archaic sense of the word: she's flippant, merry, a bit boozy. She's a good-time gal with unlimited wealth and a fabulous wardrobe, and any gay man worth his salt—any gay man *d'un certain âge*, that is—would happily imagine himself in her pumps. But *Dark Victory*'s unabashedly amplified, high-stakes melodrama, especially as acted out by Bette Davis, elevates it into the pantheon of gay iconography—the impassioned and exceedingly imitable realm of the drama queen. It's not just that the queen of both fact and fiction reigns melodramatically, though in this case, of course, she's awarded a brain tumor and a splendid, heartrending death. More essentially, it's the pent-up energy of concealment and its imminent breakdown that provide the gay regent with much of her authority. The question of who knows what about one lies at the heart of gay men's experience—gay men of the twentieth century, at least. The queer theorist Eve Sedgwick calls it "the epistemology of the closet."

In this light, it's little wonder that Bette Davis became a gay icon. As the playwright, actor, and actress Charles Busch notes, "She's wonderful at playing someone with a secret—like the scenes in *Dark Victory* where she knows she's dying, and she's being a horrible bitch to everybody."[22] *Cabin in the Cotton*'s seductive and bizarre "I'd love to kiss ya but I just washed my hair" may have been her first camp-worthy bit of dialogue, but Davis's delivery of Judith Traherne's grandest line is precisely that of the flamboyant gay queen of the dramatic arts. Having discovered the truth about her own mortal illness, Judith lets her doctor and best friend in on the secret they have kept from her by snatching the menu out of the waiter's hands and, her nostrils flaring, declaring, "I think I'll have a large order of *prognosis negative!*" From these glorious moments of subterfuge and its destruction, concealment and revelation, twentieth-century gay men forged their own culture.

That Edmund Goulding asked Ronald Reagan to play gay in *Dark*

Victory adds a minor grace note to the proceedings—*minor* in both senses of the word. Not only is Reagan's faintly asexual character, Judith's sodden friend, not terribly important to the film's nature, but the performance is soured by Reagan's lack of talent. The future president wasn't enough of an actor to play someone fundamentally unlike himself. As Reagan too euphemistically put it, "The director wanted it to be kind of a—well, as he described it once, a fellow that could sit down in the room while the gals were changing clothes and they wouldn't mind. And I didn't really see it that way." Didn't, couldn't, no matter. Goulding's biographer, Matthew Kennedy, goes so far as to call Reagan's objection a kind of homosexual panic. "He comes off as a greenhorn actor giving a poor imitation of drunkenness," Kennedy adds. "His character is watery and forgettable, and Reagan's refusal to take chances makes him appear insecure both as an actor and as a man."[23]

Reagan is unimpeachably straight in the worst possible way—stilted even when drunk. The drama queen, on the other hand, knows exactly when to pour it on and when to play it subtly. She saves herself for her best, most attention-grabbing moments. At other times, it's all about restraint. In the scene when Judith wanders through Dr. Steele's emptying office, discovers her own medical file on his desk, and sees the "prognosis negative" conclusion in letters from other consulting doctors, Davis abandons almost all activity and simply lets the camera register her face—slightly tense and sober but nothing more. She permits the celluloid to do the work rather than taking over the job herself. Even when she confronts Steele's nurse about the meaning of *prognosis* and *negative*, thereby confirming her own impending death, she underplays it. The buoyant Judith—partying with her aristocratic friends and parrying with Humphrey Bogart's strangely Irish horse trainer, Michael—is Davis being mannered; the serious, private Judith is much more the result of Bette's knowing when to leave well enough alone.

DARK VICTORY BEGAN shooting on October 10, 1938, under the hawklike eyes of Hal Wallis. Two weeks later, the producer was irate. The film was falling behind schedule. He complained bitterly to Goulding about what he considered to be the abominably long time it took to film two shots. One of them, representing only nine seconds of screen time, took Goulding and his cinematographer an hour and a half to shoot. "You can tell Ernie Haller for me that any other cameraman on the lot could have made the shot in half the time or less," Wallis fumed.[24]

There was also a fresh chill in the air between Goulding and Davis, Bette considering her director to be artistically irresolute. According to the *New York Times*, Goulding also kept Bette in the dark, as it were, about the nature of Judith's illness, the theory being that she would appear more believably happy during the first part of the film. Bette is said to have been annoyed, and justifiably so; a director of Goulding's experience might have given an Oscar-winning actress more credit for being able *to act*.[25] Then again, the detail itself is suspect. Bette presumably had read the play before pitching it again and again to Warner Bros. In any event, Judith is acutely if secretively aware that there's something awfully wrong with her from the beginning. She enters the film in failed denial.

Prunella Hall was pleased to report in her *Screen Gossip* column not only that Bobby Davis Pelgram's two English setters, Daffy and Don, but Bobby herself were all appearing in the film. According to Prunella, the volatile Daffy refused to let anyone else handle her, so Bobby donned a maid's uniform, went before the cameras, and was so nervous about her performance that she yanked her older sister's zipper in the wrong direction and momentarily choked her.[26] (Coincidently, Louella Parsons informed her readers—erroneously, of course—that Warner Bros. had cut a deal with Sigmund Freud to be a consultant on the film.)[27] Bobby's scene must have ended up on the cutting-room floor, but the dogs play a key role: they humanize Judith, who responds to them with more consistent affection than she displays toward any of her other friends, including the man she marries.

It was no secret that filming *Dark Victory* was nerve-wracking for Bette almost to the point of debilitation. She didn't start off well in any sense of the word. The columnist Dorothy Manners reported that after the divorce, Bette tried to recuperate from the stress at "La Quinta, at Palm Springs, at all the other hideaways she sought," but that these escapes didn't really help. When Davis began shooting the film, Manners noted, "she was a sick girl mentally and physically."[28] Then, after just a week of filming, and having pleaded for the role for months, she begged Hal Wallis with equal gusto to find someone else. The role was too much for her, she told him; she was ill, upset, hysterical; she couldn't bear it; he simply had to replace her. But Wallis, having seen the dailies, knew that the camera—in its cold, close, mechanical way—was picking up something ineffably honest about Davis's own anguish. "Stay sick," he said.[29]

She never was one to hide her neurosis successfully, if she was able to hide it at all, and everyone connected with the production was aware that she was especially fragile. "It's up to you guys to keep the lady on an even keel," Wallis told Goulding and her costar, George Brent. "Eddie, you work with her—and George, you play with her—and it'll keep her excited, amused, and on the ball."[30]

She missed at least three days of filming in late November because of an unspecified illness. And on December 3, the day the company filmed the gardening scene, in which Judith comments that the sky is clouding over but feels the warmth on her hand and realizes that she is going blind and will die within hours, Bette became particularly overwrought. As one production manager reported to another, "Miss Davis was taken hysterical in this scene and they had difficulties in getting it. She cried very heavily and it was very difficult and very trying for everybody to get the scene."[31] By this point late in the filming Bette empathized with Judith so overpoweringly that she couldn't help sobbing at her imminent death, knowing all the while that histrionic tears were all wrong for the character. And her intensely frustrating inability to get it right only made her all the more hysterical. Goulding didn't pressure her but instead let her play the scene again and again until finally, dry-eyed, Davis gave the result they both wanted.[32] Bette was characteristically hard on herself when describing her performance in this scene to Gladys Hall: "I went into the scene and knew that it was *putrid*. I wasn't being the character of the girl in *Dark Victory*, you see. I was just being Bette Davis weeping over my own heartache."[33]

"WHY, THE TEAR jerker is an art in itself!" Goulding declared to the *New York Times* around the time of the film's release. "There is a certain psychiatric technique to it. You see, no one will cry about anyone who cries about himself. In *Dark Victory*, I wrote into the picture a character in the person of Geraldine Fitzgerald who did all the crying for Miss Davis. If Miss Davis had wept, no one would have wept with her, but Miss Fitzgerald was in the position of the audience, weeping behind Miss Davis' back, and that gave Miss Davis a clear course of martyrdom."[34] (Judith has a good friend in the play, but Fitzgerald's character is indeed Goulding's creation.)

For all his talent and gay sensibility, Goulding's "psychiatric technique" fails him as far as the ending of *Dark Victory* is concerned. As finely, honestly heartbreaking as the ending is—it's certainly one of the most emotionally commanding last reels in American film—its heart and its art owe infinitely more to Davis than to Goulding, who keeps trumping up sentiment in all the wrong places. Once she realizes the end is imminent, Judith methodically sends Dr. Steele, now her husband, off to Philadelphia. (George Brent's sluggishness actually works to his character's advantage here, since it makes it possible for audiences to believe that this dedicated neurosurgeon remains oblivious to his wife's swiftly oncoming blindness. Casey Robinson had advocated casting Spencer Tracy as Dr. Steele instead of Brent, and one can only wonder how Tracy, much the better actor, would have handled the role.)[35] She also dispatches Ann, who goes running tearfully down the street toward an unspecified destination. Alone, as she has planned to be at the end, Judith feels her way into the house and begins to climb the stairs.

Geraldine Fitzgerald, who plays Ann, recalled that the set "had been beautifully lit with a kind of heavenly glow shining on Bette as she slowly climbed the stairs. Suddenly she stopped and turned around and came down the stairs, this time very matter-of-factly (almost clumping down, you could say) and said to Eddie Goulding, 'Is Max Steiner going to underscore this scene?' 'Oh, no,' said Goulding. 'Of course not! We all know how you feel about that!' '*Good*,' said Bette, 'because either I'm going up the stairs or Max Steiner is going up the stairs, but we're goddamn well not going up together!'" ("I hate to remember," Fitzgerald added, "but I think the scene *was* underscored and she had the Vienna Boys Choir accompanying her.")[36]

In fact, Steiner's underscoring is mercifully quiet—at first—as Judith ascends the stairs, gripping the banister for support. She crosses to her bedroom and closes the door behind her. But neither Goulding nor Judith's maid, Martha, takes the hint. Judith wishes above all else to be supremely alone, but Goulding cuts from the heroine sequestering herself in her bedroom to die to a shot of Martha looking stricken on the landing. He even tracks forward on this heretofore undistinguished character, giving her much more emotional weight than she either deserves or requires. If Judith's best friend, Ann, has been the audience's surrogate thus far, Goulding proceeds—most unfairly—to turn her maid into a gawking neighbor craning to get a better look at who's being carted into the ambulance at the house next door.

Goulding still doesn't let up. After Martha stares at the closed bedroom door, not only does she open it and enter, but her first impulse is, ridiculously, to draw the drapes—in the room of a woman who obviously no longer cares and can no longer see.

Goulding then pans with Martha as she crosses right to reveal a final surprise. Flying in the face of everything we know about her until this moment, Judith Traherne suddenly becomes religious: there she is, on her knees at the side of the bed, devoutly praying. It's Hollywood piety at its most intolerably phony. The free-spirited Judith has evinced absolutely no interest in God throughout the film, but now Goulding forces her to experience death as the foxhole in which atheism vanishes.

And Geraldine Fitzgerald was only partially correct: *this* is when the angelic choir comes in. That a sense of authenticity survives such hokum is a testament to Bette Davis's measured, sure-footed performance.

Judith pulls herself onto the bed and says, "I don't want to be disturbed," but Martha persists in trying to make herself useful and begins removing what she considers to be extraneous items from the bed: a jacket, a sweater, a blouse. Martha then tucks Judith in with a comforter Judith has not requested and, at long last, makes her exit.

But Goulding's inexplicable fixation on his heroine's extraneous maid is so overpowering that he simply can't resist cutting to yet another shot of her. We see her looking stricken again, this time at the door. Finally, she closes it with herself on the other side. Good riddance, and amen.

With his heroine alone at last, Goulding gets to the heart of the matter in just a few seconds: a brilliant head-and-shoulders shot of Judith lying on her side, in solitude and at peace. A close-up would have been intrusive, the visual equivalent of Martha's pestering. A more distant shot would have lacked depth of feeling. The shot holds for only a few moments before—in an inspired touch—the image goes out of focus and blacks out, a visual trope that precisely expresses Judith's diminishing experience of vision, light, and life.

Cut to the racetrack.

In one of Goulding and Robinson's least inspired ideas, *Dark Victory* originally had a happy ending. Judith still died, of course; there was no miraculous cure. But her death did not originally serve as the final scene. No, Goulding and Robinson cut away from Judith dying quietly, in dignity and solitude, to a horserace, with Judith's horse charging down the stretch in the lead. Cut to Bogart's Michael in out-of-character tears. Cut to the triumphant Challenger with a wreath of flowers around his neck. Cut to Ann and Steele in Judith's old box at the track, where Ann urges the dispirited Steele to return to his medical mission. "Your work can't stop now!" she insists. "We can't let her courage have stood for nothing!" Making a bad scene even worse, Casey Robinson gave Steele one of the most ineloquent final lines in all cinema: "All right," he says.[37] The end.

As David Lewis described it in a November 4 memo to Hal Wallis, Goulding wanted "to take the edge off Judith's death and [let audiences] leave the theatre with the feeling of entertainment and optimism."[38] To his profound discredit, Wallis concurred, and they shot the scene. After seeing what appears to have been a fairly polished rough cut, Wallis offered some guidance. For one thing, he counseled, "shorten the long shot holding on Davis at the bed after the maid leaves." In that he was right. But there was more: "See if you can find some close-ups of a dark horse that we can cut into the race where Ann says 'Look, he's winning,' and where the boy talks to the Colonel about the horse—about three cuts of him in the proper spots"—as though *Dark Victory* was really the tale of a conquering steed. But even Wallis found one shot to be overly jubilant: "Take out the cut of putting the wreath on the horse," he advised.[39]

The film previewed on March 7, 1939, complete with the Challenger and "all right" ending. Lo: it didn't work. Wallis's assistant made the point simply, even plaintively to his boss two days later: "I do not know how the picture could end any better than by having the girl die as she did."[40] It was that ending, the truncated one, that Warner Bros. released to extraordinary acclaim and tears of melodramatic fulfillment. If only they could have edited out the maid.

THE TRAILER FOR *Dark Victory* proved to be something of a milestone. Against a close-up of an assertively unglamorized Bette looking solemnly to the right, the crawl began: "In the career of every great actress, one role lives forever as her finest creation. Warner Bros. now proudly present [sic] the most exciting star on the screen in a story that lights the full fires of her genius. The portrait of a free soul!" Beyond trumpeting the earnestness and depth of Davis talent, which was by then irrefutable, the studio was finally fully exploiting what it had tried so hard to dampen or deny: the "free soul" in question could have just as easily been Bette as Judith Traherne. Warners at last appreciated and was willing to sell a film based on the fact that its fierce and neurotic star was indeed the rebellious and unconventional woman the public well knew her to be offscreen as well as on-.

At the same time, Warner Bros. could only go so far. "Which type of make-up for you?" the *Dark Victory* pressbook asked. "With medium skin and light blonde hair, Bette Davis is an outstanding example of this type beauty. Below are her make-up suggestions: powder—peach; rouge—blush; mascara—brown; lipstick—blush; eye shadow—purple." And: "'A clear, lovely skin is the blonde's most precious beauty asset,' states Bette Davis, the exquisite blonde star of *Dark Victory*, which will open at the Radio City Music Hall on Friday."[41] Apparently nobody told Warners' publicists that Bette hadn't been blonde, either onscreen or off-, for several years.

Then again, Warners was only following cultural convention in continuing to sell Davis as an offscreen fashion plate. The following year, for example, the New York–based Fashion Academy named Bette one of America's twelve best-dressed women. Bette won, naturally, in the "Screen" category. Mrs. Alfred Gwynne Vanderbilt won for "Society." And in the "Adventure" category, the winner was the naturalist Osa Johnson, "selected for using scientific knowledge of jungle attire in practical everyday fashion."[42]

10

FEUDS

*D*ARK *VICTORY* WRAPPED ON DECEMBER
5, 1938, and despite Davis's precarious emotional state, the studio gave
her only a week off before beginning her scenes for *Juarez* on the twelfth.
Juarez was, for Warners, an Important Picture. The script was two years
in the making; 372 sources were consulted. The production designer Anton Grot and his team drew 3,643 sketches and 7,360 blueprints for fifty-
four sets including several Mexican villages, the throne room and living
quarters of Chapultepec Palace, rooms in a castle on the Adriatic, and
rooms in a castle in France.[1] A total of fourteen women were said (by
Warners' publicists) to have provided the black hair used to concoct
Bette's wig at a cost of $2,500.[2] Shooting began almost two months be-
fore Davis set foot on a soundstage and continued until February 8, 1939.

Mexico elects as its president Benito Juarez (Paul Muni), the brilliant
Zapotec who rose from illiterate fieldworker to lawyer, judge, governor
of Oaxaca, and radical reform politician, but Louis Napoleon (Claude
Rains) installs the glamorous Maximilian von Hapsburg (Brian Aherne)
as emperor. Catastrophically liberal for an emperor, poor Max just
doesn't get it. He arrives in Mexico with his wife, Carlota (Bette), expecting great popular support, figures out that he's a dupe, but soldiers
on. He refuses to suppress Juarez, but Juarez stubbornly insists on a
Hapsburg-free democracy and keeps on rebelling. Maximilian considers

abdicating, but Carlota, not a great political adviser, convinces him not to on the theory that he can save Mexico from its real enemies in Europe if he remains in charge. Maximilian holds an olive branch out to Juarez in the form of the prime ministership. Juarez refuses. Napoleon then undercuts Maximilian by ordering his troops out of Mexico. Carlota travels to Paris and confronts Napoleon but loses her mind, a shift in temperament Orry-Kelly expresses by way of an all-black gown. Juarez and his forces capture Maximilian, who nobly ends up facing a firing squad for the good of Mexico.

Juarez was directed by William Dieterle, who had directed *Fashions of 1934*, *Fog Over Frisco*, and *Satan Met a Lady* and who nearly took over *Jezebel*. Dieterle was, as Brian Aherne described him, "a very tall, precise German with dark, burning eyes and strictly formal manners [who] always wore white cotton gloves on the set in case it should be necessary, in getting the exact angle he wanted, to touch the face of a player."[3] The director certainly had the getup; he just didn't have much talent.

Aherne didn't have kind things to say about his leading lady: "I even found Bette Davis attractive when I played Maximilian to her Carlota and, brilliant actress though she is, surely nobody but a mother could have loved Bette Davis at the height of her career."[4] He didn't elaborate. Perhaps he didn't have to.

Juarez is hampered by its most dramatic attempt at scrupulous authenticity: Paul Muni's makeup. In a misguided quest for strict realism, Muni insisted on precisely mimicking the real Juarez. He and the film's producers, Hal Wallis and Henry Blanke, traveled to Mexico in August 1938 on a fact-finding mission. Somebody even managed to dig up a 116-year-old man who had fought under Juarez. But Muni went much further than listening to an old soldier's tales. He demanded that he appear onscreen looking exactly like Juarez. Perc Westmore described the laborious process: "We started by taking photographs of Muni, then painting the likeness of the Indian Juarez over them. We took plaster casts of his face. We had to accentuate his bone structure, make his jaws appear wider, square his forehead, and give him an Indian nose. He had to be darker than anyone else in the picture, so we used a dark reddish-brown makeup, highlighted with yellow." After seeing the makeup tests, Jack Warner remarked, "You mean we're paying Muni all this dough *and we can't even recognize him?*"[5]

Warner was right, but he missed the more critical problem: Muni can barely move his mouth under all the glop, let alone register even the broadest facial expressions. The otherwise brilliant actor forced himself to play the entire film from under an inflexible Zapotec mask, and the result is disastrous.

Bette was complimentary about Muni in a backhanded kind of way: "Muni was brilliant. Utterly. Articulate. A real intellectual. But he was his own worst enemy. Why did he hide behind the characters so much? . . . He could have accomplished his purpose without that rubber face."[6]

Bette's three mad scenes are measured, altering between shifty-eyed paranoia and filtered-lensed catatonia with makeup by Perc Westmore. Agitated, she storms into the chambers of Louis Napoleon (Claude Rains) and demands that he revoke his orders to pull his troops out of Mexico. She's elegantly dressed in a dark velvet gown with white fur collar and cuffs, but it's the gauzy, trailing scarf that falls from her hat that enhances her distracted quality as it flies around her head with every gesture. When she sees that Napoleon is set in his plans and has betrayed Maximilian, she hautily shrieks, "What *else* might a Hapsburg have expected from a *bourgeois Bonaparte*!" Her voice cracks: "*You charlatan!*"

She then faints, wakes up crazy, and accuses Louis Napoleon of trying to poison her; she comes to believe that Napoleon is Satan in a subsequent scene. Finally, in her last scene, Dieterle cuts away from Maximilian about to face the firing squad to an evocative shot of Carlota in her chambers, wandering to the window, throwing it wide, and reaching out, saying and then screaming, "*Maxl!*"

There was originally to be more of Maximilian and Carlota, but it was Muni's picture all along—the title makes that point succinctly—so when Muni demanded more scenes to tip the balance in his favor, Warner Bros. acquiesced, and a number of Davis's and Aherne's scenes ended up on the proverbial cutting-room floor.

*T**HE** **O**LD **M**AID* started shooting on March 15, 1939. It's a complex Edith Wharton plot: On the day Delia Lovell (Miriam Hopkins) is to marry the stiff Jim Ralston (James Stephenson) at the dawn of the Civil War, her old fiancé, the reckless Clem Spender (George Brent), returns from a two-year absence. He's crushed by the wedding, so Delia's sister Charlotte (Bette) consoles him—intimately. Clem joins the Union army and dies. Charlotte turns a stable into a home for war orphans, including a little girl named Tina (who grows up to be played by Jane Bryan). Tina is short for Clementina; she's Charlotte's illegitimate daughter, but it's a big secret. Delia invites Charlotte and Tina to live at the Ralston mansion. Fifteen years pass. Charlotte has become a carping biddy. Tina, who calls Delia "Mummy" and her real mother "Aunt Charlotte," falls in love with someone presentable. Delia adopts her to give her propriety and a fortune; Charlotte threatens to reveal the truth on the eve of the wedding. But at the brink she realizes she can't go through with it, and so, like the great Stella Dallas, she masochistically effaces herself and lets her daughter wed in ignorance.

In *The Lonely Life*, Bette was delightfully catty about her costar: "Miriam is a perfectly charming woman socially. Working with her is another story. On the first day of shooting, for instance, she arrived on the set wearing a complete replica of one of my *Jezebel* costumes. It was obvious she wanted me to blow my stack at this. I completely ignored the whole thing. Ensuing events prove she wanted even more to be in my shoes than in my dress." And: "Miriam used and, I must give her credit, knew every trick in the book. I became fascinated watching them appear one by one. . . . Keeping my temper took its toll. I went home every night and screamed at everybody." And: "Once, in a two-shot favoring both of us, her attempts to upstage me almost collapsed the couch we were sitting on. . . . If her back had had a buzz saw that allowed her to retreat beyond it, I wouldn't have been in the least surprised."[7]

On Monday, April 17, Bette fainted at 3:50 p.m. A doctor was summoned; he found her pulse to be abnormally high and sent her home. Davis stayed out Tuesday and Wednesday as well, at which point Miriam declared that she was sick, too, damn it, and departed for home. Friday, April 28 saw a discussion between Hopkins, Goulding, and the unit manager, Al Alleborn. The subject: Hopkins's evolving, rejuvenating makeup. Goulding had noticed that Miriam was coming onto the set looking younger and younger by the day, and he wasn't pleased. Hal Wallis responded by ordering Perc Westmore not to deviate from the makeup design that he and Goulding had originally approved. Hopkins registered her displeasure by showing up on time the next day but immediately claiming illness and leaving for home.[8] The film finally wrapped on Saturday, May 6, ten days behind schedule.

The tension between Hopkins and Davis was no secret at the time. Indeed, Warners used it for the sake of publicity. As *Life* reported in August 1939, "The fact that Davis and Hopkins dislike each other intensely not only added to their pleasure in making the picture, but also proved so mutually stimulating that Hal Wallis, Warner Bros. production chief, plans to team them again in *Devotion*."* *Life* was astute in appreciating that both actresses used their enmity as a kind of recreation. Davis herself was quoted as saying, "The jealousy was completely one-sided. I have never been jealous of an actor I was working with in my life."[9]

She went much further about Hopkins later: "Actors went through torture working with her because she was a pig about it."[10]

*T*HE *PRIVATE* *LIVES* of *Elizabeth and Essex* is the protracted title with which Warner Bros. saddled Davis's next film, an expensive ersatz-historical costume drama filmed in Technicolor. Davis plays Elizabeth I, Errol Flynn her arrogant sometime consort Robert Devereaux, the Earl of Essex. The production was fraught with tensions, breakdowns, and ill feelings. Flynn—whose name Michael Curtiz tended to pronounce as "Earl Flint"—drunkenly crashed his car midway through filming and came away with facial scars. Olivia de Havilland, fresh from the pressure of filming *Gone with the Wind*, threw a fit on the set one day and caused much memo writing. In one pivotal scene Bette slapped Errol on the face so hard, her fist laden with jewelry, that he never forgave her. The film is at best a curiosity.

Elizabeth and Essex is based on Maxwell Anderson's 1930 blank-verse play, *Elizabeth the Queen*, which ran on Broadway for 147 performances and starred Alfred Lunt and Lynn Fontanne. Like Fontanne, Bette Davis could have torn into the role of Elizabeth and still have spoken the poetry, but Flynn—whom Bette called "the only fly in the ointment"—was out of his depth.[11] "I can't remember lines like that," he complained to Curtiz, so the screenwriters Aeneas MacKenzie and Norman Reilly Raine rewrote them out of verse and into fairly inelegant Hollywood prose. Davis had advocated casting Laurence Olivier to no avail. She later claimed that during her scenes with Flynn she was playing in her mind to Olivier.

Davis had just turned thirty-one when she began filming *Elizabeth and Essex*. Having been aged to about fifty for the later scenes of *The Old Maid*, she was now prepared to let Perc Westmore transform her not only into a sixty-year-old but a most recognizable sixty-year-old with a forehead

---

*Devotion wasn't made until 1946 and ended up starring Olivia de Havilland and Ida Lupino. Davis and Hopkins were paired together in 1943 in *Old Acquaintance*.

even higher and bonier than Bette's own. The press reported at the time that Westmore "was horrified" at Davis's insistence on being completely bald in one scene—she was evidently talked out of it—but he later took some of the credit for Davis's radical transformation, though he was quick to praise Bette's gumption: "Here was a gal—I don't care what the part—who would go along with the make-up I decided on. When she played Queen Elizabeth I in *Elizabeth and Essex* I shaved her head halfway back!"[12]

With less than a week of rest after wrapping *The Old Maid*, Bette was back at the studio on May 11 to start shooting *Elizabeth and Essex*. According to her lawyer at the time, Oscar Cummins, Hal Wallis promised her not only a long rest period after she finished but also "a modern picture" as her next project. Wallis contentiously responded that he'd promised nothing, it was just a discussion, there was no formal agreement about anything.[13] (In fact, Davis took a long, restorative, life-changing trip East after finishing the film.)

Some of the difficulties surrounding *Elizabeth and Essex* might have been diminished, or at least played out at a lower volume, had Davis been given more than five days off between pictures. An imbroglio about the film's title was already raging at the end of April. Warner Bros. wanted to change Anderson's *Elizabeth the Queen* to *The Knight and the Lady* to give Errol Flynn more prominence, but that presented a contractual problem: if the film was considered to be a "man's picture," Flynn got top billing over Davis. Bette took an extreme position on the matter: syntactically, she argued, the title *The Knight and the Lady* indeed made it a man's picture, so she really couldn't appear in it at all. "The present title is obviously one to give the man first billing. I feel so justified in this from every standpoint that you force me to refuse to make this picture unless the billing is mine," she wrote to Jack Warner. Warner offered to give Davis top billing but still wanted to keep *The Knight and the Lady*. Davis refused: "I could not accept first billing with the present title as it is a man's title. Therefore the title will have to be changed." Warner telephoned Davis at her table at the studio commissary on May 6, the day she finished *The Old Maid*, and informed her that she would get top billing, that *The Knight and the Lady* would definitely not be used, and that the picture might end up being called *Elizabeth and Essex*. This was not the end of the discussion.

Davis was also fighting with Hal Wallis about a dress: "I forgot to

drop you a line before I left about the costume you turned down for Elizabeth. I insist on wearing it."

Robert Lord, the film's associate producer, was concerned enough
about Bette's emotional state that he suggested that the studio take out an
insurance policy on her health. Miss Davis, Lord wrote, "is in a rather serious condition of nerves. At best she is frail and is going into a very
tough picture when she is a long way from her best." Jack Warner vetoed
the idea.[14]

Bette didn't show up for filming on Monday, June 19; she phoned in
complaining of a sore throat. Her physician—now a Dr. Culley—told
her that it was laryngitis and that she'd be out until Thursday at the earliest. The production shut down completely. As a production manager
noted, "We can do absolutely nothing on this picture until Miss Davis
returns." On Wednesday, Dr. Culley informed the studio that Miss
Davis was still ill and, by the way, she'd read about Flynn's having
wrecked his car off Sunset Boulevard and not being able to appear before the cameras for a week or maybe two because of facial abrasions.
The studio informed the doctor "that most of it was publicity and that we
expected Flynn by Saturday or Monday at the latest," at which point Dr.
Culley acknowledged that "it would be possible for Miss Davis to be in
by Saturday or Monday." This innocuous statement led to a testy conversation between Oscar Cummins and Warners' counsel Roy Obringer,
with Cummins forced to assure Obringer that Flynn's injury had nothing
to do with Bette's absence, that Culley's remarks were "uncalled for,"
and that although Bette felt truly terrible about being unable to work, the
studio surely must appreciate that it wasn't mere laryngitis but ruptured
blood vessels in her throat that kept her from being able to perform.[15]

With both Davis and Flynn indisposed, each in his or her own special
way, the production didn't get back into gear until the twenty-seventh.
The title issue reared up again on the thirtieth. Warners, evidently fix-
ated on certain crucial words, was now proposing *The Lady and the
Knight*. And Bette was having none of it, dramatically: "I find myself so
upset mentally and ill physically by the prospect of this title," she wired
Jack Warner, "that unless this matter is settled in writing I cannot without serious impairment to my health finish the picture."

There were only a few more days to go as far as wrapping the troubled production was concerned, and Flynn's lack of professional training wasn't helping. It hadn't helped all along. The production reports

are peppered with such notations as "If Flynn knows his lines today we should finish" and "[Mr. Flynn had] considerable difficulty with his lines" and "Mr. Curtiz can make fast time until he gets with Errol Flynn, and then we slow down to a walk."

Flynn's difficulties had begun with the impossible verse of the script and worsened when Bette slapped him with a fistful of rings. In the finished film, the slap occurs very quickly; Curtiz immediately cuts in to a closer shot of Flynn, and it appears in the take he used that Davis's hand is free of jewelry. In any case, Flynn chronicled the initial slap in his marvelously titled memoir, *My Wicked, Wicked Ways*: "Joe Louis himself couldn't give a right hook better than Bette hooked me with. My jaw went out. I felt a click behind my ear and I saw all these comets, shooting stars, all in one flash. . . . I felt as if I were deaf." Flynn claimed that he approached Bette privately in her dressing room, but that she cut him off before he had a chance to complain: "Oh, I know perfectly well what you are going to say. If you can't take a little slap, that is just too bad! If I have to pull punches, I can't do this. That's the kind of actress I am—and I stress *actress*! Would you mind shutting the door?" According to Flynn, he went back to his dressing room and threw up.[16]

In the scene between Elizabeth and Essex in the Privy Chamber before Elizabeth orders his head chopped off, Elizabeth having had enough of Essex in much the same way Davis had of Flynn and Jack Warner had of Davis, Flynn found it impossible to speak his already simplified dialogue. "We lost considerable time because of Mr. Flynn's continual blowing up in his lines," the production manager noted with despair. "We made 20 takes, all on account of Flynn. Mr. Curtiz dismissed him at 5 pm as it was absolutely impossible to accomplish any more than he had already done."[17]

The gossip columnist Harrison Carroll was quick to report that Flynn, rising after delivering the line "Am I not as worthy to be king as you to be queen?" had caught his cape under his heel and landed on his ass.[18]

Olivia de Havilland, who plays Lady Penelope Gray, was creating her own havoc as well. She'd shown up on the set on May 24 but immediately announced that she couldn't film anything because she was too caught up with shooting retakes for *Gone with the Wind* and she certainly couldn't play two characters simultaneously. Shouting ensued. Jack Warner himself finally convinced her to shoot at least some of her scenes on schedule. "I had another display of temperament late Saturday afternoon from

Miss de Havilland," the exasperated production manager wrote on June 10, "to wit—at 5:15 pm when we started to rehearse a scene between her and Miss Fabares [Nanette Fabray playing the girlish Margaret Radcliffe under the original spelling of her name], she informed Mr. Curtiz that she positively was going to stop at 6:00 pm, but Mr. Curtiz told her that unless she stayed and finished the sequence he positively would cut it out of the picture. Miss de Havilland expressed herself before the company, and Mr. Curtiz came right back with the result that she made a display of hysterics before the company and it became necessary for me to dismiss the company at 6:15 without shooting the sequence." The production manager dryly added that "inasmuch as this sequence was inserted at Miss de Havilland's request, I believe we should not shoot it and uphold Mr. Curtiz in the matter."

If *The Private Lives of Elizabeth and Essex* matched in art what it provided in stress for its director, actors, and producers, these gossipy tales would give way to more profound pleasures. But despite Davis's nervy, complex performance, the film doesn't hold together. Orry-Kelly outdoes himself with a jewel-toned metallic satin gown with a severely cinched waist and great volumes of hooped hemline in the scene in which Davis plays a testy game of chess with de Havilland. Erich Wolfgang Korngold's score is nothing if not majestic. And Anton Grot's set design is charmingly perverse, ranging from an expectedly grand throne room to Elizabeth's bizarre quarters in the Tower, which call to mind a vast and gloomy mausoleum. The world Grot created for Elizabeth is a distorted magic kingdom, the deformity reaching its apogee in the Tower scene when a mysterious, orange-lit staircase suddenly unfolds in the stone floor to provide access to the dungeon in which the queen's lover lies. Given that this love story ends in an execution, Grot's design is especially inspired.

But Flynn, adept at derring-do, is a simple Essex, a pinup schemer. His one-dimensionality is especially striking compared to Davis's weighty if fidgety Elizabeth. Whether she's imperiously flicking her wrist or waving her arm, displaying flashes of melancholy as well as rage, Davis inhabits the difficult, iron-willed monarch even (or perhaps particularly) when she's expressing the character's profound self-doubts. She leans ungainly against the arm of Elizabeth's throne, making herself look awkward and her character exhausted under the weight of her authority. She gives Elizabeth a slight, elderly shake of the head, the natural tremble of declining health, all the while delivering her lines with supreme confidence and a masterly, elegant vocal inflection that registers as the queen's English without being a Streep-like technical tour de force. It is to Mildred Rogers's Cockney as silk is to linen.

There is a particularly vivifying moment toward the end of the film in which the wormish courtier Cecil (Henry Daniell) pleads to his politically threatened, romantically torn queen, "If we do nothing, both you and your kingdom are at the mercy of Essex!" And Davis decides to play it down. With dismissive flutters of her heavily bejeweled hands, and with a tone of superb distraction, she turns away from him and replies, with an acidic calmness, "Little man, little man—leave me alone." It's instants like this that turn a coloring-book Tudor epic into something truly regal, however momentarily. As for Davis's contempt for Flynn's putative ineptitude, she ended up changing her mind. He may not have been Laurence Olivier, but he was still Errol Flynn. After seeing the film again late in life, Bette told Olivia de Havilland, "Damn, he's good! I was wrong about him."[19]

On her first day as a teacher in New York City, prim Henriette Deluzy-Desportes (Davis) becomes slightly unhinged when she learns that her spoiled students know her secret shame: she was once a notorious French jailbird. ("How do you spell *Conciergerie*?" one especially snotty girl demands.) She cancels the day's French lesson and tells them her sad tale. In flashback, Henriette becomes the governess for the children of the Duc de Praslin (Charles Boyer) and his wife (Barbara O'Neil), a beautifully groomed harridan. Monsieur le Duc hates the crazy Duchesse and falls in chaste love with Henriette. The mad Duchesse accuses Henriette of having an affair with the Duc, and after a series of screamingly tight close-ups, the Duc kills the Duchesse and drinks poison. Thanks to a kindly Methodist minister, Henry Field (Jeffrey Lynn), Henriette finds a teaching job in New York, and this regeneration brings us back to the present, by which point Henriette's schoolgirls are all weeping uncontrollably and begging Henriette's forgiveness. The film ends with the promise of Henriette's marriage to the minister: *All This and Heaven, Too.*

Budgeted at $1,075,000, the melodrama was written—lengthily—by Casey Robinson and directed just as time-consumingly by Anatole Litvak. The producer David Lewis had wanted Greta Garbo to play Henriette; others at Warners advocated Helen Hayes.[20] Litvak considered casting his estranged wife, Miriam Hopkins, as the Duchesse, saying, "The Duchesse de Praslin is a heartless and venomous bitch. Miriam will be perfect."[21] But Barbara O'Neil—who plays Scarlett's mother in *Gone with the Wind*—was cast instead. As Bette points out, this "didn't help matters. As she was conceived for the film, the Duc's revulsion with her was not convincing. His wife was in actuality a sloven and a horror with none of the exterior beauty that was Miss O'Neil's."[22]

Shooting began on February 8, 1940. Hal Wallis told Litvak the following day that he'd gotten off to a good enough start but that Davis looked "pasty and tired" in the scene in which Henriette interviews for the governess job, and, by the way, Wallis didn't like the way Davis kept moving her hands in that scene, either. That night, Jack Warner saw Litvak and Olivia de Havilland coming out of the studio café together at 2:15 a.m. "I told him it would be very funny if Goulding had to finish his picture," witty Warner told Wallis. Warner thought it would be a good idea to have another director ready to go on the picture because of Litvak's characteristically slow pace.[23]

Bette and Litvak clashed often. They had wildly different conceptions of Henriette, for one thing. *All This and Heaven, Too* is based on a novel by Rachel Field, Henriette's great-niece; her great-uncle was the kindly minister. Field, Robinson, and Litvak all believed in Henriette's innocence, but in *The Lonely Life* Bette claimed that she'd read the Marquis de Sade's book about the case as well as Field's novel and that despite her growing friendship with Field, Bette thought de Sade had it right. Henriette and the Duc "must have been lovers," Davis wrote. "It was impossible for me to believe that they were not." Sandford Dody, who helped Davis write *The Lonely Life*, reiterated the point in his own memoir: "She informed me that she didn't for one moment believe that they were not lovers. Though in fairness to Bette, who preferred using the Marquis de Sade as a historical source and not the governess' niece, Rachel Field, who was only the author, there was precedent for such a conceit."[24] (What neither Davis nor Dody explain, however, is the fact that the Marquis de Sade had been dead for thirty-two years before Henriette met the Duc.)

There was another point of tension between Litvak and Davis. Litvak showed up every day with elaborate written plans for shooting. Davis, without a trace of irony, later commented that Litvak's shot designs were, "more times than not, not the way *I* had envisioned it. He was a very stubborn director."[25]

Litvak was already prone to raising his voice, but according to the actor Basil Rathbone, Bette Davis "was the only one who could give him as good as he gave. A friend of mine told me you could hear Davis and Litvak screaming at each other all the way to Santa Monica when they got going."[26]

All This and Heaven, Too was Bette Davis's forty-second motion picture. Not only did she think she knew best how to make movies, but she was unable to keep herself from letting everybody know it, including her director, her producer, and the head of the studio.

Charles Boyer, meanwhile, kept listening to war news on his dressing room radio—France and Great Britain had declared war on Germany in early September 1939—and became so agitated that Litvak had no choice but to mention it on the set. "Yes," Boyer admitted, "the war news is destroying my ability to concentrate." He got rid of the radio, but his mood didn't improve. A doctor had to be called to the set on two occasions to treat his nervous condition, and he lost ten pounds during the production. But although Boyer eventually decided that he liked neither the film nor his own performance, he did appreciate that his misery fit the role.[27]

With *All This and Heaven, Too*, Warner Bros. had in mind a vast, romantic epic. *Gone with the Wind* was released at the end of 1939, and Jack Warner wanted the world to know that he could produce a picture every bit as gargantuan as Selznick's blockbuster, albeit without Technicolor and the Civil War. Not only did the budget skyrocket to a reported $2.5 million, but Warner insisted that in all internal memos the film be referred to as *ATAHT*, a shameless attempt to ape Selznick's *GWTW*. Warner publicists put out the fact that *ATAHT* featured sixty-seven sets, whereas *GWTW* had but fifty-three.[28] "The picture was overproduced," Litvak later acknowledged. "You couldn't see the actors for the candelabra, and the whole thing became a victory for matter over mind. Bette Davis was the world's most expensively costumed governess. I'll tell you what was wrong with the picture: *Gone with the Wind* was wrong with it."[29]

Hal Wallis decided early on that he didn't like what he thought was Bette's overly precise enunciation, and in the second week of shooting he told Litvak to coax her out of it. Almost a month later he was still complaining about Bette's speech, which in point of fact is not as radically clipped as Wallis found it to be. Wallis's broken record still wasn't fixed by the first of April. "I'm certainly surprised at her insistence and persistence in doing this," he wrote to Litvak, "when she knows of our objections and when it is so obviously a forced manner of speaking." Wallis wasn't wild about Litvak's pace, either, though Goulding was never brought in to replace him, as Warner had threatened. The production was already behind schedule on February 19, in part because the children kept flubbing their lines. "I don't like the way things are going at all," Wallis complained in mid-March. "One and two scenes a day, doing things over and over again from many angles, etc." By mid-April, Wallis was even more impatient and fired off a memo to the producer David Lewis about how upset he was that Litvak had spent an entire day on crane shots of the gendarmes escorting Bette into the Duc's mansion and up the stairs to see the dying Boyer. The picture wrapped on April 20, 1940—a full twenty days behind schedule.[30]

"Warners are in a quandary," Louella Parsons announced in her *Examiner* column on May 9. "And they'd like to ask your advice, Mr. and Mrs. Public! *All This and Heaven, Too*, previewed today, runs 20,000 feet in length—approximately 23 reels. Bette Davis and Charles Boyer and Jeffrey Lynn are so good that Warner bosses hesitate about cutting a foot from Rachel Field's book. What to do is the question." If Parsons's figures are correct, this initial cut of *All This and Heaven, Too* ran at least three hours and twenty minutes. The film was previewed again in June with only twenty minutes having been cut. By the time of its general release in July, it ran 144 minutes. And it still drags under the weight of its own sense of significance.

All This and Heaven, Too's gala world premiere took place at a 1,500-seat, mission revival heap called the Carthay Circle Theatre on June 13, 1940. It was the first premiere Bette had attended since *Seed* in 1931, which was also, coincidentally, held at the Carthay Circle. (Not coincidental for *ATAHT*'s publicity purposes was the fact that *GWTW* also received its West Coast premiere at the Carthay Circle.) A crowd estimated at 15,000 cheered as Bette arrived accompanied by Ruthie, her cousin John Favor, Bobby and Robert Pelgram, Warners' publicity chief Robert Taplinger, and her old friend Robin Byron. (Byron was the former Ogunquit waitress Marie Simpson, who had changed her name to Robin and married Arthur "Bunny" Byron Jr. in 1930, divorcing him in 1939. In an odd coincidence, Bunny Byron's father, the actor Arthur Byron, had appeared as Bette's father in *Fog Over Frisco*; he's the one who refers to Bette's "escapade.")

Bette's putative escort for the evening was Ham's friend and her own current agent, Lester Linsk. The *Los Angeles Times* chronicled Davis's outfit in swooning detail: She was "gowned in a white organdy Holoku, copied from a native Hawaiian costume, fashioned with a high neckline, with full skirt and train carried over one arm and posed over a white taffeta slip. A white ermine bolero, white shasta daisies in her hair, and a necklace and bracelet of rubies set in antique gold made up her accessories."[31] "There's no question that the Hollywood premiere, so often satirized, is an exciting affair," Bette later commented. "If you are in the picture being premiered, it is difficult not to feel like a queen. Certainly it wasn't difficult for Ruthie to be the Dowager Empress."[32]

MORE BATTLES AND
TWO RETREATS

AT THE BEGINNING OF *THE LETTER*, William Wyler's moody camera stalks laterally to the right past the tamed jungle foliage of a rubber plantation's garden. A white cockatoo perches on a fence. A gunshot shocks the bird into flight as, in the far background, a man staggers out of a colonial bungalow and onto the porch. A woman closely follows him—a woman holding a gun. She fires again as he staggers down the steps. For reasons that aren't clear, Wyler cuts to some startled but irrelevant plantation workers before cutting back to a closer shot of the porch and steps. The man falls out of focus toward the camera as the woman, now sharply revealed to be Bette Davis, strides across the porch and halfway down the steps, her face a mask of determination as she fires again and again, six times in all. Her arm is outstretched, her unwaveringly locked elbow preventing any recoil. The camera tracks forward as she drops the gun. She stares at the body until the close-up, her mouth a frown of contempt and spent rage.

Somerset Maugham's play *The Letter* opened in London in 1927, starring Gladys Cooper as the killer, Leslie Crosbie. The first Broadway production opened in 1929 with Katharine Cornell in the lead. There was a Paramount film that year as well: the great and greatly troubled Jeanne Eagels played opposite Reginald Owen, with Herbert Marshall in the small but key role of Geoffrey Hammond, the man Leslie kills. It's a story of adultery, murder, and deceit set in the exotically unnerving world of a Malaysian rubber plantation outside of Singapore. Leslie Crosbie shoots Geoff Hammond and claims she was defending her honor against his drunken advances. Her naive, hardworking husband, Robert, convinces his friend Howard Joyce to defend her, but Joyce is suspicious of her story. Joyce's Chinese legal clerk connivingly mentions a letter Leslie wrote to Geoff telling him to meet her the night of the killing—a stark contradiction of Leslie's earlier claim that Hammond had shown up that night, both unannounced and drunk. Against his better moral judgment, Joyce agrees to buy the letter for $10,000. The seller is (depending on the version) either Li-Ti, Hammond's carnal Chinese mistress, or Mrs. Geoffrey Hammond, his tarted-up Eurasian wife. In every rendition, the Other Woman insists that Leslie personally bring the money to her. To no one's surprise, Leslie is acquitted of murder, but Robert doesn't know that she has spent all his savings on the letter. Joyce sets him straight; only then does Leslie confess.

The rarely screened 1929 version, directed by Jean de Limur, provides a remarkable contrast to Wyler's 1940 film. Made well before the imposition of the Production Code, Limur's *The Letter* has all the moody exoticism and much of the visual elegance of Wyler's, and it isn't forced to downplay the lurid and the depraved. The scene in which Jeanne Eagels's Leslie Crosbie has to deliver the money in person to Li-Ti takes place in Li-Ti's disreputable saloon, which features a graphic snake fight, drunken sailors, and a bamboo cage full of women. It's expressly about Leslie's racial and sexual humiliation at the hands and, literally, the feet of Li-Ti, who not only brings in a Chinese john during the transaction just to make Leslie feel her own prostitution more keenly but who, after throwing the damning letter on the floor, cries out, "White woman at Chinese woman's feet!" She cackles as Leslie stoops to pick it up, all to the rich amusement of the whores in the bamboo cage. At the end of Limur's film, Leslie asks Robert to send her away, but he refuses, saying that her punishment is to stay with him in a world she detests.

In April 1938, when Warner Bros. first thought of buying the film rights from Paramount, the studio asked Hollywood's chief censor, Joseph Breen, for his reaction before cutting the deal. Two days later, Breen rejected the property in its entirety. After all, Maugham's play as well as Limur's film contained "adultery without compensating moral values," not to mention miscegenation and an unpunished murder brought about by a perversion of justice.[1] Actually, these were easy problems to solve.

Turning the Chinese mistress into a Eurasian wife would minimize the miscegenation, not to mention eliminating the illicit nature of the relationship, and punishing Leslie in some definitive manner or other would solve the Production Code's chief concern by demonstrating to any audience members considering killing their lovers in a fit of enraged jealousy and unfulfilled lust that such a crime would not ultimately pay.

At the end of 1939, Edmund Goulding was briefly considered to direct *The Letter*, but Warners found his ideas "a trifle radical."[2] Bette was announced as the film's star in January. (According to her grandson and biographer, Sheridan Morley, Gladys Cooper was, however misguidedly, "more than a little irritated" that she didn't win the role she'd originated onstage, though at the age of fifty-two Cooper should have realized she was a bit long in the tooth for Leslie Crosbie.)[3] The other players were in flux. George Brent was offered the role of Robert Crosbie, but he preferred the role of the lawyer, Howard Joyce, which was taken by James Stephenson. Raymond Massey was considered briefly. The role of Robert Crosbie was eventually given to Herbert Marshall—a nice twist, given that he'd been Geoff Hammond in the Paramount version.

By April 1940, Wyler had signed on. He made two requests: to work with Howard Koch on the script for ten days, and to borrow the cinematographer Gregg Toland from Goldwyn. He got the first but was denied the second; *The Letter* would be shot by one of Warners' best cinematographers, Tony Gaudio (though Ernie Haller was always Bette's favorite).

Shooting began on May 27, 1940, with the exterior of the Crosbie bungalow on Stage 7, and it proceeded smoothly and certainly more swiftly than Wyler's filming of *Jezebel*. At first, the only real tension had to do with Wyler's having directed Herbert Marshall and James Stephenson to play one of their scenes in such low-key tones that Jack Warner couldn't hear their dialogue.[4] They had to retake the final close-up of Gale Sondergaard (as the Eurasian wife) because, after viewing the rushes, everyone could plainly see her wig line. Hal Wallis also asked Wyler to reshoot the scene in which Mrs. Hammond views her husband's dead body in the rubber drying shed because, according to Wallis, it looked like it took place in a laundry.[5]

This time, it was the pace of the piece rather than Wyler's endless retakes that began to annoy Hal Wallis, who, at the end of June, urged Wyler to pick up the tempo: "The action of the principals seems to be almost labored," he memoed, "and so slow [as to be] self-conscious." Wallis could scarcely complain about the production falling behind schedule because it was precisely on-target until July 15. When the production wrapped on the nineteenth, it was only three days behind schedule and was, remarkably, $35,000 under its budget of $700,000.

The last-minute delay was caused by Bette, who chronicled the battle she launched with Wyler over the script's most quotable line: "With all my heart, I still love the man I killed!" As the film historian John Simons has noted, the line applies equally well to Pat Garrett's feelings for Billy the Kid in Sam Peckinpah's 1973 western, but in this case it's Leslie Crosbie telling her husband that she can no longer endure their marriage—that the fact that she plugged Hammond with all six rounds from a pistol has changed nothing in terms of her desire. "I couldn't conceive of any woman looking into her husband's eyes and admitting such a thing," Davis explained. "I felt it would come out of her unbeknownst to herself, and therefore she would not be looking at him."

Wyler disagreed. Shouting ensued. Bette responded by walking off the set.

"I might have been Hollywood's Maria Callas, but Willy Wyler was the male Bette Davis," she later commented. "I could not see it his way, nor he mine. I came back eventually—end result, I did it his way. I lost, but I lost to an artist. *The Letter* was a magnificent picture due to Willy. . . . So many directors were such weak sisters that I would have to take over. Uncreative, unsure of themselves, frightened to fight back, they offered me none of the security that this tyrant did."[6]

Davis may not have been able to imagine a woman looking directly at her husband and declaring her undiminished desire for the lover she murdered, but Jeanne Eagels certainly did. Vindictively and bordering on hysteria, Eagels spits the line as a vicious curse on both herself and her husband. As the critic Dan Callahan describes her, she's "a wild animal in a steel trap howling at her captors."[7] It's much more disturbing than either Davis's original impulse or Wyler's more conventional staging. And it's the clincher line of the film; Limur fades out immediately after Eagels hisses it.

Davis's initial interpretation does make a certain marital sense—but not as Davis herself has played Leslie all along. She once said that "the big trick is don't do too much emotion as the character, because your audience will never feel as much. You've taken all of it away from them by doing too much."[8] Leslie Crosbie either represses her guilt or doesn't feel much of it at all; in either case, Davis's restraint leaves her audience free to supply it on their own. The critic Lawrence O'Toole claims that Davis "did not want to repeat Jeanne Eagels' extraordinary turn as the plantation owner's wife—a performance on the verge of hysteria due not only to Eagels' genius but also to the fact that she was suffering from the last stages of heroin addiction at the time she played it." But O'Toole gives Eagels's smack habit too much credit; her performance is more nuanced and controlled than any a truly strung-out junkie could give.

Davis's control in *The Letter* is only in part a matter of repression. She plays Leslie Crosbie as a bored, stifled housewife forced to expend her libido in the creation of a crocheted white coverlet. Still, her Leslie is also a sociopath, a calculating killer and remorseless liar, ceaselessly putting on acts for those around her because authentic emotions—other than murderous rage, that is—are not part of her psychological makeup. Even as Leslie fires the gun repeatedly at Hammond's dead body in the opening moments of the film, her face is stonelike, her feelings impossible to penetrate, and it's this ambiguity that makes it possible for audiences to question Leslie's motives from the beginning, even while we give her some benefit of the doubt.

There is a marvelous extended moment when Leslie's cold sociopathology, her wish to appear sympathetic while lacking all feeling, and Davis's generosity as an actor come together in overlapping, complementary silhouettes. When Joyce tells Robert that he has paid $10,000 for the letter, Wyler handles much of the scene in a single shot lasting about a minute and a half. Joyce is slightly out of focus on the left, with Robert sitting in the middle of the couch and Leslie slumped in the corner on the right. With the camera remaining static, Leslie performs the role of both the exhausted but exonerated innocent and the cunning killer, all with a minimum of gestures or words. A slight shift of the eyes, a studied rearrangement of the hands, even an absence of movement altogether—all reveal the inner workings of Leslie's mind as the truth of her duplicity finally dawns on her gullible husband. And the balletlike interaction of Davis and Marshall demonstrates the difference between, on the one hand, two fine screen actors playing off each other toward a mutually satisfying end, and Miriam Hopkins–like upstaging on the other. Bette's subtle gestures compel our attention—and she's literally upstage of Marshall while she's performing them—but not at the expense of her costar, who plays it all with equal understatement. If anything it's Marshall's scene more than Davis's.

This is William Wyler's direction at its unobtrusive best as well. He lets the audience see the couple's imminent destruction without breaking them up into crass individual shots. We see the marriage collapse in a shower of tacit lies and their tense exposure in what is effectively a ninety-second two-shot, with an out-of-focus third wheel on the side serving as catalyst.

Curiously, Wyler himself had second thoughts about *The Letter* once he saw it in an assembled cut. The normally resolute director was convinced that he'd created a far too thoroughly unsympathetic Leslie Crosbie, and he was worried that audiences would react badly to his film as a result. The film's production notes reveal that after seeing the film with Hal Wallis, Wyler requested permission to reshoot and reconstruct the whole ending, and Wallis was inclined to let him do it as long as he stuck to a prearranged plan and didn't "start wandering [and] bringing in four or five alternate things."[9] Wyler asked the screenwriter Howard Koch (who was working with the uncredited Anne Froelick) to rewrite these final scenes to provide a more compassion-inspiring Leslie.

This time it was Davis who prevailed. Alarmed that he was tinkering with something she knew was working fine as it was, she requested a screening of Wyler's initial cut. If Bette Davis was going to soften the character she'd struggled to make hard-edged, at least she wanted to see what she'd done before it was destroyed.

To what she oddly calls her "shame," she burst into tears at the end. After composing herself, she argued that what she called "the intelligent audience" would understand what she and Wyler were doing, and that if they filmed the rewritten scenes they would risk losing everyone.[10] They did reshoot the final bedroom scene between Davis and Marshall on October 16 and 17, as well as a scene involving James Stephenson and Frieda Inescort (who plays Stephenson's wife, Dorothy Joyce), but this was scarcely the wholesale new ending Wyler had proposed.

When the annual Oscar nominations were announced, Davis found herself nominated for a third year in a row. After winning in 1938 for *Jezebel*, she was nominated in 1939 for *Dark Victory* but lost, of course, to Vivien Leigh for *Gone with the Wind*. The critic Janet Flanner describes the logic: "As Hollywood abbreviates the paradoxes, in *Victory*, which was Davis's tops, she had to lose the Oscar to Leigh, who got it on *The Wind* because Davis had just got it on *Jezebel* because she hadn't got it on her next-to-tops *Bondage* because she had to lost it to Colbert in *One*

Night, which was why Davis had got her original Oscar on *Dangerous* in the first place."[11]

Warners didn't do much campaigning for Davis this time. Its own gigantic-budget *All This and Heaven, Too* was up against *The Letter* in the Best Picture category, though Bette did get a nod as "Best Dressed Gal of the Week" for her "clever, self-designed slacks suit with a new kind of military aspect."[12] At the ceremony, which was held at the Biltmore Hotel on February 27, 1941, the emcee Bob Hope noticed Bette in the audience and quipped, "Bette drops in on these affairs every year for a cup of coffee and another Oscar." But she didn't walk away with one that year. Ginger Rogers snared it for *Kitty Foyle*.

Tony Gaudio had faced an unexpected problem during the filming of *The Letter* in the summer of 1940. Like any fine cinematographer, he had a sharp eye for shapes and shadows. So it wasn't surprising that he noticed that Bette was pregnant.

Gaudio "kept looking at me sideways," Davis later told her confidant, Whitney Stine. "Obviously, I couldn't have the baby, and I was upset as hell. I had already had two abortions. I was only 32 and thought to myself that, if I married again and wanted to have a baby, my insides might be in such a mess that I couldn't. I cried and cried, but I knew what I had to do. (Where was that damn pill when I needed it?) I went to the doctor on a Saturday and showed up for scenes on Monday wearing a formfitting white eyelet evening dress for a scene. And that damn Tony said, 'Jesus, Bette, it looks like you've lost five pounds over the weekend!'"[13]

Davis never revealed the identity of the father, but that may be because she didn't know herself.

Bette reserved her most consistent affections for her dogs, who could be trusted to provide her a constant flow of all the simple love in dogdom. In the late 1930s she acquired a Pekingese she named Popeye after a fan magazine applied the cartoon moniker to Bette.[14] (Actually Bette told the writer Gladys Hall that she herself thought her eyes resembled those of a bullfrog.)[15] There was also Sir Cedric Wogs, a white Sealyham terrier sometimes called "Ceedie," sometimes "Wogs."[16] Her favorite remained Tibby, the female black Scottish terrier. No wonder. A guide to dog breeds describes the Scottie: "This breed has unusual variable behavior and moods—it can get moody and snappish as an adult. It is inclined to be stubborn and needs firm, gentle handling from an early age or it will dominate the household."[17] Bette once had a director's chair made for Tibby, complete with the pooch's name emblazoned on the back. A poodle, too, arrived sometime along the way. Ham's Doberman moved out along with Ham.

In "Divorce Is Making Her Miserable," Gladys Hall reported that Bette left the Coldwater Canyon house after splitting up with Nelson and moved into a furnished rental in Beverly Hills with her friend Ruthie Garland. An unsourced clipping in one of Davis's scrapbooks identifies Garland as "an old friend from Boston"; check the credits for *The Sisters* and you'll find that Bette got her an acting job: the small role of Laura Watkins. (It's Garland's only screen credit.) Every Wednesday they had dinner at the counter at Steven's, a diner near the Warners lot that was operated by another Bostonian, Steven Draper.[18]

What Gladys Hall failed to report was that the other Ruthie, Bette's mother, had moved in with Bette first. But their relationship was fraught with tension, and Mother quickly moved out again in a huff. There were two different postdivorce rentals: one on North Rockingham and one on Beverly Grove.[19] And the January 1939 *Screen Guide* claimed that Bette had moved in with Bobby and her husband.[20]

Wherever she was living, the Yankee-est girl who ever came down the pike had let loose. Bette finally launched the affair she'd always wanted with George Brent—whose second marriage had ended, as it had begun, in 1937—but it didn't last very long. "Our secretaries were so busy courting each other for us that it was inevitable that they would take over our romance," Davis wrote.[21]

She also had a brief fling with Anatole Litvak, of all people; after the shouting matches came lust. The ever-overheated Lawrence Quirk has Miriam Hopkins, "still riddled with lesbian hankerings for Davis," telephoning Bette in a fury and threatening to name her as correspondent in Hopkins's divorce proceedings against Litvak.[22] The only indication in Davis's personal scrapbooks that Litvak was anything more than just one of her many directors occurs in a graffito added to a clipping about Bette attending the Warner Club Sixth Annual Dinner Dance at the Biltmore Hotel on February 17, 1940. Her escort was Litvak, after whose name Bette has appended a handwritten "!"[23]

In the late summer of 1939, a more long-lasting relationship began. In late July, after finishing *The Private Lives of Elizabeth and Essex* (and before starting *All This and Heaven, Too*), Bette headed for Mountainville, New York, to spend two weeks with her friend Peggy Ogden. On August 14, the two women left by car for New England. *The Boston Globe* caught up with her on the Cape, in Dennis. "Mostly I am eating lobsters and clams," Bette declared. Davis also said that she was blissfully free of Warners' publicity department, going so far as to claim that her contract contained a clause that forbade any studio publicists to come within one hundred yards of her when she wasn't shooting a film.[24]

"After two weeks of roaming, seeing old friends whom I no longer had anything in common with, nor they me, I went to an inn in Franconia, New Hampshire," Bette later wrote. "It was called Peckett's."[25]

Franconia was, and remains, a small Yankee village about two-thirds of the way up New Hampshire toward Quebec. It's about ten miles from the Connecticut River, which divides New Hampshire from its neighbor, Vermont. About three miles in the other direction is the northwestern edge of White Mountain National Forest. Robert Frost once had a farmhouse there. The closest town of any size is Littleton, the population of which was then 5,000.

The assistant manager at Peckett's Inn was a thirty-three-year-old divorcé named Arthur Farnsworth. Handsome, cultured, manly but refined, Farnsworth was more than just the assistant hotelier; he was an experienced pilot and aeronautic engineer—rather like Howard Hughes, only not crazy. He was also an accomplished violinist. Descending from praiseworthy Yankee stock and bringing along equally fine manners, Farney was a most acceptable beau for Bette during her time in Franconia.

The more stable relationship Bette began while in Franconia was with the land itself. She bought what she called "one hundred and fifty acres of rocky, rolling land" on Sugar Hill. (She later revised the figure upward to two hundred acres.)[26] "It was here that I came out of my blue funk—here that I felt happy for the first time in years. New Hampshire and Farney were a tonic for me. I kept extending this rare vacation, hating to leave."[27] The property had a name, which Bette kept: Butternut.

In March 1940, the Hollywood press was all abuzz. Arthur Farnsworth and his sister were currently Bette's houseguests, and the sweet promise of nuptials filled the gossip columns. But one famous scribe wasn't so sure: "It wouldn't surprise me if she does marry, but I doubt it will be to Farnsworth," Louella Parsons noted.[28]

Louella may have been on to something. In late April, after finishing work on *All This and Heaven, Too*, Bette set sail on the *Monterey* for a ten-day vacation in Hawaii. Initially, the press reported that she was accompanied only by her friend Robin Byron.

Dateline: Honolulu, April 29: "Hundreds of people" greeted Bette Davis as the ship pulled into the dock. "Take off those dark glasses, Bette!" reporters shouted. "And Bette did and shouted back, 'Hello, everybody!' Wearing a white linen sailor dress with navy blue trim and a pert little sailor hat, Bette repaid her fans for waiting long on the hot crowded dock. She stood out on her lanai suite so everybody could see her, talked across to the crowds, jingled her gobs and gobs of charm bracelets, and smiled for pictures." "She wants to take hula lessons," one reporter announced. Still another tracked Bette down a few days later and found her in "a bright red and white Tahitian print holoku she had purchased that afternoon." Davis had taken "a trip around the island, with a stop at Janet Gaynor's beach home for a swim, and of course a luau," at which Bette sampled poi with lomi lomi salmon. She'd also purchased a carved ivory pikake necklace for Ruthie.[29]

The journalists quickly discovered a much juicier detail: Bette was traveling with another friend besides Robin Byron. "Just the publicity director, not a boyfriend," Bette announced when asked who the short, good-looking, dark-haired man was—the one who was hanging around Bette's lanai. Thirty-one-year-old Robert Taplinger was indeed Warners' head of publicity. But with Farney having gone back East, and with Bette in the middle of the Pacific Ocean, she was free to explore her coworker's other talents.

One member of the fourth estate was less than impressed with Bette's latest choice. "From outward appearance, you might think he was just a shoe clerk or something."

Dorothy Kilgallen, May 6: Warners is "tearing its hair over Bette Davis's sudden and serious romance with Robert Taplinger, the press agent, but she just giggles, and what can they do?"

Jimmie Fidler, May 8: "Arthur Farnsworth, Boston hotel Midas, is burning wires to Bette Davis in Hawaii, checking her 'romance' with a studio press agent."

Reporters swarmed when Davis and Taplinger—and Robin Byron—arrived back in Los Angeles on May 13. Bette flatly denied that the couple was planning to be married.[30]

Hedda Hopper noted that she was still going out on the town with Taplinger on June 1. Toward the end of the month, Sidney Skolsky broke the news that a single gardenia was arriving for her on the set of *The Letter* every day; there was no card, no note, but everybody knew it was from Taplinger.

After *The Letter* wrapped, Bette headed east for a three-month vacation. She arrived at Boston's South Station at noon on July 27 and was promptly greeted by what the *Boston Traveler* described as a crowd of 1,000 "unruly autograph seekers and hero-worshippers, mostly young girls." With a ten-man police escort, she was swept along by the crowd to a waiting car and "whisked to the Ritz Carlton" for a press conference, at which she announced that her next film would be *Calamity Jane*. Davis was apparently of two minds about *Calamity Jane*. She wrote in *Mother Goddam* that she "would have adored to play this character. Always one of my dreams, one that didn't come through."[31] At the time, however, she told *Modern Screen*, "There's been some talk of *Calamity Jane*, which I politely trust I shall *not* do."[32]*

Bette had taken the train east with Robin Byron. Bob Taplinger had arranged for a special dinner on board with champagne, an empty chair for Bob, and a note: "Don't wait for me." Davis didn't. The affair was over.

THE GREAT LIE isn't great as much as it's outlandish: The dashing multimillionaire flier Peter Van Allen drunkenly marries the tempestuous concert pianist Sandra Kovak, but Sandra is a little vague about legalities; her divorce papers haven't actually been filed yet, so they aren't really married after all. Pete, sober for a change, goes on to marry his old sweetheart, the plain but wealthy Maggie, only to disappear over the jungles of Brazil, never having been told that during his weekend of inebriated illegal marriage he has impregnated Sandra, who is convinced by Maggie to bear the child, little Pete, who is raised by Maggie as her own son until Pete the father turns up alive, and Sandra threatens to reveal the truth to win both Petes back, and Maggie actually tells the truth and wins both Petes back, and Sandra loses the ball game. Surprisingly, Bette plays Maggie rather than Sandra.

---

*Jerry Wald's script for *Calamity Jane*, although written with Ann Sheridan in mind, was handed instead to Bette, but the film didn't get made until 1953, by which point it had become a Doris Day musical.[33] Another of Bette's abortive projects around this time was the crime drama *Danger Signal*, which she emphatically didn't want to do; it was eventually made by Robert Florey in 1945.

"Before I started *The Great Lie* I wasn't very excited about it," Davis told an interviewer at the time of the film's release in the spring of 1941. "I had just come back from a vacation in New Hampshire [and] was still wondering what to do when I got some of my fan mail. A lot of it ran in this vein—'Why can't you be nice for a change?' I also remembered [that] someone, while I was in New Hampshire, said, 'Why, you're *young*!' Everyone apparently had the idea that I was an old woman due to the many older characters I played. . . . I guess I do need happier roles for a change. I don't kill anyone in this picture."[34]

It was scarcely news that Davis wasn't thrilled by *The Great Lie*. Hal Wallis was enraged when he read in Harrison Carroll's syndicated column in mid-November 1940—the film was then in the middle of shooting—that Bette didn't think it was terribly important: "This is just another motion picture," she blithely told Carroll. Wallis advised Jack Warner thenceforth to have the publicity department "keep people away from her."[35]

Warners had been developing the property—Polan Banks's best-selling potboiler, *January Heights*—since early that year. Warners was all over the map in terms of choosing a director. In late January, Hal Wallis was considering two: Curtis Bernhardt and William Dieterle.[36] Less than a month later, Jack Warner was adamant: "Let us have it definitely understood that Vincent Sherman will be put on *January Heights* as the director."[37] Bette added her two cents sometime later: she wrote to Wallis that yet another choice, Lloyd Bacon, simply wasn't right for the picture. Maybe they could borrow Garson Kanin from RKO, but "Eddie G. is the one if he would do it."

Goulding needed convincing. In late September Wallis ordered Henry Blanke to "keep after Goulding and have him start active preparation." Goulding started working on it later that week.[38]

Warners originally assigned the script to the writer Richard Sherman, but Sherman took so long with it that they handed it over to Lenore Coffee in June. And still nobody liked it very much. Blanke was afraid that the story was so contrived that any alteration in the already-unstable plot might cause the whole thing to collapse. At one point they even killed little Pete.

George Brent was cast, appropriately enough, as the flier, Peter Van Allen. (The critic Matthew Kennedy describes Brent's character all too well: "He isn't much more than a hard-drinking sperm donor.")[39] But the part of Sandra was up for grabs. Rosalind Russell met with Goulding over cocktails in late September. Warners' casting director, Steve Trilling, scheduled a meeting with Joan Crawford and tried to sell her on the project by telling her the story verbally, pointedly avoiding showing her the script itself.

Tallulah Bankhead was mentioned. So was Vivien Leigh. Barbara Stanwyck turned it down because she didn't want to play an unsympathetic character at that particular time. "I'm dying to do Sandra!" Constance Bennett wired Hal Wallis in mid-October. Sylvia Sydney and Jane Wyatt were screen-tested, as was Anna Sten.

According to Mary Astor, Bette called her on the phone in December 1940 and asked her to play the role. "She personally wanted me for the part, she said, and she apologized for asking me if I would mind taking a test. 'A few idiots have to be convinced.' "[40]

Astor is slightly off on her chronology. *January Heights*, aka *Far Horizon*, aka *The Great Lie*, began filming on November 1 with the role of Sandra yet to be cast, though Astor's screen tests had taken place the previous week. Astor started shooting on November 15.

Thanks to Davis's intervention, Astor's Sandra Kovak is by far the juicier role. As Goulding described her, "She is brandy, men, and a piano"—the last on which she persistently pounds the thunderous chords of Tchaikovsky's Piano Concerto No. 1 in B flat Minor as a way of burning up her overabundant energy. She's flamboyant, catty, and gorgeously gowned. Brent's Pete tells Bette's Maggie in contrast, "You smell of hay and horses and sunshine," a signal to stop breathing if there ever was one.[41]

As Astor wrote in her memoirs, Davis "was sullen and standoffish" at first. She watched nervously as Davis "smoked furiously and swung her foot in the angry rhythm of a cat's tail."[42] After a few days of shooting, Davis just couldn't take it anymore. "Hey, Astor!" she announced. "Let's go talk a minute." They adjourned to Bette's dressing room. "She flopped on the couch and said, 'This picture is going to *stink*! It's too incredible for words. . . . I've talked to the writers and to Eddie, and everybody's satisfied but me, so it's up to us to rewrite this piece of junk to make it more interesting. All I do is mewl to George about "that woman you married when you were drunk" and "please come back to me" and all that crap. And that's just soap opera.' "[43]

Davis's idea was frankly self-effacing. It meant building up the fiery, elegantly nasty Sandra character at the expense of her own. "Bette and I [became] as simpatico as a pair of dancers as we worked out the story," Astor wrote.[44] When Astor won the Best Supporting Actress Oscar for her performance, Bette sent her a cable: "We did it. Congratulations, baby." "People have said that I stole the picture from Bette Davis, but that is sheer nonsense. She handed it to me on a silver platter."[45] Which is why, no doubt, Astor thanked two people in particular in her Oscar acceptance speech: Bette Davis and Tchaikovsky.[46]

The title continued to be a matter of contention. Bette hated the last one the studio settled on. "I beg you not to call it *The Great Lie*," Bette told Jack Warner, because "the lie is not a great one" and "it gives away the whole story before anyone sees the picture." Goulding suggested one she thought she'd pass along to Jack: *Aren't Women Fools?* Warners stuck with *The Great Lie*.[47]

The Great Lie is great fun to the extent that Mary Astor is a great bitch. Orry-Kelly went out of his way to make Bette look dowdy—at one point he sticks her in a bizarre bonnet that makes her look like a cross between Little Bo Peep and Elvira Gulch—but he gives Astor the full treatment, with innumerable chic hats and furs and slinky black gowns. Her high international style only adds to her bite; the emotional stakes are always raised just that much higher when the vicious bitch looks fabulous.

Amusingly, when Maggie and Sandra adjourn to Arizona for Sandra's pregnancy—it looks a lot like the set for *The Petrified Forest*—they become a bickering married couple squabbling over ham and pickles, cigarettes and sleeping pills. Maggie even takes to wearing pants. As Sandra delivers her baby, the trousered Maggie paces back and forth on the porch like any other anxious father-to-be.

It's a fine moment onscreen as far as lesbian subtexts go, but the drama queen takes center stage in Sandra's mad scene, which comes complete with a howling desert windstorm, a well-barked "You make me sick!" directed at Maggie (the killjoy certainly deserves it), a marvelously histrionic attempt to set the house on fire by hurling a kerosene lamp against the wall, and an excellent full-volume shriek. Unfortunately, down-to-earth Maggie methodically slaps Sandra twice in the face, and it's all over.

I N 1940, FLUSH with home ownership in New Hampshire and a raise to $4,500 a week, Bette bought a house in Glendale. As an article in *Look* noted, Davis had lived in at least twenty-five different places over the course of the last decade alone. Evidently it was time to alight. The house she chose, located at 1705 Rancho Avenue, was a Tudor located on the banks (what banks there were) of the Los Angeles River, where a flood two years earlier had "washed the neighbors away."[48] She reportedly paid $50,000 for it and dubbed it Riverbottom.[49]

Riverbottom wasn't a large house. Janet Flanner pointed out in the *New Yorker* that it was "probably the only two-bedroom, two-acre estate in the film colony."[50] It was homey, not grand—Flanner called it a "peak-roofed Hansel and Gretel" house—and featured exposed beams holding up a high ceiling on the first floor; a brick patio; and a cozy breakfast room with a white dinette set. Davis's scrapbooks are rife with pictures of the house, one of which Bette charmingly labeled "my first home in California." One photo shows a brick sidewalk with a floral border; another a circular brick raised planter in the backyard. The house sported not only a swimming pool but a stable, so naturally Bette bought a horse to go along with it. She labeled one scrapbook picture "Laddie, my Arabian horse, Ruthie, and me, riding ring at Riverbottom"; Bette and her mother are seen being pulled around the driveway in a carriage.[51]

But her domestic preoccupation remained Butternut and its complete renovation. Ruthie had been supervising things for several weeks by the time Bette arrived in August 1940 to see what had gone on in her absence. She traveled with Robin Byron and stayed at the nearby estate of the novelist Ernest Poole.

When it was completed, Butternut became a rambling, three-sectioned white house with a relaxed living room with a white couch and a red brick fireplace; a large, functional kitchen with wood cabinetry painted white; and an unfortunate early American dining room with overly quaint wallpaper featuring a Huck Finn–like boy repeated ad infinitum all over the room. The living room fireplace chimney was unusual in that it served to heat the kitchen; the flue traveled under and across the kitchen floor before heading to the roof. Bette's bedroom had its own 3,500-pound fireplace suspended by girders from the ceiling and a big couchlike bed in the center of the room. There was a large screened-in porch, too, along with servants' quarters. Bette loved it. Her nearest neighbor was a quarter mile away.[52]

Davis arrived back in Hollywood in early October. After filming the revised scenes for *The Letter*, she began making *The Great Lie*.

She married Farnsworth on New Year's Eve, 1940, at her friend Jane Bryan's ranch in Rimrock, Arizona. (Jane Bryan was now Mrs. Justin Dart.) Farney had been proposing for quite some time, and finally Bette agreed. Whitney Stine describes the scene: "Three cars left Los Angeles on Monday morning, December 30, occupied by Davis, Ruthie, her hairdresser Margaret Donovan, [Donovan's] boyfriend Perc Westmore, dog Tibby, Lester Luisk [sic], cousin John Favor, and houseguest Ruth Garland. They picked up the marriage license in a driving rain in Prescott, Arizona. The weary travelers finally drove into the ranch on Tuesday afternoon. Sister Bobby and her husband flew in from Los Angeles with Dart in his private plane. The wedding was held that night." Farney had flown himself in from New England.[53] There was no honeymoon. Davis had to start work on her next picture.

As a publicity stunt, The Great Lie's world premiere took place on April 5, 1941—Bette's thirty-third birthday—in Littleton. ("Warner Bros. did this for me at my request. The purpose of the premiere was to raise money for the Littleton Hospital," Davis later wrote, but the studio got great press no matter what.)[54] Warner Bros. installed Davis-themed street signs all over town. For the duration of the gala, the All Saints Episcopal Church, for instance, was located at the corner of Dangerous and Dark Victory. Whitney Stine, always with an eye toward wardrobe, reports that "Davis, in a white blouse and felt skirt, and Farnsworth, in a plaid shirt, and brown corduroy suit, hosted a cocktail party at the Iron Mine Inn in the afternoon."[55] The New York Times rather snidely claimed that "crowds of celebrities and curious swelled this quiet community five times its normal size of 4500, and everybody stayed up way past the usual bedtime and liked it a lot."[56] The governors of both New Hampshire and Vermont turned up. Life chronicled the event with a four-page spread. ("A birthday ballet is rendered by nervous Shirley Walters of Littleton, aged 5," one caption reads.) The prescreening stage show featured a 200-pound plaster of paris birthday cake, which was perilously suspended by safety cables above certain unnamed dancers—possibly including nervous little Shirley Walters—and then lowered to the stage. There was also a 103-pound edible cake baked by a man named Gerald Corkum.[57] But "the birthday gifts she most appreciated were cookies, candy, and preserves bestowed on her by Littleton people," Life glowed. And the town mortician gave Bette a bag of butternuts.[58]

BREAKDOWN AND
RECOVERY

"I

T WAS CALLED A COMEDY," DAVIS WRITES
dismissively of *The Bride Came C.O.D.*[1] And for once her assessment of
humor is correct. *The Bride Came C.O.D.* is the worst screwball comedy
ever made.

It's a classic, abrasive screwball setup: a madcap heiress (Davis) becomes engaged to the wrong guy, a slick and conceited bandleader (Jack
Carson). Her father is Eugene Pallette. (Pallette, whose voice is like an
adenoidal foghorn, plays Carole Lombard's father in *My Man Godfrey*
and Henry Fonda's father in *The Lady Eve* and Gene Tierney's father in
Heaven Can Wait.) Croaking, three-hundred-pound Dad hires a fast-
talking, in-debt flier (James Cagney) to kidnap his dizzy daughter to
keep her from getting married. Heiress and flier bicker and, by bickering, end up falling in love.

The Epstein brothers, Philip G. and Julius J., certainly knew how to
fashion a script; they wrote *Casablanca* the following year, and they'd already written two little-known but perfectly serviceable screwball comedies, both for Barbara Stanwyck: *The Bride Walks Out* and *The Mad Miss
Manton*. They'd even adapted *No Time for Comedy*, one of the higher-
toned S. N. Behrman plays that Bette found preferable to *It's Love I'm After*. But with *The Bride Came C.O.D.*, they fail to provide a single funny
line. The closest they come to comedy is a near obsession with Bette's

rump. They keep landing her, squarely and gluteally, on prickly pear cacti. She jumps off the plane after Cagney crash-lands it in the desert—ha ha, she parks her rear on a prickly pear. She crashes an old jalopy, goes flying out of the vehicle, and lands bottom-down on, yes, a cactus. In the meantime, Cagney has sling-shotted a rock directly at her behind. And guess where she comes to rest after parachuting from an airplane? It's demeaning, and not because Bette's ass is sacrosanct. It's demeaning because nobody—not Davis, nor Cagney, nor the Epsteins, nor the director, William Keighley—can figure out a way to make any of it funny. Ernie Haller's silvery, high-contrast desert cinematography is the only reason to see the film.

Davis began shooting *The Bride Came C.O.D.* on January 8, 1941, a week after marrying Farney. He was protected from the press and Warners' publicists at first—he could stay home at Riverbottom while Bette was at the studio—but when the production moved to Death Valley in mid-January for the desert and western ghost town location shooting, he accompanied his bride and was much more on public display. It was his first exposure to the intrusive necessities of Hollywood stardom, but according to Davis he handled it with aplomb.

The company stayed at the Furnace Creek Inn, the 1927 mission-style hotel built by the Pacific Borax Company in the desert basin below the western slopes of the Funeral Mountains. The ghost town location was forty miles away. They filmed in the heat of the day, which makes it all the more remarkable—and implausible—that Davis is forced to wear a fur-collared coat through much of the film, though that's not nearly as far-fetched as the extraordinary smokeless campfire that Davis's character builds deep in an abandoned mine. The production wrapped on March 13, and the film was released in July.

THE LITTLE FOXES, Lillian Hellman's acidic play about an avaricious southern family in the 1900s, had opened on Broadway in February 1939 and played just shy of a year. Tallulah Bankhead led the cast as the heartless Regina Giddens who schemes with—and against—her two brothers for controlling interest in a new cotton mill. Davis's old friend Frank Conroy played Regina's sickly husband, Horace. Regina was a role tailor-made for Tallulah, but like *Dark Victory* it was also perfect for Bette, and by the summer of 1940, word had gotten out in

Hollywood that Sam Goldwyn was planning to borrow Davis from Warner Bros. to play Regina under the direction of William Wyler. Louella Parsons claimed to have known it all along. "I printed some six months ago that Sam was literally moving heaven and earth to get Bette to play the role that Tallulah Bankhead created on the stage," Louella crowed on July 22.[2]

Goldwyn struck a rather complicated deal with Warner for Bette's services, and Warner agreed at least in part because he owed his rival a gambling debt. These men didn't play penny ante; Jack owed Sam a whopping $425,000.[3] At first, it was a simple transaction. Goldwyn would lend Gary Cooper to Warner Bros. for *Sergeant York*, and Warner would lend Davis to Goldwyn for *The Little Foxes*; Warners would pay Davis, Goldwyn would pay Cooper, and that was it. But Goldwyn suddenly threw Miriam Hopkins into the mix. Goldwyn wanted Warner to take over his commitment to Hopkins, and so, Goldwyn reasoned, if he paid Cooper $150,000 and Hopkins $50,000, then Davis would end up costing him $200,000. But what would Warner Bros. do with Hopkins? Jack wanted to know. Goldwyn was vague, telling Warner, "You have a big studio and should have no difficulty" in finding something for Miriam to do.

On August 2, more than a week after Louella's bugle alert, Warner impatiently told Goldwyn it was Cooper for Davis as they had originally agreed or no deal. The final agreement was a slight compromise: Cooper went to Warners for $150,000, Davis went to Goldwyn for $150,000, and one or the other studio could use Hopkins under her existing contract with Goldwyn.[4]

But according to Davis and other sources, Goldwyn ended up paying her $385,000 for *The Little Foxes*. Not only that, but "Mr. Warner, on my steely request, gave me Warners' share of the deal."[5] As the Hollywood historian Arthur Marx explains, "At the time, the standard practice was for the star to pocket the difference between the loan-out fee and the amount that the studio was paying the star," but Bette apparently got to keep it all.[6]

Tallulah's shadow loomed much larger than it had over *Dark Victory*. "I hadn't seen her in *Foxes*," Davis told James McCourt, "and when they signed me, I didn't want to." But Goldwyn told her and Farney to stop in Cleveland on their way back to Los Angeles from New Hampshire and see Bankhead perform the play. Unfortunately, they ended up getting lost en route and saw the play one evening later than planned.

Bankhead was not pleased. "I had to go back and see her," Davis told McCourt, "and she was just *livid*."[7]

From Bette's perspective, Bankhead played Regina as a coldly greedy conniver, sinister from the start—an interpretation that made perfect sense, given the merciless thrust of Hellman's cleverly mean-spirited script. But Davis thought that Wyler wanted her to see Bankhead's Regina precisely so that she would come up with something different—something softer, easier to take. In Bette's version of the story, both Goldwyn, a hardheaded mogul, and Wyler, an equally tough director ("ruthless" was how the *New York Times* described him at the time), were terrified of this supremely toxic character—a woman who, by virtue of her vile nature, possessed the immoral authority to threaten ticket sales.[8] Wyler and Goldwyn were convinced, Davis believed, that audiences would reject *The Little Foxes* unless the antiheroine of the piece—a woman who sits notoriously still in the climactic scene while her husband suffers a fatal heart attack, deliberately refusing to fetch the medicine that would save his life—wasn't just a little bit likable.

Davis had already had this argument with Wyler over Leslie Crosbie in *The Letter*; they would be pandering to the stupid by tenderizing the killer dame, and she was sick of it. That Wyler indeed wanted to take the edge off *The Little Foxes* gets some support from the fact that Hellman herself added the character of David Hewitt, the love interest for Regina's daughter, Alexandra, to the screenplay, specifically as a way of adding a touch of youthful romance to the otherwise harsh story. Goldwyn asked for opinions: Wyler loved it, but everyone else thought the juvenile love story just watered the whole thing down.[9]

"She thought I was making her play the part like Tallulah Bankhead," Wyler later argued.

> I was not. It was the story of this woman who was greedy and high handed, but a woman of great poise, great charm, great wit. And that's the way Tallulah had played it on the stage. But Bette Davis was playing it all like a villain because she had been playing bitches and parts like that. This is what made her at Warner Bros.—*Jezebel* and things like that. But she was playing Regina with no shading . . . all the villainy and greediness of the part but not enough of the charm and wit and humor and sexiness of this woman. So, anyway, she thought when I tried to correct her that I was trying to make

her imitate Tallulah Bankhead, which I was not. . . . We had terrible disagreements over the way we saw Regina, so things were kind of cool between us.[10]

Wyler was wrong on two points: Davis doesn't play Regina as a one-dimensional villain, and his relations with Davis weren't "cool." Not at first. They were fiery hot, like the late Santa Ana winds that blew through Los Angeles in late April and early May 1941, when *The Little Foxes* went into production. Raymond Chandler once described the Santa Anas as burning, parching currents that "come down through the mountain passes and curl your hair and make your nerves jump and your skin itch. On nights like that every booze party ends in a fight. Meek little wives feel the edge of the carving knife and study their husbands' necks. Anything can happen."[11] Add to Chandler's list of Santa Ana jitters, itches, and murderous women the heat of blazing movie lights in a barnlike sound studio; the pressure of a running, whirring camera; and a series of ten-pound period-piece Edwardian gowns, and the result for Bette was catastrophic.

The temperature skyrocketed as early as the wardrobe and makeup tests, when Bette was subjected to unhelpfully contradictory advice. Wyler would voice one opinion, someone else quite the opposite, and Bette was caught in the middle, a position that preyed on her insecurities. When Wyler criticized her, she took it personally. Which is the way he meant it. She'd brought Perc Westmore along to Goldwyn to do her makeup, and she showed up one day with her face covered with aging makeup made of calcimine, a whitewash made of zinc oxide and water. "You look like a clown," Wyler told her.[12]

"Later on they photographed a dinner scene," Warners' Roy Obringer reported to Jack Warner—because of the loan arrangement, Warner Bros. had a stake in Bette's ability to complete the picture—

> and Davis, on account of her sick and hysterical condition, didn't get into the scene properly, and Wyler criticized the scene and . . . stated it was the lousiest dinner scene he had ever witnessed and possibly they had better get Bankhead.
>
> Davis gradually got more hysterical and ill due to the constant change of makeup and wardrobe and the criticism and finally made up her mind that she had better get off the lot. [The source of his information was Davis's lawyer, Dudley

Furse.] However, this situation was quieted down, and Goldwyn stated he would not need her from May 12 up until last
Wednesday, the 21st. At this time Davis actually became ill
and nervous and was much exhausted. Her doctor, Dr.
Moore, advised her that she should not attempt to work but
needed rest. It then appears that Goldwyn and Espy [Gold-
wyn's controller, Reeves Espy] stated that they actually
didn't need Davis and could shoot around her from the 21st
[until] June 5.[13]

Whitney Stine reported that Davis actually did walk out on May 12—
Furse was putting the best face on the situation—and when she did,
Hollywood lit up with rumors: "(1) She was pregnant. (2) She was divorcing her husband. (3) She was feuding with Wyler. (4) She was feuding with Sam Goldwyn. (5) She was being replaced by Miriam Hopkins.
(6) She was being replaced by Katharine Hepburn. (7) She was taken off
the film because she could not stack up to the original New York actors.
(8) It was 100 degrees on the sound stage, and the star collapsed from
the heat. (9) She walked off the set because Wyler disliked her long eye-
lashes."[14] "It's a sit-down strike, not a nervous collapse," Erskine Johnson declared in the *Los Angeles News*. And Mayme Ober Peake was
emphatic: Bette was definitely not expecting a visit from the stork.[15]

Douglas Churchill of the *New York Times* took the long view: "The outbursts were little different from those that marked the filming of *Jezebel*."[16]

But they *were* different. Two earlier pictures and a failed love affair
with the "ruthless" Wyler; a high-profile performance riding on an extreme amount of money; a most frustrating inability to blame Jack Warner
for anything that went wrong; and most of all a lack of confidence in her
director's vision coupled with her own Yankee intransigence—all con-
spired together to hurl Bette Davis into another nervous breakdown, Erskine Johnson's bland claim of a "sit-down strike" to the contrary
notwithstanding. It took several doctors as well as personal assurances
from both Wyler and Goldwyn, offered directly over the phone, to calm
her down and enable her to go back to work.

The *New York Times*'s Thomas Brady was on the set the third week of
June, and his description of Davis's performance casts doubt on *both*
Davis's and Wyler's accounts of the core dispute: Regina's nature. "Miss
Davis seemed intent last week on interpreting her role with gayety and
daring; Wyler wanted subtle repression. . . . Miss Davis was icy in

deferring to his wishes, and each was monstrously patient with the other. When one scene reached its eighth or ninth take, Mr. Wyler told Miss Davis she was rattling off her lines. Her response was cool enough to make the set suitable for a Sonja Henie skating spectacle."[17]

Perhaps Wyler was right after all; the Santa Anas had passed, and an Arctic chill moved in for the duration of the filming. Davis finished shooting on July 3.[18] "I ended up feeling I had given one of the worst performances of my life," Davis recalled.[19]

Lillian Hellman was evidently ambivalent about the film. She wrote to Arthur Kober after seeing the film and called it a "fine picture as pictures go, but it should have been better, and I think Willy did a bad job."[20] It didn't "hit hard enough," she felt. But late in life, she told Austin Pendleton, who directed a 1980 Broadway production with Elizabeth Taylor, that "the one that came closest to what I intended was Willy Wyler's film."[21]

Davis is noticeably less self-assured in *The Little Foxes* than she should be. Her clashes with Wyler produced a kind of nervous indecision in place of the calculatedly suppressed drive that is both Regina's hallmark and Bette's own. After Horace (Herbert Marshall) returns from an extended hospitalization in Baltimore with the pallor and physical slackness of the imminently dead, Regina greets him by bursting gaily through a pair of enormous sliding doors and dismissing his illness by remarking with a forcedly mild tone, "It sounds almost like a holiday. . . . And here I was, thinking you were in *pain*."

"I was thinking about us," Horace feebly replies, to which Regina responds, clipping her words like scissor shears as she rises to leave, obviously bored: "About *us*. About *you* and *me*. After *all these years*." She is literally looking down on him when she concludes, "*Well*. You can tell me everything you thought. *Some day*." It's one of Davis's most effective line readings precisely because it's so unredeemably nasty—glib sarcasm about the future directed at a man she knows is actively dying.

The matter-of-fact tone Davis deploys when delivering one of the film's most quotable lines is terrifying in its simplicity: "I hope you *die*. I hope you die *soon*. I'll be *waiting* for you to *die*." Revenge may be a dish best served cold, but Davis correctly understands in this instance that poison works best at room temperature.

The film's set piece—Regina gazing in lethal passivity while Horace suffers his heart attack—derives at least some of its force from Davis's and Wyler's contradictory approaches to Regina. Bette is lounging, even slouching on the couch when Horace drops the medicine bottle and gasps for her help. From the time Horace forces himself up from his wheelchair, Wyler handles the sequence in only two shots, both of which focus on Regina, the second somewhat closer than the first. Critics who describe this sequence as deep focus miss the point; the cinematographer Gregg Toland, obviously at Wyler's behest, keeps his lens focused on Davis and her murderous gaze while Marshall—remaining visible throughout— increasingly loses clarity as well as physical strength in the background.

The philosopher Stanley Cavell, appreciating the thrust of Davis's performance, nevertheless errs when he describes Regina as "watching her husband die, as if her gaze deprives him of life." Cavell's larger point about the power of the female gaze is right on the money, but in fact Regina isn't watching Horace at the moment in question. (Moreover, he doesn't die—not yet, anyway.) She's depriving him of vitality by refusing him any human connection at all—not his medicine, not her attention. Her authority comes from her steadfast refusal to engage him by watching him suffer.

Louella Parsons noted in October 1940 that Bette had dined twice with the playwright George S. Kaufman during a stopover in New York on her way back to Hollywood from Butternut. They talked about adapting *The Man Who Came to Dinner*, his current Broadway comedy hit, into a film. Upon her return to Hollywood, Bette began lobbying for Warner Bros. to cast her in the picture, but she was told rather peremptorily that her request was premature.[22] She wanted to play a central role but an unusually sober one for her: that of the eponymous houseguest's secretary, a sophisticated New Yorker who falls in love with a small-town midwestern newspaperman.

Bette had to meet with Kaufman in New York because, as Ann Kaufman Schneider notes, "my father, of course, never bothered to go out to California. He never had anything to do with movies. He'd had quite a lot of trouble in 1935 with Mary Astor—their affair and all that stuff. He fled, literally, and didn't go out there again for years. He sold the picture rights [to *The Man Who Came to Dinner*] and that was it. It was a very good, unglamorous, unneurotic part for Bette."*

---

*In 1935, during a bitter custody battle with her recently divorced husband, portions of Mary Astor's personal diary, including intimate details of her ongoing affair with the then-married Kaufman, were released to the press, and Kaufman was all but hounded back to New York from Hollywood.

According to Parsons, Davis and Kaufman discussed the possibility of building up the part of the secretary, Maggie Cutler, so it more closely matched that of Sheridan Whiteside, the imperious radio commentator and critic who slips and falls on the icy front steps of a businessman's house in Ohio and ends up staying for a month and commandeering everyone's personal lives in addition to the living room, dining room, and library. The actual film adaptation would not be done by Kaufman and Hart, though; as Ann Schneider notes, her father and his writing partner took the rights money and banked it and left the rewriting to others, namely Julius and Philip Epstein.

Hal Wallis and Jack Warner floated various ideas for the cast and director; Bette's winning the role of Maggie Cutler was far from certain. Wallis wanted Jean Arthur or Myrna Loy. On Broadway, Sheridan Whiteside was being played to rave reviews by Monty Woolley, but nobody knew who Woolley was outside of New York and Yale, where he taught drama, so he wasn't considered for the film. Bette strongly advocated John Barrymore and took it upon herself to write to Spencer Berger, the Barrymore family's factotum: "I'd love to do that play with Mr. Barrymore—any play with Mr. Barrymore—but I think this one would be excellent for the screen with him. So let's hope my bosses agree."[23] The idea of the great, thundering John Barrymore was appealing enough for Warners to give him a screen test in May 1941, but as Hal Wallis later noted, "I couldn't risk it. The dialogue . . . was tremendously complicated, and Barrymore was drinking so heavily that he had to read his lines from cue cards."[24]

Charles Laughton was eager to do the role and was screen-tested, too, but as his agent told Warners, he knew "that the test wasn't up to par."[25]

Cary Grant was interested. In fact, he said, he'd do the film for free as long as Warner Bros. kicked in $125,000 to the British War Relief Fund. Grant's participation piqued the interest of Howard Hawks in directing the picture.[26]

Others considered for Sheridan Whiteside, if only by their press agents, were Fredric March and Robert Benchley. Charles Coburn put himself out of the running by refusing to make a screen test.[27] Mary Astor was tested for the role of Lorraine, the flashy actress who tries to steal Bert Jefferson, the reporter, away from Maggie. Ronald Reagan was considered for Bert, and Danny Kaye was mentioned as Banjo, the antic Hollywood comedian modeled after Harpo Marx.

At the end of March, Jack Warner invited a young hotshot actor-director to dinner at his house to discuss the project. *The Man Who Came to Dinner* rather than *The Magnificent Ambersons* might well have been Orson Welles's second film. Welles had finished shooting *Citizen Kane*—it hadn't been released yet—and was nosing around for a new project. The dinner went well, and Warner and Welles came to a tentative agreement: Welles would play Sheridan Whiteside for $100,000, but if he also directed the film he'd get $150,000. The two men mapped out the rest of the cast: Ann Sheridan would play Lorraine, and Barbara Stanwyck, Paulette Goddard, or Carole Lombard would be Maggie. If he didn't direct it himself, Welles said, he wanted either Hawks or Leo McCarey.

Jack Warner and Hal Wallis gave the role of Maggie to Bette at a meeting in June while Davis was still shooting *The Little Foxes*, and the film started shooting the following month. Grant was out; Monty Woolley was in. Reagan was out; Richard Travis was in. Danny Kaye and Mary Astor were out; Jimmy Durante and Ann Sheridan were in. Welles, of course, was very much out, and in his place, absurdly, was William Keighley: from *Citizen Kane* to *The Bride Came C.O.D.*

"I felt the film was not directed in a very imaginative way," Davis later noted with remarkable understatement. "For me it was not a happy film to make."[28]

Asked if she had any trouble with Bette during the making of *The Man Who Came to Dinner*, Ann Sheridan was dismissive: "Oh, no. Very, very little. She wasn't happy about a lot of things . . . but this had nothing to do with me. I adored her. Wouldn't dream of fighting her at all—so she got very nice. She was just temperamental. Who isn't now and then?"[29]

This was a period of physical as well as emotional distress for Davis; she kept suffering mishaps. In April she's said to have mildly poisoned herself by drinking household ammonia in the mistaken belief that it was potable spirits of ammonia. In May was the nervous breakdown. In late July she fell down some steps leading to a soundstage and broke a small bone. And however temperamental she may have been during the production of *The Man Who Came to Dinner*, the greatest uproar was caused not by Bette but by a dog. Mike, a Scottie, got a little too boisterous in mid-September and bit Bette Davis squarely on the nose.

"The dog was too highly bred," Ruthie Davis told the press. "He was strange to us, and it just happened." Mike seems to have had a thing for noses; he'd bitten Farney's the week before just after Farney climbed into bed at night.[30]

Bette's injury was severe enough to send her home—all the way to Butternut. She left Los Angeles around September 17. Warners expected her back at the beginning of October, but the bite marks were slow to heal. "Scab not off nose yet," Bette wired Wallis from Butternut on the second, "and nose still very red. Am hoping it will be all right by Thursday when I get in."[31] She returned to the studio on Friday, the tenth, and the production wrapped at the end of the following week.

The Man Who Came to Dinner is disappointing even without imagining what Orson Welles would have done with it. Monty Woolley is quite amusing as the hammy Whiteside, but Keighley has a penchant for cutting to medium shots or close-ups of him just when he's at his stage-training broadest. Still, Woolley's acerbic verbal delivery is up to Kaufman and Hart's snappy dialogue. Asked by Bert how he thinks Ohio women "stack up," Sheridan Whiteside responds, "I've never gone in for stacking women up so I really can't say." (Woolley had a sharp wit of his own. One night while cruising the New York streets for trade with his friend Cole Porter, they pulled the car up next to a sailor, who asked with superb candor, "Are you two cocksuckers?" "Now that the preliminaries are over," Woolley quickly replied, "why don't you get in and we can discuss the details?")[32]

For Bette, Maggie Cutler was a refreshing change from the needling neurotics, suppressed hysterics, and cold sociopaths she'd been playing for several years. Her restraint plays well against Ann Sheridan's showy, divine Lorraine. Hal Wallis made an apt observation: "It was like her first film, *Bad Sister*, in a way—here she was, the drab wren up against the flashy peacock! Bette was full of surprises, and her not minding her status on this picture was one of them."[33] For Bette, the problem is not Maggie Cutler's little-brown-wrennishness; in fact, the urbane Maggie sports some of Orry-Kelly's most wearable suits. The trouble is that she's forced to fall in love with Richard Travis, whose toothy grin is as annoyingly omnipresent as Maria Schell's in *The Brothers Karamazov*. Travis is a blandly handsome blond, not muscular enough to be beefcake, not magnetic enough to be watchable. As Maggie notes while munching on a hot sweet potato at a fake-looking soundstage skating pond, "Funny thing is—you *are* sort of attractive in a" (pause) "*corn-fed* sort of way." She's right. Whether or not he's enough to give up her career and move to Ohio for is something else again.

James McCourt and Bette Davis were discussing the distinctive swing-stride of her walk when McCourt mentioned James Baldwin's famous line: "Bette Davis walks like a nigger." "Yes, they told me," Davis replied. "What do you say back to *that*?"[34]

Unlike Davis herself, Baldwin was a great admirer of *In This Our Life*, in which Davis's toxic belle frames a black legal assistant–chauffeur for her own hit-and-run. "Bette Davis, under the direction of John Huston, delivered a ruthlessly accurate (and much underrated) portrait of a Southern girl," Baldwin wrote. "She thus became, and, indeed, remained, the toast of Harlem because her prison scene with the black chauffeur was cut when the movie came uptown. The uproar in Harlem was impressive, and I think that the scene was reinserted; in any case, either uptown or downtown, I saw it. Davis appeared to have read, and grasped, the script—which must have made her rather lonely—and she certainly understood the role. Her performance had the effect, rather, of exposing and shattering the film, so that she played in a kind of vacuum."[35]

"It was one of the worst films made in the history of the world," said Bette.[36]

In This Our Life—which is indeed rent apart by Davis's willfully foul performance—is saddled with a title that seems at first notice to mean something but, upon reflection, does not. Based on Ellen Glasgow's Pulitzer Prize–winning novel, it's the story of two Virginia sisters, each of whom has, for no discernible reason, a man's name: Stanley and Roy. (Manly names for women were all the rage in 1941: Hedy Lamarr was a Johnny and a Marvin that year, and the eponymous heroines of Frank Borzage's *Seven Sweethearts* were called Victor, Albert, Reggie, Peter, Billie, George, and most outrageous of all, Cornelius.) Stanley (Davis) is the wild one, Roy (Olivia de Havilland) the good girl. The potboiler story has Stanley running off with Roy's husband (Dennis Morgan), who descends rapidly into shame and despair and ends up killing himself. Stanley returns home after a brief period of convalescent hysteria and brazenly comes on to the earnest lawyer she'd jilted (George Brent), but he's now romancing Roy, however tepidly, so in a fit of pique Stanley gets drunk at a roadhouse, speeds away in her flashy car, runs over and kills a little girl, stops and looks back momentarily before speeding away again, and blames Parry (Ernest Anderson), the black chauffeur, after the police identify her car. (Parry is studying law while working both as the family's driver and George Brent's legal assistant.) The truth outs, Stanley engages in a terrifically overwrought scene with her corpulent, all-too-loving uncle (Charles Coburn), and drives her car over a cliff. "Yeah, she's dead," an inappropriately bored cop sighs at the end.

Sure, the film is on the silly side despite its liberal racial politics and daring suggestion of the uncle's incestuous desire for Stanley; he actually tells her he's got something in his pocket, and she goes rooting around looking for it. And yet under Huston's sharp-eyed direction (and with Howard Koch's smart screenplay and Ernie Haller's moody, shadowy cinematography), the film rises above its material, as does Davis, who repeatedly voiced her contempt for the thing but left it curiously unexplained other than to say that the novel was better. What James Baldwin admired about Davis in *In This Our Life* still retains its bite. By "a ruthlessly accurate . . . portrait of a Southern girl," Baldwin means a superficially charming, mercilessly selfish tramp who drives her husband to suicide, ends her mourning by dancing a rhumba, and lays the blame for a crime she knows she committed on an innocent black man, all with a sickening degree of viperish southern narcissism. There is nothing in Davis's performance to convey the slightest sympathy for this spoiled white woman, and Baldwin clearly approved. If Davis became "the toast of Harlem," it was precisely because Stanley Timberlake is one of her most uncompromisingly nasty creations, the epitome of evil white privilege, and, as such, she is enormously entertaining. Listen to her deliver this diatribe to her character's overly indulgent uncle when the scoundrel announces, stunned, that he has been given only six months to live:

"All *right*, so you're going to *die*!" Stanley rises in a fury of frustrated greed, the unbridled rage of an egomaniac denied her rightful attention. "But you're an *old man*! You've *lived* your life! I haven't lived mine— mine's hardly begun! Think of *me*, Uncle! Think of what'll happen to *me* if you don't get me out of this. You're not even listening! You don't care what happens to *me* any more than the others! You'd let me go to *prison*! All you're thinking about is your *own miserable life*! Well you can *die* for all I care! *Die*!" Scenes like this make life worth living.

"Bette fascinated me," Huston wrote in his autobiography. "There is something elemental about Bette—a demon within her which threatens to break out and eat everybody, beginning with their ears. The studio was afraid of her—afraid of her demon. They confused it with overacting. Over their objections, I let the demon go."[37]

Davis was not the only passionate player involved in the production. "Huston was and is a most attractive man," Jack Warner recalled, "and during the filming of this Davis–de Havilland epic anyone could see that it was cold outside but Valentine's Day on the set. When I saw the first rushes I said to myself: 'Oh-oh, Bette has the lines, but Livvy is getting the best camera shots.'" Huston and de Havilland weren't just having a torrid affair. They were openly living together at the time, and de Havilland herself was showing signs of anxiety, not only about her relationship with the volatile Huston but about constantly finding herself in front of the cameras, having just finished two other films back-to-back before starting *In This Our Life* without a break. Davis had top billing, but de Havilland was getting the bulk of Huston's lavish photographic attention, and Warner warned him that he'd better "get back on track."

"Huston has a huge heart of lead beneath that fine gray head of his, and in a few hand-picked words he told me to go you know where," Warner noted.

Warner's solution was ingenious if abstruse. He escorted Bette, Huston, de Havilland, and the producer David Lewis into a studio screening room and showed them some rushes, after which he told them,

> "Tell you what—you all go ahead and finish the picture as is. We'll get our money out of it because these kids will draw, but I won't go to the preview."
>
> "You won't go to the preview?" Bette snapped.
>
> "No," I said.
>
> And Bette caught my little pop fly to the infield, and suddenly she used all the four-letter words, and some that were new to me, on Lewis. She came close to tearing out every seat in Projection Room No. 5, and she would have given everyone a punch in the nose if I hadn't interfered.[38]

Living on the emotional edge had become as natural to Bette Davis as her means of coping with it: shouting and swearing. But there was an added reason for panic as the production got under way. Farney, in Minnesota doing some consulting work for Minneapolis Honeywell on the basis of his aviation expertise, had developed a bad case of lobar pneumonia, his second in less than a year. He was rushed to Abbott Hospital, where, on Monday, October 20, his fever spiked to 106.

Bette was called at the studio, and she quickly left for Minneapolis. With the help of Howard Hughes, who provided an airplane on short notice, she flew via Kansas City and Des Moines before reaching Rochester, Minnesota; she drove the rest of the way. She found Farney in critical condition but beginning to respond to the sulfa drugs his doctors were administering. She and Farney's mother, Lucille—a sturdy, stocky Yankee gal with spectacles—checked into the Curtis Hotel.[39]

"Farney not out of danger yet—doctor thinks by end of week will definitely know," Davis cabled Warners. "Am so sorry about Farney and of course understand," Hal Wallis replied. At first, she planned to take the *Super Chief* back to Los Angeles, but then she decided to fly, which she hated to do, so much so that Farney's doctor forbade her to get back on a plane. As Dr. J. C. Davis of Minneapolis explained in a wire to the studio, her trip to Minnesota had "exhausted her due to her inability to relax in the plane with the result that it has required four days for her to recuperate." She arrived on the *Super Chief* on the thirtieth and proceeded straight to the studio in Burbank.[40]

Because of Farney's illness, *In This Our Life* was behind schedule even before Huston started shooting it, and by mid-December, Jack Warner was irate. Referring to the footage Huston was cranking out every day, Warner told the director on the seventeenth, "[I think you] can just exactly double what you are taking."[41] That was the day Bette caused a further delay by falling ill. "She is confined to bed with the flu," Dr. Paul Moore told the studio.[42] For reasons that remain unclear, Raoul Walsh took over for Huston in early January, and Bette adamantly refused to play at least one scene according to Walsh's direction. The production wrapped on January 8, 1942, thirteen days behind schedule.

Testiness reigned. Wallis reprimanded Davis for causing so many delays on her last three pictures—the breakdown, the dog bite, Farney's pneumonia, the flu—and Bette was indignant. "I am sorry your plans were delayed," she crisply observed in a handwritten response, "but I didn't ask the dog to bite me, nor did I have much fun during the process." Wallis forwarded the letter to Warners' legal counsel with the comment, "Just put it in your files with the accumulation of other nasty notes."

Wallis was similarly displeased by the comment cards he read in February after an early preview, and he responded by blasting Perc Westmore for radically changing Davis's makeup without clearing it with him first. Mayme Ober Peake announced as early as November that Bette had "hit the peroxide trail" again for *In This Our Life*, and to Wallis's dismay she also appeared to have acquired a new set of lips—as though he hadn't been seeing the rushes all along.[43] (Mayme wasn't entirely accurate; Davis's hair is much darker and more natural looking than it had been early in her career.) As Wallis told Westmore, there were "far too many [cards] commenting on Bette Davis's makeup and in most uncomplimentary terms. They thought she looked badly, and they didn't like the hairdress nor the new style of Cupid's bow lips on her."[44]

Always the voice of the braying middlebrow, Bosley Crowther of the *New York Times* took a swipe at Davis when the film opened in May 1942: "She is forever squirming and pacing and grabbing the back of her neck. It is likewise very hard to see her as the sort of sultry dame that good men can't resist. In short, her evil is so theatrical and so completely inexplicable that her eventual demise in an auto accident is the happiest moment in the film. That, indeed, is what probably provoked the audience to cheer." The twitchiness that so annoyed Crowther is a physical expression of her character's base and supremely uncontrollable carnality, the salty funk that emanates from a woman who can't stop moving, and in point of fact there are men who appreciate that musk. One imagines de Havilland's Roy chairing some committee of the Junior League; Davis's Stanley gets her kicks in more provocative ways and in sleazier surroundings. What "good men" see in her is also what they smell: the unquenchable energy that enables her to keep going for hours. John Huston and James Baldwin were more perceptive critics. They saw, even though Bette herself did not, that *In This Our Life* gives full voice to Davis's obdurate honesty. Should she really have played this racist bitch as having a softer, more lovable side?

Two ITEMS FROM the wire services in November 1941:

HOLLYWOOD, Nov. 7 (U.P.)—Bette Davis, twice winner of the Movie Academy award [*sic*], today became the first actress-president of the Academy of Motion Picture Arts and Sciences. Miss Davis was elected by the board of governors to succeed Walter Wanger, producer, the academy announced today. Another actress, Rosalind Russell, was elected third vice president.

CALDWELL, Idaho, Nov. 15 (A.P.)—Calamity Jane, with wings aflutter, raced down a dusty asphalt track today to fleeting fame and the Thanksgiving dinner table of Bette Davis, the actress. For Calamity, shooed by Ellen Gregory, proved herself the "runningest" bird in Caldwell's annual Turkey Derby. Miss Gregory, a bookkeeper, competed against heavy-footed businessmen. The winning bird had been promised to Miss Davis.

There is no record of how Calamity Jane tasted or whether she was even roasted and served at Riverbottom, where Bette and Farney were sharing space with a total of seven Scotties: Tibby, of course; the rather recent arrival Peckett's; and Peckett's's new litter of five. (The puppies were eventually given away.)[45] There is, however, some documentation of Bette's brief but stormy tenure as president of the Academy. Her mistake was in believing that she had the authority to make a few changes.

Davis went into it as a smart, capable, dynamic leader—the Girl Scout troop commander grown into a movie star. She was an avid reader if not an intellectual; she knew her way around the film business in Hollywood as well as the larger popular culture from which her films sprang. And she was accustomed not only to being taken seriously but to having her way as often as possible. She was an inspired choice to lead the Academy—on paper.

It took less than a month before a group described by one reporter as the Academy's "old-timers" began demanding that Wanger take over again. It wasn't exactly that they didn't like Bette. It was that "no woman, especially no actress, is in a position to successfully direct Academy affairs." By the first week of January, she was out.[46]

"I have reached the conclusion that probably I am a very disagreeable person," Davis wrote in "Uncertain Glory," her first memoir (published in the *Ladies Home Journal*), and it is clear that she rubbed the Academy's old guard the wrong way for reasons that went beyond her sex, though it's equally obvious that had Walter Wanger or any other Hollywood male acted in the same commanding manner, he wouldn't have been forced out after only sixty days.[47]

From her perspective, Bette just made a few practical suggestions, that's all. "I was the first to suggest that they abolish votes by extras, which they all thought was the wildest thing they'd ever heard," she later said. "Well, three quarters of the Hollywood extras at that time couldn't even speak English. . . . If you were up for an Oscar and you bought them ice cream every Saturday afternoon, you'd get it."[48]

And another thing: because of the impending war, Davis felt that holding the annual Oscar ceremonies—which then included cocktails and dinner—at the Biltmore Hotel would "seem frivolous in the midst of national austerity."[49] Instead, Davis proposed, the Academy should hold the event in a grand theater, invite the public and charge admission, and donate the proceeds to the British War Relief Fund. By the time Bette got around to suggesting that Rosalind Russell take over from Mervyn LeRoy as chair of the committee that ran the event, the die was cast. Walter Wanger went so far as to ask her what she had against the Academy, as though Davis's sensible suggestions were a deliberate attempt to tear the organization apart.

Darryl Zanuck, who'd sponsored her for the presidency in the first place, told her melodramatically that if she resigned she would "never work in Hollywood again," but Bette quit anyway, knowing that her career wasn't even up for discussion, let alone on the line.[50]

There was some consolation: in December 1941, the Hollywood Women's Press Club named Bette as Tinseltown's most cooperative star along with Bob Hope. (The least cooperative? Fred Astaire and Ginger Rogers.)[51] The award was a bit of sweet revenge for Bette, who had seen herself publicly reprimanded by Hedda Hopper earlier that year for the grievous sin of failing to take a call from the women of the Studio Club.[52]

O<small>N</small> F<small>EBRUARY</small> 1, 1942, Louella Parsons reported that Hal Wallis had bought the film rights to Ben Ames Williams's novel *The Strange Woman* for Bette, but the film, a melodrama, didn't get made until 1946 and ended up starring Hedy Lamarr. Warners considered starring Davis as a would-be murder victim in the noirish *Danger Signal*, but Faye Emerson ended up in the role when the film was finally made in 1945.[53] In July 1942, the *Hollywood Reporter* fell for somebody's tale that both Bette and Greta Garbo were interested in playing the lead in *Dishonored Lady*, but that one didn't get off the ground until 1947, with Hedy Lamarr once again taking the role in question.[54]

The *Reporter* also announced in October the renaming of the Hollywood Theatre to the "Bette Davis," and in November the same paper declared, as the headline put it, "Bette Davis to Play Self in Film," the autobiopic said to be based on her *Ladies Home Journal* piece.[55] Neither was true.

It's unclear whether Bette herself even heard of any of these projects, the trade papers and gossip columns tending to claim things based not on facts but rather on producers' and agents' schemes. But there was one film Warners really did want her to do, and she fought it. In early 1941, Warners paid $35,000 for the rights to Stephen Longstreet's novel *The Gay Sisters*, a tale of intrigue between two prominent New York families, the Gaylords and the Barclays. The Gaylords were thinly veiled Rockefellers, the Barclays Vanderbilts. Bette Davis was to play the stubborn Fiona Gaylord, with Mary Astor playing her younger sister.

Bette read the novel while resting at Huntington Beach during her tense, emotional absence from *The Little Foxes*, and as she wrote to Wallis she had "only one reaction—my character in the book is so much like Regina in *Little Foxes*." In addition, she wrote, she did not want to play yet another forty-year-old woman. "There's so much time for that," she observed. (Davis was then thirty-three.) Another stumbling block was Mary Astor. Henry Blanke clarified Davis's objection to Astor's casting to Hal Wallis: Davis held nothing against Astor personally, but Astor necessarily looked older than Davis on celluloid, so Davis would be required to be aged—again—in order to make it plausible that she was the oldest of the three sisters. Wallis sent Davis Lenore Coffee's script anyway, but as Bette noted in a letter to Jack Warner, she still didn't want to do the film and that casting Astor as her younger sister would be "very foolish [and] just not right."[56] Irene Dunne was considered; MGM was asked to loan Norma Shearer; an offer was made to Katharine Hepburn; Barbara Stanwyck ultimately took the role opposite George Brent. Mary Astor, meanwhile, was cast in another picture: *The Maltese Falcon*.[57]

Bette proposed to Warner Bros. in the summer of 1941 that she, Alfred Lunt, Lynn Fontanne, and Richard "Dicky" Whorf film Chekhov's *The Seagull*. She'd spoken to Whorf, who told her that Lunt and Fontanne were interested in doing a picture of one of their plays; they'd done *The Seagull* on Broadway in 1938. But the project went nowhere.[58] Also in 1941, Bette expressed interested in *Mrs. Parkington*, then only a one-page treatment written by the Pulitzer Prize–winning novelist Louis Bromfield: Susie Graham runs a cheap boardinghouse in Leaping Rock, Nevada, until she marries Major Augustus Parkington, moves to New York, enters high society, travels to Paris, meets the Prince of Wales. . . .

But MGM won the bidding war for the property in July, and the film was eventually made in 1944 with Greer Garson.[59] In addition, Edmund Goulding considered casting Bette as the jealous wife in *The Constant Nymph*, but the part was ultimately taken by Alexis Smith.[60] Bette turned down *The Hard Way* for Vincent Sherman and was replaced by Ida Lupino.[61]

It may seem obvious, but it bears stating directly: sustaining the stardom she fought for was at least as emotionally draining for Bette as scrapping her way into it in the first place. Hollywood filmmaking is often called a high-stakes game, but Davis never thought of it that way. It was high stakes, all right, but it was never a game. It was a *crusade*, with all the righteousness and potential for glory the word carries with it. And as in a military battle, one false move—another bad script, an intransigent and misguided director, an unflattering wig, a silly costar—could result in a mortal injury.

One role Bette particularly coveted was that of wild Cassandra Tower in the melodrama *King's Row*. It's a lurid small-town story set in the nineteenth century: Cassie, who was eventually played by Betty Field, has a hot affair with Robert Cummings, but her father, Claude Rains, thinks she's insane and poisons her. (We learn only by reading Henry Bellamann's racy novel that Cassie's father has been having an incestuous relationship with her for years.) Then he shoots himself. Later in the film, Ronald Reagan famously gets his legs vengefully and pointlessly amputated by Charles Coburn. As Hal Wallis reported to Roy Obringer, "Bette Davis pleaded to be allowed to play this part," but as Wallis explained later, "We all felt the picture would be thrown off balance because of her fame and talent." *King's Row* ended up being one of Reagan's favorite pictures, so much so that he titled his autobiography after a line he delivers in the film: *Where's the Rest of Me?* (After her divorce from Reagan, Jane Wyman was heard to say, "At least I'll never have to see that damn *King's Row* again.")[62]

Radio dramas continued to provide something to do in Bette's off hours, which were few. On a Sunday night in March 1941, for instance, Davis was heard opposite Brian Aherne in a thirty-minute adaptation of *Jane Eyre* on CBS's *The Gulf Screen Guild Show*. She'd done several earlier *Screen Guild Shows*—including *Can We Forget* with George Murphy and Robert Montgomery in January 1939, and *Ballerina, Slightly with Accent* with William Powell in March 1940—with all the stars' salaries going to the Motion Picture Relief Fund.[63] In April 1942, Davis returned to the

Screen Guild Show airwaves for an adaptation of the Joan Crawford melodrama *A Woman's Face*; her costar was Warren William.

In January 1942, Bette did a episode of the DuPont Company's *Cavalcade of America*, which aired on NBC. The series's point was to soften the public image of the large munitions company by way of stirring dramas about American history; Bette's program, *An American Is Born*, concerned a refugee who wanted her baby to be born in the United States. She'd also been heard on *Lux Radio Theater* at least once a year since 1936. Notable performances included *Another Language* with Fred MacMurray in 1937 and *Forsaking All Others* with Joel McCrea in 1938, after which she began reprising some of her film roles in radio adaptations: *Dark Victory* with Spencer Tracy in 1940, *The Letter* with Herbert Marshall, and *All This and Heaven, Too* with Charles Boyer and Bea Benaderet, both in 1941.

As far as her public image was concerned, Bette was still putting up with a lot of bullshit. As the Hollywood correspondent Ann Masters asserted, "Bette Davis says that a fine exercise for slimming the ankles and strengthening the arches is to walk pigeon-toed."[64]

13

A PRESCRIPTION
FOR INDEPENDENCE

IN 1925, THE NOVELIST OLIVE HIGGINS
Prouty suffered an emotional collapse. She had been conflicted about
her life as a writer for some time. Despite her commercial successes with
novels and short stories, Prouty was nonetheless forcing herself to hew
to a strictly conventional life as wife and mother, taking pains to make it
seem as though her popular fiction had been, as she described it, simply
"dashed off at spare moments" during days devoted to making a suitable home for her husband and kids in Brookline, Massachusetts. But
the creative spark that enlivened her wouldn't be stifled, and indeed its
ceaseless ignition was so great that after her daughter Olivia died of en-
cephalitis in 1923, Prouty fought through her grief by writing *Stella
Dallas*, the story of the world's most embarrassing but ultimately self-
sacrificial mother. Still, nagging guilt over her daughter's death and her
own insistent creative drive finally cornered her, and she broke down.
She sought treatment at a sanitarium, which she later called "an educa-
tional institution from which I 'graduated.'" Her psychiatrist discharged
her with a prescription for independence: he advised Prouty to rent office space outside her house and work five days a week on her writing.
She went on to chronicle the agony of a nervous breakdown and the
painful struggle for recovery in two subsequent novels: *Conflict*, which
was published in 1927; and *Now, Voyager*, which came out in 1941.[1]

Like *Stella Dallas*, *Now, Voyager* was a hit, though not as much of one as Prouty and her publisher had hoped. When Warner Bros. made its bid for the film rights on the basis of an advance copy and the recommendation of its West Coast story editor, Irene Lee, the studio offered $50,000 if the book sold 50,000 copies by May 1, 1941, or, as Prouty later wrote, "$40,000 if it didn't. It didn't!"[2]

She drew her title from Whitman's two-line poem "The Untold Want" in *Leaves of Grass*.

> *The untold want by life and land ne'er granted,*
> *Now voyager sail thou forth to seek and find.*[3]

For Prouty's heroine, psychotherapy launches her on a journey of self-discovery that leads her out of common, drab, imposed expectations— and their concomitantly fierce, necessarily unfulfilled desires—and onto a ship of her own making and guidance. *Now, Voyager* is a coming-out story.

Hal Wallis sent a copy of the book to Ginger Rogers, hoping to interest her in the leading role: Charlotte Vale, who begins the story as a repressed Boston spinster stifled into a state of neurotic agitation by the hateful, spiteful mother who never wanted her in the first place, and ends it as an independent, self-knowing woman of the world. But Edmund Goulding, whom Warners assigned the task of writing the first treatment in preparation for directing the picture, preferred Irene Dunne. One can only imagine Bette Davis's rage when she picked up the *Herald-Examiner* one day and read in Louella Parsons's column that Dunne was being loaned to Warners by Columbia for *Now, Voyager*. "I became apoplectic," she later wrote.[4]

Ginger Rogers kept pushing for the role, commenting later of Bette's irritation, "One thing that really irked her was that I was getting more money per film than she was."[5]

Goulding then became ill and was replaced, inaptly, by Michael Curtiz, who wanted either Rogers or Norma Shearer. "*I'm under contract here!*" Bette raged to Hal Wallis. "Why can't *I* play Charlotte Vale? As a New Englander, I understand her better than anyone else ever could!" Wallis took the idea to Jack Warner, and Warner wisely agreed.[6] *Now, Voyager* is as unimaginable without Bette Davis as *Gone with the Wind* is with her.

Curtiz dropped out—possibly because he didn't want to work with

Davis again, or maybe he just didn't like the idea of directing a weepie. His replacement, a former dialogue director named Irving Rapper, held to the latter view: "My great teacher Michael Curtiz was originally supposed to have directed this picture but didn't like it as a subject and preferred to do an action picture." Rapper went on: "I insisted upon casting *Now, Voyager* myself; I was starting to sail high, and they gave me my head. So I hired Claude Rains to play the psychiatrist [Dr. Jaquith] and Gladys Cooper, whom Hal Wallis had never heard of, to play the mother."[7]

Although he had appeared in a number of pictures since emigrating in the mid-1930s, Paul von Hernreid—who had recently de-Germanized his name to Paul Henreid—was a newcomer to Warners. According to Henreid, Jack Warner got it in his head to turn Henreid into a continental-accented cross between George Brent and Leslie Howard, with Bette correctly describing Warner's proposed concoction as also including a smidgen of Charles Boyer. Henreid's screen test for the role of Jerry Durrance, the unhappily married man with whom Charlotte falls in love, was thus a fiasco, the studio hairdresser having been advised to pomade Henreid's hair down to the scalp, with Perc Westmore adding lipstick, rouge, and mascara, and the costumer topping off the ensemble with a satin smoking jacket. Henreid was mortified.

Bette "hit the ceiling" when she saw the tests. "She turned to Rapper and Hal Wallis and shouted, 'What did you *do* to that man? *How* can I act with him? He looks *ghastly*—like some floorwalker in a department store! You are two of the most miserable bastards!' "

Davis was more than relieved to learn that Henreid himself hated the way he looked, too, and a strong, enduring friendship resulted—one of the few Davis enjoyed with a male co-star. (Another was with Claude Rains.) "There was something about her manner, flirtatious and friendly, flattering and yet honest, that made you think of her as an immediate friend and a solid master of her craft," Henreid later wrote. "I found her a delight to work with, and we got along famously. . . . She has remained a dear, close friend—and always a very decent human being."[8]

To round out the cast, Ilka Chase was hired to play Lisa Vale, Charlotte's sympathetic sister-in-law, with Bonita Granville playing Lisa's casually cruel daughter, June. (Granville also appears as the shrill and obnoxious child in *It's Love I'm After*.) Juanita Quigley, who had appeared in such films as John Stahl's *Imitation of Life*—under the name "Baby Jane," coincidently—was tested for the role of Tina, Jerry Durrance's troubled daughter, but the part went instead to plain Janis Wilson, an unknown.[9] In fact, Wilson was *so* unknown that her appearance in *Now, Voyager* is uncredited.

Three of the central dramatis personae have claimed credit for the excellence of the unashamedly melodramatic script:

Bette Davis: "It was a constant vigil to preserve the quality of the book as written by Olive Higgins Prouty. . . . I used Miss Prouty's book and redid the screenplay in her words as we went along. . . . My script was scratched to pieces. I'd sit up nights and restore scenes [that] were right just the way she had written them."[10]

Olive Higgins Prouty: "I took part in the writing of the film. . . . There wasn't a single page that escaped my comments in red type. Sometimes I added an extra page or two. . . . The few portions of my suggestions that were accepted made the effort worthwhile."[11]

Casey Robinson: "There was a small annoyance in the beginning in that Hal Wallis kept sending the material back to the author, and we used to get a few letters from Prouty picking on this little point or that. . . . As I say, this was an annoyance, but it was no more than a mosquito bite. . . . I've never read Bette Davis's book, but there was never, *never* one word changed in any of the scripts that I wrote for her—by Miss Davis, by a director, by anybody—and that is a flat statement, a true statement, and final."[12]

Now, Voyager began shooting on April 7, 1942, and finished on June 23, with some retakes on July 3. The production went fairly smoothly. Bette missed a day or two of shooting a week and a half into the production because of laryngitis, but there seem to have been no major tantrums. Minor ones, yes. Practically daily. Ilka Chase describes Davis as "a fine, hard-working woman, friendly with members of her cast, forthright and courteous to technicians on her picture, and her director's heaviest cross. She will argue every move in every scene until the poor man is reduced to quivering pulp." Dark storm clouds hovered on only one particular day; Chase calls it "a morning of heavy weather." They were shooting on the Vale mansion set. Davis was inevitably out of makeup fifteen minutes ahead of schedule, Chase reports, and "the occasion of which I speak was no exception. She was ready but remained closeted in her portable dressing room, a brooding Ajax, while the set simmered in a miasma of gloom." Irving Rapper "sat in his canvas chair staring moodily at his fingertips" as everyone else milled around trying not to make the situation worse. Finally Bette emerged from her dressing room. "Gone the comradely smile, the cigarette breezily proffered. Hers was a mien blighted yet austere. Here, you said to yourself, is one who has suffered; here is a woman who has sampled the dregs and found them bitter."

The assistant director explained Davis's despondency to Chase sotto voce: "Last night she saw *In This Our Life*."[13]

World War II intruded briefly on the production of *Now, Voyager*. During some location shooting at Laguna Beach in May, a navy officer appeared to be stalking the star. Davis was a bit concerned but decided to approach him directly and ask if he wanted an autograph. "No," young Edward Hubbell replied; "I'm sorta here to censor the Pacific Ocean." Hubbell's job was to make sure that the film didn't reveal any details of the shoreline.[14]

Davis begins *Now, Voyager* looking hideous. Warner Bros.' theatrical trailer for the film featured only the glamorous swan phase of Charlotte's life, pointedly leaving out the ugly duckling overture, so contemporary audiences had no preparation for the mess they were about to encounter. Rapper reveals Charlotte Vale first by her hands as they nervously dispose of two cigarette stubs in a wastebasket, then by her orthopedically stockinged legs and frumpy, flat-heeled shoes as she ventures tentatively down her mother's imposing staircase. These isolated body parts hesitate and start to turn back before proceeding—an effective way of getting across Charlotte's fearful shyness. Rapper's slow revelation is a clever tease for what's to come, but more subtly the sequence fragments Charlotte visually as a way of expressing her disjointed emotional state. Only then does Rapper reveal her wholly in long shot as she comes around the corner and into the drawing room. And oh, she's a fright. Here's Bette Davis with bushy eyebrows and mouse-colored hair pulled back in a hank. She's wearing an ugly oversized print dress filled out by cotton batting. It's the most extreme uglification that Davis had ever done, and it's gasp inducing. It's also a point of intense audience identification, since most of us feel precisely that way at one point or another in our lives.

Now, Voyager is much more astute about the positive healing effects of psychotherapy than it is about the process. When Dr. Jaquith enters the Vale mansion, he taps his pipe against a vast urn to remove ashes and bits of unburned tobacco. The racket greatly disturbs the elderly Mrs. Vale, but Dr. Jaquith doesn't care. What he tells the butler neatly sums up his vision of psychiatry: "Messy things, pipes. I like 'em." But the film's depiction of Charlotte's actual treatment at Cascade, Dr. Jaquith's country club–like sanatorium, elides the raw, even filthy work of regaining mental health in favor of a productive weaving session. Still, Robinson in his screenplay, Rapper in his direction, and Davis in her performance all appreciate the tentative nature of the results. Charlotte emerges from Cascade looking fabulous on the outside but remaining wobbly within. Hal Wallis wisely had Rapper cut a scene he'd filmed of a newly discharged Charlotte being refashioned at a beauty salon, thereby intensifying the big reveal at the top of the gangplank of a cruise ship heading for South America. In an echo of Charlotte's introductory sequence, Rapper begins with a fragment—her feet and legs, now shapely and clad in fine silk stockings and high heels—only this time he unveils her in a single, unified shot that cranes up rapidly past a tailored black suit all the way to Charlotte's newly plucked eyebrows, shaped lips, and chic new broad-brimmed hat. And yet as the shot and the costuming make clear, she's still Charlotte Vale, with all the homonym implies; far from being fully brought to light, this is a woman still partially hidden, her eyes only briefly visible, her face concealed not only by the hat's brim but also through a veil of exquisite fine black netting.

A bit of business in *Now, Voyager* became an instant sensation when the film was released in the fall of 1942 and remains one of the most delightful screen gimmicks of all time. According to Paul Henreid, Casey Robinson's script instructed him at one point "to offer Bette a cigarette, take one myself, light mine, then take her cigarette out of her mouth, give her mine, and put hers between my lips." Henreid practiced the routine with his wife, Lisl, but neither of them could get it right, and it became farcical. Then they tried it the way they did it themselves when driving: Henreid put two cigarettes in his mouth, lit them both, and handed one to his wife.

Bette went for the idea. The bit was not only simpler and cleaner but also a hell of a lot more romantic. They took it to Irving Rapper, who hated it. Bette, always prone to overruling her director, insisted that Hal Wallis come down to the soundstage right away and see it for himself. Wallis appeared, witnessed it, and approved it. In fact—at least according to Henreid—Wallis liked it so much he had Casey Robinson add two more occasions for the couple to perform it later in the film. In the completed *Now, Voyager*, the double cigarette lighting occurs three times: first at the airport in Rio when Charlotte and Jerry part after their five-day affair (and as the film historian Tom Phillips points out, we're all mature enough to assume that they've slept with each other); next when Charlotte agrees to marry the pleasant but bland Elliot Livingston and Jerry inadvertently proves to Charlotte how wrong her decision is by putting two cigarettes in his mouth and lighting them; and finally in the film's closing moments, just before Jerry asks Charlotte if she will ever be happy, and Charlotte responds with one of the most eloquent expressions of sublimated desire in all cinema: "Oh, Jerry—don't let's ask for the moon. We have the stars!"

My mother tells me that my grandfather, like many men around the country in 1942, began lighting two cigarettes at a time thanks to the suave Paul Henreid. (Unfortunately for my grandfather, my grandmother didn't smoke.) Equally charmed by the routine, fans grew pushy and began accosting Henreid, demanding that he perform the cigarette routine for them on the spot. A drunken woman charged up to him at the New York restaurant Voisin and noisily called for a command performance. Henreid told Bette about the incident later, and Bette gave him a piece of blunt advice: "I tell people like that, 'Leave me alone. I don't know you, and you don't know me.'" Henreid was aghast. "But that's so rude!" To which Davis replied matter-of-factly, "Believe me— rudeness is the only thing that works in a situation like that."[15]

But as with many tales of Hollywood glory, there is another version of the double-lighting bit. "Mr. Wallis did not come onto the set at all," Irving Rapper insisted. "And it was my idea, not that of Henreid, who has gone on taking credit for it ever since."[16]

Rapper, who had just directed *The Gay Sisters*, was one himself. Like Edmund Goulding, Rapper appreciated, with whatever degree of consciousness, that so-called women's pictures were also appealing to a certain strain of man. *Now, Voyager* suggests a gay man's quest for self-acceptance as much as it explicitly tells of an independent, free-thinking woman's emergence from a state of self-loathing and sexual inhibition. Bette Davis is his embodiment as well as hers.

Because overt expressions of homosexuality were explicitly forbidden by the Production Code, Hollywood had to inscribe gayness delicately, if at all. Here, it's an oh-so-proto-gay character actor, the ever-fluttering Franklin Pangborn, who scurries onto the scene just in time to introduce Charlotte to Jerry. Like Eric Blore's many onscreen performances (including that of Leslie Howard's manservant in *It's Love I'm After*, whom Bonita Granville spies through the keyhole declaring his love to Howard—they're really acting out a theatrical scene), Pangborn's appearance is a wink at a knowing gay audience. He's the ship's busy-bee social director, as gay a job as a hairdresser or florist. "Ah, Miss Beauchamps! Here you are! We've been waiting for you!" Pangborn squeals. (Charlotte is traveling under an assumed name.) Then, in a flurry: "Miss Beauchamps! Miss Beauchamps? Allow me to introduce Mr. Durrance. . . . You're travelling alone, and he's travelling alone, and, and so, that's *splendid!*" Pangborn pops up at the end of the cruise, too. As Lisa and June stand by at the pier, flabbergasted by Charlotte's transformation from dowdy spinster to chic socialite, a couple starts to bid Charlotte good-bye, but Pangborn scurries into the shot and stops them: "Don't anybody say good-bye! *Not anybody!* Just 'au revoir!'" His rapid-fire line delivery is breathless and funny, like a machine gun shooting violets: "It *is* a sad time, isn't it, but I want to tell you one thing—there was no lady on this cruise that was as popular as you were. Au revoir!"

Eve Sedgwick may have founded queer theory on the concept of the epistemology of the closet, but gay men know the ontology of theater equally well—the being of acting, the essential reality that only stylization can fully reveal. Bette Davis remains its prime exemplar in the cinema, with fussy, prissy, witty character actors like Pangborn and Blore serving as grace notes. In *Now, Voyager*, as elsewhere, Davis's theatricality hints at something existentially honest; her mannerisms express core emotional truths. Charles Busch describes it in the practical terms of a working actor and playwright: "What I find interesting about her is that while she's the most stylized of all those Hollywood actresses, the most mannered, she's also to me the most psychologically acute. You see it in *Now, Voyager* in the scene on the boat when she starts to cry, and she's playing it in a very romantic style. Henreid says, 'My darling—you are crying,' and she says, 'These are only tears of gratitude—an old maid's gratitude for the crumbs offered.' It's very movie-ish, but the way she turns her head inward, away from the camera, is very real."[17]

In the instance Busch so perceptively describes and appreciates, Davis uses her melodramatic mannerisms and breathy, teary vocal delivery as well as her seemingly spontaneous nuzzling into Henreid's chest to express the undeniable legitimacy of self-pity. It's not a pretty emotion, but Davis somehow makes it so. Through Davis's elevating, sublimating stylization, this woman's secret shame becomes beautiful.

Stanley Cavell, referring to melodramas of female abnegation, *Now, Voyager* in particular, astutely asks, "Is it that the women in them are sacrificing themselves to the sad necessities of a world they are forced to accept? Or isn't it rather that the women are claiming the right to judge a world as second-rate that enforces this sacrifice; to refuse, transcend, its proposal of second-rate sadness?"[18] In light of Cavell's observations, it's little wonder that Bette Davis became an icon for several generations of gay men, who learned through bitter experience the severe limits mainstream culture imposes on rebellious selves. But gay men also learned that they could, through wit and style and camp, rise above this oppressive, second-rate world and, inside at least, be the men they were meant to be. Bette Davis helped make this transcendence possible. They knew they couldn't shoot for the moon, but they didn't have to. They had a star.

IN MAY 1942, while Bette was filming *Now, Voyager*, the columnist Sidney Skolsky put out an amusing tidbit: Farney had begun speaking to Bette in an Austrian accent to counter the European charms of Paul Henreid.[19] The Henreids and the Farnsworths socialized often. Henreid found Farney to be "the perfect husband for Bette. He didn't interfere with her professional life but let her do as she pleased, and we could sense the warmth and love between them."[20] "Our light was a low one but steady," Davis wrote in *The Lonely Life*. "He didn't have an ounce of jealousy. He never questioned me about anything I did. He let me run my own life."[21]

In January, after spending their anniversary in the California desert, in part to improve Farney's health, Bette and Farney had headed for Butternut, with a stopover in New York for a Red Cross benefit radio broadcast with Helen Hayes. Also that month, the trade gossip columnist Harrison Carroll debunked what he called "stork rumors" for Bette.[22]

The renovation of Butternut continued with the building of an immense barn. The structure was designed for neither livestock nor hay, though it did feature a windowed circular silo on the side. There was a large picture window on the end, and an open balcony ran along half the structure. Inside was one great room on the first floor with a kitchen area on one end and a living room space on the other. The kitchen had a huge brick fireplace, the living room a squared, built-in couch done up in red upholstery. The second floor was more traditional in look and furnishings: there were defined bedrooms as well as a library. The Farnsworths had moved some of their furniture from Riverbottom, including a large four-poster bed. Their caretaker, Phil Bilodeaux, and his family now lived on the property in the cottage Davis built for them.

The Farnsworths returned to New York in time for a huge benefit for the Navy Relief Fund at Madison Square Garden on March 10; the party was still rocking at midnight and raised over $160,000. Bette also showed up at the Stage Door Canteen on West Forty-fourth Street. Taking the mike from a wisecracking comedian, she announced, "I can't sing or tell stories, but I'll be glad to dance with anyone who cares to dance with me." Scores of the soldiers and sailors took her up on the offer for about half an hour.

The Farnsworths planned to stop in Chicago to see Ethel Barrymore appear in the Emlyn Williams play *The Corn Is Green*—it was more of a professional call than a social one—but Bette got so sick to her stomach that she had to be carried off the train. She and Farney checked into the Blackmore Hotel, where she was examined by doctors who diagnosed the malady as ptomaine poisoning; evidently she'd eaten something contaminated. To make matters worse, one of her trunks went missing. She reported the loss of a fur coat, several suits and dresses, and lingerie she valued at $2,000. After more than a year went by with neither the trunk being found nor restitution having been offered; she ended up suing the New York Central Railroad and the Pullman Company.

Farney and Bette parted in Chicago, Farney heading back to Minneapolis, Bette for Los Angeles.

Bʜᴇᴛᴛᴇ Dᴀᴠɪs ᴡᴀs finally earning the money she deserved. According to the studio's annual report filed with the Securities and Exchange Commission in May 1942, Warner Bros. had paid her $271,083 the previous year. (Satisfyingly for Bette, this was $11,000 more than Hal Wallis earned.) She was still making less than the top male stars— Cagney took in a whopping $362,500 in 1941, $5,000 more than Clark Gable—but it was a vast improvement over what she'd made earlier.[23] Still, these top wage earners actually banked little of their earnings. The Revenue Act of 1941 capped the top tax bracket at $200,000, at which point anyone earning that or more would owe a whopping 90 percent of his or her income to the government. To avoid what would have amounted to working for the U.S. Treasury, major movie stars had a choice: they could reduce the number of films they made, thereby reducing both their income and their tax liability, or they could move away from contracts and salaries toward one-picture deals with profit-sharing plans. Their income would thus be taxable as capital gains at a rate of 25 percent.[24] Indeed, Bette made far fewer pictures per year after 1941, and she did eventually launch her own production company.

After finishing *Now, Voyager*, Bette traveled in June to Bates College in Lewiston, Maine, to accept an honorary Doctor of Laws degree in the name of her father, who had graduated from Bates thirty-five years earlier. Naturally, Harlow had been valedictorian of his class.[25]

Characteristically outspoken, and scarcely intimidated by any petty instructions she might have been given by Warners' publicity men, she'd been offering opinions on the war's impact on American culture, not to mention Americans' love lives, for some time already. "What the moving pictures need is more sex and fewer preachments," she preached to the *Oakland Tribune*. Hollywood was turning out blunt propaganda, and Davis had confidence in little of it. "There are too many war and Nazi pictures," she declared. "It's sex—or at least a reasonable facsimile thereof—that the public wants."[26]

Meanwhile, the monthly advice column she wrote and signed for *Photoplay* often answered questions about how far young American women should go in the war effort. It's likely that these columns were actually penned by publicists or *Photoplay* staffers, but they do put across Davis's voice and tough-mindedness. "Don't Be a Draft Bride" was the title of her column in January 1941. "The kindness you think you were doing [by marrying a soldier on his way into the military] would turn into a hideous boomerang for both," Bette advised an anxious letter writer. "Far kinder—and wiser—to say no now, thereby serving your country as well as your two selves."[27] (By which she meant the girl and the boy, not that the girl had multiple personality disorder.) She gave similar advice to "Eleanor J." in December 1942, though this time the letter writer had already married the draftee only to find that she wanted to date her old flame in his absence. "It seems selfish for a boy to want to marry just before he leaves for camp," Davis wrote. "This is just a man's way of putting a girl on the shelf for the duration although he can do nothing for her—not even offer her companionship. It is, in fact, a type of hoarding." As for Eleanor's old flame, Bette advised, "Beware of propinquity."[28]

She'd helped sell $40,000 worth of war bonds during her trip to New England in January, but the September tour aimed much higher. A coordinated effort between the Treasury Department and the Hollywood

War Activities Committee, September's "Stars Over America" was the culmination of a nine-month drive by such big names as Davis, Walter Pidgeon, Adolphe Menjou, Ralph Bellamy, Ronald Colman, Janet Gaynor, Ginger Rogers, Edward Arnold, Gene Tierney, Andy Devine, James Cagney, Fred Astaire, Dorothy Lamour, Jane Wyman, Greer Garson, Veronica Lake, Hedy Lamarr, Irene Dunne, Paulette Goddard, Myrna Loy, and Charles Laughton. In September alone, "Stars Over America" sold $775 million worth of bonds, including $86 million raised at a huge rally at Madison Square Garden.

Bette Davis was righteously angry about what she saw as the nation's lack of commitment to the war effort, and she didn't hesitate to let the public know it. "I think it is outrageous that movie stars have to wheedle and beg people into buying bonds to help their country," she told one reporter. "But if that's the way it is, I'm going to squeeze all I can out of everyone."[29] She visited cities and towns in Iowa, Illinois, Missouri, Oklahoma, and Kansas, appearing in large civic auditoriums, schools, Rotary meetings, and even private homes. She was on a mission, and Bette Davis on a mission was unstoppable. She badgered a group of factory workers into buying more bonds by informing them that they had better give at their "top level—or you're not my idea of an American." Advised to be little more discreet, Bette held even faster to her approach: "It lights fires under their asses," she declared.[30]

Jack Warner told her she was taking the wrong tack, but his pleading was to no avail. "Jack," she responded, "you and your brother in New York just sit around and count the money I make for you. I'm the one who has to deal up front with the public, and I know what I'm doing."[31]

Her stop in St. Joseph, Missouri, brought in $177,000. She appeared before a crowd of 250 at the Hotel Robidoux, gave a short speech, and raised $77,000 in the first ten minutes; the rest of the pot came pouring in at the town auditorium. "Isn't this a wonderful country to fight for?" she asked the enthusiastic crowd. In Kansas City alone she helped raise as much as $650,000. Her pace was frenetic. She arrived in Tulsa from Springfield on Monday, September 14, and immediately drove to Muskogee for a speech at an ironworks and a rally at a movie theater, then back to Tulsa that afternoon for a visit to a Douglas Aircraft factory, where she sold a portrait of herself as *Jezebel*'s Julie Marsden for $250,000. In the evening was another rally at the 18,000-seat Skelly Stadium, where she sold a single autograph for $50,000. On Tuesday morning she drove two hours to Oklahoma City for a civic luncheon, stopped by the offices of a publishing company in the afternoon, and appeared at a bond rally at the Municipal Auditorium that evening. She took the train back to Los Angeles on Wednesday morning, promptly came down with a bad cold, and had to be hospitalized.[32]

She adored Franklin Roosevelt and hated anyone who didn't. And she was deeply, morally offended: by Hitler, by fascism, by complacency. As Bette wrote to a friend, despite the fact that she found "great enthusiasm" and "raised millions of dollars" and enjoyed "probably the most satisfying experience I've ever had," she was still disheartened. It wasn't the fact that the temperature hovered around one hundred degrees; nor was it "the strain of being polite and charming 24 hours a day—you know, a rebel can't bear that!" It was that the midwesterners she met struck her as being profoundly out of touch: "In spite of this outward show of 'God Bless America,' such *nonsense* they are hanging on to with the belief that the war will never touch them personally, so why worry?"[33]

At the time she wrote those words, Bette Davis was about to see her own major work for the war effort come to fruition. She and John Garfield began imagining the Hollywood Canteen at a table in the Warners commissary soon after the war started. "Johnny Garfield sat down at my table during lunch," Bette later wrote. "He had been thinking about the thousands of servicemen who were passing through Hollywood without seeing any movie stars. Garfield said something ought to be done about it. I agreed, and then and there the idea for the Hollywood Canteen was born."[34] New York's Stage Door Canteen was up and running, but there was no similar venue for the GIs who shipped out through Los Angeles. So with the help of Jules Stein, the head of the Music Corporation of America, many other stars, and—as Davis was always quick to point out—"the forty-two unions and guilds that made up the motion picture industry," they took over a building at 1415 Cahuenga Boulevard and set up a large nightclub for service members. Alfred Ybarra, an MGM art director, supervised the decoration and provided items that (in his view anyway) MGM no longer needed. Other studio artists also chipped in with time, labor, and studio property. Bob Taplinger, who had moved from Warners to Columbia, organized a fund-raiser: the premiere of Columbia's comedy-drama *The Talk of the Town*, followed by dinner at Ciro's.

On opening night, October 3, 1942, spectators paid one hundred dollars each to sit on bleachers and watch 2,000 servicemen enter through

THE DAVIS GIRLS ▦ Ruth Elizabeth "Betty" Davis (holding Margaret, her favorite doll), Ruth Favor Davis, and Barbara Davis on a summer day

HARLOW MORELL DAVIS ▦ A formal portrait of Bette's strict, stonily intellectual father

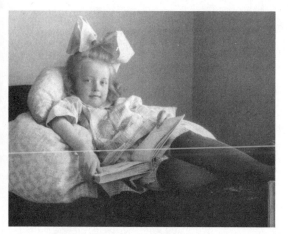

WITH A RIBBON IN HER HAIR ▦ Bette's mother, Ruthie, was fond of adorning her hair with elaborate ribbons.

BETTE, BY RUTHIE Ruthie had become a successful commercial photographer by the time she took this portrait of Bette at the time of her high school graduation.

DELICATE FLOWER Though her beauty was always unconventional, Bette gives the lie to Carl Laemmle Jr.'s comment "She has about as much sex appeal as Slim Summerville."

BEAUTY IN THE EYES Despite what some might consider her face's flaws, Davis was every bit as lovely as any Hollywood star.

UNUSUAL PORTRAIT ▦ Bette Davis's beauty was both odd and unmistakable enough to accommodate even this extreme lighting treatment, reminiscent of Elsa Lanchester's in *The Bride of Frankenstein*.

"I ALWAYS USED TO WIPE MY MOUTH!" ▦ Despite the attempt to glamorize Bette's vulgar Mildred Rogers in *Of Human Bondage* in this publicity shot, one can still see that Davis didn't care how repulsive she had to look onscreen when the role demanded it.

HAM AND SPUDS ▦

Ham and Spuds: Bette's first husband, Harmon O. "Ham" Nelson, nicknamed her "Spuds." They are seen here at Pebble Beach in 1935.

BETTE AS RASPUTIN? ▦

Unconcerned with convention even in her leisure time, Davis appeared as a bearded lady at William Randolph Hearst's circus-themed birthday party held on the beach at Santa Monica in May 1937. From left: Leslie Howard, Ronald Howard, Mrs. Leslie Howard, and bearded Bette.

JEZEBEL ▦ A Warner Bros. stills photographer's striking rendition of the moment when Julie kneels before Preston (Henry Fonda), begging his forgiveness

"HOMELY DYNAMO" ▦ That was Davis's description of William Wyler, her director on *Jezebel* (depicted here), *The Letter*, and *The Little Foxes*, and her lover at the time this publicity still was taken.

WEDDING DAY NUMBER 2 ▦ Bette, caught unaware of the photographer, celebrates her marriage to Arthur Farnsworth as her sister, Bobby, looks on.

SISTERS ON THE SET ▦ Bette and Bobby on location in Death Valley during the filming of *The Bride Came C.O.D.*

"LIKE A MINK" ▦ Bette Davis was a popular attraction among the servicemen at the Hollywood Canteen, which she cofounded with John Garfield in 1942.

WEDDING DAY NUMBER 3 ▦ Bette and William Grant Sherry celebrate their marriage in Riverside, California, in 1945.

THE EVIL EYE ▦
Gale Sondergaard, as Mrs. Geoff Hammond, shoots Bette a suspicious glance in *The Letter*—and rightly so, since Bette's sociopathic character has murdered Hammond.

PERITONITIS SETS IN ▦
Rosa Moline (Bette, wearing what Edward Albee's Martha calls a "fright wig") is beginning to get feverish in *Beyond the Forest*, a film Davis despised. She's ignoring the ministrations of her husband (Joseph Cotton).

MAUDLIN AND MAGNIFICENT ▦ Davis, Marilyn Monroe, and George Sanders exchange pleasantries before the night becomes bumpy in *All About Eve*.

TWO'S COMPANY
▦ Bette parodies Jeanne Eagels's performance as Sadie Thompson in *Rain*, complete with a broken umbrella, in Davis's ill-fated musical revue, which closed on March 8, 1953.

A BETTE DAVIS WESTERN?
▦ In "The Elizabeth McQueeny Story," an episode of *Wagon Train*, Davis plays what she calls an "impresario." Yes, of a whorehouse.

DESIGNED BY BETTE ▦

For her role in *What Ever Happened to Baby Jane?*, Davis designed her own makeup; her theory was that her character, Jane Hudson, never washed her face — she just applied a new layer of powder every day.

ON BROADWAY ▦

Davis played the earthy, salty Maxine Faulk in Tennessee Williams's *The Night of the Iguana*, which opened in December 1961.

"LET'S CLEAR OUT. I DRAW THE LINE AT THIS CROWD." ▦
A previously unpublished cartoon by the great Charles Addams celebrating the release of *What Ever Happened to Baby Jane?*

JOAN, BY BETTE ▦ Davis doctored this 8 x 10 glossy of Crawford and pasted it into one of her scrapbooks around the time of the *Hush...Hush, Sweet Charlotte* contretemps.

LUSH LIFE ▦
Bette and Gary
Merrill — each
looking a little
lulled — dancing
together, circa 1950

POETRY ONSTAGE ▦ Bette Davis, Carl Sandburg, and Gary Merrill enjoy the success of *The World of Carl Sandburg*, a stage adaptation of Sandburg's poetry.

BETTE, HER DAUGHTER MARGOT, AND DINNER ▦ Bette had a lobster pit specially built into her Bel Air patio to bring a bit of her beloved Maine to Southern California.

MOTHER, DAUGHTER, AND SON ▦ Bette, B.D., and Mike at Honeysuckle Hill, circa 1964

IT WORKS ▦ Davis loved playing the horrendous mother in *The Anniversary*; here, in the last scene, she toys with a model of the Mannekin Pis.

MISS MOFFAT ▦ Davis reprised her role as the schoolteacher who helps one of her students rise above his station in life in this stage adaptation of *The Corn Is Green*, though the action is transferred from Wales to the American South.

MADAME SIN AND HER PET HAWK ▦
Davis attempts to steal a Polaris submarine in this 1972 ABC *Movie of the Weekend* thriller, costarring (and co-produced by) her friend Robert Wagner.

LAST PICTURE SHOW ▦
Not counting *Wicked Stepmother*, which she didn't complete, *The Whales of August*, costarring Lillian Gish (left) was Davis's last film.

THE WORLD'S MOST FAMOUS SMOKER ▦ Bette Davis, 1979, New York City

P.S. BETTE DAVIS ▦ Davis's fearless-fighter spirit is captured well in this portrait, taken after her stroke and mastectomy. Note that she's still smoking.

a door over which was inscribed "Through these portals pass the most beautiful uniforms in the world." Five thousand soldiers had to be turned away for lack of room. Civilians, stars included, had to use the side entrance.[35]

Just as she'd been as a Girl Scout leader in New York City, Davis was a taskmaster, but she only worked others as hard as she pushed herself. As Hedy Lamarr later recalled, "One night after a rough day at the studio, I went right home and to bed. I was dozing off when Bette called. Several actresses who had promised to work that night for one reason or another couldn't make it. I protested, but Bette was insistent. I told her that the way I looked I'd do more harm than the enemy." Bette brushed Lamarr's exhaustion aside, and Lamarr soon found herself reporting for duty at the Canteen. "I went to the kitchen and helped put some sandwiches together, and then I saw about two hundred unwashed cups piled in the sink. Bette smiled and said, 'I washed the last few hundred. Now it's someone else's turn.' "[36] Davis handed the job over to Lamarr, telling her that a guy standing nearby would dry them, thereby introducing Hedy to her next husband, John Loder. They married within the year.

Bette's can-do or, better, *must*-do style engendered some resentment among the Canteen's leaders, just as her take-charge attitude had inspired antipathy at the Academy. The Hollywood Victory Committee, led by Jimmy Cagney, insisted that Davis's policy of calling stars herself was inappropriate and that henceforth she would have to go through the committee to get celebrities to show up. Bette pointed out that the committee had agreed to let her and her team call people at the last minute if necessary, and that the terms of this agreement were clearly spelled out in the past minutes. "Regrettably," Cagney replied, "the minutes of that meeting have been lost." Bette responded with a volley of unveiled threats: unless the committee reversed its idiotic decision, she'd call the press, call the unions, call the guilds, close the Canteen. . . . She got her way.[37]

Marlene Dietrich generally worked the cooking detail, though Johnny Carson, then a navy cadet, fondly recalled dancing with her. Dietrich once appeared fresh from the set of *Kismet*, still clad in gold paint. "I had never seen two thousand men screaming in a state of near mass hysteria," Bette observed, adding that "Marlene was one of the most generous in the amount of time she spent at the Canteen." The Gabor sisters were waitresses, as were Kay Francis and Greer Garson. (Zsa Zsa once commented of Bette's taste in clothing, "Vell, she doesn't have very much dress zense.")[38] Joan Crawford showed up one night and was instantly surrounded by fans and autograph seekers. Davis broke it up: "Hello, Joan," she said after muscling her way through the crowd. "We need you *desperately* in the kitchen. There are dishes to be washed."[39] It was nothing personal. That would come later. Bette merely saw the need to clean up stacks of dirty plates and glasses, and Crawford happened to be nearby.

Bing Crosby and his three small sons showed up and sang on Christmas Eve. "There was not a dry eye in the Canteen," Davis remembered. "Roddy McDowall came night after night, helping us out as a busboy. Mrs. John Ford, the director's wife, was in charge of the kitchen from the night the Canteen opened to the closing night. Saturday was Kay Kyser's night. I cannot remember Kay and his band ever missing one Saturday, even though sometimes it was necessary to fly the band back from some distant engagement."[40]

Davis issued instructions to the Canteen's volunteer hostesses on how to treat the men, particularly the wounded ones. "Forget the wounds, remember the man," Davis's printed instructions read. "Don't be over-solicitous, nor too controlled to the point of indifference. Learn to use the word 'prosthetics' instead of 'artificial limbs.' Never say, 'It could have been worse.' And when he talks about his war experiences, *listen*, but don't ask for more details than he wants to give."[41]

One soldier showed up the day before the Canteen opened and found a familiar-looking woman sweeping the floor. "Say," he said, "you look like you were Bette Davis." Bette told him that she still was. "Well, lady," the GI replied, "your pictures certainly stink, but you look like sweetness and light now."[42]

DAVIS MAY HAVE urged other stars and studio to eschew war-themed propaganda in favor of sex, but she herself agreed to appear in Warner Bros.' adaptation of Lillian Hellman's play *Watch on the Rhine*, and she did so largely as a favor to the studio; her presence certainly helped sell the overtly political film. Tactlessly, she made her pronouncements about the national need for onscreen sex in June, just as the sex-free *Watch on the Rhine* began shooting.

The play, which opened on April 1, 1941, and ran for 378 performances (closing in February 1942), is set in 1940, before the United

States entered the war, and it concerns an ardently anti-Nazi German, Kurt Muller; his American-born wife, Sara; their three children; Teck de Brancovis, an oily Rumanian count who has been currying favor with the Nazis; and Teck's wife, the pretty but naive Marthe.

Although both Paul Henreid and Charles Boyer were screen-tested for Kurt, the role ultimately went to the Hungarian-born Paul Lukas (né Pál Lukács). Margaret Sullavan and Irene Dunne were briefly considered for Sara, but Hal Wallis ultimately asked Bette to play the part—"for name value," she later explained.[43] There was, however, a contretemps about her casting. Bette argued, strenuously, that she should *not* get top billing. *Watch on the Rhine*, she said, belonged to Paul Lukas, so his name should come first. On May 14, Warner Bros.' Roy Obringer reported to Jack Warner that he had been arguing about the issue with Dudley Furse, Bette's lawyer, and that Furse had taken Warners' case to Bette once again but had failed to change her mind. "While she is willing to do the picture, Lukas has the choice part and she does not want to appear ridiculous by taking first position billing," Obringer reported. "I am sure she will permit us to bill her first," Hal Wallis confidently told Obringer the following day.[44] Eventually, she did.

Dashiell Hammett wrote the script with some help from Hellman, and it stuck closely to the plot of the play. The Production Code office voiced a choice objection: Kurt's killing of Teck—in other words, a member of the Resistance killing a Nazi sympathizer—not only went without punishment but was clearly justified. This, to the Production Code Administration, was wrong. That the wormy Teck deserves what he gets is the moral linchpin of the play, but the vigilant Hays Office, consumed with its own sense of dumbed-down propriety, was compelled to find a way around Hellman's hardheaded ethical question. The hero of the piece could still kill the villain, the PCA ruled, as long as Warners made it crystal clear that the Nazis ended up murdering the hero in the end. Hellman thought the suggestion was inane and offensive. Warner Bros. agreed.[45]

Herman Shumlin, who had directed the Broadway production, was signed to direct the film, which was shot between June 9 and August 22. The part of Marthe went to Geraldine Fitzgerald; George Coulouris reprised his portrayal of Teck. Bette had taken an interest in young Janis Wilson during the filming of *Now, Voyager* and recommended her for the role of Babette, Sara's daughter.[46]

"It was not ever my favorite part, except for one speech about being alone at night," Davis told Dick Cavett in 1971, whereupon Cavett played the clip: "I don't like to be alone at night. I guess everybody in the world has a time they don't like. Mine is right before I go to sleep. And now it's going to be for always—all the rest of my life."[47] It's the understated Davis we see throughout *Watch on the Rhine*, and never more so than when she's delivering these lines with a sad smile. There are no hand-wringing, hair-clutching, neck-bending revelations of inner turmoil; just a woman letting herself know that she will forever spend her life's worst moments alone.

"STORIES OF WOMEN are always box-office," Bette declared in a 1945 note to Jack Warner. "Witness the lousy picture *Old Acquaintance*. (I'm sure you agree with this opinion privately and not for publication.)"[48]

Davis may have been a bit hyperbolic with the word *lousy*, and Warner's private opinion of the movie is unrecorded. But Bette's assessment is more or less on target. Given Davis's pairing with Miriam Hopkins, *Old Acquaintance* ought to be livelier, pricklier. Hopkins and Davis were more than capable of generating the crackling onscreen chemistry born of authentic, deep-seated hatred, and yet the picture is sluggish in a paradoxically brittle sort of way. *Rich and Famous*, George Cukor's 1981 remake starring Jacqueline Bisset in the Davis role and Candice Bergen in Hopkins's, is much snappier.

The production didn't get off to an easy start. Warner Bros. bought the screen rights to John Van Druten's play about two old friends, each a successful writer, for $75,000. Rosalind Russell and Irene Dunne are said to have been briefly considered for the role of Kit Marlowe, the more cerebral of the two authors, but the role was clearly Davis's almost from the start.

Her clout was greater than that of the film's first director. Originally assigned to direct *Old Acquaintance*, Edmund Goulding worked on early drafts of the script (which is credited to Van Druten and Lenore Coffee), but Davis's demands got to him, as did the prospect of dealing with an encore performance of the Davis-Hopkins feud. What had animated Goulding's *The Old Maid* artistically had debilitated Goulding personally. As Vincent Sherman, who ended up directing the picture, said, "I was told later that Goulding had gone through *The Old Maid* with these two ladies, and he just felt he wasn't up to it."[49] Goulding dreaded the bickering and one-upwomanship, Hopkins's upstaging and Davis's complaints, and according to Matthew Kennedy he tried to avoid the whole thing by suggesting Constance Bennett or Janet Gaynor or Margaret Sullavan instead of Hopkins for the role of Millie, to no avail.[50]

Bette called Norma Shearer personally and asked her to costar with her. Shearer talked with Goulding about it, assuming she was to play Kit, but Goulding corrected her—"But, Norma, Bette wants you to play the bitch who writes the trash!"—and Shearer wanted no part of it.[51] One story has it that Davis herself became exasperated and said, "Get Miriam. At least she can *do* it."

Goulding, says Sherman, was also chafed by Davis's ability to overrule his choice of cinematographer. Henry Blanke told Goulding he was going to assign Tony Gaudio, only to turn around and give the job to Bette's choice, Sol Polito. Irritated and unnerved, Goulding sent a telegram to Jack Warner: "This is no temperamental or childish whim but very solid and businesslike conviction that I am either working for Warner Bros. or Miss Davis, and there is a difference."[52] Goulding appears to have realized, however, that the picture hinged on Davis, not himself, and he became so upset that, as Kennedy writes, "he stressed himself right into another health crisis. In October, he was hospitalized with a bad flu, had his contract suspended, recovered his health, then suffered a relapse in December. There was a rumor circulating through studio gossip that he faked a heart attack, but he didn't fake anything. It's true that he left *Old Acquaintance* with nary a backward glance, but he was genuinely sick."[53] Irving Rapper was briefly mentioned as Goulding's replacement, but Sherman ended up taking the job.

There's a bland, underwritten male role in *Old Acquaintance*—that of Millie's husband, Preston Drake—so naturally George Brent was announced for it. But Brent joined the Coast Guard, and the part was handed to Franchot Tone, who turned it down.[54] (The Warner Bros. archives contain Tone's unsigned contract for $60,000.) John Loder—Elliot Livingston, Charlotte Vale's short-term fiancé in *Now, Voyager*—was cast instead.

Sherman began shooting *Old Acquaintance* on November 11, 1942, starting with scenes between Hopkins and Loder. Bette was finishing up a vacation in Palm Springs. A few days later she appeared at the studio with her new agent, Lew Wasserman. ("I've had most of them from time to time," Bette once said of agents. She had at least eighteen of them during her career.[55]) They watched Hopkins's rushes, and according to

Sherman, Bette called him an hour later from the projection room, saying, "I just think it's marvelous! I don't know how you got Miriam to do all those things—they were wonderful!"[56] She reported to the studio the following morning and began shooting. That's when the fun and games started.

"I hadn't been in the business long enough to realize that there were so many tricks that could be played," Sherman later admitted. "Let's say for instance the two of them were sitting on the sofa in the living room. I'd make an over-the-shoulder scene. Well, Miriam came to me once and said, 'Do you mind if I use this long cigarette holder for this character?' I said no, I think that's right for her. Well, the camera's back of her and I'm shooting across her shoulder on Davis, and Miriam would take a puff of the cigarette and hold the cigarette right across Davis' face. And I said, 'Oh, Miriam, please, honey.' She said, 'Oh! I was just trying to match up what I did before.' And Davis knew, of course, and would burn."

At one point, Hopkins suggested that she and Davis figure out their own blocking for a scene. Sherman agreed to try it. "The two ladies played the entire five pages practically riveted to the center of the room," said Sherman, neither of them providing the other with a chance to do anything unchoreographed. They were literally unwilling to give an inch, a fact Sherman found entertaining but unproductive. He pointed out to them their five-page-long immobility. "Bette, realizing it was true, broke into a hearty laugh. Miriam did not find it the least bit amusing."

"Ladies," Sherman announced, "sometimes I feel I'm not directing this picture, I'm *refereeing* it! Bette roared with laughter, which only endeared her to me. Once again, Miriam was not amused."[57]

"I can, in all honesty, say I never lost my temper with Miriam on the set," Davis wrote. "I kept it all in until I got home at night. Then I screamed for an hour at least."[58] Farney seems to have taken it with aplomb and alcohol.

There is a scene toward the end of *Old Acquaintance* in which Kit's long-simmering and well-earned frustration with Millie's self-dramatization becomes intolerable. Violence ensues. Davis described it in *The Lonely Life* as a slap, but in fact it's an extended shake of Millie's shoulders. "Now, Vincent," Bette said on the morning the scene was to be shot, "I'm going to shake Miriam just as I have to do it. There's no way I can fake that. I hope she doesn't try to pull anything and start complaining about it, so just warn her that I'm going to do it."

"Vincent," Hopkins said to her director, "I know that she has to shake me, but I got up this morning with this terrible thing in my neck, and I hope she won't overdo it because I know she doesn't like me, but she doesn't have to overdo it."[59]

According to Bette, spectators gathered on the catwalks above the soundstage. A reporter from *Life* got wind of it and tried to cover the story with a photographer, but they were barred from the set.

As Humphrey Bogart said of Bette and her wallop, "Unless you're very big she can knock you down."[60] Hopkins was not very big, and to make matters worse, she relaxed her body so completely when Bette began to shake her that, as Sherman describes it, "her head began to wobble about grotesquely like a doll with a broken neck."[61] Davis stormed off the set in a rage and slammed the door for good measure but was coaxed back for a second take, during which Hopkins, at Sherman's insistence, forced herself to resist the shaking enough to look human. As Sherman notes, "it was done well enough to be all right, and that's all there was to it."[62]

But that is exactly the problem with the scene, and with the film as a whole: it was done well enough to be all right, but that's *all* it is. Sherman plays that particular scene for comedy, but it's not very funny. And the notorious enmity between the two actresses, which might have lent their characters' rivalry some real bite, ended up being so controlled that it barely registers at all. The joyous contempt the two actresses felt for each other, the recreational loathing *Life* had appreciated in 1939, was reined in to get the picture in the can, and *Old Acquaintance* suffers for its absence.

Jack Warner asked Sherman, Davis, and some crew members to work late on a Saturday in mid-February and finish the whole thing up. They agreed and worked till 2:00 a.m. Davis asked Sherman to drop her off at Ruthie's house on Laurel Canyon, but as they were driving down Ventura Boulevard toward the canyon they spotted an open hamburger joint and stopped for a bite to eat. "It's been fun working with you in spite of the trouble with Miriam. But you handled her beautifully, and I love you!" Bette said. "I love you, too," Sherman replied. "Then her voice changed. She became subdued and solemn as she took my hand. 'You don't understand. I mean, I really love you.'"[63] Bette was infatuated.

And married. Sherman, a good-looking and intelligent man, was interested and married. Nothing came of it—yet.

Sherman dropped Bette off at Ruthie's house around 3:00 a.m. and was astounded to see Ruthie appear on her doorstep in her bathrobe the minute the car pulled up and call out, "Is that you, Bette Davis? *Do you know what time it is? Get into this house at once!*"

"Yes, Mother."[64]

14

FOR THE BOYS

WHILE *OLD ACQUAINTANCE* WAS IN the early stages, still under the direction of Edmund Goulding, Warners arranged for Bette to see Irving Rapper's *The Gay Sisters* with an eye toward casting the role of Rudd Kendall, the young navy lieutenant with whom Kit Marlowe enjoys an affair and, toward the end, decides to marry. There is a character in *The Gay Sisters* named Gig Young; the role was played by an actor who was born with the name Bryant Fleming, and who had acted under the name Byron Barr. The trouble was, there was another young actor in Hollywood named Byron Barr—the second Byron Barr appears as Nino Zachetti in *Double Indemnity*—so Bryant Fleming decided to take his character's name in *The Gay Sisters* and began a long career under the name Gig Young.

Goulding approved of Young's casting in *Old Acquaintance*, but Vincent Sherman didn't see his appeal and tried to get someone cast in his place. But Davis had taken a liking to him and insisted that he play Rudd Kendall. She also seduced him.

Farney was often out of town working for Honeywell and the war effort, and though Young was also married, he convinced his wife, Sheila, that the reason he was staying late at the studio was because of delays caused by Davis and Hopkins and their tempers, an excuse Sheila certainly found plausible. Although *Old Acquaintance* did run significantly behind schedule, Gig Young was actually spending his off hours in Bette's dressing room at the studio or at Riverbottom when Farney was in Minneapolis.

The affair was rather brief; it ended when Young joined the Coast Guard shortly after *Old Acquaintance* wrapped in mid-February, though the two remained good friends for the rest of Young's life. They greeted each other with a particular shtick: "*Gig Young!*" Bette would cry upon seeing him. "*Bette Davis!*" Young would respond. "She's not a professional charmer," Young said of Davis many years after their affair was over. "I like that kind of honesty."[1]

Soon after *Old Acquaintance* wrapped, Bette departed, without Farney, for a vacation in Mexico.

Bᴇɢɪɴɴɪɴɢ ᴡɪᴛʜ Pᴀʀᴀᴍᴏᴜɴᴛ's *Star Spangled Rhythm*, released at the tail end of 1942, Hollywood gave wartime America a spate of puttin'-on-a-show movies featuring a given studio's stable of stars playing themselves. In *Star Spangled Rhythm*, Bob Hope, Bing Crosby, Fred MacMurray, Dorothy Lamour, Paulette Goddard, Veronica Lake, Alan Ladd, and other Paramount leading lights turned up onstage at a navy benefit, with Eddie Bracken playing a sailor and Betty Hutton playing the Paramount switchboard operator with whom he falls in love. MGM got in line with *Thousands Cheer*. Described by the critic Damien Bona as "arguably the worst A picture of the 1940s," *Thousands Cheer* featured Gene Kelly as an army private and the "MGM Star Parade," including Judy Garland, Mickey Rooney, Red Skelton, Eleanor Parker, Lucille Ball, Lena Horne, Donna Reed, June Allyson, and "introducing in his first appearance on the screen, José Iturbi." Universal weighed in with *Follow the Boys*, which, as Bona points out, remains notable for being the only film in history to star both Orson Welles and Maria Montez. Marlene Dietrich, W. C. Fields, and the Andrews Sisters also appeared.

Warner Bros. brought forth two such cavalcades: *Thank Your Lucky Stars*, which began filming in October 1942 but wasn't released until the following September; and *Hollywood Canteen*, made in two batches and released on December 31, 1944. The latter film had gone into production in November 1943, but the Screen Actors Guild put a stop to the filming by demanding that all the stars be paid their full salaries no matter how brief their appearances were. The issue was settled in late April 1944 when the Guild agreed that a week's salary was a reasonable minimum payment for those actors who worked on a per-picture basis. The problem was, *Hollywood Canteen* was not originally designed to showcase only Warners' talent, and other studios refused to loan their stars to Warners under the new conditions. What's more, the *New York Times* reported, a total of nine other all-star films had been in the planning stages at other studios, but all were dropped thanks to the new rules. Filming on *Hollywood Canteen* resumed on June 5, 1944.[2] Davis filmed her sequence during the last week of June.[3]

Hollywood Canteen finds Bette acting more or less unself-consciously as herself at the Canteen, introducing acts and presenting prizes and a cake to the lucky "Slim," the millionth man to enter the club. According to the actress Joan Leslie, with whom "Slim" wins a date, Davis had trouble being Davis. "I just can't do this!" Bette cried after repeatedly flubbing lines that had been scripted to make her sound like herself. "If you give me a gun, a cigarette, and a wig, I can play any old bag. But I can't play myself!" "Everyone laughed," Leslie continued. "This broke the tension on the set and allowed the scene to proceed smoothly, as this super, sophisticated lady probably knew it would."[4]

"A very pleasant pile of shit for wartime audiences" is how Joan Crawford described *Hollywood Canteen*.[5] A group of enlisted men responded with even less praise. The film, they wrote to Warners, was "a slur on the intelligence and acumen of every member of the armed services."[6] Still, *Hollywood Canteen* was a huge hit and became one of Warners' top-grossing films of 1945.[7]

Thank Your Lucky Stars is by far the more entertaining of the two films, if for no other reason than Bette Davis enters it singing.

The movie strings itself along on a plot, but it's deliberate twaddle involving hard-to-take Eddie Cantor and his equally excruciating look-alike, a Hollywood tour guide who helps two fresh-faced kids (Joan Leslie and Dennis Morgan) break into showbiz. That the comedy is mainly about how wretched Cantor is—how stale his routines are, how bug-eyed and "repulsive" he is physically—is a testament to Cantor's self-deprecating good nature, though toward the end of the film when he turns up in a psycho ward and gets strapped to a gurney, you might find yourself hoping that the onscreen surgeon will actually go through with the lobotomy he threatens to perform. In any event, *Thank Your Lucky Stars* features Edward Everett Horton and S. Z. "Cuddles" Sakall playing a pair of producers who enlist Warner Bros.' stars as entertainment for the big war benefit they're throwing at a Hollywood theater—the kind of marvelous, supernatural stage that quadruples in size when necessary to accommodate vast cinematic musical numbers. John Garfield, Humphrey Bogart, Hattie McDaniel, Errol Flynn, Olivia de Havilland, Ida Lupino, Dinah Shore, Ann Sheridan, Jack Carson, and Alan Hale all appear as themselves.

Nothing in Bette Davis's career to this point can prepare you for the sublimely ridiculous moment when she opens her dark lipsticked mouth and—well, okay: *sings* is not the right word. Davis *delivers* Frank Loesser and Arthur Schwartz's witty, forced-rhymed "They're Either Too Young or Too Old." As she remarked about her singing voice to Dick Cavett many years later, "It has more personality than vocal ability, shall we say."[8]

However little she appreciated it on a conscious level, her appearance in *Thank Your Lucky Stars* marks the first time in her career that Bette Davis knew that to get the job done, to make the sequence work—to be bedrock honest as an actress—she had to turn herself into self-parody:

> They're either too young, or too old,
> They're either too gray or too grassy green,
> . . .
> The battle is on, but the fortress will hold,
> They're either too young or too old.

The sheer ghastliness of Davis's singing voice is precisely what sells the song. It's not that she's gamely attempting to sing while acknowledging that she can't. No, she transcends mere singing by parodying her speaking voice at its most mannered and italicized, all the while hovering toward but generally missing the musical notes that, for a lesser talent, would have formed the structure of the song. Davis played it smarter. To give an honest performance of herself playing a musical comedienne, Davis knew she had to turn cartoonish. The absurd jitterbug she does with a GI in the middle of the routine is so fast and frenzied—he hurls her around with utter abandon, lifting her far off her feet and flinging her around like a yo-yo—that it might as well serve as a Looney Tunes sequence.

In terms of Bette Davis caricatures, Warners' animation department had already beaten her to the punch. The enormity and depth of Davis's well-like eyes had attracted the attention of Friz Freleng and his Merrie Melodies crew as early as 1936 with *The CooCoo Nut Grove*, which catches a brief glimpse of Davis seated at her own table at the eponymous night-club. (Freleng took it easier on Davis than he did with Katharine "Miss Heartburn" Hepburn, whom he depicts as a whinnying horse complete with elongated equine teeth and hooves.) The following year, in *She Was an Acrobat's Daughter,* Freleng drew a vast-eyed Bette overplaying a scene from *The Petrified Florist* with an effeminate Leslie Howard before an audience of rude and boorish animals until an obnoxious duck-child commandeers the projector and sends *The Petrified Florist* unspooling into chaos. Freleng brought Bette into his 1940 *Malibu Beach Party* as well, along with Jimmy Cagney, George Raft, Ginger Rogers, Greta Garbo, and Spencer Tracy.

In Fred "Tex" Avery's animated 1941 *Hollywood Steps Out,* Cary Grant, Clark Gable, Bing Crosby, Jimmy Stewart, and the inevitably mocked Leopold Stokowski all appear at Ciro's, but Davis's reserved table is notably empty. They're waiting for her, but she doesn't show up; as the film critic and animation expert Hank Sartin notes, Avery is slyly riffing on Bette's frequent absences from the studio owing to suspensions.[9] In Chuck Jones's 1942 *Fox Pop,* released under the Looney Tunes label, Bette shows up briefly in the window of the chic Hollywood restaurant Chiro's wearing a fashionable silver fox fur.

Davis's last appearance as a Warner Bros. caricature came in 1946 with *Hollywood Daffy,* in which Daffy jumps off a bus at Hollywood and Vine and jubilantly cries, "*Hollywood!* The *thit*-y of the *thin*-ema at *latht*!" He immediately heads to "Warmer Brothers Studios" and attempts, with increasingly violent results, to crash the front gate. Animated Bette, of course, has no such difficulties. "Good morning, Miss Davis!" says the security guard (in one of Mel Blanc's most nasal voices). "So you *think* I'm *mean to you*," the cartoon Bette snaps, clutching a script as she marches through the gate. "You think I'm *cruel. Mad. Selfish. Domineering!* (To the guard:) Good morning. *Well.* You're *right.* I'm *all that. And heaven, too.*" (Bette's voice was most likely not provided by Mel Blanc, but rather by Bea Benaderet, Warners' go-to gal for female cartoon voices in the 1940s.)[10]

But the funniest Davis-related moment in any Warner Bros. cartoon occurs without Davis herself being onscreen. In Bob Clampett's 1946 Bugs Bunny–starring *The Big Snooze,* in the middle of a speech in which a theatrically desperate Bugs begs a fed-up Elmer Fudd not to leave him, he looks straight at the audience and confides, "Bette Davis is going to hate me for this."[11] The joke is doubly comical. Not only is Bugs playing an overwrought Bette Davis scene—the drag-loving Bugs is almost as much of a gay icon as Bette—but Elmer is threatening not only to leave Bugs but to leave Warner Bros. Disgusted with his deal, especially the fact that he's constantly playing the same role, Elmer has ripped up his contract and thrown it on the ground. Fudd had an excellent role model in Bette Davis.

HAVING RENOVATED BUTTERNUT to their satisfaction, Bette and Farney turned their decorating attentions to Riverbottom. They hired the designer Mac Mulcahy to redo almost everything; Mulcahy finished his work in the spring of 1943. The breakfast room was done over in Early American style with a corner cupboard and dark wood table and chairs. The sitting room was made even more informal than it had been before, with new built-in bookshelves and overstuffed chairs, although the large full-color map of the world hanging on one wall was a bit schoolmarmish.

The original dining room design had featured all-too-scenic wallpaper—horses on a hunt running through fields—and a long, dark dining table set off by white chairs. Mulcahy installed knotty pine paneling and a matching dining table and chairs and added cheerful pink and white draperies and a huge breakfront displaying china and pewter cups. The living room's original layout—two long couches facing each other—was transformed into a more casual room by way of easy chairs surrounding a large circular coffee table. The master bedroom, which once featured a high four-poster bead with white cover and canopy, now sported a new, long, low bed with a plaid bedspread and matching drapes, wall-to-wall carpeting, and a recovered chaise.[12]

Riverbottom was newly homey, but it wasn't the home of a traditional couple. After completing Old Acquaintance, Bette went off to Mexico with her friend the Countess Dorothy di Frasso while Farney continued to spend time in Minneapolis and elsewhere on the road doing notably unchronicled work for the military. (Di Frasso was the daughter of the millionaire Bertrand Taylor. Known for giving lavish parties, she was a fixture on the Hollywood scene in the 1930s and '40s. Her title came from her second marriage, to Count Carlos di Frasso.)

Bette, meanwhile, was battling Warners for a new contract. "My trip to Mexico was of long duration," she wrote. "I was in contractual difficulty with Warner Bros. I had never demanded a salary raise or limitation of films per year, and I felt the time had come. I informed the studio I would not return until my contract met these demands."[13]

The contract she won, dated June 7, 1943, covered nine films over five years at $115,000 per film for the first five and $150,000 for the final four. In a separate pact, Warner Bros. and Davis agreed that five of these films would be produced by her new production company, B.D. Inc., with Davis finally achieving some measure of contractually based control over the selection and development of stories and, indeed, all production matters, though the final decisions would remain the studio's. For the first three B.D. Inc. pictures, Davis would get the first $125,000 of gross receipts, with Warners getting the next $232,000; any remainder would be split as follows: 35 percent to Davis and 65 percent to Warner Bros. For the remaining two B.D. Inc. films, Davis would get the first $150,000.[14]

There were the usual number of misfires and false alarms. The *Hollywood Reporter* announced that Bette was set to star in the romance *One More Tomorrow* opposite Paul Henreid; the film was actually made in 1943 with Ann Sheridan and Dennis Morgan but wasn't released until 1946.[15]

She was offered a role in *Battle Cry*, a propaganda epic to be directed by Howard Hawks, whose biographer Todd McCarthy describes it as an action film dealing "with virtually every front on which the war was being fought, from China and the Soviet Union to North Africa and the French underground. It would have run eighteen reels and cost $4 million." Writers included Clifford Odets, Lillian Hellman, Ben Hecht, Pearl Buck, Edna Ferber, Maxwell Anderson, George Kaufman, and Moss Hart, with William Faulkner as the orchestrating author of the piece. Jerome Kern was commissioned to write the score. Bette's segment would have cast her most improbably as "Ma-Ma Mosquito," described by McCarthy as "a tough old Chinese grandmother recognized by Chiang Kai-Shek for leading resistance against Japanese occupation."[16] Not only did Bette turn down the role, but *Battle Cry* went into turnaround at practically the last minute and never got made.

She did appear in a seventeen-minute Fox short called *Show Business at War*, along with everyone from Eddie "Rochester" Anderson, Louis Armstrong, Ethel Barrymore, John Garfield, and Irving Berlin to Irene Dunne, Marlene Dietrich, W. C. Fields, Alfred Hitchcock, Myrna Loy, Walt Disney, Frank Sinatra, and Orson Welles.[17]

Davis expressed some interest in an adaptation of Edith Wharton's

Ethan Frome with an eye toward appearing opposite Raymond Massey, who had played the title role on Broadway in 1936. Matthew Kennedy reports that Joan Crawford had encouraged Edmund Goulding to approach Bette for *Ethan Frome*, but Goulding had had enough: "I wouldn't go near her with a ten-foot electric pole," he told Crawford.[18] And as Louella Parsons announced in March, "along came the war, taking Massey to Canada—and along came *Mr. Skeffington* for Bette."

Farney died on August 25. He had collapsed while walking down Hollywood Boulevard two days earlier and never regained consciousness.

The death of a movie star, or a movie star's spouse, usually engenders dark speculations about mysterious circumstances and all-too-tidy cover-ups, and the death of Arthur Farnsworth at the age of thirty-seven is no exception, particularly because Bette brought to the case the suspicious habit of killing her onscreen husbands. Add to her murderous melodramas Farney's cryptic war work, and the case remains ripe enough to be covered on E! Network's *Mysteries and Scandals* series more than a half century after the fact. But Bette was not Leslie Crosbie or Regina Giddens, and Farney was not James Bond. As disappointing as it may be to the morbidly nosy, there is no indication that Farney died from any reason other than a brain hemorrhage resulting from a skull fracture that was caused by a fall. The most sober explanation is that he was drunk and fell off a moving train.

On Monday, the twenty-third, Farney left Riverbottom for the Walt Disney Studios in Burbank, where he was serving as a technical consultant on aeronautics for some government films Disney was producing. From there he went to Hollywood to do some shopping. Davis wrote in *The Lonely Life* that "he had been forgetful, disorganized, as he went off to work. He had seemed almost tipsy and I joked about the possibility that he'd spiked his orange juice. We'd laughed about it. Later on, he'd ordered me a leopard stole at Magnin's."[19] He then paid a visit to their lawyer, Dudley Furse. On his way to his car, he suddenly cried out and hit the pavement in front of a tobacco store on the 6200 block of Hollywood Boulevard, between Vine and Argyle. The store owner called an ambulance, and Farney was taken first to a receiving hospital and then to Hollywood Presbyterian Hospital, where he died two days later.

Bette had gone shopping that day with Margaret Donovan, her

longtime hairdresser and the wife of Perc Westmore, and had returned to Riverbottom by the time the phone call came in. She's said to have called Dr. Moore, who told her to meet him at Hollywood Presbyterian.

Rehashing the case luridly in 1951 for *American Weekly*, Adela Rogers St. Johns, the overrated grande dame of Hollywood journalists, wrote that "after the coroner's autopsy report, the Hollywood Homicide Bureau and the District Attorney's office took over. The autopsy revealed that the skull fracture had not resulted from the fall that day. According to medical authorities, it had taken place some time before and the sidewalk hadn't caused it, but possibly 'a blunt instrument such as a blackjack or the butt end of a gun.'" Swiftly abandoning the blackjack and gun for lack of evidence, St. Johns moved on to quote Bette: "Then I remembered a fall Farney had at our New Hampshire home late in June. Coming downstairs in his stocking feet to answer the telephone, he slipped on the first landing and slid the full length of the stairs. He landed on his back, struck the back of his head and scraped his back severely. He suffered the usual lameness for some days but not being the complaining kind he said nothing, so I thought no more about it."

St. Johns, needing to spice up her story in the blackjack's continuing absence, plunged on: "Still, there were complications about the time element. Dr. Homer R. Keyes, assistant county surgeon, thought it couldn't have been more than two weeks since the original injury occurred." Eventually, though, St. Johns was forced to admit that "following conferences, investigations, hearings, and further medical reports, Bette's explanation was finally accepted as the true one." How accurate St. Johns's reporting is on any point remains questionable, however, since she went on in the same story to credit William Wyler for directing the great, sardonic tale of Hollywood murder, *Sunset Boulevard*.[20]

Lawrence Quirk brings Lucille Farnsworth to the scene: "Farney's bossy mother came immediately from New York and demanded [the] autopsy." Then he drops the bombshell. Farney's briefcase, which supposedly went missing when he collapsed, turned up later, and "in it were bottles of liquor. Then [Bette] learned that he had been hit over the head two weeks before he died by a cuckolded husband who had found Farney in bed with his wife."[21]

James Spada goes so far as to place Bette herself at the scene of Farnsworth's collapse, but his source is Davis's notorious third husband, William Grant Sherry, who told Spada long after the couple's acrimonious divorce that he and Bette had been walking along Hollywood Boulevard once when "all of a sudden Bette started shaking and looked frightened. I said, 'What's the matter?' She pointed down to the ground and said, 'That's where I pushed Farney. I thought he was drunk and I pushed him and he fell and hit his head on the curb." What better way to get back at one's ex than to have her privately confess to killing her previous husband, especially after she's safely in her grave and can't sue? The generally reliable Spada proceeds to theorize: "She could have pushed him and stalked away so quickly that she never realized he had hit his head." (Davis was so busy stalking away that she never heard what one of Spada's own witnesses describes as "a terrifying yell.") Or: "she could have realized he was hurt and remained without being recognized in her sunglasses, then slipped away unnoticed to avoid a scandal once she was sure Farney was being cared for." (Disguised a few steps short of a Groucho nose and glasses, Bette Davis remained unrecognized in a crowd that gathered just off the corner of Hollywood and Vine.) "Or she might have remained with Farney at all times and Warner Bros. was able to use its formidable power to cover up the facts, coach the witnesses with their stories, and ram through the inquest verdict." (Jack Warner, aka Satan, was so commanding and manipulative that he bought off the press, the justice system, and every bystander in the heart of Hollywood.) These speculations are all dismissable.[22]

Vincent Sherman provided the most credible account of the cause of Arthur Farnsworth's death. According to Sherman, Davis had urged him to accompany her on the trip to Mexico after *Old Acquaintance* wrapped back in February. Although he was flattered—and interested—Sherman nevertheless hesitated to accept the invitation. The day before Bette was to leave, Farney showed up at Sherman's office at Warner Bros. and told him that he knew about Bette's infatuation. The couple had had a drunken fight about it the night before. Sherman quotes Farney as saying, "She's very emotional and not aware of how bad it could be for both of you if you meet her in Mexico. . . . So I'm begging you—don't go! Please don't go to Mexico." Sherman described Farney as "a gentle soul" who understood his wife's overly emotional nature very well.

Bette phoned Sherman twice from Mexico—once from Mexico City and once from Cuernavaca—to see if he was coming to join her, but Sherman begged off, citing work commitments. It's not that he didn't find Bette attractive. In fact, he was fascinated by her and quite susceptible to her charms. But even if he hadn't been married, which he was, he knew that an affair with the mercurial Bette Davis would have been unavoidably messy. And so he demurred, hoping that by the time they began work on *Mr. Skeffington* in the fall, Bette's ardor would have cooled.

It hadn't. One Sunday afternoon in late 1943 or early 1944, after filming some scenes for *Skeffington*, the soundstage having emptied, Davis invited Sherman to her dressing room for a scotch. "I've been a perfect bitch," she told him. "I feel guilty about what I am doing to you and what I did to Farney." Bette then told him that on the morning she'd left for Mexico, she and Farney had had a few more drinks and another fight, after which Farney had followed her to the train station. They'd continued arguing on the train, and Farney told Bette that Sherman had agreed not to meet her in Mexico. The train began to move. "I begged him to get off, but he went on, saying he'd had a long conversation with you. . . . I screamed at him to get off before it was too late, and I pushed him toward the platform. Finally, he took the last few steps down and jumped, but by this time the train was moving rapidly. I ran down to the bottom step, held onto the bar at the side to look back and see if he was all right. He had fallen and was holding his head."

Davis and Sherman began their affair that night.[23]

"Farney and I had a good life together," Davis wrote in *The Lonely Life*. "Classically European in tradition, I believed it would have gone on forever. We made few demands on one another, and still he was always there. So was I. He filled the house with his sweetness and consideration of me. Now I was alone again. I will always miss him."[24] It's an amiable if overly discreet literary send-off to a man whose worst fault may have been a tendency to drink too much, but it leaves many issues unresolved. Since everyone who had a meaningful relationship with the couple is now dead, these questions will remain unanswered, though it is safe to assume that if Davis indeed shoved Farney hard enough on the train steps and helped cause the fatal injury, however inadvertently, the guilt she felt must have been powerful and long-lasting.

The only further aspect of the case that deserves reporting is that during the inquest, when Bette was asked if anything had happened recently to cause Farney's head injury, Bette lied and said no.

"A TEMPERAMENTAL STAR for whom sex was an artistic necessity" is how Vincent Sherman described Davis. "She was very sexy," Sherman said, "but sex for her was an act of physiological need. It was a pile up of energy, and she had so damn much of it. She was pent up. And that was relaxing for her."[25] But Davis was "pent up" even during sex; she couldn't fully let herself go. She was a sexual athlete, but an inhibited one. "Because of her repressive nature and her attitude toward sex, I think she rarely allowed herself to indulge her sexuality fully," Sherman explained. "As a result she was plagued by a misdirected energy that often turned into nervousness, emotional outbursts, and at times cruelty. I say this because she limited her warmth and affection before the deed, and afterward seemed only to want to forget that it had ever occurred. It was as though from hunger she had stolen food but felt guilty about it."[26]

According to Quirk, it was only a few days after Farney died that Bette began showing up again at the Hollywood Canteen and defying one of the central rules laid down by Jules Stein: no fraternization between hostesses and servicemen. As the director Delmer Daves pointed out, "Some of these kids were prize specimens—real catnip for the gals. I'm not saying she disappeared with any of them, but I would not have blamed her if she had. She was in a real intense, uptight mood at times, and some romantic quickies might have filled the bill for her—might have calmed her down." As for the stars, starlets, and volunteers who served as Canteen hostesses, they, too, were often young beauties, and yet it was Bette Davis who commanded the most attention. Jack Carson once noted, "There were some real lookers at the Canteen—knockouts like Dolores Moran and Julie Bishop and Dorothy Malone. But Bette was the one they clustered around." Carson asked a hunky marine why: what did Bette possess that was so magnetic for the men? One young soldier had a simple reply: "I hear she screws like a mink." Carson was indignant at first, taking it as a slur on Bette, especially since Davis had earned a less lurid reputation as one of the Canteen's hardest workers. But then, Carson realized, there was nothing wrong with Bette's having a little fun on the side. "Well, ain't it the truth," he thought to himself.[27]

It was also at the Hollywood Canteen that she met the composer and lyricist Johnny Mercer, with whom she had a brief and unpublicized affair.[28]

The Hollywood Canteen didn't serve just as an easy pickup joint for the widow Farnsworth. She continued to wash dishes, organize the staff, and perform for the service members who flocked there to get their minds off the war. Perc Westmore recalled one evening when he showed off his makeup skills by transforming Mickey Rooney into Clark Gable and Bette into Bela Lugosi as Dracula.[29] Another night, with Westmore's help, Bette became Groucho Marx. Westmore then selected a brawny soldier and turned him into a woman. Groucho and his pretty date then danced to the great amusement of the crowd.[30]

Among the many books, records, photos, and ephemera archived at the Academy of Motion Picture Arts and Sciences' Margaret Herrick Library is a fascinating record of day-to-day, or rather evening-to-evening life at the Hollywood Canteen. It's a diary written by one of the volunteer hostesses—a civilian, not a starlet. Here's Jane Lockwood Ferrero's entry for February 27, 1943. (*Old Acquaintance* had just wrapped, and Farney was still alive.)

> The Canteen was jammed again tonight. . . . Bette Davis sang the song she sings in her new Warner Bros. picture called *Thank Your Lucky Stars*—same idea as Paramount's *Star Spangled Rhythm* and Columbia's *Tales of Manhattan*. The name of the song was "They're Either Too Young or Too Old"—very cute, altho it's very evident that Bette is a much better actress than singer. Her husband Wm. Farnsworth [*sic*] was there, too. She also greeted and had her picture taken with the lucky fellow who was the 500,000th serviceman to cross the Canteen's threshold. He was a sailor stationed at Port Hueneme.

A slightly later entry notes, "She's no singer—she sounds like a broken-down Dietrich."

Davis doesn't make too many appearances in the diary until late October—she had spent some time at Butternut after Farney's death as well as having taken her Mexico vacation beforehand—when Ferrero writes, "Bette Davis was back—smiling but careworn. Wore black simple tailored suit and black snood." And again in late November: "Bette Davis was there signing and working behind the snack bar. Her hair is quite dark for her new picture *Mr. Skeffington*, I guess."[31]

*M*R. *SKEFFINGTON* WAS A difficult picture for all concerned with its making. It had nothing to do with the fact that the star and the director were carrying on behind the scenes. (As Sherman wryly observed, "The only way I could finish the picture was by having an affair with her."[32] When the film wrapped, so did the affair.) The chief reason was Bette's compulsion to wrangle about points that required no argument, and Sherman wasn't Wyler enough to withstand the pressure. She couldn't help herself but battle. "In these years I made many enemies," Davis wrote. "When I was most unhappy I lashed out rather than whined. I was aggressive but curiously passive. I had to be in charge, but I didn't want to be. I was hated, envied, and feared, and I was more vulnerable than anyone would care to believe. It wasn't difficult to discover that when people disliked me they really detested me. And they couldn't do any more about me than they could about death and taxes."[33]

Mr. Skeffington began as a novel by the Australian-born, English-educated Elizabeth von Arnim. It was published in 1940, and Warner Bros. quickly bought the film rights with an eye toward turning it into a vehicle for Davis. But Bette, who was preparing to start shooting *The Letter* at the time, expressed her displeasure at the property in a hand-written note to Jack Warner: "I have also heard rumors that *Skeffington* with Mr. Goulding was my next. This, I would be forced, for my own future career, to refuse. It is physically impossible for me to play this woman of fifty."[34] She was then thirty-two and certainly enough of an actress to handle the challenge. She'd played Elizabeth I at sixty, after all.

Mr. Skeffington is the story of Fanny Trellis, a vain young beauty whose family is on the skids, whose brother commits securities fraud, and who marries the wealthy but all-too-Hebrew Job Skeffington mostly as a financial transaction, only to put him through hell. He takes it, to a point, at which time he leaves for Europe, gets caught up in the Nazis' roundup of Jews, is sent to a concentration camp, goes blind, and returns to Fanny's guilt-filled, last-minute-salvation ministrations.

Warners approached Katharine Cornell, who turned it down. "Tallulah Bankhead finally agreed to confirm the deal J.L. offered—$50,000 to do *Mr. Skeffington*," Steve Trilling wrote excitedly to Hal Wallis. "Definite rejections on *Skeffington* from both Dunne and Colbert," Hal Wallis telegrammed Jack Warner; "Under circumstances do you want me close deal for Bankhead as I promised?"[35] By mid-April 1941, Wallis called a halt to it. "The Bankhead thing is off indefinitely," he wrote to Trilling. "I have taken the picture out of production until we can get the script into proper shape, and we don't want to make any commitment now."[36]

David Lewis was talking to Dorothy Parker and Alan Campbell about preparing a script, but they apparently weren't interested. Wallis sent some material to Herman Shumlin to try to convince him to direct the picture, but Shumlin turned it down; he didn't like the story. Warners commissioned a script from John Huston, and Huston obliged. But nothing much happened until early 1943, by which point Bette understood that she could—*should*—take the risk of appearing as old as Fanny Skeffington needed to look by the end of the film, and *Mr. Skeffington* was slated for a fall shoot under the direction of Vincent Sherman.

Davis began by rejecting Huston's script, perhaps because she'd so detested *In This Our Life*, and another draft had to be written. Warners hired Julius and Philip Epstein, whose deal elevated them to the role of producers as well as screenwriters. It was a promotion they came to regret.

Jack Warner wanted to cast the elegant if bland John Loder to play Job Skeffington, Fanny's appropriately if obviously named husband. Davis, Sherman, and the Epstein brothers advocated Claude Rains precisely because, as Sherman put it, "he was not supposed to be a romantic character."[37] (To say the least. Fanny marries him out of maliciousness and greed, though the film itself downplays her viciousness in a misguided effort to make Fanny less atrocious.) Rains was cast.

Warner then suggested one small change. He called Sherman and the Epsteins into his office one day and asked, evidently seriously, "Is it necessary that Skeffington be Jewish?"[38]

Warner, of course, was Jewish, as were most of the moguls with the exception of the goyish Darryl Zanuck. As such, the brothers Warner were on the alert for any undue attention being called to that fact. "They were very sensitive about any character in any film who was Jewish," Bette later wrote. "We had many requests from the front office during the filming of *Mr. Skeffington* to add lines that would make Job appear a saint. Claude and I fought the good fight. We were never forced to say these lines."[39] Still, the film plays Job's Judaism extremely subtly, just as it does the anti-Semitism of Fanny's felonious brother, Trippy (Richard Waring). At one point, Trippy haughtily calls Job "a cheap, common little . . ." but Fanny cuts him off before he can supply the obvious missing word.

Job Skeffington's Judaism was the least of the problems with the production. Warners considered filming *Mr. Skeffington* in Technicolor. Bette put up a fuss about the color palette, and the studio decided to film in black and white.[40] But by and large, Davis's outbursts were as irrational as they were constant. "We did not get along too well on *Skeffington*," Vincent Sherman later reflected. "I thought she went overboard. . . . It was a very difficult time in her life."[41]

Davis challenged him as she had challenged him on *Old Acquaintance*, but with a new, more biting edge and with much less reason. Simply reading the unit production manager Frank Mattison's daily reports is enough to require a stiff scotch with a chaser of Pepto Bismol. Even when Davis was home ill, her shadow loomed large and menacing. "Yesterday afternoon [Monday, October 18] there was quite a hullabaloo on the set when the producers [the Epsteins] came to the stage with Mr. Warner and Mr. Trilling. The producers protested against Mr. Sherman changing the dialogue and cutting out the guests that appeared in the first part of the picture. However, after discussion pro and con, we got some extra people in a hurry and the guests are in the set as per the script. Mr. Sherman feels that Miss Bette Davis would not like this and we may have a blow up on account of it this morning."

The following week: "Sherman goes on at his slow pace. . . . I can readily see why Bette Davis wants him to direct her—for the same reason Ida Lupino likes Sherman. He lets them do as they please, and in fact they are really the director when you come right down to it."

Two days later, Bette caused a fuss when she intervened in Sherman's attempt to film a close-up of Richard Waring. "How can you do it when we haven't played the master scene?" Bette demanded. She was referring to one of the most conventional—and dull—ways of composing a scene on celluloid: the director plunks the camera down at the greatest possible distance from the action and runs the scene in its entirety so that later, in the cutting room, the editor will have something to fall back on if the director is so inept that shots taken from closer distances don't match with one another. Some directors *never* play the master scene. But Bette thought she knew how everyone should do everything and didn't hesitate to say so.

October 30: "Today Bette Davis was opposed, and still is, to our shooting the interior of the café with Rains and the child until they have shot more script preceding this. It seems as though they sit down and rewrite and rehearse each scene before it is shot, and I suppose she wants to have her finger in even the scenes in which she does not appear."

November 4: "There was absolutely no progress made on this set yesterday afternoon except to establish a new entrance for Bette Davis into this scene. The producers were familiar with the sequence and were on the set but they seemed just about as able to do something as nobody. I surely would not want to have my own money in any picture being made the way this picture is being made for Warner Bros. There isn't a damn thing that can be done about it as long as Bette Davis is the director."

By November 9, the production was ten days behind schedule: "I am wondering if it would be possible to speed up the next Bette Davis picture by making it a Bette Davis production, where she would understand that all these delays and slowly progressing through a script at one page or less a day would cost her a little bit of money. . . . If you don't like the suggestion just forget I made it, but it sure is tough on a unit manager to sit by with a show that goes like this where she is the whole band—the music and all the instruments, including the bazooka."

By the end of the week, Mattison reported a new glitch: "We are in somewhat of a dilemma concerning the matter of our producers refusing to have anything to do with the picture. Miss Davis is not only the director, but she is now the producer also. Nevertheless, we will keep on going."

By the beginning of December, Claude Rains was getting cranky. He objected to the nasal, hoarse voice of the child actor Sylvia Arslan; "It seems Mr. Rains is getting to be an old woman," Mattison remarked.[42]

Bette was felled by a very serious eye problem on December 9. "I prefer to believe that on the set during *Skeffington* my eyewash was filled with aceteyne by mistake," she coldly noted in *The Lonely Life*. "Aceteyne is a corrosive liquid that dissolves adhesives. It almost dissolved my eyes. I screamed in agony." Perc Westmore rushed to her aid and washed her eyes out with castor oil.[43] She couldn't film that day, which Sherman spent rewriting more of the Epsteins' now thoroughly disfigured screenplay.

By January 7, the production was a full month behind schedule. Shooting continued at its snail's pace, and according to Mattison, "the air was very tense. However, Miss Davis warmed up in the afternoon," and the pace picked up. "The balance of the script is now out, and there have been scenes added. I am sure that when the Epsteins see it they will be spinning on their heads like tops."

Julius Epstein, asked later about how it was to work under Vincent Sherman on *Mr. Skeffington*, replied with a laugh, "No, actually, it was Bette Davis who directed it. She took control of everything." Jack Warner sent the Epstein brothers an angry memo during the production asking why the picture was taking so long to film. "Because Bette Davis is a slow director" was their response. At one point, Sherman and the Epsteins requested some retakes, but Bette refused. The three men took the matter to Jack Warner, who responded by shouting, "Who the fuck does she think she is?" and storming onto the soundstage in a rage, shouting about having built the studio from the ground up—until he saw Bette. "Bette, darling!" Warner said, giving her a warm hug, and that was the end of the retakes controversy.[44]

Mr. Skeffington required Bette to age from a young beauty to a pathetic old woman who cannot accept her physical decline. Davis demanded not only to achieve the effect through performance but by way of increasingly cumbersome makeup. At first, Sherman let her have her way. She tested the makeup on January 11, 1943. But the layers of rubber and powder soon began to look absurd, and Sherman was compelled to talk to Perc Westmore about it.

> I said, "Perc, she's getting to look like a mummy, for God's sake, and it's wrong. I have to stay away from the close-up stuff, and I shouldn't be away from it. Please ease up on it. Don't say anything to her." Well, next morning I hear *click, click, click*—her heels coming onto the stage the way she walks, you know, and I can feel her standing on the edge of the set behind me. I looked round, and she said, "How dare you speak to Perc Westmore behind my back and tell him to change my makeup?! Why did you do it? Why didn't you speak to me about it?" I said, "For the same reason that you're acting this way now. It's gotten so difficult to talk to you. You seem to resent anything that I tell you. You challenge me and I don't want to go through the arguments, so I went to Perc and I told him that I think it's getting too heavy and I want him to go easy on the makeup, and Mr. Warner agrees with me." Well, she got angry and she walked away.[45]

"We came to the elderly part after Fanny Skeffington had had the illness," Sherman continued. "That morning when she came down she looked so hideous I said to her, 'Bette, I'm very upset. I think that the woman should be affected, but I don't think she should become so hideous that it's hard to look at her.' She said, 'Don't worry about it. My audience likes to see me do this kind of thing.' I said, 'Well, I think it's hideous—it's too much.' "[46]

Davis persisted with the monstrous makeup even in the face of the physical toll it took on her. Around this time someone—Hal Wallis? Jack Warner himself?—lit into Sherman, a fact recorded by Frank Mattison as follows: "You can tell by the report of pages covered and setups made yesterday that it did pay to slap Vince Sherman's ears down. Perhaps if someone had the guts to sit down on him a little more often we could even improve our schedule and shooting."

By the nineteenth, despite the fact that she was the one who insisted on its use, Davis was complaining about the makeup and how irritating it was to her skin. It didn't help matters when, the following day, she took her rubber face home with her at the end of the day and forgot to bring it back in the morning. By February 1, she was out sick again, no doubt from the effects of the latex.

The mask and foundation and cakey powder were brutally uncomfortable, especially under the bright lights. Her face began to itch, but she had to suppress any reaction while the cameras were rolling. "Toward the end of the day," Sherman later recalled, "as we'd complete the last shot, she'd often tear the makeup from her face hysterically."[47]

Davis then lodged objections to certain Orry-Kelly gowns, which Kelly redesigned to her satisfaction.

On Valentine's Day 1944, Frank Mattison was in despair: "I hope to hell this picture gets over pretty soon—it's driving me nuts!"

Hell responded positively to Mattison's wish: *Mr. Skeffington* wrapped on February 21, two months behind schedule. Mattison called Davis in her dressing room after shooting was over. She told him she was pleased with the way everything turned out, but, according to Mattison, she was "depressed because it had come to an end."

15

COMMANDERS IN CHIEF

Aᴀ ғᴛᴇʀ ʀᴜɴɴɪɴɢ ʜᴇʀ sᴄᴇɴᴇs ɪɴ *Hollywood Canteen* at the end of June 1944, Bette began shooting Warners' adaptation of Emlyn Williams's play *The Corn Is Green*, a melodrama about a middle-aged woman, Miss Lily Moffat (Davis), who inherits property in a hardscrabble Welsh mining town and sets herself to the task of educating its children. She takes a particular liking to young Morgan Evans, whose intellect impresses her, and whose life she considers far too valuable to be spent hacking coal out of the earth. But the youth's seemingly inexorable path to a scholarship at Oxford is blocked when, in a moment of indiscretion, he kisses a floozy, the daughter of Miss Moffat's housekeeper. Soon enough, she's with child.

Irving Rapper was assigned to direct the picture, and Rapper wanted Richard Waring for the role of Morgan Evans. Waring had made a great impression as the obnoxious Trippy in *Mr. Skeffington*, but he was drafted before *The Corn Is Green* began filming. According to Davis, Warners "tried in every way" to delay his entry into the service so he could appear in it, but to no avail. John Dall was cast in his stead.

With *Mr. Skeffington* safely behind her, and the traumatic guilt over Farney's death receding, Bette began *The Corn Is Green* in a better frame of mind. But no Davis picture could be free of tension, and in this case, she became convinced, obstinately, that her own hair was all wrong for

Miss Moffat, and she refused to shoot any scenes without first filming tests of a wig. Rapper thought she was far too vexed about her character's appearance and attempted to convince her not to wear the hairpiece Perc Westmore concocted at her behest—a rounded red affair with streaks of gray. Rapper lost the battle, of course; there was simply no arguing with her on the point. Even after the wretched rubber Fanny Skeffington mask, Davis was determined to alter her natural appearance in the mistaken belief that in order to get into certain characters she needed to wear a disguise. The wig is attractive but unnecessary, though if it helped Davis achieve the precision and honesty she sought for Miss Moffat, perhaps it was indispensable after all. What Davis really needed, Rapper snapped to the production manager Eric Stacey, was a psychiatrist, not a director.[1]

Davis also insisted that the film be shot in strict continuity. Stacey advised Rapper to go along with this demand, saying that he didn't think it was "worthwhile upsetting her for such a small item since she is so much better on this picture than she has been on former pictures." (He was referring to her behavior, not the quality of her performance.) And continuity shooting was easy enough to achieve on *The Corn Is Green*, since despite a number of scenes set out of doors, there was no location filming to schedule around. In fact, there wasn't even any back lot construction. The town of Glansarno was built indoors on Soundstage 7, an odd decision that partially explains the film's hermetic and stagebound quality.

Adding to the artificiality, Glansarno's miners are a peculiarly energetic and musical lot. Early in the film, Miss Moffat asks the minister, Mr. Jones (Rhys Williams), how many children under seventeen there are in the town, and Jones replies, "Around here they're only children until they are 12. Then they are sent away to the mine. And in one week, they are old men." But Rapper doesn't direct the boys to play it that way. *The Corn Is Green* presents these prematurely "old men" as a pack of cheerful and boisterous teenagers who burst rousingly into song at every opportunity, even on their way home at the end of a long, tough shift in the coal mine. To cap it all, Warners insisted on dubbing in a professional Welsh choir, the Saint Luke Choristers, over the real boys' voices. This, to Davis, rightly, "was wrong. It made the film very 'Hollywood.' A direct recording of the actors who played the miners, many of whom did not have perfect voices, would have given reality to the songs."[2] The filthy, ought-to-be-exhausted young miners merrily end their grueling workdays in what sounds like a recording studio. The audible presence of a particularly bright soprano doesn't help.

Shooting went reasonably smoothly, mainly because Rapper let Davis have her way on most issues. But on the afternoon of Saturday, August 5, a barn door (the hinged metal flap used to focus a lighting unit) fell off a small light and hit Bette on the head. Complaining of a headache, Davis was sent home, but she was well enough to attend a party at Jack and Ann Warner's house that night.

Still, on Monday morning she called in sick. She showed up on Tuesday but talked of having some X-rays done—not by the studio's doctors but by her personal physician, who then reported that she had suffered a slight concussion and needed to rest. She called in sick again on the tenth. "I have had a little talk with Miss Davis," Eric Stacey reported to the front office, "and she seems to be in a mental condition that looks pretty good. In other words, she has realized that the best thing to do about a situation like this is to go back to work and not think about it too much."[3] They all agreed that she would film until the seventeenth at noon and then take four or five days off.

The Corn Is Green appeared either near the end or at the very end of Orry-Kelly's tenure at Warner Bros.; there's a dispute. He's credited as the costume designer for her next picture, *A Stolen Life*, but Davis herself claimed that he didn't actually design her wardrobe for that film.

Kelly served in the army after designing Davis's costumes for *Old Acquaintance*—Milo Anderson designed Hopkins's wardrobe—and returned to do *Mr. Skeffington* at Bette's request. But he quarreled with Jack Warner once too often upon his return and found that he'd lost his base of support. Kelly was known for having a hot temper anyway, and there was nothing like a year's absence to call his indispensability into question. Kelly left Warners in 1946, joined Twentieth Century-Fox in 1947, and later opened his own couture studio. He went on to design one more film for Davis: *The Star* in 1952.

According to Milo Anderson, who worked with Kelly at Warners, Bette "didn't like him as a person, but she kept using him to design her films because she knew she needed him." "She and Kelly did not like each other," David Chierichetti agrees. "They fought a lot. One of the things they fought over was her bras. She had these long breasts that hung down to her waist. He wanted to give her bras that had underwires in them to push them up, but she thought that the metal would give her breast cancer."

The lengthy shape of Davis's bosoms was certainly not lost on Jack Warner, who once ordered the producer Sam Bischoff to "be sure that Bette Davis has her bulbs wrapped up. If she doesn't do it, we are either going to retake, or put her out of, the picture—and if you talk with her you can tell her I said so."[4] (Since the film in question was *The Case of the Howling Dog*, which she refused, her unwrapped bulbs were the least of Warner's problems.) "Leah Rhodes said that one time Kelly bought a boned bra for Bette and tried to get her to wear it, but she threw it at him," says Chierichetti. "One day Kelly came back to the office and said to Leah, 'Oh, if somebody could just give me some idea how to break her bust!' He'd push it up as much as he could, but then he'd put something above it to take away attention. She wore a lot of corsages. In *The Petrified Forest* she's not wearing a bra underneath that waitress outfit. The outfit has a very loose waist. It looks like it's just fullness in the dress, but actually that's where her breasts were."[5]

John Dall, who went on from *The Corn Is Green* to give a more convincing performance in Alfred Hitchcock's perverse *Rope*, was complimentary to Davis in a 1945 interview: "In that scene where I had to tell her off, for instance, in some shots the camera was on me alone. But Bette always stood right behind the camera, facing me, giving the scene the same acting as if she were before the camera. She really listened to what I was saying and fed me my lines with the same intensity she would have if the camera had been on her."[6]

Davis had wanted Ida Lupino to play the role of the floozy, which ultimately went to the less subtle but suitably appalling Joan Lorring. "Bette fought like mad," Lupino later said, "but I was committed to another picture—I'd already done wardrobe fittings and things. It would have been very exciting to do a picture with her. I didn't know her very well. I met up a couple of times with her and some people. Tremendous wit, this woman has. Great sense of humor—and about herself, too. I found her to be a charming woman, you know—not a frightening dragon lady or the queen."[7]

Davis finished shooting *The Corn Is Green* on September 13, 1944. When the film was approaching its release in March 1945, Warners' publicity department created an especially absurd advertisement, given Miss Moffat's sensible, tailored wardrobe: "I remember my battle to keep Warners from displaying *The Corn Is Green* with ads consisting of a picture of me playing the Welsh schoolmistress in black satin décolletage."[8]

Irving Rapper was also flattering to Davis in an interview, but he was even more complimentary to himself, and with less reason: "At the end of the second act, which we retained in the film, there is a moment when the schoolteacher in the Welsh mining village conveys to the audience that she has dreamed—that she somehow clairvoyantly knew—that her star pupil's main historical question in the big examination would be all about Henry VIII. . . . Bette tossed the moment away, and there was a bit of an argument. I simmered down for five days, and finally I said to her, 'Bette, I saw the cut stuff, and I am very sorry to tell you that wasn't the way it should have been done.' And she said, 'Do you really think so?' And I said, 'Yes.' And she agreed to do it again. You could get through to her even though she had enormous power at the studio; she was its queen."[9]

But Rapper's self-congratulation inadvertently points out the central problem with *The Corn Is Green*: its staginess. Given that Miss Moffat's clairvoyance is scarcely the point of that scene, Davis's less drastic delivery was the right choice to make. Morgan Evans wins a scholarship to Oxford because of his own intellect and his teacher's diligence in developing it, not because Miss Moffat possesses powers of divination. Rapper, who had been so spot-on in his direction of *Now, Voyager*, plays the scene too theatrically, tracking in so quickly on Davis's too-triumphant line reading that Miss Moffat appears to be the recipient of a direct communication from God. Rapper then tracks forward on Dall only to turn and aim the camera pointlessly out the window.

The Henry VIII incident illustrates the way Davis's instincts—the dramatic impulses that bypassed conscious decision making and personal antagonisms and went straight to vocal delivery and physical gesture—deserved more trust, not only by Davis's directors but by Bette herself. When she bickered over directions, she was often wrong. When she played a scene without intervention, including her own, she was on surer ground.

On Thursday, September 21, 1944, 20,000 people—including Bette, Orson Welles, Helen Keller, Sinclair Lewis, and the current vice president of the United States, Henry Wallace—gathered at Madison Square Garden for a pro-Roosevelt rally. Roosevelt was running for an unprecedented fourth term of office, this time against the former federal prosecutor Thomas E. Dewey, who was then governor of New York. (Dewey was the model for Humphrey Bogart's character in *Marked Woman*.) Fredric March read several telegrams from movie stars, including this one from Eddie Cantor: "I once sang a song, 'Brother, Can You Spare a Dime?' I don't want to sing it again. That's why I am voting for Roosevelt!"

When Bette took the stage, she told the roaring crowd that all the women who remembered the desperate poverty they'd suffered during the 1930s must surely hope that those days remained in the past. The war's tide had turned, and although fighting would continue another eight months in Europe and another eleven months in Asia, the Allies were clearly making headway at last. Bette made the point that by winning the war "against those bloody, wicked villains who would relegate women to the bawdy slavery of the brothel or the humdrum inferiority of the kitchen," American women were learning a lesson in independence. Women no longer hesitated to use their hard-won voting rights, she declared, and they knew that to protect their own newfound freedom and security they would certainly vote for Roosevelt.[10]

On October 19, Davis was the Roosevelts' guest at the White House, along with a crowd of other ardent Democrats. Tea, followed by dinner, began at 5:30 p.m.[11] As Davis later wrote, she found herself "in line with hundreds of others. At last I reached the great man. As I prepared to file past him, I felt like a little girl being given a diploma. I wanted to curtsy as he automatically extended his hand. When his eyes met mine, he threw back his head in that famous gesture of his and laughed. 'And how did *you* get into this mob, Miss Davis?' 'I wrote, Mr. President, asking to meet you and I received this invitation.'" Roosevelt, Davis claimed, was appalled that Davis hadn't received a more personal summons, one that hadn't been solicited by the guest herself, and he asked if she would be in Washington a while. Bette told him she was heading to Georgia to visit friends.[12]

The "friends" Bette planned to visit in Georgia were singular, not plural: Corporal Lewis A. Riley of the Army Signal Corps, the unit in charge of military communications and the production of training films. Davis had met Riley in Los Angeles. Now he was stationed at Fort Benning. "He's a nobody," Ann Warner warned her. "You are a famous woman. Why throw yourself away on a good-looking set of muscles in khaki?"[13] The question need not be dignified with an answer.

Dateline Atlanta, September 27 (AP): "Bette Davis, screen actress, was quoted by the *Atlanta Constitution* today as denying published reports that she came South to marry Cpl. Lewis A. Riley, who is stationed at Fort Benning. 'I am not going to marry anyone,' the newspaper quoted her in a story from Phenix City, Alabama, which is near the Army post."[14]

Davis's presence on the outskirts of Fort Benning was hardly a secret to the locals. According to *Photoplay*'s Pauline Swanson, autograph seekers

> camped at Bette's gate once the address of her vacation home was printed in the papers. Even the padlock and the owner's four dogs roaming the premises failed to daunt their enthusiasm. One enterprising fan made friends with one of the dogs—a collie—and sent a note to Bette attached to its collar. Bette has a sense of humor, and such enterprise deserves recognition, so she sent the dog back to the gate bearing the coveted autograph.
>
> Otis Taft, a Columbus grocer, bragged that Bette had ordered supplies from his store. By nightfall everyone in town knew that Miss Davis had ordered "twenty-five dollars worth of groceries for one day! Fancy groceries, too!"[15]

Bobby Pelgram joined Bette in Georgia for a time. According to Pauline Swanson, Bobby "tried valiantly to discourage the reporters and photographers who descended on the house, but Bette at last had to make an appearance and posed for photographs wearing a red and white plaid shirt and navy blue knee-length shorts. . . . Bette took to life in Phenix City like a native. She carried wood from the back yard for the fireplace and the wood-burning cook stove. She learned to make biscuits on the old iron stove without burning them and mastered a wood-smoked steak. She bought hip boots and overalls and joined her farmer neighbors in fishing expeditions and coon and possum hunts."[16] What with the overalls and the possums and Riley's muscles, it was all terribly rustic.

On November 6, the evening before the election, Davis was back in Hollywood, where she took part in a pro-Roosevelt radio broadcast produced by Norman Corwin, along with Tallulah Bankhead, Judy Garland, Paulette Goddard, Humphrey Bogart, and Olivia de Havilland. The broadcast is said to have pushed a million votes to Roosevelt, who went on to win handily with over 53 percent of the popular vote and 81.5 percent of the electoral vote.[17]

Davis quickly returned to Georgia and Corporal Riley. At the end of November, she received an invitation to join the president for Thanksgiving dinner at his Warm Springs estate, about thirty-five miles north of Fort Benning. Many of the guests were wheelchair-bound. Some were navy men with war wounds, but most suffered from polio or infantile paralysis. Much to the annoyance of White House staffers as well as the head of the Georgia Warm Springs Foundation, Basil O'Connor—but to the retrospective surprise of no one—Bette managed to seat herself next to the president for most of the evening and couldn't be pried away.[18] As Roosevelt's personal aide, William D. Hassett, put it in his diary entry for November 28, 1944, "A movie actress managed to ingratiate herself past the administrator of the Foundation and sat beside the President to the amazement of all. She was accompanied from Columbus by a hunky escort whom she introduced as Corporal Reilly [*sic*], to the disgust of the authentic Michael [F. Reilly, head of the Secret Service], who declared with heat that he [Lewis Riley] did not belong to the Montana-Irish Reillys. Doc O'Connor furious. We suppressed all the pictures."[19]

Davis never names Riley in any of her memoirs, but she does include this comment: There was, she writes, "a man I thought I might marry. He had been in Europe for the duration and was being transferred from the European theater to Japan. . . . Before he left he asked me to wait for him. I said if that was what he really wanted, he should put a diamond on my finger. Which he did not, and as I knew I would, I grew tired of living my life in a mailbox . . . and did the 'Dear John' thing. A friend of my ex-beau was with him when he received the letter and told me he was very upset. I was pleased."[20]

IN NOVEMBER OF 1945, Ruthie finally remarried. The sixty-year-old divorcée chose Robert Woodbury Palmer, a fifty-three-year-old businessman from Belmont, Massachusetts. A Boston newspaper clipping in the Davis archives offers several eyebrow-raising details: Palmer "was divorced 10 days ago in Reno from Mrs. Helen Bush Palmer" and "is reported to have met Mrs. Davis only a few weeks ago." The clipping goes on to report that the former "Mr. and Mrs. Palmer resided for several years in Belmont. They were married 32 years. They have two children." And then the final kick: "News of the engagement announcement came as a complete surprise to the Palmer friends here, many of whom did not know he had divorced Mrs. Palmer."

The wedding took place in Palm Springs on November 24 at 4:00 p.m. at the Smoke Tree Ranch. Bette, the matron of honor, wore a white Hawaiian print with a lei.[21] The couple honeymooned at the legendary Hotel del Coronado in San Diego.[22]

Bette Davis to Wed on Coast Tomorrow

Hollywood, November 28 (UP): Bette Davis, screen star, will be married on Friday at Laguna Beach to William Grant Sherry, 30-year-old artist and former professional prizefighter, whom she met for the first time a month ago, her studio announced today. The ceremony will be performed by the 37-year-old actress' uncle, the Rev. Paul Gordon Favor, in St. Mary's Episcopal Church in the presence of a few relatives and friends. . . . Miss Davis will be given in marriage by her stepfather, Robert Woodbury Palmer, it was made known here yesterday. Mr. Palmer wed Miss Davis' mother last week. Miss Davis' sister, Barbara Pelgram, will be an attendant."[23]

Bette Davis Wedding Barred by a Church

Hollywood, November 29 (AP): Forbidden the use of an Episcopal church for the ceremony because she was once divorced, Bette Davis will marry William Grant Sherry tomorrow noon in the Chapel of Mission Inn, a hotel at Riverside. Miss Davis and Mr. Sherry obtained a marriage license at Santa Ana this afternoon. . . . The ceremony will be performed by Rev. Francis C. Ellis, pastor of the First Congregational Church of Riverside."[24]

Bride Flustered at Ceremony in Chapel of Mission Inn

Los Angeles, November 30; Special to the *New York Times*: Bette Davis, film actress, and William Grant Sherry, artist and erstwhile pugilist, were married at 3:30 P.M. today in the St. Francis Chapel of the Mission Inn at Riverside. . . . The bride, whose only attendant was her sister, Mrs. Barbara Pelgram of Laguna, appeared somewhat flustered as she was escorted to the altar by her new stepfather, Robert Woodbury Palmer of Palm Springs and Boston. Although she has appeared before motion picture cameras in many wedding scenes, she admitted to a friend at the ceremony that "this is altogether different."

Bette met Sherry at Ruthie's house, Windswept, in Laguna Beach in October, Sherry having recently been discharged from the marines. When Hedda Hopper got a look at him sometime after the wedding, she was delighted with what she saw: "In a suit you couldn't possibly guess what a handsome Greek god he was. Now he'd run up fresh from the sea with the water still glistening on his mahogany tanned skin. He has an even, confident, ingratiating smile, kindly but masculine as a left hook."[25] Hopper's final metaphor was sadly prophetic. Sherry used that left hook, and more, on Bette with some regularity. It began on their honeymoon when he hurled a trunk at Bette and threw her out of the car.[26]

The manly beauty that entranced both Davis and Hopper is not evident in photographs, which show a tall trim man with a sharp, lengthy nose, a forehead even more prominent than Bette's, a drastically receding hairline, and a jutting and slightly upturned chin. Sherry resembled Fearless Fosdick, only with Bob Hope's nose. But by all accounts he was muscular, as was Corporal Riley, to whom Davis sent her Dear John letter after deciding to marry Sherry.

The press got wind of the movie star's impending marriage to the ex-marine thanks to Sherry's mother, an elevator operator at the Pantages Theater Building in San Diego. Mrs. Sherry saw no need for secrecy when her son privately declared his intention to marry Bette after the first of the year, so naturally she told her friends, some of whom called reporters. The wedding was pushed up to late November.

Ruthie was, as Bette put it, "aghast" that Sherry's mother was an elevator operator, though Ruthie of all people should have appreciated the practical problems faced by working women. Hitting closer to the mark, Ruthie also thought that Sherry was a dangerous golddigging hustler. Ruthie "was violently against our marriage," Davis wrote. "It turned out she was right. But for the wrong reasons."[27]

Bette's sister agreed with Ruthie. "I was furious when I heard that Bobby had hired a detective to investigate Sherry behind my back," Bette writes. "It was as if my family were saying that at the grown-up age of thirty-five I could not make up my own mind. Bobby finally told me she had had Sherry investigated and I must not marry him. I refused to read or hear about the report the detective gave her; one can only guess at what it discovered: his temper, his inability to support himself, his desire to marry money. After we were married, a friend said that Sherry had told his Marine buddies in San Diego that his ambition when he left the Marines was to marry a wealthy woman. This information came a little late."[28]

Bette's anger at her mother and sister was misplaced; Ruthie and Bobby weren't questioning Bette's decision-making skills in general but rather the specific—and disastrous—course of action she was taking by marrying a man she barely knew. But everyone made nice at the wedding in Riverside. Bobby attended Bette like the dutiful sister she was. Bette's stepfather of less than a week was indeed the father substitute who escorted her down the aisle, with Bette wearing a simple checked suit with a netting-trimmed hat. Sherry's mother was there, as was his eleven- or twelve-year-old brother. Bette's cousin John Favor and his wife were guests. So were the Westmores: the chubby makeup man Perc and his volatile wife, the hairdresser Maggie Donovan.

Frank Westmore, Perc's brother, recalls Perc telling him about being at Bette's house just before Bette was to marry Sherry. Donovan spied the handwritten guest list and noticed that it said only "Perc Westmore." With a shriek, Donovan yanked Bette into a nearby closet and locked her in. As Bette pounded on the door demanding to be released, Maggie forced Perc to amend the offending document to read "Mr. and Mrs. . . . ," and only then did she let Bette out of the closet. "I was afraid of that Maggie," Bette later admitted.[29]

In 1944, WARNERS bought the film rights to James M. Cain's 1941 novel *Mildred Pierce* and offered it to Bette, but she turned it down; she's said to have disliked the idea of playing the mother of a sixteen-year-old.[30] Others considered for the role of the hardworking pie baker and excessively indulgent mother were Claudette Colbert, Barbara Stanwyck, and Rosalind Russell.[31] Warners eventually settled on Joan Crawford, who won an Oscar for her performance. Davis was more intrigued by the prospect of filming *Anna and the King of Siam*, but Warners refused to loan her to RKO, and the role went instead to Irene Dunne opposite Rex Harrison.[32]

Michael Curtiz wrote to Mrs. Sherry in care of the Plaza Hotel in Laredo, Texas, in mid-December 1945; the Sherrys were still on their honeymoon. Curtiz had just returned from New York, where he showed

Howard Lindsay and Russel Crouse the screen test Bette had made for the role of the amiable but iron-willed Vinnie Day, the mother in Lindsay and Crouse's long-running Broadway comedy *Life with Father*. Curtiz was "heartbroken" to have to tell her that they'd rejected it—and Bette—calling the performance (in Curtiz's words) "too powerful, too dominating, too superior and without any naiveté."[33] After testing Rosalind Russell, Rosemary DeCamp, and even Mary Pickford, Curtiz ultimately made the film with Irene Dunne and William Powell.[34] Bette was also considered for the lead in Jean Negulesco's *Humoresque*, but by the time the film went into production in December of 1945, Joan Crawford had taken that role as well.[35]

In 1944, shortly after *Mr. Skeffington* was edited and screened for Jack Warner, Bette ran into Vincent Sherman and told him that Warner was pleased with the way their film had turned out. "I'm glad he was, but I'm not," Sherman said. *Mr. Skeffington* had turned out to be *nobody's* picture, he told her—not hers, not his. They had been talking about teaming up again on a remake of *A Stolen Life*, a 1939 British melodrama starring Elizabeth Bergner as twin sisters and Michael Redgrave as the man who marries the wrong one, but Sherman insisted they'd have to reach some kind of understanding before proceeding. "She said something about 'Do you want me to be like one of those little girls who's just starting and you tell them everything to do?' I said no, no, I've never been that kind of director, I don't have that kind of ego. . . . Well, she got very upset, and I said I wouldn't work that way, and we just never did anything together after that. I'm sorry about it."[36]

Bette saw an early studio screening of *My Reputation*, a Barbara Stanwyck melodrama, and she liked the way the German émigré Curtis Bernhardt had directed it. (Although *My Reputation* wasn't released until 1946, it finished shooting in January 1944.) She decided he'd be perfect to direct *A Stolen Life*. "A producer at Warner called me and said that Miss Davis had insisted on having me as director," Bernhardt later said. "I read the script and thought it was godawful. I went back to the producer and said that it was awful for this, this, and this reason. He said, 'You know, you're right.' I don't recall now what the original problems with the script were, but when the producer went up to Jack Warner and asked for a new writer, Miss [Catherine] Turney, Warner asked why. He gave the reasons, and Warner asked how long he had been on the script. When he answered, 'about four months,' Warner said, 'You're fired.'"[37] (Bernhardt didn't name either the producer or the original screenwriter in question.)

In mid-December 1944, while Bette was just outside the gates of Fort Benning with Corporal Riley, Warner sent her a telegram in care of the Williams Lumber Co., Columbus, Georgia. He suggested assigning the producer Mark Hellinger to *A Stolen Life*. In addition to being the proposed star, Bette was the film's producer, the deal for *A Stolen Life* having been inked as the first production under the B.D. Productions label. But as Warner pointed out in his telegram, "Your not being here makes it rather awkward in getting this film prepared." "Hope you're having a wonderful time and that everything is really the life of Riley with you," he cutely added. But Bette was displeased at the Hellinger suggestion, perhaps because she believed she could handle the producer's function herself when she returned to Hollywood, and so *A Stolen Life* was left adrift without an executive in charge.[38]

After Davis returned from the South, she began looking at wardrobe designs. "I went to a showing of Miss Davis's costumes," Bernhardt later recalled.

> The whole staff that she'd assembled was there, and I walked in as the new director. The costume designer was a friend of hers. [Bernhardt appears to be referring to Orry-Kelly, but Davis, in *Mother Goddam*, insisted that she "did not have Orry-Kelly to help" her on *A Stolen Life*.[39] Precisely who designed the dual wardrobes for the twins remains unclear.] Whenever a new costume would come out, she would rave, "Isn't that wonderful! It's glorious!" etc. After the third time of "wonderful, glorious," I asked her very softly, "Excuse me, Miss Davis. Don't you think these costumes are a little theatrical?" I thought I was very diplomatic, but my words had the opposite effect. She burst out in a flood of insults. "Theatrical? *Theatrical!* Let's stop talking that way, Mr. Bernhardt." She went on for ten minutes until I finally said, "Thank you, Miss Davis," and got up and walked out. She asked me where I was going. I said, "You don't need a director, you need a yes-man." She said, "That's not true," ran after me, grabbed me firmly by the hand, and led me back. That was my first encounter with Miss Davis. After that, her attitude was a little more demure.[40]

When confronted by Bernhardt's anecdote, Davis offered the following objection: "I never believed in yes-men. I despised them."[41] True enough, but not enough. Davis despised those "weak sisters" who refused to stand up to her, but she also raged against those who did. In a way, Bette Davis thought she could walk on water, but her first step turned any lake into a sheet of exceedingly sheer ice that only she could stride upon. Others, their tread either too heavy or too timid, fell through.

"Later on," Bernhardt claimed, "Bette was fired as producer, and I produced it. It's an argument between her and me. She never did produce it, but her name is on it as producer and she claims that she produced it. For tax reasons, she had her own company, B.D. Productions. . . . It was a stupid argument because there is no producer at a major studio. Everything is handled by departments. The expenses are handled by the finance department, the cutting by the editing department, the writing by the story editor who assigns the writers."[42]

Obviously Bernhardt never worked with Hal Wallis, who oversaw virtually every aspect of the films he produced. Wallis never produced departmentally or by committee. But Wallis left Warners for Paramount in the spring of 1944.[43] And given that *A Stolen Life* was the first B.D. production, it's unlikely that Wallis would have been in charge of it even had he stayed.

If the argument over who actually produced *A Stolen Life* is, as Bernhardt put it, "stupid," it's not because Bernhardt's explanation is any sounder than Davis's. In *The Lonely Life*, Davis wrote: "I was no more allowed to be a real producer than the man in the moon," suggesting that she was somehow kept from exercising any authority by some nefarious unnamed force emanating from the Warners front office. And yet she went on to admit that "as star in the dual role, I simply meddled as usual. If that was producing, I had been a mogul for years."[44] But when faced with Bernhardt's assertion that she didn't produce *A Stolen Life* at all, she bristled: "We were coproducers," she insisted.[45] Shooting began on Valentine's Day 1945.

For the role of Bill Emerson, Bernhardt and Davis chose a twenty-nine-year-old ex-marine, Glenn Ford, whose blend of ruggedness and glamour made it possible for him to be convincing not only as a lighthouse mechanic but also as a socialite's presentable businessman husband, the former the object of Kate's love, the latter the recipient of Pat's disregard.

A Stolen Life works not despite its gimmick but because of it; it's doubly riveting to watch Bette Davis act in tandem with Bette Davis, especially at the spectacular moment when she lights a match and hands it to herself in a simple, uninterrupted two shot. She plays Kate and Pat as believable identical twins, the differences between them noticeable enough by the audience but not at all by the other characters—especially not by Bill Emerson, the man with whom both sisters fall in love. Had Davis's performances been any broader, Bill would end up looking like a fool— a too-naive husband unable to tell the difference between the woman he should have married and the one he actually did. Had her performances been any subtler, the melodrama would lose its punch, since Kate's repression and Pat's sensuality would have run together into an undefined and meaningless intermingling. As she was when at her best, Davis makes clever but restrained decisions: Pat tends to look out of the corner of her eyes, revealing her calculating nature, while Kate's brows knit in attentiveness as a way of establishing both her intelligence and her hang-ups. The Bosworth twins are two of her most nuanced performances.

A Stolen Life's production was plagued by illnesses. Glenn Ford called in sick March 3, 4, and 5; Davis went out on the sixth and stayed out so long that the whole production shut down on the twelfth and didn't pick up again until she returned on the nineteenth. Then came the boils. On April 10, Bette showed up at the studio with facial abscesses so severe that she couldn't apply her makeup. Her "face looks so bad . . . all broken out," the production manager, Al Alleborn, noted in his production log. The production ground to a halt till the fourteenth. Despite these delays, A Stolen Life was running only ten days behind schedule, but then on May 1 Bette took sick again and stayed out for three more days. Jack Warner was particularly annoyed at Bette's absence on the first because she'd managed to appear at a Hollywood Democratic Committee meeting the night before.[46]

At some point, Curtis Bernhardt walked off the picture. His dispute was with Warner Bros., not Bette. The Warners archives contain the draft of a letter from the front office to Davis informing her that Michael Curtiz was taking over the direction of A Stolen Life despite her objections. But Bernhardt resolved the dispute, returned to work, and finished the picture.

Davis credits the success of the special optical effects to the camera operators Russell Collings and Willard Van Enger. Bernhardt cites the cinematographer Sol Polito. Polito became ill late in the filming, and Ernie Haller took over; both men are named in the film's opening credits, though Polito's name is larger because he did most of the shooting.

Bernhardt didn't mince words in an interview with Mary Kiersch: "Polito was a sweetheart. Haller was a ruthless, ambitious man."[47]

There was location shooting in Monterey in mid-June—the lighthouse scenes had already been shot in Laguna Beach, where Warners actually built a Cape Cod–style lighthouse because a suitable one didn't exist on the Southern California coast—and by the time the filming concluded at the end of July, *A Stolen Life* had run over schedule by thirty-three days. Davis and Ford returned to the studio for a few days of retakes in January 1946, and the film was released in May.

A Stolen Life was an unusually expensive production for Warner Bros., but it still made money. According to studio records, its negative cost was $2,217,410. But by July 1947, the film had taken in over $4 million at the box office—by any standard a big success.[48]

THE HOLLYWOOD DEMOCRATIC Committee meeting Bette Davis attended on May 1, 1945, was not an organization devoted to advancing the Democratic Party but rather to support the broader goals of a democratic society, and as such it—and Bette—came under the scrutiny of the FBI. Davis had attracted the bureau's notice at least as early as 1943, but it amounted to little. The FBI recorded the fact that an article in the *California Eagle* ("a Negro newspaper," the entry specifies) stated that Bette—along with Ethel Waters, Clarence Muse, and Hattie McDaniel—was scheduled to appear at a war bond drive sponsored by the Negro Victory Committee of Los Angeles. Another entry in the file notes that her picture had appeared in the *Daily People's World*, "a West Coast Communist newspaper."

The file picks up a bit of steam in 1945 with duly recorded notations of Bette's having joined the Hollywood Independent Citizens' Committee of the Arts, Sciences, and Professions (HICCASP), the result of a merger between the Hollywood Democratic Committee and a similar East Coast group. Bette, Greer Garson, and Katharine Hepburn became members of another committee, the purpose of which was to award screenwriters whose work, in the FBI's words, combined "mass entertainment appeal with mature treatment of national and international issues," always a suspect endeavor. And Bette's nomination—along with Lena Horne, Orson Welles, Norman Corwin, and Eddie "Rochester" Anderson—for an Interracial Film and Radio Guild Award was the subject of another notation.

The most ludicrous entry, with names whited out by the FBI before being released through the Freedom of Information Act, runs in its entirety as follows: "_____ was present on 4/26/45 during a conversation between _____ in which _____ informed _____ that the meeting Sunday would have to be prompt as _____ has a meeting at Bette Davis's house."

The FBI file chronicles Davis's decidedly mixed feelings about the Hollywood Democratic Committee and HICCASP.[49] The bureau's informants were often wrong: one of them assumed that the "Beth Davis" who gave generously to the Communist Party in Rhode Island referred to "Bette Davis, the movie actress." Another claimed when Bette was elected as a HICCASP officer that she was "a CPA line follower" (meaning someone who rotely spouted the Communist Party line). Neither was true. More accurate is this entry: "_____ on 6/24/45 reported a conversation between _____ and Jack Lawson [a leftist screenwriter and member of the Communist Party of America who was later sentenced to prison after refusing to name names while testifying before the House Committee on Un-American Activities] in which _____ told Jack that 'this Bette Davis thing' is more serious than he thought and he was inclined to believe she thinks the Committee is too radical." (The "Bette Davis thing" appears to refer to Davis's vocalizing her opinion and, typically, causing a commotion.) In August 1945, an informant told of attending a dinner party at which someone had mentioned his surprise at the growth of communism in the film industry, prompting Davis to state that "she would not associate with any organization that has a Communist in it. She said she would leave an organization if she knew there was a Communist in it." The informant "described Davis as an emotional type who is lonely."[50]

During a studio workers' strike in October 1945, the strikers told one of the FBI's rats that they thought it would be great publicity "if they could stop some big star like Bette Davis—keep her out by a picket line." According to Jack Lawson, Bette was most unsympathetic to the plan. And Mary Ford, the director John Ford's wife and a very active worker at the Hollywood Canteen, remembered that several members of the Canteen's board, among them Bette, Jules Stein, Bob Hope, and Kay Kyser, were so concerned about a perceived leftward push by other board members (foremost John Garfield) that they held what Ford's biographer Joseph McBride calls "secret meetings at her house on Odin Street to make decisions without involving leftists."[51] Davis was a liberal Democrat, but that's as far left as she went.

With the war over, and its mission accomplished, the Hollywood Canteen closed on November 22, 1945, with a farewell celebration starring Bob Hope and Jack Benny. In recognition of her efforts, Bette was presented with a gold pin in the shape of the Canteen's crest, with her initials set in diamonds and rubies.[52] The FBI got wind of Bette's (and two or three other names, all whited out) desire to "take over one million dollars" of the Canteen's remaining funds over the objections of the Canteen's union supporters "and have themselves appointed trustees in perpetuity." According to Davis, the figure was only $500,000, and she was scarcely grabbing the money for herself and her fellow board members. In any event, the controversy ended when Jules Stein formed the Hollywood Canteen Foundation, which invested the leftover money under his supervision and continued to contribute to service members' causes and other charities as late as 2003.

A STOLEN LIFE was a financial success, but both Warner Bros. and Bette Davis understood that B.D. Productions wasn't really such a good idea after all, so on February 4, 1946, they agreed to a new set of terms for Davis's continued employment at the studio. First, Warners and B.D. Productions were released from any prior obligations; in short, Davis's company was no longer under any legal compulsion to produce more films and was now solely in the business of cashing any remaining proceeds from *A Stolen Life*. (Davis owned 80 percent of B.D. Productions; the remaining shares were divided between Jules Stein, Dudley Furse, and Ruthie; the company was finally liquidated at the end of September 1947.)[53] The new contract with Warners was to run for 172 weeks, thus ending around the middle of 1949, and it covered no more than eight films. Davis was to be paid $6,000 per week for the first sixty-six weeks and $7,000 per week for the remainder. The new contract also granted Bette the right to make an unlimited number of guest appearances on the radio as long as the programs on which Bette appeared weren't adaptations of films produced by other studios.[54]

"I am so terribly anxious for you to buy the Mary Lincoln story," Davis wrote in a note to Jack Warner around this time. "I am so desperately anxious to have you own this," she repeated. Davis pitched the heroine of the piece as a combination of a power-behind-the-throne kingmaker, Scarlett O'Hara, and "even the *Back Street* type of woman—the discarded woman." She also expressed interest in developing it as a theater piece, but she was certain that Warner wouldn't permit it.[55] The idea went nowhere.

Early in 1946, when Warners bought the film rights to Philip Wylie's novel *Night unto Night*, *Variety* speculated that the studio intended it for Bette, but the role ultimately went to Viveca Lindfors, in her American debut, opposite Ronald Reagan. In May, Warners announced that it intended to star Bette in a remake of Ernst Lubitsch's 1925 *Lady Windermere's Fan*, based on the Oscar Wilde play, but Warners sold the rights to Fox the following year, and the role eventually went to Jeanne Crain.

Liberty reported that after her current film, *Deception*, Davis's next project would be *Ethan Frome*.[56] *Liberty* also relayed some amusing details about the party Warner Bros. held for its employees at some point in 1946. The highlight of the evening was Bette's appearance, as herself, in a skit called "The Strange Career of Bette Davis." Robert Alda played the role of Jack Warner. "I can't hire you, my girl," Alda's Warner told the aspiring starlet. "You can't even spell *Betty* correctly. I'm sure you aren't very bright." But by the time the skit ended, Bette was firmly ensconced in Jack Warner's chair, her feet on his desk, and one of his cigars in her mouth. Warner himself laughed very hard at the little comedy, but then several hundred of his employees were eyeing his reaction at the time.[57]

DECEPTIONS

AVIS FILMED *DECEPTION* FROM LATE April through mid-September 1946; the production, under Irving Rapper's direction, ran well over a month beyond schedule. The property began as a two-actor play called *M. Lamberthier* by Louis Verneuil, which played on Broadway in 1928 under the title *Jealousy* and starred Fay Bainter and John Halliday. It concerned a temperamental artist who becomes madly jealous of his new bride's wealthy former lover and patron. When Paramount adapted it into a 1929 melodrama for Jeanne Eagels and Fredric March, the director, Jean de Limur, opened it up by bringing the ex-lover onto the screen as well as several secondary characters. He also introduced retribution in the form of a shooting: the artist kills the ex-lover.

Warner Bros. originally acquired the rights with the idea of casting Barbara Stanwyck and Paul Henreid, but Bette ended up in the Stanwyck role. Claude Rains rounded out the cast as the rich, witty, demonic former lover. The most significant change Warners made to the property in all its various incarnations was to make all three central characters intensely musical: Christine (Bette) is an accomplished if largely unsung pianist; Karel (Henreid) is an émigré cellist who suffered the war in Europe but survived, albeit in a weakened state; and Hollenius (Rains) is a flamboyant composer and conductor. And for once Max Steiner didn't write the score; Warners gave the commission to Erich Wolfgang Korn-gold, the Austrian émigré known for his Richard Strauss–like late romantic style, soaring melodic invention, and dense chromatic har-monies. The pulsing musicality of *Deception* is one of the film's most ef-fective devices, for at their operatic best, the three characters are guided by passions so powerful that they can't be tied down by mere words.

In his memoirs, Paul Henreid claims that the Production Code Ad-ministration was alarmed about *Deception*'s proposed ending, in which Davis's character goes back to her husband. The PCA insisted on pun-ishment for her earlier affair, Henreid insisted; it was the PCA that im-posed the violent ending in which Christine shoots and kills Hollenius, leading to what Henreid calls "a thoroughly unbelievable situation, and the entire picture suffered from it." But de Limur's film features a killing as well. What Warners shifted was the character who commits the crime, Bette already having proven herself to look magnificent while firing a pistol at a man she's loved. Davis, too, blamed the PCA, but for a slightly different problem: "*Deception* was completely ruined by censorship," she told an interviewer. "We wrote the last scene, in which I had to con-fess my crime, ten thousand ways, but they were all so phony we never did get a solution."[1]

After only a week of filming, Bette crashed her car on the way to La-guna; another car forced her off the road, and she slammed into a tree. She called the studio after getting home and said she'd have to wait to see her doctor before she knew whether she could report for work the following day. The next day, Saturday, May 4, she was having dizzy spells and didn't come in. Dr. Wilson told the studio on Monday, the sixth, that Bette was flat on her back and had to stay that way for at least two days to provide time for yet another physician, Dr. Penny, to go over the X-rays he had ordered. Irving Rapper and Henry Blanke visited her at home, but they only saw Sherry; Bette remained sequestered in her room. They reported back to Jack Warner, though, that she must have "had a terrific blow from the looks of the car," the windshield having shattered where she hit her head. But the X-rays showed nothing seri-ous, and she was back at work on Wednesday, the eighth.[2]

She was out with a cold on the twenty-third, twenty-fourth, and twenty-fifth—Davis's maid had called in to report the illness—and al-though she reported for work on the twenty-seventh, she came down with strep throat on the thirty-first. Dr. Dicke, the studio physician, was concerned that possibly the damp air of Laguna Beach was the real culprit rather than *Streptococcus pyogenes*, but Paul Henreid was sick as well.

Bette returned and worked steadily and calmly through June—until the twenty-second, that is. That's when Steve Trilling paid a visit to Davis in her dressing room. It was about 11:45 a.m., and just before Bette was to film a five-page scene. Knowing how far behind schedule *Deception* had fallen, Trilling began, would she mind being ready to shoot at 9:00 a.m. instead of 10:00 a.m. and work till 6:00 p.m., not 5:00 p.m.? Bette didn't take the suggestion well. Trilling had a hell of a nerve to ask her this, she told him, given her agreement with Warners to arrive by 9:00 a.m. and work until 5:00 p.m. And she couldn't work any harder than she was already working. Then she burst into hysterical tears.

The company was told to be ready to shoot at 9:00 a.m. the following Monday. But on Sunday, Bette's agent, Lew Wasserman, called: Bette won't be in at all on Monday morning, he said. She's sick.

Jack Warner himself sent a telegram that day to Bette's two current addresses: 671 Sleepy Hollow Lane in Laguna Beach and 134 S. Carmelina Drive in Brentwood, Bette having sold Riverbottom after her marriage to Sherry, presumably because it carried too many associations with Farney. "We are not responsible for the working hours under which the industry is making its pictures," Warner opined, creatively forgetting that as the head of a major studio it was he who set the industry's policies. Warner then ordered his accounting office to prepare a detailed report of what it cost him not to shoot any scenes for *Deception* on Monday, June 24. It came to precisely $6,474.83, including ten hours of work by the service porter at eighty-seven cents an hour.

Davis returned to work but went out again, claiming that she had hurt her finger on July 3. The finger was still sufficiently troubled on the fifth to keep her away. This time Warner slapped her on suspension.

Bette arrived on Monday, the eighth, and asked to address the company. There were things the crew ought to know, she said to the assembled camera operators, sound recordists, makeup people, costumers, electricians, and grips, as well as Rapper and Blanke, who were certainly interested in hearing what their star had to say. She had hurt her finger, she began. She had to have X-rays taken. She was surprised to discover that shooting calls had been issued on the days she had told them she wasn't able to shoot because of the injury. This, to Bette, demonstrated a complete lack of consideration for the crew, and she resented the fact that it might seem to the crew that it was her fault that they'd been called in to work when the producer, the director, and the whole front office knew she couldn't shoot anything at all.

Having gotten this out of her system, Bette spent the day working. Warners rescinded the suspension.

On one unspecified day Ernie Haller was ill and Bette refused to shoot without him. Irving Rapper was more generous to Haller than Bernhardt was; Haller was, in Rapper's words, "a cosmetician's camera-man, very concerned with making the stars look beautiful."[3] Davis was never the vainest of movie stars, but she certainly wanted to look as beautiful as possible in a film like *Deception*. Bette went out sick again on July 30 and 31, but so did Claude Rains.

On August 9, Warner Bros. denied Davis's request to do a broadcast for Cresta Blanca's radio show because Cresta Blanca was a winery and therefore might create an unsavory association in the malleable mind of the public. She took sick again on the tenth. All in all, she was out for a total of 17 days. *Deception* took 122 working days to complete—46 days longer than planned.

Aside from Claude Rains's entrance—Hollenius disrupts Christine and Karel's wedding party, held at Christine's well-appointed apart-ment, by dramatically throwing the door open and standing just inside the doorway with his overcoat draped over his shoulders like Dracula's cape—and a spectacularly funny scene at a restaurant, *Deception* is much less entertaining than it should be. "A party indeed," Rains intones after the wedding reception grinds to a halt at his abrupt and menacing ap-pearance. "That object, I presume, is a wedding cake. Champagne. All very fitting. I infer a husband."

Christine's apartment, designed by Anton Grot, is not only beautiful but prescient. It's a loft located at the top of a Manhattan industrial build-ing. To get to it, one has to take an elevator to the floor below and walk up a dimly lit flight of stairs to the penthouse. It's the height of future style. Inside are several large rooms, obviously cut from one open area, and one wall near the piano consists entirely of angled panes of glass. According to the historians of 1940s style in Hollywood Howard Man-delbaum and Eric Myers, Grot based his design on Leonard Bernstein's current apartment.[4]

Hollenius invites Christine and Karel to join him for dinner before Karel performs, his intent being to so unnerve Karel that he will play badly and humiliate himself. Rapper introduces the sequence wittily. As the threesome enters the restaurant, we see a dish being prominently and elaborately flambéed—as though Hollenius carries with him the fires of hell in the form of cherries jubilee. Rains is obviously enjoying himself as much as his character does; Hollenius relishes the calculated dithering with which he chooses the entrée, the *potage*, the proper wines. He picks up a dead partridge with the head and feathers still attached, sniffs it, and pronounces it worthy, only to worry the issue of its preparation to death. Should it be stuffed with what he pronounces "troofles" or served more simply? He selects the troofles. He orders the trout to start. Then changes his mind: woodcock, not partridge! All of this drives Karel to precisely the state of distraction Hollenius desires.

In the face of all this theatricality, Bette remains understated. As with Mary Astor's performance in *The Great Lie*, Rains isn't stealing any scenes because Davis has yielded them to him. Her Christine is remarkably calm for a woman whose lies spiral out of control, and even when she shows up at Hollenius's baroque mansion and assassinates him, her tempestuous pianist remains under an eerie sort of self-discipline. It's as though Bette played out *Deception*'s drama by way of her personal turmoil—the frequent absences from the set due to her illnesses, the car crash, the injured finger—and by the time the cameras rolled she had no theatricality left to give.

One of *Deception*'s most delightful details is the severely square-shouldered white fur cape Davis wears when she plugs Rains with the pistol shot. It's not padded as much as framed, and it sits on the back of her neck as if suspended by a curtain rod. Her new designer, Bernard Newman, sets it off by pairing it with an all-black dress. Camp at its best, it's both the height of style and risible, as chic a garment as Davis ever wore and yet as comical in its way as the curtains Carol Burnett wore in her immortal parody of Scarlett O'Hara. ("I saw it in the window and I just couldn't resist.")

"I killed him!" Christine confesses to a startled Karel on her knees, the striking fur cape gone tragically missing for the big confession. "Tonight—all the time since you first asked me about him—I've told you nothing but lies. One lie. One small lie at first—to be explained the next day, I thought. And then it was nothing but lies! You see I thought you'd leave me if you knew. I thought you'd give up the concert. I thought you'd have nothing!

"I was wrong. I see that now." That's an understatement.

"Oh, Christine! You must be the happiest woman in the world!" a bystander cries as Christine and Karel make their exit at the end of the film. Unfortunately, Rapper hammers home the irony by tracking into a close-up of Davis—one that's ill-matched to the previous shot to boot. When all is said, done, and shot, *Deception* doesn't quite work.

THERE WAS ONE other reason for Davis's spate of illnesses and absences and temper tantrums during the production of *Deception*: she was pregnant.

"The rumor on the set was that I was really the father of Bette's baby," Paul Henreid claimed, and "Bette, for reasons of her own and probably to spite her husband, encouraged the rumor. She would tell our friends, 'I have such a crush on Paul, but he just won't give me the right time. I don't know how I can get an affair going with him.' It started as a joke at first, and I took it as one, but eventually the humor, if any, began to wear thin, and it started to annoy Lisl and me, particularly since I never believed she really wanted an affair. It was simply a ploy to annoy her husband."

Bette and Henreid had been friends since *Now, Voyager*, and it was only natural that they'd spend time together in Bette's dressing room trailer. "Whenever we were there together and she saw her husband coming on the lot, she'd lock her door and, if he knocked, she would shout out, 'Paul and I are busy! Leave us alone!' The implication was that being 'busy' was more than just rehearsing lines. I began to think the 'joke' had gone far enough, because Bette's husband was not only a very jealous man, but also a very strong one." One day the trailer began to shake violently. Henreid assumed it was an earthquake, but Bette knew better: "Earthquake my ass! It's that stupid bastard of a husband of mine."

She then proceeded to invite Sherry in to join them, saying, "It's all over anyway. We've had our little affair and now we're having coffee. You might as well be civilized and join us." Sherry declined the invitation and stomped off. Perplexed, Henreid asked Bette why she'd said that. "She smiled at me with that absolute charm of hers and said, 'But we might as well have an affair, Paulie—everyone thinks we are.'"

"Thanks to you," Henreid replied. "Let's get back to work."

"And that," Henreid concluded, "was that."[5]

Sherry was a violent husband who, after all, had not only hurled a steamer trunk at her but threw her out of the car on their honeymoon.[6] That Bette goaded him scarcely excuses his actions, but it does partially explain them. It was a marriage of mutual abuse.

In October, Bette officially informed Warner Bros. that for personal reasons—obviously her pregnancy—she would not be able to work for an indefinite period beginning in the middle of December. Warners agreed that she would be kept on salary for the duration.

The Sherrys—accompanied by Bobby and her daughter, Fay—set off by train from the San Bernardino station for Butternut to await the birth of the baby. They arrived on November 1. In one of the few kind passages regarding Sherry in *The Lonely Life*, Davis recalled that although she looked forward to the baby's arrival, she didn't feel as though she was doing anything special. Sherry consoled her by pointing out that "creating a baby is the only creating for most women. You have been creating for years."[7]

The family was at Butternut on December 15 when Sheilah Graham let fly a major scoop on her radio broadcast: "Bette Davis—no matter what they say at the studio—is leaving Warners when her present contract expires in another eighteen months. And Bette is wasting no time because she is already contacting writers and directors and cameramen for her new independent movie company." Whether Davis was in fact developing any independent film projects at this time is doubtful. In any event, in a letter to Warner Bros.' lawyers, Roy Obringer called Graham an "air parasite."[8]

After spending an especially rough winter at Butternut, the Sherrys returned to Laguna Beach in March to await the baby's birth; they were concerned about being too far from an available doctor. They moved from the house on Sleepy Hollow Lane to a new one overlooking the beach at Wood's Cove—"a dream," as Bette described it, "filled with antiques, wood-paneled walls, and all my beloved books." The Wood's Cove house was not what one would call a beach house. It sat on a bluff high over the ocean and in fact appeared to climb up the cliff. It featured a large entrance hall with old English prints on the walls. To the right was a small library with floor-to-ceiling bookcases, a fireplace, a desk, and a club chair; the library served as Bette's study. Down the hall was an expansive living room, where Sherry did his painting. The living room walls were covered with his landscapes and still lifes. The kitchen and dining room were upstairs along with a porch. The bedroom was on the top floor.[9] "Keeping house does keep a woman busy," Bette remarked, "and time flew."[10]

Two snapshots in Davis's scrapbooks taken the night before she gave birth: one shows a massively pregnant Bette looking out over the ocean, the other of her leaning backward for balance and looking very, very happy.[11]

Time reported the blessed event: "Born. To Bette Davis, 39, high-strung cinemactress, and painter (ex-boxer) William Grant Sherry, 32, her third husband: her first child, a girl, on May Day, which Bette Davis chose for her Cesarean section; in Santa Ana, Calif. Name: Barbara Davis Sherry. Weight: 7 lbs."[12]

They called the baby B.D. They pronounced it "beady."

RUTHIE DIDN'T COME calling as often as she once did. Sherry forbade her to do what she'd long been accustomed to doing, namely marching in unannounced. "He convinced me that I was now sufficiently grown up to run my own life," Davis wrote. "I stopped confiding in Mother at thirty-six." Ruthie responded by escalating from "distrust" of Sherry to "loathing."[13]

Ruthie also found that she couldn't adjust to marriage after so many years of being single, so she divorced Robert Palmer.[14]

Bobby had by that point divorced Robert Pelgram; the couple separated in the spring of 1944. She'd given birth to a daughter, Ruth Favor Pelgram—always called Fay—in October 1939 and immediately plunged into a postpartum depression so severe that she had to be hospitalized. Bette cared for the baby at Riverbottom until Bobby recovered. "The baby is with me until Bobby is stronger; she's been so ill since the baby's birth," Davis told *Modern Screen*'s Gladys Hall at the time.[15]

In February 1946, *Photoplay*, covering Bette's wedding with Sherry, also gushed that Bobby "was rumored to be marrying again, this time a young doctor, also from Laguna Beach."[16] The identity of the seaside physician remains a mystery, but in June of the following year Bobby married a man by the name of David Berry. "The Davis girls were now, absurdly, Mrs. Sherry and Mrs. Berry. There was rhyme if not reason to both of our marriages," Bette later remarked.[17]

David Berry was, according to Fay Pelgram, "a nice man, but he had a problem with alcohol." Bette's wedding gift to the couple was either cruelly witty or simply cruel: a dozen cases of liquor. By the end of 1948, after one too many binges on her husband's part, Bobby threw Berry out of the house and obtained a restraining order against him, and her marriage was effectively over. The divorce was granted on March 4, 1949.

Soon thereafter, Bobby suffered another nervous breakdown and spent the next two years in a sanitarium.[18]

A<small>FTER</small> B.D.'<small>S BIRTH</small>, Davis returned to the screen in *Winter Meeting*. The film's director, the fantastically named Bretaigne Windust, came from Broadway, where his most recent production had been the musical *Finian's Rainbow*; before that he'd staged the comedy *State of the Union*. Earlier credits include the comedies *Arsenic and Old Lace* and *Life with Father*. *Winter Meeting* was his first motion picture. It was a melodrama.

According to Davis, Windust "had the idea that he would introduce a brand-new Bette Davis to the screen. He would have been smarter to leave the old one alone." She never liked the movie, which she called "a badly drawn triangle . . . a dreary film and hardly a triumphant return."[19] And there's nothing especially new about Bette; her performance is thoughtful and muted, rather like her interpretation of Kate Bosworth in *A Stolen Life*.

The story is simple: "Slick" Novak, a brooding war hero visiting New York City, is set up with a bit of flashy fluff (Janis Paige) but falls instead for Susan (Davis), a troubled poet with massive inherited wealth and a taste for tailored suits. Burt Lancaster turned down the role of Slick after telling Warners' head of production, Steve Trilling, what was wrong with the screenplay scene by scene.[20] Thirteen actors tested for Slick, including Richard Widmark, whom Davis rejected. They settled on strapping James Davis, fresh from a series of small and often uncredited roles in westerns and action pictures. His screen test was apparently excellent, and Bette insisted that he be cast, but as she later acknowledged, his performance in the film itself was lackluster. James Davis went on to appear in over 140 films and television shows, but in *Winter Meeting* he makes little impression. One almost wishes they'd cast George Brent.

Winter Meeting took forever to film. Shooting began on September 15, 1947, but the production didn't wrap until February 1948. Jack Warner made noises about seeking financial "relief" for all the time lost because of Davis's illnesses.[21]

With its combination of Windust's enervating direction, a set of underdrawn characters (with one flaming exception), and the lack of chemistry between the two Davises, *Winter Meeting* is dull. Still, a ludicrous shock comes when Slick looks down at Susan, who is kneeling by a taste-ful fire, and intones, "This is going to be tough on you, Susan, but all my life I've wanted and planned on being a priest!" (Thunderous Max Steiner chord.) "*A priest?!*" Susan cries. The revelation puts a crimp in the romance.

Winter Meeting features two notable details: the only screen appear-ance of William Grant Sherry, who appears dressed in a sailor suit in a crowded subway station (he's the one carrying a sack over his shoulder in front of Bette as she makes her way up the stairs), and the marvelous performance of John Hoyt as Susan's bitchy friend, Stacy. Hoyt is a sort of poor queen's Clifton Webb—slightly pinched and delightfully prissy. "Well, if you don't mind my saying it, I'm relieved," Stacy snaps at one point. "He may have been a hero—and the uniform is *devastating*—but that's the trouble! The really dreadful letdown comes when you see them dressed in civvies, all set to go to work in a soap factory in Akron." A lit-tle later: "Susan, dear, this is really dreadful—I'm terribly upset!—but what I simply *can't* understand is how a man like that got to first base with you! The fellow obviously has nothing inside that handsome head. Of course he probably has *other* attributes." Bette shoots him a very funny look before responding.

Why Bretaigne Windust was selected to direct Bette's next picture, *June Bride*, is unclear, given Bette's distaste for his directorial style. She'd been shocked by Windust's insistence not only on extensive rehearsals on the sets of *Winter Meeting* but on a complete dress rehearsal before the cameras began to roll. "Not since the George Arliss days had such involved preproduction rehearsals taken place," Davis later noted.[22]

Davis had mixed feelings about *June Bride*. "I had fun," she wrote in *The Lonely Life*, "as I seldom got a chance at a good comedy." But earlier in the book she damned her costar for a particularly dastardly method of hogging scenes: "Robert Montgomery and I made one picture to-gether, and it might just as well have been a ballet. An excellent actor who needn't have bothered embroiled me in a fascinating tangle of me-chanics. . . . Mr. Montgomery, resenting, I presume, my role of a woman in charge, purposely added elements to his close-up performance that did not exist in the original scene. By reacting to things I never did, he invalidated my close-ups, making them worthless. It was upstaging in its most diabolical form. Needless to say, it was thoroughly unprofes-sional as well."[23]

But *June Bride*'s sexual tensions may actually have benefited from

Montgomery's shenanigans. It's the story of a commanding New York professional woman, an editor at the popular women's magazine *Home Life*, and an international ace reporter known for ferreting out the hidden dramas and uncomfortable details of the stories he covers. Their attraction for each other is palpable in a prickly, screwball sort of way. "I never know whether you're going to kiss me or kick me," Carey (Montgomery) tells Linda (Davis) in admiring frustration toward the end. *Home Life*'s gimmick is to make over the middlest of middle-American houses and its occupants. The current task is to create a picture-perfect June wedding in a small Indiana town in the middle of the winter. The magazine has a long lead time. One editor is in charge of renovating the garish, knickknack-ridden rooms. (As Barbara Stanywck says in *Ball of Fire*, "Who decorated this place? The mug that shot Lincoln?") Another, the fat mother. The wedding plans fall into chaos when the bride elopes with the callow groom's older brother, but Carey engineers a real love match between the all-too-cutely named "Boo" (Betty Lynn) and the jilted groom, Bud (Raymond Roe).

Just before the wedding begins, you can catch a glimpse of Debbie Reynolds making her first screen appearance: she's sitting next to the fireplace watching as Bette admonishes a little boy who is bridging between the arm of the couch and the fireplace mantel. Reynolds reappears for a second during the ceremony—she's mostly blocked by the bride—as Windust's camera tracks in on a tearful Linda standing in the doorway. In her memoir, Reynolds tells of sneaking onto the set one day and climbing up to a catwalk, where she watched Davis and Montgomery film the shot of Linda lying on a fur rug and Carey kissing her neck. Reynolds was mesmerized as they took various takes until, she writes, "one of my elbows accidentally slipped from the railing, throwing me slightly off balance, and one of my shoes made the slightest knocking sound on the metal walk. Davis stopped the kiss. She threw Montgomery off and sat up ramrod straight. 'What's that?!' She looked skyward." Reynolds beat a silent retreat as Bette shouted, "This is supposed to be a closed set! *Who is up there?!*" "My heart was pounding. She was furious. I thought she was going to kill me."[24]

Creating appropriate publicity proved to be difficult. Gil Golden, a Warners publicity executive in the New York office, complained that he and his staff had had to do "a lot of fooling around and a lot of dangerous faking of heads and bodies—Montgomery from one still and Davis from another" because none of the unretouched stills conveyed the fact that *June Bride* was a comedy. The publicist Marty Weiser responded from the Burbank office: "Davis absolutely refused to pose for any laughing/happy stills and kept remarking that she didn't want to look like the 'June Bride.'" Bette seems to have been uncharacteristically uncooperative: "She acted as though she was doing us the greatest favor in the world by giving us the few stills she did. However, I asked Morgan [the still photographer on *June Bride*] to shoot Davis laughing off-stage whenever the occasion arose."[25]

Edith Head, borrowed from Paramount at Bette's request, designed Davis's wardrobe for *June Bride*. Head had helped Davis build her own wardrobe on *Winter Meeting*; she simply accompanied Bette on a shopping trip to the department store I. Magnin, though Bette herself credited her favorite Magnin saleswoman, Bertie Strauser. Head received no credit for helping Davis choose her *Winter Meeting* costumes, but the film contains an inside joke: Bette's hairstyle in the early scenes is a direct copy of Edith's.[26]

A postwar comedy, *June Bride* trades in contemporary concerns about women's newfound independence clashing with men's frustrated expectations. Carey hasn't returned from World War II; in fact his backstory tells us that he left for Berlin *after* the war ended in order to avoid settling down with Linda. But however, and whenever, he got there, Carey—like a lot of GIs—has indeed returned from Europe to find his ex-girlfriend thriving without him, both professionally and personally. Bette plays the role of a sophisticated, dynamic, intelligent New York editor as though she was born to do it. Still, the film's happy ending is anything but. It's merely sad to see Linda quit her job to become Mrs. Carey Jackson, but it's nothing short of nauseating to watch, aghast, as she literally picks up his suitcases like a Pullman porter and agrees to tote them behind her man wherever he leads.

JUST AFTER NEW YEAR'S, 1948, one of Hedda Hopper's sources told her that Bette was considering selling the house at Laguna Beach and buying a 750-acre "spot" in Hidden Valley, north of Malibu. The source also said that Ruthie said that Bette and Sherry were thinking about adopting a baby boy from a Chicago orphanage.[27] By February, Hopper's informant was hearing more accurate buzz about marital discord between the Sherrys, but he assured Hopper that he'd investigated the matter and found the rumors to be "just a bit of smog." "It is fact, however, that the Laguna house is on the market for $100,000," he went on, adding that "Bette and Bill are interested in a large ranch near Escondido—Vista to be exact."[28] Vista is south of Laguna.

The couple didn't move. Bette did. "I hoped fatherhood would be good for Sherry and for a time it was," Bette wrote in *This 'n That*, her follow-up to *The Lonely Life*.

> But the cruelty continued. The day after Sherry threw me down the stairs and onto the front lawn, I did not return home from work. I moved into my dressing room at Warners. Actually, it was a two-story apartment planned for me by Perc Westmore, my makeup man and trusted friend. It had a bedroom upstairs and a living room and a makeup room downstairs. The perfect setting, I decided, in which to kill myself. I was quite serious. I didn't want to live this way any longer. How could I deal with such a man? I was even afraid to divorce him. . . . I laid out my best nightgown. I planned every detail. The next morning, when I was due on the set at nine o'clock, there would be a dramatic moment when they broke into my dressing room and found me there. And on the set they would whisper . . . "*Bette Davis is dead.*" For years I had sometimes taken a sleeping pill when I couldn't sleep. I got out all I had and lined them up on the bedside table. And then I started laughing. I laughed myself silly. I said, "This is ridiculous."[29]

Sherry promised to see a psychiatrist, and they reconciled. But, she went on, she "left him for good when one evening, for no reason at all, he threw a silver ice bucket at me. I was holding B.D. in my arms. She was six months old. I had told Sherry if he ever showed any violence toward B.D. I would leave him. I did, once and for all."[30] Davis's chronology is off, however. If B.D. was indeed six months old when Bette left Sherry, the split would have occurred in November 1947. In fact, the couple remained unhappily married for quite some time thereafter.

Sherry, perhaps needless to say, painted a different picture of the marriage than Bette did. According to him, she thwarted his ambitions, ridiculed him, made him feel small, all in a perverse effort to provoke him into taming her. He told a story of an argument the couple had over the family's finances, with Bette needling him about his worthlessness—he was leeching off of her, he couldn't earn a dime on his own, he was basically her kept boy—to the point that he turned the dining table over on top of her. "She was under the table," Sherry said, "with dishes, lettuce, crystal on top of her. I walked out of the room, and I don't know how she got out from under that mess." They worked it out sexually later that night. "She loved it, you see," Sherry explained. "She had to dominate her men, and when they didn't let her, she liked it."[31]

BETTE VISITED NEW YORK City in October 1948. She wanted to stay at the St. Regis, but she became upset when the hotel wasn't able to provide her with four adjoining bedrooms until three days after her arrival. She had changed reservations four times by October 15, and as a frustrated Warners' employee put it in a telegram to the studio, "frankly St. Regis does not care whether she stops there or not—simply trying to accommodate her as favor to Warner Bros." (As it turned out, she spent only October 18 and 19 at the St. Regis and moved to the Hampshire House through the twenty-eighth.)[32]

Late that year, Lew Wasserman was trying to get Warner Bros. to agree to yet another new contract for her—a seven-year deal with one picture per year—even though the old contract had another year to go.[33] "Bette began showing up in my office surrounded by the MCA [Music Corporation of America] group," Jack Warner writes,

> and every time we talked about a new script she would say sweetly: "Jack, can I have a copy for Lew?" "I'd be happy to, honey," I would say, "but I did not engage Lew Wasserman to read scripts. I want *you* to read it." But Lew would get his copy, and he would come back claiming to have read it and reporting that we flunked our Wasserman test. What he really meant was that his fifth cousin Amanda had read it, and on their recommendation he would decide it wasn't good enough for Bette Davis. Before long the ten-percenters had Bette so confused that it affected her story vision, and she was laying bigger eggs than an ostrich. [If Davis was indeed laying eggs during the mid- to late 1940s, she was continuing to lay them in a familiar nest in Burbank with the assistance of Warner Bros. screenwriters, Warner Bros. producers, Warner Bros. directors, and Jack L. Warner himself.] I simply couldn't take it. Or them. I finally cracked down, and barred the MCA blackbirds from the lot—a move no one had ever

dared to make in Hollywood. I kept them outside peeking through fence knotholes for quite a while, but eventually they sneaked in with the connivance of other studio executives, or by conning my brother Harry.

When they pushed me too far, I told Bette I was through. We settled her contract, and I was relieved to see her go elsewhere with her cortege. Thereafter many of the Davis pictures were flops, and the sun went down on her shining sky.[34]

Bette's exit from Warner Bros. was much more complicated than either Warner or Davis ever publicly acknowledged. During the first week of January 1949, Lew Wasserman suggested to Jack Warner that Bette make a film called *Storm Center*, from a script by Richard Brooks. Warner thought it wasn't a bad idea—the heroine witnesses a KKK murder in the South and helps the DA solve the case—and proposed Raoul Walsh as director. Wasserman abruptly proceeded to ridicule the notion of Walsh directing the picture and offered instead to tear up Davis's contract.

Warner was willing to entertain the idea of setting Bette free—for a price. He claimed his company had advanced Davis a total of $224,000 during various times she hadn't worked over the years, and he offered to sell Davis her contract for that amount. Warner told Wasserman that he'd rather make *Storm Center* with Davis and Walsh than get rid of Bette altogether, but Wasserman responded by telling Warner that Davis actually didn't want to make *Storm Center* after all. What she really wanted, the agent said, was to be released from her contract. (The film in question was made under the title *Storm Warning* in 1951; Davis did make a film called *Storm Center* in 1956, but it was based on a different property.)

On January 6, Wasserman and Warner agreed that if Davis paid Warner $124,000 and waived her claim to the $100,000 the studio was still holding against *A Stolen Life*, she could leave Warners for good.[35]

So at the end of January 1949, Bette Davis and Warner Bros. signed a brand-new contract for four pictures at the precisely specified rate of $10,285.72 per week for "a period of not less than fourteen consecutive weeks with respect to each motion picture produced hereunder." The contract also gave Davis the right to make one outside picture per year.[36]

There was a touch of absurdity in the middle of it. "*The Octopus and*

Miss Smith is, as I'm sure you know, out of the question," Bette wrote in a note to Jack Warner in mid-January while contract discussions were taking place. "I could not possibly reconcile myself to this type of comedy. . . . For you and I to end it all over *The Octopus and Miss Smith* seems entirely unnecessary."[37] (The comedy was made as *The Lady Takes a Sailor* with Jane Wyman and Dennis Morgan.)

And meanwhile Albert Warner was obsessing over the repayment of certain expenses from Davis's October trip to New York. "If it's the last act as treasurer of W.B. I will see that she pays," he scrawled on one of the many memos written on the subject. At the end of February, the studio sent Davis a bill for $735.27.[38]

"*BEYOND THE FOREST?*" Bette Davis said in response to an interviewer's question in early 1949. "No, I haven't made it. Probably I'm not going to make it. It is a great book, a wonderful story, but they can't make a word of it—not a word. If they make it at all they'll have to change it so completely that it won't even resemble the book."[39]

Warner Bros. bought the film rights to Stuart Engstrand's racy novel in the summer of 1948, and the censor Joseph Breen immediately rejected the very idea of making a movie out of it "because of its treatment of adultery and lust."[40] Jack Warner gave the go-ahead to develop it anyway and assigned Lenore Coffee the task of writing the script. Not surprisingly, Breen summarily rejected Coffee's first draft in late February 1949. "This is a story of a woman who coldly and maliciously conspires to wreck her own marriage," Breen explained. "Pursuing these means, she employs lust in a savage and debased way. More than that, she will not stop short of murder . . . or of attempted abortion." And furthermore, Breen concluded, the ending didn't provide a strong enough voice for traditional morality.[41]

Beyond the Forest is the inflamed tale of Rosa Moline, an ambitious woman stuck in a small town in Wisconsin, her unsatisfying marriage to the bland village doctor, her lust-ridden affair with another man, and her insatiable drive to escape it all for the big city, Chicago. It's *Madame Bovary* played as pulp fiction. "That was a terrible movie," Davis flatly, wrongly, declared many years later. "It didn't have to be. Primarily it was terrible because they insisted on putting me in it. I was too old for the part, and I was temperamentally wrong. I mean, I don't think you can believe for a moment that if I was so determined to get to Chicago I wouldn't just have upped and gone years ago."[42] (She's got a point there, though the same question might also be asked about why the stifled Leslie Crosbie doesn't simply leave Herbert Marshall and his boring rubber plantation in *The Letter*.) Bette thought that Virginia Mayo would have been a better choice as Rosa Moline, and she was appalled at Warners' choice of Joseph Cotten to play the husband, Louis—not because she didn't like Cotten, but because she *did*. "Who would leave that darling, lovely man?" she once commented. "The character in the book was a Eugene Pallette type—a horrible, rich, fat man in a little town," she added.[43] In Bette's theory, Pallette would be easy to ditch; Cotten would not.

Joseph Cotten thought as little of *Beyond the Forest* as Bette did. "As for me," he wrote in his beautifully named memoir *Vanity Will Get You Somewhere*, "I will admit to having stumbled into several trashbins here and there, but never into quite such an important trashbin."

Ironically, a scene in *Beyond the Forest* became one of Bette Davis's most iconic. Edward Albee made it so.

> MARTHA: What a dump. Hey, what's that from? "What a dump!"
>
> GEORGE: How would I know what . . .
>
> MARTHA: Aw, come on! What's it from? *You* know . . .
>
> GEORGE: . . . Martha . . .
>
> MARTHA: WHAT'S IT FROM, FOR CHRIST'S SAKE?
>
> GEORGE (wearily): What's what from? [. . .]
>
> MARTHA: Dumbbell! It's from some goddamn Bette Davis picture . . . some goddamn Warner Bros. epic [. . .] Bette Davis gets peritonitis in the end . . . she's got this big black fright wig she wears all through the picture, and she gets peritonitis, and she's married to Joseph Cotten or something. [. . .] Bette Davis comes home from a hard day at the grocery store . . .
>
> GEORGE: She works in a grocery store?
>
> MARTHA: She's a housewife; she buys things. . . . And she comes home with the groceries, and she walks into the modest living room of the modest cottage modest Joseph Cotton has set her up in . . .
>
> GEORGE: Are they married?

> MARTHA (impatiently): Yes. They're married. To each other. Cluck! And she comes in, and she looks around, and she puts her groceries down, and she says, "What a dump!"

George and Martha never recall the name of the picture in Albee's *Who's Afraid of Virginia Woolf?* George suggests *Chicago*, but as Martha insultingly observes, "*Chicago* was a 'thirties musical starring little Miss Alice *Faye*. Don't you know *anything*?"[44]

But Martha, too, gets it wrong. Bette isn't coming home from a hard day at the grocery store at all but rather emerging from her upstairs bedroom. She strolls down the stairway of the finest house in town—it's nothing but the best for Rosa Moline—and she's filing her nails with an air of distraction, and she walks into the expansive living room she's decorated to the nines using every nickel of modest Joseph Cotten's meager income, and she says, offhandedly and without biting any of her words, "What a dump."

If Martha had remembered *Beyond the Forest* more distinctly, she might also have imitated one of Bette's later lines. "I know you're not interested in my work, but I just saved a woman's life," Rosa's doctor husband remarks. To which Rosa, lying on a wicker porch couch and twisting the ends of her black fright wig, responds in crisp and singsong sarcasm, "*Saved* it for *what*?"

Lenore Coffee made several key changes to the script before shooting began. First she turned Dr. Moline and his rustic friend Moose into stronger voices for morality, a shift that all but demanded the casting of someone like the saintly-looking Cotten over Eugene Pallette, a croaking tub of lard. Coffee also combined several of the men with whom Rosa has affairs into one: Neil Latimer, an industrialist from Chicago. Warners cast David Brian as Latimer. "And then the lover," Bette later raged, "that big boring blond actor—what's he called?—was so dull you could understand it even less."[45] True, David Brian is no Errol Flynn, but he's beefy enough to suggest that he satisfies Rosa sexually in ways that modest Joseph Cotten cannot. In any case, the whole point of Rosa Moline's character is that her decisions are, in every sense of the word, *bad*. As Warner Bros. put it in its twin taglines for the film, "She's a midnight girl in a nine o'clock town!" And: "Nobody's as good as Bette when she's bad!"[46]

Davis was vacationing in Sarasota Springs, Florida, in mid-March when Henry Blanke airmailed her a draft of Coffee's script; the production's proposed start date was set for May 2. Bette showed up at the studio that day, but not for filming. Instead, she told the director King Vidor along with Blanke and Steve Trilling that she liked neither the script nor her casting. When informed of the discussion's tenor as well as its content, Jack Warner took it that she was refusing to do the picture and informed Lew Wasserman that the decision was not hers to make. So on Wasserman's advice, Bette sent a telegram to Warner saying that she wasn't technically refusing the role but simply spelling out her problems with it. Shooting began on Tuesday, May 24.

Given Davis's contempt for the picture, it comes as a surprise to learn that King Vidor found her rather easy to work with: "Bette Davis was full of ups and downs as an actress. She had a temperament that changed quickly from hot to cold all through the picture. She was pleasant to work with, though. She was cooperative and helpful. There was one point where she became very high-strung and she was almost impossible to work with for two days, but once she got over this, it wasn't so bad." Vidor was amazed at "what she could do to enhance her acting performance by using her eyes. She evidently did a lot of thinking about her character."[47]

"I had rehearsed a scene where she was dancing," Vidor recalled, "and I think she was also embracing David Brian. He was rather large and I had the camera in such a way that you could just see about half of Bette Davis's face. You could just see her eyes as she turned. During the take they turned differently, and I said, 'Why don't you do it again so that we can see more of your face.' She got upset and made an absolutely tremendous speech, one of the best performances I've seen. At the end of her speech, I said, 'That's fine with me if you don't want to do it again. I'd just as soon not see your face.' That worked quite well. There was a quiet hush over the stage the rest of that day, but I got the scene shot the way I wanted to eventually. It was almost like child psychology."[48]

Vidor provides her with a most dramatic entrance. After a rather lengthy voice-over sets the scene in the small sawmill town of Loyalton, Wisconsin, and after a series of static shots of quiet, nearly empty streets, Vidor cuts to a courtroom with equally static shots of an immobile crowd of quiet, bland midwesterners all staring solemnly toward the judge. Suddenly Bette stands up into the image, and shouts, "*Why should I kill him!? Will someone tell me that? Why should I want to? It was an accident!*" She punctuates the line by impulsively scratching the back of her neck, the effect of which is to give an itchy toss to the hideous black wig.

She looks monstrous, a fact not lost on the *Hollywood Reporter*, which commented in its review that "photographically, Bette Davis has never looked worse; she affects the most grotesque makeup and the strands of stringy black hair hardly belong to a small town belle out to land a man." But the *Reporter* missed a key point of *Beyond the Forest*: Rosa Moline is scarcely a "belle." She's a tramp. Davis does look horrible, but it's not just the wig, which exposes far too much of her high forehead. Her lipstick is lurid, her mascara equally extreme. And Davis's face itself has broadened and shows its age. (Bette had turned forty-one in April.) What Perc Westmore disguised in *Winter Meeting* and *June Bride* he enhanced in *Beyond the Forest*: not only was Davis no longer oddly attractive; she'd suddenly become downright ugly while losing none of her carnality.

What Davis achieved under Vidor's direction in *Beyond the Forest* is much more intriguing and courageous than either the *Reporter* or Davis herself appreciated. As with the wretched Mildred in *Of Human Bondage*, Davis had the guts to compel audiences to see a contemptible, evil woman as being not only contemptible but repulsive and venal, too. Davis successfully makes us hate her.

And as a result, we adore her. In an early scene, Rosa picks off an innocent porcupine with a single rifle shot. Her husband's geezer friend Moose disapproves, but Rosa couldn't care less. "*I* don't *like* porkies," she cracks. "They *ir*-ritate me."

"I don't want people to like me," she informs her callow husband a little later. "*Nothing* pleases me more than when people don't like me." Then, with a smirk—"Means I don't belong." Davis's voice rises to an abnormally high pitch on the word *nothing*, and she drags it out, too—"*nuuuhhh*-thing." By way of this mannerist, showy, theatrical device, we catch the extent of Rosa's perversity. Rosa Moline is the hearty appetizer served before the main course of Baby Jane Hudson.

But perversely, as with Baby Jane, Rosa Moline presents Bette Davis at her most authentic. *Beyond the Forest* is exactly the kind of film that must be seen to be believed, and the belief it inspires is in the essential truth of camp. Like Vidor's previous film, *The Fountainhead*, *Beyond the Forest* achieves a peculiar but no less worthy goal: melodrama that periodically teeters over the edge into dark comedy. Davis appreciated the value of such a weird, on-the-precipice tone, however little she was aware of the fact. Her fidgety gestures may be tragically clownish, but they're no less tragic for it. Her vocal delivery artificially calls attention to itself as a way of conveying a more ephemeral honesty than invisible naturalism could possibly express. When Davis held a script in contempt, as she clearly held *Beyond the Forest*'s, she worked all the harder to make it work, the consequence being that by the time Rosa attempts to get an abortion, throws herself off a cliff, and comes down with the peritonitis, Davis has chewed every bit of scenery she could get her mouth around and spat it all out. The performance is electrifying.

Rosa Moline dies in feverish dementia while staggering and then crawling in the dirt toward a departing train. One pays her the greatest honor by laughing. In awe.

DAVIS MADE HER exit from Warner Bros. after a row over a medicine bottle, or, more precisely, over the direction Vidor gave her on how to hurl one. As Rosa lies in bed at the end, her temperature rising to the point of altering her skin tone to a rich, sweaty-ripe brown—it now matches that of Jenny, the Molines' surly, gum-chewing Indian maid—Louis tries to give her a shot of what one presumes is an antibiotic to combat what Albee's Martha calls peritonitis. In her delirium, she smacks the medicine away. Bette did it her way. Vidor told her to do it his way. She demanded that he be fired. Jack Warner refused. She asked to be released from her contract, won the release, returned to the set, and did it Vidor's way.

Vidor was unaware of Davis's demand that Warner fire him until later, when Harry Warner told him the story. "They didn't want to tell me because they thought I'd take it out on her or that it would affect our work together. . . . As it turned out, she came up to me at dinner on that last night of work and told me how much she had enjoyed working with me, and that if I ever had any stories she could do, to please let her know. . . . She was preparing herself for freelancing, and if I came up with a good story, she would like to play in it."[49]

According to Davis, her last professional act at Warner Bros.—after eighteen years and fifty-two pictures—was to loop the line "I can't stand it here anymore."[50] She got her wish, though by her own account she drove off the lot for the last time in tears. The trouble was, she couldn't stand it anywhere.

PART THREE

ONGOING CONFLICTS

FAST FORWARD

IN MAY 1983, BETTE, THEN SEVENTY-FIVE, stepped out of the shower, dried herself off, and felt a lump on her breast.[1] She checked into New York Hospital under an assumed name and underwent a mastectomy on June 9. Nine days later she suffered a debilitating stroke. Her doctors told her she'd never work again, but her lawyer, Harold Schiff, disagreed. "You just don't know Bette Davis," he said.[2]

The doctors were wrong. Work was to Bette Davis as human blood is to vampires: hot, fresh, nourishing, and vital for survival. She made twenty-four feature films after she left Warner Bros. in August 1949; over a dozen made-for-televsion movies; several TV pilots; and a number of guest appearances on existing series. She starred in two stage musicals: one in the 1950s, the other in the 1970s. During the latter decade she also performed a one-woman show all over the United States as well as in London, New Zealand, and Australia; and she appeared on countless talk shows until the end of her life.

The mastectomy and stroke slowed her down, but only temporarily. Davis recovered and shot three and a half more pictures before she died in 1989: Agatha Christie's *Murder with Mirrors* and *As Summers Die*, both made for television; Lindsay Anderson's *The Whales of August*; and Larry Cohen's ill-fated *Wicked Stepmother*, out of which she walked after a few weeks of filming, saying that she had no choice but to do so "for the good of my future career."

For any female Hollywood star over the age of fifty to speak without irony of her "future career" might strike one as clinically crazy. After all, Norma Desmond, the demented star of *Sunset Boulevard*, was barely into her fifties, and to put it in the kindest possible light, her comeback ("I *hate* that word!") is quixotic at best. But the octogenarian Bette Davis didn't even see *Wicked Stepmother* as the end of the line. "I'm not a vain person," she explained. Still, she'd seen some of the rushes and commented, "At 80 years old I don't want to look the way I looked. It seriously could be the end of anybody ever hiring me again."[3]

She was a hellion—on the sets of her films, at the homes of her friends, at New York Hospital at the time of the mastectomy and stroke. One can only begin to imagine the acid rage she hurled at nurses and interns, errants and innocents, in the days following her surgery and stroke. "After a stroke you have a very short fuse with people" was the excuse she offered to a visitor to her hospital suite. "Bette," the friend responded, "you've always had a short fuse with people. Don't blame it on your stroke."[4]

Still, she managed to display proper etiquette to a neighbor down the hall. Robert Lantz, the agent who represented Davis in the 1970s and '80s, tells the story: "At the end of the corridor on the 16th floor were two special suites, what we now call a junior suite at a hotel—a bedroom and a sitting area with sofas. Bette was in one. In the opposite one was Mrs. Richard Nixon. Now Bette was, like Myrna Loy, a militant Democrat. I came to visit her, and because there were so many flowers, she said to me, 'Do you think I should send some flowers to Mrs. Nixon?' I said, 'If you think you should, you should.' She told me the next day that she *had* sent the flowers with a note that said, 'We're neighbors, and I hope these please you.' Mrs. Nixon sent back a very nice letter but said she was allergic to flowers. But how nice it was of Bette to have offered. I mean, very few people would have had the manners, especially with somebody she hated as much as Bette hated the Nixons."[5]

The breast cancer metastasized; that's what got her in the end. She died on October 6, 1989, at the American Hospital in Neuilly, a suburb of Paris, where she was taken after falling ill at the San Sebastian Film Festival in late September. Her attitude all along was a mix of denial and concern for what she refused to stop calling her "future career." Before leaving for San Sebastian, she told her friend Robert Osborne, "I hope this will prove to the world I'm not dying. The only thing that's making me sick are all those awful reports and rumors about how ill I'm supposed to be. Where do they start? And how do you get them to stop?"[6]

It was the stroke, not the cancer, that defined Bette Davis's public persona in the last five years of her life. Or, more precisely, it wasn't the stroke itself that defined Bette in the end but rather her vitally stubborn persistence in the face of it—her refusal to withdraw tastefully behind a veil of privacy despite the obvious physical damage the stroke had wrought. Davis was not one to go gently into retirement. In fact, she didn't retire at all. Just as she compelled the world to look at her before half of her mouth went slack, Davis craved attention afterward with the same degree of dynamic daring. Bette Davis wasn't a quitter. "Old age is not for sissies," she famously declared.

The small woman became minuscule. By the end of 1983 she weighed only ninety-two pounds. But in spite—literally, in angry *spite*—of her wizened body, wrinkled face, and droop-mouthed speech, Bette Davis kept acting, appearing in public, showing up on Johnny Carson's *The Tonight Show* and at awards ceremonies, surviving, too ornery to die, too driven to sit still, too proud to recede into muted seclusion.

By that point she had a loyal helpmate, secretary, surrogate daughter, go-fer, adviser, factotum, and slave by the name of Kathryn Sermak, whom Davis hired in June 1979 to accompany her to London for the filming of *The Watcher in the Woods*, a trying-to-be-spooky Disney tale in which she plays a reclusive landlady.[7] Luckily, Sermak, then twenty-two, had studied psychology at UCLA before taking the job.

"I asked if you could boil an egg," Bette once recalled. "And I believe I asked you your astrological sign. You told me that you were a Libra. Almost to my own surprise, I said, 'You have the job.'"[8] Davis believed increasingly in the authority of astrology as she aged. She was, of course, an Aries. And what an Aries she was. "The fire element of Aries brings assertive *I* energy," a popular astrology guide states. "This is a flaming drive and the desire to do something! The Aries will is full of tension and passion—the *I* brings a need for independence." So far, so accurate; this description of the Aries temperament could have been written specifically as a zodiacal biography of Bette Davis. "Aries coincides with spring time," the sketch continues, "when seeds germinate in an outpouring of energy and growth. This sign has an instinctive identity, early extroversion, spontaneity, and a very direct approach." But all is not well in the garden. Aries carries with it a fundamental danger: "'Fire' can rage out of control! Aries' cardinal-sign assertiveness can become too willful. Then we have wild spring weather—a storming nature and a passion for power. Spontaneity can become impulsive, as only a sign ruled by energizing Mars can be!"[9]

Aside from weathering her boss's fiery storms, Kathryn Sermak did much more than boil Bette's eggs. She answered Bette's mail, conveyed messages, nursed. "She was wonderful with Bette," says Robbie Lantz. "I don't think she called her anything but 'Miss Davis.' She was just remarkable." During Davis's nine-week hospitalization, Sermak—whom Davis called Kath—spent every night with her until even Bette had to admit that her crankiness was "beginning to take its toll," so with Bette's encouragement she flew to Paris to visit her boyfriend. During the week she was away, Kath sent Davis a gardenia every day, each accompanied by a card with a little poetic inscription and a smiley face: "A gardenia a day while I'm away, love & kisses." "Gardenia number two, because I need understand and adore you." "Gardenia number three sends love to thee, I believe in you for I love you." "Gardenia number five, remember April five, *je vous envoyer mille braisse*." "Gardenia number seven, you are my heaven, miss you like mad, will be so glad to see you, your crazy stepdaughter."[10]

Davis's own children were decreasingly involved in her life, though at the time of the mastectomy and stroke, it was not out of malice. By 1983, B.D. had been married for nineteen years to a former film executive, Jeremy Hyman, who had recently gone into the trucking business; they and their two children had their own lives to live in eastern Pennsylvania, though it was Bette who paid many of their bills. In addition, Bette had adopted two children during the early years of her fourth marriage—to Gary Merrill, her costar in *All About Eve*. Michael Merrill, a sturdy and good-looking guy who graduated from the University of North Carolina and went on to law school at Boston University, married Charlene "Chou Chou" Raum in 1973, opened up a legal office in Boston, and had two children of his own. Another adopted child, dark-haired Margot Merrill, was discovered early on to be mentally retarded, and after much soul searching and grief, Davis and Merrill sent her away to live at Lochland, a home for the developmentally disabled in Geneva, New York, where she has remained more or less consistently ever since.

And so it was Kathryn Sermak who assumed the role of the loving and selfless daughter with the aged, increasingly needy, and cantankerous

Bette Davis for the last ten years of her life, especially after B.D. published a harsh tell-all book, *My Mother's Keeper*, in 1985. She wrote it, B.D. explained, as an act of Christian charity. That and a $100,000 advance.[11]

Sermak, who calls Bette "Miss Davis" to this day, described the way she and Bette celebrated holidays together in her portion of *This 'n That*. On Washington's Birthday, Kath wrote, "she serves cherry pie to go with dinner—and once she dressed like Martha Washington. On St. Patrick's Day we dressed like leprechauns." One Easter Kath bought Bette a rabbit. "She adored the rabbit, whom we named Mr. Brier, but the amount of traveling we did forced us to give him away."[12]

Sermak was, and remains, fiercely loyal to Davis. She was reluctant to be interviewed for *Dark Victory* and ultimately declined. She polarized Davis's friends, some of whom admired the support and care she provided Bette, while others came to distrust her immensely. From 1965 to 1977, Davis lived in Connecticut and needed a place to stay when visiting Los Angeles; she found her home away from home with Chuck Pollack, a designer and antiques dealer who lived on North Orlando Drive. "I knew Bette for about fifteen years," Pollack recalled. "We were very close. Then she brought in that terrible girl, and the girl started to cut off all of Bette's real friends. She started to cut Bette down to where Bette had only her. And Bette was desperate not to be left alone, so the girl had full control. The girl got exactly what she was after. She ended up being the recipient of half of Bette's estate."

"She was a road-show Eve Harrington," Davis's earlier assistant, Vik Greenfield, piped in. Greenfield had introduced Davis to Pollack and was living in Pollack's guest cottage at the time of the joint interview. "Yes," Pollack continued. "It was like Bette found her own Eve. The girl wormed her way into her confidence, and little by little, she got rid of almost all of Bette's close friends. I was a friend, and Vik had worked for her and was always friendly toward her. Vik was out of the picture, I was out of the picture, and several more were out of the picture. So there was nobody left but her and Bette and the adopted son. The daughter cut herself out with that book."[13]

The desperate race Davis ran throughout her life against self-doubt and a morbid fear of idleness is infectious to the point that her biographer, heaving and winded by his subject's furious pace, has found it impossible to endure the marathon without pulling a Rosie Ruiz: breaking ranks, ducking into the literary equivalent of the Boston T, speeding ahead, and crossing the finish line before the race is truly over. So we return to our place in the pursuit: Bette has just driven out of the Warners' lot in 1949 and still has forty years to go. But strict chronology doesn't necessarily reflect the life being chronicled. Cut loose from the indentured (albeit lucrative) servitude to Jack Warner and the studio system in general, Davis was if anything *too* free—free to pursue a purely domestic life for which she wasn't naturally suited; free to make movies far worse and more demeaning than any of the Warners programmers she decried; free to drink away her days when she wasn't working and become obnoxious and mean; free to be truly impossible. The story of Bette Davis's life is still a race, but it is at times a nonlinear one—a race, one might say, against time.

Before she made *All About Eve* in 1950, and the name Eve Harrington entered the language as a deadeye term for a faux innocent with a game plan, Bette filmed a melodrama called *The Story of a Divorce*; the title was changed just before its release in 1951 to *Payment on Demand*. Joyce Ramsey (Bette), the ambitious wife of a successful lawyer, is shocked when, after a long day at the office, her husband, David (Barry Sullivan), arrives home to his usual cocktail only to inform her that the marriage is over. Joyce spends the rest of the film concluding that despite the tepid affair David has launched out of boredom, it's really her fault after all. Davis told the critic Bruce Williamson that *Payment on Demand* was "among the best bloody films ever done about this driving kind of American woman—oh, that was *written* for me!"[14]

The director, Curtis Bernhardt, recalled that Bruce Manning, the screenwriter, and he "sat down to discuss writing a script for Bette Davis. . . . Bette then lived in Laguna Beach. I went down there and told her the story. I remember her response: 'I would jump through flaming hoops to make this film!' At that time Bette and I were on good terms. *A Stolen Life* had been a walloping success and she trusted me."[15]

Payment on Demand is a hard-edged, downbeat, honest film—Bette's grasping wife isn't a showy harridan, Barry Sullivan's fed-up husband isn't self-righteous about it—and Bernhardt directs it with a blend of sensitivity and technical invention. Joyce reviews her life in a series of flashbacks, and as Bernhardt described it, "When we reverted to the past, the foreground became dark, the background lit up, and the walls disappeared, because the walls were actually transparent. But you couldn't discern that when they were illuminated for foreground action. They were like screens. As soon as you took the light off them and moved into the background the walls vanished."[16]

All About Eve was shot, edited, and released to great acclaim—and Bette had divorced Sherry and married Gary Merrill—before *Payment on Demand* hit the screens in mid-February 1951. "Originally we had an uncompromising ending where the two just separate—they're finished," Bernhardt noted. "I think it stopped at the daughter's wedding—maybe while they're sitting at opposite ends of the table. But Radio City Music Hall suggested that we change it before they played it. So we had a big meeting with Bruce Manning, Mr. Skirball [one of the film's producers], myself, and Howard Hughes, who was then the owner of RKO. I could see what they meant because American audiences go for upbeat films. And this was 100 percent downbeat. So we tried to soften it by leaving it open, by letting the audience speculate on whether the man and wife ever get together again."[17]

Davis's recollections were harsher: "Howard Hughes was the producer, and he messed around with the ending. We had the perfect ending, where she's got her husband back and starts all over again telling him what he should do about his career and so forth, and he gets up and walks out. Marvelous! But Hughes wouldn't let us do that. He also insisted we call it *Payment on Demand*, a very cheap title, and made us end with a touching reunion at the front door. I begged him not to redo the ending, but I remember Hughes saying, 'Doesn't every woman still want a roll in the hay?' And I said, 'No—this is *not* her big drive after 35 years.'"[18]

The film was set to open at Radio City on February 15, 1951, but Hughes made the decision to order the new ending at practically the last minute. Davis and Sullivan were called in on February 13 to shoot the revised final scene on the front porch—a scene that is not "touching" as much as it's demoralizing, for no matter what the role demands, it's always sad to watch Bette Davis eat crow. The footage was immediately processed and edited into the last reel, which was flown to New York on one of Hughes's TWA jets and handed over to a jittery projectionist, who was already unspooling the beginning of the movie by the time the ending arrived.[19]

* * *

THE CAST AND crew of *Payment on Demand* threw Bette a party on April 5, 1950, her forty-second birthday. After cake and champagne were served, Bette was given an ostrich egg inscribed "Thanks for being a good egg." The party degenerated quickly, though, when Sherry showed up and got into a shoving match with the two security guards who'd tried to bar his entrance, Bette having requested that they keep her husband out. Then Barry Sullivan made the mistake of trying to reason with the belligerent ex-fighter and all-too-spurned husband. "Where's your sense of humor? The cast and crew are giving your wife a birthday party," Sullivan told him. "Stay out of it," Sherry answered. "I don't want to hit you because you have to be photographed tomorrow." According to Bette, "Sullivan said, 'Don't let that bother you.' Before he could say anything else, Sherry knocked him down."

The incident made the papers. Sherry sought sympathy: "I'm tired of being pushed around," he announced. "She was the breadwinner and I was the housewife. . . . I have dinner ready when she gets home. I take off her shoes and bring her slippers and a drink. I press her dresses when her maid isn't here. But . . . I'm a man who needs a lot of affection. When she comes home from work, she always says she's too tired."[20]

Sherry used to send her flowers every week, too, until Bette discovered that she was paying for them.[21] As for the lack of sex, Sherry was right. Davis admitted to Vik Greenfield that she and Sherry didn't sleep together very often. "The birth of B.D. was almost immaculate conception" was how she rather uncharitably put it.[22]

Bette later claimed that Sherry, meanwhile, was getting his daily dose of affection from B.D.'s nanny, twenty-one-year-old Marion Richards.[23]

On June 7, 1950, the Superior Court of the State of California approved an agreement giving Davis custody of B.D., with Sherry given limited visitation rights.[24] On July 3, Judge Eugenio Calzada Flores of the First District Court in Juárez, Mexico, granted Bette a divorce, the couple having already reached a property settlement in which Davis agreed to pay Sherry alimony for three years.[25]

The *Laguna Post* ran a classified ad on November 16, 1950: "Handyman—Odd Jobs Done Efficiently by William Grant Sherry— Phone 4-3626."[26] An anonymous reader sent the clipping to Hedda Hopper with a note: "From an old admirer who does not want slimy mouth Lousyella to beat you to the gun."

* * *

"DEAR BOY, HAVE you gone mad? This woman will destroy you. She will grind you down to a fine powder and blow you away! You are a writer, dear boy. She will come to the stage with a thick pad of long yellow paper. And pencils! She will write. And then she, not you, will direct—mark my words. And you may quote me, dear boy." That's Edmund Goulding warning Joseph Mankiewicz of what he was getting himself into by replacing the injured Claudette Colbert with Bette Davis in his upcoming production of *All About Eve*.

Mankiewicz told Davis about Goulding's advice near the end of the location shooting in San Francisco in April 1950. Bette was amused. As Mankiewicz put it, she emitted "that inimitable Davis snort—then she laughed. Her snort and her laugh should both be protected by copyright."[27]

To paraphrase the great theater critic Addison DeWitt: for those of you who do not read, attend the theater, watch black-and-white films, or know anything of the world in which you live, it is perhaps necessary to rehearse the story of *All About Eve*. Eve Harrington (Anne Baxter), née Gertrude Slojinsky, worms her way into the good graces of her idol, the theatrical legend Margo Channing (Davis). She's perfect, Eve is. Obvious, too, to everyone but the main characters of the film, each of whom initially falls, each in his or her own way, for Eve's overdone performance of sincerity. Only Margo's dresser, Birdie (Thelma Ritter), sees through Eve's act to the hungry but icy self-promotion at its core. Eve's tale is told in flashback form. We meet the central players, theater people, at an august banquet at which Eve receives the coveted Sarah Siddons Award. The rest of the film explains how Eve has manipulated her way there by conning Margo and Margo's friends: her director and younger lover, Bill Sampson (Gary Merrill); her longtime playwright, Lloyd Richards (Hugh Marlowe); her best friend, Karen, Mrs. Lloyd Richards (Celeste Holm); and the ascerbic Addison DeWitt (George Sanders). By the end, everyone but DeWitt has been burned by Eve.

All About Eve is one of the best, richest movies ever made, and Davis gives one of her finest performances in it. As a consequence, critics have chronicled the film with an unusual degree of detail. It is a masterpiece that deserves to be treated like a fine single-malt scotch, aged in wood and served neat, but, instead, tales of its making have been dumped in quantities more suited to Thunderbird. Still—and speaking as a Davis drunk—one can never get enough.

There are, for instance, the eminently repeatable Tallulah Bankhead anecdotes, Bankhead being self-evidently one of Davis's models for Margo Channing. On her radio show, Tallu announced, "Don't think I don't know who's been spreading gossip about me and my temperament out there in Hollywood, where that film was made—*All About Eve*. And after all the nice things I've said about *that hag*. When I get a hold of her I'll tear every hair out of her mustache."[28]

It was all a joke, Bankhead later explained: "The gossips and the gadabouts made a great to-do about Bette Davis's characterization of a truculent actress in *All About Eve*. These busybodies said Miss Davis had patterned her performance after me, had deliberately copied my haircut, my gestures, my bark, and my bite. For comedy reasons this charge was fanned into a feud on my radio show. I was supposed to be seething with rage over the alleged larceny. In superficial aspects Miss Davis may have suggested a boiling Bankhead, but her over-all performance was her own." All very gracious, until the zinger: "I had seen Miss Davis play Regina Giddens on the screen, thus knew I had nothing to worry about."[29]

"Bette and I are very good friends," Bankhead once said. "There's nothing I wouldn't say to her face—both of them."[30]

As it happened, Bankhead was enraged to find that the literary Margo Channing wasn't actually based on her. Mary Orr, who penned the short story "The Wisdom of Eve," from which Mankiewicz built his film, told of performing a *Theatre Guild on the Air* radio adaptation of the piece with Bankhead as Margo in November 1952. During a rehearsal, Tallulah asked Orr whether she had in fact been the inspiration for Margo. No, the writer said; she'd based Margo on the actress Elisabeth Bergner, who had indeed suffered her own compliant-factotum-turned-ruthless-competitor. As Orr later said, "This made her so mad she never spoke to me again, except on the air."[31] For the record, Mankiewicz claimed improbably that he based *his* Margo on the eighteenth-century actress Peg Woffington.[32]

Darryl Zanuck's biographer, George Custen, covered the film's casting saga: Marlene Dietrich was Zanuck's first choice for Margo Channing, though his handwritten notes on a script draft also mention Claudette Colbert and Barbara Stanwyck. Mankiewicz was adamantly against Dietrich, so Zanuck signed Colbert in February 1950. Colbert then ruptured a disc on the set of the film *Three Came Home*—her character was supposed to be fighting off a prison guard rapist, and Claudette fought a little too hard—and had to bow out, at which point they approached the

English musical-comedy star Gertrude Lawrence, who responded by demanding that Margo's drunk scene be removed or rewritten. "Rather than listen to the endless versions of *Liebesträume* the self-pitying (but always theatrical) Margo keeps asking her hired pianist to play, Lawrence insisted on singing a torch song," Custen reported. "Mankiewicz refused."[33]

Ingrid Bergman was briefly considered, but the role went to Davis, Colbert's broken back being one of the best things that ever happened to world cinema.

Zanuck wanted his contract actress Jeanne Crain to play Eve, but Crain had the nerve to get pregnant, leaving Mankiewicz free to cast his own choice, Anne Baxter. Zanuck also reportedly advocated putting John Garfield in the Bill Sampson role and José Ferrer in Addison DeWitt's; the parts were taken by Gary Merrill and George Sanders.

Davis stepped into the role at next to the last minute—the Curran Theatre in San Francisco had been rented for two weeks of location shooting and had a show already booked thereafter—but she immediately hooked into the character, planning bits of business and line deliveries in advance. For one of the Curran Theatre scenes, Edith Head designed for Bette what David Chierichetti calls a "gray suit with a high white collar and a big bow of the same material. This replaced a simpler blouse, which Edith had made and tested, because Davis knew ahead of time that she wanted to fiddle with the collar during an angry scene. She also instructed Edith to make the suit loose enough so Gary Merrill could push her over onto a bed on the stage of the theater. At a meeting in Edith's office, Davis suddenly ran across the room and threw herself onto a divan. When Edith protested that there was no such action in the script, Davis said, 'Yes, but that's what I'm going to do.' "[34]

According to Sam Staggs in *All About "All About Eve,"* the junkie's guide to the movie, Edith Head did base Margo's wardrobe on Tallulah Bankhead and her style. Staggs quotes Head as saying, "I steeped myself in Tallulah, and everything looked as if it was made for her, yet the clothes complimented Bette. She is such a good actress that she makes clothes belong to her." He also has Head colorfully remarking of Bette, "She has a walk like a whiplash."[35]

Gary Merrill told a comical story about Marilyn Monroe, who plays Addison DeWitt's eye-popping, dumb-as-dirt escort to the grand party at Margo's colossal apartment and also shows up briefly at the theater for an audition. Bette hosted a dinner party in San Francisco the night before she and Marilyn filmed their brief encounter in the theater lobby. "The party went on quite late," Merrill said, "but Marilyn excused herself early because she had to work the next morning. We all knew the scene Marilyn had to work on the next morning was really Bette's scene and that Marilyn had only a few lines. . . . Bette had more, but she was an experienced actress and accomplished the scene with little bother. It had to be done in ten takes, however—Marilyn kept forgetting her lines."[36] Marilyn's lines are, in toto: "Like I just swam the English Channel. Now what?" and "Tell me this, do they have auditions for television?"

There was some bitchiness during the production of *All About Eve*, but compared to the grinding agitation, sabotage, reaction formation, and development of hysterical physical symptoms that characterized Bette at her worst, *All About Eve* was actually made without much fuss. Despite Fox-generated publicity to the contrary, Davis got on well with Anne Baxter during the shoot. "The studio tried to play that up all during the filming," Baxter later declared, "but I liked Bette very much. She'd come on the set and go 'Sssssssss' at me, but it was just a joke between us."[37] Bette had no reason to fly off the handle at anyone for any reason. She knew the role was great, the dialogue superb, the director expert and resolute. "You know as well as I that there is nothing more important to an actress than a well-written part—and a director who knows what he wants and knows how to ask for it," she told Mankiewicz at the time. "*This* [*Eve*'s script] is heaven. But as often as not the script has been a compromise of some sort. And the director can't make up his mind whether we're to stand, sit, run, enter, or exit. He hasn't the foggiest notion of what the scene is all about or whether, in fact, it's a scene at all."[38]

Margo Channing is Bette Davis at her smoky best. Mankiewicz introduces Margo sitting at a table at the Siddons Awards. She reaches for a cigarette, taps it twice on the table, lights it, and inhales deeply in the first few seconds of her first shot. She then reaches offscreen for a bottle of booze, pours a couple of healthy glugs in a glass only partially visible on the lower right corner of the screen, and dismissively pushes away with the back of her hand her unseen tablemate's attempt to water it down. Then she smirks.

Tallulah aside, Margo is Bette Davis. It's as efficient an introduction to her character as her opening shots in *Jezebel*, only this time the director is introducing Davis herself as well as the character she is playing: a boozy, tobacco-stained broad who's not so much past her prime as proudly attenuating it. The only thing missing is the foul mouth.

When Karen Richards escorts Eve into Margo's dressing room, Margo extends her hand dramatically to Eve, the cold cream smeared all over her face unable to dim her theatrical grandeur. "How do you *do*, my dear," she regally announces, prompting Thelma Ritter, as Birdie, to mutter "oh, brother," the first of her many sober commentaries. "Oh, *brother*!" Birdie repeats a moment or two later after Margo introduces her preposterously as her "*dear* friend and companion." An old vaude-villian, Birdie has seen Margo play the role many times before. "All of a sudden she's playin' Hamlet's mother," Birdie observes.

The party Margo throws in honor of Bill's birthday is not only one of *All About Eve*'s highlights but as seminal a scene in movie history as Rhett Butler's parting shot to Scarlett O'Hara. Margo is already breathing fire early in the scene when she asks the producer Max Fabian (Gregory Ratoff) what would happen if he dropped dead, a line Bette delivers, casually dragonlike, while exhaling cigarette smoke. Lloyd Richards observes that there's something "Macbethish" in the air. "What *is* he talking about?" Margo asks, Bette giving the simple line a poisonous edge. "We know you," the well-bred Karen remarks. "We've seen you like this before. Is it over or is it just beginning?" Margo responds by gulping down her fourth martini with the same hand that holds a half-smoked cigarette, while in the other an olive lies impaled on a toothpick. She plops the olive into the emptied glass, turns to leave—leading with a broad sweep of the shoulder—and the camera pans with her as she heads for the stairs. She climbs a few and, with her hands on the bannister, turns, smirks again, pauses for dramatic effect, and issues her classic advisement: "Fasten your seatbelts—it's going to be a bumpy night."

After a brief, rich scene with Marilyn Monroe and her walker, George Sanders, Birdie enters with a look of concern and a hefty cup of coffee. She offers it to a morose Margo, who is seated on the piano bench, her eyes cast down into the abyss of yet another martini glass as the strains of Liszt's *Liebesträume* lend the party a funeral touch. Birdie's coffee becomes the receptacle into which Margo drops another toothpicked olive with a flamboyantly drunken gesture. Later, when Margo and Lloyd emerge from the kitchen, Bette inflects Margo's drunkenness with a more hostile tone. Margo confronts Eve and bites her with what appears to everyone else to be an outrageously rude remark, but to the audience at this point in Eve's increasingly tedious humble act, it's more than justified: "Please stop acting as if I was the Queen Mother." This prompts Bill to provide Margo with a setup: "Outside of a beehive, Margo, your behavior would hardly be considered either queenly or motherly." "You're *in* a beehive, pal, don't you know?" Margo retorts, Bette slurring her words just slightly. "We're all busy little bees, full of stings, making honey day and night." She faces Eve and snaps, "*Aren't* we, *honey?*"

Addison DeWitt's eyes are shining. As a gay man (albeit of the Hollywood-enforced closeted type), he's riveted by Margo and everything she stands for. "You're maudlin and full of self-pity!" he cries with golden admiration. "*You're magnificent!*"

Davis always said she understood Margo Channing, but she cited the wrong reasons. "Though we were totally unalike," she wrote in *The Lonely Life* in a failed attempt to deflect the obvious parallels, "there were also areas we shared." She brings up the scene with Karen Richards in the front seat of the Richardses' out-of-gas car in which "Margo confesses that the whole business of fame and fortune isn't worth a thing without a man to come home to. . . . And here I was again—no man to go home to. The unholy mess of my own life—another divorce, my permanent need for love, my aloneness. Hunched down in the front of that car in that luxurious mink, I had hard work to remember I was playing a part. My parallel bankruptcy kept blocking me, and keeping the tears back was not an easy job."[39]

But she got it wrong, her continual assertions of the emptiness of single womanhood serving as a cover for other less culturally acceptable deficiencies. For one thing, she was scarcely alone at the time she filmed that scene, immersed as she was in a torrid affair with her costar. It's the other half of the scene that registers as clinically autobiographical on Davis's part:

"So many people," Margo begins. "*Know* me," she adds, with Davis concluding the sentence peculiarly after a full stop. "I wish I did. I wish someone would tell me about *me*."

"You're Margo—just Margo," Karen, Mrs. Lloyd Richards, graciously offers.

"What is that? Besides something spelled out in lightbulbs, I mean. And something called a 'temperament.' That consists mostly of swooping about on a broomstick and screaming at the top of my voice. Infants behave the way I do, you know. They carry on and misbehave. They'd get drunk if they knew how. When they can't have what they want. When they feel unwanted. Or insecure. Or unloved."

Flashes of unwantedness and insecurity and a craving for love plagued Bette Davis her entire life and propelled her into the dueling self-medications of liquor and acting. She believed that she could fulfill herself with marriages, but they never worked. Again, it's curious that the passage Davis cites as mirroring her own emotional state was filmed at precisely the hot beginning of her relationship with Merrill. She was divorcing, yes, but she was far from being alone and unloved at the time. More self-revealing of Davis is Margo's "temperament," the witchlike cruelty, the acting out, the shouting at family and friends, the drinking. One wishes for her own sake that she'd have been able to calm down, but then she wouldn't have been Bette.

If there is one thing wrong with *All About Eve*, it's that Margo's decision to marry Bill at the end of the film depressingly represents the triumph of marital convention over what we've loved about the character all along: her aggressive independence, her boozy wit, her prickliness, her hands-off-me-I'll-do-it-myself spikiness. There's logic behind the nuptials; the career Margo promises to curtail to marry Bill isn't like law or medicine, jobs in which middle-aged practitioners are at the height of their authority and prowess. It's acting, where the roles for women begin to dwindle just as the humiliation of losing them grows. The sequence in which Margo eyes a bowl of chocolates and finally yields to one with a ravenous chomp remains the most effective demonstration ever filmed of the price actresses pay in hunger alone. In this light, Margo's choice to marry Bill is more reasonable—self-protective, even. And convincing. It's little wonder that Bette Davis saw it as her own personal solution as well as Mankiewicz's artistic one. And yet, given Davis's own thorny nature, it's even less surprising to discover that her much coveted domesticity led to an artistic decline. As bittersweet as it is, the closure offered by Margo's marriage with Bill at least has the virtue of being somewhat satisfying.

AFTER MAKING AN initial screen test with Anne Baxter for *All About Eve*, Gary Merrill showed up again at the Fox lot for a makeup test. That's when he met his future wife: "There, being turned this way and that on a stool, as though she had just been picked up from a counter at a jewelry store, was the Queen, Bette Davis. I was appalled. The makeup people should have been pampering her, remarking on her abilities and skills, but instead they were twirling her around, rather callously examining her facial lines. I guessed they were trying to see if our age difference would be too noticeable."[40] By the time they'd spent a day shooting *All About Eve* on location in San Francisco, the two actors were in love.

As Celeste Holm later recalled, "That first night we all went for drinks at the Fairmont, where they had a bar that went around and around. Everybody was showing off. Bette had taken one look at Gary and Gary had taken one look at Bette, and something had happened."[41] "And from then on she didn't care whether the rest of us lived or died," Holm continued. "Why, I walked onto the set the first or second day and said, 'Good morning.' And do you know her reply? She said, 'Oh, shit—good manners.' I never spoke to her again—ever. Bette Davis was so rude, so constantly rude. I think it had to do with sex."[42] "It was not a very pretty relationship," Holm said on another occasion. "They laughed at other people. Bette and Gary formed a kind of cabal, like two kids who had learned to spell a dirty word."[43]

"I started falling in love with him when I observed how he could relax in bed all day long for two solid weeks," Bette later said.[44] She was aroused by Merrill's laziness but enraged by it, too. He was erotic but passive. He worked up a sweat when he had to and slacked off the rest of the time. His headstrong nature, which matched her own, went hand in hand with a fuck-it-all attitude toward his career. This she could never understand. His contradictions provoked her. For his part, Merrill found Davis at age forty-two to be an intensely erotic woman. "From simple compassion, my feelings shifted to an almost uncontrollable lust," Merrill declared. "I walked around with an erection for three days." The writer Kenneth Geist once asked Merrill about his attraction to Davis, and Merrill replied, "Don't you understand? I thought if I got a hard-on I had to marry the woman!"[45] The wedding took place in Juárez in July 1950, after *All About Eve* was in the can, after which the Merrills headed for a honeymoon in Maine.

Gary had a much greater desire to forge a family than did any of Bette's other husbands. He made their marriage contingent upon having more children. As Bette later wrote, Sherry's three-year alimony payments were almost up when Merrill offered to adopt B.D. "He tried to get Sherry's permission. Sherry said for $50,000 he would give his approval. When we refused, he sued to get custody of her. A judge in Maine, a stern, old-fashioned Yankee judge, threw the case out of court when he learned that Sherry had received alimony from me. . . . I asked my lawyer what options we had left. He suggested I withhold Sherry's last month's alimony check. For that final check, Sherry gave Gary permission to adopt B. D. Sherry married the nursemaid, had children, and now has grandchildren."[46]

RUTHIE DAVIS PALMER, meanwhile, had sent a telegram to Bette in April: "Married Captain O. W. Budd in Immanuel Community Church, Las Vegas."[47] But Mother's second and third marriages were even shorter than her daughter's; this one was over by the end of 1951.

Bette and Gary stayed for part of their honeymoon in a primitive cabin on Westport Island off the midcoast of Maine. The blacklisted screenwriter Walter Bernstein, a friend of the oddball-loving Gary's, had arranged the deal with the landlord, whom Bernstein described as "an old Communist." Bernstein prepared the cabin by hiding the landlord's collected editions of Marx, Engels, Lenin, and Stalin in a closet and stacking firewood in front of the door to bar entry, his theory being that "this was not exactly movie star reading, at least not in that day and age." After Bette and Gary arrived, Bernstein and Merrill went out for about two hours and returned to find that Bette had turned the ramshackle cabin into a model 1950 home, albeit with a leftist twist. The aproned Bette—full of domestic fury built upon a kindling of characteristic nervous energy—had built a fire, polished the furniture, dug up doilies from somewhere and draped them on the couch, prepared "martinis and a plate of canapés," and restocked the bookcase with all the Marxist classics, which she had painstakingly unearthed by restacking the firewood away from the closet door. "I don't know whether she even read the books; it was more as if she had simply accepted the challenge of disinterring them," Bernstein commented.

"They stayed for two weeks," Bernstein recalled, "drinking a lot, fighting when they drank too much. . . . Once, awakened late at night, I heard loud, drunken voices from a boat on the water and asked Bette the next day if they were the ones. She was furious at me for thinking she would be that loud in public. She told me icily that she had better manners than that. Before they left, she got down on her hands and knees and scrubbed the cabin floor. They thanked me for the cabin and said they had had a swell honeymoon."[48]

Davis and Merrill were a mismatch well suited to each other. Bernstein described the couple's bristlingly complementary nature: "Gary was passive and easygoing and a thinker; Bette was a doer. He dampened his fires with drink; liquor only aroused her. He had no ambition, but he had an integrity she admired and respected." Bette Davis's marriage to Gary Merrill would be her longest lasting as well as the most disruptive to her career.

WIFE AND MOTHER

I N NOVEMBER 1950, THE TRADES IN BOTH
Hollywood and London announced that Gloria Swanson, whose career
had just been revitalized by Billy Wilder's *Sunset Boulevard*, would take
the leading role in the British murder mystery *Another Man's Poison*. But
in December Gloria went into a Broadway revival of *Twentieth Century*
opposite José Ferrer. She asked for a postponement of *Another Man's Poison* but was released from her contract instead. By February 1951, Bette
not only had taken the role (for what one British paper called a "staggering salary" estimated at £40,000, which included a stake in the film's
profits) but had also demanded that the male lead, originally to have
been played by Leo Genn, be given to Gary Merrill.[1]

Neither Bette nor Gary was fond of the script they'd been sent. "Then
[the producer] Daniel Angel appeared on our doorstep," Merrill wrote.
"He walked with canes because he had been afflicted with polio; this
made him seem Rooseveltian, which quite affected us."[2] The presence of
the playwright and actor Emlyn Williams (*The Corn Is Green*) in the cast
impressed them, too. According to Merrill, "Bette was going to involve
herself in some script revision with Emlyn Williams's help." The director, at Bette's behest, was Irving Rapper, whom Merrill later dismissed
as "a real run-of-the-mill talent."[3]

The Merrills, accompanied by four-year-old B.D., the newly adopted, two-month-old Margot, two nannies, and Bette's longtime housekeeper Dell, traveled to England on the *Queen Elizabeth*, arriving to harsh words from the British press. One reporter called Bette a "middle-aged matron"; another set Gary off by calling him "Mr. Bette Davis."[4] Merrill was especially annoyed because Davis had welcomed these reporters into their *Queen Elizabeth* suite when the ship docked at Southampton and plied them full of drinks and hors d'oeuvres, only to be shocked when the same reporters sniped "about rich American actresses with hundreds of pieces of luggage, fur coats, and a mention or two about the kids and 'Mr. Davis.' "[5]

Another Man's Poison began shooting in April 1951 and continued through June. Interiors were shot at Nettleford Studios in Walton-on-Thames, just southwest of London, with exteriors shot on location in the North Yorkshire villages of Settle, Malham, and Tarn. The Merrills took up residence at Great Fosters, the landmark hotel in Surrey that Elizabeth I and her father, Henry VIII, had used as a hunting lodge.[6]

During the production, Bette and Gary dined at the Lord Chancellor's apartment at the Houses of Parliament, the current Lord Chancellor being Sir William Jowitt, who had represented her in the 1936 Warner Bros. lawsuit. They also went to John Gielgud's house one evening for dinner, showing up late because of filming. Alec Guinness was upstairs when they arrived. Guinness made his appearance sporting a mustache for the title role in *Hamlet*, and Davis didn't recognize him, thanks to Merrill's having told her that he was the ale heir.[7]

"Emlyn rewrote many scenes for us, which gave it some plausibility, but we never cured the basic ills of the story," Bette wrote of *Another Man's Poison*. The *New Statesman* called Davis's performance "a blaze of breathtaking absurdity." Merrill, the *Socialist Leader* sniped, "wanders about looking like a cross between Tarzan and Frankenstein."[8]

Bette and Gary were in England standing around a radio on the night the Oscars were awarded for the previous year's films. Bette was nominated for *All About Eve*, Gloria Swanson for *Sunset Boulevard*. Davis was also competing against Anne Baxter for *All About Eve* as well as Eleanor Parker for *Caged* and Judy Holliday for *Born Yesterday*. When Broderick Crawford opened the envelope and announced that Holliday had won, Davis was magnanimous: "Good," she said. "A newcomer got it. I couldn't be more pleased."[9]

* * *

THE MERRILLS WERE back in Hollywood in 1952 when Bette filmed *The Star*, a melodrama about an on-the-skids Hollywood actress. It should have been tailor-made for a post–Margo Channing Bette Davis at her most scenery ripping, but aside from two or three scenes it's pretty drab. Davis plays Margaret Elliot, an Oscar-winning star who's gotten a bit long in the tooth for the romantic leading roles that made her famous and now has trouble finding work. She's spent her fortune incautiously on her needy sister and belching brother-in-law and her twin nephews' saxophone lessons, not to mention the three films she financed personally to ruinous returns. Having not made a movie in three years, she's forced to auction off her property, after which, in the film's best scene, she returns to her cheap apartment, throws her sister and brother-in-law out the door, grabs her Academy Award as though it was her only friend, takes a few quick breaths, and announces, "Come on, Oscar—let's you and me get drunk!"

Cut to a shot taken from the backseat of her car. Her hand reaches away from the steering wheel and dips below the bottom of the image. When it reemerges it's clutching Oscar, which it wedges onto the dashboard behind the rearview mirror. The hand disappears but quickly returns, this time grasping a bottle of whiskey. "To absent friends," Maggie toasts before swigging from the bottle.

As her sheets blow ever more swiftly to the wind, Maggie takes us on a tour of the movie stars' homes: Mitzi Gaynor's, Jeanne Crain's, Barbara Lawrence's. ("*Thaaaat* looks like the kind of monstrosity that Barbara *Law*-rence would choose!") She pulls up at her own former mansion and delivers a maudlin, self-pitying speech, roars off in the car, sideswipes a convertible, and gets pulled over by the cops. Next thing you know, she's in the slammer. "Everybody knows who I am—I'm Margaret Elliot!" she testily, drunkenly informs her cell mate as she clutches the bars as though she's in a women's prison picture. "What a coincidence," the fellow jailbird remarks. "I'm Snow White."

Salvation is found in the form of Jim Johannson (Sterling Hayden), a former builder turned actor turned shipyard owner, who bails her out. After some disappointingly calm melodrama—Maggie's short-lived attempt to earn a living as a lingerie shopgirl at May's; a shoplifting episode involving eau de cologne; and a disastrous screen test ("I've rented a small chicken farm from some people named Garfield, and I run it alone, and there's been a murder, and I've seen it, and the Garfield family is involved in it, and I know it ... and that's the test scene!")—Maggie rushes back to Jim's place along with her all-too-unscarred teenage daughter, Gretchen, played by Natalie Wood, and another happy 1950s family forms at the expense of a formerly strong woman's character and career.

Natalie Wood claimed that her fear of deep water began when making *The Star*; she was all of fourteen at the time. There's a scene on Jim Johannson's yacht; Jim takes Maggie and Gretchen out for some redemptive fresh air. The director, Stuart Heisler, insisted that Wood herself, not a stunt double, dive off the yacht. "I went into hysterics that must have been heard all the way to Catalina," Wood later recalled. "Bette Davis heard me screaming and came out of her dressing trailer to find out what the commotion was. It was the only time I ever saw Bette's legendary temperament surface, and it was not in her behalf. When she discovered what was going on, she shouted at the director, 'If you make Natalie do that, I'll walk off the picture. Who do you think she is— *Johnny Weissmuller*?' A double was sent for pretty fast."[10] Wood's sister, Lana, later noted that Natalie "always said that it was Bette Davis who first caused her to realize that speaking up—and out—wasn't a bad thing to do."[11] Whatever diving footage was shot ended up on the cutting-room floor.

Davis—much later—asserted that Margaret Elliot was a thinly veiled Joan Crawford. *The Star*, she pointed out, "was written by the Eunsons— Katherine Albert and Dale Eunson, two of the best writers in the business. She, in particular, was a fan magazine writer who'd done most of the stories about Crawford." Bette claims to have played up the in-joke on the set: "I kept saying 'Bless you' to the crew—all that sort of thing she did. Oh, yes—that *was* Crawford. I often wondered if she ever realized it, but I never, never knew."[12] But there's something slightly suspicious about Davis's glee: her feud with Crawford hadn't really begun at that point. The two women's mutual loathing didn't achieve its full force until the 1960s. They were rivals in the 1940s and '50s, true, but only to the extent that every major star saw every other major star as a threat. Crawford and Davis actually had a lot in common: each had left the studio that had been her bedrock (Crawford's was MGM); each had achieved a monumental, vindicating success afterward (Crawford's was *Mildred Pierce*).

In any case, Maggie Elliot is as much Bette herself as she is Joan. When preparing for the catastrophic screen test, Maggie redoes her makeup to her own specifications (including high, thin, Crawford-like eyebrows); claims to know what the screenplay should be about despite the fact that her ideas contravene the screenplay; refuses to take direction from the director. . . . As Dale Eunson observed, "With Bette Davis and a director like Stuart Heisler, *he* didn't direct—*she* directed."[13]

The Star opened on Christmas Day, 1952. "I liked it. The public was lukewarm," Davis writes. She was nominated for another Academy Award for Best Actress—as was Joan Crawford for *Sudden Fear*—but they both lost to Shirley Booth for the pathos-laden melodrama *Come Back, Little Sheba*, in a role Bette had turned down.

The Star was the last picture Bette Davis made before moving with Gary to Cape Elizabeth on the coast of Maine to raise their children, with results both rejuvenating and disastrous. She felt she needed the break artistically, and she loved the bitter beauty of northern New England. But according to Davis, it hurt her marriage to pent up her professional energies. "For three years I was solely a wife and mother and Gary fell out of love with me," she wrote.[14] She finally had the domestic life she thought she'd craved, but her drive scarcely abated. Now, in place of the blood she'd sweated to create *Jezebel*, *The Letter*, *Now, Voyager*, *Mr. Skeffington*, and even *Beyond the Forest*, she found herself scooting the kids off to school and feverishly polishing the silver.

Clippings from the scrapbooks:

> Mrs. Franklin F. Ferguson of Surf Rd., Cape Cottage, entertained at coffee Tuesday to meet Mrs. Gary Merrill, a newcomer to the Cape Shore.

> Pourers at the silver tea sponsored by the Waynflete Alumnae Association Thursday afternoon at the residence of Mr. and Mrs. Gary Merrill on Ocean House Road will be Mrs. Kenneth C. M. Sills, Mrs. S. Allan Howes, Mrs. Howard R. Ives, and Miss Mildred Owen.

The Merrills emceed the Community Chest's twenty-fifth birthday party. Bette Merrill was seen attending a rehearsal of the South Portland Lion's Club play *The Red Mill*. Mrs. Merrill made a theatrical appearance in the Portland Junior League Follies of 1954.[15] She also assisted Mrs. William Kirkpatrick in applying makeup for the cast of the Waynflete Christmas Program on December 19, 1956; the pageant began at 11:00 a.m. under the direction of Mrs. Hugh L. Bond IV and featured Lord

Waynflete, lords and ladies of the court, carolers, tumblers, shepherds, and Mary and Joseph, with angels supplied by grades 9, 10, and 11.[16]

One of the scrapbooks contains a handwritten name tag for the Democratic State Convention, held March 23–24, 1956, in Brewer: "Bette D. Merrill, Cape Elizabeth, Me." An accompanying newspaper photo shows Bette waving a Cumberland County convention placard.[17]

The rural life appears to have affected the Merrills' minds. They got into their heads the cockamamie plan of building a movie studio in Portland, the first production of which was to have been a little number called *Angel Manager*. They were scouting Catholic orphanages in Biddeford, Saco, and Lewiston as possible locations for the film, which was to be . . . well, a local newspaper reported the facts: "She said her husband would play the part of a wounded veteran and former baseball player who assists a nun, played by Miss Davis, in forming an orphanage baseball team."[18]

M ARGOT M OSHER M ERRILL—NAMED, of course, after Margo Channing—was born in January 1951 to an unmarried alcoholic who immediately put her up for adoption. Gary came to believe that the birth mother's alcoholism contributed to Margot's developmental problems, which only became evident over time; Bette wondered if the mother had taken drugs to induce an abortion. But at the time of her adoption within days of her birth, Margot was to all appearances a normal, healthy baby. "She was so beautiful that Gary and I scarcely could believe our good fortune," Bette said. All was not quite so rosy, though. At the time of Margot's adoption in 1951, Bette and B.D. were staying in Westport, Connecticut, with Bette's friend Robin, now married to Albert "Brownie" Brown, a New York advertising executive; Merrill was filming *Frogmen* on Key West. "It was here that I got a call from Bette," he wrote. " 'You're the proud father of a beautiful baby girl.' Our plan had been to adopt a boy next, then a girl, then a boy. So my response to her announcement was, '*Wrong fucking sex*.' "[19]

The new parents began to notice problems early on, but a blend of acceptance and denial kept them from facing the extent of their infant daughter's brain damage. As Bette described Margot's behavior and their reactions, "She cried a great deal as a baby, but she cried differently than I remembered B.D. crying. But as we told each other, knowledgably enough, children differ. We were to remark this more and more frequently and with less and less conviction."[20]

Margot learned to run as any normal child would, but she ran unusually fast for a toddler. "She seemed driven," Bette observed, though for a mother as driven as Bette was, that can't have been all that odd. Once Bette left her in the car for a short time, and when she came back, Margot had stripped off all of her clothes. Bette and Gary's tolerance of their children's individuality turned out to be misguided in Margot's case; it contributed to their failure to face the reality, let alone the extent, of Margot's problems. Other children did things like this, they told themselves, but Margot somehow did them differently, more disturbingly.

She was slow to learn to talk. At age two she didn't have much of a vocabulary, and what she said she repeated: "Hi hi hi hi hi hi hi hi . . ." "Five minutes after we had put her to bed she would be up shaking the crib bars and screaming," Bette said, describing the sort of unrestrained rage that parents of a two-year-old might excuse from time to time but which would necessarily become more troubling the more it became routine. "I remember the day she tried to choke her kitten."[21]

Bette and Gary brought their second adopted child, Michael Woodman Merrill, directly home from the Los Angeles hospital in which he was born on February 5, 1952. Michael, whom they threatened to call Woody but mercifully never followed through, was a pretty baby and grew into a handsome man, having passed through a knock-'em-dead-blond-boy phase between the ages of five and sixteen. Bette described him at ten as "devastating," and her scrapbooks have the photos to prove it.[22]

"Compared to me he has turned out pretty square," Mike Merrill's father once observed—an understatement made even greater when one considers his parents' volatile eccentricities; their regular absences and the family's frequent uprootings (Hollywood, New York, Maine, Beverly Hills, New York again . . .); and the multiplicity of schools to which he was sent, sometimes for as little as a few months.[23] By all accounts Michael Merrill emerged unscathed from a difficult, unenviable childhood and grew into a stand-up fellow.

Gary, Bette wrote, "claimed that I could study my lines, polish the silver, prepare dinner, and still discover in a rage that Michael had been wearing gym pants without knees when he had assured me that he didn't need new ones."[24] The word that gives pause, of course, is *rage*. Over a boy's torn sweats?

In 1953, when Michael was one, the Merrills hired a nanny, Elsa "Coksie" Stokes. Coksie "no doubt took a psychological beating during the years she spent with us," Gary Merrill later admitted, but she did give "Michael much of the mothering of which he was deprived. . . . Coksie said she couldn't understand girls. Fortunately for Michael and me, she did understand men and boys, which offered security for Michael when I was away from home."[25]

The onus was certainly not solely on Bette. Gary was a heavy drinker and thus an absent father even when he was around. But in terms of a little boy's needs, Gary got it in a way Bette didn't. "When Michael went to school the year we moved to Maine, he came home after the first day crying," Bette recalled. The reason: "I never believed that a five-year-old boy should wear long pants, and that day he was wearing shorts. And he was a new boy in school, with hair a beautiful golden blond. All these ingredients were definitely a problem for him. One of the boys called him a sissy and tried to beat him up." What James McCourt calls Davis's "rectitude" in this case took the form of a steadfast but out-of-time belief in short pants for school-age boys, "I never believed" being a startling locution to employ when discussing little boys and long trousers. Having dressed B.D. with similarly religious rigor as her idea of a model child, Bette tried to do the same with Michael, but this time the results were disastrous. Still, it was Bette, not Gary, who taught Michael how to fight back—according to Bette, that is.[26]

Snapshots from Michael's childhood:

"Our first family boat trip, Casco Bay, 1953"—a grumpy eighteen-month-old boy sits on his father's lap on the deck of a sailboat.[27]

"Daddy as Santa, 1954"—Gary making a slightly bizarre St. Nick with the requisite red jacket with white trim and a full white paste-on beard and an unusual black leather belt tied midway up his chest.[28]

"Fall of 1954, when Mother visited us"—Michael and B.D. standing in the crook of a tree, with Ruthie standing next to a sweetly clowning Margot mimicking the photographer by holding an imaginary camera in front of her face.[29]

Margot loved to play dress up; "the customary perplexed look in her eyes was dissipated by her excitement." But then she began to pull out her little brother Michael's hair. One day, Bette found Margot standing near the bar calmly watching toddler Michael staring at his bleeding hands and crying. There was broken glass all over the floor, Margot having destroyed the barware.

Beginning to fear for Michael's safety, Bette and Gary took the three-year-old Margot to Presbyterian Hospital in New York in 1954 for a week of diagnostic tests, at the end of which the doctors reported that Margot was brain damaged and had an IQ of 60. (An IQ of 65 or below places one in the lowest percentile of the population.) One of the physicians recommended the Lochland School, a home for the developmentally disabled located on Seneca Lake in the Finger Lakes region of New York State. Bette cried on the way home and told Gary they couldn't send Margot away. Gary resisted the idea as well. So as Merrill described it later, "A little vest was made for her, which could be attached to the bed to keep her in, and when she finally understood that she was secure, unable to climb out of bed, she began to nap."[30] Ruthie, meanwhile, was coldly advocating that they just give Margot back to the adoption agency and start again with a fresh baby.

When Margot's harness proved to be ineffective in the long run, the Merrills invited the founder of Lochland, Florence Helene Stewart, to come to their house for a two-day visit, at the end of which Stewart gently laid out the facts.

"The most difficult day of my life was the day I was dressing Margot, three years old, in a sailor suit and a sailor hat [and told her] about the lovely school she was going to," Bette said. Gary escorted Margot to Lochland by plane; Bette stayed home with B.D. and Michael. "The setting was lovely," Merrill later recalled—"a big old Victorian house on a sloping lawn near a lake. But God it was depressing."[31]

19

ONSTAGE, ONSCREEN, AND ON TV

IN THE SPRING OF 1952, BETTE, GARY, AND the children were still living near the heart of Hollywood in what Gary called "a terrific, old, wooden California-style house" at the corner of Camino Palmero and Franklin. The *Los Angeles Times*'s Radie Harris wasn't nearly as impressed, dismissing the neighborhood as "unfashionable."[1] In any case, it was there that a friend of Gary's, the theatrical designer Ralph Alswang, called from New York with an idea: his office mates, Jimmy Russo and Mike Ellis, wanted to produce a revue called *Two's Company*. They wanted someone like Beatrice Lillie or Gertrude Lawrence or Mary Martin—none of whom they could get. Alswang suggested Bette. "I had been approached to follow Judy Garland into the Palace, and I gave it some serious thought," Bette told Radie Harris in August after she signed on to *Two's Company*. "I knew I didn't want to do the usual 'in-person' appearance of reenacting scenes from my movies, nor did I want to do anything heavy and dramatic. I thought it would be fun to try a variety act—*if* I could get the right material. Famous last words!"

"Vernon Duke played me the score he had written to Ogden Nash's lyrics, and I adored it," Davis went on. "Jerome Robbins, than whom there is none better, is going to stage the show." Costumes would be done by Miles White. "We won't come in until we're sure it's in perfect shape. That's why we're trying it out first in Detroit—far from the Sardi's scuttlebutt."[2]

The Merrills left Los Angeles for New York in September and moved into a Beekman Place triplex. Bobby Davis came along. "Bless her heart," Gary Merrill wrote—"always reliable in emergencies. In times of stress, Bette had a tendency to take out her frustrations on whomever she ran into first. Frequently this was Bobby, who, by her presence, enabled the children to be once removed from Bette's short circuits."[3]

Bette and Gary invited everyone over to the triplex for cocktails to get acquainted. The evening appeared to go very well and eventually everyone left, except for Ralph Alswang, whereupon Bette abruptly announced that she couldn't possibly work with Jerome Robbins. As Merrill later explained, Davis thought that Robbins would concentrate "on the ballet numbers and forget about her."[4]

Robbins stayed on, but tensions between him and Davis soon became obvious. "They were rehearsing a big production number based on Sadie Thompson from Somerset Maugham's *Rain*," recalled Sheldon Harnick, who wrote one of *Two's Company*'s songs.

> It was a big musical number with Bette and other dancers and singers onstage. Jerome Robbins was trying to teach her a very simple dance step. Robbins . . . could be so severe with his people that many of them hated him. I was not one of them; I liked him a lot. But he created a lot of hostility in the company. So anyway, he was trying to teach Bette how to do this simple step, and finally he said, "Let me demonstrate it for you."
>
> I think it was because of nervousness, but she just started to scream at him, "You're trying to make me look like a horse's ass, and I won't stand for it!" And she stomped offstage and went to her dressing room. I looked at the company, and because so many of them disliked Robbins, I could see them trying to conceal their giggles. They were very pleased by the whole thing. Mike Ellis came out and said, "Jerry, you have to go apologize to her." Robbins said, "What did I do? I was just . . ." "You've got to go apologize to her." It was not an easy thing for Robbins to do. But he did. He went offstage and shortly after that she came back out and began to rehearse again.

Two's Company set out on a preview tour in mid-October. The first stop was Detroit. "I only had one song in the show," Harnick continued,

> and they didn't pay for me to go out of town. I paid for myself so I could be there opening night. Davis had a song—her first song—called "Good Little Girls." It was the kind of song like "Old MacDonald Had a Farm," where each additional chorus had an additional couple of lines in it, so it got very long. I never saw her get through the song. She always fumbled at some point—she blew it. So I was worried about it. The way she was introduced, she was in a magician's cabinet, and the magician opened the door to the cabinet and showed the audience it was empty, and then he closed the door, waved his wand over it, said some magic words, he opened the door, and there was Bette. She stepped out of the cabinet, and everybody applauded. Then she went into "Good Little Girls."
>
> As she got to about the third or fourth chorus, where it began to get longer, I detected a sense of hesitation. I thought, "Oh my God, she's going to blow it again. She doesn't know it well enough. And she's nervous—it's opening night." And suddenly, she fainted. She just fell to the floor. I thought, "Oh, what is this? Is this new staging?"
>
> The audience thought that it was part of the show—until the lights went up and a stagehand came out in his shirt-sleeves. Shortly after that, Mike Ellis came out and announced to the audience that Miss Davis had fainted. She claimed that the magician's cabinet was so airless that she was suffocating, and that's why she fainted. But I'm sure it was because she got to the part where she knew she didn't know the lyrics and just collapsed. It was very smart.
>
> Then she did something even smarter. Mike told the audience she needed just a little bit of rest and then she would go on with the show, and everybody applauded. He then went into the wings and brought her out, and she looked at the audience and said, "Well, you can't say I didn't fall for you," which was charming.[5]

Two's Company still wasn't working for reasons that went beyond Davis's opening-night jitters, and Robbins asked her for permission to bring Joshua Logan and the writer Paul Osborn to Detroit to try to help.

"The show started and continued, and I kept waiting for Bette Davis to appear," Logan recalled in his memoirs. "Finally, the first act was over and she had still not appeared onstage once, although in the program she had been listed at least six times. I couldn't decide whether I was more frustrated or infuriated." During the intermission, Robbins explained to Logan what the matter was: "She won't come on. She says her first-act scenes aren't good enough, so she just told the stage manager to cut them tonight."

"In the second act she appeared three times and was marvelous each time," Logan continueed. "She was all that I dreamed Bette Davis might be in a musical." Logan and Osborn went backstage to see Bette after the show, "but the only one we got to see was Gary Merrill." Davis refused to meet with them. So they headed back to New York.[6]

Ogden Nash took a more felicitous tone.

> It happened in Detroit,
> And let who will be clever.
> The passion in my life came late,
> But Bette late than never.[7]

The troupe moved to Pittsburgh, where the *Press* was unimpressed: *Two's Company* "lacks two main essentials for a show of its type—comic punch and zingy tunes." New cast members came and went; sketches were shuffled around or dropped altogether. The troupe moved to Boston.

Enter, or reenter, John Murray Anderson, Bette's flaming drama teacher from 1926. Anderson, who had directed many circuses over the years and harbored a particular fondness for freaks, was an inspired choice to pull *Two's Company* together.[8] "Murray was the king of revues," said Harnick. "He had done many of them, and he'd been around for decades—a man of great taste. You always pictured him with a glass of champagne in his hand—or a martini."[9] Gary Merrill remembered that Anderson took one look at *Two's Company* in its present form and pronounced it "more amateurish than a Princeton Triangle show."[10] Trimming, tweaking, cutting, reigniting ensued, all voiced with what Harnick called Anderson's "aspish wit." "What he did was miraculous," Bette declared.[11]

"I was never able to do the original opening song again," Bette later admitted. "I was just plain frightened of it. . . . Jerome Robbins planned a new opening for me finally. We rehearsed it for a day or so and then put it in the show after the Boston opening. It was a success—'Just Turn Me Loose on Broadway' became my opening number."[12]

Collier's covered the production with a photo spread: "In haglike garb, Miss Davis crouches before the footlights, brings down first-act curtain of *Two's Company* singing rowdy hillbilly ballad." The picture shows Bette looking like an Ozarks witch with long tangles of gray hair poking out from beneath a raggedy black hat. Another photo presents her in the hag getup sitting in a chair next to an "XXX" jug of corn likker. Another caption: "In song and dance parody 'Roll Along Sadie,' Bette Davis cuts loose in hip-swinging, gum-chewing take-off on tropic siren Sadie Thompson." The photo shows Davis wearing a brilliant yellow hat and skirt set off by an orange and black feather boa and a long string of pearls.[13]

After a delay of almost two weeks, *Two's Company* opened at the Alvin Theater in New York on December 15. Congratulatory telegrams flew in: Irving Rapper; Joshua Logan; Kim Hunter; Janis Paige ("your number one fan"); Edith Head; "Ruthie, B.D. and Margot and Michael and Klaus and Tinker Belle and Aunt Bobby"; "Lenny Bernstein"; Joan Blondell; Yul Brynner; Richard Widmark; Don Siegel; Bob Taplinger; Jule Styne; Abe Burrows; Glenda Farrell; Kay Thompson; Kay Francis; "Lilli and Rex"; Gary ("All I can say is that I love you and I think you are wonderful in this show—your husband"); Moss Hart and Kitty Carlisle; Michael Todd; and one most surprising one: "Believe me, I wish all that is fine for you tonight!—Miriam Hopkins."[14]

Walter Winchell went out of his way to plug *Two's Company*. One of Bette's scrapbook pages contains a total of nine Winchell columns praising the show. "One sourpuss fussed, 'She can't sing or dance,'" Winchell reported, but "that's worth the price of admission!" "There is no coincidence in the two Ts in the star's first name," another column roared. "They stand for Terrific Trouper! There are two Ts in Bette and two in Talent."[15]

The New York run played to sold-out houses and mild if not downright hostile reviews. "The ovation was, to say the least, heartwarming. The reviews were bloodcurdling," Davis wrote.[16] Greta Garbo showed up to see the show one night, Marlene Dietrich another.

Appearing as the high-profile star of a Broadway revue was taxing enough, but Davis felt an unusual exhaustion and kept popping Dexedrine to get her through the performances. She sought medical help, but her physicians found no reason for her lack of energy until, on March 7, one of her wisdom teeth became inflamed. She was examined by Art Carney's dentist brother; Dr. Carney referred her to Dr. Stanley Behrman, who diagnosed her with osteomyelitis, an acute bone inflammation of the jaw. *Two's Company* closed the following night.

Walter Winchell promptly reported that Bette Davis had cancer.

"Your recent statements about me are utterly without foundation," an enraged Bette wired Winchell. "Have authorized my physician at NY hospital to answer any questions you may care to put to him, and to examine hospital's and pathologist's reports. I am sure you have no wish to hurt me. Accept my assurances that I do not have cancer. Please retract on broadcast. Bette Davis."[17] By way of a retraction, Winchell printed the telegram in his column.

Two's Company has developed a reputation as one of Bette Davis's stinkers, a humiliation, a camp classic of the mean-spirited-cackle variety. But according to Sheldon Harnick, that's unjustified. "I felt that the show was mixed. It wasn't brilliant, but it had a number of things in it that were great, including three absolutely wonderful dances that Jerome Robbins choreographed. They starred Maria Karnilova, who later became our Golde in *Fiddler on the Roof*, and Nora Kaye. The dances alone would have made this show worth seeing. I guess they hadn't found as much terrific material as they wanted, and consequently there were letdowns in the show—sketches or songs that didn't work. But it was not a bad show. I think if she had been able to do the show, just her name alone would have kept it running, and they would have had a very good run. There was a lot that was entertaining."[18]

BOREDOM AND A dual need for cash and attention brought Davis back to Hollywood from Maine in 1955.

"You must be out of your mind to work with Bette Davis," Curtis Bernhardt told the director Henry Koster after reading in the trades in early 1955 that Koster and the producer Charles Brackett had cast Davis in *The Virgin Queen*. Bernhardt ranted in a way he never did in public: "I worked with her—the most impossible thing! I was ready for the insane asylum—for the sanitarium!" Koster wanted to know what exactly Davis had done to enrage Bernhardt, and the director of *A Stolen Life* and *Payment on Demand* answered, "Well, she argues and she's impossible!

Don't take the picture! Tell them you don't feel well or something, because if you like your health, you won't work on a picture with Bette Davis."[19]

Davis invited Koster to tea, and Koster informed her that if there was to be trouble, he'd rather not do the picture at all. "She laughed," Koster later reported, "and said, 'If you know your business, there won't be any arguments. But if I feel a director guides me into something where I think he's absolutely wrong, then I'll argue 'til my last drop of blood.'" Evidently Davis approved of Koster's vision, because Koster came away from the experience saying that he and Davis "were the best of friends all the way through."[20]

She reserved her enmity for *The Virgin Queen*'s cinematographer, Charlie Clarke. According to Koster, Davis "couldn't stand" him. She was justifiably annoyed by Clarke's tendency to make what Koster called "funny remarks" during rehearsals. "She had had her head shaved" for the role, Koster said, and Clarke would say such things as 'Gee, you scare me with that billiard-ball head.' She got mad, because she was trying to get into the mood of the scene."[21] One can hardly blame her, though at the same time she'd had her hairline shaved back precisely to be unnerving.

The Virgin Queen finds Elizabeth at forty-eight; Davis herself was on the brink of forty-seven in March 1955, when she shot her scenes. (She'd played the monarch at sixty in *The Private Lives of Elizabeth and Essex*.) The film concerns Walter Raleigh's quest to convince Elizabeth to fund his exploration of the New World, Elizabeth's unrequited love for Raleigh (played by Richard Todd), and her jealousy of one of her ladies-in-waiting (Joan Collins), who eventually marries the explorer. "It had been three years since I'd been in front of a camera," Davis noted. "I was sure of nothing. Least of all myself. The first day was a nightmare for me. I heard Henry Koster, the director, say, 'Okay, let's try a take,' and I heard my voice: 'Mistress Throckmorton, is this your pet swine? I see you cast pearls before him.'"[22] (Joan Collins is ticking off pieces of advice for Richard Todd using a strand of pearls to make her points. She breaks the strand and sends the pearls cascading to the floor just as Elizabeth enters.)

Davis gives a thoughtful, muted performance, except for one self-defeating decision. *The Virgin Queen* gives the lie to an old saying: if it walks like a duck and acts like a duck, it isn't a duck at all but rather Elizabeth I as portrayed by Bette Davis, whose bandy-legged waddle was compared by one critic to that of Groucho Marx. Another wag had her "walking not on one artificial leg but on three," while two others compared her to "a saddle-sore jockey" and "an overhearty lacrosse captain in a red wig."[23] It's a shame she felt the need to add such a pointless tic to an otherwise restrained rendition.

Little Michael Merrill paid his first visit to a movie set on one of the eleven days Bette worked on *The Virgin Queen*. Gary brought him over to the Fox lot to see what his parents did for a living. "I was doing a scene in which I, as Queen Elizabeth, had to rant and rave at Sir Walter Raleigh, played by Richard Todd," Davis wrote in *Collier's* just before the film's release. "After a few minutes of listening to my tirade, Mikey turned to Gary with a puzzled face and asked, 'Why is Mummy yelling at that man instead of you?' "[24]

The Virgin Queen received its world premiere in Portland, Maine, on July 22, 1955, a benefit for the Portland Children's Theater, in which the Merrills had taken an interest. The newspaper magnate Jean Gannett threw a clambake in the afternoon. Guests included Bette's *Bad Sister* costar Conrad Nagel; the comedian Tom Ewell, fresh from *The Seven Year Itch*; the former pinup girl Jinx Falkenberg; and the actress Faye Emerson.[25] After the clams came cocktails at Witch Way, the Merrills' rambling house on the shore, followed by a buffet dinner—cold cuts and potato salad—at the Eastland Hotel. (Why Bette and Gary dubbed their house Witch Way requires no explanation.)

The film was to start at 9:00 p.m. at the Strand Theater, which held 1,900 people. A half an hour before showtime there were 10,000 people milling around in front of the Strand. Unfortunately, the planned gag of a fan blowing up Bette's skirt when she introduced Tom Ewell failed to come off.[26]

Dᴀᴠɪs ꜰɪʟᴍᴇᴅ ꜰᴏᴜʀ more feature films in the 1950s: Richard Brooks's *The Catered Affair*, with Ernest Borgnine, and Daniel Taradash's *Storm Center*, both in 1956; and John Farrow's *John Paul Jones* and the British film *The Scapegoat*, with Alec Guinness, both in 1959. She found more employment on television dramas, with decidedly mixed results. She was still big; it was the picture that got small, and for the most part Davis plays her television roles that way. They're performances designed for the living room rather than the movie palace.

Davis's role in *The 20th Century-Fox Hour*'s "Crack-Up," billed at the time (February 8, 1956) as marking her television drama debut, was actually just reused footage from *Phone Call from a Stranger*. But in the spring of 1957, Bette appeared in two new television dramas: *General Electric Theatre*'s "With Malice Toward One" and *Schlitz Playhouse*'s "For Better, for Worse." The malice of the former's title is wholly understandable: Bette plays an unpublished novelist, an accountant by day, who attends a writer's conference only to have her beloved manuscript savaged by a pretentious and mean-spirited New York editor. So, following the lead of her fictional protagonist, she buys a gun and threatens to shoot him if he doesn't publish it. "The editor was really the murderer," Bette's character thoughtfully explains. "He took the work I loved and threw it in my face like a piece of trash." It's an inspirational tale.

"For Better, for Worse" features Davis as John Williams's compulsively lying new wife, a former actress who finds that the simplest way out of a touchy situation is to make up a tale. First it's half a bottle of scotch gone missing; later there's the little matter of a hit-and-run accident. Ray Stricklyn plays Davis's stepson; Stricklyn had played her son in *The Catered Affair* and went on later to become her friend and publicist.

After making "Footnote on a Doll" for *Ford Theatre* (in which she played Dolley Madison) and "Stranded" for *Telephone Time*, both in 1957, Davis returned to *General Electric Theatre* in 1958 for "The Cold Touch," which aired on April 13. Set in Hong Kong, filmed in Hollywood, it's a convoluted drama about a kidnapped husband. "Oh, you'll never get away with it—*never*!" Davis cries as she attempts to understand the plot. Highlights include Bette climbing out on an eighth-story ledge in high heels and a hilarious performance by Jonathan "Dr. Smith" Harris—in full Fu Manchu makeup—as "Hong Kong Sam," a shady figure from whom Davis's distraught character seeks assistance. Also in 1958 was *Studio 57*'s "Starmaker," the tepid tale of a Broadway agent (Davis) and one of her clients, a nervous young actor whose father, a Barrymore-like ham, intimidates him into giving a terrible opening-night performance. Gary Merrill plays Davis's playwright husband. "Starmaker" was designed as a pilot for a series called *Paula*, named after Davis's character, but it wasn't picked up. It might have ended even earlier: "The night before Gary and I started the actual filming on *Paula*," Bette recalled, "our living room at the Chateau Marmont, where we were staying, caught on fire. Had not someone in a nearby room seen the smoke billowing out our window, we would have been asphyxiated by morning. I often wondered why I was saved."[27]

In early 1959, Davis filmed an episode of *Alfred Hitchcock Presents*. Called "Out There—Darkness," the tale features Bette as an Upper East Side matron who falsely accuses her elevator operator of mugging her. It's not one of the series's best programs; the story is muddled, through no particular fault of the director, Paul Henreid. "It was the first time I directed Bette," Henreid remembered. "She was remarkably easy to work with, intelligent and very quick to grasp what you had in mind."[28] Perhaps because of the weakness of the teleplay, Davis is even more prone than usual to delivering line readings eccentrically, laying peculiar stresses on odd words and breathing before she finishes her sentences. It was a strategic way of putting her personal stamp on a generic script, but it could veer toward the absurd. At one point, Eddie, the elevator operator, calls her "Ma'am." "Oh, *Ed*-die," Bette enunciates. "You make me feel so *an*-cient! Like *some*-thing *out* of *Charles*."

Breath.

"*Dickens!*"

The mind reels at the fact that Bette Davis appeared in three episodes of *Wagon Train*. In the legendary "Ella Lindstrom Story," she plays a widowed mother of seven with an eighth on the way, except it turns out to be a malignant tumor. Legend has it that the episode begins with a covered wagon's flap opening and a familiar face popping out, saying, "I *yoost* want to get my *gir*-ls to Californ-eye. *A*!" The reality is less camp but still fun. Ella is in fact the Boston-born widow of a Swede; Mr. Lindstrom died on the wagon train about a month before our story begins. As if the premise needed any more sentimentality, the last of the seven children, little Bo, is deaf and dumb on account of Ella's having come down with the measles while carrying him. After a doctor in Dodge City diagnoses the supposedly eighth pregnancy as cancer, Bette asks Ward Bond, "How much time did . . . how much time did he say I would have to live?" "Five or six weeks, maybe less," says Bond. "He was sure?" "He was sure," at which point Davis hurls herself to the dusty ground and wails, "*My babies! My babies!*"

The heroic but pragmatic Ella insists on going on with the wagon train and forces the kids to ingratiate themselves among various families who will then become their foster parents. She's terribly upset over the fate of little Bo, however: "As for *school*, or *board*ing him *out*,

I'd *ra*-ther *see* him *dead*!" (The critic Brigid Brophy captured this tendency well when she described Davis's "unique method of expelling the words as though snubbing them.")[29] Bond then acts as unlikely cupid for the oldest girl, Inga, and an attractive cowboy named James; they become engaged at the end and pledge to raise little Bo. There's no death scene for Bette. We simply see the wagon train heading off into the distance at the end.

Bette appeared on *Wagon Train* again in "The Elizabeth McQueeney Story," playing what the script delicately calls "an impresario." Yes—of a whorehouse. She introduces herself to Ward Bond as "Madame Elizabeth McQueeney" and says she's heading out West to start "a girl's finishing school." Asked why girls would want to go out West, she flatly answers, "*men*." "I am an impresario," she announces; "any woman is an impresario if she chooses to entertain a man." "You'll be entertaining a lot of men," Bond remarks. "I am a lot of woman," Bette replies.

She did a third episode of *Wagon Train* in 1961, "The Bettina May Story," and an episode of *The Virginian* in 1962 in which she appears in the first shot as a bank teller, nose upturned in disgust at the robbers who are cleaning out the bank. Bette's expression also registers as personal contempt for the sad fact that she's stuck in yet another TV western.

Davis's DRINKING, in play since the Farney years, deepened during her marriage to Merrill. One August early in the relationship Bette threw a surprise birthday party for Gary—a barbecue. At the end of the meal she presented him with an iced cardboard-prop cake that said, instead of "Happy Birthday," "Fuck You!" "I think that was the party where Jim Backus and I wound up in Margot's playpen," Merrill managed to recall.[30]

As Walter Bernstein so accurately described it, drinking lulled Gary but inflamed Bette. Her compulsion to cause scenes worsened with liquor. Davis always painted herself as the rare kind of star who simply had no use for the Hollywood social scene, but that was not the only problem; the producer William Frye claims that Bette caused so many public scenes upon her return to Hollywood in 1957 that she simply wasn't welcome in the social whirl. She kept to herself in part because she wasn't interested in glad-handing but also because regular glad-handers were afraid of her. One evening Frye escorted Bette, Gary, and the director Herschel Daugherty to a restaurant, the Ready Room. Cocktails were served. Daugherty, a little tipsy, made the mistake of pointing his finger at Bette to reinforce a point. The Ready Room wasn't a top-drawer establishment, unlike the staid, country-clubby Chasen's; it was the kind of place that might accommodate a liquor-fueled temper tantrum, which Davis swiftly supplied. "Don't you *dare* put your finger in my face!" she shrieked at Daugherty. "*I never want to see you again!*" Gary Merrill beat a hasty exit with an exasperated "I've had it," but Davis stayed in her seat, deviously pleased with what she'd wrought. "Cleaned this place out pretty good, didn't I? Now let's go someplace!" She and Frye kept the evening alive by heading to Mocambo.[31]

According to Merrill, the move back to Los Angeles was meant to "let it be known we were on the scene. Our professional lives were enhanced by this move, but our personal lives weren't."[32] To say the least. In June 1957, Davis filed a separation action in Santa Monica Superior Court through her lawyer David Tannenbaum, charging "grievous mental suffering" and "extreme cruelty." She sought custody of the children and support for herself and the kids. Bette, asked to confirm the breakup, gave one reporter a bit of verse from James Russell Lowell's "Legend of Brittany": "Fit language there is none for the heart's deepest things." Asked to respond, Gary echoed Othello: "Rude am I in my speech and little blessed with the soft phrase of peace." The accompanying photo was captioned "Just ten days ago Bette Davis visited hubby Gary Merrill on Hollywood set with daughter Barbara and son Michael."[33]

Merrill returned to Maine.

Bette, on the other hand, prepared to stay in Los Angeles for rehearsals for a theatrical adaptation of *Look Homeward, Angel*; she was to play Eliza Gant with Anthony Perkins cast as the son Eugene. She rented a house on Bundy Drive in Brentwood. But on the day she moved in, she opened a door and plunged forward into what she thought was a closet but was in fact the stairs to the basement, breaking her back. Three years later, Bette sued for damages; the jury awarded her $65,700. As the *Examiner* put it, "The Oscar-winning film star burst into tears as the jury's verdict favoring her was read in the courtroom of Superior Court Judge Carlos. M. Teran."[34]

She had been offered a guest spot on a *Lucy and Desi Comedy Hour* episode called "The Celebrity Next Door," but the staircase accident prevented her from appearing in it. The accident cost Davis a reported $20,000 fee, not to mention equal billing with Ball and Arnaz. "First she wanted a lot of money, which we gave her," Lucy later said. "Then she wanted a private plane to take her out here from Connecticut or Maine or wherever the hell she lived. And then she wanted this, that, and the other thing. She knew I wanted her, and she knew I'd give her anything she wanted. So after everything was all set, she went ass over teakettle in her house and broke something, and that was the end of that."[35] Bette was replaced by Tallulah Bankhead at her most obnoxious; after calling Desi a "fat pig," Tallulah actually spat at the director, Jerry Thorpe.[36]

("There's a great story about Lucy and Bette Davis on a flight together," Ball's friend and biographer Jim Brochu says. "There was a lot of turbulence. And all these stars from Warner Bros. and Columbia—*everybody*—was on this plane. Bette said to Lucy, 'My god, with all these stars on board, who would they list first if we all died?' And Lucy said, 'Don't worry, Bette. It'll be you.' ")[37]

Davis spent four months in the hospital, then recuperated at Bobby's house in Laguna Beach until she was ready to make the trip back to Maine, and Gary.[38]

"That was the end of our trial separation," Merrill wrote. "It was an extremely painful time for her, but she was a tough lady."[39]

In the scrapbooks, pictures of Gary disappear around 1958.

The Merrills returned to Hollywood in the early spring of that year. During the first week of April, a realtor showed them an oddly familiar-looking house; they quickly realized that it was the house in which Lana Turner's daughter had stabbed her mother's lover to death only a few days before. "The real estate agency had been so anxious to rent it that the bloodied mattress hadn't been removed before people began to troop through," Merrill writes. (Point of information: Johnny Stompanato died on the floor, not the bed.)[40] They took, instead, an Art Deco mansion on Hanover Drive in Brentwood at $750 a month. It offered, Merrill writes, a "living room, a den, bar, and tennis court—typical Hollywood excess."[41] After attending a producer's party, Bette wryly remarked to her husband that "they're all fatter and richer and stupider than ever."[42]

One of the first projects Davis was offered was an episode of the television series *Suspicion* called "Fraction of a Second." John Brahm directed; Bill Frye produced. On the first day of shooting, Bette called Frye at five in the morning and said she couldn't film that day because she was sick. The so-called illness was in fact a mass of bruises and scratches, the result of a violent physical struggle between the Merrills the previous night. Bette scraped her face on the driveway—or Gary scraped it for her—and was in no shape to go before the cameras.[43]

She showed up for filming the following day, the cameraman shot her good side, and she continued making the picture.

Frye was later appalled to see in the rushes that Brahm had shot a critical scene of Bette with her back entirely to the camera. Bette had insisted, Brahm insisted. Frye complained to Bette, who answered, "Goddamn it, I was acting before you were even thought of!" Still, they reshot it Frye's way for the sake of comparison. Davis remained silent during the screening of the two versions, then left the screening room without a word. Things remained chilly between them thereafter, but she ultimately agreed to use Frye's take.

Variety's critic was hardly on the edge of his seat: "This *Suspicion* spends close to sixty minutes telling events that never occurred—events apparently imagined by a woman in the 'fraction of a second' before she's killed by a load of lumber which falls on her. They call this a suspense series, but the only note of suspense arising here is why they ever made the picture."[44]

The final shooting day of "Fraction of a Second" was April 5, 1958—Bette's fiftieth birthday. When the production wrapped at 5 o'clock, Frye heard a familiar voice cry, "Where's that producer who thinks he knows everything? Tell him to get his ass into my room for a drink!" Frye, along with Brahm and the camera operator, enjoyed tension-free cocktails in Bette's dressing room until Frye realized that she had no other plans for the evening, at which point he organized an impromptu birthday party for her at his Coldwater Canyon house. Gary Merrill, it seems, was nowhere to be found.[45]

Merrill acknowledged a pronounced level of violence in the marriage, but one gets the sense that he still understated it: "Some of our arguments were whoppers, the noise level so intense that I'm surprised we could speak the next day. Once, she threatened to call the police, and I told her to go ahead. When they arrived I was sitting at the bottom of the stairs, laughing, while she screamed at them to do something. They said they didn't get involved in domestic quarrels."[46] Another time, back East, they were "walking along a snowy path. Somehow an argument started. I don't recall what it was about, but I do remember that I just got tired of having her scream in my ear. She slapped me, so I pushed her into a snow bank. I am not a wife beater, but ours was not a smooth marriage."[47] Michael Merrill said, "I don't doubt that there was physical violence. She was very volatile and could get angry at a moment's notice. . . . By the same token, when he was in that manic period, he could be exactly the same way. People go, 'Oh, he was so laid back.' Are you kidding? Sometimes he was *not* laid back."[48]

Neither of them knew how to manage money and so were continually strapped for cash. She never invested hers; she never got a chance to do so, so busy was she buying gifts for her family: Ruthie, mostly, but Bobby, too, not to mention B.D., who—according to practically everybody who knew the family—got almost anything she asked for. One of her many agents, Jules Stein, had once offered to manage her money for her, but she declined: "You can handle my jobs; I'll handle my money."[49] The family finances were further strained when the IRS socked Gary for $50,000 in back taxes. It wasn't malfeasance on Merrill's part; he simply hadn't gotten around to paying them.[50] When they were living at the Chateau Marmont, Davis recalled, "At least once a day, or so it seemed, I would answer a knock on the door and find a bill collector standing there. Some poor young man who would hang his head and stammer, 'I hate to do this to you.' I would hold out my hand and say, 'Quite all right.' "[51]

On April 28, 1958, Louella Parsons noted that "Bette Davis had no more set foot in her home in Maine after weeks on the Coast than she started packing to be ready to sail May 6 on the S.S. *Independence* for Spain and *John Paul Jones*. The bid from producer Sam Bronston for her to play Catherine the Great—$50,000 in nonrecession money—was too much to turn down. . . . Bette has just four days' work as Catherine. It's called a guest appearance, such as Mike Todd introduced in *80 Days*."[52]

In a little more than two hours, the film traces John Paul Jones's rise from an impoverished family in Scotland, where he hurls an egg in the face of a British officer, to the commander of the first U.S. ship to be saluted by a foreign country (France) during the American Revolution. He scuttles a major portion of the British fleet; utters his most famous line, "I have not yet begun to fight!"; and travels to Russia, where Catherine the Great offers to hire him.

Mikey cried on Bette's departure from Maine on May 3—his mother had been there only a week—but the trip to Europe was as much a vacation from Gary as it was a girls' retreat for Bette, B.D., and Bobby—"the three Bs," as Bette called them in her travel diary. "Heaven to have Bobby—am really so happy." This was one of Bobby's stable periods, and, tellingly, she devoted it to the care of her sister and niece.

The crossing was pleasant—"drank multitudinous martinis," "had nap." Bette called Ruthie ship to shore on Mother's Day. The *Independence* landed at Gibraltar, after which the three Davis girls traveled to Córdoba and Seville ("really magnificent—linen sheets! The works! Birds, flowers, donkeys. All *so* as it should be") before arriving in Madrid. Bette's diary is full of praise for B.D.'s behavior ("fantastic," "absolutely terrific"), though on at least one occasion she felt the need to give the eleven-year-old a sleeping pill to put her down for the night. B.D. attended a bullfight in Madrid: "a horse was gored, but all in all she loved it."[53]

Bette met John Farrow and Robert Stack, the director and star of *John Paul Jones*, on May 15. May 16 began with a meeting with the film's dressmaker, after which Davis was off to the studio to select her wig, then back to the hotel for lunch with Bobby and B.D., and then they all embarked on a tour of the city. A side trip to see Cervantes's birthplace occurred the following day. They drove to Toledo the day after that. Davis was in her element in Spain, enthusing about everything she experienced: the art, the architecture, the flowers . . .

Her Catherine the Great costume dress wasn't finished by the morning of the twenty-second—"have never been so nervous"—but it was completed by 7:00 p.m. and shooting began. Work went on until 9:00 p.m. and continued the following day and the twenty-fourth as well.

The Bs then flew to Rome; "had doctor give me pills for flight," Bette noted; they made her feel "lousy." It was sightseeing all day on the twenty-ninth. The Pantheon, the Coliseum, Vatican City: "Saw the Pope from Vatican Square at noon—a goose pimply experience! Like an angel on high!" The thirtieth brought a trip to Cinecittà to see the chariot race being filmed for *Ben-Hur*, after which she enjoyed dinner with her old Warners producer Henry Blanke and Anna Magnani. "Divine!"

By the third of June they were in Venice; on the sixth they drove to Milan, saw the cathedral, then headed to the airport and flew to London. They ended up in Henley-on-Thames.

Diary entry, June 9: "Invited to Monaco for the week-end—big do with the Grimaldis—think I'll skip it!"

There was a press party on the twelfth, lunch with Michael Balcon at Ealing Studios on the thirteenth. On June 15 Bette noted how much she enjoyed Irish coffee: "can't wait to make it at home for Gary." (This is an odd notation, considering the fractious state of the marriage at that point.)

She was in Paris on June 18, where she had dinner with Alec Guinness and the director Robert Hamer in preparation for her next film, *The Scapegoat*, in which she was to play Guinness's drug-addicted mother. Guinness was a changeling genius, a supreme technician whose most notable tour de force was to play all eight members of the doomed d'Ascoyne family in the great Ealing Studios comedy *Kind Hearts and Coronets*.

Davis, Guinness, and Hamer returned to London, where makeup and fittings for *The Scapegoat* occurred on June 23 and 24. Shooting began on the twenty-fifth.

"My costar is a terror," Davis reported in her diary. Guinness "never looks or gives a reaction," she complained. There was slight improvement by July 1: "Still get panicked working with A.G.," she wrote, though she did admit that playing one scene was "a pleasure." But later, she went on, she "did all close-ups at 6 o'clock and had a terrible time. Can never explain to anyone why it bothers me so much. . . . Ached so much that evening—thought I would die."

The magic of Europe was wearing thin. She was getting sick of European food, Bette wrote in her diary. She longed for a hamburger.

By July 9, Bette's shooting for *The Scapegoat* was completed. She purchased an eleven-month-old red Yorkshire puppy for Mike. She picked him up in Kent and named him Lord Mountbatten before sailing home with Bobby and B.D. on the *Queen Mary* on July 10.

The Scapegoat was never one of Bette's favorite films. Alec Guinness "cut my part into such shreds that my appearance in the final product made no sense at all," she claimed. "This is an actor who plays by himself, unto himself. In this particular picture he played a dual role, so at least he was able to play with himself."[54]

Matters weren't helped by her director's pronounced alcoholism. According to Piers Paul Read, Guinness's biographer, Robert Hamer went on a particularly hard bender when Davis arrived. As Guinness himself wrote in his diary at the time of Bette's death,

> I loaded her with flowers—which she accepted. But she refused all invitations to dinner etc. and had no desire to chat.

> She despised all the British film crew, told me Robert Hamer
> wasn't a director and knew nothing of films (admittedly
> Robert was on the way down and deep in drink trouble) and
> she obviously considered me a nonentity—with which I
> wouldn't quarrel greatly. But she was not the artist I had ex-
> pected. She entirely missed the character of the old Count-
> ess, which could have been theatrically effective, and only
> wanted to be extravagantly over-dressed and surrounded,
> quite ridiculously, by flowers. She knew her lines—and spat
> them forth in her familiar way—and was always on time.
> What is called a professional. A strong and aggressive per-
> sonality. After the film was shown (a failure) she let it be
> known that she considered I had ruined her performance
> and had had it cut to a minimum.[55]

But it wasn't just Guinness who thought Davis's part deserved to be
truncated. Apart from the fact that he was mostly drunk, Robert Hamer
didn't think Davis was very good: "May I say that in my opinion any
modification in the performance of Bette Davis will be to our advantage," he wrote in notes to Michael Balcon; Hamer suggested cutting the
Countess's court testimony by half. Daphne du Maurier, who wrote the
novel on which the film was based, agreed: she requested that "the scenes
in which Miss D appears [be] reduced in length if possible."[56]

I T'S AUGUST 28, 1960, and the panelists are blindfolded: time
for the Mystery Guest segment on *What's My Line?* A white-gloved
hand graced by a diamond bracelet appears and signs a famous name
on the chalkboard, and, to a fine ovation, Bette strides to her seat. Joey
Bishop asks the first question: "Are you in the entertainment business?"

A high-pitched "*Oui.*"

"Are you in pictures?" Arlene Francis inquires.

"*Oui.*"

Bennett Cerf is next: "Have you also appeared in the legitimate theater?"

"*Oui.*"

"Are you in a picture that is currently appearing on Broadway or in
the major first-run houses?" Dorothy Kilgallen wants to know.

"*Non.*"

Arlene Francis follows up: "Are you in a show that is about to appear on Broadway?"

Bette, amused, answers, "*Oui.*"

And Bennett Cerf gets it: "Would the show that you are going to do have anything to do with Mr. Carl Sandburg?"

"*Oui!*"

Unfortunately, despite the *What's My Line?* plug and related bally-hoo, the Broadway run of *The World of Carl Sandburg* lasted only twenty-nine performances. It opened at Henry Miller's Theatre on September 14 and closed on October 8.

Norman Corwin had approached Davis and Merrill in April 1959 with the idea of adapting the popular poet's work for the stage. But by the time the play was ready for rehearsals at a grange hall in Cape Elizabeth, Maine, the couple had essentially parted. "We'd meet in the morning, rehearse all day, then go our separate ways," Merrill reported.[57]

After previews at Bowdoin College in September, *The World of Carl Sandburg* had its world premiere at the State Theater in Portland. It played to a sold-out crowd, including Edmund Muskie and Carl Sandburg himself, who commandeered the stage after the show and went on so long with one of his tales that Merrill privately told him afterward to stick to the writing and let Gary and Bette do the performing.

Mr. and Mrs. Merrill continued with *The World of Carl Sandburg*, how-ever, and took the show on tour: Lowell, Massachusetts, and upstate New York, and all the way west to Los Angeles and San Francisco, thirty-two cities in all. The strain of appearing as a loving couple onstage while be-ing unable to bear each other's presence off—they stayed in separate wings of hotels while touring—wore thinner and thinner. It finally snapped when Bette had Gary served with divorce papers. The separa-tion agreement gave Gary visitation rights with the children but took away his right to appear in *The World of Carl Sandburg* in New York. Barry Sullivan took over initially for a swing through Florida before the show opened in New York with Bette and Leif Erickson.[58] The show's married-couple appeal vanished, and *The World of Carl Sandburg* closed. For Gary, though, it was good while it lasted: "It was the high spot in my career."[59]

Though the Merrills might have endured another reconciliation after splitting again in the summer of 1959, the stresses of *The World of Carl Sandburg* set a match to the couple's long-smoldering pile of used-up and discarded passion. Bette filed for divorce on May 3, 1960.[60] "Not long after our divorce, I ran into Joe Mankiewicz at a party," Bette recalled. "For years I had been asking him to write a sequel to *All About Eve*, telling what had happened to Margo and Bill. I said, 'You can forget about the sequel, Joe. Gary and I played it and it didn't work.' "[61]

TROUBLES AND A TRIUMPH

T HE GHOSTWRITER SANDFORD DODY, WHO got to know Bette's children as well as Bette herself while he was working with her on *The Lonely Life*, offered this precise description of Michael Merrill at ten: "If B.D. had her mother's confidence and outgoing personality, manly little Michael kept his own counsel. Though amiable, he seemed a rather grave little boy and perhaps a trifle tentative. I felt a depth in him, a self-containment unusual in one so young." By that point, Michael's parents had divorced, and Gary was a visitor rather than an active father. "Bette adored both kids and enjoyed roughhousing with Michael," Dody went on, "partially to give him the kind of tough, physical affection a father who was not absent might supply, and also, I'm certain, because she enjoyed it." And then this: "Mother and son would sometimes roll all over the floor, wrestling and laughing gaily, though I always felt that the boy was conscious that he was romping with a leopardess simply in the mood for play, a leopardess who might in a change of mood devour him."[1]

After the divorce, Gary took up with Rita Hayworth, a romance that sparked a particularly jealous and threatened sort of rage in Bette, who acted out by attempting to revoke Gary's visitation rights. After escorting Mike and B.D. to see *The Sound of Music* onstage along with Rita and her children, Yasmin Khan and Rebecca Welles, Gary pulled up in front of Bette's house to drop the kids off only to encounter Bette leaning out an upstairs window and screaming, "using language a hardened sailor would have thought music to his ears, 'That's not a fit woman for my children to be with! You and that whore shouldn't be together with young children,' and on and on."[2]

According to Merrill, Florence Stewart of the Lochland School had once advised him to "keep that little boy away from his mother as much as possible."[3] But now Bette was bent on keeping Mike away from his father. "The following day," Merrill continued, "Bette went off to see her lawyers to try to get my visitation rights with Mike revoked. And she did." For a time. After protracted legal wrangling, a judge awarded Gary visits with Mike every other weekend in addition to half of Mike's school vacations.

Losing her quest to deny Gary any visitation rights at all, Bette responded with drastic theatricality by sending Mike to live with him permanently. By the end of the school year, however, Bette changed her mind, and Michael Merrill was returned to her custody.[4]

That summer, the summer of 1962, Mike spent a month with his father in New England. "And while he's been with the boy, he promised to stop drinking," Hedda Hopper bleated, obviously getting her information from Davis. "Rita has not been with him for the month," Hopper added.[5] At one point, father and son found themselves in Maine. "We looked across the cove at our old house. I glanced at Michael and saw tears in his eyes," Gary recalled.[6]

IN THE LATE spring and early summer of 1961, Frank Capra remade his 1933 film *Lady for a Day* as *Pocketful of Miracles*. Based on a Damon Runyon story, the film traces the exploits of a benign bootlegger, Dave the Dude (Glenn Ford), who helps transform a beggarwoman, Apple Annie (Davis), into a presentable society matron when Annie's daughter, Louise (Ann-Margret), arrives from Europe. Louise has grown up in a Spanish convent, you see, and has no idea that her mother lives on the streets.

Ford, with whom Bette had made *A Stolen Life*, made an inopportune remark that set Bette off. "During the third week of shooting," Capra recalled, "Glenn Ford gave a columnist an interview, to wit: He felt so grateful to Bette Davis for having started *him* on *his* path to success that *he* had demanded Miss Davis be rescued from obscurity and be given the role of Apple Annie in *his* starring film. Well, I don't know what Bette Davis did the day she started Glenn on his career, but I sure know what she did when she read Glenn's interview. She flashed, and sparked, and crackled like an angry live wire thrashing in the wind: 'God*dam*dest insult . . . that sonofabitch Ford . . . helping *me* make a comeback . . . that shitheel . . . wouldn't let him help me out of a *sewer* . . . shouldn't have come to Hollywood . . . I hate it . . . hate Apple Annie . . . hate the picture . . . hate you most, Capra, for bringing me out here.' "[7] Bette also mentioned to a reporter visiting the set—a soundstage at Paramount—that she had seen *Lady for a Day* and didn't understand why Capra didn't simply rerelease it.[8]

Davis was in the final stages of shooting *Pocketful of Miracles* when Ruth Favor Davis, briefly Palmer, briefly Budd, died on July 1, 1961. It would have been her fifty-third wedding anniversary had she not divorced Harlow Davis and married and divorced Robert Palmer and married and divorced Otho Budd.

Ruthie's caregiver in her final months was Bobby, of course; Bette had to work.

Ruthie was in labor for twenty-one hours before she gave birth to Bobby and never let Bobby forget it. It wasn't until the mid-1940s, according to Bette, that Bobby grew deaf to the "oft-repeated horror" story. As Bette saw it, Ruthie never identified with Bobby in any way. "Love, yes," Bette noted less than convincingly, but not empathy.[9] But Ruthie's distance was a defensive posture, her identification with Bobby too powerful to be conscious. Ruthie herself had suffered from depression during her marriage to Harlow and at one point checked herself into a sanitarium when the girls were very small.[10] Bobby's psychological troubles always threatened to shine an unwelcome light on Ruthie's darkest corner. It was easier for her to take credit for Bette's success and remind Bobby of how difficult she'd been to produce.

Except for a brief time in East Hampton, New York, in the late 1940s, Ruthie lived on Ramona Avenue in Laguna Beach in an elegant home that was bought, paid for, and lavishly furnished by Bette, who always said publicly that she owed her mother everything, given the toils Ruthie endured to pay for her daughters' clothing, let alone their private school education.[11] ("I didn't want a career for myself," Ruthie told an interviewer once. "I wanted money to give the girls things. . . . A girl can so easily acquire an inferiority complex if she is shabbily dressed.")[12] But Bette overstated Ruthie's case drastically. Her mother was an emotional drain as well as a financial one, Lady Bountiful in reverse. By any reasonable measurement, the rewards flowed *to* Bette's mother, not from her, for most of her life.

Bette maintained, both in private and in public, that Ruthie's early sacrifices for her daughters were commensurate in anguish and strain with thirty years of high pressure, do-or-die acting work on her own part. In fact, of course, Bette paid a far greater price psychologically than Ruthie paid physically, photographic chemicals not being nearly as caustic as movie reviewers, directors, and studio bosses. One can only wonder at the degree of conscious irony in Davis's mind when she showed up at Ruthie's seventy-second birthday party in 1957 dressed as an aproned maid.[13]

Ruthie adored being the mother of a superstar, attending premieres, giving interviews, receiving gifts and money from Bette. In May 1957, she was herself the star of an episode of *This Is Your Life*, the sentimental journey into the lives of ordinary as well as famous people conducted by Ralph Edwards. Bette flew in with B.D. from Maine; Bobby was there, along with her daughter, Fay; Mrs. Robert Peckett, of Peckett's Inn, showed up from New Hampshire, too. (Mrs. Peckett bought Butternut from Bette shortly thereafter.)[14]

When Ruthie died, Sandford Dody recalls, he and Davis were in the middle of composing *The Lonely Life*. Bette telephoned him, hysterical. She couldn't go on with the project, she said, weeping. She couldn't bear it. She did, of course. But she toned down the more ambivalent passages about her mother—an understandable response on the one hand, a mother's death leading to idealization, but incomprehensible on another. Bette was finally free to speak her mind about the selfless-turned-selfish woman who had dominated her life through four marriages, but Ruthie's departure for eternity only served to kick in Bette's guilt.[15]*

Davis appears to have felt no similar guilt about Bobby. If anything, age made her increasingly hostile to her younger sister. "Bette was angry a good part of the time, and I really can't tell you why," Chuck Pollack said. "She didn't trust anybody; that was one of the worst things. She had no one, not even her sister. Her poor sister. She treated her like a dog."[16]

Bobby had her own daughter, Fay, to care for in the 1940s and early 1950s, but even then Bobby found time—and the presence of mind—to

---

* *The Lonely Life* was published in 1962 to positive reviews and solid sales.

care not only for Bette's children but for Bette herself. It was Bobby who escorted B.D. to Maine to spend part of Bette and Gary's honeymoon with them, Bobby who accompanied Bette and B.D. to Europe in 1958.

Bobby was there, too, when Bette became ill during the last night of *Two's Company*; it was Bobby who accompanied Bette to the hospital. And when Ray Stricklyn, who appeared with Davis in *The Catered Affair* and "For Better, for Worse," tells in his memoirs of how, during the filming of the latter in 1957, when Bette took a palpably seductive attitude toward him despite their considerable difference in age, Bobby hovers in the background of the tale: at 10:00 p.m., when the director finally called it a night, there was Bobby in Bette's dressing room, dutifully packing the star's clothes and preparing the star for her exit.[17]

By 1971, Bobby was living in Phoenix. She showed up for Bette's own episode of *This Is Your Life* (which was taped on February 2, 1971, and aired on March 7), along with Edith Head, William Wyler, Robert Wagner, Benny Baker (who'd been onstage with Bette in one of the Cukor plays in Rochester), Olivia de Havilland, Sally Sage Hutchinson (Bette's longtime stand-in), and Ted Kent (the editor of *Bad Sister*).[18] But the two Davis girls became increasingly estranged as the 1970s went on. Bette was living in Hollywood when she was told that Bobby was dying of cancer in Arizona. "Let her come and visit me," Bette responded. The sisters never saw each other again. Bobby died in 1979.[19]

Cigarettes were to Bette Davis what a bottle of Southern Comfort was to Janis Joplin or a half-unbuttoned black shirt is to Tom Ford: a mundane prop elevated by sheer force of personality to the level of a stylized autograph. Davis smoked eminently onscreen—Charlotte Vale's romanticized oral fixation in *Now, Voyager*; the pungent fumes of Margo Channing—but, if anything, she was even better known in real life as the world's most famous nicotine addict. Only Winston Churchill and his cigars could come close, but Davis takes the prize if only because she inhaled.

Her friends, family, and coworkers necessarily grew accustomed to Davis's acrid exhalations, but they put up with them because, after all, she was Bette Davis, and cigarettes—the gestures they enabled, the attention they called to the hands and mouth, the full fire-breathing drama—were her stock-in-trade. "She used smoking in a way I'd never seen before. It was a signature," said Dr. Ivin Prince. Dr. Prince knew Davis intimately. He was her dentist.[20]

She came to him first in the mid-1950s with a mouth full of out-of-position teeth, many of which were loose. She couldn't close her mouth because the uppers hit the lowers. The cause of this dental disaster was the osteomyelitis that had forced *Two's Company* to close. Years of smoking hadn't helped.

Dr. Prince's office was located on the ground floor of the Imperial House, an apartment building on the Upper East Side. He also treated one of the Imperial House's most famous residents. "I never mentioned to Bette that I was also treating Joan," Dr. Prince said, though he did eventually reveal the fact after Crawford died. Bette was amused.

"When she laughed, you could hear it half a block away. Patients in the waiting room would hear Bette Davis laughing—there was no mistaking her. She was the kind of person who—when she liked and trusted you—was wonderful. But there weren't many such people in her life. She was always lovely with my staff. She wasn't always lovely with *her* staff." Dr. Prince remembered that Davis smoked not only in the waiting room but even in the dentist's chair. "She pretty much did what she wanted," he noted.

One day, Dr. Prince recalled, he heard dramatically raised voices emanating from the waiting room. Bette was scheduled for an appointment, as was another of the dentist's high-profile patients: Tennessee Williams. "I remember them screaming and shouting at one another, oblivious to the fact that there were other people around." According to Dr. Prince, Williams actually employed the most exhausted of tired clichés. "You'll never work in this town again!" the playwright yelled at the star.

Davis had, by that time, ended her run on Broadway as Maxine Faulk in Williams's *The Night of the Iguana*. "I don't think she enjoyed the experience," Dr. Prince lightly observed. "She told me she would get so nervous before the curtain that she would throw up." But, Bette's dentist added, "She *used* it. She said she thought her nervousness made her better."

The Night of the Iguana concerns a drunken defrocked minister, Shannon (Patrick O'Neal), who has descended ignominiously to driving a tour bus in Mexico; Hannah Jelkes (Margaret Leighton), a Yankee spinster; and Maxine Faulk, the earthy owner of an Acapulco hotel. Frank Corsaro directed. Rehearsals began in New York in October 1961, and according to Williams's agent, Audrey Wood, they went well. Davis let her feelings about Maxine Faulk be known, however. During one rehearsal, for example, Margaret Leighton entered carrying a suitcase. Bette took it as directed and headed upstage only to stop in her tracks, whirl around, and call out to the dark theater, "Tennessee! I don't think this bitch for one moment would pick up her bag and carry it. I just don't think she would. What do *you* think?" Williams let her do it her way.[21]

Trouble started when the company traveled to Rochester for previews. The first performance was, as Wood described it, "rough, but the audience was receptive. . . . There was an opening night party which we all attended, including Bette, and we all went to bed."

The company manager called Wood in her hotel room the following morning to announce that "Bette Davis is being taken in a wheelchair to an ambulance and then to a hospital." It seems she had fallen during the performance but suffered no symptoms until the following day. After two performances with the understudy taking Davis's place, the company moved on to Cleveland. She was driven there by limousine. "Bette recovered, and we went on. Finally, the tour brought us to Chicago," Wood recalled.[22]

In December, *The Night of the Iguana* faced the critics. *Time* was downright mean: "A big, ugly edible lizard called the iguana is, in Mexico, more or less what the Thanksgiving turkey is in the U.S. Mexicans catch iguanas, fatten them up, and serve them on festive occasions. Tennessee Williams' latest play, now in Chicago and headed for Broadway this month, is called *The Night of the Iguana*. And from all indications last week, despite impressive performances by Margaret Leighton and Bette Davis, it is indeed a massive turkey. Chicago critics have carved it up." *Time* quoted some choice remarks of the Chicago papers: "*The Tribune*, for example, found the play 'bankrupt . . . barren . . . bleakly dull.' And the *Sun Times* called it 'something of a dud . . . a swollen vignette . . . vulgarity for the sake of vulgarity, padding for the sake of fill, waterfront humor to patch the gaps and the pulpit for preaching.' "[23]

Williams wrote a note to Bette while the show was still in Chicago. He advised her, "Everything about [Maxine] should have the openness and freedom of the sea. I can imagine she even smells like the sea." He didn't like Bette's wig at all, and he told her so: "It is too perfectly arranged, too carefully 'coiffed.' It ought to be like she had gone swimming without a cap and rubbed her hair dry with a coarse towel and not bothered to brush or comb it." And, he commented, "when she says, 'I never dress in September,' I think she means just that.

"There is so much that's wonderful in your characterization that it seems a crime to risk its total effect by neglecting the final touches. Yours devotedly, Tennessee."[24]

"It was there in Chicago that Bette Davis said she'd not take further direction from Frank Corsaro and ordered him barred from the theatre," Williams later recalled in his *Memoirs*. "He stayed out of the theatre but stayed in Chicago; but Bette said she could sense his lingering presence in Chicago and that he must be returned to New York and that goddam Actor's Studio, which had spawned him."[25] Williams and Charles Bowden took over the direction, though Corsaro remained on the bill.

The Night of the Iguana opened on Broadway at the Royale Theatre on December 28, 1961. The director Joshua Logan saw the show and admired it, particularly Davis: "She was svelte, handsome, voluptuous, wicked, wise, raffish, slightly vulgar—in fact, she was ideal for the part and gave the play an added dimension."[26]

Bette kept an autograph book to register those who came backstage during the New York run. The first signatory is "Mike Merrill, your ever loving son." Others include Anita Loos, Dakin Williams, Natalie Schafer, B. D. Merrill ("your ever lovin' daughter"), Glenda Farrell, Kaye Ballard, Teresa Wright, Ann Sheridan, Joan Bennett, Olivia de Havilland, Fredric March, Margot Merrill (who printed her name in a legible but childish hand), Mike Merrill again, right below Margot, and, in an outsized flourish that dominates the lower half of one page, "Love to Bette—Joan Crawford."[27] Telegrams flew in, too, from such notables as Ray Stark, Leland Hayward, Spencer Tracy, Dore Shary, Terence Rattigan, Bobby ("Hang this above the steam pipes and know that I am there with you and only you on this opening night . . . I love you for all the greats you are. Great mother, great aunt, great great sister, great dad and my best friend. Pocket full of miracles for you on opening night and every night thereafter"), Johnny Dall, Farley Granger, Mike Levee, and finally one that reads, "Darling Bette—Please let me do the movie version. Bless you—and love—Tallulah."[28]

Despite the mean if funny critical fanfare in Chicago, *The Night of the Iguana* was a success in New York, but Bette began missing performances—according to Audrey Wood, without explanation. Wood's theory is that Davis began to resent the amount of time her character was offstage: "When you have been a great film star, it must be difficult to sit backstage in your dressing room for protracted periods in which there is nothing to do but to wait for your next entrance."[29]

Shelley Winters saw the show after hearing some negative buzz. "Bette Davis seemed to be shooting her lines right at the audience, facing squarely front and not talking to Margaret or Patrick at all," Winters later wrote. "She was getting uproarious laughs, but I knew she wasn't that kind of actress. What the hell was going on? Only in the scenes when Bette was alone with Patrick was there any communication. Those scenes were powerful. Why had she just stood on the stage and shouted out her jokes?"

Davis left the show in disgust in early April 1962, and Winters agreed to take over the role. She attended a matinee during the interim, when Maxine Faulk was being played by Davis's quite experienced understudy, Madeleine Sherwood. When the announcement was made that Sherwood was appearing that afternoon in Davis's place, "half of the audience stood up simultaneously and rushed to the box office to get their money back." (Sherwood had the guts to yell out from the stage, "Come on, ladies! Give me a chance! I'm really very good, and the play is terrific!")

"The first time I walked into my dressing room backstage at the Royale," Winters continued, "written on the mirror in very red lipstick were the following words: 'SHELLEY—AFTER YOUR FIRST OR POSSIBLY SECOND PERFORMANCE YOU WILL FIND OUT WHY I LEFT THIS SHOW. BETTE DAVIS.'" Winters noted that Sherwood hadn't "washed Bette's message to me off the mirror. So whatever was going to happen to me must have happened to Madeleine, too."

She figured it out soon enough. As Winters explained it, Williams had written Maxine Faulk as a comic role to relieve the relentless sadness of an alcoholic going to "his almost certain death, like the iguana that is tied up under our stage veranda." And the laugh lines Williams gave to Faulk depended on timing—everyone's, not only the actress delivering them. According to Winters, "Margaret Leighton or Patrick O'Neal would say the *setup* of my joke and then move slightly for a few seconds, keeping the eye of the audience so the audience was not looking at me or even listening. . . . It's a wicked British stage trick." It took Winters about three performances to understand exactly why Davis had gotten fed up enough to leave the show.[30]

Williams saw things differently. "Bette Davis quit the show and Shelley Winters went in," the playwright wrote to his friend Maria St. Just. "It is hard to say which was worse but at least La Davis drew cash and La Winters seems only to sell the upper gallery."[31]

But Shelley got the last laugh. At one performance she became so enraged at her fellow actors' antics that she pushed a cocktail cart across the stage so hard that it "knocked Patrick O'Neal over and he knocked Margaret Leighton over as he fell. The audience either liked this stage business or felt they deserved it," she wrote.[32]

NEUROSIS, HYSTERIA, AND paranoia are defining features of Davis's acting style, the film scholar Martin Shingler points out—"the fidgity fingers; the cracks in her voice and leaps to a shrill, high pitch; the roving eyes suspiciously scanning her immediate environment." But Davis's performance style is complicated, as was her psyche. "In contrast," Shingler adds, "there's the absolute restraint, the steady, steadfast glare; the straight back; the ability to subdue all the tics and mannerisms, suggesting a high level of self-control." Davis's public image was similarly split: "Her star persona shifts from her famous furies to her absolute level-headedness about herself and the industry she worked in."[33]

To put it in psychiatric terms, Davis's torn nature suggests that she may have had a borderline personality, one that shifts been the commonly neurotic—anxiety, depression, emotional outbursts—and a baldly psychotic inability to perceive the point at which reality stops and paranoid fantasy takes over. Davis's temper was, it might go without saying, legendary, and behind it lay not only a deep-seated rage against authority, at root antipaternal, but also a compulsion to disrupt the outside world so that it matched her convulsive interior. A history of unstable relationships with men; an impulsive streak; a raw incapability to control anger; a destructive tendency to undercut her directors' interests purely for the sake of undercutting them; a disrupted, itinerant childhood; paternal abandonment; increasing alcoholism . . . Davis's character traits come straight out of a diagnostic manual.*

Davis also shifted drastically between two other poles: the obsessive-compulsive and the hysterical. The woman who recalled with candor her childhood upset at the uneven seam in the circus's red carpet was the same woman whose hot crying jags led to the shutting down of *The Little Foxes*. The Bette Davis who routinely polished all the silver and brass in her house as a way of expending nervous energy was the same

* The manual happens to be *Disordered Personalities* by David J. Robinson, M.D., second edition.

Bette Davis who threw fits, swore filthily, called people vile names. Rob-bie Lantz recalled meeting Bette Davis for the first time in Westport: "She showed us the house. On the landing, she had railings made of brass—very shiny. I said, 'Somebody comes to keep this spotless?' And she said, 'No. I do it.' This gave me a clue to certain things."[34] Did the suppression of her hysteria lead to the compulsive brass polishing, or did the unquenchable need to keep everything in perfect order lead to the regular breakdowns?

The origins of Bette Davis's double nature are clear enough—Ruthie on the one hand, Harlow on the other—but Ruthie was herself a mix of obstinacy and neurosis. In their unpublished, jointly written memoir, her brother Paul Favor asks Ruthie to name the traits that led Ruthie to "see drama in Bette," and Ruthie tellingly responds: "What he really means is that she had a very bad temper. Yes, this is true, but I know now that I did not understand how to manage it. We were too much alike. She cannot take correction. She is perfectly sure she is right, and so am I. They just do not mix. Many people have asked me why did I let her have her own way. Well, I couldn't help it."[35] In other words, Bette's the-atricality went hand in hand with its diametric opposite: unshakable conviction.

As Shingler notes, Davis's mix of righteousness and combustibility served to "make her a frightening figure for those who worked with her. It also made her more enigmatic and intriguing for audiences and fans. It probably also frightened her."[36] Bette Davis was scarcely easy to live with, perhaps least of all by herself. Still, her nuttiness led directly to one of the greatest performances of her career, an all-stops-pulled portrait of degenerated talent and family resentment spun out of control. And for better or worse (mostly worse), the performance was so brilliant that it set the tone of the rest of her career.

"I've written. A letter. To Daddy! His address is heaven above. . . ."

IT'S TIME FOR *What's My Line?* again. Now it's November 11, 1962. The first guest, Mimmi Paulsen, is a shipboard radio operator in a black cocktail dress. The second, Dell Winders, is a toothy, outdoorsy type from Philadelphia. He's a porpoise trainer. Nobody gets either of them.

After a pitch for the folks at home to get tested during Diabetes Week, the panelists—Dorothy Kilgallen, Bennett Cerf, Arlene Francis, and Art Linkletter—put on their blindfolds before Bette Davis makes her entrance. This time, the signing arm is clad in long-sleeved velvet and graced by a charm bracelet. So far so good, but to loud applause from the audience, Davis strides to her seat and we see that the dress is a disaster: a full-length gown with a drastic Empire waist combined with a plunging neckline. The sleeves are tightly fitted, a satin bow calls further attention to the too-high waist, and the skirt is of densely gathered chiffon. It's too girlish for a woman of fifty-four, mutton dressed as lamb in a prom dress. She has gotten thick.

And yet . . . although she looks every year of her age, she's also glamorous and attractive. There are big bags under her eyes, but the neck and face are fine. The hair, thinner and coarser than it was when she was in her prime, is cut just short of her shoulders and suggests Margo Channing with soft waves around her face. She's undeniably sexy and vibrant. Bette Davis has been a movie star for thirty years.

Bennett Cerf knows who she is even before she sits down, probably because Joan Crawford had been on the show a few weeks earlier promoting the same movie. "Well," he says, "that was a spectacular ovation that you received, Mr. or Miss Mystery Guest! Uh, would it be possibly because you have made a great name for yourself in motion pictures?"

"Yes," Davis replies in a weirdly squeaky voice.

"Do you have a new picture just out?" Linkletter asks.

"Yes."

Arlene Francis knows the answer, too: "Boy, try to fake that voice—the most impersonated voice in America! Have you just done a picture with a vis-à-vis who is also a big name in the picture business?"

"Yes," squeals Bette, who clearly knows what's coming.

Cerf provides the coup de grâce: "Would the vis-à-vis be a lady who has also been a Mystery Guest here within the past month named Miss Joan Crawford?"

"Altogether now," the host, John Daly, says—"one, two, three . . . ," and the panelists cry in unison, "Bette Davis!"

"I've just come back from Miami," Cerf remarks (pronouncing it *Miama*), "and it seems to me your picture's playing in every motion picture theater in Florida—it's all over the place!"

"Well, you know," Bette replies, "we were chosen by motion picture theater owners as a sort of a test run—what they call preview engagements. We were very fortunate we were chosen. We opened in 137 theaters in Manhattan alone, 22 of which I have done in three days in a Greyhound bus."

"You have won two Academy Awards, if memory serves me right," says Daly.

"Very old boys and very tarnished," Davis modestly replies, "a long time ago—oh, they're so tarnished!" (She'd probably polished the gold plate right off of them.)

"I think a bright, shiny new one is what is necessary and will be forthcoming," Daly adds.

"Well, I think my two old boys would be pretty pleased," Davis responds, "but you never know."

The picture in question is, of course, *What Ever Happened to Baby Jane?*

The night Joan Crawford signed Bette's autograph book backstage after a performance of *Night of the Iguana*, she told Davis of a novel she had just read—one that could be adapted into a film for both of them. It was written by Henry Farrell and concerned two strange sisters, one considerably stranger than the other. The Hudson girls had once been movie stars but now live in simple baroque despair on the fringes of Hollywood. Blanche is in a wheelchair, the result of a car accident; Jane is off her rocker, the result of the American film industry.

As Davis recalled of Crawford's suggestion, "She said she had sent it to Robert Aldrich with hopes that he would direct it. He had phoned her from Italy, where he was finishing a film, to say he had acquired the rights to the book."[37] Several weeks later, Aldrich arrived at Bette's townhouse on East Seventy-eighth Street. Bette first asked him which part was hers.[38] Then she asked him whether he'd ever fucked Joan. "If you had," Davis stated, "then you couldn't be fair to both of us." "The answer is no—not that I didn't have the opportunity," Aldrich responded.[39]

Davis was between agents at the time, said Martin Baum: "I was Bob Aldrich's agent, and Bob suggested her for the part of Jane Hudson. I volunteered to be her agent for that job, and she allowed me to sign her."[40]

Bill Frye claims some credit for the genesis of *What Ever Happened to Baby Jane?* He came across Farrell's novel while searching for new material for his new series *Thriller*. It was too complex for a TV show, he decided, but it would make a great feature. According to Frye, he gave a copy of the novel to Davis and to Olivia de Havilland as well, with the idea of casting de Havilland as the invalid sister; Frye thought Ida Lupino would be an ideal director for the project. He took the package to Lew Wasserman at Universal (Wasserman had ceased being an agent and became head of MCA, which bought Universal), but when Wasserman learned that Frye wanted to cast Davis, he declined to give the project the go-ahead. (Wasserman had recently seen Davis in "The Bettina May Story" on *Wagon Train* and, according to Frye, disliked her performance.) "You'll never believe it," Davis told Frye later, "but Crawford gave me a copy of the book with a note suggesting I play the younger sister. I told her *never*. The only part I'm interested in is Baby Jane."⁴¹*

"I hadn't the faintest idea what to do with her until I saw the wardrobe," Davis told James McCourt. "The minute I did, she came to me *like that*."⁴² In one way, at least, Davis appreciated the finer, creepier points of Jane Hudson better than Aldrich. She insisted not only on applying her own makeup but on designing it. "What I had in mind no professional makeup man would have dared to put on me," she remarked in *This 'n That*. "One told me he was afraid that if he did what I wanted, he might never work again. Jane looked like many women one sees on Hollywood Boulevard. . . . I felt Jane never washed her face—just added another layer of makeup each day. I used a chalk-white base, lots of eye shadow—very black—a cupid's-bow mouth, a beauty mark on my cheek and a bleached blond wig with Mary Pickford curls."⁴³ The effect is hideous.

After three days of filming, Aldrich told her to tone it down; it was too much. "If you change my makeup," Bette claimed she told her director, "you'll have to recast me, because if I play Jane *I will continue to wear this makeup*."⁴⁴ Aldrich relented, though according to him, when Davis herself saw the film she was aghast at what she'd wrought. "She'd never seen the complete picture before seeing it with me at Cannes, and I don't think she was prepared for the experience of seeing it among lots of people," Aldrich said. "About five minutes into the picture I heard this quiet but kind of desperate sobbing beside me and turned to her wondering what the hell was the matter. 'I just look awful,' she wept. 'Do I really look that awful?'"⁴⁵

According to Bette, Joan had precisely the opposite impulse. Crawford wanted to look glamorous: "her hair well dressed, her gowns beautiful, and her fingernails with red nail polish. For the part of an invalid who had been cooped up in a room for twenty years, she wanted to look attractive!" Crawford launched an argument with Aldrich the morning

---

*It's at best unclear whether Blanche is younger than Jane. The opening scene suggests that she is older.

they were set to film Blanche hobbling her way down the stairs. Aldrich wanted her to remove her nail polish. "You have taken everything else away from me," Joan moaned, bereft. *"You're not taking away my nail polish!"*[46]

"In her vanity she was consistent," Davis observed. She offered an especially ludicrous example: "As part of her wardrobe, Miss Crawford owned three sizes of bosoms. In the famous scene in which she lay on the beach, Joan wore the largest ones. Let's face it—when a woman lies on her back, I don't care how well endowed she is, her bosoms do not stand straight up. And Blanche had supposedly wasted away for twenty years. The scene called for me to fall on top of her. I had the breath almost knocked out of me. It was like falling on two footballs."[47]

B.D., who plays the Hudson sisters' teenage neighbor in a bit of stunt casting (apart from an uncredited appearance as a toddler in *Payment on Demand*, this was her only professional acting job), told *Look* that, as the reporter described it, "the most revealing difference in the personalities of the two women is that Miss Crawford lights her cigarettes with a dainty, ultrafeminine gold lighter, whereas her mother fiercely strikes enormous cowboy matches on the sole of her shoes."[48]

Bob Thomas, one of Crawford's biographers, overheard the following dialogue on the set one day.

> DAVIS: Of course you know, Joan, that everybody is trying to work up a feud between us.
>
> CRAWFORD: I know, dear, and isn't that ridiculous? We're much too professional for anything like that.[49]

As conventional as the observation may be, the fact is that the tortures the Hudson sisters inflict upon each other in the film—Blanche applies graciousness in the face of infirmity as though it was a painful wrestling hold while Jane, more elemental, chains her sister to the bed and starves her to death—played out in precisely the way Crawford politely denied. Davis fondly told of the day she and Joan were sitting together on the set—Joan serenely knitting—when Bette industriously began crossing out huge portions of the screenplay. "Whose dialogue are you cutting, Bette?" Joan asked. "Yours," Bette answered, whereupon Joan burst gratifyingly into tears.[50] She wasn't really eliminating Joan's lines, Bette confessed to Vik Greenfield; she only performed the routine to upset Joan.

Joan, meanwhile, was driving Bette crazy with kindness. Someone began sending a single rose to Davis on the set every day. "If you're going to send roses, for God's sake send a dozen or more," Bette muttered. When she found out they were coming from Crawford, she thought she'd retch.[51]

She retaliated by signing Crawford's copy of *The Lonely Life* with the following inscription: "Joan, Thanks for wanting my autograph. Bette."[52]

Sheilah Graham reported that Joan, always the company gal, showed up one day with a cooler full of Pepsi for the cast and crew; the next day Bette appeared with an even larger cooler full of Coke.[53]

Bette was blunt: "We were polite to each other—all the social amenities, 'Good morning, Joan,' and 'Good morning, Bette' crap. Thank God we weren't playing roles where we had to like each other. She was always so damn proper. She sent thank you notes for thank you notes!' "[54]

As Curtis Bernhardt once observed, the two actresses employed opposing strategies to get to a similar place onscreen: "Crawford was a typical film actress. When she needed to play an emotional scene, the director had to take her aside and tell her a sad story. Tears came to her eyes and you let her go out and play the scene. Bette would immediately use tears if I said I wanted them. She was completely professional. I would call Crawford an amateur actress. But Crawford was very good as such. Bette, of course, never shed real tears in an emotional scene. Crawford shed real tears."[55]

Sexually, they were opposites as well. Vincent Sherman, who slept with each of them, tells the story of Crawford watching her own film *Humoresque* in a screening room with him in preparation for Sherman's *The Damned Don't Cry* and becoming so "stimulated by her own eroticized image" that she stood up in the middle of the film, "raised her dress, and quickly pulled off a pair of silk panties she was wearing." "Was it possible," Sherman asks, "despite my efforts to keep it quiet, that someone had whispered to her that Bette Davis and I had had an affair and she was out to accomplish what Davis had not: have me get a divorce and marry her?" Sherman sums it up: "Sex for Bette was a biological need, while for Joan it was primarily an ego trip."[56]

IN *SUNSET BOULEVARD*, Max von Mayerling (Erich von Stroheim), Norma Desmond's chauffeur and former husband, drives her—in her lengthy and fabulous Isotta Fraschini—through Paramount

Pictures' ornate Bronson Avenue gate, the elegant architectural symbol of one of world cinema's preeminent institutions. *What Ever Happened to Baby Jane?*—filmed on the cheap—was shot across the street.

The Producers Studios, on the other side of Melrose Avenue from Paramount, has been described as "ramshackle," but that's overstating the case.[57] Now called Raleigh Studios, it has been a working lot since 1914, providing relatively inexpensive accommodations to independent filmmakers such as Aldrich and Stanley Kramer as well as television series such as Ronald Reagan's *Death Valley Days*. Aldrich and company shot *Baby Jane* there from July 9 through September 12, 1962, with the exteriors of the Hudsons' two-story Spanish Revival house filmed on location in the Wilshire district at 172 South McCadden Place near the corner of Highland and Beverly.[58]

According to Bob Thomas, Joan got $40,000 and 10 percent of the producer's net profit, but Bette had a more immediate need for cash and agreed to $60,000 with only 5 percent of the profit.[59] Aldrich's biographers Alain Silver and James Ursini disagree; according to them, Crawford got 15 percent while Davis got 10 percent.[60] And Aldrich himself cited a different base figure for Joan: $25,000.[61] No matter; the point is, *Baby Jane* was relatively cheap to shoot, and the two stars settled for less up front than they had earned in their prime.

Baby Jane was made so inexpensively that Aldrich couldn't afford process shots for Jane Hudson's drive through Hollywood, so Bette herself got behind the wheel one day and drove, with Ernie Haller crouched in the backseat or perched on the hood with his camera.[62] But artistic considerations played into Aldrich's decision, too. It was a full twelve years after Eve Harrington and Addison DeWitt strolled toward the camera on a soundstage floor while images of a New Haven sidewalk were projected behind them, and by 1962, rear projection was beginning to look more than a tad artificial. By placing the preposterous Jane Hudson in a real car wending her way in traffic down real Los Angeles streets, Aldrich renders her even more terrifying: the drive visually forces Jane to be plausible in her demented absurdity.

Aldrich struck a distribution deal with Warner Bros. Jack Warner recalled in his memoirs that he caught a preview of the film in New York at the RKO Theater on Eighty-sixth Street. "There were perhaps 3,000 people in the house, and I thought they'd blow the roof off. I hadn't heard such screaming and yelling at a preview in years. *Baby Jane* lit up the skies like a paint-factory fire."[63]

The film was an immediate hit upon its release, first in New York on October 31, 1962, a week later in Los Angeles. As the *Hollywood Reporter* trumpeted, "*What Ever Happened to Baby Jane?* made film history by amassing through the weekend $1,600,000 in film rental, putting the Warner–Seven Arts Association and Robert Aldrich picture into the profit column in less than two weeks."[64] Although the trades reported the film cost $825,000, the actual negative cost was $1,075,664.28.[65] Still, the film made money; by the end of August 1963, *What Ever Happened to Baby Jane?* had grossed $3,898,568.55.[66] Davis herself claimed that by the late 1980s *Baby Jane* had pulled in about $10 million.[67]

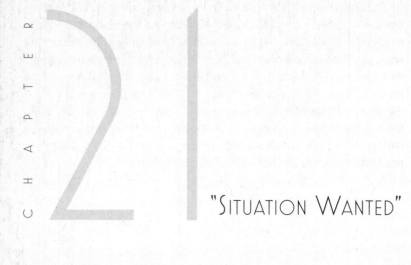

"SITUATION WANTED"

IT WAS ONLY NINE DAYS AFTER *WHAT EVER Happened to Baby Jane?* wrapped that Bette Davis placed her notorious want ad in the trades. Listed under "Situation Wanted, Women" was the following:

> MOTHER OF THREE — 10, 11 & 15 — DIVORCEE. AMERICAN. THIRTY YEARS EXPERIENCE AS AN ACTRESS IN MOTION PICTURES. MOBILE STILL AND MORE AFFABLE THAN RUMOR WOULD HAVE IT. WANTS STEADY EMPLOYMENT IN HOLLYWOOD. (HAS HAD BROADWAY.) Bette Davis, c/o Martin Baum, G.A.C. REFERENCES UPON REQUEST.[1]

As Martin Baum described his bemused reaction in retrospect, "I was an important agent, she was a big star, and I wasn't going looking for work for her. That was not exactly the position I expected to be in at that point in my career—or *her* career. She was never out of work, but she was concerned about where her career was going. So she placed the ad. Everyone was laughing—it was a joke. *Bette Davis looking for a job?* It didn't make sense! But she was serious about it. She felt she needed work. It just wasn't as dire a circumstance as she portrayed it in the ad.[2]

"I had a good three years representing her," Baum concluded, "but then she left. She wanted to work more consistently." (The last film he repped for her was *Hush . . . Hush, Sweet Charlotte*.) "She was a lovely human being—feisty, a fighter all the way, and had great pride in the work she did. As she grew older, and parts became more difficult to get, she still went in there fighting for what she believed in. I loved her, and I'm honored to have represented her for a little while."[3]

"Actually the ad was tongue-in-cheek, but a deep dig as well," Bette later commented. "The ad was half playful and half serious. After all, I had left a hit play, had finished *What Ever Happened to Baby Jane?*, and my book *The Lonely Life* was just out, so my career was not in jeopardy. If I was truly unemployed, I could never have taken the advertisement."[4]

The ad is a prime example of how Bette's sense of humor could misfire—a less extreme, eminently more comprehensible version of the baskets of rotten vegetables Chuck Pollack says she'd send to friends as her peculiar way of apologizing for her drunken hostility at dinner parties in later years.[5] She meant the ad to be a serious joke, a goof with a chip on its shoulder. (How she meant the rotten vegetables remains inexplicable.) But Hollywood took it as an inadvertent joke, and Bette ended up looking foolish in the eyes of fools.

The ad was clearly still on the *machers'* minds when, in early 1963, the Academy nominated Bette Davis as Best Actress for *Baby Jane*. Bette blamed not the Academy but Crawford for her loss. "Joan did everything she could possibly think of to keep me from winning," Bette bitterly recalled. "She campaigned openly in New York, contacting all the Oscar nominees who were in plays in New York that year."[6] By "all," Bette is referring to two: Geraldine Page, nominated for *Sweet Bird of Youth*, who was appearing in a revival of O'Neill's *Strange Interlude*; and Anne Bancroft, who was nominated for *The Miracle Worker* and was starring in Jerome Robbins's production of Brecht's *Mother Courage and Her Children*. The other two nominees were Katharine Hepburn, for *Long Day's Journey into Night*, and Lee Remick, for *Days of Wine and Roses*.

Crawford somehow convinced Bancroft to allow her, Joan, to accept the award on her behalf should she win. And she did, the Academy predictably choosing Helen Keller's heartwarmingly devoted teacher over an atrocity-committing wackjob who, were she real, could herself have been a member of the Academy.

The honors were awarded at the Santa Monica Civic Auditorium on April 8, 1963, with Frank Sinatra serving as the emcee. According to Davis, all the nominees or their surrogates were backstage in dressing rooms, each with its own television monitor. The Oscar historians Mason Wiley and Damien Bona specify that Bette was ensconced in Sinatra's dressing room with Olivia de Havilland. Joan was down the hall. Wiley and Bona quote the show's director, Richard Dunlap, on why he refused to show the television audience the scene backstage: "I couldn't. It would have been cruel."[7]

"When Anne Bancroft's name was announced, I am sure I turned white," Bette wrote. "Moments later, Crawford floated down the hall past my door. I will never forget the look she gave me. It was triumphant. The look clearly said, *You didn't win and I am elated!*"[8]

Bill Frye was Bette's escort that night. Watching Crawford standing there receiving an ovation for an award she hadn't even won was too much for Davis to bear. "Let's get out of here!'" she demanded and asked to be taken home. But Frye convinced her to go to a party at the Beverly Hilton, where they were joined by Bobby, B.D., Robert Aldrich and his wife, and Olivia de Havilland. All the tables were graced with fifths of booze, and Bette immediately dove for the scotch, filling a glass to the brim. "This is for La Belle Crawford," she announced. When told that Joan drank vodka, not scotch, Bette replied, "I don't care what she drinks. This is going into her *fucking face.*"

Bette didn't throw the drink but said "I refuse to be in the same room with her. I don't care how big the room is." So they all went to Bette's house, whereupon she began to make scrambled eggs and toast. She was slicing a loaf of bread when Frye, casually seated in a rocking chair, tactlessly remarked on Crawford's elegant appearance. "What did you say?" asked Bette, who stopped slicing the bread and proceeded to advance upon the startled Frye with the knife in her hand. "*What did you say?*" she repeated, aiming the blade at his heart. "You make me sick," she told him and calmly went back to making breakfast.[9]

AFTER *BABY JANE*, Davis filmed her episode of *The Virginian*—"The Accomplice," which aired on December 19, 1962—and didn't work again until the fall of 1963, when she agreed to make a film in Italy. "The name of the film was *The Empty Canvas*," Bette remarked. "Empty it was."[10]

The film's producer, Carlo Ponti, promised Davis to add more scenes with Davis's character—the extravagantly wealthy, no-named mother of a depressed young painter (Horst Buchholz)—to give her more pizzazz as well as screentime. But as Davis described it, "[I] arrived in Italy to find that nothing had been done to the script at all. In desperation I decided to use a Southern accent to give some kind of flavor to this extremely dull woman. The blonde wig was also my idea, a further attempt to make her at least a noticeable character in the film. My costar, Horst Buchholz, was anything but easy to work with; in fact, he went out of his way to thwart me at every turn.[11]

"My first day on the set, I arrive, and here is this completely naked girl—and I mean completely naked—walking around, and the grips and the electricians are ogling her and naturally not getting any work done at all, and I thought I'd taken leave of my senses," Bette declared a few months after *The Empty Canvas*'s American release. "Then somebody thinks to introduce me, and the naked lady turns out to be my costar, Catherine Spaak, who has a scene in the picture where her nude body is covered by Mr. Buchholz with ten-thousand lire notes. Quite a change, you see, from the good old days on the Warner lot. . . . Never again. Never another picture in Italy! Remember the Italian title, *La Noia*? Well, it means *The Bore*."[12] On that point she's not trying to be funny, though *La Noia* actually translates as *Boredom*; the film is based on the novel by Alberto Moravia.

Bette took one look at her costumes and rejected them all, prompting Carlo Ponti's wife, Sophia Loren, to escort Davis on a shopping spree at the couture house of Loren's friend, Simonetti.[13] The results range from the fashionable to the ludicrous—the elegant effect of Simonetti's mid-1960s dresses and suits is destroyed by a hideous fur-trimmed dressing gown that would have looked more at home on Milton Berle.

The Empty Canvas is overripe; Davis's character is literally introduced in a hothouse sniffing "the most *heh*-venly dahlias." Other rank moments include Bette lying bare-shouldered on a massage table receiving a muscular rubdown while smoking, and her casual but hilarious delivery of the line "For godsakes be careful, Dino—there are all *kahnds* of diseases floatin' aroun'!"

Davis was baffled by the fact that after shooting each master shot, the director, Damiano Damiani, made no attempt to match anything when shooting different angles and closer distances. "Not only do they not *know* how to match, the whole *concept* of matching to a master scene is foreign to them. I began to realize the kind of trouble I was in." This is what Davis said in public; in private, she called Damiani "an idiot, impolite, boor of an untalented director."[14]

"Mr. Buchholz plays my son, you see—an American—with an accent that just screams 'unter-den-Linden.' And Miss Catherine Spaak—I never did understand what nationality her character was."[15] The man playing Spaak's father solved the accent problem easily; his character is mute.

Bette's out-of-nowhere southern accent caused enough postproduction distress that one of Ponti's assistants flew to London and asked Davis to return to Rome to redub herself. "He nearly left this room through that window, let me tell you," she told a visiting journalist. The reason Ponti's assistant was unnerved was Bette's response: she would be willing to consider doing the redubbing, she told him—for $50,000. Ponti ultimately decided that Bette's accent was just fine.

"In a blonde Dutch-boy bob, Bette looks like a degenerate Hans Brinker," *Time* claimed in its review.[16] Perhaps, though in this case the role of Hans Brinker is being played by an aging drag queen with heavy black lashes, dark red lips, smears of eye shadow, and dramatically shaped brows that are many shades darker than his wig. Hans also waves a long cigarette holder around and wears metallic harlequin glasses.

The Legion of Decency awarded *The Empty Canvas* a C rating— "Condemned"—calling it "a peep-show excursion with a special appeal to the prurient-minded."[17] But that's what's *good* about the picture. The film's philosophical aspects are dreary and irrelevent—Michelangelo Antonioni inadvertently parodied by Damiano Damiani. "That's it," says Dino (Buchholz) as he gazes moodily at a stretched piece of white cloth. "That's my masterpiece. There's nothing worth painting in the whole damn world. The empty canvas says everything worth saying." Dino has anomie. It's catching.

Much more entertaining is the abundant sleaze: watching Bette playing Dino's mother as she pimps her son with a serving girl whose ass he squeezes while she serves him lunch on a silver platter; Cecilia (Spaak) hitching her skirt up to the tune of a 1963 bubble-gum pop song; Dino sporting a tight European swimsuit while morosely regarding a corpse-like piece of driftwood on the beach. . . . All the while Cecilia tortures Dino with her affairs with both a formerly elderly, now-dead artist and a muscular Nordic blond whose name, absurdly, is Luciani. At one point, Dino pays Cecilia for a near rape and calls her a slut; she loves it. Later, they strip for a toss on Mother's bed—the bed in which Dino was born. That's where Cecilia's naked body serves as the second eponymous canvas for Dino's lira-based conceptual art. By the time Dino rams his sleek Italian sportscar into a convenient cinder-block wall, you, too, are ready to call it quits.

ALSO IN 1963, Bette covered for Raymond Burr on an episode of the television series *Perry Mason* when Burr got sick; Davis's show was called "The Case of Constant Doyle." The thriller *Dead Ringer*, filmed in 1963 but released in 1964, was a smooth production. Directed by Paul Henreid, it features Bette killing her twin sister, also played by Bette. And in 1964, she made the film version of Harold Robbins's pot-boiler *Where Love Has Gone*, the most notable aspect of which is that she fought bitterly with her costar, Susan Hayward, to the point that after the last take Bette ripped her wig off, pitched it straight at Hayward's face, and shouted, "*Fuck you.*"[18]

"What film isn't a struggle? I am so *sick* of the struggle." This is Bette writing to Paul Henreid in August 1964, from Honeysuckle Hill, her home at 1100 Stone Canyon Road in Bel-Air. (She moved to Honeysuckle Hill in 1962 from the town house on East Seventy-eighth Street in New York in which she had composed *The Lonely Life*, after spending a brief interlude in a house on Heather Road in Beverly Hills.) "The history of our film would really fill a book—and it's an idea—it would be quite a story of a *real* villainess—Miss C.—*unbelievable.*"[19] She is referring to *Hush . . . Hush, Sweet Charlotte*, her second Robert Aldrich horror film—one that costarred, for a while, Joan Crawford. But Crawford, in a noto-rious act of cowardice, checked herself into Cedars of Lebanon Hospital and refused to come out. During the entire month of July Crawford worked only four days.[20] "I played no scenes with '*her*' before she retired into the hospital," Bette told Henreid. Crawford was eventually replaced by Olivia de Havilland.

There are those who favor Davis's performance in *Hush . . . Hush, Sweet Charlotte* over hers in *What Ever Happened to Baby Jane?*—among them Robert Aldrich. His reason is technical: Aldrich's use of multiple cameras on *Charlotte* enabled less of the performance to be lost. "Now, Bette—never mind the picture—is much better in *Hush . . . Hush* than she is in *Baby Jane*, but only for that reason: that every reaction—and that's what film is, really—every reaction is recorded. It's not lost in transition because you have to be on somebody else. That's very, very tough to do. But with two cameras you can do it and still not lose it. And you're not often going to be that lucky to work with people as intelligent and as knowledgeable as Davis, so from *Baby Jane* on I said, 'Oh, fuck it, I'll use two cameras all the time.' "[21]

The filming of *Charlotte*—based, like *Baby Jane*, on a novel by Henry Farrell—began on June 1, 1964, but was suspended not only by Crawford's phantom illness but by a lawsuit against Bette, who had refused to shoot additional scenes for *Where Love Has Gone* and had to be forced back to Paramount. Whitney Stine quoted at length from *Boxoffice*, Monday, June 15, 1964; the article is headlined "Drama, Confusion Too, in Joan-Bette Affair."

> A two-pronged decision issued Friday [June 12] in Superior Court forbids Bette Davis from appearing in any picture until she first completes added scenes in Paramount's *Where Love Has Gone* and at the same time requires Paramount to put up a bond of $175,000 to be used to pay Miss Davis's salary in the event she is prevented from working in Robert Aldrich's *Hush . . . Hush, Sweet Charlotte* underway at Twentieth Century-Fox. Miss Davis already has received the first $125,000 on payment of $200,000 pledged by Aldrich. Meanwhile, an upper respiratory infection landed Joan Crawford, who also stars in *Charlotte*, in the Cedars of Lebanon Hospital.
>
> Both events focused attention on the "Joan Crawford–Bette Davis Day" luncheon at the Twentieth-Fox commissary, which Mayor Sam Yorty had proclaimed in honor of the two actresses for Monday, the 15th. Robert Aldrich was host at the affair, a bit confused perhaps, but the luncheon went on despite the absence of Miss Crawford.[22]

The dual delays forced Aldrich to suspend filming from July 2 to July 21 and from July 29 to September 9. The production, which was shot partly on location in Louisiana but mostly on the Fox lot in what is now Century City, finally wrapped on November 23, 1964, at a cost of $2,265,000. It was released on December 24.[23]

Crawford's ostrichlike plunge into a suite at Cedars, together with her insatiable need for glamour and sex, has provided much merriment over the years, all of it at her expense. Bette wrote, "The rest of the cast and I kept up with her condition by reading Hedda Hopper, who received frequent bulletins from Joan's hospital room. She had clothes fitted every day. The Brown Derby catered her food.[24]

"The only thing I will say about Miss Crawford is that, when Olivia replaced her in the film, Crawford said, 'I'm glad for Olivia—she needed the part.' Joan issued these daily releases from her oxygen tent."[25]

Vincent Sherman, upon learning that Joan had landed in the hospital, sent flowers. Joan invited him over for a visit, whereupon, says Sherman, "she confided that there was nothing wrong with her and that she was merely trying to get out of doing *Sweet Charlotte* because Bette was maneuvering Aldrich to reduce her role down to nothing. After we talked for a few minutes, she got up from the bed, walked over to the door, locked it, and asked me to get into bed with her." Always a gentleman, Sherman obliged.[26]

Bob Thomas reports that Crawford learned of her replacement by de Havilland from the columnist Dorothy Manners, who called her on the phone at Cedars and asked for her opinion. "I cried for nine hours," Crawford was quoted as saying at the time. "I still believe in this business, but there should be some gentleness." Yes, she told a reporter, she would continue to make motion pictures. "But I'm going to make them with decent, gentle people."[27] The films she went on to make include *Berserk!* and *Trog*.

Crawford's faux-hurt attitude further fueled Bette's rage. As she told a publicist, "The widow Steele has had her say, now I'll have mine." But disappointingly, Bette simply expressed regret over Joan's condition, the only zinger being Davis's employment of the word *reported* as the modifier to *illness*.[28]

Crawford simply couldn't take the strain of challenging Bette for primacy again, both on- and offscreen, particularly after she'd provoked Davis's undying enmity with the Oscar incident the year before. In short, Bette Davis was a far better actress than Joan Crawford, they both knew it, and by faking infirmity in such an obvious and theatrical way, Crawford proved it. At least Davis actually *had* osteomyelitis when she left *Two's Company*.

Davis enjoyed working with Aldrich a second time, but she claimed to have disliked certain aspects of their second collaboration. "He had strange lapses of taste. I thought the scene in *Charlotte* in which the head bounces down the stairs was a bit much. *Baby Jane* had some shocks and high drama, but no heads bouncing down the stairs."[29] At the time, however, she told *Sight and Sound*'s John Russell Taylor that Charlotte was (in Taylor's words) "incomparably better than *Baby Jane*." Still, she said, "the role is a cheat. . . . Charlotte really has to be played dishonestly, because though she didn't do the murder and knows that she didn't, she has to keep doing things in such a way that you think she might have, though there is no reason inherent in her situation in the story why she should. I tell you, it was one of the most difficult parts I have ever played; I just had to try to construct some sort of reality for the character in my own mind so that I could do it at all."[30]

Kenneth Tynan, a discerning critic, was impressed with *Charlotte*, though he was dismissive of the material: "An accomplished piece of Grand Guignol is yanked to the level of art by Miss Davis's performance as the raging, aging Southern belle; this wasted Bernhardt, with her screen-filling eyes and electrifying vocal attack, squeezes genuine pathos from a role conceived in cardboard. She has done nothing better since *The Little Foxes*."[31]

As central as *Charlotte* to Bette's experience of 1964 was the January 4 wedding of her daughter B.D. to Jeremy Hyman. The groom was twenty-nine, the bride sixteen. B.D. obviously wanted to get out from under Bette's thumb as quickly as was legally possible.

Bette planned everything, from the selection of B.D.'s bridal gown— a sleeveless, white cotton velvet number with a guimpe and a veil made of Marseilles lace—to the lavish reception at the Beverly Wilshire Hotel and even beyond. She arranged for the couple to spend their wedding night at the Beverly Hills Hotel. As she herself blithely described it in *This 'n That*, she went into the nuptial chamber earlier in the day and pulled some pranks—iced tea in a bottle of scotch, tape on all the faucets. Then she made the bed: "Jeremy had once mentioned that he thought black satin sheets were the sexiest background for a roll in the hay. I must say they were hard to come by for a king-size bed, but find them I did. My new son-in-law obviously had extravagant tastes, Dom Perignon and black satin sheets included. Of course, champagne was waiting for them in a cooler, along with masses of flowers."[32]

Bill Frye and his associate Jim Wharton were invited to the wedding as escorts for Rosalind Russell and Hedda Hopper. As the reception began, they attempted to order glasses of champagne but were told that no champagne would be served until the bride and groom were toasted. Frye asked the waiter to put a bottle of champagne on his account, whereupon an enraged Bette descended on the table and declared, "There is to be no champagne until the toasts are made, *do you understand*?" After she walked away, Hopper announced that she'd had quite enough, thank you very much; Russell agreed, and the four of them adjourned to the Bistro for dinner. According to Frye, Bette never spoke to him again.[33]

When the child bride departed the latest of her homes, she left behind her extensive collection of miniatures, which filled three long shelves at Honeysuckle Hill: little giraffes, some cutesy fawns and does, little playful puppies; many porcelain dolls; a tiny gondola fitted with even tinier passengers.[34]

B.D.'s rejection of her mother in favor of an older man was a stinging rebuke to Bette, though Bette never acknowledged it as such. Until B.D.'s all-but-matricidal betrayal with *My Mother's Keeper* Davis reserved all of her resentment for Jeremy, who made his independence clear even before the wedding by marrying B.D. in a civil ceremony the week before. Bette never forgave him.

A<small>FTER A SERIES</small> of short-term schools, Michael Merrill was sent to Gary's alma mater, Loomis, a prep school in Windsor, Connecticut, from which he graduated in 1968. Both of his parents attended the ceremony; Gary and Bette chatted, but only briefly. The most notable aspect of Mike's high school graduation was his father's outlandish getup: Gary showed up for his son's rite of passage not having shaved for several days and wearing a watermelon colored jacket graced by a roaring yellow print tie, with gold shoes and a red plastic water pistol completing the ensemble. This attention-grabbing stunt was designed, Merrill told reporters, to publicize his most recent film, *Cycad*, which ended up never being released. Whatever humiliation Mike suffered at the hands and clothing of his strange father was partly offset by his graduation present: a brand-new MG.

Mike proceeded to the University of North Carolina at Chapel Hill. It was the late 1960s and early 1970s, and his mother took a puritanical approach to the prevailing haze: "During Michael's college years," Davis recalled, "the primary problem was marijuana. I could find no excuse for it, or for the parents who ignored how dangerous a habit it was. I flatly stated, 'If ever he or a friend indulge in marijuana in my house, they are not welcome in the future.' And I made it clear to Michael that no more college tuition would be paid."[35]

The house in question was the one on Crooked Mile in Westport, Connecticut, where Mike increasingly tended to take walks without revealing his destination. He wasn't going off to smoke pot in the woods, as it turned out, but rather to visit a girl down the street. Her name was Charlene Raum; everyone called her Chou Chou. Michael announced his intention to propose, and Bette, who had approved B.D.'s decision to marry at sixteen, now advised a postponement for her son. He should wait until he finished law school, she told him. "As is usually the way with parental advice, he did not take it. A few months later, Michael proposed to Chou Chou and she accepted. I always promised him one of my rings as an engagement ring when the time came, and this he gave to Chou Chou."[36]

Mike had just graduated from Chapel Hill only a week or two before marrying and was preparing to start law school at Boston University in the fall. Gary threw Mike and about fifty of his college buddies a bachelor party the night before the wedding. For the main event, Chou Chou wore a satin gown finished with pearls and lace and gold threads on the sleeves, and the groom's mother wore a floor-length electric blue silk organza gown.[37] Tempers had tempered since the custody battle. Of her ex-husband, Bette writes, "We stood side by side at the head of the reception line. Gary had obviously regained control of his life and was once more the attractive man I had met during the filming of *All About Eve*. I often wished that my feelings toward Gary had been less hostile and that he had not given me such good reasons for having them."[38]

After graduating from law school in 1976 and passing the bar exam the following February, Michael Merrill and his wife moved to Frankfurt for a year while Mike worked as a lawyer for the military. They returned to Boston after three years, and Mike set up his own legal practice, at which he still works. He and Chou Chou are the parents of two sons: Matthew Davis Merrill, born on April 27, 1981; and Cameron S. Merrill, born on September 22, 1984.[39]

"I think she has been fantastic with us," Michael Merrill once said in a rare interview. "She doesn't impose at all. She will ask if we want to come visit with her, and if we do, we do. If we don't she says, fine, there will be a better time. You know, we do like to stay close."[40]*

---

*To me, he wrote the following: "I am pleased that you intend to write a book about my mother. She was a great actress and a loving mother. I have not cooperated with any writers on the past books, and I see no reason to change my position. Best of luck, and I hope your book is both sympathetic and successful. Very truly yours, Mike."[41] His brief note speaks volumes about his temperament.

* * *

IN THE FALL of 1959, Bette told Margot Merrill's story to the writer Adele Whitely Fletcher for a magazine article titled "The Story of Our Daughter, Margot, Retarded!" Margot was then eight years old, but as Bette described her, in "all other ways, except for her size, she is about four." "She still deeply resents authority," Bette told Fletcher. "She still is destructive. She cannot read. And she cannot write."[42]

Davis announced in the article that she planned to bring Margot home to live with her and Gary once B.D. was married and Michael was away at prep school. At the time, Lochland generally didn't house girls over sixteen or boys over twelve. But Margot's return to family life was a pipe dream. Not only did Bette and Gary divorce the following year, but Bette herself was constitutionally unable to put up with Margot for anything longer than a brief visit for the rest of her life. Fortunately, Lochland expanded its mission and began providing ongoing care for adults as well as children.

As Gary Merrill acknowledged, "Miss Stewart once said that she was the most pathetic child at the school because she was just bright enough to know what she was missing. She wanted to have babies, hold a job, get married—all the things normal people do—and she knows she can't."[43]

"Margot weaves and makes things," Bette said in 1964. "She writes letters—though it takes hours, of course—and she truly adores coming home for visits. With her, one must be very quiet, though firm. I must talk to her in short sentences, or it becomes too complicated. Right now, Margot has a passion for the Beatles. John Lennon is her favorite. However, the children at school finally told her to stop talking about the Beatles or they'd never speak to her again. I can understand why. I spent two weeks with her on the Beatles."[44]

In public, Bette always credited Florence Stewart and her staff for providing Margot with a stable, caring home. But sometime in the early to mid-1960s, and for unexplained reasons, she pulled Margot out of Lochland. "Margot isn't here," Bette told Hedda Hopper. "She's having a whole new life with a family in Pennsylvania and adoring it. She is happy and I am thrilled for her."[45] One detail Davis failed to tell Hedda was that she hadn't informed Margot's father of the move. She and Gary spoke infrequently at that point—they were locked in their bitter, years-long custody battle—but changing Margot's living situation was worthy of at least a brief conversation.

Gary found out about it when he returned from Europe and called Lochland to check on things. He was enraged. "I was told that Bette had consulted a psychologist, who, without any real understanding of the matter, had convinced Bette that Margot would be better off living with a family," Merrill wrote. "So Bette had found a family on a farm outside of Philadelphia and had taken Margot there." Merrill got the address and arrived unannounced only to find that Bette had moved Margot again, this time to somewhere outside of Pittsburgh. Merrill called Lochland again and asked if anyone knew why Margot would be living near Pittsburgh, and one of the teachers mentioned that a former employee of Lochland had in fact moved to western Pennsylvania.

Merrill tracked down his daughter, and according to him she seemed happy. She liked living in the country, she said. But when Merrill returned to Pennsylvania for another visit sometime later, he found that Bette had moved Margot yet again, this time to a Devereux Foundation home in Santa Barbara.

Later, in one of their rare conversations, Bette called Gary and told him that Margot was unhappy at Devereux. A shouting match ensued after Merrill demanded to know why Bette had moved her out of Lochland in the first place. "If you're so set on Lochland, all right!" Bette yelled. "You take her back there, and you pay for it!" "What were you looking for, a bargain?" Merrill shouted in response. Bette hung up on him.[46]

"Margot is past thirty now," Bette benignly wrote in *This 'n That*. "She has come home often, and our times together have been happy. On one of her birthdays, I took her to New York and pulled out all the stops—nightclubs, theaters, the works. Wherever we went I was asked for my autograph. In the car going back to the hotel, Margot said, 'Mummy, may I have your autograph?' Sometimes you laugh to keep from crying."[47]

Bette's former personal assistant Vik Greenfield remembers Margot well. Davis, said Greenfield, would periodically lose her temper at Margot, though of course Margot couldn't help her behavior. "But you could hold a conversation with her," Greenfield recalled. "She was very pretty. Huntington Hartford, who liked young girls, once struck up a conversation with her at a party. She held her own."[48]

Still, Bette's visits were far less frequent than she suggests in her books. Lochland's housemother Mary Beardsley once said that Margot's visits to her mother generally ended abruptly and prematurely. If

Margot was scheduled to be with Bette for two weeks, it would usually turn out to be only one. And, Beardsley added, "Whenever Margot got back from Bette's, she always had a new vocabulary of curse words. And she'd be crushed that her mother treated her that way."[49]

Bette Davis made no provision for her second daughter in her will; she left everything to Michael Merrill and Kathryn Sermak. Gary Merrill paid for Margot's care until his death in 1990 and bequeathed a trust for Margot, who still resides at Lochland. The trust is administered by Michael.

DAVIS FILMED *THE NANNY* at Elstree Studios in London in the spring of 1965. She threw a party for the press at the Ritz Hotel. ("Where else?" she quipped. "It's just like home.") Asked by a reporter why she continued to work so hard, Bette was bluntly bitter: "I'm a single woman with kids to bring up, and I've only made ten cents out of every dollar I've earned in this goddamn business."[50]

The Nanny is a thriller, the tale of a dysfunctional family: a histrionic mother (Wendy Craig) and a cruelly indifferent father (James Villiers) who try without much success to recover from the drowning death of their little girl, possibly at the hands of their disturbed son (William Dix). Davis plays the title character.

"I got on with her very well," Wendy Craig recalled.

> We were all very nervous, because we'd heard she could be quite tough. But when she met us and realized that we were all out to help her—that there was going to be no attempt at scene stealing or anything of that nature—she relaxed and began to enjoy it. And I think she really did enjoy it. She was very happy.
>
> She took being the nanny very seriously. She dressed right down to her underwear—she wore these big navy blue bloomers that came down to her knees with elastic at the bottom. Sometimes she used to lift up her skirt and do the can-can and show us her terrible old knickers!
>
> [The two actresses discussed technique.] She said you should go straight into a scene. You don't have to muck around behind the scenery trying to get into the mood, but instead just go instantly into what you've got to do. It was something *she* did. She didn't do the Method thing of working

herself up into a state before she could do a scene but rather went straight into it.[51]

Michael Merrill came over for a visit while Davis was shooting *The Nanny*, and one day Bette and her son took in a greyhound race at White City Stadium. Bette put all her hope on a dog called I'm Crazy. As one reporter described it, "There was pandemonium in the box. Avocado pears and prawn cocktails positively wilted under a din of decibels as La Davis screamed '*I'm Crazy!*'" The dog won, and Bette collected £16 5s.[52]

While Davis was in England, John Gielgud asked her if she'd like to do a play with him; she suggested a revival of *Design for Living*, with Gielgud as the husband and Michael Redgrave as the lover.[53] But it didn't work out, and she returned from England to do an episode of *Gunsmoke*. "The Jailer" aired on October 1, 1965. The following week she gamely appeared on *The Milton Berle Variety Show* in a skit called "The Maltese Chicken."[54]

Davis RETURNED TO Europe in 1968 to make *The Anniversary* for Hammer Films. Jimmy Sangster, who wrote and produced *The Nanny*, performed the same functions for *The Anniversary*. "Oh, I just adore that film," Davis told Lawrence O'Toole. "This is a woman who puts her glass eye on the pillow when her son is going to bed with his new girlfriend. Oh, she was an adorable woman. But they were all idiots. Weak nothings. One son is definitely homo. And he loved women's underwear. Oh, it's a fun picture."[55] In point of fact, though, the homo son is not a homo. He does, however, love women's underwear. Bette clearly failed to appreciate the distinction.

"I was a very young director," Alvin Rakoff reflected,

> and she was certainly the alpha female—very dominant. That sort of star finds it very difficult when the director comes along. With an alpha male directing an alpha male, you get conflict, but usually it's resolved. To carry on the analogy, which is wearing thin: the alpha male meeting the alpha female can result in trouble.
>
> When we first met we got on very well. We had lots of dinners together at the Brown Derby. She couldn't believe some of the films I saw. She kept saying, "How old are you?" I'd say, "I was five then, or six." *The Bride Came C.O.D.*—she

was intrigued that I'd seen it. We went through various scenes; she was taken aback that I could remember them. The scene where she smells pickles on Cagney's breath—she was amazed that I could recall it. We talked about *Mr. Skeffington*. We talked about Claude Rains a great deal.

She was worried about her accent. I said, "You played the queen in *Elizabeth and Essex*. I've seen your work, and I know you can do an English accent. Don't worry about it."

Still, a fly flew all but unnoticed into the ointment. "On the night we met in Hollywood she immediately said to me that I reminded her of Gary Merrill. I took it as a 'how nice' sort of thing. I should have taken it as an omen." The relationship deteriorated when they met again in London before filming began. In the script, said Rakoff,

her son's girlfriend (played by Elaine Taylor) doesn't like revealing her ears because she thinks they're not what the world demands in terms of beautiful ears. A psychological hangup about some part of your anatomy is fairly common, but Bette insisted that the ears be *scarred*. And so the ears were duly scarred. I protested like hell, but they were disfigured. I kept saying, "It isn't necessary—It's a psychological hangup." But Bette insisted. . . . It was an old Hollywood joke. When the poor actress arrived on the set with the disfigured ears, Bette said, "Oh, aren't they horrible! Cover them up with your hair!" I knew then that we were in for some fun and games.

The producers did say, when we first started to disagree with each other, "In the event of a row, Alvin, you're not going to be the survivor." And the row did happen. The megastar and the young director have a row, and the megastar wins. It's not really very surprising when you think about it.

Rakoff was replaced with Roy Ward Baker after only a week. "I was on the floor shooting and was told to go see Jimmy Sangster," Rakoff said. "[Sangster informed me] that Miss Davis was not coming on the set as long as I was there. I asked if I could see her and was told she didn't want to see me. So I was driven home."[56]

Susan Sontag famously argued that camp was failed seriousness, but *The Anniversary* is failed camp—a metafailure. It supposes itself to be sickly amusing, but its own self-consciousness kills it. Mrs. Taggart (Davis, playing to the rafters) utters this foul remark: "Shirley, my dear, would you mind sitting somewhere else. Body odor offends me." She's wearing the fuschia eye patch for that one, a touch we're expected to find droll. To her shame-filled transvestite son, Mrs. Taggart advises, "You can't go to dinner dressed like that. You *know* nylon brings you out in a rash." Haw! To son Thomas she declares, "If I could stuff you I'd put you in that cabinet there, with all my other beautiful po-sessions. And that's love." That one's delivered with the black patch.

It wasn't a good dramatic decision for Bette to screech the hymn "Rock of Ages" in a forcedly off-key manner. Given the thudding obviousness of *The Anniversary*, let alone Davis's singing voice, she scarcely needed to force anything. The film concludes with Bette laughing maniacally in freeze frame while playing with a working model of the Manneken Pis.

FAILED FILM PROJECTS, PLAYS SHE DE-
clined, television series that didn't work out; the chronicle of things
Bette Davis didn't do after *All About Eve* is as fascinating as what she
did. In April 1955, for instance, she and Paul Henreid discussed remak-
ing *The Affairs of Anatole*, Gloria Swanson's 1921 comedy-drama based
on an Arthur Schnitzler play. Henreid owned the rights, which Max
Ophüls and, later, Joseph Mankiewicz had each tried to buy. Henreid
saw it as a vehicle for the Merrills, with Gary playing Anatole and Bette
his wife. But only a month later, Henreid's interest turned instead to two
other projects, each with madness at its core: *The Bad Seed*, the tale of a
sociopathic child; and *The Stubborn Wood*, Emily Harvin's autobiographical account of her time in a women's asylum.[1] Mervyn LeRoy ended up
making *The Bad Seed*; Henreid went through two screenwriters on *The
Stubborn Wood* over the course of a year and a half, but it never got farther off the ground.

Bette considered returning to Broadway in 1957 for George Roy
Hill's adaptation of *Look Homeward, Angel*, but Hill cast Jo Van Fleet
instead.[2]

Gore Vidal, who wrote the screenplay for *Suddenly Last Summer*,
Joseph Mankiewicz's 1959 adaptation of the Tennessee Williams play,
pushed the idea of casting Bette as Mrs. Venable with Joanne Woodward

as Cathy, the role ultimately taken by Elizabeth Taylor. "I lost on both parties," Vidal stated. "Shrewd Sam [Spiegel, the producer]—he said, 'Baby, Davis has played it, Hepburn hasn't.' In other words, you would know that Bette Davis would cut out the girl's brain, and you wouldn't think that Katharine Hepburn—such a healthy person—would."[3]

Also around that time John Huston offered Davis the role of Mrs. Zachary in *The Unforgiven*, but she turned it down; she wasn't ready to admit she was old enough to play Burt Lancaster's mother.[4]

She was seriously considered for the role of Martha in the film adaptation of *Who's Afraid of Virginia Woolf*. "Let's get the story straight," Edward Albee declared.

> When I went out to talk to Jack Warner, who wanted to buy *Who's Afraid of Virginia Woolf?*, my major interest was, "Who do you plan to put in it?" I knew, even then, that when you sell a play to Hollywood you don't retain any rights in casting or anything—they do what they want with it. They could have made it a swimming flick for Esther Williams— which would have been interesting. And I remember Jack Warner saying to me, "I'm buying your play for Bette Davis and James Mason." I remember him saying that to me. And I said, "Well, that sounds pretty good to me." Bette was exactly the right age. And James Mason seemed absolutely right. I was delighted, and I signed the deal.
>
> Now we all know about verbal agreements not being worth the paper they're written on. The next thing I knew, Davis and Mason had become Burton and Taylor.
>
> I remember talking to [Davis] afterward, and I got the impression—though she was drunk and I was drunk when we were talking—that she thought she had the role. And I think it would have been extraordinary [with Davis]—in a somewhat different way, of course. We wouldn't have had the two superstars, and that problem that you have when you have a couple like Burton and Taylor: is it Burton and Taylor up there, or is it the characters? There were such similarities between Burton and Taylor's home life and George and Martha's, as we read in the newspaper gossip columns, and it's hard to know what's being acted up there. I think with Mason and Davis you would have had a less flashy and ultimately, I think, a deeper film. And gee, to have watched

Bette Davis do that Bette Davis imitation in the first scene—
that would have been so wonderful. To have her do a Bette
Davis imitation on purpose, rather than later, when she did
them without intending to.[5]

Davis doing Davis in Albee makes great sense, but one can only
pause in wonder at the revelation that she was one of Walt Disney's first
choices for the role of Mary Poppins.[6]

In the mid-1960s, Bette was offered what would have been a landmark role onstage, but she declined it. The agent Lionel Larner tells the
tale:

They were looking for a replacement for Carol Channing in
Hello, Dolly!, and I suggested Bette Davis. I thought it was an
exciting and challenging idea. The head of my department
dismissed it, saying "She'll never do it, and [the producer]
David Merrick will never go for it." The next thing I knew, I
got a call from David Merrick, saying "was I serious?" And I
said, "Very." He said, "Well, I am seriously interested, and
I'd like to pursue it." She would have made it her own, and
she would have had a success. It would have done phenome-
nal business, and Merrick was smart enough to know that.

I forwarded David Merrick's interest to her agent, Martin
Baum, who called me and said that Miss Davis wanted to
meet me. We went out for dinner to talk about it. We went to
a place called The Leopard. It was a townhouse in the East
50s—very elegant. The lady who owned it was an Italian
princess named Goia Cook. She'd been married to an actor,
Donald Cook. [Cook appears with Davis in *The Man Who
Played God*.] When we arrived, she took Bette Davis's coat,
and she kept coming over to chat. Miss Davis got very irritated and said, "*Who* is that *hat check girl?*" I said, "Miss
Davis, she's not the hat check girl. She's the owner of the
restaurant, and she's a princess." That didn't wash. As far as
Bette was concerned, she was the hat check girl.

I asked for the wine list and ordered wine. Apparently
that was an enormous break-through. She was having dinner with some friends, including [her lawyer] Harold Schiff,
the following night, and she said to me, "Oh thank God! You
ordered wine! I know [Schiff] won't order wine. It's so nice
to go out with a young man who takes control." At the end

of the dinner, she said I could bring Gower Champion to see her. [Champion was the director and choreographer of *Hello, Dolly!*]

She was very nice to Gower, though she treated him rather like a schoolboy. She told him she'd seen the play, she'd loved it, she loved his work, she loved him, and then she said, "But I'm not going to do your musical. It's a fifteen-minute show. But I would like to work with you some other time. Good afternoon." And that was that. She thought it was a fifteen-minute show—the "Hello, Dolly!" number. *My* feeling was, "but what a fifteen minutes it would have been."[7]

The Killing of Sister George was another no-go for Davis. "The producers told me that they were going to make a movie of it," Dame Eileen Atkins remembered.

And they said, "We're not going to use Beryl Reid [who costarred with Atkins on Broadway], but we want to use you, and we want a big American Hollywood star for Beryl's part." Katharine Hepburn turned it down out of hand. I was also supposed to meet Angela Lansbury, only it never got far—she also turned it down out of hand. The only person who didn't turn it down out of hand was Bette Davis. They wanted her to meet me to see if she would like to work with me.

It was at a party. My producers brought me over. Andy Warhol was standing there as well. [As Atkins approached, Bette let fly a zinger:] She looked at Andy Warhol and said, "Why the *hell* don't you do something about your *skin*?"

I was just stunned that anyone could be that rude. But the thing was, I can remember thinking that she was quite right to be rude to Andy Warhol.

I think Bette Davis made a big mistake by not doing *The Killing of Sister George*. I think she'd have been wonderful in the part. But none of them would play a lesbian. I think they all thought they'd ruin their reputations by playing a fully blown, male-type lesbian. She was an out-and-out "Eat my cigar! Drink my bathwater!" lesbian, and they got very nervous. In the end they had to have Beryl, so therefore they had to find a star for my part.[8]

Susannah York took Atkins's role in the movie, which was directed by Robert Aldrich.

I<small>N</small> 1965, D<small>AVIS</small> filmed a pilot for a sitcom series to be called *The Decorator*. The gimmick, apart from Bette herself, was that her character, Liz, moves into her clients' homes and solves their personal problems while redesigning their rooms—a blend of *June Bride*'s Linda Gilman with a more overtly benign Sheridan Whiteside from *The Man Who Came to Dinner*. Mary Wickes played Liz's wisecracking assistant, Viola. In the first (and only) episode, we meet Liz in the darkened bedroom of her chic Malibu beach house. Viola is trying to rouse her from a hangover. "My head feels like an old combat boot," Liz groans. "It was a di-*vine* party. I liked everything about it after the second martini—especially something British with a lot of gray going for it in the temples." Her new client soon shows up—an Oklahoma judge played by Ed Begley— and before the half hour is over, Liz has defied the judge's wishes by convincing his daughter to sneak away by bus and elope with her hunky but impoverished boyfriend. We later learn that Liz has sent them to honeymoon at her own house in Malibu, where, in the final scene, Mary Wickes delivers a line seemingly written with the express purpose of propelling a mouthful of coffee out of one's nose: "It was quite unnerving having to meet your honeymooners at the terminal. All those sailors, my dear! I've never been in a bus station in my life!"

The end credits go a long way toward explaining how that line got there. Before he wrote *The Boys in the Band* in the late 1960s, the playwright Mart Crowley was working as Natalie Wood's secretary. As the writer Dominick Dunne told the critic Michael Giltz, "I was the vice-president of Four Star, this studio owned by Charles Boyer, Dick Powell and David Niven—three of the classiest guys ever in Hollywood." [The fourth star was Ida Lupino.] "The script came in by a famous writer and she [Davis] hated it—she *hated* it. We were supposed to start shooting two days hence, and I went to Mart Crowley because he's hilarious and camp and I said, 'Mart, rewrite this.' He had written before; he wasn't going to be a secretary to Natalie forever. And he rewrote it, and it was so hilarious and so exactly right for Bette Davis. It was a great pilot but it didn't sell."[9]

Dunne was overly generous in calling the original scriptwriter "famous." Cy Howard is best known for having written *My Friend Irma*. But he was correct in his assessment of *The Decorator*. If one can ignore the distracting canned laugh track, the show is genuinely amusing. Most remarkable of all is Davis's relaxed, in-your-living-room performance. Still, within the confines of a 1960s sitcom on the small screen, her Liz is certainly flamboyant. In the precredits sequence, the designer—hiding behind fashionably oversized sunglasses, still trying to get over the hangover—charmingly bullies a little girl into adding a moat to the sandcastle the child has built on the beach outside Liz's fabulous house. "I don't need a decorator," the girl pouts. "Don't be absurd," the snood-wearing Bette snaps. "*Ehhh*-vrybody needs a decorator!"

Mart Crowley remembered many entertaining details:[10] "The lot itself had been Republic Studios. Outside my office window were Trigger's hoofprints, just to let me know where I was.

"I wrote the assistant as a man," Crowley casually dropped. "I suggested Paul Lynde. She thought it was funny, but the network said, 'No way are we having a gay character on the screen.' They didn't even call him gay; they called him much worse things. I just did it to take the edge off the Eve-Arden of it all, you know? Yet another wisecracking sidekick?"

As for the sailors-at-the-bus-station line, Crowley could barely believe it either. "Good God! What was the state of my brain by the time I got to that line? It's funny for a woman who has a profile that looks like it belongs on a nickel to say it, but it would have been hilarious for Paul Lynde."

The *Decorator* pilot was actually shot, clearly at Davis's insistence, by her favorite Warner Bros. cinematographer, Ernie Haller. And of course she brought in her own makeup person—a man who specialized in temporary rejuvenation. As Crowley recalled:

> She had a very famous makeup man, Gene Hibbs, who invented the glue-on tabs with the hooks in them. You smash all the hair down under a wig cap, then glue these awful gauzes with hooks in them all around, and then attach rubber bands over the top and back of the head and the neck to pull everything back, and then you slap a wig on top of it.
>
> The set was tense as hell, because she was just not moving as fast as you have to move in television. It was going over schedule and over budget. She was slow to get out of the dressing room; she was slow between shots. She was used to the director saying "Cut" and then they'd light for an hour. In TV, they're ready to go in ten minutes, and she just could

not work at that pace. [Her attitude was] "I'm gonna show *them*. I'll be out when *I'm* ready—don't knock on that door *one more time*." It's like Judy Garland's line in *I Could Go On Singing*: someone says, "Jenny, Jenny, they've been waiting an hour," and Judy screams, "I don't care if they're *fasting*!"

She was very disappointed that *The Decorator* didn't go. No, not disappointed—hurt. Very hurt.

The Viola character in *The Decorator* didn't come by her name accidently. "Bette had a manager called Violla Rubber," Lionel Larner explained.

> Violla was tied into all her deals. [If they wanted Bette Davis,] they also had to take Violla Rubber for $400 a week. Martin Baum would say to me, "Trust me. She'll earn her money—it will be worth it."
>
> She was like a gym mistress—a sort of old maid British spinster. She wore tweed skirts and brogue shoes like those ladies you see in British movies of the 1940s with feathers in their hats going 'round the park. Violla was also kind of tricky. She was manipulative—that would be the word. A little two-faced and manipulative. And controlling. She had two sides: one that Miss Davis would see, and one that other people would see.[11]

Alvin Rakoff remembered Violla Rubber well from his initial meeting with Bette about *The Anniversary*. "Violla was very much her protector; that's what she was there for. Every time I said something that she thought Bette would disagree with, Violla would kick me under the table. I left that evening with a lot of bruises."[12]

Bette's closest friendships were both enduring and strained in equal measure. Her friends were loyal to her, by and large, though they had to put up with a lot, particularly when alcohol came into play. "She wasn't the nicest person to be friends with," Vik Greenfield admitted. "It was fine when *she* was fine, but if she felt lousy or mean, she took it out on you. As a friend of mine once said, 'Bette defies friendship.' She *defied* it. How she had *any* friends I don't know, to be quite honest."[13]

Davis's oldest friend was Robin Brown—the former Marie Simpson, from West Virginia via Ogunquit. "I knew Robin very well," Greenfield said. "She was a very nice woman. Quiet, intelligent, small—she was only about 5'2"." Robin's size may have helped; she could look Bette directly in the eye. "Robin was a very good friend to Bette. And Bette wasn't awfully nice to her at times. Her husband, Albert Brown— everybody called him 'Brownie'—was a very nice man. Bette always be- haved herself more when Brownie was around. Robin told me once that she used to say to Brownie, 'We're going to dinner with Bette tonight,' and he'd say, 'Do we *have* to?' You had to guard every word you said around her. It was tough."

"Robin spent a lot of time with her over the years," said Brown's sis- ter, Reggie Schwartzwalder (the widow of the legendary Syracuse foot- ball coach Ben Schwartzwalder). "She was always very cautious about what she said about Bette; she never admitted anything that wasn't admirable about her."[14]

"My sister was a private nurse," Greenfield continued.

> Bette asked her to nurse her after the mastectomy. I said to Stephanie, "Don't do it. *Don't do it*. You'll rue the day." And of course she rued the day. Bette wouldn't allow Stephanie to ring her husband from the hospital. Robin asked Stephanie if she should come up and see Bette, and Stephanie said of course. When Robin got there, Bette *shrieked* at her: "What are *you* doing here? *Get out!*" That's to her oldest friend in the world.
>
> They fell out when Bette, after the operation, went up to Connecticut to stay with Robin in her house, and she ac- cused Robin of trying to get rid of her by not setting the heat high enough. That more or less ended the friendship.

The actress Ellen Hanley, who had met Bette during the run of *Two's Company* (John Murray Anderson brought her into the show), became friendly again with Bette when they both lived in western Connecticut in the late 1960s and '70s. Hanley saw the best in Bette: "She was very proud of being a Yankee. She loved American holidays, so every time there was a holiday like Memorial Day or the Fourth of July, she wanted to do things. She loved to cook and be a homemaker. Her homes were beautiful; everything was lovely, lovely. I still use some of her recipes.

There's a meatloaf: it's got poultry seasoning in it, and red wine and eggs and all that stuff."[15]

Hanley fondly remembered visiting Twin Bridges, the Westport house Bette lived in from 1965 to 1973, and Bette's contribution to the surrounding landscape. A river ran behind the house, but a merely natural body of water wasn't enough for the industrious Davis. As Hanley noted, "She and Vik Greenfield had physically moved rocks and stones and made a swimming hole there. My kids loved to go there."

But there was tension, too, and it usually appeared with the first drink of the day. "I saw that if she had a drink at lunch—I think it was screwdrivers she liked to have at lunch—there would be an instant personality change. Not into any kind of meanness at that point. It's difficult to describe. My point is that she would have a snap change when she drank. But she was still the Bette I knew and loved.

"She was getting older, and her stardom days were over—that had to be difficult. It caused her a lot of anxiety."

Hanley described the day Bette was left at Hanley's place while Hanley helped her brother move into a new house nearby. "When we got back, Bette was annoyed with me because we had been gone so long and she wasn't included. While we were gone, she had emptied my food closet and had gone through all my spices and said to my daughter, 'Why does your mother have *two* jars of rosemary? She only needs *one*!' She went through all kinds of things and cleaned out my closet. I was very annoyed. It was noontime, and I think she'd had a drink or two."

It was to Ellen Hanley that Bette turned at a particularly dark moment in the early 1970s. It's a story Hanley never before told anyone outside her immediate family, and it goes a long way toward explaining the increasing bitterness and rage that Bette felt—and expressed—from that point on. "One morning in 1973 she called me [wanting] to know if I could come down and be with her. She said she had to do something, and she didn't want to be alone to do it. I said, 'What is it? What's the matter?' " Someone had sent Bette a liquor-sized carton of letters written over many years by Ruthie to a friend—one of Edna St. Vincent Millay's sisters. The box had been found in the attic by the new owners of the Millay sister's house in Maine, and they thought that Bette would want them.

According to Hanley, Bette was terrified of what she would find in that carton.

> The closer it came to arriving, the more frightened she got. Their relationship must have been very complicated, but you never got an inkling of that from Bette, really. She never said a word against her mother—and we talked about a lot of things over the years. She never said, "Ugh, my mother was *this*, my mother was *that*." Never. Actually, she rarely talked about Ruthie.
>
> It was a very upsetting morning. It was really frightening for her to open that box. I said to her, "Do you want *me* to open it?" and she said, "No. *I* will open it." And then she started reading the letters to me. Bette was *extremely* devastated. Some of them were just about what Ruthie was doing that week, but there were others of a sarcastic nature. She wrote as though Bette was a chore and a pain, calling her "the Queen Bee" and other things. Bette was so upset. She never came across this before—that her mother was writing so critically about her and in such a derogatory sense to someone she herself didn't know.
>
> She was devastated, and hurt, and angry. In the midst of it she fixed herself a screwdriver. She was furious—absolutely furious. The whole thing came falling in on her that morning. She looked across the room at me and screamed, "*Can you believe this? Can you believe this?! After all I did for her!*"

LATER THAT YEAR, Bette Davis sat for several portrait sessions with Don Bachardy. The first occurred in Westport on November 1, several weeks after Davis met Bachardy at a party thrown by Roddy McDowall in Hollywood. "I realized right away that if I was going to get on with her, if I wasn't going to become one of her victims, I had to stand up to her," Bachardy remembered.[16] "She had contempt for people who gave way to her." Bachardy's stance didn't stop Davis from issuing an ultimatum for the second sitting; she gave him precisely one hour and not a minute more. "She did relent," Bachardy reported. She saw that I was trying to keep to the limitation she set, and she said, 'Well, you know, you can go on working.' But she didn't tell me soon enough.

"I didn't dare to ask her to look directly at me because, when I began to peer into her face, I saw her intense shyness and uncertainty. She hides her vulnerability with an outward show of strength and independence, but I suspect that if anyone made the mistake of cowering before her, she would be merciless."

There was initial tension—"she managed to be restless *and* rigid"— but she loosened up with cigarettes and drinks. But the liquor continued to loosen her beyond what Bachardy needed; it killed her concentration. She began chatting and moving her head constantly. "As I gradually lost control of my drawing, it became a sad, almost mournful version of her," Bachardy noted. Bette thought it captured her well: "That's the best," she told the artist.

"There was one drawing of her that she wouldn't sign—which was so odd coming from Bette Davis, who was so eager to make a grotesque out of herself for a part, and in fact she was likely to go way too far. I was surprised that she would object to the second drawing as 'cruel,' but it was just a bit more factual than the other two I did that day."

Davis then proceeded to prepare one of her prized homemade dinners: a frozen chicken pot pie and canned beets, which she boiled for half an hour before serving.

"Drink eased her shyness, and it also brought out her susceptibility to self-pity," said Bachardy. "She complained of loneliness but cited her own perversity as the cause. She was often too impatient to endure having other people around her, and she sent them away, only to find that she was alone again. Narrowing her eyes and fixing them on a slim white cat sleeping on a kitchen chair, she exclaimed: 'I *never* thought I'd wind up with a cat!'

"I'd imagined that in her movies she exaggerated herself for the camera. Now I realized she was keeping herself down."

Another sitting took place on December 4, at Chuck Pollack's house on North Orlando Drive in West Hollywood. "I kept my drawing simple and was determined not to worry about a flattering likeness. But the uncompromising face that gradually formed on the paper scared me." The drawing shows precisely the steely look masking vulnerability that Bachardy describes, the familiar painted mouth a dark crescent, the set jaw, the heavy, weary eyes. Davis took one look at the rendering and declared, "Yup—that's the old bag."

The sittings went well enough for Bachardy to invite Davis to dinner with him and his lover, Christopher Isherwood. But she turned him down. "I think she was, like a lot of bullies, also a coward," Bachardy reflected. "I think she was scared of meeting Chris—of being in company that might outdistance her." There was no reason to think that Isherwood would have been anything less than friendly to her. "He wasn't a combative person, but she most certainly was. I think she was just afraid of meeting a literary figure who might make demands on her—I mean, just asking her what she'd read lately. She took cover when she felt threatened, and she didn't have any idea what he was like, and rather than find out, she just refused to come."

"THEY SHOULD HAVE changed the title to *The Corn Was Green*," Emlyn Williams quipped of the ill-fated *Miss Moffat*, Joshua Logan's 1974 musical adaptation of Williams's play.[17] Originally planned for Mary Martin, *Miss Moffat* became a Bette Davis vehicle after Martin's husband, Richard Halliday, died suddenly and Martin withdrew. Logan sent a script to Katharine Hepburn, who, according to Logan, "felt it wasn't right for her."[18] (Hepburn did go on to film George Cukor's nonmusical film adaptation of *The Corn Is Green* in 1979.) Williams, Logan, and the composer Albert Hague then drove to Weston, Connecticut, where Davis was living in a house she called "My Bailiwick," and pitched the idea to Davis, who agreed to do it after hearing the songs. "She thought it was her answer to Katharine Hepburn doing *Coco*," Chuck Pollack explained.[19]

The show's topical, mid-1970s gimmick was to shift the setting from the Welsh mining town to the South, and to turn Morgan Evans into a young African-American. Davis was more than interested. "We had numbers of conferences, talks on the phone, and I began to realize her true brilliance, her originality of thought," Logan wrote in his memoirs.[20]

Logan's account of the tanking of *Miss Moffat* is credible, albeit in a self-serving way. He begins by insisting that he cast Bette Davis in a musical and expected her to speak her songs the way Rex Harrison did in *My Fair Lady*, but by his own account he didn't tell Davis about this strategy until well into the show's development—whereupon, to Logan's apparent astonishment, Davis responded contrarily and testily. She insisted on singing, he reported.

Two weeks into rehearsals she changed her mind. One of her numbers was called "The Words Unspoken Are the Ones That Matter."

"Without any warning, she began to act the song—gave it the full Bette Davis hot talent—and the cast and I were moved to tears and applause. . . . None of us could have believed then that she would never perform it that way again."

When *Miss Moffat* was ready for its first run-through, Logan invited more than a dozen people to come and watch, including some of the show's investors. The problem was, he didn't bother to inform his notoriously high-strung star. Davis reacted poorly to the surprise audience and, no surprise, ended up giving a terrible performance.

That's when the first hysterical symptoms appeared: Bette started walking around with a pronounced limp. The next day she saw a doctor, who suspected a slipped disk and had her check into Columbia Presbyterian. "As it turned out, we never really found what was causing her pain," Logan noted, unable to imagine that one source might have been himself.

Davis's doctors put her in traction for three weeks, but after a few days she called Logan, invited him to the hospital for a visit, and told him that she wanted to continue with the show. The hospital actually permitted them to schlep a piano into her room so she could work on her songs.

Rehearsals continued without the show's star for another week, after which the company took a two-week break before setting up shop in Philadelphia for the first tryouts. Bette, released from the hospital, was able to perform the first preview as scheduled on a Friday night in early October. As Logan described it, she "entered without her script for the first time and got an ovation at the end of the performance that I had never heard before for anyone. The entire audience rose as one, calling out, applauding, whistling, cheering, and they would have gone on for an hour had she allowed them to. But she bowed slightly and left the stage, only to be forced to return three or four times before they would quiet down. It was almost like a revivalist meeting."

Davis gave another great performance on Saturday. "Her music was handled in a much better way," according to Logan. "She spoke a bit, sang a bit, spoke a bit, sang a bit, close to the way we had agreed." Robbie Lantz agrees that Davis was on target in *Miss Moffat*: "I saw it in Philadelphia. She was good. She was *always* good. She was sometimes over the top—she needed a good director—but she was unendingly interesting."[21]

But, Logan claimed, *Miss Moffat*'s opening night—Monday, October 7,

1974—was disastrous owing to an acute attack of stage fright. Davis mumbled lines and repeated lyrics or skipped them altogether, he writes. "She forgot dialogue she had never forgotten before, then giddily repeated what she had just said. At one point she turned to the audience and said, to our horror, 'How can I play this scene? Morgan Evans is supposed to be onstage. Morgan Evans, get out here!'" Dorian Harewood, playing Morgan, is said to have rushed onto the stage "prematurely, as he knew, and a surprised Bette then turned to the audience and said, 'I was wrong. I want you to know that. It wasn't his fault.' The audience, under her spell, cheered and applauded and laughed all through it, forgiving, even enjoying, any slip, any mistake. Bette went on. 'It was my own stupid fault, and Dorian had nothing to do with it. Go back, Morgan, and we'll start over.'"

Later in the show, a child actor, thinking that she needed help, whispered one of her lines to her. "Don't you tell me my line!" Bette shouted at the kid. "I know it! You're a naughty little boy!"

Things improved, however, climaxing on Thursday evening with a truly magnificent performance. Logan went backstage to see her after the final curtain and found her "in a state of euphoria. The audience could always get her into this mood. In her dressing room she told me how much she loved the play, how she wanted to tour it all year and then play at least a year in New York and a year in London, and she said, 'And then we'll make the picture. We'll make this whole picture all over again, with music.'"

"Thank God for this play," Davis declared. "It's going to save me from those flea-bitten films. The last one I read they had me hanging in a closet. *Miss Moffat* has saved me—*saved me*."

Except that the next morning Logan was called to her suite and found her lying flat on her bed refusing to move, let alone perform the show that night, or ever again. Doctor's orders. "I was walking naked through hell," Logan observed.

They summoned a well-known orthopedist, who announced, "It is absolutely impossible for her to walk onto the stage tonight or to think of continuing playing or even getting to her feet for another six weeks to three months. During that time she mustn't move." And so *Miss Moffat* closed.

A muddy-sounding bootleg recording of *Miss Moffat*'s opening night floats around the twilight netherworld of Bette Davis collectors. One clearly hears the audience rooting for Davis; she gets a sustained round of applause at her entrance and appreciative laughs and clapping throughout the show. But the relative weakness of the score and one young actor's cutesy sing-song delivery leave sour notes in the ear even without Davis flubbing her lines. The extent of that particular aspect of the disaster is difficult to confirm; audience members' coughs come across more clearly on the recording than any of the dialogue. The songs are faint; the dialogue is unintelligible.

Fish run in schools, geese in gaggles, but theater queens come in shrieks, and *Miss Moffat*, like *Two's Company*, has provided superbly amusing schadenfreude to shrieks of queens who never saw or heard the show. But Dorian Harewood sells his bluesy numbers with passion, and Davis is so predictably off-key when she sings that it's not only forgivable but lovable. It's a charming sort of croaking, and it's precisely what audiences wanted—and expected—to hear from her. Had it not been for Davis having been seized with extreme attacks of anxiety that manifested themselves in back pain horrific enough to convince two orthopedists of its authenticity, the show might well have been one of her greatest tours de force. But Davis herself killed it, and that's a fact.

"The audience stood up cheering and screaming every night," she told Rex Reed about a year after *Miss Moffat*'s failure, "but I knew it wasn't what they wanted. They wanted me to be a bitch, not a middle-aged schoolteacher." (This is preposterous. They simply wanted her to be Bette Davis.) "The songs were wonderful. I sang them all and I was good at it, but it was nothing but hell. I had to carry the burden of the rewrites, and I spent three weeks in a hospital traction from the nerves and tension." Routinely, she blamed her director: "Joshua Logan finished me off in two weeks. He was terrified of the critics and started changing things on opening night in Philly. I had one year on the road to do those changes, but I couldn't work ten hours a day and play a different show at night. They wanted me to learn forty pages in four days. I had to get my health back before I could concentrate on that kind of work. So we closed it down. I will never go near the stage again as long as I live." (Vik Greenfield, who ran lines with Davis in Philadelphia, confirmed that Logan kept throwing script changes at her throughout the play's short run.)

"I think theater is a dog's life—grueling," Davis told the critic Bruce Williamson seven years later. "And I'm too selfish. I find eight shows a week absolutely inhuman, plus I cannot be replaced. Someone like me, from motion pictures, cannot have an understudy because the box office for picture people is astronomical. *Astronomical*. If you don't appear, customers just get up and turn in their tickets. Therefore, you have a monkey on your back and aren't allowed even a small case of flu. It's frightening. So you sit around between shows and worry about your health—I find that a very stupid way to live."[22]

SHE HAD MUCH more success the year before *Miss Moffat*—and for several years thereafter—with *An Evening with Bette Davis*, the first of a series dreamed up and produced by the veteran film publicist John Springer: *Legendary Ladies of the Movies*. It debuted at New York's Town Hall on West Forty-third Street on February 11, 1973. The idea was to present classic film clips from the star's career for the first half of the program and then bring the star herself out onstage to field questions from her adoring fans.

John Springer's son, Gary, remembers Bette's opening night vividly.

> My dad came out and did a little introduction, and then there was a good hour or so of film clips that he'd put together, then intermission, and then there were maybe fifteen more minutes of film clips, ending of course with, "Fasten your seatbelts, it's going to be a bumpy night." And onstage walked Bette.
>
> Later on we had people write questions and pass them through, but on opening night, as soon as Bette walked onstage, every gay man in the audience ran to the stage screaming, '*Bette! Bette!* I want to *be* you!' They had Baby Jane dolls. They had Bette dolls. Some were dressed as Bette. It was the campiest thing!
>
> They managed to quiet everybody down, and my dad did maybe a twenty minute interview with Bette. Then they opened it up to questions, and again it was just mass hysteria. They were laying palm fronds at her feet—it was such an experience.[23]

She had only to stand there in velvet and satin, her hair in a blond pageboy, her lips done in a bright shade of red, and bask in her own glory. "What can I say?" she asked after the crowd finally grew quiet. "You have had a long session with me. Some of them were bad years, and some were glorious years. But, oh . . . I would go through all the bad times again for what you just did for me."[24]

Springer and Davis knew they were onto something good, and they began booking tours around the country, to England, and to Australia. Whatever she said onstage got laughs and applause.

> QUESTION: How do you stay so young?
>
> ANSWER: I'm really 14 years old half the time.
>
> QUESTION: How do you think of yourself as a legend?
>
> ANSWER: In a coffin.[25]

During the question-and-answer portion of the show at the Palm Springs High School auditorium, a voice called out from the audience, "Who was your favorite producer at Warner Bros.?" "She got off her stool, walked to the edge of the stage, peered into the darkness, and called back, 'Hal Wallis? Is that you, Hal?'" Wallis's widow, Martha Hyer Wallis, continues:

> She said, "You know you gave me my best roles at the studio," and she named them and thanked him.
>
> We had drinks with her after the show and, later, she came to dinner at our home in Rancho Mirage. Age had mellowed both Bette and Hal, but she still seemed driven—typically wired. I made sure that she was the center of attention, respected, revered—no other guests better known or with bigger egos. But she never seemed to relax. She was wound so tight she seemed to vibrate—tense, taut, very Margo Channingish.[26]

While in London on the *Legendary Ladies* tour, Davis cut a record with the help of the composer Roger Webb and the lyricist Norman Newell. After an afternoon's worth of studio time, Webb invited Davis to dinner along with his wife. "She arrived with two cartons of cigarettes, drank her way through an awful lot of booze, and totally ignored me," Margot Webb remembered. "She got on very well with the boys, Roger and Norman, but she didn't speak a word to me through the dinner. I thought, 'This is awful, I feel I ought to say something to her.' I wasn't allowed to call her Bette, though Roger and Norman were, so I said, 'Miss Davis, during the show, a young man asked you what

I thought was quite an impertinent question.' She said, 'What was that?' 'Well,' I said, 'he asked you if you wore underwear during love scenes on a film.' She turned around to me and said, '*You stu-pid ——— cow.*' (I won't tell you the language she used, but you can imagine what the word was.) She said, 'You've been in the business long enough. You should know.' And that was all she said to me."[27]

Mrs. John Springer recalled a similar antagonism toward women, particularly spouses. She accompanied her husband into the VIP lounge at Kennedy Airport on one occasion only to be greeted by Bette angrily shouting, "*No wives! No wives!*"[28]

Late Bette Davis offers few pleasures. For every delicate, watchable *The Whales of August* there are five *Scream Pretty Peggy*s. Jimmy Sangster cowrote the script for that one, a made-for-television horror movie starring Davis as the reclusive mother of a creepy, Norman Bates–like sculptor (Ted Bessell) who hires coeds to clean their mansion. The film, described by its own director as "a second-rate thriller based on cliché ideas," aired on ABC in November 1973.[29] Bette herself was succinct: "*Scream Pretty Peggy*? She never even screamed."[30]

She was equally dismissive of another schlocky-scary effort: "I was in one really bloody film, which turned out much bloodier than indicated in the script. That was *Burnt Offerings*, and if you haven't seen it, congratulations."[31]

The Judge and Jake Wyler, another failed series pilot, aired as a made-for-television movie in early December 1972. Davis played a hypochondriacal retired judge-turned-private-investigator; Doug McClure was Judge Meredith's ex-con sidekick. Vik Greenfield, who accompanied Davis to a number of shoots during his employment as her assistant, recalls only one occasion when she blew up: During the filming of *Jake Wyler*, McClure showed up late one day and was obviously hungover and having a hard time. But Davis didn't take it out on him. She took it out (naturally) on the director, David Lowell Rich.[32]

Davis's interminable filmography certainly presents her biographers with a challenge. Barbara Leaming, for example, solves the problem by covering *The Anniversary, Connecting Rooms, Bunny O'Hare, Lo Scopone Scientifico* (an Italian comedy), and *Burnt Offerings* as well as the TV pilots *Madame Sin, The Judge and Jake Wyler,* and *Hello Mother, Goodbye!* in a single paragraph. In the same spirit, then, and with the same literary goal . . .

In January 1970, she turned up on an episode of her friend Robert Wagner's hit series *It Takes a Thief*, in which she played the world's greatest lady jewel thief who was then reduced to poverty. This led to 1972's *Madame Sin*, which costarred Wagner (who also served as executive producer) and concerned Bette's character's diabolical attempt to take over the world. As the title character, Bette is made up rather like Gale Sondergaard in *The Letter*.

As the Davis encyclopedist Randall Riese drily puts it, "*The Dark Secret of Harvest Home* was shot on location in Mentor, Ohio, and starred Bette as a witch with a pitchfork in a very strange neighborhood."[33] There's a cult involved. The five-hour, two-part made-for-television movie aired on NBC on January 23 and 24, 1978.

In 1980 she made *White Mama*, the story of an aging white woman and her friendship with an African-American boy from the ghetto. *A Piano for Mrs. Cimino* and *Right of Way* were both made in 1982. The former found Bette as the aging owner of a music store; the latter costarred Jimmy Stewart and was about the right of an elderly couple to end their lives on their own terms.

In *Agatha Christie's "Murder with Mirrors"* Miss Marple, played by Helen Hayes, helps her old friend Carrie (Davis) save her family's estate—and herself—from covetous, murderous forces. *Murder with Mirrors* aired on CBS on February 20, 1985. *As Summers Die* aired on HBO on May 18, 1986. Jamie Lee Curtis has said that her primary motivation in taking the role in *As Summers Die* was to play opposite Bette Davis; "How many actors of my generation can say that?" Curtis asked. Someone once asked her what first came to mind when hearing Davis's name, and Curtis answered, "Heat. I have to qualify this. I was president of the homeowners association at the Colonial House in West Hollywood where she lived. I would get calls from her. 'Hello. Jamie. This is Bette Davis. It's too cold. I want the heat.' I'd say, 'Miss Davis, I understand you are chilly, but it's July. I can't in good conscience go to the board of directors and say that we're going to turn on the heat and charge people for heat in July in Southern California. I really would suggest you get a heater or plug ins.' She'd answer, 'It's too expensive on my electric bill.' "[34]

Although it's one of Davis's more highly regarded made-for-television dramas and in fact won her an Emmy Award, *Strangers: The Story of a Mother and Daughter* is just an even more lackluster *On Golden Pond*. Bette is the ornery, resentful mother; Gena Rowlands is the daughter who ran away from home twenty-one years earlier and returns with terminal cancer. Given the film's reputation, Davis's performance is surprisingly uninspired. Mistaking shouting for emotional depth, she punches her lines and stomps around in sensible Yankee slacks and milks a predictable breakdown scene of the sort that earns honors for familiar actresses whose best years are behind them. *Strangers* aired on CBS in May 1979.

"I wanted badly to win that Emmy," Davis admitted. "I felt I deserved it, if not for the performance I gave, then for the difficulty of the part and the hardships of the filming. The setting was a Rhode Island summer, but we worked in the bitter winter cold of Montecito, in northern California."[35] The older Davis got, the better Warner Bros. looked in retrospect.

"They claim it's cheaper to shoot on location," Bette griped to Bruce Williamson. "I claim that we're all stunt people today—we're not actors anymore. When we shot *Family Reunion*, we were outdoors, with the temperature 22 below, trying to *act* of all things!"[36] The four-hour, two-part miniseries, which aired on NBC on November 11 and 12, 1981, finds Davis as a retired Yankee schoolteacher who goes on a genealogical odyssey. Its gimmick was the casting of stars' offspring: Eli Wallach and Anne Jackson's daughter Roberta; Don Murray and Hope Lange's son Christopher; John Garfield's daughter Julie; Victor Borge's daughter Frederikke; and Bette's grandson, J. Ashley Hyman. Bette had been impressed by Ashley's ability to mimic movie stars, particularly Peter Sellers as Inspector Clouseau. Still, Davis writes, "The day we rehearsed our first scene I had no idea what to expect. He was terrific. He hit his marks, remembered his lines, did all the right things."

Davis grew concerned, however, about the fact that when Ashley was some distance away from the director, Fielder Cook, he couldn't hear his instructions. She called B.D. and told her that she wanted to take Ashley to a specialist, to which B.D. is said to have replied, "If you want to waste your money, go ahead." It turns out Ashley had an eraser jammed up his nose. "Finding this eraser did away with the many headaches he had had for years. No more aspirin daily." Unfortunately, the misplaced eraser led to partial deafness in Ashley's left ear.[37]

* * *

"You tell her."

"No, *you* tell her."

This is the conversation Mike Merrill and Vik Greenfield had on the sidewalk of Bette's Westport house in 1971 after they saw a screening of *Bunny O'Hare*. Bette, aware of trouble, had sent them as scouts. The news they bore wasn't encouraging.

With its inane premise, tacky costumes, irritatingly bouncy early 1970s score, and execution that makes the word *shoddy* seem like a compliment, *Bunny O'Hare* really ought to be delightful. But it's a plain bore, the rock-bottom nadir of Davis's career. The eponymous Mrs. O'Hare (Bette) awakes one morning to find a bulldozer about to demolish her house at the insistence of the bank. Ernest Borgnine shows up as a used toilet dealer and spirits Bunny's commode away before the bulldozer knocks the house down, and together they take off in Borgnine's ramshackle camper. "I betcha didn't always sell second-hand toilets," Bunny pleasantly remarks. No, he used to be a bank robber. So they dress up as hippies—Bette in a Peggy Lipton wig and Peggy Cass sunglasses, Borgnine bearing an uncanny resemblence to Jerry Garcia—and launch a late-in-life of crime. "This is a stickup," Bunny comments to a startled teller. "I've got a gun in my purse. Howdja like to have your guts spilled all over the floor?" It's not just crap; it's dull crap.

There was a preview screening at the Picwood Theatre in Los Angeles on June 24, 1971, but as Whitney Stine remarked, "the showing was poorly attended, probably because many Davis admirers were attending a Gay Liberation Parade on Hollywood Boulevard at the time."[38]

Rumors grew, and Bette, to her professed shock, discovered that *Bunny O'Hare*'s artistic integrity had been violated—that the producer, Samuel Z. Arkoff, had peremptorily spirited the film away from its auteur, Gerd Oswald, and had recut it and ordered that additional scenes be shot. Farcically, the case of *Bunny O'Hare* ended up in litigation when, on August 23, 1971, Davis filed suit in the New York Supreme Court against American International Pictures. She asked for $3.3 million in damages. As Stine phrased it, "AIP made fraudulent misrepresentation to induce her to star in a film designed to be a social documentary with humorous undertones"—Stine reported this with the prose equivalent of a straight face—"and, after the film was finished, transformed it into a substantially different film." But the feisty Samuel Z. Arkoff was not one to sit idly by and let himself be sued, so on November 1, AIP countersued for $17.5 million.[39] The suit was settled out of court for undisclosed terms.

The auteur took Bette's side. "I feel that they mutilated the picture completely after I turned in my final cut," Gerd Oswald told an interviewer as though he were Orson Welles lamenting *The Magnificent Ambersons*. "They made a different film from that which we had conceived."[40] *Bunny O'Hare* did, however, find one prominent admirer. The generous and genial Vincent Canby of the *New York Times* wrote, "Certainly not since *What Ever Happened to Baby Jane?* have I admired [Davis's] wit, courage, discipline, talent, and guts in quite the same degree as I did yesterday. . . . The gimmick is dreadful, [but] Miss Davis gives a performance that may be one of the funniest and most legitimate of her career."[41]

23

BETRAYAL

IN THE SUMMER OF 1976, BETTE DAVIS traveled to Colorado to play Mildred Pearce—not the old Crawford role (which is spelled *Pierce*), but rather the mother of Aimee Semple McPherson, the Pentecostal preacher who faked her own kidnapping in 1926, suffered a nervous breakdown in 1930, and committed suicide in 1944. *The Disappearance of Aimee* is essentially a courtroom drama, the story of McPherson's trial on charges relating to the ersatz kidnapping. McPherson was originally to have been played by Ann-Margret, but she dropped out and Faye Dunaway took the role.*

"I can imagine no circumstances under which I would work again with Miss Dunaway," Davis sniffed in *This 'n That*. "It is possible she feels the same about me, but I believe I have the stronger claim." According to Davis, she'd wanted to play Aimee herself twenty-five years earlier, but "at the time no studio would touch the story; the censors would never permit a film about a woman who was the head of a church and was also a whore. So I ended up later playing her mother.

"We filmed *The Disappearance of Aimee* in Denver, in the summer, and day after day Miss Dunaway kept the cast and crew waiting. She had a

---

*McPherson's mother's nickname was Minnie and she married James Kennedy; thus Davis's character is called Minnie Kennedy in the film.

fondness for riding around town all night in a chauffeur-driven limousine, sipping champagne in the back seat. [Dunaway showed up late] while nearly two thousand extras sweltered in a church that could not be air-conditioned. . . . To help pass the time, I went onstage and sang 'I've Written a Letter to Daddy' from *Baby Jane*."[1]

The film's director, Anthony Harvey, had been a Davis fan since his youth in Britain. He and his mother would see any Davis picture that came out, so he was especially excited by the prospect of directing her. "I just loved working with Bette," Harvey said,

> because she had a wonderful, dark sense of humor—gritty, gritty, very straightforward. The very first time I met her, she said, "You know something? That cameraman of yours— we'll have to get someone else." And I said, "Bette, if you get someone else *I* have to leave." Then she saw some of the tests and thought they were pretty good. She said, "I don't know if he's a great photographer, but he sure is a looker." He was a marvelous cameraman, actually—Jim Crabe.
>
> We were shooting in this exhausting place, but she was always there at 6 in the morning, long before anyone else; knew all her lines; tremendous![2]

Predictably, there was one other altercation. Davis's hairdresser, Peggy Shannon, had concocted—obviously at Davis's behest—what Harvey described as an "*All About Eve* wig," and it wasn't at all right for the part. "My fans expect me to look like that," Davis argued, but Harvey stood his ground. Harvey sat outside her trailer reading a book for about two hours, and finally Peggy Shannon came out and said, "Miss Davis would like you to see her." "And there she was looking absolutely great, with perfectly marvelous hair of her own, and that was that. In both occasions—the cameraman and the wig—I thought, you know, she admired you if you were stubborn and stood up to her."

Davis plays McPherson's mother understatedly, giving the charismatic Dunaway the lioness's share of the histrionics. But Aimee's mother does have one notable moment. Standing in front of her daughter's vast congregation while Aimee goes missing, she leads the crowd in a hymn, and she's remarkably on-key: "In the *sweet. By* and by. We shall *meet*—on that *byoo*—*tee*—*ful*—*shore*." *The Disappearance of Aimee* aired on NBC in November 1976. Harvey last saw Davis sometime in the

1980s. He was driving down Sunset Boulevard on the western edge of West Hollywood, and there she was—standing right in the middle of traffic. "It was near Doheny, down from where she used to live, and she was looking for a taxi. So I pulled up. She said, 'Oh, I'm fine—don't worry about me.' And, very reluctantly, I drove off."

Two adorable snub-nosed children, Tia and Tony (Kim Richards and Ike Eisenmann), arrive from outer space in a large metal frisbee in the opening scene of *Return from Witch Mountain*, an unremittingly bad Disney picture from 1978. The villains, Letha (Bette) and Dr. Victor Gannon (Christopher Lee), kidnap the kids to utilize their skills at levitation in a terroristic attempt to take over a plutonium plant. The boy executes his tricks without apparent strain, but whenever Tia wants to make something move, she jams her hands against her temples and squints as though she's suffering a terrific migraine.

The children get separated when Davis whisks Tony away for kinky experimentation—she strips the boy to the waist before binding him to a table—leaving Tia stranded in a bad part of town. Tia promptly gets involved in a gang fight among multiracial nine-year-olds, all of whom are quite amazed when she telekinetically clobbers the bad ones with a bunch of garbage cans. Later, after being chloroformed, Tia, too, finds herself strapped to a gurney. "I've put her into a state of comatose neutralization," says Christopher Lee, referring inadvertently to most of the audience as well. Luckily, Tia manages to escape and enlists the aid of Alfred the friendly goat, who runs off to Tia's new friends and communicates a necessarily obscure message.

Bette participates gamely in this awful exercise, and it's just plain sad to see a great star working at such sorry stuff solely for the sake of employment. The cute kids levitate her at the end of *Return from Witch Mountain*, which features neither a witch nor a mountain. They hoist her up and hang her in midair. "I've lost my faith in science," the star of *Of Human Bondage, Jezebel, The Letter, Now, Voyager*, and *All About Eve* sadly remarks, aloft.

Bette had one reservation about accepting the role of Mrs. Van Schuyler in the 1978 *Death on the Nile*: the director, John Guillermin, planned to shoot on location in Egypt. "But what if they start a war while I'm there?" she asked her agent, Robbie Lantz. "They wouldn't dare," Lantz replied.[3]

"She was a terrific pro," said Guillermin.[4] "I just adored her. The first day, we were shooting on location in a real boat on the Nile. (That's how we started; we finished up at Pinewood Studios later.) And Bette was sitting there, all made up and ready in costume, and I was sitting on the rail of the riverboat. I was in shorts, naturally. She was looking at me. I said, 'What's up, Bette?' And she said, 'You've got nice legs.' From that moment on, she was a darling. Everybody liked her and had a lot of laughs with her."

Death on the Nile, adapted by Guillermin and Anthony Shaffer from Agatha Christie's novel, presents a collection of disparate characters dying from a series of creatively lethal acts. It features, in addition to Bette, an international cast of stars: Maggie Smith, Peter Ustinov, Mia Farrow, David Niven, Angela Lansbury, George Kennedy, and Jack Warden.

Davis was seventy years old in 1978. "She had a little bit of a problem sometimes remembering her dialogue," Guillermin continued. "She'd make pauses that didn't exist in the script. But she was such a consummate pro that they were pregnant pauses, and she got away with it. She did it so well you'd think it was the way the damn thing was written." Guillermin didn't approach *Death on the Nile*'s screenplay as though it had been written by God or Billy Wilder: "It didn't matter whether she got the fucking dialogue right. If the *scene* is right, the dialogue doesn't mean a fuck if it's saying the same thing."

Given the number of stars crammed together on a Nile riverboat, there was bound to be friction among the all-star egos, but as Guillermin saw it the tensions weren't generated by Bette. "Maggie was difficult," Guillermin noted. "She had had a very expensive wig made in London and got terribly upset after Mia saw the wig and said that it was the color of *her* hair. I had to tell Maggie that she couldn't wear that wig, and she hated me for the rest of the film." Was there tension between Olivia Hussey and Bette? "No, not with Bette. With *Mia*." Hussey is said to have reprimanded Farrow's child, "and Mia got really angry and went for her physically. I don't know—I think it was the girl that Woody married later. Anyway, Mia wasn't pleased, and I don't blame her. If anybody smacked my child I'd give them a smack back." (Bette herself claimed that Hussey stopped speaking to her after Davis complained about having to listen to Hussey's Eastern religious chanting.) What about B. D.

Hyman's claim that there was trouble between Davis and Ustinov? "That's absolute bullshit. I never saw Bette and Peter having anything but fun together. He was very much a gentleman and had a wonderful sense of irony. They used to kid each other mercilessly.

"She had this heavy period stuff on, you know—her wardrobe. And of course it was Egypt—115 in the shade some days and no breeze. I'm amazed that she was on time every day at her age, never missed a day, never was sick, never complained. As you can see, I liked Bette," Guillermin concluded.

"I especially enjoyed working with Maggie Smith, who played the companion to my rich dowager," Davis wrote in *This 'n That*. "Maggie and I felt a few more scenes between us would have been an addition to the film. The relationship between our characters was hilarious." The aristocratic Bowers (Smith) has been reduced to servitude—she's Mrs. Van Schuyler's companion, nurse, and prison matron—and she takes her frustrations out on Mrs. Van Schuyler. Guillermin's firm denial to the contrary notwithstanding—"no, no, absolutely not!"—there really is a hint of sadomasochism to the mistress-slave relationship. Not only do they enjoy mutual verbal abuse at every opportunity, but the mannish, suited Bowers wrenches the femme-y old lady roughly by the arm toward what she calls her "massage" and yanks her again when it's time for bed. These precious moments are the closest Bette Davis ever came to playing any kind of lesbian, let alone a kinky one.

IN *SKYWARD*, A made-for-television movie directed by Ron Howard in 1980, Davis plays an aging pilot who teaches a paraplegic girl (Suzy Gilstrap) how to fly against the wishes of her overly protective parents. It was shot at an airstrip outside of Dallas. "The film was a pleasant one to make except for the intolerable heat and electrical storms," Davis wrote. Pleasant for her, perhaps, but not for everyone else. "Goddamn!" one of Davis's Texan drivers later declared. "I drove her for one day and asked for somebody else. That mean ol' gal—she was the nastiest thing we had down here since we drove the snakes out."[5]

"I got my first taste of hell with her," drawled *Skyward*'s production co-ordinator, Betty Buckley. Before Davis arrived in Dallas, Anson Williams, Howard's sidekick from the sitcom *Happy Days* and one of *Skyward*'s producers, asked Buckley to stock Davis's refrigerator.

She drank Belle scotch and Belle vodka—it's imprinted on my brain, since I had to get what she wanted. Anson was kind of pacing up and down going, "I've got better demographics than she does" because of *Happy Days*. As he was running out the door, I asked him what she smoked, and he said, "I don't know—Columbian?" At one point Paul Lynde was in town and called to invite her to something, so I picked up the phone and said, "Miss Davis, you have an invitation . . ." I never even got to the Paul Lynde part. She just screeched, *"There will be no social engagements on this picture!"* [Then she threw the telephone.] I could actually hear it hitting the wall. At other times I'd call her to say that dailies were at 7:30 or 6:00 or whenever they were, and she would say, "Oh, *thank* you—thank you so much," and be just delightful and lovely. She was either gracious or terrifying.

John Kuri, another of *Skyward*'s producers, has more positive memories.

We were working outside at an airport. It was so hot that the legs of the director's chairs were sinking into the tarmac. [Davis was quite anxious, since she was in her seventies, and every day's newspaper featured accounts of elderly people dying from the heat.] She gave us an edict: "I will not work when the temperature gets over 100." It was kind of funny because the temperature never got *under* 100.

Our special effects guy created a wonderful air conditioning rig which sat right behind her director's chair. We got one of the taller chairs for Bette, and a large umbrella, and Bette would sit there and hold court. [Cocktail hour began at 11:00 or 11:30.] She enjoyed martinis. She was just a major diva sitting there in the sun under the umbrella with the air conditioning going, her cigarette in one hand, her drink in the other.

I'm not trying to imply that she was inebriated. By no means was she that. She was very professional. But she did enjoy her drinks and made no bones about it. She was a tremendous pro. She hit her marks, she did everything we needed, she did it beautifully—she was a real sport and a pleasure to work with.[6]

Betty Buckley remembered the way it all ended: "On the last day of the shoot she told the producers she was going to leave the set when it got to be noon or 100 degrees, whichever came first. The producers got hysterical and were calling Lloyd's of London to figure what to do. They were filming the climax when the parents pull up and jump out of their car yelling and screaming at her character. There was drama all over the set—in front of the camera, behind the camera. . . . We got everything filmed by noon and said a collective, 'Goodbye, Miss Davis,' and she was gone."

Davis later let it be known that she thought the idea of casting Suzy Gilstrap, herself a paraplegic, was "cruel if not exploitative." Not only did she deplore "this kind of realism," but she felt it was wrong of Ron Howard to give Gilstrap a taste of a world "it was obvious she could never be a part of."[7] Gilstrap went on to become a vice president at Howard's production company, Imagine.

IN HIS 1982 interview with Davis in *Playboy*, Bruce Williamson asked her whether she thought Hollywood's golden age was better than the contemporary world of American moviemaking. The old days were a lot of hard work, Davis replied, then added, "Maybe the difference is that the *world* is less golden. We're in a mess, and our scripts reflect it. Everything gets bigger and more vicious: terror in the streets, dismembered hands floating around. I am truthfully horrified by all the violence and blood on the screen."[8]

One can see why she was attracted to *Little Gloria . . . Happy at Last*, an old-fashioned costume melodrama about the deliciously trauma-ridden early years of Gloria Vanderbilt. Directed for television by Waris Hussein, *Little Gloria* stars Angela Lansbury as Gloria's aunt, Gertrude Vanderbilt Whitney; Christopher Plummer as her charming but derelict father, Reggie Vanderbilt; Glynis Johns as her flamboyant maternal grandmother, Laura Fitzpatrick Morgan; Maureen Stapleton as her nanny; and Lucy Gutteridge as Gloria's mother. Bette plays Gloria's paternal grandmother, Alice Gwynne Vanderbilt.

"Say horrible things about Bette Davis? That's the last thing I would do!" Waris Hussein declared in a shocked tone of voice when asked to spill some dirt.[9] "She was not in any way horrendous. The problem is that she was a hugely professional woman. And anybody who crossed her on an amateur level, or gave her false information, or made bad excuses, got the bad end of her professional anger."

When Hussein and his producers were trying to cast the leads, Hussein suggested Bette Davis. Nobody took the suggestion seriously because Davis's character had only eighteen pages in a two-hundred-page script. "Look," Hussein proposed, "let's see what she says. All she can do is turn us down." When they met, he asked her what tempted her to take the role. "And she said, 'I'll tell you this: I've never accepted an 18-page script in my life, but Alice Gwynne Vanderbilt was one of the richest women in America—that was a huge temptation. And the script appeals.'"

They rehearsed for ten days in New York, but without Bette; Hussein was told that Davis didn't want to rehearse. Bette arrived from Los Angeles on the first day of shooting and checked into the Wyndham Hotel. Hussein got a phone call—would he go and see her after finishing the shoot? He said he would as soon as he wrapped.

> I went over and—I'll never forget—I was walking down this long corridor from the elevators, and there framed against the doorway, standing there waiting for me, was Bette Davis. For me, this was a legend.
>
> She doesn't say hello, she doesn't say anything. She walks me into the room; we sit down; and I'm looking at her hair—she's got a silver-gray wig on with huge sort of bouffant rolls on either side. She said, "What are you looking at?" I said, "I'm looking at your hair, Miss Davis, because it looks very . . . I can see what you're . . . you're trying to show me how Alice Gwynne Vanderbilt would look. . . . But it's very '40s to me." And she said, "40s? *40s?!* I *was* the 40s!"
>
> So I said, "Miss Davis, I appreciate that. The thing is, I suggest that the hair would be much closer to the face, because we're dealing with the '20s." Without further ado, she said, "Did you hear what the man said?" And there, hiding in the corner, was her assistant. They went off and fussed around for around fifteen minutes and came back with her hair pushed much closer to the head. I said, "That's perfect. That's really right." And she said, "Good. Now I know what you're doing."

"Why didn't you ask me to come to rehearsals?" Davis demanded. Hussein responded that he'd been told that she didn't want to rehearse.

"That's absolute *nonsense*. That is the producers trying to economize on bringing me over and keeping me in a hotel for ten days. Did anyone ask *me* whether I wanted to do it? I understand now what kind of people you're working for." She bore a robust resentment against the producers for the rest of the production; after she determined precisely who the enemy was, she was firmly on Hussein's side.

Davis had an agreement in her contract that at six o'clock precisely she would leave the set, whether or not she was in midsentence. "I was told to understand that, and I did," Hussein said.

> Except one day we had a very elaborate banquet scene, and we were shooting in the Flagler mansion [the Henry Morrison Flagler Museum in Palm Beach], and we had only one day to shoot this very expensive scene, and I had to progress from a lengthy long shot toward her. She watched me setting the whole thing up, and she summoned me over and said, "Mr. Hussein." She never called me Waris—only Mr. Hussein—and I called her Miss Davis. She said, "Can I have a word with you? You're not going to finish with me by 6 o'clock, you know." I said, "I think I can." She said, "You can try. But I can tell you right now you're not going to finish it." I jokingly said, "What time do you think I'll finish with you, Miss Davis?" She said, "10 o'clock."
>
> At 6 o'clock precisely—we had not gotten anywhere near finishing—she summoned me over and said, "Now, look. I could get up and leave—right now—and that would screw up your entire schedule. But I'm not going to. Because I think you deserve to finish this scene. However. I do not want those men over there"—she pointed to the producers, who were in a huddle—"I don't want *them* to think I am doing *them* any favors." And, you know, at exactly 10 o'clock she finished.
>
> She knew her lights; she knew her situation. She even said to me, "The right side of my face is not my best side because it's falling down. If you'd be kind enough to ask the cameraman to be aware of that, and I'll also talk to him." She would walk on the set and say, "I love it, Tony [Tony Imi, the cinematographer]—that's great. Just help me with a little bit of light over here, and there." That's a lady who knew her art.

There are long-standing rumors that Davis was difficult on the set, especially to Angela Lansbury, but that wasn't the case, said Hussein.

> If ever there was a more difficult person to work with, it wasn't Bette Davis—it was Glynis Johns. She was a bundle of neuroses. We had a sequence where they were all at a lunch table together. Glynis was playing an extravagant South American woman and was very over the top, and I had to keep bringing her down. There was a storm brewing, and we had an exterior shot, and I thought "I have to just get through this quietly, quietly," and Bette sat there watching Glynis do her number. She had all her reaction shots to do with Glynis. The looks on her face, the subtle variations of contempt for this character—as well as the actress—were all in the film! She utilized the situation as it grew. Later, she took me aside and said, "Mr. Hussein. I want to let you know that I thought you were magnificent with Miss Johns. I thought she was being *very* difficult in view of the fact that we were about to be *rained on*."

Little Gloria aired on NBC on October 24 and 25, 1982. Davis has two particularly delightful lines—one for her delivery of it, the other for its irony. "These Morgan girls have, as I believe the expression has it, *been around*," Davis tells Plummer over tea, pronouncing *been* as *bean*. And at the end of the tracking shot Hussein describes as having taken until 10 o'clock to shoot, the camera ends up on Bette, draped in yet another of the designer Julie Weiss's all-black gowns. "When a family's divorces begin to outnumber its marriages," Davis says, "we must question the intelligence of its romantic choices."

IN 1983, DAVIS starred in the pilot of *Hotel*, Aaron Spelling's trashy TV series. The series got picked up, but the mastectomy and the stroke and Bette's irascible distaste for the scripts she read kept her from continuing with it. She told Spelling that she would return to *Hotel* in January 1984 but later wrote, "[My] decision, while sincere, was motivated by my desire to go back to work, not by my opinion of the product. . . . After watching the episodes each week I thought that *Hotel* should have been called *Brothel*."[10] Bette's daughter was outraged at her mother's intransigence: "I cringe thinking that she turned down $100,000 a day," B.D. Hyman told the Hollywood columnist George Christy in 1985. "I did everything but physically shake her."[11]

"I DON'T BLAME the daughter—don't blame her at all," Bette said in the early 1980s, referring to Christina Crawford. "She was left without a cent living in a motor home in Tarzana, and I doubt she could have written this if it weren't true. One area of life Joan should never have gone into was children. She bought them—paid thousands for them—and here was a role she was not right for. No, I don't blame Christina Crawford. I don't think anyone would *invent* her book. You couldn't just make it up." Then: "I've never behaved like . . . well, I doubt that *my children* will write a book."[12]

My Mother's Keeper came out in the spring of 1985, just in time for Mother's Day. It was, as *People* magazine reported at the time, a "portrait of Davis as a mean-spirited, wildly neurotic, profane and pugnacious boozer who took out her anger at the world by abusing those close to her." B.D. was clear about her motives in writing it: "After I found the Lord," she said, "I realized there was a chance of a miracle in the literal sense with Mother. For Mother to change, she has to discover God through facing herself in this book. I want her to go to heaven."[13] B.D. and her husband, Jeremy, went on to write a sequel, *Narrow Is the Way*, chronicling their religious awakening and bad-mouthing Bette at every opportunity.

It was Robbie Lantz and Harold Schiff who broke the news to Bette that B.D. had written the tell-all.

> Harold and I agreed that we could not tell her on the phone. We had to go there. I have to tell you it was one of the worst moments of my life. To tell any mother, whether it's Bette Davis or not, that her child has written a book like that—to tell any mother that her child has turned on her. But Bette was one of those people who had to hear the truth. You could only tell her the truth, pleasant or unpleasant. Harold and I were absolutely flat and direct about it. She was shocked and distraught in equal measure, but she also appreciated that she had two friends who understood.
>
> I wouldn't want to suggest . . . that I would have liked her for a parent. She must have been overwhelming. But she did love the girl. She made enormous financial sacrifices for her.[14]

Davis, her cancer seemingly in remission but still debilitated from the stroke, was preparing to leave for England to film the made-for-television film *Murder with Mirrors* when she learned that B.D. had betrayed her in the name of the Lord. According to B.D., Bette responded by calling and writing angry letters, all the while insisting on seeing the manuscript, a request B.D. denied. "How dare you do this to me? I'm a very famous woman," B.D. claims Bette said, though clearly Davis's fame was only one of her concerns at that point. "Did you do it for the money?" Bette inquired.

B.D. and Jeremy had been receiving lavish gifts and direct financial support from Bette for years. Gary Merrill, who doesn't come off very well in *My Mother's Keeper*, thought that B.D. wrote the book to get back at her mother for refusing to pay for something: "I surmised that B.D. must have wanted something Bette couldn't afford," a thought that occurred to Robbie Lantz and Chuck Pollack as well.[15] "As long as Bette was making money and she could get things from her, she took, took, took," Pollack said of B.D. "She had no taste—no sense. To write the book while her mother was still alive! Bette was very ill. She probably was hoping that she would die before the publication, but who knows? She's not a very nice person."[16] Ellen Hanley remembered, "Harold Schiff called me on the phone one time and said, 'Ellen, you've got to tell Bette that she cannot let B.D. charge any more on her credit card.' He said, 'There is no money. She *cannot* keep doing it.' "[17]

Gary Merrill acknowledged at the time that "there are kernels of truth in [the book], but multiplied. Bette and I were both big drinkers, and sure—I slapped her and B.D. We had physical fights, but not much more than the average family. Usually Bette pushed me first or something. I'm a lazy slob. I wouldn't start a fight." Merrill also made a point of denying that he ever called B.D. "a little slut,"as B.D. claimed. "Christ!" Merrill said. "She doesn't have enough gumption to be a slut."[18]

My Mother's Keeper is a sour, whiny book written by a spoiled child who grew up and found Christ. B.D.'s accounts of Bette's temper, her drinking, her ill treatment of Bobby and Margot are believable enough, but her sanctimoniousness and take-it-for-granted privilege counterbalance whatever Bette or Gary did or didn't do to her. For instance, Bette never hid the fact that she, like most parents of her generation, used spanking as punishment. "Be a fanny-spanking disciplinarian until your kids are ten—then they'll turn out all right," Bette told *Look* in 1962, a point on which she was quite evidently wrong.[19] B.D., though—like many parents of *her* generation—saw it as child abuse.

"B.D. had fastened on an item on display which she thought she must have," Gary recalled, "but Bette refused to buy it. Aware that people were noticing her famous mother, B.D. decided a tantrum might help change Bette's mind—and proceeded to perform. Bette yanked her around, gave her a good one, and marched B.D. out of the store. It was a mother's appropriate reaction to an embarrassing scene created by a manipulative eight-year-old."[20]

"If you have never been hated by your child, you have never been a parent," Bette once said.[21]

B.D.'s prolific accounts of the abuse she endured—from the harrowing (Bette's theatrical threats to commit suicide, threats that were issued in front of her children) to the laughable (the museums and churches B.D. was forced to tour while accompanying Bette to Spain)—have been echoed by enough people that, on whole, one has to agree with certain aspects of B.D.'s characterization: Bette Davis could be a drunk, and a nasty one; she picked fights for the hell of it; and she could be very mean.

An independent observer—Don Owens, Kaye Ballard's manager—establishes that B.D. didn't have it easy. Owens was invited, along with Ballard and the composer Fred Ebb, to a dinner party at Bette's East Seventy-eighth Street town house in 1960 or 1961. B.D. was about thirteen. Owens describes Bette drinking so heavily—martinis—that her sister Bobby had to wipe Bette's lipstick off her nose, where she had drunkenly smeared it. Then, at the dinner table, in front of Michael, Bobby, and the guests, Bette humiliated B.D. by forcing her to tell everyone what her current career aspiration was. B.D., knowing what was coming, clearly didn't want to, but Bette forced her to say it—"a horse doctor"—whereupon Bette threw her head back and cackled. B.D. quickly asked to be excused from the table. (Bobby then ended the meal by handing out checks to the guests. Bette told her that, no, they weren't giving out checks that night, after which Bobby told the guests to go into the kitchen and wash the dishes. Bette explained that Bobby had just been released from a mental hospital.)[22]

In short, one ends *My Mother's Keeper* feeling sorry for everyone, but B.D.'s spectacular breaking of the fifth commandment ends up backfiring. We feel sorrier for Bette than for B.D. in the end.

Knowing the end of the story gives a certain poignance to various items in Davis's scrapbooks: An elaborate hand-made Valentine with cut-out, pasted-on red hearts: "Dear Mommy—Valentine's Day is loads of fun, if only you think it is, and if you think so, I will think so too! To the sweetest mother in all the world, from B.D."[23] A 1964 photo of the dining room at Honeysuckle Hill, the house in Bel-Air; the room is dominated by an enormous portrait of B.D. in an evening gown, her hair piled high. Photos of Christmas at Twin Bridges, 1967—Mike putting an angel at the top of the tree, Bette roasting her traditional goose—and a notation in Bette's daybook: "Wednesday December 27: order 4 doz white roses—for Hymans anniversary—wrap presents for *them*—make goose a la king."[24] "Wednesday August 11, 1971—Ashley's outfit, steak knives for Jeremy, nightgowns."[25]

Here are a few shots of B.D.'s twenty-first birthday party: balloons are tied to an overhead light; B.D. wears a pink top hat.[26] There's the baby shower Bette threw for B.D. before the birth of B.D.'s first son, Ashley; B.D. is in a flowing chartreuse gown with matching eye shadow.[27] (Ashley was born on June 19, 1969; B.D.'s second son, Justin, was born on August 7, 1977.) And finally photos of the extravagant twentieth anniversary party Bette threw for B.D. and Jeremy at La Scala in Beverly Hills; guests included R. J. Wagner and Rock Hudson.[28] The party took place on January 4, 1984. By the end of that year, Bette had found out about B.D.'s book and had stopped talking to her.

After *My Mother's Keeper* was published, letters of support and sympathy came in from friends such as Burt Reynolds, Meryl Streep, and Sally Field, but Bette was consoled only so much. At first she was deeply hurt. Then, characteristically, she got mad—very, very mad. She devoted a sizable portion of *This 'n That* to telling B.D. off. (*This 'n That* was published in 1987 by G. P. Putnam's Sons; it was written with the assistance of Katheryn Sermak and Michael Herskowitz.)

There are no mind-blowing wire hanger scenes in B.D.'s book, but that doesn't mean it has no camp value. "There's one funny part in *My Mother's Keeper*," Charles Busch pointed out. "B.D. tells her mother about letting Jesus into her life, and Davis says something like 'I wouldn't let *any* man run my life!'—as though Jesus was an agent at William Morris."[29]

Davis had an equally good line outside the book. "Jeremy's become a Christian, too, right?" she asked B.D. one day while they were still speaking. "That means he'll go to heaven, too, right? Well," she said, "if that bastard wants to be there, I'm not going."[30]

WAR'S END

For BETTE DAVIS, ALCOHOL AND CIGA-rettes were PROPS in both senses of the word: they buttressed her against her nerves and served equally well as reliable bits of business, things to do with her hands. According to her friend Chuck Pollack, "We had a lot of fun, especially early in the day before she started drinking."[1] When did she start drinking? "Early in the day. She would drink orange juice with vodka, and by the time it got around to lunch it was just vodka, and it was vodka for the rest of the afternoon until cocktail hour, when she switched to what she considered the hard stuff—scotch."

The good times, Pollack went on to say, were mostly times when Bette wasn't drinking. When she had a job to do, an appearance on *The Tonight Show* with Johnny Carson, for instance, she didn't touch a drop all day long. Instead, she'd spend the time preparing herself to appear as the grand movie star she was. "She came off beautifully on all those shows," Pollack observed. "She'd done them a million times, and she knew exactly what the answers were. When she was working, she was a different person because she didn't drink. She was much easier to cope with."

Liquor made her feel better, but her behavior got exponentially worse. Pollack offered some examples:

She would offer to help in the garden—I'd be pruning—and she'd just chop up a plant and kill it. People would send over bouquets of flowers. She'd sit there drinking and smoking, with those nervous little hands twitching away, and she'd start picking the buds off, one by one. By the end of the day there would be no flowers left.

She would pick fights with people and be absolutely horrible. She'd ask me to have people over for cocktails, and then she couldn't wait to attack somebody and make a scene. People in the movie business, friends of mine—it didn't make any difference to her. If they looked cross-eyed and she decided she wanted to attack them, she did—for no reason. She'd become argumentative, insulting, sarcastic. Finally she'd just say, "Why don't you go home?" We'd all sit there with our mouths hanging open thinking, "My god, what just happened?"

One such evening occurred when Pollack invited Carroll O'Connor and his wife to dinner along with Louis B. Mayer's granddaughter, Barbara Wyndham. Bette was filming a television movie at the time—Pollack didn't recall which one—and she brought home a birthday cake from the set. Having been baked to serve as a prop, it was a gaudy affair, iced in bright Technicolor. Barbara Wyndham made the mistake of calling it ugly. The remark provoked Davis into an instant and violent rage; she screamed at Wyndham about what a rude and ungrateful person she was. Carroll O'Connor tried to calm her down, but to no avail.

When Pollack invited Mae West one evening, it proved to be just as disastrous, if much less loud. For whatever reason, the prospect of meeting Mae West frightened Bette; she was anxious all day, started drinking early, and was violently drunk—falling-down drunk—by the time West arrived. It was August in Los Angeles, but Bette insisted that Pollack light a fire in the fireplace. "I tried to stop her," he recalled, "but two minutes later there was a fire blazing. She was so drunk that she picked up a paper napkin—not a cracker—and smeared it with caviar and handed it to Mae." As was often the case, however, once dinner was served and she got some food into her, she returned to a state that approximated presentability.

The writer Dotson Rader, who interviewed her for *Parade* in 1983, experienced Bette's extended cocktail hours at her apartment from time to

time. "She'd call me up and say, 'Can you come over for dinner tomorrow night?' " Rader remembered.

> She'd call at 10:00 or 11:00 o'clock in the morning and say,
> "*I've* been up since *six*. *Cooking*. For *dinner*!" Well, I'd show
> up, but there was never any dinner.
>
> Once there was an old lady there—Bette Davis's hair-
> dresser. She opened the door—Bette was off getting ready—
> and offered me a drink and hors d'oeuvres, "hors d'oeuvres"
> being Ritz crackers with a roll of American cheese on them
> and a stuffed olive on a toothpick—and not even standing
> up straight but lying on its side. Anyway, she brought me
> this little plate and a vodka, and then she sat in a little
> French chair against the wall and never said another word.
> That's the only time I ate anything at Bette Davis'.
>
> Miss Davis came into the living room where I was sit-
> ting with this mousy little hairdresser. Bette was a tiny little
> woman, but she had this sort of Death Ray Look that was
> terrifying. She walked in, paused a moment to give you
> time to collect yourself—you were supposed to be
> awestruck at the vision that presented itself. So she paused,
> smiled at me, and then That Look came over her face—a look
> of ill-contained rage. She marched over, grabbed the hors
> d'oeuvres plate with two hands—not one hand, but two, the
> way you'd grab a tray—and marched back over to the table
> where the hors d'oeuvres were, slammed the plate down,
> and turned on the poor little hairdresser and started scream-
> ing at her. "This is *my* party! He's *my* guest! *I'm* the hostess!
> This is *my* house! How *dare* you? *How dare you*?!" She put the
> olive back where it was, paused a moment, and came back
> over to me carrying the original hors d'oeuvres tray, and
> asked if I'd like one.
>
> There are a couple of other people who could drink me
> under the table, but she was the only woman who could. Her
> capacity for booze was just amazing. She would insist on
> pouring the drinks. She'd pour you a tumbler—not a
> highball—of pure vodka with a piece of ice.[2]

Mart Crowley vividly recalled a dinner party he attended at Natalie
Wood and Robert Wagner's place, with Bette in an increasing state of
hostile inebriation.

They had to be careful who they asked to dinner with Bette Davis. They'd ask me—she knew me, she'd worked with me, she liked to dance with me! But Natalie knew what a handful she was, and she didn't have a lot of patience with it. [One night] it was just Bette, R.J., Natalie, and me. Davis was very much in her cups and flirting like mad with R.J., and Natalie was rolling her eyes and about to say "I've got to go to bed" and get out of there. And Bette, who was well on her way and in a cantankerous mood, said something about the only roles she was being offered at the time were actresses. She said, "I played a movie star once—a washed-up movie star—in a picture called *The Star*." And then she said to Natalie in the most condescending, sarcastic way: "Of course *you're* too *young* to re-*mem*-ber." And Natalie very cooly said, "Bette. I played your daughter in that movie." Bette was so stunned and shocked. She didn't have the Noël Coward savoir faire to plunge right on with an "Of course you did, my dear." She didn't know what to say. In fact, I don't even think she knew if it was true or not.[3]

"Bette Davis was very funny," Roddy McDowall once observed, "but she didn't have a sense of humor."[4] McDowall knew that she was fully capable of coming out with hilarious statements, but according to him she didn't even know they were a scream, let alone why. Chuck Pollack, too, insisted that Davis generally didn't realize that what she said was funny. "She wasn't really witty," he said. "She would give incorrect responses to questions, which turned out to be what people thought was amusing. Like those shows she did. The audience would ask questions, and she would misunderstand them. She'd get it totally off, and the answer would be disconnected. As far as the audience was concerned, they were fans, so she could have stood there and read the telephone book and they would have loved it." Pollack was present at one of the London shows. "They loved her—everything she said. She never let herself be stumped. She'd just give preposterous answers to questions she hadn't understood, and the audience loved it. But after the show, she said to me, 'Chuck, I have no idea why they laughed.'"[5]

James McCourt described it more cerebrally: "She had intuitive thrusts." She was a natural performer, and she'd feed off her audience's reaction. "She'd say something, and some time along the line she'd get that it was funny."[6] Vik Greenfield put it another way: "She'd get a bee in her bonnet. But it would be *the wrong bee*."[7]

Greenfield related the story of accompanying Davis to a political rally at Madison Square Garden that had been organized by Shirley MacLaine. Carol Channing came toddling over and greeted her, saying, "Bette! I'm Carol Channing!" To which Bette replied, *"Of course you are,"* and marched right past her.

Martha Wallis told a signal anecdote.

> I remember one evening when Hal was honored by the industry at some event that took place at the old Palace Theatre near Hollywood and Vine. Bette was to introduce and present him with the award. She stood at the podium while Hal sat directly behind her onstage. She talked on and on, praising him and telling wonderful stories about their working together. She finished to great applause, then went back to Hal, took him firmly by the hand, and led him off the stage.
>
> He stopped, pulled away from her gently, and said, "Uh, Bette? I think I'm supposed to say something, too."
>
> The audience roared. Grinning from ear to ear, Bette went back to the podium and said, "Now you see what he had to put up with at Warner Bros.!"[8]

Bette's response certainly proved that she could think on her feet, let alone joke her way out of a bad situation. But the laughter she generated was rooted in inadvertence.

Not always, though. "I suppose the dead birds with mayonnaise *were* kind of unattractive," Bette once acknowledged, referring to the famous scenes in *Baby Jane*. "And the rat," she added. But they played well into her own sense of humor. "Not long after *Baby Jane* opened," Davis continued, "I gave a cocktail party in New York and had the head chef at the Plaza Hotel make a pate for me in the shape of a rat. Everyone got a big laugh out of it—this awful rat made of pate served on a huge silver platter, looking a lot like the one in the film. Oh, I tell you, it was *heaven* when I lifted the top off."[9]

Davis's wit was as extraordinary as her presence of mind, but as often as not the laughs she pulled resulted from gaffes, illogical twists that made sense anyway. At other times she knew damn well what she was saying. Anthony Harvey, her director on *The Disappearance of Aimee*, fondly recalled her delight in telling friends during the 1980s, "*Lit*-tle *Ron*-nie *Rea*-gan. *Terrrrr*-ible actor. Now he's *Pres*-ident. *God!*"[10]

"The *laaaaaast* movie I made with Joan was *What Ever Happened to Baby Jane?*" she used to say. "I played Baby Jane. She played whatever."

What difference does consciousness of comedy make in the end? Bette Davis was highly quotable and, in her own way, brilliantly funny. One evening during the filming of *The Whales of August*, the cast and crew were sitting around the dinner table when Davis started ragging on Crawford. After a while, Lindsay Anderson decided he'd heard enough, and he slammed his hand on the table and told Davis bluntly that Crawford had been a friend of his and he wasn't going to listen to any more. To which Davis, not missing a beat, calmly replied, "Just because a person's *dead* doesn't mean they *changed*."

ON MARCH 1, 1977, the American Film Institute awarded Bette Davis with its Life Achievement Award at a black-tie ceremony at the Beverly-Hilton Hotel. She was the first female recipient of the award; the previous winners were John Ford, James Cagney, Orson Welles, and William Wyler. Over a thousand people watched clips of Davis's films and heard tributes from such notables as Jane Fonda, who emceed the event; Henry Fonda; Olivia de Havilland; George Stevens Jr.; and Cicely Tyson. After accepting the award, Davis credited four men who particularly helped her career: George Arliss, Jack Warner, Hal Wallis, and William Wyler. She concluded by honoring Ruthie: "How her eyes would have sparkled if she could have been here tonight."[11]

Davis's escort that night was Ray Stricklyn, who had played her son in *The Catered Affair* and who was then working as a publicist in the Hollywood office of John Springer and Associates. "She adored Ray," Stricklyn's lover, David Galligan, said. "She was an absolute harridan with me, but she was a pussycat with him." Galligan, who also worked at Springer, recalled that there were innumerable requests for interviews at the time of the AFI award. Stricklyn told him to decline them all on Davis's behalf, with one exception: Galligan was to call Davis about doing an interview for a charity for mentally retarded children.

"She answered: 'Hel-*lo?*'" Galligan remembered. "As soon as I started talking I knew I was losing steam. I could feel my voice shaking. 'Oh, hi, Miss Davis, this is John Springer Associates . . .' '*What* do you *want?*' And I said, 'I was wondering—I have all these requests . . .' '*Why* did you *call* me?' 'Well, there's one in particular that's from a retarded children's . . .' '*Why* would you *think* I'd be *in*terested in *that?!* Don't *ever* *call* me a*gain!'* And she slammed down the phone."[12]

Stricklyn accompanied Davis not only to the AFI award but also, the following evening, to the opening of Geraldine Fitzgerald's nightclub act at Studio One, a gay club in West Hollywood. Chuck Pollack, Olivia de Havilland, Robert Osborne, and Mr. and Mrs. Paul Henreid were also there to witness Bette being mobbed by a group of gay fans.[13]

As early as 1942, in an extraordinary article in the *Ladies Home Journal*, Bette openly wished that she had a "sissy" husband—one who would do the housework and shopping and cooking for her, all the while appreciating the finer things in life.[14] By the 1970s, she was much more explicit. "Let me say, a more artistic, appreciative group of people for the arts does not exist," Bette Davis told the *Advocate* in 1977. She was referring, of course, to gay men. "And conceited as it may sound, I think a great deal of it has to do with their approval of my work—the seriousness of my work. They are more knowledgeable, more loving of the arts. They make the average male look stupid."[15]

When visiting Los Angeles in the dozen or fifteen years before she moved back to Hollywood in 1977, she usually stayed with Chuck Pollack. "She liked to sit in the kitchen—a big country kitchen. That was what she considered her style," Pollack remembered. "She loved to play housewife—dressing very plainly and wearing no makeup unless she was being interviewed. In the morning, she was plain old Ruth Elizabeth. By noon, she had become Bette Davis. By cocktail hour, she was the imperial Bette Davis. One morning I said to her, 'You're all your characters rolled into one.' She couldn't stop laughing."

But despite the title of her first book, Bette Davis found solitude difficult if not impossible to bear. "She couldn't be left alone—couldn't stand to be by herself," observed Pollack. "She had to have attention every second, like a child. She was very, very needy." She proposed marriage to Pollack, who she knew was gay. Was she serious? "She was," said Pollack—"at the moment." From time to time she would even present herself sexually to Pollack, who never responded the way she wanted him to. "She never got clear about why a man would want a man. She didn't understand that it wasn't a choice." She did, however, tell Pollack about a female magazine writer Bette had known for a long time—a writer who had offered Davis the chance to experiment with a lesbian relationship. Bette declined.

Davis also proposed marriage to her equally gay personal assistant, Vik Greenfield. Once again, she was perfectly serious—at the moment. "But she'd have gotten cold feet" before going through with it, Greenfield insisted.

Whitney Stine claimed that Davis proposed to him as well. Stine also declined. (Stine suffered a heart attack and died on October 11, 1989, five days after Davis.)

Davis's need for gay men's companionship—with Davis being only semiconscious of the men's sexual orientation—was long-standing. While living at Twin Bridges, Davis involved herself with any number of younger men far beneath her in intelligence and, certainly, wealth. The task of informing Bette that one or another was obviously gay fell to her oldest friend and current Westport neighbor Robin Brown. "Oh, no!" Bette would protest; "I'm going to be the one to change him."[16]

Dotson Rader recalled the evening they got to talking about *Making Love*.

> I'd seen it on cable. I was crazy about Michael Ontkean, and I asked her if she'd met him. She said no. I said, "Oh, he's so gorgeous. There's a movie you've got to see—*Making Love*." I told her what it was about. "Oh, *that* movie! I know *that* movie!" She said she could only watch it up to a point— "when they started doing whatever it *is* that they *do*!" She said she appreciated the fact that she had a big gay following—she didn't understand it, but she appreciated it— and she realized that one of the reasons for the longevity of her career was that gay men found her sympathetic. She was aware that drag queens "did" her, and she thought it was all rather jolly. But she never understood what gay men saw in her.
>
> She also didn't understand what they actually did in bed. She said, "I find it *shocking*. Do they actually *do* that?" From that point, there was a discussion—in a very specific, explicit way—about what two men do in bed. There was an undeniable prurience in her interest, but at the same time she assumed a posture of almost Puritanical shock and disgust. It wasn't "deer in the headlights" exactly, but . . . She couldn't stand what she was seeing, but she couldn't look away either. I don't know how much of a pose it was, but I do remember she was very emphatic about the fact that until *Making Love*

she had no idea what gay men did. Which I find impossible to believe. I was surprised at the vividness of her questions. She was very keenly interested in the physical mechanics of male sex.

. . . I think that's pretty much how she continued to see the world: there were men who were prissy, and there were men who were pansies, but she didn't connect the word "pansy" with a sexual act.

On several occasions she tried to put the make on me. She had a big chaise, where she would sit. Someone else would have patted the cushion. She would *slap* it. "Oh, come and sit over *here*." I'd go over and sit down, and her hand would end up on my thigh—which was fine with me.[17]

"The very first celebrity I heard from when *The Boys in the Band* was a success was Bette," Mart Crowley declared. "I was out of money and staying on a friend's couch. God knows how Violla tracked me down, but the phone rang, and a voice said, '*Bette Davis!* Oh, I'm so *happy* for you—all the reviews—*divine!* What are you doing right now? We've got to have a drink!' " Crowley went over to the Plaza, where Bette was staying. "She said, 'What have you read?' I said '*Myra Breckenridge.*' '*What's that?*' 'It's a novel by Gore Vidal, and by the way, there's a very good part in it for you—a woman agent. Her name is Letitia, and she could be very funny. . . .' 'Vi-*ol*-la! *Vi!* Gore *Vidal!* (What's it called?)' '*Myra Breck . . .*' '*Myyyyy-ra Breck-en-ridge! Get a copy!*'" And yet, Crowley said, with all this, the subject of homosexuality was never discussed between them.[18]

"THE END WAS a remarkable Bette Davis movie, with a really good part in it for her," said Robbie Lantz.

She got an invitation to the San Sebastian Film Festival. They were going to honor her. I have a photo of her that was taken there. It's heartbreaking—she was so frail. The second or third night of her stay—it was a triumph for her, that festival—she became ill. And Kathryn Sermak called the hotel doctor, who came and examined Bette and said to Kathryn, "Miss Davis is dangerously ill. She should go to the hospital."

Bette said, "I'm not going to any hospital in San Sebastian. You must be *crazy*."

So they hired a plane to take her to the American hospital in Paris. The doctors examined her. Kathryn was waiting, and they told her, "Miss Davis is going to die. She has only hours to live. What should we do?" Kathryn knew the only way to deal with Bette. So the doctors went in and said whatever they had to say. Bette thanked them. They left the room. And Bette said to Kathryn, "We have a lot to do. I have to sign all the checks. You have to cancel the dinner date on Friday night. You have to get Harold Schiff on the phone, and that will be difficult because he's away from New York. . . ."

When she finally got Harold on the phone, she said, "I won't be able to get out of this one."

And then she died. "Fasten your seatbelts," James Woods told the crowd at her memorial service. "It's going to be a bumpy eternity."

Davis's last film was *Wicked Stepmother*, which she only half completed before walking out; the director, Larry Cohen, replaced Bette by having her witchy character turn herself into Barbara Carrera.

Her penultimate film provides a far more fitting send-off. In September 1986, seventy-eight-year-old Bette Davis and ninety-two-year-old Lillian Gish traveled to Cliff Island off the coast of Maine to film *The Whales of August* with Lindsay Anderson. The film is both slight and majestic—a slender story magnified by two superb actresses with thunderingly resonant histories and the weathered, iconic faces to prove it. Ann Sothern, Vincent Price, and Harry Carey Jr. rounded out the cast.

It was on board an airplane to Maine when Bette was about to start shooting *The Whales of August* that she last saw Gary Merrill. She came over to his seat to say hello, but he wouldn't look up from the book he was reading. He died of lung cancer on March 5, 1990, five months after Bette.

"Bette Davis could be extremely difficult, extremely funny, demanding, eccentric, thoroughly professional, irritating, and even charming when she wanted to be," one of the film's producers, Mike Kaplan, observed.

> In the beginning, we spoke about going back to Maine, and she was just filled with glee and delight. Once we got there, though, things changed. It wasn't the Maine she remembered, and she got temperamental. And the closer we got to shooting, the more insecure and competitive she became.

She insisted on first billing. She was always concerned about her star position. We did get into a bit of a row because Lillian's contract had her in second position on the title card but raised slightly above Bette. We went back and forth. She said she'd never shared a title card with anyone in her life, and I had to point out that she had second position with James Cagney in *The Bride Came C.O.D.*

[There was a scuffle over her dressing room trailer:] We had Winnebagos for the four stars, and they were placed on a ball field down the road from the set house. Bette's was first, then Lillian's. Lillian didn't care. They were all parallel. Bette was there for about a week before she wanted hers turned in a perpendicular direction from the others. So we turned the Winnebago around so it was at a right angle to everyone else's. She used it for about two days and never went back into it. [Instead] she commandeered the spare room on the set—the one her character used all the time.[19]

"Half of Bette Davis is a real solid trouper, and half is the victim of some temperamental compulsion," Lindsay Anderson shrewdly observed. "She's difficult because she's Bette Davis, not because she's a star. She has an initial hostility to life and people that she has had all her life."[20]

During the first weeks, Kaplan admitted, Bette was prickly and difficult toward Gish. "No one had ever been difficult with Lillian in her entire career," said Kaplan. But he refused to call it feud, in large measure because it was entirely one-sided. Davis was simply anxious: *The Whales of August* was her first important picture in quite some time; her role was slightly less important than Lillian's; and the familiar compulsion to compete reared its head.

John Springer's son Gary recalled that "at one point Miss Gish said, 'Why doesn't she like me?' It was hard to watch. She even yelled at my father. She said, 'I know you like Miss Gish better than me.' He said, 'That's not true at all, Bette.' And she said, 'Well you didn't say hello to me.' And he said, 'Well, that's because you were yelling at somebody else and I didn't want to get near you.' He felt bad at the end, because she was closing off everybody."[21]

Still, as Mike Kaplan noted, Davis immersed herself fully in the production. She loved the gossip and the grind, and she was never more alive than when the cameras were rolling and she was doing the work she loved. Davis was the only one of the major actors who went to dailies; according to Kaplan, Gish never watched dailies in her life, and at this point in her long life she needed to rest after shooting. Davis, however, attended the screenings every night. Once she saw how good they were in general—and how good Gish was in particular—she realized the impossibility of stealing anything from her costar, and her behavior improved. Somewhat.

"She always needed a foil," said Kaplan, echoing countless other producers, writers, directors, and fellow actors through the course of Davis's career. "Lindsay became the foil she needed for about a month during shooting. She would invariably question things he wanted to do, they'd discuss it, he'd suggest something, and she'd say no, and then she'd do it in the end. There were serious tiffs and not-so-serious tiffs. I think she needed the drama to get through it." For instance, Davis argued with Anderson about whether or not her character, Libby, should move to the window at one point. Anderson didn't see why, since Libby was blind, but Davis insisted. "*Lindsay*," she stated emphatically. "Blind people are sensitive to *heat*. She's drawn to the *heat*."[22]

As Anderson later commented, "Lillian's first instinct is to try to give the director what he asks for. Her professional attitude comes from those days with D. W. Griffith. Bette tries to dismiss the director."[23] "Lillian just shakes her head," Anderson noted in his diary. " 'Poor Bette,' she says. 'How she must be suffering. What an unhappy life she's led.' "

"In fact," Ann Sothern said, " 'poor Bette,' who wasn't well, was a holy terror, crabby and irascible."[24]

Several of Davis's more repeatable comments during the production of *The Whales of August* have assumed a legendary air. "Lillian doesn't need to rest," Davis declared one day. "She was in *si*-lent pictures." Her meaning remains obscure.

Charles Busch recalled another of Davis's bon mots: "There's that famous quote when Gish did a close-up and Davis said, 'Why of course it's good—she invented it!' " But as Busch went on to note, "People use that as an example of her being bitchy, but I'm sure she meant it as a compliment. In a way, Lillian Gish *did* invent the close-up."[25]

She paid her respects to Ann Sothern, too, in her own strange way. "She would call and compliment me," Sothern told Aljean Harmetz of the *New York Times*. "She would say abruptly, 'Ann, I just saw the rushes—it's the nuts!' and hang up."[26]

It had been nearly forty years since she left the security of Warner

Bros., not only the long-term contracts that guaranteed both work and income, but the comfort and security of vast soundstages in which exteriors could be constructed and filmed. As Lindsay Anderson's friend and biographer Gavin Lambert wrote, "She was not used to going out on location, as she reminded anyone who would listen, because 'locations always used to come to *me*.' Her most frequent response to any suggestion that Lindsay made was an emphatic 'Rubbish!' Occasionally she agreed with a grudging nod, and once announced to the crew, 'That's twice I've given in to the director today. I must be slipping.' Finally she provoked Lindsay to say, 'You're not taking over this picture, Bette,' which provoked her to walk off the set and refuse to come back until he apologized."[27]

Anderson sent Lambert a postcard from Maine after six weeks of shooting: "Bette has gone full circle, from suspicion and hostility to paranoia to (proclaimed) friendship and admiration. I think she is essentially mad."[28]

"In the end," Kaplan concluded, "after all the 'This isn't the Maine I knew,' and 'The house isn't as big as I thought it was going to be'—all the little scrambles we had with her that weren't so little when we were going through them—she was the last actor to leave the island."

All this tension and drama was put to the service of a small movie that climaxes with the addition of a picture window to an old cottage. If the anxiety, if not downright agony, of filming *The Whales of August* yielded but one lasting image of Bette Davis, it is this: Libby lying in bed, skeletal, her face hollow, the late afternoon sun blasting in through the window as she caresses her own cheek. Davis's brutal boniness slices cleanly through the gesture's sentimentality, as she no doubt knew it would. She gets up and walks, limping, to a chest of drawers, removes and opens a box of keepsakes, clutches a pocketwatch, then a lock of dark hair, which she touches to her face. Her character's gesture is as delicate and intimate as the lock itself, but her command of the luminous silver screen—the sheer might of Bette Davis photographed in motion—is as purely, grandly overpowering as ever.

OBITUARY

A WARRIOR TO THE END, BETTE DAVIS died on the night of Friday, October 6, 1989, at the American Hospital in Neuilly, a Paris suburb. She was eighty-one years old. The cause of her death was metastasized breast cancer.

Plaques, citations, and statuettes were not rarities for Miss Davis, who fought her way to a total of ten Academy Award nominations in the Best Actress category. They were for her leading roles in *Dangerous*; *Jezebel*; *Dark Victory*; *The Letter*; *The Little Foxes*; *Now, Voyager*; *Mr. Skeffington*; *All About Eve*; *The Star*; and *What Ever Happened to Baby Jane?*— though she won for only *Dangerous* and *Jezebel*. In addition to the Oscar nod for *All About Eve*, Miss Davis was nominated as Best Actress by the British Academy of Film and Television Arts and the New York Film Critics Circle, which actually awarded her the prize, as did the Cannes Film Festival.

In later years, she earned three Emmy nominations for her work in television: *Strangers: The Story of a Mother and Daughter* in 1980; *White Mama* in 1981; and *Little Gloria . . . Happy at Last* in 1983; she won the Emmy for *Strangers*.

Miss Davis was never the recipient of a Golden Globe, though she was nominated for both *All About Eve* and *What Ever Happened to Baby Jane?* The Hollywood Foreign Press Association did, however, present

Miss Davis with its Cecil B. DeMille Award in 1974—an irony, since Mr. DeMille was one of Hollywood's most notoriously reactionary figures and Miss Davis one of its most consistently liberal.

Her honors stretched from the 1930s through the 1980s. In 1937, the Venice Film Festival awarded her the Volpi Cup for best cinema actress of the year for her performances in *Kid Galahad* and *Marked Woman*. She snared both the *Redbook* Trophy and the Popularity Crown "Queen of the Movies" award in 1939. In 1941, she won the Golden Apple, the Women's Press Corps' coveted citation for "Most Cooperative Actress" in Hollywood. Participating in Hollywood's publicity machinery was simply part of the battle for Miss Davis, who fought to maintain her career long after a less combative celebrity would have been content to rest on her laurels and call it quits.

Miss Davis was the recipient of the American Film Institute's Life Achievement Award in 1977—the first woman so honored—and an honorary César Award, France's most prestigious national film award, in 1986.

The year 1989 not only saw Miss Davis win the lifetime achievement award at the San Sebastian Film Festival only days before she died but also the American Cinema Award, an event organized by the impresario David Gest. The ceremony was held on January 6 at the Beverly Hilton Hotel. Miss Davis's unlikely fellow honorees were Clint Eastwood and Julio Iglesias. Veteran hoofers from the Hollywood Canteen, which Miss Davis cofounded in 1942, danced a salute to her; they included Buddy Ebsen, Eddie Bracken, Joan Leslie, June Haver, Donald O'Connor, George Murphy, and June Allyson. Also performing that evening were Robert Goulet, Donna Summer, Toni Tennille, and Kim Carnes, who sang her 1981 hit single, "Bette Davis Eyes," which celebrated the mysterious allure of the actress's most notable features.

On April 24, 1989, Miss Davis was the subject of yet another gala tribute, this one from the Film Society of Lincoln Center. Stylists at an elegant Manhattan hair salon were jittery with excitement that day when they learned that a 3:30 p.m. appointment had been secured by Miss Davis. At precisely 3:30, a hatbox appeared at the salon's door, containing Miss Davis's wig and a set of precise instructions. James Stewart, Ann-Margret, Geraldine Fitzgerald, and Joseph Mankiewicz were on hand at Lincoln Center's Avery Fisher Hall to toast her at the ceremony. Miss Davis later attended the after-party at the celebrated Tavern on the Green restaurant in New York's Central Park. According to one eyewitness, the moment Miss Davis stood up from the table and turned her back in preparation for departure, a shriek of queens descended upon the detritus she left behind and seized every lipstick-and-cigarette-ash-stained item they could lay their hands upon. The eyewitness, the actor and literary agent Edward Hibbert, snatched the coffee cup.

Characteristically for a woman who forcefully spoke her mind even when she was out of it, Miss Davis's last will and testament, dated September 2, 1987, minced no words: "I give, devise and bequeath . . . Fifty (50%) of my residuary estate to my son, Michael Woodman Merrill [and] Fifty (50%) of my residuary estate to Kathryn Sermak. . . . I declare that, except as otherwise provided in this will, I have intentionally and with full knowledge omitted to provide herein for my daughter, Margot Mosher Merrill, my daughter, Barbara Davis Hyman, and/or my grandsons, Ashley Hyman and Justin Hyman." There were, in fact, no other provisions in the will pertaining to Miss Merrill, Mrs. Hyman, or Mrs. Hyman's sons.

Miss Davis bequeathed her jewelry to Miss Sermak, her clothes to her son's wife, the former Chou Chou Raum (though the will curiously misspells her name as "Shu Shu"). She left a painting, a pearl and sapphire watch, and a portrait of herself to her oldest friend, Robin Brown, from whom she had become more or less estranged in the years immediately preceding her death. Her silver flatware was divided between the two principal heirs: two place settings went to Miss Sermak, the rest to Mr. Merrill. Miss Davis left to her niece, Fay Forbes—the daughter of Miss Davis's troubled younger sister, Barbara—a set of six silver condiment holders that had been a gift from Miss Davis's mother, Ruth Favor Davis Palmer Budd. Most of the actress's furniture and other possessions, specifically including her cookbooks and handwritten recipes, were left to Miss Sermak.[1]

Miss Sermak sold the most valuable of those possessions: Miss Davis's two Oscars. The restaurant chain Planet Hollywood initially bought the one Miss Davis won for *Dangerous*, but the director Steven Spielberg later purchased it for $207,500 at a 2002 Sotheby's auction and promptly donated it to the Academy of Motion Picture Arts and Sciences. Mr. Spielberg went on to buy the *Jezebel* Oscar for $578,000. It, too, was returned to the Academy.[2]

PROLOGUE

1. Warner with Jennings, p. 147.
2. Bogart, p. 230, quoting a 1953 *London Daily Mirror* interview.
3. Ellen Hanley to Ed Sikov (ES), June 2, 2006.

CHAPTER 1. AN INFANT'S ALBUM

1. The Bette Davis Collection, the Howard Gottlieb Archival Research Center, Boston University (BU), scrapbook 62: Ruth Elizabeth Davis's baby book.
2. BU, box 22.
3. BU, scrapbook 32.
4. Bette Davis, *The Lonely Life*, p. 19. (Hereafter cited as *Lonely Life*.)
5. Ibid.
6. Williamson, p. 72.
7. BU, box 9: Paul Favor, "Bette Davis," section 2, by Ruth Favor Davis, p. 16.
8. *Lonely Life*, pp. 12–13.
9. Bette Davis, "Uncertain Glory," p. 17.
10. BU, box 9: Paul Favor, "Bette Davis," section 2, by Ruth Favor Davis, p. 16.
11. Ibid., p. 17.
12. BU, scrapbook 17: Lyle Rooks, "I'm Tired of Hag Roles," unsourced, undated.
13. *Lonely Life*, p. 20.
14. BU, box 9: Paul Favor, "Bette Davis," section 2, by Ruth Favor Davis, pp. 17–18.
15. Leaming, p. 24.
16. BU, scrapbook 32.
17. Ibid.

18. *Lonely Life*, p. 23.
19. Ibid., p. 22.
20. Ibid., p. 21.
21. Ibid.
22. Ibid.
23. Ibid., p. 22.
24. Madsen, p. 73.
25. *Lonely Life*, p. 22.
26. Ibid., p. 23.
27. Ibid., p. 20.
28. Ibid., pp. 12, 24.
29. Ibid., pp. 24–25; BU, box 9: Paul Favor, "Bette Davis," section 2, by Ruth Favor Davis, p. 19.
30. *Lonely Life*, p. 24.
31. BU, scrapbook 52.
32. BU, scrapbook 17: Gladys Hall, "Bette Davis's True Life Story," undated.
33. *Lonely Life*, p. 25.
34. Ibid.
35. BU, scrapbook 32.
36. BU, box 3, folder 8: *Boston Sunday Globe*, April 5, 1936.
37. *Lonely Life*, p. 26; Bette Davis, "Uncertain Glory," p. 107; Leaming, p. 31.
38. *Lonely Life*, p. 27.
39. Ibid.
40. Ibid., p. 28.
41. BU, box 4.
42. *Lonely Life*, pp. 28–29.
43. Brophy, p. 225.
44. *Lonely Life*, p. 29.
45. Ibid., p. 30.
46. Leaming, p. 33.
47. *Lonely Life*, pp. 33–34.
48. Leaming, p. 42.
49. *Lonely Life*, p. 37.
50. Bette Davis, "Uncertain Glory," p. 108.
51. BU, scrapbook 57.
52. BU, box 2, folder 3: program for Alice D. Miller and Robert Milton, *The Charm School*.
53. BU, scrapbook 63.
54. BU, scrapbook 57.
55. James McCourt to ES, January 3, 2005.
56. BU, box 9: Paul Favor, "Bette Davis," p. 15.
57. *Lonely Life*, p. 23.
58. Leaming, p. 25.
59. McCourt, *Queer Street*, p. 505.
60. Leaming, p. 25; Davis with Davidson, November 25, 1955, p. 99.
61. Davis with Herskowitz, *This 'n That*, p. 97.

62. *Lonely Life*, p. 34.
63. BU, scrapbook 57.
64. *Lonely Life*, p. 38.
65. Ibid., p. 46.
66. Ibid., p. 47.
67. Fonda and Teichmann, p. 35.
68. BU, box 1: Bette Davis's speech at Loomis School.
69. BU, scrapbook 57.

CHAPTER 2. LESSONS

1. BU, box 9.
2. Sheldon Harnick to ES, October 15, 2003.
3. BU, scrapbook 23: *Boston Transcript*, April 22, 1939; *Lonely Life*, pp. 51–52.
4. Leaming, p. 59.
5. http://www.peterboroughhistory.org/new_page_3.htm; Leaming, p. 46.
6. *Lonely Life*, pp. 42–43.
7. Leaming, p. 47.
8. http://www.npg.org.uk/live/search/person.asp?LinkID=mp55949.
9. http://www.dancespirit.com/backissues/march02/legends.shtml.
10. Bette Davis, "Uncertain Glory," p. 109.
11. *Lonely Life*, p. 54.
12. *The Dick Cavett Show*, ABC, November 17, 1971.
13. *Lonely Life*, p. 54.
14. Ibid., p. 55.
15. Ibid.
16. Bette Davis, "Uncertain Glory," p. 110.
17. *Lonely Life*, p. 54; Shingler, "Malevolence"; http://www.marthagrahamdance
    .org/us/; and Dawn Lille, "Martha Graham's Legacy," http://www.arttimes
    journal.com/dance/grahamfour.htm.
18. McCourt, *Queer Street*, p. 490.
19. *Lonely Life*, pp. 55–56.
20. Leaming, p. 60.
21. New York Public Library for the Performing Arts at Lincoln Center (NY-
    PLLC), *The Earth Between* clippings file.
22. *Lonely Life*, p. 77.
23. BU, scrapbook 4: Paul G. Favor to "Gail," undated letter.
24. *Lonely Life*, p. 82.
25. Spada, *Bette Davis*, p. 51.
26. Leaming, p. 65.
27. Bette Davis, "Uncertain Glory," p. 111.
28. Ibid.
29. *Lonely Life*, p. 74.
30. Ibid.
31. Spada, *Bette Davis*, p. 57.
32. *Lonely Life*, p. 75.
33. Williamson, p. 73.

34. Bette Davis, "Uncertain Glory," p. 112.
35. Spada, *Bette Davis*, p. 59.
36. Graham, p. 27.
37. Reggie Schwartzwalder to ES, September 19, 2006.
38. *Lonely Life*, pp. 93–94; BU, scrapbooks 4 and 5.
39. BU, scrapbook 5.
40. *Lonely Life*, p. 98.
41. *Boston Evening American*, February 21, 1939.
42. *Lonely Life*, p. 98.
43. NYPLLC, *Solid South* clippings file.
44. *New Republic*, October 29, 1930.
45. BU, scrapbook 5: unsourced clipping.

CHAPTER 3. A YANKEE IN HOLLYWOOD

1. Hanson, *AFI Catalog, 1931–1940*, pp. 111–12.
2. Meyers, *Bogart*, p. 41.
3. Stine and Davis, *Mother Goddam*, p. 7.
4. Bogart, p. 52.
5. Ibid., p. 182.
6. Stine and Davis, *Mother Goddam*, p. 13.
7. Margaret Herrick Library, Academy of Motion Picture Arts and Sciences (AMPAS), clippings file for *Bad Sister*: *Variety*, undated clip.
8. *Lonely Life*, pp. 109–10.
9. Williamson, p. 70; *Lonely Life*, pp. 109–10; *The Dick Cavett Show*, ABC, November 17, 1971.
10. *Lonely Life*, p. 113.
11. BU, scrapbook 4: *Boston Traveller*, June 29, 1931.
12. Stine and Davis, *Mother Goddam*, p. 13.
13. *The Dick Cavett Show*, ABC, November 17, 1971.
14. Bette Davis, "Uncertain Glory," p. 117.
15. Warner with Jennings, p. 8.
16. Kennedy, p. 162.
17. Warner with Jennings, p. 6.
18. Gabler, p. 191.
19. Ibid., p. 190.
20. Gussow, *Zanuck*, p. 49.
21. Warner Bros. Archives, University of Southern California (USC), legal files, May 21, 1931, to December 19, 1933.
22. Ibid., January 2 to September 30, 1936.
23. Stine and Davis, *Mother Goddam*, p. 20.
24. *Lonely Life*, pp. 124–25.
25. Ibid.
26. Ibid., p. 135.
27. Gabler, p. 196.
28. *Lonely Life*, pp. 135–36.
29. LeRoy and Kleiner, pp. 115–16.

CHAPTER 4. AN ACTRESS IN MOTION

1. *Lonely Life*, pp. 40, 52, 59–60; Leaming, p. 52.
2. Ibid., p. 60.
3. Ibid., p. 113.
4. Ibid., p. 130.
5. USC, legal files, May 21, 1931, to December 19, 1933.
6. Leaming, p. 103.
7. Stine and Davis, *Mother Goddam*, p. 41, quoting Gladys Hall, *Modern Screen*.
8. BU, box 2, folder 5: *Boston Post* clipping, undated; *Boston Globe*, March 8, 1933.
9. *Lonely Life*, p. 133.
10. USC, legal files, January 2 to September 30, 1936: interoffice memo, September 24, 1936.
11. Leaming, p. 98.
12. *Lonely Life*, p. 131.
13. USC, legal files, May 21, 1931, to December 19, 1933.
14. *Lonely Life*, p. 135.
15. Stine and Davis, *Mother Goddam*, p. 42.
16. Swindell, *Tracy*, p. 102.
17. Andersen, *Affair*, pp. 79–80.
18. Cagney, pp. 118–19.
19. Baldwin, p. 7.
20. *Lonely Life*, p. 136.
21. Fairbanks, p. 192.
22. *Lonely Life*, p. 138.
23. AMPAS, clippings file for *The Working Man*, Warner Bros. accounting sheet dated April 6, 1933.
24. Vieira, pp. 220–21; Warner Bros. accounting sheet dated April 6, 1933.
25. BU, scrapbook 108.
26. BU, scrapbook 63; *Boston Sunday Globe*, June 21, 1931.
27. USC, legal files, May 21, 1931, to December 19, 1933.
28. *Lonely Life*, p. 132.
29. Leaming, p. 103.
30. Ibid., p. 107; Sikov.
31. Stine and Davis, *Mother Goddam*, p. 44.
32. O'Brien, p. 183.
33. Davis with Davidson, November 25, 1955, p. 29.
34. *Lonely Life*, p. 141.
35. Bergman, p. 49.
36. Ibid., p. 48.
37. Cagney, p. 60.
38. Ibid.
39. Warren with Cagney, p. 102.
40. Stine and Davis, *Mother Goddam*, p. 54.
41. Leaming, p. 108.
42. Stine and Davis, *Mother Goddam*, p. 42.
43. Cagney, pp. 52–53.

44. *Lonely Life*, p. 141.
45. Stine and Davis, *Mother Goddam*, p. 57.
46. *Stardust: The Bette Davis Story*, dir. Peter Jones, Turner Classic Movies, 2006.
47. *Lonely Life*, p. 142.
48. Howard, p. 208.
49. *Lonely Life*, p. 141.
50. Shingler, "Malevolence."

CHAPTER 5. THE FIRST OSCAR
 1. Stine and Davis, *Mother Goddam*, p. 55.
 2. Leaming, p. 109.
 3. Ibid., p. 110.
 4. Ibid., p. 111.
 5. Behlmer, *Inside Warner Bros.*, p. 15: Wallis to Mayo, September 13, 1934.
 6. Bette Davis, "Uncertain Glory," p. 119.
 7. Jerome Lawrence, p. 357.
 8. *Lonely Life*, p. 147.
 9. Quirk and Schoell, p. 70.
10. *Lonely Life*, p. 149.
11. Brophy, pp. 227–28; http://encycl.opentopia.com/term/Curate's_egg.
12. http://www.thanhouser.org/people/eagelsj.htm.
13. Sperber and Lax, p. 53.
14. USC, *The Petrified Forest* file: daily production and progress report.
15. Caine, pp. 227–28.
16. USC, legal files, January 2 to December 29, 1935.
17. *New York Times*, July 23, 1936.
18. Stine and Davis, *Mother Goddam*, p. 76.
19. Ibid., p. 35.
20. USC, legal files, January 2 to September 30, 1936; Berg, *Kate Remembered*, p. 124; Eyman, p. 168; *New York Times*, February 23, 1936; Hanson, *AFI Catalog, 1931–1940*, pp. 1335–36; Stine and Davis, *Mother Goddam*, p. 121.
21. *Lonely Life*, p. 156.
22. Hanson, *AFI Catalog, 1931–1940*, p. 796.
23. USC, legal files, January 2 to September 30, 1936.
24. Ibid.
25. Leaming, p. 115.
26. *Lonely Life*, p. 150.
27. Wiley and Bona, p. 65.
28. Ibid.
29. *Lonely Life*, p. 154.
30. Stine and Davis, *Mother Goddam*, p. 74.
31. Ibid.
32. BU, scrapbook 23: *Boston Globe*, February 26, 1939.
33. *Lonely Life*, pp. 154–55.
34. Hanson, *AFI Catalog, 1931–1940*, pp. 68, 779.
35. Stine and Davis, *Mother Goddam*, p. 72.

36. Ibid., p. 76.
37. BU, scrapbook 11.
38. Huston, p. 187.
39. Warner with Jennings, p. 247.
40. USC, legal files, January 2 to December 29, 1935.
41. Ibid., January 2 to September 30, 1936.
42. Wiley and Bona, p. 65.
43. Leaming, p. 111; Schatz, p. 202.
44. BU, scrapbook 13: *Motion Picture Daily*, January 18, 1937. Finler, p. 244. There is a discrepancy between the *Motion Picture Daily*'s reporting of the star's 1935 income and a Warner Bros. internal accounting sheet, which claims that between 1931, when she first signed on at Warners, and late 1936, the studio paid Davis $74,941.67 while working and $71,583.33 while not working (which is to say, while she wasn't clocking in on a particular film), for a total of $146,525.00, or about $30,000 per year. Still, Davis clearly earned less for herself than she earned for the brothers Warner.
45. *New York Times*, February 26, May 1, and May 26, 1936.

CHAPTER 6. UP IN ARMS

1. Stine and Davis, *Mother Goddam*, p. 76.
2. *Lonely Life*, pp. 156–57.
3. USC, legal files, January 2 to September 30, 1936.
4. Warner with Jennings, p. 248.
5. BU, scrapbook 11: Louella Parsons, *Los Angeles Examiner*, June 20, 1936.
6. Slide, p. 238.
7. USC, legal files, January 2 to September 30, 1936.
8. John T. McManus, "Bette Davis Here: Stop," *New York Times*, March 29, 1936.
9. BU, box 3, folder 8: *Boston Globe*, April 3, 1936. BU, box 2, folder 8: *Boston Post*, April 4, 1936; *Boston Herald*, April 4, 1936.
10. BU, box 1: telegram from Harlow M. Davis, April 5, 1936.
11. USC, legal files, January 2 to September 30, 1936: Martin Gang to Roy Obringer, April 6, 1936.
12. USC, legal files, January 2 to September 30, 1936.
13. Ibid.
14. Ibid.
15. Ibid.
16. Ibid., October 1 to December 24, 1936.
17. Stine and Davis, *Mother Goddam*, p. 77.
18. *The Dick Cavett Show*, ABC, November 17, 1971.
19. USC, legal files, January 2 to September 30, 1936.
20. Ibid.
21. Bette Davis to Jack L. Warner, June 21, 1936; USC, legal files, January 2 to September 30, 1936.
22. USC, legal files, January 2 to September 30, 1936.
23. Ibid.
24. Ibid.

25. *Daily Mail*, September 16, 1936.
26. Warner with Jennings, p. 248.
27. BU, scrapbook 11.
28. *Lonely Life*, p. 159; Stine and Davis, *Mother Goddam*, p. 77.
29. BU, scrapbook 10: *British Daily Express*, August 18, 1936.
30. BU, scrapbook 10: *Glasgow Evening Citizen*, August 18, 1936.
31. *Lonely Life*, p. 160.
32. *Today's Cinema*, September 9, 1936; *Referee*, September 13, 1936.
33. *Sunday Express*, September 13, 1936.
34. BU, scrapbook 11: *Daily Express*.
35. BU, scrapbook 13.
36. Warner with Jennings, p. 250.
37. *Lonely Life*, p. 162.
38. "Law Report, Oct. 16," *Times* (London), October 17, 1936.
39. "K. C. Calls Contract a 'Life Sentence' on Film Star," *Daily Telegraph*, October 16, 1936.
40. *Evening News*, October 14, 1936.
41. *Lonely Life*, pp. 163–64.
42. "K. C. Calls Contract a 'Life Sentence' on Film Star," *Daily Telegraph*, October 16, 1936.
43. *Lonely Life*, p. 164.
44. Ibid., pp. 167–68.
45. USC, legal files, October 1 to December 24, 1936.
46. Freedland, *Warner*, p. 84.
47. BU, box 1: Ludovico Toeplitz to Bette Davis, August 27, 1936.
48. BU, scrapbook 10: card from George Arliss dated October 27, 1936.
49. Stine and Davis, *Mother Goddam*, p. 82.
50. "Miss Bette Davis Judgment on Monday," *Daily Telegraph*, October 17, 1936.
51. USC, legal files, October 1 to December 24, 1936.
52. Stine and Davis, *Mother Goddam*, p. 81.
53. USC, legal files, October 1 to December 24, 1936: Roy Obringer to Eric Fletcher of Denton, Hall & Burgin, November 20, 1936.
54. USC, legal files, October 1 to December 24, 1936.
55. BU, scrapbook 11: *Standard* and *Daily Telegraph*, October 19, 1936.
56. BU, scrapbook 10.
57. Thanks to Martin Shingler for this observation.
58. Martin Shingler to ES, August 20, 2004.
59. Anon., "Freedom Fighter."
60. BU, scrapbook 67.

CHAPTER 7. "IN THE WARNER JAIL"
1. BU, scrapbook 17.
2. *Lonely Life*, p. 169.
3. Leaming, p. 134.
4. Dotson Rader to ES, February 18, 2004.
5. Leaming, p. 134.

6. Ibid., p. 135.
7. Spada, *Davis*, p. 130.
8. Powell, p. 69.
9. Ibid., p. 127.
10. Hanson, *AFI Catalog, 1931–1940*, pp. 1329–30.
11. *Lonely Life*, p. 171.
12. BU, scrapbook 17: "Glamorous Bette—Marked Woman," unsigned fanzine article.
13. Behlmer, *Warner*, p. 39.
14. Spada, *Davis*, pp. 130–31.
15. Sperber and Lax, p. 105.
16. Wallis and Higham, p. 47.
17. *Lonely Life*, p. 172.
18. Sperber and Lax, p. 203.
19. *Lonely Life*, p. 172.
20. McGilligan, *Backstory 1*, p. 300.
21. *Variety*, June 9, 1937.
22. Leaming, p. 37.
23. Ibid., pp. 37, 41–42, 92–93, 98–99.
24. Ibid., pp. 110, 121.
25. *Lonely Life*, p. 153.
26. *Los Angeles Examiner*, June 13, 1937.
27. *Lonely Life*, p. 153.
28. Ibid., p. 170.
29. Leaming, p. 136.
30. USC, legal files, January 8 to June 30, 1937: Obringer to Perkins, January 14 and March 10, 1937.
31. Hanson, *AFI Catalog, 1931–1940*, pp. 942–43.
32. *Lonely Life*, p. 157.
33. Stine and Davis, *Mother Goddam*, p. 96.
34. Warner with Jennings, p. 253.
35. *Lonely Life*, p. 174.
36. Hanson, *AFI Catalog, 1931–1940*, p. 803.
37. Ibid.
38. *Lonely Life*, p. 174.
39. BU, scrapbook 13.
40. Ibid.
41. Lambert Gavin, "The Making of *Gone with the Wind*," *Atlantic Monthly*, February 1973.
42. Warner with Jennings, p. 253.
43. *Lonely Life*, p. 174.
44. Behlmer, *Selznick*, pp. 164–67.
45. USC, legal files, January 8 to June 30, 1937: Bette Davis to Jack Warner, July 17, 1937.
46. Ibid.: Bette Davis to Jack Warner, July 26, 1937.
47. Flanner, p. 23.

48. USC, legal files, July 6 to December 6, 1937: Bridget Price to Jack Warner, July 30, 1937.
49. Radie Harris, "The Fear That Is Haunting Bette Davis," November 1937.
50. Leaming, p. 139.
51. *Boston Globe*, January 16, 1933.
52. *Lonely Life*, p. 152.
53. Ibid., p. 173.
54. Leaming, p. 122.
55. BU, scrapbook 9.
56. Spada, *Bette Davis*, p. 110.
57. Ibid., p. 116.
58. Williamson, p. 79.
59. Spada, *Bette Davis*, p. 138; *Screen Guide*, "Home Life of a Movie Hellcat," undated.
60. Spada, *Bette Davis*, p. 135.
61. Bette Davis, "Uncertain Glory," p. 118.

CHAPTER 8. THE SECOND OSCAR
1. Herman, pp. 118, 174–75.
2. Hanson, *AFI Catalog, 1931–1940*, pp. 1064–66.
3. Higham, p. 98.
4. Hanson, *AFI Catalog, 1931–1940*, pp. 1064–66.
5. Herman, p. 174–75.
6. Ibid., p. 176.
7. *Lonely Life*, p. 175.
8. Hanson, *AFI Catalog, 1931–1940*, pp. 1064–66.
9. Herman, p. 177.
10. *Lonely Life*, p. 175.
11. Higham, *Bette*, p. 107.
12. Wallis and Higham, p. 50.
13. Spada, *Bette Davis*, p. 134.
14. Herman, p. 178.
15. *Lonely Life*, p. 175.
16. Ibid.
17. Herman, p. 178.
18. Ibid.
19. Ibid., p. 180.
20. Ibid.
21. USC, *Jezebel* file: daily production and progress report.
22. David Chierichetti to ES, January 23, 2006.
23. USC, legal files, July 6 to December 6, 1937; memo dated November 30, 1937.
24. Higham, *Bette*, p. 108.
25. Malcolm, pp. 8–9.
26. www.ibdb.com; *Lonely Life*, p. 82; Bette Davis, "Uncertain Glory," p. 113.
27. *Lonely Life*, p. 82.
28. Ibid., p. 83; Bette Davis, "Uncertain Glory," p. 113.

29. BU, box 2, folder 3.
30. *Lonely Life*, p. 83.
31. Ibid., pp. 83–84.
32. Ibid., p. 85.
33. Ibid., pp. 85–86.
34. Leaming, p. 49.
35. Ibsen, p. 196.
36. Higham, *Bette*, p. 33.
37. Spada, *Bette Davis*, p. 64.
38. Martin Shingler to ES, August 20, 2004.
39. *Lonely Life*, pp. 12, 24.
40. Ibid., pp. 88–89.
41. *Boston Post*, January 3, 1938; USC, *Jezebel* file: daily production and progress report.
42. *Boston Post*, January 3, 1938.
43. USC, *Jezebel* file: daily production and progress report.
44. Schatz, p. 225.
45. Herman, p. 182.
46. Ibid.
47. *Photoplay*, January 1938.
48. The Academy changed its regulations in 1944 to allow only five films to be nominated for Best Picture.
49. *Boston Globe*, February 26, 1939.
50. *Lonely Life*, p. 178.

CHAPTER 9. "A GIRL WHO DIES"

1. USC, legal files, August 3 to December 16, 1938. Retakes were shot on August 22.
2. *The Dick Cavett Show*, ABC, December 31, 1969.
3. Westmore and Davidson, p. 84.
4. *Lonely Life*, pp. 180–81.
5. Thomson, p. 522.
6. *Lonely Life*, p. 181.
7. Ibid.
8. Higham, *Bette Davis*, pp. 110–11.
9. Higham, p. 111.
10. BU, scrapbook 21.
11. Spada, *Bette Davis*, pp. 143–45.
12. Vik Greenfield to ES, August 9, 2004.
13. BU, scrapbook 21: various clippings dated August 30, 1938, and later that fall.
14. BU, box 2, folder 4: Complaint for Divorce, dated November 22, 1938, Harmon Oscar Nelson Jr., plaintiff, versus Ruth Elizabeth Nelson, defendant.
15. BU, box 1: anonymous letter dated November 27, 1938.
16. BU, scrapbook 17: Gladys Hall, "If I Had Six Months to Live."
17. *Lonely Life*, p. 182.

18. NYPLLC, *Dark Victory* (play) clippings.
19. Zierold, p. 212; Swanson, p. 450.
20. Hanson, *AFI Catalog, 1931–1940*, p. 465.
21. *Lonely Life*, p. 183.
22. Charles Busch to ES, May 26, 2004.
23. Sperber and Lax, p. 104; Kennedy, pp. 179–80.
24. USC, *Dark Victory* files: Hal Wallis to Edmund Goulding, October 27, 1938.
25. Douglas Churchill, *New York Times,* November 6, 1938.
26. BU, scrapbook 43: *Screen Gossip*, undated.
27. Kennedy, p. 178.
28. BU, scrapbook 17: Dorothy Manners, "Hollywood's Next Great Love Story."
29. *The Dick Cavett Show,* ABC, March 11, 1971.
30. Kennedy, p. 181.
31. Meyers, p. 102, quoting production memos in the Warner Bros. archive at USC.
32. Stine and Davis, *Mother Goddam*, p. 112.
33. AMPAS, Gladys Hall Collection, folder 141: "Bette Davis," *Modern Screen*, January 28, 1939.
34. Mann, *Behind the Screen*, p. 171, quoting Ezra Goodman, *New York Times*, June 28, 1942.
35. USC, *Dark Victory* files: Casey Robinson to Hal Wallis, August 19, 1938.
36. BU, box 28: Geraldine Fitzgerald to Harold (Schiff?), undated.
37. USC, *Dark Victory* files: "Story—Changes" file.
38. Ibid.: David Lewis to Hal Wallis, November 4, 1938.
39. Ibid.: Hal Wallis's cutting notes, December 9, 1938.
40. Ibid.: A. C. Blumenthal to Hal Wallis, March 9, 1939.
41. Ibid.: *Dark Victory* pressbook.
42. *New York Times*, March 19, 1939.

CHAPTER 10. FEUDS

1. Meyer, p. 127.
2. Stine and Davis, *Mother Goddam*, p. 116; BU, scrapbook 22: unsourced clipping.
3. Aherne, p. 280.
4. Ibid., p. 255.
5. Stine and Davis, *Mother Goddam*, p. 115.
6. Jerome Lawrence, pp. 353, 356.
7. *Lonely Life*, pp. 186–87.
8. USC, *The Old Maid* files: daily production and progress report.
9. *Life*, August 21, 1939.
10. *Wide World Special: The Dick Cavett Show*, ABC, September 19, 1974.
11. *Lonely Life*, p. 188.
12. *Pittsburgh Press*, May 17, 1939.
13. USC, legal files, January 4 to August 31, 1939.
14. Ibid.
15. Ibid.
16. Flynn, pp. 260–61.
17. USC, *Private Lives* file: daily production and progress report.

18. Harrison Carroll, *Herald Express*, June 10, 1939.
19. Olivia de Havilland, interviewed in *The Adventures of Errol Flynn*, dir. David Heeley, Turner Classic Movies, 2005.
20. Hanson, *AFI Catalog, 1931–1940*, pp. 41–42.
21. Swindell, *Boyer*, p. 158.
22. *Lonely Life*, p. 200.
23. USC, *All This and Heaven, Too* files.
24. Dody, p. 156; *Lonely Life*, p. 200.
25. Stine and Davis, *Mother Goddam*, p. 130.
26. Quirk, *Colbert*, p. 100.
27. Swindell, *Boyer*, pp. 160–61.
28. Ibid., p. 158.
29. Ibid., p. 163.
30. USC, *All This and Heaven, Too* files; Swindell, *Boyer*, p. 158.
31. *Los Angeles Times*, June 14, 1940.
32. *Lonely Life*, p. 201.

CHAPTER 11. MORE BATTLES AND TWO RETREATS

1. USC, *The Letter* files: Walter MacEwen to Breen and Breen to MacEwan, both April 16, 1938.
2. Ibid.: Bob Lord to Wallis, December 20, 1939.
3. Morley, *Cooper*, p. 116.
4. USC, *The Letter* files: Warner to Wallis, June 8, 1940, and June 20, 1940.
5. Ibid.: Wyler to Wallis, June 12, 1940.
6. *Lonely Life*, p. 204.
7. Callahan, http://www.toxicuniverse.com/review.php?rid=10005377.
8. See O'Toole, "Whatever Happened to Bette Davis?"
9. USC, *The Letter* files: Wallis to Lord, October 11, 1940.
10. Stine and Davis, *Mother Goddam*, p. 140.
11. Flanner, p. 20.
12. Wiley and Bona, p. 105.
13. Stine, *Kiss*, p. 126.
14. BU, scrapbook 21.
15. Shingler, "Masquerade," quoting Gladys Hall in *Modern Screen*, undated.
16. BU, box 25: "Home Life of a Movie Hellcat,"*Screen Guide*, 1938.
17. http://www.dogbreedinfo.com/scottishterrier.htm.
18. BU, scrapbook 17: Gladys Hall, "Divorce Is Making Her Miserable," undated.
19. Spada, *Bette Davis*, p. 148.
20. BU, box 25: *Screen Guide*, January 1939.
21. *Lonely Life*, p. 197.
22. Quirk, *Fasten*, p. 179.
23. BU, scrapbook 32.
24. BU, scrapbook 43: *Boston Globe*, August 20, 1939.
25. Stine and Davis, *Mother Goddam*, p. 127.
26. *Lonely Life*, p. 199; Stine and Davis, *Mother Goddam*, p. 127.
27. BU, scrapbook 33: Louella Parsons, *Los Angeles Herald Examiner*, March 6, 1940.

28. *Lonely Life*, p. 199.
29. BU, box 2, folder 6: Zaida, "Bette Davis," (Honolulu) *Ka Moae*.
30. BU, scrapbook 27: various clippings, including Peggy Bairos, "Bette Davis Receives Rousing Island Welcome"; James T. Hamada, "On the Screen," *Honolulu*, May 1, 1940; Jimmy Fidler, *Los Angeles Times*, May 8, 1940; Dorothy Kilgallen, *New York Journal American*, May 6, 1940; Sidney Skolsky, *Citizen News*, June 21, 1940.
31. Stine and Davis, *Mother Goddam*, p. 138.
32. BU, scrapbook 17: "It's Idle Gossip," *Modern Screen*, January 1941.
33. Schultz, p. 19.
34. Stine and Davis, *Mother Goddam*, p. 140, quoting contemporary interview with Jack Holland.
35. USC, *The Great Lie* files: Wallis to Warner, November 18, 1940.
36. Ibid.: Wallis to Blanke, January 29, 1940.
37. Ibid.: Warner to Blanke, February 20, 1940.
38. USC, legal files, September 5 to December 30, 1940: Davis to Wallis, undated; Wallis to Blanke, September 21, 1940.
39. Kennedy, p. 200.
40. Astor, *My Story*, pp. 201–2.
41. Ibid., p. 202.
42. Astor, *A Life on Film*, p. 152.
43. Ibid., p. 153.
44. Astor, *My Story*, p. 203.
45. Ibid., p. 204.
46. Wiley and Bona, p. 120.
47. USC, legal files, September 5 to December 30, 1940: Davis to Warner, undated.
48. Stine and Davis, *Mother Goddam*, p. 117.
49. Flanner, p. 22.
50. Ibid.
51. BU, scrapbook 52.
52. BU, box 25: *Boston Sunday Post*, August 4, 1940.
53. Stine and Davis, *Mother Goddam*, p. 146.
54. Ibid., p. 143.
55. Ibid.
56. *New York Times*, April 6, 1941.
57. BU, box 2, folder 6: *Manchester Union*, April 5, 1941.
58. "Life Goes to a Birthday Party," *Life*, April 28, 1941, pp. 126–29.

CHAPTER 12. BREAKDOWN AND RECOVERY

1. *Lonely Life*, p. 208.
2. Louella Parsons, *Los Angeles Herald-Examiner*, July 22, 1940.
3. Berg, *Goldwyn*, p. 357.
4. USC, legal files, January 1 to August 31, 1940, and September 5 to December 30, 1940.
5. *Lonely Life*, p. 206.
6. Marx, "In Hollywood," pp. 206–7.

7. McCourt, *Queer Street*, p. 498.

8. Thomas Brady, "Peace Comes to *The Little Foxes*," *New York Times*, June 22, 1941.

9. Berg, *Goldwyn*, pp. 355–56.

10. Marx, *Goldwyn*, p. 280.

11. http://www.atmos.ucla.edu/~fovell/ASother/mm5/SantaAna/winds.html.

12. Marx, *Goldwyn*, p. 281.

13. USC, Bette Davis legal files, January 8 to December 31, 1941: Obringer to Wallis and Warner, May 22, 1941.

14. Stine and Davis, *Mother Goddam*, pp. 150–51.

15. BU, scrapbook 30: various clippings.

16. Douglas Churchill, "A House Divided," *New York Times*, June 1, 1941.

17. Brady, "Peace Comes to *The Little Foxes*."

18. USC, Bette Davis legal files, January 8 to December 31, 1941.

19. *Lonely Life*, p. 207.

20. Rollyson, p. 180.

21. Wright, p. 179.

22. USC, legal files, September 5 to December 30, 1940: memo dated November 12, 1940.

23. Peters, p. 448.

24. Wallis and Higham, p. 97.

25. USC, *The Man Who Came to Dinner* files, legal file.

26. Hanson, *AFI Catalog, 1941–1950*, pp. 1484–85.

27. Ibid.

28. Stine and Davis, *Mother Goddam*, p. 154.

29. Kobal, p. 423.

30. BU, scrapbook 37: various clippings.

31. USC, Bette Davis legal files, January 8 to December 31, 1941: Davis to Wallis, October 2, 1941.

32. http://www.musicals101.com/gay5.htm.

33. Quirk, *Fasten*, p. 236.

34. McCourt, *Queer Street*, p. 494.

35. Baldwin, p. 60.

36. *The Dick Cavett Show*, ABC, March 11, 1971.

37. Huston, p. 81.

38. Warner with Jennings, p. 255.

39. BU, scrapbook 37: *Minneapolis Star-Journal*, October 22, 1941.

40. USC, Bette Davis legal files, January 8 to December 31, 1941.

41. USC, *In This Our Life* files: Warner to Huston, December 17, 1941.

42. Ibid.: Wright to Warner and Wallis, December 18, 1941.

43. BU, scrapbook 37: Peake clipping, November 8, 1941.

44. USC, *In This Our Life* files: Wallis to Perc Westmore, February 11, 1942.

45. BU, scrapbook 37: clipping, mid-November 1942.

46. Ibid.: undated clipping.

47. Bette Davis, "Uncertain Glory," p. 17.

48. Williamson, p. 75.

49. *Lonely Life*, p. 205.

50. Ibid.

51. BU, box 25: *Boston Post*, December 15, 1941.

52. AMPAS, Hedda Hopper Collection, file 506 (Bette Davis).

53. Hanson, *AFI Catalog, 1941–1950*, p. 537.

54. Ibid., p. 616.

55. *Hollywood Reporter*, October 19 and November 30, 1942.

56. USC, Bette Davis legal files, January 8 to December 31, 1941; Behlmer, *Warner*, p. 150: Blanke to Wallis, June 7, 1941.

57. Hanson, *AFI Catalog, 1941–1950*, p. 868.

58. USC, Bette Davis legal files, January 8 to December 31, 1941.

59. Troyan, p. 177.

60. Hanson, *AFI Catalog, 1941–1950*, p. 471.

61. Swindell, *Garfield*, p. 175.

62. Hanson, *AFI Catalog, 1941–1950*, pp. 1285–86; Behlmer, *Warner*, p. 140; Wallis and Higham, p. 101.

63. www.audio-classics.com.

64. BU, scrapbook 28: Ann Masters, *Chicago Herald American*, August 3, 1940.

CHAPTER 13. A PERSCRIPTION FOR INDEPENDENCE

1. http://www.uua.org/uuhs/duub/articles/olivehigginsprouty.html.

2. Sperber and Lax, p. 178; Prouty, p. 195.

3. Whitman, p. 379.

4. *Lonely Life*, p. 210.

5. Ginger Rogers, p. 248.

6. Stine and Davis, *Mother Goddam*, p. 163.

7. Ibid.

8. Henreid with Fast, pp. 111–12.

9. Hanson, *AFI Catalog, 1941–1950*, pp. 1729–30.

10. *Lonely Life*, pp. 210–11; Williamson, p. 73.

11. Prouty, p. 198.

12. McGilligan, *Backstory 1*, pp. 303–4.

13. Chase, p. 21.

14. *Boston American*, May 20, 1942.

15. Henreid with Fast, pp. 115–16.

16. Freedland, *Now, Voyager*, p. 139.

17. Charles Busch to ES, May 26, 2004.

18. Cavell, pp. 226–27.

19. BU, scrapbook 40: clipping.

20. Henreid with Fast, p. 114.

21. *Lonely Life*, p. 206.

22. BU, scrapbook 40: various clippings.

23. *New York Times*, May 30, 1942.

24. Schatz, p. 299.

25. *New York Times*, April 23, 1942.

26. *Oakland Tribune*, June 5, 1942.

27. *Photoplay*, January 1941, pp. 26–27, 67.
28. *Photoplay-Movie Mirror*, December 1942.
29. Hoopes, p. 110.
30. Ibid., p. 122.
31. Ibid., p. 129.
32. *Lonely Life*, p. 211; BU scrapbooks 1 and 41: various clippings.
33. Wisconsin Historical Society, Herman Shumlin Papers: Davis to Shumlin, September 1942.
34. Davis with Herskowitz, *This 'n That*, p. 123.
35. Hoopes, pp. 169–70; Schultz, p. 63.
36. Hoopes, p. 179.
37. Davis with Herskowitz, *This 'n That*, pp. 126–27.
38. Vik Greenfield to ES, September 18, 2006.
39. Hoopes, p. 170.
40. Davis with Herskowitz, *This 'n That*, pp. 127–28.
41. Hoopes, p. 172.
42. Flanner, p. 24.
43. *The Dick Cavett Show*, ABC, November 17, 1971.
44. USC, Bette Davis legal files, January 7 to December 28, 1942: Obringer to Warner May 14, 1942, and Wallis to Obringer, May 15, 1942.
45. Hanson, *AFI Catalog, 1941–1950*, p. 2724.
46. Stine and Davis, *Mother Goddam*, p. 165.
47. *The Dick Cavett Show*, ABC, November 17, 1971.
48. USC, Bette Davis legal files, January 4 to November 8, 1945: Davis to Warner, February 20, 1945.
49. Kobal, p. 559.
50. Kennedy, p. 210.
51. Quirk, *Norma*, pp. 229–30.
52. Kennedy, pp. 209–10.
53. Ibid., p. 210.
54. Hanson, *AFI Catalog, 1941–1950*, p. 1741.
55. Riese, p. 5.
56. Kobal, p. 560.
57. Sherman, pp. 122–24.
58. Stine and Davis, *Mother Goddam*, p. 176.
59. Kobal, p. 561.
60. Bogart, p. 230.
61. Sherman, p. 125.
62. Kobal, pp. 561–62.
63. Sherman, p. 126.
64. Ibid., p. 128.

CHAPTER 14. FOR THE BOYS

1. Eells, pp. 63–64.
2. Hanson, *AFI Catalog, 1941–1950*, pp. 1069–70.
3. USC, *All This and Heaven, Too* files.

4. Quirk, *Fasten*, p. 268.
5. Hoopes, p. 176.
6. Ibid.
7. Hanson, *AFI Catalog, 1941–1950*, pp. 1069–70.
8. *The Dick Cavett Show*, ABC, March 11, 1971.
9. Hank Sartin to ES, December 30, 2005.
10. http://forum.bcdb.com/forum/gforum.cgi?do=post_view&post=57466.
11. Thanks to Hank Sartin, David Germain, and Ethan Minovitz for their observations about Bette Davis's appearances in Warner Bros. animation.
12. BU, scrapbook 52.
13. Stine and Davis, *Mother Goddam*, p. 180.
14. USC, Bette Davis legal files, January 20 to June 24, 1943: contract dated June 7, 1943.
15. Hanson, *AFI Catalog, 1941–1950*, p. 1759.
16. McCarthy, pp. 352–57.
17. Beaver, p. 116, and www.imdb.com.
18. Kennedy, p. 221.
19. *Lonely Life*, p. 213.
20. Rogers St. Johns.
21. Quirk, *Fasten*, p. 261.
22. Spada, pp. 205–15.
23. Sherman, pp. 130–45.
24. *Lonely Life*, p. 214.
25. Vincent Sherman, interviewed on *Mysteries and Scandals: "Bette Davis,"* E! Entertainment Television, 2000.
26. Sherman, p. 147.
27. McDougal, p. 98; Hoopes, p. 174.
28. Riese, p. 294.
29. Westmore and Davidson, p. 137.
30. Stine and Davis, *Mother Goddam*, p. 184.
31. AMPAS, Jane Lockwood Ferrero's Hollywood Canteen diary, entries dated February 27, 1943, October 23, 1943, and November 20, 1943.
32. Hoopes, p. 173.
33. *Lonely Life*, p. 214.
34. USC, legal files, January 1 to August 31, 1940.
35. Ibid.: Wallis to Warner, March 7, 1941.
36. Ibid.: Trilling to Wallis, March 1, 1941, and Wallis to Trilling, April 14, 1941.
37. Sherman, p. 139.
38. Ibid.
39. Stine and Davis, *Mother Goddam*, p. 186.
40. Ibid., p. 181.
41. Kobal, p. 562.
42. USC, *Mr. Skeffington* file: daily production and progress report.
43. *Lonely Life*, pp. 214–15.
44. Freedland, *Warner,* p. 163.
45. Kobal, p. 563.

46. Ibid., p. 562.
47. Sherman, p. 148.

CHAPTER 15. COMMANDERS IN CHIEF

1. USC, *The Corn Is Green* files: daily production and progress report.
2. Stine and Davis, *Mother Goddam*, p. 190.
3. USC, *The Corn Is Green* file: progress reports.
4. Behlmer, *Warner*, p. 17.
5. David Chierichetti to ES, January 23, 2001.
6. Stine and Davis, *Mother Goddam*, p. 190, quoting Dall's interview with Dorothy Hasking in *Movie Story*, August 1945.
7. Kobal, pp. 542–43.
8. *Lonely Life*, p. 252.
9. Higham and Greenberg, *Celluloid Muse*, pp. 199–200.
10. Anon., "Wallace Calls Roosevelt Better Fitted than Dewey," *New York Times*, September 22, 1944.
11. Ward, p. 335.
12. *Lonely Life*, pp. 215–16; Ward, p. 335.
13. Hoopes, p. 175.
14. *New York Times*, September 28, 1944.
15. Stine and Davis, *Mother Goddam*, p. 186.
16. Ibid.
17. Billingsley, p. 97; http://en.wikipedia.org/wiki/Image:ElectoralCollege1944 Large.png.
18. Lippman, pp. 13–14.
19. Hassett, pp. 300–302.
20. Davis with Herskowitz, *This 'n That*, pp. 173–74.
21. BU, box 25: various clippings, including *Boston Post*, November 26, 1945.
22. BU, scrapbook 68.
23. *New York Times*, November 29, 1945.
24. Ibid., November 30, 1945.
25. Staggs, *All About*, p. 69, quoting *Modern Screen*.
26. Riese, p. 389.
27. *Lonely Life*, p. 218.
28. Davis with Herskowitz, *This 'n That*, p. 174.
29. Westmore and Davidson, p. 177.
30. Thomas, *Crawford*, p. 151; Madsen, p. 222.
31. Schatz, p. 417.
32. O'Toole, "Whatever Happened," p. 170.
33. Behlmer, *Warner*, p. 269.
34. Hanson, *AFI Catalog, 1941–1950*, p. 1375.
35. Swindell, *Garfield*, p. 204.
36. Kobal, pp. 563–64.
37. Bernhardt and Kiersch, p. 110.
38. USC, Bette Davis legal files, January 5 to December 18, 1944.

39. Stine and Davis, *Mother Goddam*, p. 195.
40. Ibid., pp. 195–96.
41. Bernhardt, p. 112.
42. Ibid., p. 110.
43. Steven DeRosa to ES, January 17, 2006.
44. *Lonely Life*, p. 219.
45. Stine and Davis, *Mother Goddam*, p. 195.
46. USC, Bette Davis legal files, January 4 to November 8, 1945.
47. Bernhardt and Kiersch, p. 113.
48. USC, Bette Davis legal files, February 26 to December 29, 1947: *A Stolen Life* accounting statement to July 5, 1947, dated August 11, 1947.
49. Sperber and Lax, p. 310.
50. "SAC, Los Angeles" to "Director, FBI," FBI office memorandum dated December 12, 1951.
51. McBride, *Ford*, p. 370.
52. BU, box 25: Jack Ashland, "Invitation to the Wedding of Bette and William Grant Sherry," *Photoplay*, February 1946, p. 27.
53. USC, Bette Davis legal files, February 26 to December 29, 1947.
54. Ibid., January 4 to July 31, 1946: contract dated February 4, 1946.
55. Ibid., January 4 to July 31, 1946.
56. Elizabeth Wilson, "Battling Bette," *Liberty*, February 1947, pp. 32–33.
57. Ibid.

CHAPTER 16. DECEPTIONS

1. Stine and Davis, *Mother Goddam*, p. 209.
2. USC, Bette Davis legal files, January 4 to July 31, 1946.
3. Higham and Greenberg, *Celluloid Muse*, p. 203.
4. Mandelbaum and Myers, p. 64.
5. Henreid with Fast, pp. 176–77.
6. *Lonely Life*, p. 218.
7. Ibid., p. 220.
8. USC, Bette Davis legal files, August 9 to December 28, 1946.
9. BU, box 2, folder 7: Hedda Hopper, "Welcome Stranger!" *Modern Screen*.
10. *Lonely Life*, p. 220.
11. BU, scrapbook 52.
12. *Time*, May 5, 1947.
13. *Lonely Life*, p. 219.
14. Ibid.
15. AMPAS, Gladys Hall Collection, folder 141 (Bette Davis): manuscript of "What Has Happened to Bette Davis?" *Modern Screen*, January 14, 1940.
16. BU, box 25: Jack Ashland, "Invitation to the Wedding of Bette and William Grant Sherry," *Photoplay*, February 1946, p. 27.
17. *Lonely Life*, p. 219.
18. Spada, *Bette Davis*, p. 252.
19. *Lonely Life*, p. 222.

20. Buford, p. 90.
21. USC, Bette Davis legal files, February 26 to December 29, 1947, January 5 to October 15, 1948, and January 15 to December 7, 1949.
22. Stine and Davis, *Mother Goddam*, p. 211.
23. *Lonely Life*, pp. 194, 195, 222.
24. Reynolds, pp. 53–54.
25. AMPAS, Marty Weiser Collection, correspondence, 1948: Gil Golden to Weiser, September 24, 1948, and Weiser to Golden, November 5, 1948.
26. Chierichetti, p. 87.
27. AMPAS, Hedda Hopper Collection, file 506 (Bette Davis): Ted Hodges to Hopper, January 2, 1948.
28. Ibid.: Ted Hodges to Hopper, February 1, 1948.
29. Davis with Herskowitz, *This 'n That*, p. 175.
30. Ibid., p. 176.
31. Spada, *Bette Davis*, pp. 254–55.
32. USC, Bette Davis legal files, January 5 to October 15, 1948.
33. Ibid.
34. Warner with Jennings, p. 251.
35. USC, Bette Davis legal files, January 5 to December 7, 1949.
36. Wisconsin Historical Society archives, United Artists Corporation records, series 1.7, Warner Bros. contract and legal files, box 6: *Beyond the Forest* contract dated January 27, 1949.
37. USC, Bette Davis legal files, January 15 to December 7, 1949: Davis to Jack Warner, January 14, 1949.
38. USC, Bette Davis legal files, January 15 to December 7, 1949.
39. Ibid.
40. Hanson, *AFI Catalog, 1941–1950*, pp. 197–98.
41. Ibid.
42. Arkadin (John Russell Taylor), pp. 151–52.
43. O'Toole, "Whatever Happened," p. 169.
44. Albee, pp. 3–5.
45. Arkadin (John Russell Taylor), pp. 151–52.
46. USC, *Beyond the Forest* file, pressbook.
47. Vidor, Dowd, and Shepard, p. 242.
48. Ibid., p. 243.
49. Ibid., pp. 242–43.
50. *Lonely Life*, p. 222.

CHAPTER 17. FAST FORWARD

1. Staggs, *All About*, p. 102.
2. Davis with Herskowitz, *This 'n That*, p. 44.
3. BU, scrapbook 100: *Los Angeles Times Calendar*, undated clipping.
4. Davis with Herskowitz, *This 'n That*, p. 26.
5. Robert Lantz to ES, November 20, 2003.
6. BU, box 28: Robert Osborne, *Hollywood Reporter*, September 1, 1989, p. 4.

7. Riese, p. 386.
8. Gina Piccalo, "Celebrity Personal Assistants Win Time in Spotlight," *Orlando Sentinel*, December 14, 2003.
9. http://astrology.yahoo.com/us/astrology/profile/aries.html.
10. BU, scrapbook 79.
11. *Stardust: The Bette Davis Story*, dir. Peter Jones, Turner Classic Movies, 2006.
12. Davis with Herskowitz, *This 'n That*, p. 42.
13. Charles Pollack and Vik Greenfield to ES, April 4, 2004.
14. Williamson, p. 79.
15. Bernhardt and Kiersch, p. 148.
16. Higham and Greenberg, *The Celluloid Muse*, p. 52.
17. Bernhardt and Kiersch, pp. 150–51.
18. Williamson, p. 79.
19. Stine and Davis, *Mother Goddam*, pp. 238–39.
20. Ibid., p. 228.
21. Greenfield to ES, April 4, 2004.
22. Greenfield to ES, August 9, 2004.
23. Davis with Herskowitz, *This 'n That*, p. 177.
24. *New York Times*, June 8, 1950.
25. Ibid., July 4, 1950, and Davis with Herskowitz, *This 'n That*, p. 177.
26. AMPAS, Hedda Hopper Collection, file 506 (Bette Davis).
27. Staggs, *All About*, pp. 113–14.
28. Israel, p. 269.
29. Bankhead, p. 278.
30. Kanfer, p. 198.
31. Hanson, *AFI Catalog, 1941–1950*, p. 50.
32. Ibid.
33. Custen, p. 339.
34. Chierichetti, p. 114.
35. Staggs, *All About*, p. 84.
36. Merrill, p. 90.
37. Staggs, *All About*, p. 104.
38. Ibid., pp. 113–14.
39. *Lonely Life*, p. 227.
40. Merrill, p. 88.
41. Staggs, *All About*, p. 78.
42. Ibid., pp. 73, 88.
43. Geist, p. 169.
44. Staggs, *All About*, p. 89.
45. Kenneth Geist to ES, May 27, 2004.
46. Davis with Herskowitz, *This 'n That*, pp. 177–78.
47. Riese, p. 136.
48. Bernstein, pp. 224–26.

CHAPTER 18. WIFE AND MOTHER

1. British Film Institute (BFI), Special Collections, Val Guest Collection, scrapbook, item 3, box 3: various clippings, including *Sunday Dispatch*, February 18, 1951.
2. Merrill, p. 97.
3. Ibid., p. 98.
4. Stine and Davis, *Mother Goddam*, p. 240.
5. Merrill, p. 99.
6. http://www.greatfosters.co.uk/pdfs/history_house.pdf.
7. Merrill, p. 100.
8. BFI, Special Collections, Val Guest Collection, scrapbook, item 3, box 3: *Socialist Leader*, December 1, 1951.
9. Wiley and Bona, pp. 209–10.
10. Warren G. Harris, *Natalie and R.J*, p. 24.
11. Wood, pp. 11–12.
12. Williamson, p. 79.
13. Finstad, p. 100.
14. *Lonely Life*, p. 238.
15. BU, scrapbook 52: various clippings.
16. BU, scrapbook 53: clipping.
17. BU, scrapbook 53.
18. Ibid.: unsourced clipping.
19. Merrill, pp. 96–97.
20. BU, box 1, manuscript of "The Story of Our Daughter, Margot, Retarded!" by Bette Davis, as told to Adele Whitely Fletcher, November 20, 1959.
21. Ibid.
22. *Lonely Life*, p. 243.
23. Merrill, p. 108.
24. *Lonely Life*, p. 243.
25. Merrill, pp. 121–22.
26. Davis with Herskowitz, *This 'n That*, pp. 164–65.
27. BU, scrapbook 71.
28. Ibid.
29. Ibid.
30. Merrill, p. 127.
31. Ibid., p. 128.

CHAPTER 19. ONSTAGE, ONSCREEN, AND ON TV

1. Merrill, p. 105; Radie Harris, *Los Angeles Times*, August 17, 1952.
2. Radie Harris, *Los Angeles Times*, August 17, 1952.
3. Merrill, p. 111.
4. Ibid., p. 113.
5. Sheldon Harnick to ES, October 15, 2003.
6. Logan, p. 288.
7. BU, scrapbook 51: undated note from Ogden Nash to Bette Davis.
8. NYPLLC, John Murray Anderson clipping file, unsourced clipping.

9. Sheldon Harnick to ES, October 15, 2003.
10. Merrill, p. 114.
11. *Lonely Life*, p. 234.
12. Stine and Davis, *Mother Goddam*, p. 248.
13. BU, box 2, folder 7: *Collier's*, undated clipping.
14. BU, scrapbook 51, and BU, box 1.
15. BU, scrapbook 51.
16. *Lonely Life*, p. 234.
17. Stine and Davis, *Mother Goddam*, p. 251.
18. Sheldon Harnick to ES, October 15, 2003.
19. Koster and Atkins, p. 139.
20. Ibid., p. 140.
21. Ibid.
22. *Lonely Life*, p. 239.
23. Stine and Davis, *Mother Goddam*, p. 258.
24. Davis and Davidson, *Collier's*, p. 29.
25. Ibid., p. 257.
26. BU, scrapbook 53: various clippings.
27. Stine and Davis, *Mother Goddam*, p. 267.
28. Henreid with Fast, p. 226.
29. Brophy, p. 225.
30. Merrill, p. 163.
31. Frye, p. 226.
32. Merrill, p. 142.
33. BU, scrapbook 53: various clippings.
34. Stine and Davis, *Mother Goddam*, p. 276.
35. Brochu, pp. 152–53.
36. Warren G. Harris, *Lucy and Desi*, pp. 230–31.
37. Jim Brochu to ES, April 1, 2004.
38. Stine and Davis, *Mother Goddam*, p. 266.
39. Merrill, p. 142.
40. Ibid., p. 143.
41. Ibid.
42. Ibid.
43. Frye, pp. 226–28.
44. Stine and Davis, *Mother Goddam*, p. 267.
45. Frye, pp. 226–28.
46. Merrill, p. 154.
47. Ibid.
48. *Stardust: The Bette Davis Story*, dir. Peter Jones, Turner Classic Movies, 2006.
49. Merrill, p. 154.
50. Ibid., p. 145.
51. Davis with Herskowitz, *This 'n That*, p. 184.
52. Stine and Davis, *Mother Goddam*, p. 267.
53. BU, box 4: diary of trip to Europe.
54. *Lonely Life*, p. 195.

55. Read, p. 310.
56. BFI, Special Collections, Michael Balcon Collection.
57. Merrill, p. 156.
58. BU, box 2, folder 6: *Miami Herald*, January 25, 1960.
59. Merrill, p. 156.
60. Stine and Davis, *Mother Goddam*, p. 275.
61. Davis with Herskowitz, *This 'n That*, p. 186.

CHAPTER 20. TROUBLES AND A TRIUMPH

 1. Dody, pp. 134–35.
 2. Merrill, p. 176.
 3. Ibid., p. 199.
 4. Ibid., p. 185.
 5. AMPAS, Hedda Hopper Collection, file 506 (Bette Davis): transcript dated July 16, 1962.
 6. Merrill, p. 192.
 7. Capra, p. 477.
 8. Riese, p. 352.
 9. *Lonely Life*, p. 219.
10. Leaming, pp. 21–23.
11. BU, box 25: *Boston Globe*, August 28, 1949.
12. BU, scrapbook 17: Virginia Maxwell, "Ruthie Was Right," circa late 1930s.
13. BU, scrapbook 71.
14. BU, scrapbook 53: clipping dated May 23, 1957; BU, scrapbook 71.
15. Dody, p. 161.
16. Charles Pollack to ES, April 4, 2004.
17. Stricklyn, pp. 90–91.
18. BU, box 18: "This Is Your Life—Bette Davis," bound script.
19. Riese, p. 128.
20. Dr. Ivin Prince to ES, June 10, 2004; all subsequent quotes from this interview.
21. Dody, p. 168.
22. Wood, p. 181.
23. *Time*, December 8, 1961, p. 82.
24. Williams and St. Just, p. 176.
25. Williams, pp. 182–83.
26. Logan, p. 289.
27. BU, scrapbook 76.
28. Ibid.
29. Wood, p. 183.
30. Winters, pp. 389, 395, 455 (paperback edition).
31. Williams and St. Just, pp. 179–80.
32. Winters, pp. 389, 395, 455 (paperback edition).
33. Martin Shingler to ES, August 20, 2004.
34. Robert Lantz to ES, November 20, 2003.
35. BU, box 9: Paul Favor, "Bette Davis," section 2 by Ruth Favor Davis, p. 25.
36. Martin Shingler to ES, August 20, 2004.

37. Davis with Herskowitz, *This 'n That*, pp. 134–35.
38. Ibid., p. 135.
39. Ibid.
40. Martin Baum to ES, December 1, 2004.
41. Frye, p. 230.
42. McCourt, *Queer Street*, p. 494.
43. Davis with Herskowitz, *This 'n That*, p. 137.
44. Ibid., pp. 137–38.
45. Greenberg, p. 49.
46. Davis with Herskowitz, *This 'n That*, p. 138.
47. Ibid., pp. 138–39.
48. *Look*, December 18, 1962.
49. Thomas, *Crawford*, p. 226.
50. Vik Greenfield to ES, August 9, 2004.
51. Frye, p. 230.
52. Ibid.
53. Graham, p. 29.
54. Quirk and Schoell, p. 205.
55. Bernhardt, p. 121.
56. Sherman, pp. 200, 218.
57. Thomas, *Crawford*, p. 225.
58. Silver and Ursini, pp. 256–57; Alleman, pp. 92–93.
59. Thomas, *Crawford*, p. 223.
60. Silver and Ursini, p. 24.
61. Bogdanovich, p. 789.
62. Stine and Davis, *Mother Goddam*, p. 290; Davis with Herskowitz, *This 'n That*, pp. 140–41.
63. Warner with Jennings, p. 252.
64. Stine and Davis, *Mother Goddam*, p. 293, quoting *Hollywood Reporter*, undated.
65. USC, Bette Davis legal files: accounting statement dated June 1, 1963.
66. Ibid.: accounting statement dated August 31, 1963.
67. Davis with Herskowitz, *This 'n That*, p. 141.

CHAPTER 21. "SITUATION WANTED"
1. Stine and Davis, *Mother Goddam*, pp. 291–92.
2. Martin Baum to ES, December 1, 2004.
3. Ibid.
4. Stine and Davis, *Mother Goddam*, p. 291.
5. Charles Pollack to ES, August 9, 2004.
6. Davis with Herskowitz, *This 'n That*, p. 141.
7. Wiley and Bona, p. 352.
8. Davis with Herskowitz, *This 'n That*, p. 141.
9. Frye, p. 230.
10. Davis with Herskowitz, *This 'n That*, p. 150.
11. Stine and Davis, *Mother Goddam*, p. 302.
12. Marchant, p. 84.

13. Warren G. Harris, *Loren*, p. 193.
14. AMPAS, Paul Henried Collection, Bette Davis file: Davis to Henreid, September 16, 1963.
15. Marchant, p. 84.
16. "Existential Momism," *Time*, April 17, 1964.
17. Ibid., p. 305.
18. Staggs, *All About*, p. 102.
19. AMPAS, Paul Henried Collection, Bette Davis file: Bette to Paul, August 18, 1964.
20. Silver and Ursini, p. 24.
21. Sauvage, p. 62.
22. Stine and Davis, *Mother Goddam*, pp. 308–9.
23. Silver and Ursini, p. 264.
24. Davis with Herskowitz, *This 'n That*, p. 142.
25. Stine and Davis, *Mother Goddam*, p. 313.
26. Sherman, p. 216.
27. Thomas, *Crawford*, p. 231.
28. Ibid.
29. Davis with Herskowitz, *This 'n That*, p. 144.
30. Arkadin (John Russell Taylor), pp. 151–52.
31. Stine and Davis, *Mother Goddam*, p. 313.
32. Davis with Herskowitz, *This 'n That*, pp. 152–53.
33. Frye, p. 257.
34. BU, scrapbook 59.
35. Davis with Herskowitz, *This 'n That*, pp. 165–66.
36. Ibid., p. 160.
37. BU, scrapbook 79: *Westport News*, June 8, 1973.
38. Davis with Herskowitz, *This 'n That*, p. 161.
39. Intellius.com.
40. Davis with Herskowitz, *This 'n That*, p. 86.
41. Michael Merrill to ES, July 2, 2004.
42. BU, box 1: Bette Davis, as told to Adele Whitely Fletcher, "The Story of Our Daughter, Margot, Retarded!" November 20, 1959 (unedited manuscript).
43. Merrill, p. 201.
44. BU, scrapbook 59: Jerry Asher, "It Could Happen to You," undated clipping.
45. AMPAS, Hedda Hopper Collection, file 506 (Bette Davis).
46. Merrill, pp. 199–200.
47. Davis with Herskowitz, *This 'n That*, p. 164.
48. Vik Greenfield to ES, August 9, 2004.
49. Spada, p. 397.
50. BU, scrapbook 59: *Daily Mirror*, April 1, 1965.
51. Wendy Craig to ES, December 16, 2004.
52. BU, scrapbook 59, unsourced clipping.
53. Arkadin (John Russell Taylor), pp. 151–52.
54. Stine and Davis, *Mother Goddam*, p. 318.

55. O'Toole, "Whatever Happened," p. 170.
56. Alvin Rakoff to ES, November 20, 2003.

CHAPTER 22. LOSSES

1. AMPAS, Paul Henreid Collection, Bette Davis file: letters from Henreid to Davis dated April 15 and May 18, 1955.
2. Baskette, p. 32.
3. Fraser-Cavasson, p. 206.
4. Meyer, p. 197.
5. Edward Albee to ES, July 12, 2006.
6. Interview with Richard Sherman, *San Francisco Chronicle,* December 26, 2005.
7. Lionel Larner to ES, November 3, 2004.
8. Dame Eileen Atkins to ES, October 30, 2003.
9. http://www.michaelgiltz.com/articles/Dominick_Dunne_transcript.htm.
10. The following recollections are from Mart Crowley to ES, May 1, 2006.
11. Lionel Larner to ES, November 3, 2004.
12. Alvin Rakoff to ES, November 20, 2003.
13. The following recollections are all from Vik Greenfield to ES, September 18, 2006.
14. Reggie Schwartzwalder to ES, September 19, 2006.
15. Ellen Hanley to ES, June 2 and July 21, 2006.
16. Don Bachardy to ES, April 12, 2004, and Bachardy, pp. 15–26.
17. Ann Kaufman Schneider to ES, December 6, 2003.
18. Logan, p. 295.
19. Chuck Pollack to ES, August 9, 2004.
20. The following account is from Logan, pp. 296–309, including interview with Rex Reed.
21. Robert Lantz to ES, November 20, 2003.
22. Williamson, p. 80.
23. Gary Springer to ES, September 26, 2004.
24. Anon., "What a Dump," *New Yorker,* February 17, 1973, p. 32.
25. "Bette Davis Launches British Tour," *Times* (London), October 3, 1975.
26. Martha Wallis to ES, February 9, 2006.
27. Margot Webb to ES, December 16, 2004.
28. Gary Springer to ES, September 26, 2004.
29. Riese, p. 384.
30. Mel Gussow, "Bette Davis: One of the First to Look Like 'a Real Person,'" *New York Times,* January 19, 1977.
31. Williamson, p. 88.
32. Vik Greenfield to ES, August 9, 2004.
33. Riese, p. 118.
34. www.findadeath.com.
35. Davis with Herskowitz, *This 'n That,* p. 88.
36. Williamson, p. 88.
37. Davis with Herskowitz, *This 'n That,* pp. 103–6.
38. Stine and Davis, *Mother Goddam,* p. 328.

39. Ibid., p. 331.
40. Ibid., p. 332, quoting *Film Facts*, vol. 19.
41. Vincent Canby, *New York Times*, October 19, 1971.

CHAPTER 23. BETRAYAL

 1. Davis with Herskowitz, *This 'n That*, pp. 77–78.
 2. The following recollections are all from Anthony Harvey to ES, March 31, 2006.
 3. Davis with Herskowitz, *This 'n That*, p. 78.
 4. The following recollections are all from John Guillermin to ES, June 29, 2004.
 5. This anecdote, and all others from Betty Buckley, are from Betty Buckley to ES, October 20, 2004.
 6. John Kuri to ES, October 26, 2004.
 7. Davis with Herskowitz, *This 'n That*, p. 102.
 8. Williamson, pp. 88–90.
 9. Waris Hussein to ES, October 17, 2003.
10. Davis with Herskowitz, *This 'n That*, p. 29.
11. Riese, p. 230.
12. Williamson, p. 79.
13. Chambers, p. 40.
14. Robert Lantz to ES, November 20, 2003.
15. Merrill, p. 256.
16. Charles Pollack to ES, April 4, 2004.
17. Ellen Hanley to ES, July 21, 2006.
18. Chambers, p. 40.
19. *Look*, December 18, 1962.
20. Merrill, p. 257.
21. *Lonely Life*, p. 243.
22. Owens, pp. 6–7.
23. BU, box 1.
24. BU, scrapbook 79; BU, box 4.
25. BU, box 4: 1971 daybook.
26. BU, scrapbook 79.
27. Ibid.
28. Davis with Herskowitz, *This 'n That*, p. 166.
29. Charles Busch to ES, May 26, 2004.
30. Chambers, p. 40.

CHAPTER 24. WAR'S END

 1. This and all other Pollack recollections are from Charles Pollack to ES, April 4 and August 9, 2004.
 2. Dotson Rader to ES, February 17, 2004.
 3. Mart Crowley to ES, May 1, 2006.
 4. Bob Hofler to ES, October 30, 2003.
 5. Charles Pollack to ES, April 4 and August 9, 2004.
 6. James McCourt to ES, January 3, 2005.

7. This and all other Greenfield recollections are from Vik Greenfield to ES, April 4 and August 9, 2004, and September 18, 2006.
8. Martha Wallis to ES, February 9, 2006.
9. Williamson, p. 90.
10. Anthony Harvey to ES, March 31, 2006.
11. Robert Lindsey, "Film Institute Honors Bette Davis," *New York Times*, March 3, 1977.
12. David Galligan to ES, April 2, 2004.
13. Stricklyn, p. 198.
14. "Could Your Husband Take It," *Ladies Home Journal*, April 1942, p. 18.
15. Dickman, pp. 30–31.
16. Leaming, p. 300.
17. Dotson Rader to ES, February 17, 2004.
18. Mart Crowley to ES, May 1, 2006.
19. This and all other Kaplan recollections are from Mike Kaplan to ES, September 22, 2004.
20. Harmetz, p. 621.
21. Gary Springer to ES, September 26, 2004.
22. James McCourt to ES, January 3, 2005.
23. Harmetz, p. 621.
24. Lambert, *Lindsay Anderson*, p. 293.
25. Charles Busch to ES, May 26, 2004.
26. Harmetz, p. 621.
27. Lambert, *Lindsay Anderson*, p. 293.
28. Ibid.

OBITUARY

1. Last Will and Testament of Bette Davis (copy), dated September 2, 1987, and admitted to probate on February 15, 1990.
2. Ken Hall, "Ken's Korner," *Antiques and Collecting Magazine* 108, no. 1 (March 2003): 18, and Heathcliff Rothman, "I'd Really Like to Thank My Pal at the Auction House," *New York Times*, February 12, 2006.

BIBLIOGRAPHY

Affron, Charles. *Lillian Gish: Her Legend, Her Life.* New York: Scribner, 2001.

Aherne, Brian. *A Proper Job.* Boston: Houghton Mifflin, 1969.

Albee, Edward. *Who's Afraid of Virginia Woolf?* New York: Atheneum, 1978.

Aldrich, Robert. "Care and Feeding of 'Baby Jane.' " *New York Times*, November 4, 1962.

Amburn, Ellis. *The Most Beautiful Woman in the World: The Obsessions, Passions, and Courage of Elizabeth Taylor.* New York: HarperCollins, 2000.

———. *The Sexiest Man Alive: A Biography of Warren Beatty.* New York: Harper-Collins, 2002.

Andersen, Christopher. *An Affair to Remember: The Remarkable Love Story of Katharine Hepburn and Spencer Tracy.* New York: William Morrow, 1997.

———. *A Star, Is a Star, Is a Star! The Lives and Loves of Susan Hayward.* Garden City, N.Y.: Doubleday, 1980.

Ankerich, Michael G. *Broken Silence: Conversations with 23 Silent Film Stars.* Jefferson, N.C.: McFarland, 1993.

Ann-Margret, with Todd Gold. *My Story.* New York: G. P. Putnam's Sons, 1994.

Anon. "B. D. Merrill: Bette Davis's Daughter." *Look*, December 18, 1962.

———. "Freedom Fighter." *Economist*, October 14, 1989, p. 107.

———. "Life Goes to a Birthday Party." *Life*, April 28, 1941, pp. 127–29.

———. "Movie of the Week: *All This and Heaven Too.*" *Life*, July 1, 1940.

———. "Movie of the Week: *The Old Maid.*" *Life*, August 21, 1939, pp. 58–59.

———. "Popeye the Magnificent." *Time*, March 28, 1938, pp. 33–36.

Arkadin (John Russell Taylor). "Film Clips." *Sight and Sound*, Summer 1965, pp. 151–52.

Arliss, George. *By Himself*. London: John Murray, 1940.

Arnold, Edwin T., and Eugene L. Miller. *The Films and Career of Robert Aldrich*. Knoxville: University of Tennessee Press, 1986.

Astor, Mary. *A Life on Film*. New York: Delacorte Press, 1967.

———. *My Story: An Autobiography*. Garden City, N.Y.: Doubleday, 1959.

Babener, Liahna. "Haywire in Hollywood." *Journal of Popular Film and Television* (Winter 1989): 138–47.

Bachardy, Don. *Stars in My Eyes*. Madison: University of Wisconsin Press, 2000.

Baldwin, James. *The Devil Finds Work*. New York: Dell, 2000.

Bankhead, Tallulah. *Tallulah: My Autobiography*. London: Victor Gollancz, 1952.

Barrymore, Lionel, and Cameron Shipp. *We Barrymores*. New York: Appleton-Century-Crofts, 1951.

Bartlett, Donald J., and James B. Steele. *Empire: The Life, Legend, and Madness of Howard Hughes*. New York: W. W. Norton, 1979.

Baskette, Kirtley. "Bette Davis' Biggest Victory." *Good Housekeeping*, August 1963, pp. 30–38.

Beaver, James N., Jr. *John Garfield: His Life and Films*. South Brunswick, N.J.: A. S. Barnes, 1978.

Behlmer, Rudy. *Inside Warner Bros*. New York: Simon and Schuster, 1985.

———. *Memo from David O. Selznick*. New York: Grove Press, 1972.

Berg, A. Scott. "Bette Davis: Best Actress for *Jezebel* and *Dangerous* at Witch Way." *Architectural Digest*, April 1990, pp. 248–49, 310.

———. *Goldwyn: A Biography*. New York: Ballantine Books, 1989.

———. *Kate Remembered*. New York: G. P. Putnam's Sons, 2003.

Bergman, Andrew. *James Cagney*. New York: Galahad Books, 1973.

Bernhardt, Curtis, and Mary Kiersch. *Curtis Bernhardt: A Directors Guild of America Oral History*. Metuchen, N.J.: Scarecrow Press, 1986.

Bernstein, Walter. *Inside Out: A Memoir of the Blacklist*. New York: Alfred A. Knopf, 1996.

Billingsley, Kenneth Lloyd. *Hollywood Party: How Communism Seduced the American Film Industry in the 1930s and 1940s*. Rocklin, Calif.: Forum/Prima, 1998.

Birdwell, Michael E. *Celluloid Soldiers: Warner Bros.'s Campaign Against Nazism*. New York: New York University Press, 1999.

Bishop, Jim. *The Mark Hellinger Story*. New York: Appleton-Century-Crofts, 1952.

Bogart, Stephen Humphrey. *Bogart: In Search of My Father*. New York: Penguin Books, 1995.

Bogdanovich, Peter. *Who the Devil Made It*. New York: Alfred A. Knopf, 1997.

Boller, Paul F., and Ronald L. Davis. *Hollywood Anecdotes*. New York: William Morrow, 1987.

Bonanino, Margaret Wander. *Angela Lansbury: A Biography*. New York: St. Martin's Press, 1987.

Brochu, Jim. *Lucy in the Afternoon: An Intimate Memoir of Lucille Ball*. New York: William Morrow, 1990.

Brophy, Brigid. *Don't Never Forget*. New York: Holt, Rinehart and Winston, 1966.

Brouwer, Alexandra, and Thomas Lee Wright. *Working in Hollywood*. New York: Crown, 1990.

Brown, Peter Henry, and Pat H. Broeske. *Howard Hughes: The Untold Story*. New York: Dutton/Penguin Group, 1996.

Bruck, Connie. *When Hollywood Had a King: The Reign of Lew Wasserman, Who Leveraged Talent Into Power and Influence*. New York: Random House, 2003.

Buford, Kate. *Burt Lancaster: An American Life*. New York: Alfred A. Knopf, 2000.

Buhle, Paul, and Dave Wagner. *Radical Hollywood: The Untold Story Behind America's Favorite Movies*. New York: New Press, 2002.

Busch, Noel F. "Bette Davis." *Life*, January 23, 1939, pp. 52–58.

Cagney, James. *Cagney by Cagney*. Garden City, N.Y.: Doubleday, 1976.

Caine, Michael. *What's It All About*. London: Century, 1992.

Callahan, Dan. "The Letter." ToxicUniverse.com, December 23, 2003: www.toxicuniverse.com/review.php?rid=10005377.

Callahan, North. *Carl Sandburg: Lincoln of Our Literature*. New York: New York University Press, 1970.

Campo, Carlos. "The Role of *Beyond the Forest* in Albee's *Who's Afraid of Virginia Woolf? Film Literature Quarterly* 22, no. 3 (1994).

Capra, Frank. *The Name Above the Title*. New York, Macmillan, 1971.

Cavell, Stanley. "Ugly Duckling, Funny Butterfly: Bette Davis and *Now, Voyager*." *Critical Inquiry* (Winter 1990): 213–47.

Chambers, Andrea. "All About Bette." *People*, May 6, 1985, p. 40.

Chase, Ilka. *Free Admission*. Garden City, N.Y.: Doubleday, 1948.

Chierichetti, David. *Edith Head: The Life and Times of Hollywood's Celebrated Costume Designer*. New York: HarperCollins, 2003.

Christy, George. "Bette Davis and the White Extension Cord." *Interview*, July 1986, pp. 92–93.

Coghlan, Frank "Junior." *They Still Call Me Junior: Autobiography of a Child Star; with a Filmography*. Jefferson, N.C.: McFarland, 1993.

Collins, Joan. *Second Act*. New York: St. Martin's Press, 1996.

Considine, Shaun. *Mad as Hell: The Life and Work of Paddy Chayefsky*. New York: Random House, 1994.

Cooper, Jackie, with Dick Kleiner. *Please Don't Shoot My Dog*. New York: William Morrow, 1981.

Corwin, Norman. *The World of Carl Sandburg: A Stage Production*. New York: Harcourt, Brace and World, 1961.

Cotten, Joseph. *Vanity Will Get You Somewhere: An Autobiography*. San Francisco: Mercury House, 1987.

Cotton, Patricia Medina. *Laid Back in Hollywood*. Los Angeles: Belle, 1998.

Crawford, Joan. *My Way of Life*. New York: Simon and Schuster, 1971.

Crawford, Joan, with Jane Kesner Ardmore. *A Portrait of Joan: The Autobiography of Joan Crawford*. Garden City, N.Y.: Doubleday, 1962.

Cunningham, Ernest W. *The Ultimate Bogart*. Los Angeles: Renaissance Books, 1999.

Custen, George F. *Twentieth Century's Fox: Darryl F. Zanuck and the Culture of Hollywood*. New York: Basic Books, 1997.

Davis, Bette. "The Actress Plays Her Part." In *We Make the Movies*, ed. Nancy Naumberg. New York: W. W. Norton, 1937.

———. *The Lonely Life: An Autobiography*. New York: G. P. Putnam's Sons, 1962.

———. "Uncertain Glory." *Ladies' Home Journal*, July 1941, pp. 16–17, 107–22.

———. "When I Was Sixteen." *Good Housekeeping*, October 1968, p. 99.

Davis, Bette, with Bill Davidson. "All About Me." *Colliers*, November 25, 1955, pp. 27–29, 98–101, and December 9, 1955, pp. 36–40, 44–46.

Davis, Bette, with Michael Herskowitz. *This 'n That*. New York: G. P. Putnam's Sons, 1987.

Davis, Ronald L. *The Glamour Factory: Inside Hollywood's Big Studio System*. Dallas: Southern Methodist University Press, 1993.

Dewey, Donald. *James Stewart: A Biography*. Atlanta: Turner, 1996.

Dickman, Ken. "This Is Bette Davis! How Did You Get My Number?" *Advocate*, February 9, 1977, pp. 30–31.

DiOrio, Al. *Barbara Stanwyck*. New York: Coward-McGann, 1983.

Dmytryk, Edward. *It's a Hell of a Life but Not a Bad Living*. New York: Times Books, 1978.

Dody, Sandford. *Giving Up the Ghost: A Writer's Life Among the Stars*. New York: M. Evans, 1980.

Donati, William. *Ida Lupino: A Biography*. Lexington: University Press of Mississippi, 1996.

Dunaway, Faye, with Betsy Sharkey. *Looking for Gatsby: My Life*. New York: Simon and Schuster, 1995.

Dunning, John. *On the Air: The Encyclopedia of Old-Time Radio*. New York: Oxford University Press, 1998.

———. *Tune in Yesterday: The Ultimate Encyclopedia of Old-Time Radio 1925–1976*. Englewood Cliffs, N.J.: Prentice-Hall, 1976.

Durgnat, Raymond, and Scott Simmon. *King Vidor: American*. Berkeley: University of California Press, 1988.

Edelman, Rob, and Audrey E. Kupferberg. *Angela Lansbury: A Life on Stage and Screen*. New York: Birch Lane Press, 1996.

Edwards, Anne. *A Remarkable Woman: A Biography of Katharine Hepburn*. New York: William Morrow, 1985.

Eells, George. *Final Gig*. San Diego: Harcourt Brace Jovanovich, 1991.

Elliott, Susan, with Barry Turner. *Denholm Elliott: Quest for Love*. London: Headline, 1995.

Eyles, Allen. *James Stewart*. Thorndike, Maine: Thorndike Press, 1984. Large-print edition.

Eyman, Scott. *Print the Legend: The Life and Times of John Ford*. New York: Simon and Schuster, 1999.

Fairbanks, Douglas, Jr. *The Salad Days: An Autobiography*. Garden City, N.Y.: Doubleday, 1988.

Finler, Joel W. *The Hollywood Story*. New York: Crown, 1988.

Finstad, Suzanne. *Natasha: The Biography of Natalie Wood*. New York: Harmony Books, 2001.

Fishgall, Gary. *Gregory Peck: A Biography*. New York: Lisa Drew/Scribner, 2002.

———. *Pieces of Time: The Life of James Stewart*. New York: Scribner, 1997.

Flanner, Janet. "Cotton-Dress Girl." *New Yorker*, February 20, 1943, pp. 19–25.

Flynn, Errol. *My Wicked, Wicked Ways*. New York: G. P. Putnam's Sons, 1959.

Fonda, Henry, and Howard Teichmann. *My Life*. New York: New American Library, 1981.

Fowler, Karin J. *Anne Baxter: A Bio-Bibliography*. Westport, Conn.: Greenwood Press, 1991.

———. *David Niven: A Bio-Bibliography*. Westport, Conn.: Greenwood Press, 1995.

Francisco, Charles. *Gentleman: The William Powell Story*. New York: St. Martin's Press, 1985.

Frank, Sam. *Ronald Colman: A Bio-Bibliography*. Westport, Conn.: Greenwood Press, 1997.

Fraser-Cavasson, Natasha. *Sam Spiegel*. New York: Simon and Schuster, 2003.

Freedland, Michael. *Errol Flynn*. London: Arthur Barker, 1978.

———. *The Two Lives of Errol Flynn*. New York: William Morrow, 1979.

———. *The Warner Brothers*. New York: St. Martin's Press, 1983.

Friedrich, Otto. *City of Nets: A Portrait of Hollywood in the 1940s*. New York: Harper and Row, 1986.

Frye, William. "The Devil in Miss Davis." *Vanity Fair*, April 2001, pp. 222–36, 257.

Fuller, Samuel, with Christa Lang Fuller and Jerome Henry Rudes. *A Third Face: My Tale of Writing, Fighting, and Filmmaking*. New York: Alfred A. Knopf, 2002.

Fultz, Jay. *In Search of Donna Reed*. Iowa City: University of Iowa Press, 1998.

Gabler, Neal. *An Empire of Their Own: How the Jews Invented Hollywood*. New York: Crown, 1988.

Gansberg, Alan L. *Little Caesar: A Biography of Edward G. Robinson*. Kent, England: New English Library, 1983.

Gardner, Ava. *Ava: My Story*. New York: Bantam Books, 1990.

Garfield, Kim. "All About Bette." *Advocate*, March 27, 1990, pp. 60–62.

Geist, Kenneth L. *Pictures Will Talk: The Life and Times of Joseph L. Mankiewicz*. New York: Charles Scribner's Sons, 1978.

Gelman, Barbara, ed. *Photoplay Treasury*. New York: Crown, 1972.

Gill, Brendan. *Tallulah*. New York: Holt, Rinehart and Winston, 1972.

Goldberg, Lee. *Unsold TV Pilots: The Almost Complete Guide to Everything You Never Saw on TV*. New York: Citadel Press, 1991.

Golden, Harry. *Carl Sandburg*. Cleveland: World, 1961.

Goodman, Ezra. *The Fifty-Year Decline and Fall of Hollywood*. New York: Simon and Schuster, 1961.

Goodman, Susan. *Ellen Glasgow: A Biography*. Baltimore: Johns Hopkins University Press, 1998.

Goodwin, Cliff. *Evil Spirits: The Life of Oliver Reed*. London: Virgin Books, 2000.

Graham, Sheilah. *Hollywood Revisited*. New York: St. Martin's Press, 1984.

Gray, Beverly. *Ron Howard: From Mayberry to the Moon . . . and Beyond*. Nashville: Rutledge Hill Press, 2003.

Greenberg, Joel. "Interview with Robert Aldrich." *Sight and Sound*, Winter 1968–69, pp. 8–13. Reprinted in *Robert Aldrich Interviews*, ed. Eugene L. Miller Jr. and Edwin T. Arnold, Jackson: University Press of Mississippi, 2004.

Grobel, Lawrence. *The Hustons*. New York: Charles Scribner's Sons, 1989.

Guiles, Fred Lawrence. *Marion Davies*. New York: McGraw-Hill, 1972.

Gussow, Mel. *Don't Say Yes Until I Finish Talking: A Biography of Darryl F. Zanuck.* Garden City, N.Y.: Doubleday, 1971.

——. *Edward Albee: A Singular Journey.* New York: Simon and Schuster, 1999.

Hack, Richard. *Hughes: The Private Diaries, Memos and Letters.* Beverly Hills: New Millennium Press, 2001.

Hadleigh, Boze. *Bette Davis Speaks.* Fort Lee, N.J.: Barricade Books, 1996.

Hancock, Sheila. *Ramblings of an Actress.* London: Hutchinson, 1987.

Hanson, Patricia King, ed. *The American Film Institute Catalog of Motion Pictures Produced in the United States, Feature Films, 1931–1940.* Berkeley: University of California Press, 1993.

——. *The American Film Institute Catalog of Motion Pictures Produced in the United States, Feature Films, 1941–1950.* Berkeley: University of California Press, 1999.

Harmetz, Aljean. "Placating the Stars of 'Whales.'" *New York Times*, October 22, 1987.

Harris, Daniel. "The Death of Camp: Gay Men and Hollywood Diva Worship, from Reverence to Ridicule." *Salmagundi* (Fall 1996): 166–91.

Harris, Warren G. *Lucy and Desi: The Legendary Love Story of Television's Most Famous Couple.* New York: Simon and Schuster, 1991.

——. *Natalie and R.J.: Hollywood's Star-Crossed Lovers.* New York: Doubleday, 1988.

——. *Sophia Loren: A Biography.* New York: Simon and Schuster, 1998.

Hassett, William D. *Off the Record with FDR, 1942–1945.* New Brunswick, N.J.: Rutgers University Press, 1958.

Hayes, Helen, with Katherine Hatch. *My Life in Three Acts.* San Diego: Harcourt Brace Jovanovich/Helen and Kurt Wolff, 1990.

Hazlitt, William. *Selected Essays of William Hazlitt.* New York: Random House, 1948.

Head, Edith, with Jane Kesner Ardmore. *The Dress Doctor.* Boston: Little, Brown, 1959.

Head, Edith, and Paddy Calistro. *Edith Head's Hollywood.* New York: E. P. Dutton, 1983.

Heimann, Jim. *Out with the Stars: Hollywood Nightlife in the Golden Era.* New York: Abbeville Press, 1985.

Henreid, Paul, with Julius Fast. *Ladies' Man: An Autobiography.* New York: St. Martin's Press, 1984.

Herman, Jan. *A Talent for Trouble: The Life of Hollywood's Most Acclaimed Director, William Wyler.* New York: G. P. Putnam's Sons, 1995.

Heymann, C. David. *Liz: An Intimate Biography of Elizabeth Taylor.* New York: Birch Land Press, 1995.

Higham, Charles. *Bette: The Life of Bette Davis.* New York: Macmillan, 1981.

——. *Errol Flynn: The Untold Story.* Garden City, N.Y.: Doubleday, 1980.

——. *Lucy: The Life of Lucille Ball.* New York: St. Martin's Press, 1986.

——. *Sisters: The Story of Olivia de Havilland and Joan Fontaine.* New York: Coward-McCann, 1984.

Higham, Charles, and Joel Greenberg. *The Celluloid Muse.* London: Angus and Robertson, 1969.

Hill, Ona L. *Raymond Burr: A Film, Radio and Television Biography*. Jefferson, N.C.: McFarland, 1994.

Holston, Kim R. *Susan Hayward: Her Films and Life*. Jefferson, N.C.: McFarland, 2002.

Hoopes, Roy. *When the Stars Went to War: Hollywood and World War II*. New York: Random House, 1994.

Hopper, Hedda. "Welcome Stranger." *Modern Screen*, August 1947, pp. 35, 104–6.

Hopper, Hedda, and James Brough. *The Whole Truth and Nothing But*. Garden City, N.Y.: Doubleday, 1963.

Howard, Leslie Ruth. *A Quite Remarkable Father*. New York: Harcourt, Brace, 1959.

Hunt, George. "Of Many Things." *America* 161, no. 11 (October 21, 1989): p. 250.

Hunter, Allan. *Alec Guinness on Screen*. Edinburgh: Polygon Books, 1982.

Hunter, Jack. *House of Horror: The Complete Hammer Films Story*. London: Creation Books, 2000.

Huston, John. *An Open Book*. New York: Alfred A. Knopf, 1980.

Hyman, B. D. *My Mother's Keeper*. New York: William Morrow, 1985.

Ibsen, Henrik. *Ibsen: Four Major Plays*. Vol. 1. New York: Signet, 1992.

Israel, Lee. *Miss Tallulah Bankhead*. New York: G. P. Putnam's Sons, 1972.

Jackson, Carlton. *Hattie: The Life of Hattie McDaniel*. Lanham, Md.: Madison Books, 1990.

Johnson, Nora. *Flashback: Nora Johnson on Nunnally Johnson*. Garden City, N.Y.: Doubleday, 1979.

Kaminsky, Stuart. *John Huston: Maker of Magic*. Boston: Houghton Mifflin, 1978.

Kanfer, Stefan. *Ball of Fire: The Tumultuous Life and Comic Art of Lucille Ball*. New York: Alfred A. Knopf, 2003.

Kanin, Garson. *Remembering Mr. Maugham*. New York: Atheneum, 1966.

———. *Tracy and Hepburn*. New York: Viking Press, 1970.

Katz, Ephraim. *The Film Encyclopedia*. New York: HarperCollins, 1994.

Kear, Lynn. *Agnes Moorehead: A Bio-Bibliography*. Westport, Conn.: Greenwood Press, 1992.

Kelley, Kitty. *Elizabeth Taylor: The Last Star*. New York: Simon and Schuster, 1981.

Kempson, Rachel. *Life Among the Redgraves*. New York: William Abrahams/E. P. Dutton, 1986.

Kennedy, Matthew. *Edmund Goulding's Dark Victory*. Madison: University of Wisconsin Press, 2004.

Kernberg, Otto. *Severe Personality Disorders: Psychotherapeutic Strategies*. New Haven, Conn.: Yale University Press, 1986.

Kinsey, Wayne. *Hammer Films: The Bray Studio Years*. London: Reynolds and Hearn, 2002.

Klaprat, Cathy. "The Star as Market Strategy: Bette Davis in Another Light." In *The American Film Industry*, ed. Tino Balio, pp. 351–76. Madison: University of Wisconsin Press, 1985.

Kobal, John. *People Will Talk*. New York: Alfred A. Knopf, 1985.

Kolin, Philip C., ed. *Conversations with Edward Albee*. Jackson: University Press of Mississippi, 1988.

Koster, Henry, and Irene Kahn Atkins. *Henry Koster: A Directors Guild of America Oral History*. Metuchen, N.J.: Scarecrow Press, 1987.

Laffel, Jeff. "Interview with John Springer." *Films in Review*, January–February 1993, pp. 2–7, and March–April 1990, pp. 94–106.

LaGuardia, Robert, and Gene Arceri. *Red: The Tempestuous Life of Susan Hayward*. New York: Macmillan, 1985.

Lamarr, Hedy. *Ecstasy and Me: My Life as a Woman*. New York: Bartholomew House, 1966.

Lambert, Gavin. *Mainly About Lindsay Anderson*. New York: Alfred A. Knopf, 2000.

———. *Natalie Wood: A Life*. New York: Alfred A. Knopf, 2004.

———. *Norma Shearer: A Life*. New York: Alfred A. Knopf, 1990.

———. "Portrait of an Actress: Bette Davis." *Sight and Sound*, August–September 1951, pp. 12–19.

Lawrence, Greg. *Dance with Demons: The Life of Jerome Robbins*. New York: G. P. Putnam's Sons, 2001.

Lawrence, Jerome. *Actor: The Life and Times of Paul Muni*. New York: G. P. Putnam's Sons, 1974.

Leaming, Barbara. *Bette Davis: A Biography*. New York: Simon and Schuster, 1992.

Lee, Sonia. "The Untold Story of Bette Davis." *Screen Play*, November 1935, pp. 32–33, 57.

Leonard, William Torbert. *Broadway Bound: A Guide to Shows That Died Aborning*. Metuchen, N.J.: Scarecrow Press, 1983.

LeRoy, Mervyn, and Dick Kleiner. *Mervyn LeRoy: Take One*. New York: Hawthorn Books, 1974.

Levy, Shawn. *King of Comedy: The Life and Art of Jerry Lewis*. New York: St. Martin's Press, 1996.

Linet, Beverly. *Ladd: A Biography*. New York: Arbor House, 1979.

———. *Susan Hayward: Portrait of a Survivor*. New York: Atheneum, 1980.

Lippman, Theo, Jr. *The Squire of Warm Springs: FDR in Georgia, 1924–1945*. Chicago: Playboy Press, 1977.

Logan, Joshua. *Movie Stars, Real People, and Me*. New York: W. W. Norton, 1978.

Long, Robert Emmet. *George Cukor Interviews*. Jackson: University of Mississippi Press, 2001.

Lord, Graham. *Niv: The Authorised Biography of David Niven*. London: Orion Books, 2003.

Loy, Myrna, and James Kotsilibas-Davis. *Myrna Loy: Being and Becoming*. New York: Alfred A. Knopf, 1987.

Madsen, Axel. *Barbara Stanwyck*. New York: Coward-McCann, 1983.

Malcolm, Janet. *The Silent Woman: Sylvia Plath and Ted Hughes*. New York: Vintage Books, 1995.

Mandelbaum, Howard, and Eric Myers. *Forties Screen Style: A Celebration of High Pastiche in Hollywood*. New York: St. Martin's Press, 1989.

Mann, William J. *Behind the Screen: How Gays and Lesbians Shaped Hollywood, 1910–1969*. New York: Viking Press, 2001.

———. "Butchered Bette." *Metroline*, October 28, 1992, p. 37.

Marchant, William. "Lesson in Survival." *Holiday*, August 1964, pp. 83–86.

Marill, Alvin H. *Movies Made for Television*. New York: Zoetrope, 1987.

Marx, Arthur. *Goldwyn*. New York: W. W. Norton, 1976.

———. "In Hollywood, You Don't Get Mad . . ." *Los Angeles*, November 1988, pp. 206–11.

Maxford, Howard. *Hammer, House of Horror: Behind the Screams*. Woodstock, N.Y.: Overlook Press, 1996.

Maychick, Diana, and L. Aron Borgo. *Heart to Heart with Robert Wagner*. New York: St. Martin's Press, 1986.

McBride, Joseph. *Filmmakers on Filmmaking*. Vol. 2. Los Angeles: J. P. Tarcher, 1983.

———. *Frank Capra: The Catastrophe of Success*. New York: Simon and Schuster, 1992.

———. *Searching for John Ford: A Life*. New York: St. Martin's Press, 2001.

McCarthy, Todd. *Howard Hawks: The Grey Fox of Hollywood*. New York: Grove Press, 1997.

McCarty, John, and Brian Kelleher. *Alfred Hitchcock Presents*. New York: St. Martin's Press, 1985.

McCourt, James. "Davis." *Film Comment*, March/April, 1978, pp. 46–48.

———. *Queer Street: Rise and Fall of an American Culture, 1947–1985*. New York: W. W. Norton, 2004.

McDonagh, Don. *Martha Graham: A Biography*. New York: Praeger, 1973.

McDougal, Dennis. *The Last Mogul*. New York: Da Capo Press, 1998.

McGee, Tom. *Betty Grable: The Girl with the Million Dollar Legs*. Vestal, N.Y.: Vestal Press, 1995.

McGilligan, Patrick, ed. *Backstory. 1: Interviews with Screenwriters of Hollywood's Golden Age*. Berkeley: University of California Press, 1986.

———, ed. *Backstory 2: Interviews with Screenwriters of the 1940s and 1950s*. Berkeley: University of California Press, 1991.

———. *Film Crazy: Interviews with Hollywood Legends*. New York: St. Martin's Press, 2000.

McGilligan, Patrick, and Paul Buhle. *Tender Comrades: A Backstory of the Hollywood Blacklist*. New York: St. Martin's Press, 1997.

Meikle, Denis. *A History of Horrors: The Rise and Fall of the House of Hammer*. Lanham, Md.: Scarecrow Press, 1996.

Menard, Wilmon. "Somerset Maugham in Hollywood." *Michigan Quarterly Review* 7, no. 3 (July 1968).

Merrill, Gary. *Bette, Rita, and the Rest of My Life*. Augusta, Maine: Lance Tapley, 1988.

Meyer, William R. *Warner Brothers Directors*. New Rochelle, N.Y.: Arlington House, 1978.

Meyers, Jeffrey. *Bogart: A Life in Hollywood*. New York: Fromm International, 1997.

———. *Inherited Risk: Errol and Sean Flynn in Hollywood and Vietnam*. New York: Simon and Schuster, 2002.

Miller, Eugene L., and Edwin T. Miller. *Robert Aldrich Interviews*. Jackson: University of Mississippi Press, 2004.

Mills, John. *Up in the Clouds, Gentlemen Please*. New York: Ticknor and Fields, 1981.

Mitgang, Herbert, ed. *The Letters of Carl Sandburg*. New York: Harcourt Brace Jovanovich, 1988.

Morella, Joe, and Edward Z. Epstein. *Jane Wyman: A Biography*. New York: Delacorte Press, 1985.

Morgan, Ted. *Maugham*. New York: Simon and Schuster, 1980.

Morley, Sheridan. *Gladys Cooper*. New York: McGraw-Hill, 1979.

———. *The Other Side of the Moon: A Biography of David Niven*. New York: Harper and Row, 1985.

———. *Tales from the Hollywood Raj*. New York: Viking Press, 1983.

Mosley, Leonard. *Zanuck: The Rise and Fall of Hollywood's Last Tycoon*. Boston: Little, Brown, 1984.

Mothner, Ira. "The Pro." *Look*, March 9, 1965, pp. 20–24.

Munn, Michael. *Charlton Heston: A Biography*. New York: St. Martin's Press, 1986.

Neal, Patricia, with Richard DeNeut. *As I Am: An Autobiography*. New York: Simon and Schuster, 1988.

Newquist, Roy. *Conversations with Joan Crawford*. New York: Berkley Books, 1981.

Niven, Penelope. *Carl Sandburg: A Biography*. New York: Charles Scribner's Sons, 1991.

Nott, Robert. *He Ran All the Way: The Life of John Garfield*. New York: Limelight, 2003.

O'Brien, Pat. *The Wind at My Back*. Garden City, N.Y.: Doubleday, 1964.

O'Connor, Gary. *Alec Guinness, The Unknown: A Life*. London: Sidgwick and Jackson, 2002.

Oderman, Stuart. *Lillian Gish: A Life on Stage and Screen*. Jefferson, N.C.: McFarland, 2000.

O'Toole, Lawrence. "Bette Davis." *Us*, May 1, 1989, pp. 40–45.

———. "Whatever Happened to Bette Davis?" *Sight and Sound*, Summer 1990, pp. 168–70.

Owens, Don. "Meeting a Legendary Dame." *Hollywood Studio Magazine*, January 1990, pp. 6–7.

Parish, James Robert, and Steven Whitney. *Vincent Price: Unmasked*. New York: Drake, 1974.

Parker, John. *Five for Hollywood*. New York: Carol Publishing Group, 1991.

Perry, Lilla S. *My Friend Carl Sandburg: The Biography of a Friendship*. Metuchen, N.J.: Scarecrow Press, 1981.

Peters, Margot. *Design for Living: Alfred Lunt and Lynn Fontanne—A Biography*. New York: Alfred A. Knopf, 2003.

———. *The House of Barrymore*. New York: Alfred A. Knopf, 1990.

Pickard, Roy. *Jimmy Stewart: A Life in Film*. New York: St. Martin's Press, 1992.

Powell, Hickman. *Ninety Times Guilty*. New York: Harcourt, Brace, 1939.

Price, Victoria. *Vincent Price: A Daughter's Biography*. New York: St. Martin's Press, 1999.

Prouty, Olive Higgins. *Pencil Shavings*. Cambridge, Mass.: Riverside Press, 1961.

Quirk Lawrence J. *Claudette Colbert: An Illustrated Biography*. New York: Crown, 1985.

———. *Fasten Your Seat Belts: The Passionate Life of Bette Davis*. New York: William Morrow, 1990.

———. *James Stewart: Behind the Scenes of a Wonderful Life*. New York: Applause, 1997.

———. *Norma: The Story of Norma Shearer*. New York: St. Martin's Press, 1988.

Quirk, Lawrence J., and William Schoell. *Joan Crawford: The Essential Biography*. Lexington: University Press of Kentucky, 2002.

Read, Piers Paul. *Alec Guinness: The Authorised Biography*. London: Simon and Schuster, 2003.

Reagan, Ronald, with Richard G. Hubber. *Where's the Rest of Me?: The Autobiography of Ronald Reagan*. New York: Katz, 1981.

Reed, Oliver. *Reed All About Me*. London: W. H. Allen, 1979.

Reynolds, Debbie. *Debbie: My Life*. New York: William Morrow, 1988.

Riese, Randall. *All About Bette: Her Life from A to Z*. Chicago: Contemporary Books, 1993.

Rimoldi, Oscar A. "Interview with Vincent Sherman." *Hollywood Studio Magazine*, May 1990, pp. 15–17, and June 1990, pp. 16–19, 36.

Robbins, Jhan. *Everybody's Man: A Biography of Jimmy Stewart*. New York: G. P. Putnam's Sons, 1985.

Roberts, Randy, and James G. Olson. *John Wayne: American*. New York: Free Press, 1995.

Robinson, David J. *Disordered Personalities*. Port Huron, Mich.: Rapid Psychler Press, 1999.

Robinson, Edward G., with Leonard Spigelgass. *All My Yesterdays: An Autobiography*. New York: Hawthorn Books, 1973.

Rogers, Ginger. *Ginger: My Story*. New York: HarperCollins, 1991.

Rogers, Peter. *What Becomes a Legend Most?: The Blackglama Story*. New York: Simon and Schuster, 1979.

Rogers St. Johns, Adela. "The Hollywood Story: Bette Davis' Darkest Hour." *American Weekly*, August 5, 1951, pp. 8–9.

Rollyson, Carl. *Lillian Hellman: Her Legend and Her Legacy*. New York: St. Martin's Press, 1988.

Sauvage, Pierre. "Aldrich Interview." *Movie*, Winter 1976–77.

Schaefer, George. *From Live to Tape to Film: Sixty Years of Inconspicuous Directing*. Los Angeles: DGA, 1996.

Schatz, Thomas. *The Genius of the System*. New York: Pantheon Books, 1988.

Schultz, Margie. *Ann Sheridan: A Bio-Bibliography*. Westport, Conn.: Greenwood Press, 1997.

Shapiro, David. *Neurotic Styles*. New York: Basic Books, 1965.

Sharp, Kathleen. *Mr. and Mrs. Hollywood: Edie and Lew Wasserman and Their Entertainment Empire*. New York: Carroll and Graf, 2003.

Sherman, Vincent. *Studio Affairs: My Life as a Film Director*. Lexington: University Press of Kentucky, 1996.

Shingler, Martin. "Bette Davis: Malevolence in Motion." In *Screen Acting*, ed. Alan Lovell and Peter Krämer. London: Routledge, 1999.

———. "Breathtaking: Bette Davis's Performance at the End of *Now, Voyager*." *Journal of Film and Video* (Spring/Summer 2006): 46–58.

———. "The Fourth Warner Brother and Her Role in the War." *Journal of American Studies* (April 1996): 127–31.

———. "Interpreting *All About Eve*: A Study in Historical Reception." In *Hollywood Spectatorship*, ed. Melvyn Stokes and Richard Maltby. London: British Film Institute, 2001.

———. "Masquerade or Drag? Bette Davis and the Ambiguities of Gender." *Screen*, Autumn 1995, pp. 179–92.

Sikov, Ed. "Bette Davis," *Architectural Digest*, March 2006, pp. 154–58, 250.

Silver, Alain, and James Ursini. *What Ever Happened to Robert Aldrich? His Life and Films*. New York: Limelight, 1995.

Slide, Anthony. *The American Film Industry*. New York: Limelight, 1990.

Soister, John T., with JoAnna Wioskowski. *Claude Rains: A Comprehensive Illustrated Reference to His Work in Film, Stage, Radio, Television and Recordings*. Jefferson, N.C.: McFarland, 1999.

Spada, James. *More than a Woman: An Intimate Biography of Bette Davis*. New York: Bantam Books, 1993.

———. *Peter Lawford: The Man Who Kept the Secrets*. New York: Bantam Books, 1991.

Sperber, A. M., and Eric Lax. *Bogart*. New York: William Morrow, 1997.

Sperling, Cass Warner, and Cork Millner, with Jack Warner Jr. *Hollywood Be Thy Name: The Warner Brothers Story*. Rocklin, Calif.: Prima, 1994.

Spoto, Donald. *The Kindness of Strangers: The Life of Tennessee Williams*. Boston: Little, Brown, 1985.

———. *Notorious: The Life of Ingrid Bergman*. New York: HarperCollins, 1997.

Stack, Robert, with Mark Evans. *Straight Shooting*. New York: Macmillan, 1980.

Staggs, Sam. *All About "All About Eve."* New York: St. Martin's Press, 2000.

———. "Everything about Eve." *Vanity Fair*, April 1999, pp. 284–94, 302–6.

Stapleton, Maureen, and Jane Scovell. *A Hell of a Life: An Autobiography*. New York: Simon and Schuster, 1995.

Steen, Mike. *Hollywood Speaks! An Oral History*. New York: G. P. Putnam's Sons, 1974.

Stempel, Tom. *Screenwriter: Nunnally Johnson*. San Diego: A. S. Barnes, 1980.

Stine, Whitney. *"I'd Love to Kiss You . . .": Conversations with Bette Davis*. New York: Pocket Books, 1990.

Stine, Whitney, and Bette Davis. *Mother Goddam: The Story of the Career of Bette Davis*. New York: Hawthorn Books, 1974.

Stricklyn, Ray. *Angels and Demons: One Actor's Hollywood Journey*. Los Angeles: Belle, 1999.

Styron, William. "Mrs. Aadland's Little Girl, Beverly." *Esquire*, November 1961, p. 142.

Suskin, Steven. *More Opening Nights on Broadway*. New York: Schirmer Books, 1997.

Swanson, Gloria. *Swanson on Swanson*. New York: Random House, 1980.

Swindell, Larry. *Body and Soul: The Story of John Garfield*. New York: William Morrow, 1975.

———. *Charles Boyer: The Reluctant Lover*. Garden City, N.Y.: Doubleday, 1983.

———. *Spencer Tracy: A Biography*. New York: New American Library, 1969.

Tannen, Lee. *I Loved Lucy: My Friendship with Lucille Ball*. New York: St. Martin's Press, 2001.

Taylor, John Russell. *Alec Guinness: A Celebration*. Boston: Little, Brown, 1984.

Thomas, Bob. *Clown Prince of Hollywood: The Antic Life and Times of Jack L. Warner*. New York: McGraw-Hill, 1990.

———. *Joan Crawford*. New York: Simon and Schuster, 1978.

Thomson, David. *The New Biographical Dictionary of Film*. New York: Alfred A. Knopf, 2002.

Todd, Richard. *In Camera: An Autobiography Continued*. London: Hutchinson, 1989.

Troyan, Michael. *A Rose for Mrs. Miniver: The Life of Greer Garson*. Lexington: University Press of Kentucky, 1999.

Vidal, Gore. *Palimpsest: A Memoir*. New York: Random House, 1995.

Vidor, King. *On Film Making*. New York: David McKay, 1972.

Vidor, King, Nancy Dowd, and David Shepard. *King Vidor: A Directors Guild of America Oral History*. Metuchen, N.J.: Scarecrow Press, 1988.

Vieira, Mark A. *Sin in Soft Focus: Pre-Code Hollywood*. New York: Harry N. Abrams, 1999.

Walker, Alexander. *Joan Crawford: The Ultimate Star*. New York: Harper and Row, 1983.

Wallis, Hal, and Charles Higham. *Starmaker*. New York: Macmillan, 1980.

Walsh, Frank. *Sin and Censorship: The Catholic Church and the Motion Picture Industry*. New Haven, Conn.: Yale University Press, 1996.

Ward, Geoffrey C., ed. *Closest Companion: The Unknown Story of the Intimate Friendship Between Franklin Roosevelt and Margaret Suckley*. Boston: Houghton Mifflin, 1995.

Warner, Jack L., with Dean Jennings. *My First Hundred Years in Hollywood*. New York: Random House, 1964.

Warren, Doug, with James Cagney. *Cagney: The Authorized Biography*. New York: St. Martin's Press, 1983.

Warwick, Christopher. *The Universal Ustinov*. London: Sidgwick and Jackson, 1990.

Wayne, Jane Ellen. *Crawford's Men*. New York: Prentice Hall Press, 1988.

Weaver, Tom. *Interviews with B Science Fiction and Horror Movie Makers*. Jefferson, N.C.: McFarland, 1988.

Westmore, Frank, and Muriel Davidson. *The Westmores of Hollywood*. New York: J. B. Lippincott, 1976.

Whitman, Walt. *Leaves of Grass*. Philadelphia: David McKay, 1891–92.

Wiles, Buster, with William Donati. *My Days with Errol Flynn: The Autobiography of Stuntman Buster Wiles*. Santa Monica, Calif.: Roundtable, 1988.

Wiley, Mason, and Damien Bona. *Inside Oscar*. New York: Ballantine Books, 1993.

Williams, Esther, with Digby Diehl. *The Million Dollar Mermaid*. New York: Simon and Schuster, 1999.

Williams, Tennessee. *Memoirs*. Garden City, N.Y.: Doubleday, 1975.

Williams, Tennessee, and Maria St. Just. *Five O'Clock Angel: Letters of Tennessee Williams to Mona St. Just, 1948–1982*. New York: Alfred A. Knopf, 1990.

Williamson, Bruce. "*Playboy* Interview: Bette Davis." *Playboy*, July 1982, pp. 67–94.

Winters, Shelley. *Shelley II: The Middle of My Century*. New York: Simon and Schuster, 1989.

Wood, Audrey, and Max Wilk. *Represented by Audrey Wood*. Garden City, N.Y.: Doubleday, 1981.

Wood, Lana. *Natalie: A Memoir by Her Sister*. New York: G. P. Putnam's Sons, 1984.

Wright, William. *Lillian Hellman: The Image, The Woman*. New York: Simon and Schuster, 1986.

Zierold, Norman. *The Moguls*. New York: Coward-McCann, 1969.

Zollo, Paul. *Hollywood Remembered: An Oral History of Its Golden Age*. New York: Cooper Square Press, 2002.

ACKNOWLEDGMENTS

My deepest appreciation goes to my trusty psychotherapist, Dr. Gerald Perlman, who had to listen to a lot of the unpleasant muck this book stirred up. Thanks also to my psychiatrist, Dr. Barry Richman, who kept me on medication. And a round of applause certainly goes to the prescient Dr. Scott Goldsmith, who warned me, as both a psychiatrist and a friend, that I might feel some of the emotions I imagined my subject probably felt. As Miss Davis would have said, *Oh, brother!*

I relied, as usual, on a group of thoughtful and supportive readers, chief among them Chris Bram, to whom I dedicate this book. Others included my ace research assistant, Gregor Meyer; Tom Phillips, Bette fan extraordinaire, who also provided the *What's My Line?* material; Matthew Mirapaul, who never fails to prop me up in times of need; and Martin Shingler, the world's greatest Davis scholar. David Boxwell, Dan Callahan, and Jim Aquino lent me hard-to-find films and recordings. My pals in the New York Independent Film Critics Circle—Damien Bona, Howard Karren, Joe Smith, George Robinson, Andy Dickos, Adam Orman, Michael Giltz, M. George Stevenson, Daryl Chin, Jeff Zeitlin, Alex Lewin, and Jace Weaver—all contributed a mix of arcana and wit.

I thank the many friends, acquaintances, associates, and admirers of Bette Davis who spent time helping me to understand her better: Edward Albee, Dame Eileen Atkins, Don Bachardy, Martin Baum, Jim

Brochu, Betty Buckley (not *that* Betty Buckley), Charles Busch, Dick Cavett, David Chierichetti, Roy Christopher, Wendy Craig, Mart Crowley, Jon Dosa, Bryan England, John Epperson, David Galligan, Kim Garfield, Vik Greenfield, John Guillermin, the late Ellen Hanley, Sheldon Harnick, Anthony Harvey, Robert Hofler, Waris Hussein, John Kane, Mike Kaplan, John Kuri, Jack and Elaine LaLanne, Robert Lantz, Lionel Larner, James McCourt, Lynda Pearl, Charles Pollack, Dr. Ivin Prince, Dotson Rader, Alvin Rakoff, David Rothenberg, Ann Kaufman Schneider, Reggie Schwartzwalder, Tom Smothers, Gary Springer, Tulip Traber, and Margot Webb.

Biographies couldn't be written without the librarians and archivists who care for the infinitely valuable records in which famous people's lives are chronicled, in this case: J. C. Johnson, Sean Noel, and the staff of the Howard Gotlieb Archival Research Center at Boston University; Haden Guest and the staff of the Warner Bros. Archive at the University of Southern California; Barbara Hall and her colleagues at the Academy of Motion Picture Arts and Sciences' Margaret Herrick Library; Michael Neault and Jim Healy at George Eastman House; and Vicky Hedley, Ayesha Khan, Anastasis Kerameos, and the other librarians at the British Film Institute.

I also thank the many people who helped me with this project in less definable ways: Christopher Anderson, Per Åsberg, John Belton, Steven DeRosa, Judy Englander, Ron Fried, Kenneth Geist, David Germain, Warren Goldfarb, Chris Gorman, Dr. Nathaniel Hupert, Dr. Rainu Kaushal, Neal Leibowitz, William J. Mann, Patrick Merla, Ethan Minovitz, Evan Mirapaul, Eric Myers, S. I. Newhouse IV, Gregory Orr, Robert Rees, Tom Rhoads, Hank Sartin, Dulcie and Walter Schackman, Draper Shreeve, Jason Simos, Frances Smith, Linnell Smith, and James Yaffe.

My editors, Jennifer Barth and David Patterson, had confidence in me when I did not, and I'm enormously grateful for their continuing support, not to mention their sharp critical skills. I also thank my expert copy editor, Vicki Haire; Kenn Russell, the executive managing editor at Henry Holt; and Lindsay Ross and Patrick Clark.

As always, I'm in awe of my agent, the superb Edward Hibbert, who relayed details of the contract negotiations for this book in the uncannily precise voice of Bette Davis. Finally, I owe a profound debt of gratitude to my shockingly stable family, particularly my mother, Betty Sikov; my brother, Costas Karakatsanis; and my partner, Bruce Schackman.

ILLUSTRATION ACKNOWLEDGMENTS

The Davis Girls: From the Bette Davis Collection in the Howard Gotlieb Archival Research Center, Boston University

Harlow Morell Davis: From the Bette Davis Collection in the Howard Gotlieb Archival Research Center, Boston University

With a Ribbon in Her Hair: From the Bette Davis Collection in the Howard Gotlieb Archival Research Center, Boston University

Bette, by Ruthie: From the Bette Davis Collection in the Howard Gotlieb Archival Research Center, Boston University

Delicate Flower: Photofest

Beauty in the Eyes: Photofest

Unusual Portrait: Collection of the author

"I always used to wipe my mouth!": Photofest

Ham and Spuds: Photofest

Bette as Rasputin? Photofest

Jezebel: Collection of the author

"Homely Dynamo": Photofest

Wedding Day Number 2: Photofest

Sisters on the Set: From the Bette Davis Collection in the Howard Gotlieb Archival Research Center, Boston University

"Like a Mink": Photofest

Wedding Day Number 3: From the Bette Davis Collection in the Howard Gotlieb Archival Research Center, Boston University

The Evil Eye: Collection of the author

Peritonitis Sets In: Photofest

Maudlin and Magnificent: Collection of the author

Two's Company: Photofest

A Bette Davis western?: Photofest

Designed by Bette: Photofest

On Broadway: Photofest

"Let's clear out. I draw the line at this crowd.": © Tee and Charles Addams Foundation

Joan, by Bette: From the Bette Davis Collection in the Howard Gotlieb Archival Research Center, Boston University

Lush Life: From the Bette Davis Collection in the Howard Gotlieb Archival Research Center, Boston University

Poetry Onstage: Photofest

Bette, her Daughter Margot, and Dinner: From the Bette Davis Collection in the Howard Gotlieb Archival Research Center, Boston University

Mother, Daughter, and Son: From the Bette Davis Collection in the Howard Gotlieb Archival Research Center, Boston University

It Works: Photofest

Miss Moffat: Photofest

Madame Sin and her pet hawk: Collection of the author

Last Picture Show: Photofest

The World's Most Famous Smoker: Photofest

P.s. Bette Davis: Photofest

INDEX

ABOUT THE AUTHOR

ED SIKOV is a film historian whose other biographies include the critically acclaimed *On Sunset Boulevard: The Life and Times of Billy Wilder* and *Mr. Strangelove: A Biography of Peter Sellers*. He has taught at Columbia University, Haverford College, and Colorado College, and lives in New York City.

www.edsikov.com